CHRISTIANITY IN THE TWENTIETH CENTURY

The Princeton History of Christianity

Christianity in the Twentieth Century

A WORLD HISTORY

Brian Stanley

PRINCETON UNIVERSITY PRESS

PRINCETON & OXFORD

Copyright © 2018 by Princeton University Press

Published by Princeton University Press,
41 William Street, Princeton, New Jersey 08540

In the United Kingdom: Princeton University Press,
6 Oxford Street, Woodstock, Oxfordshire OX20 1TR

press.princeton.edu

Library of Congress Cataloging-in-Publication Data
Names: Stanley, Brian, 1953– author.
Title: Christianity in the twentieth century : a world history / Brian Stanley.
Description: hardcover [edition]. | Princeton, NJ : Princeton University Press, 2018. |
Includes bibliographical references and index.
Series: The Princeton history of Christianity
Identifiers: LCCN 2017039619 | ISBN 9780691157108 (hardcover : alk. paper)
Subjects: LCSH: Church history—20th century.
Classification: LCC BR479 .S7155 2018 | DDC 270.8/2—dc23
LC record available at https://lccn.loc.gov/2017039619

British Library Cataloging-in-Publication Data is available

Editorial: Ben Tate and Hannah Paul
Production Editorial: Debbie Tegarden
Jacket/Cover Design: Derek Thornton, Faceout Studio
Jacket image: Courtesy of Shutterstock
Production: Jacquie Poirier
Publicity: Jodi Price and Katie Lewis
Copyeditor: Terry Kornak

British Library Cataloging-in-Publication Data is available

This book has been composed in Miller

Printed on acid-free paper. ∞

Printed in the United States of America

10 9 8 7 6 5 4 3 2 1

To Andrew F. Walls

CONTENTS

LIST OF MAPS

LIST OF ABBREVIATIONS

ABCFM	American Board of Commissioners for Foreign Missions
AIC	African Instituted/Initiated Church
ANC	African National Congress
AOC	African Orthodox Church
AUCECB	All-Union Council of Evangelical Christians and Baptists
BEDC	Black Economic Development Conference
BMS	Baptist Missionary Society
CARC	Council for the Affairs of Religious Cults
CAROC	Council for the Affairs of the Russian Orthodox Church
CCC	China Christian Council
CCP	Chinese Communist Party
CCPA	Chinese Catholic Patriotic Association
CEBS	Base Ecclesial Communities
CECB	Council of Evangelical Christian Baptists
CI	Christian Institute
CICCU	Cambridge Inter-Collegiate Christian Union
CIM	China Inland Mission
CMS	Church Missionary Society
CNI	Church of North India
CONFAB	National Conference of Chinese Christian Churches
CSI	Church of South India
ECPNG	Evangelical Church of Papua New Guinea
ECUSA	(Protestant) Episcopal Church in the United States of America
DRC	Dutch Reformed Church
FCC	Federal Council of Churches of Christ in America
HKBP	Huria Kristen Batak Protestan

ICT	Institute of Contextual Theology
IFES	International Fellowship of Evangelical Students
ISAL	Iglesia y Sociedad en América Latina
IURD	Igreja Universal do Reino de Deus
KISA	Kikuyu Independent Schools Association
LMS	London Missionary Society
MCC	Metropolitan Community Church
MRND	Mouvement Révolutionnaire National pour le Développement
MSCC	Missionary Society of the Church of England in Canada
NAE	National Association of Evangelicals
NCC	National Council of the Churches of Christ in the USA
NGK	Nederduitse Gereformeerde Kerk
NHK	Nederduitsch Hervormde Kerk
NSDAP	Nationalsozialistische Deutsche Arbeiterpartei
PCR	Programme to Combat Racism
PCUSA	Presbyterian Church (U.S.A.)
PKI	Partai Komunis Indonesia
RPF	Rwandese Patriotic Front
SACC	South African Council of Churches
SASO	South African Students' Organisation
SCA	Students' Christian Association
SCM	Student Christian Movement (in South Africa: Students' Christian Movement)
SIUC	South India United Church
SNCC	Student Nonviolent Coordinating Committee
SPG	Society for the Propagation of the Gospel
SVD	Societas Verbi Divini (Society of the Divine Word)
TSPM	Three-Self Patriotic Movement
UCM	University Christian Movement
UFM	Unevangelized Fields Mission

UMC	United Methodist Church
UNAR	Union National Rwandaise
UNIA	Universal Negro Improvement Association
USSR	Union of Soviet Socialist Republics
WCC	World Council of Churches
WSCF	World's Student Christian Federation (later, World Student Christian Federation)
YMCA	Young Men's Christian Association
YWCA	Young Women's Christian Association

ACKNOWLEDGMENTS

THIS BOOK HAS BEEN six years in the making, during which time many different people have contributed, wittingly or unwittingly, to the process of its construction. Historians depend on the willing cooperation of an army of librarians and archivists, and I owe a debt of gratitude to all those who have made available to me the wide range of resources on which this book draws. The staffs of New College Library, Edinburgh, the National Library of Scotland, Cambridge University Library, and the Cambridge Centre for Christianity Worldwide have been unfailingly helpful. Martha Smalley, who until her retirement in the summer of 2017 presided with impeccable grace and efficiency over the Special Collections department of Yale Divinity School Library, and her colleague Joan Duffy, merit particular mention as those for whom no request has ever been too troublesome. The Yale Divinity School Library remains a uniquely rich treasure-store for all scholars who work in the field of world Christianity. I am also grateful to the Overseas Missionary Fellowship, the Billy Graham Evangelistic Association, and to the Provost and Fellows of Kings College Cambridge for permission to access or cite material from their respective archives. I am very grateful to the Ecclesiastical History Society and its then president, Professor John Wolffe, for the invitation to deliver a plenary lecture at their 2014 summer conference, subsequently published in volume 51 of *Studies in Church History*. The lecture, on the churches in the Islamic environments of Egypt and Indonesia, became the basis of chapter 8 of this book, and I thank the Society for its kind permission to include a revised and expanded version of that paper in this volume.

There is quite a long list of scholarly colleagues and friends who have been gracious enough to read, or patient enough to listen to, draft chapters that fell within their respective areas of expertise and have improved the finished product by their pertinent questions, constructive comments, and valid criticisms: David Bebbington, S. J. Brown, Alexander Chow, Philippe Denis, Rick Elphick, Robert Forrest, Paul Freston, Bob Frykenberg, James Grayson, Naomi Haynes, Arkotong Longkumer, Brian Macdonald-Milne, Athanasios Papathanasiou, Ian Randall, Joshua Ralston, David Reimer, Heather Sharkey, the late Jack Thompson, and Iain Whyte. I hope that they all will feel that their labors have not been in vain. Dana Robert, who has been a faithful friend and academic collaborator over the years, revealed her identity as one of the two readers appointed by Princeton University Press: I am deeply grateful for her strongly affirmative and constructive response to the draft manuscript. The other appointed reader turned out to be another old friend, Mark Noll; I am equally indebted to him for his insightful comments and constructive suggestions. Kyo-Seong Ahn of Presbyterian University and Theological Seminary in Seoul was kind enough to answer my depressing question about the number of separate Presbyterian denominations in South Korea by the end of the twentieth century. I am also greatly indebted to Mrs. Liesl Amos for compiling the index.

Al Bertrand of Princeton University Press first invited me to consider writing this quite impossible book, a task that I would never have attempted on my own initiative, and in retrospect I am glad that he did. His colleagues, Ben Tate, Hannah Paul, and Debbie Tegarden, and my copyeditor, Terry Kornak, have been a pleasure to work with.

My wife, Rosey, has lived with this book through the joys and sorrows of two daughters' weddings, parental illness, and bereavement. She has helped me to remember that there are more important things in life than writing books, and yet has always been a source of deep encouragement and love.

I should like to acknowledge my enormous debt to the many students I have taught over the years, at Spurgeon's College, London; Trinity College, Bristol; the University of Cambridge, the Cambridge Theological Federation; and finally at the University of Edinburgh. Their questions and insights have forced me to clarify my own ideas. During the years in which I have been researching and writing this book, my academic home has been the School of Divinity in the University of Edinburgh, and in particular its Centre for the Study of World Christianity, of which I have had the privilege to be the Director. The Centre's postgraduate students have contributed more to this book than they will ever appreciate. The serious academic study of Christianity outside of Europe and North America remains a fragile enterprise in British universities, fixated as they too often are on the pursuit of those areas of study that appear to offer the best prospects for short-term financial gain. It is essential for public awareness and understanding of the changing role and increasing (not diminishing) prominence of Christianity in the contemporary world that high-level scholarly activity focused on the expanding churches of the Global South is brought closer to the heart of academic work in theology and religious studies. The Centre for the Study of World Christianity, founded in the University of Aberdeen in 1982 by Professor Andrew F. Walls, OBE, under the title,

"Centre for the Study of Christianity in the Non-Western World," is needed today more than ever before. All scholars working in the field of world Christianity owe to Andrew Walls a quite incalculable debt. This book will appear in the year in which he reaches his ninetieth birthday, and therefore I gladly dedicate this book to Andrew, with gratitude and affection.

Brian Stanley
Edinburgh,
October 2017

Introduction

AS THE TWENTIETH CENTURY DAWNED, many Christians anticipated that the coming decades would witness the birth of a new era. Their expectation was that the accelerating global diffusion of Christianity from its Western heartlands to the rest of the globe would usher in the final phase of human history—the climactic millennial age of international peace and harmony. Protestants in Europe and North America confidently predicted the universal triumph of the Western civilizing creed of technological and scientific progress, democratic and liberal political values, and broadly evangelical versions of the Christian religion. In the United States, this optimistic mood was symbolized by the revival in 1900 of *The Christian Oracle*, originally a house magazine of the Disciples of Christ, with the new and extravagantly aspirational title *The Christian Century*. From its new base in Chicago and under new ownership from 1908, the reconstituted magazine rapidly established itself as the principal interdenominational organ of mainline American Protestantism. The magazine retains that status, and its hubristic title, to this day, long after the "mainline" has lost its preeminent status in American religion.

Protestants were not alone in anticipating that the new century held out bright hopes for the triumph of Christian faith and values. Roman Catholics disseminated their own distinctive vision of a coming global transformation based on the spread of Christian revelation. "The civilization of the world is Christian," confidently pronounced Pope Pius X in his encyclical *Il Fermo Proposito* in June 1905: "The more completely Christian it is, the more true, more lasting and more productive of genuine fruit it is."[1] Pius was asserting, not that the task of civilizing the world had been completed, but that only in dutiful submission to the authority of the Catholic Church and to the Holy See could any efforts at civilization achieve permanence. In particular, he was referring to a movement of Italian lay Catholics known as Catholic Action that sought to irradiate secular society through the agency of distinctively Catholic confraternities and youth organizations. While Pius commended such aspirations, he was concerned to make it abundantly clear that no lay association could be allowed to usurp priestly authority. The Catholic hierarchy, in contrast to Protestant organs of opinion, saw no prospect for global transformation through a host of voluntary Christian mission and reform organizations. Only the formation of exclusive partnerships between the Roman Catholic Church and the State could ensure what *Il Fermo Proposito* termed "the subordination of all the laws of the State to the Divine laws of the Gospel." Nevertheless, Pius's encyclical exuded its own more qualified brand of Christian optimism. It anticipated that, if only such happy marriages between Church and State could be concluded, "what prosperity and well-being, what peace and harmony, what respectful subjection to authority and what excellent government would be obtained and maintained in the world if one could see in practice the perfect ideal of Christian civilization."[2]

With the cheap benefit of hindsight, these contrasting strands of Christian expectation that under the leadership of either the Western Protestant nations or the Holy See the globe was about to enter a golden age of universal Christian charity and international harmony display a pitiable cultural hubris. Even at the time, there were aggressively secular voices in Europe, the United States, and China who with equal confidence of faith predicted precisely the opposite—namely, that the coming century would be one in which scientific rationalism and modernization would finally dispatch the superstition of religious belief to the garbage heap of history. Observers from the twenty-first century are better able to see the fragility of both sets of confident predictions. They are also only too aware that the twentieth century turned out to be, not simply one marked by the two world wars, but also a period in which the perennial narrative of human beings' apparently ineradicable propensity for inhumanity entered a new and peculiarly ugly phase. From a Christian theological perspective, such renewed evidence of human perversity is neither surprising nor problematic. As the neo-orthodox and realist theologians of the middle decades of the century correctly discerned, the fond hopes of human improvement espoused by liberal Protestants in the early years of the century represented a gross distortion of Christian eschatology, whose central narrative is not in fact the steady upward progress of human civilization but the intervention of divine grace as the only solution to human sin. The problem that the twentieth century poses to the Christian mind is not the apparent resurgence of human propensity for atrocity but rather the seeming theological inadequacy of much of the Christian response.

In April–May 1939, as the world lurched for a second time in three decades toward the precipice of global conflict, the American realist theologian Reinhold Niebuhr (1892–1971) delivered the Gifford lectures in the University of Edinburgh on the theme of "The Nature and Destiny of Man." The first volume of the lectures, published by Scribner's in March 1941, appropriately expounded the somber theme of "human nature" in all its fallen state. However, Niebuhr struggled to complete the second volume with its more optimistic subject matter of "human destiny" in Christ, and it did not appear until January 1943. Niebuhr's difficulty in wartime conditions in making the paradoxical case that human history both "fulfils and negates the Kingdom of God" symbolizes the challenge that the century poses to much Christian theology.[3] Whereas evidence of the negation has been plentiful, convincing evidence of the tangible fulfillment of the values of the Kingdom of God in actual human societies characterized by a majority Christian presence has been decidedly patchy. When subjected to intense pressure from rampant nationalism and ethnic hostility, the European varieties of Christendom that supplied the foundations for the hopes of world transformation expressed at the opening of the century frequently turned out to be less authentically Christian than their advocates had supposed. Furthermore, while the century did indeed witness the unprecedented and extensive global diffusion of the Christian faith that they had anticipated, the theological and cultural contours that world Christianity had thereby assumed by the close of the century were very different in character from what they had imagined.

While taking due note of the relevant perceptions of outstanding thinkers such as Reinhold Niebuhr, this one-volume world history of Christianity in the twentieth century makes no claim to be an intellectual history of either theology or biblical scholarship. Theology and biblical interpretation of an applied kind will properly be the object of attention in those chapters where the focus is on the ways in which Christian thinkers have reflected on how the churches should frame their missionary strategies in response to the challenges posed by the modern world, including that of systemic economic or racial injustice. Theologies of mission, liberation, and Christian engagement with human rights ideologies will thus occupy a prominent place (chapters 9, 10, 11, and 12). But a comprehensive history of Christian doctrine in the twentieth century is a wholly different enterprise that must await the attention of a theologian with historical interests. Rather, this book provides a historian's perspective on the multiple and complex ways in which the Christian religion and its institutional embodiment in the Christian churches have interacted with the changing social, political, and cultural environment of the twentieth century. For Christian readers the approach taken may at times be disturbing in its insistence on the disconcerting extent to which Christians have allowed their theology and even their ethics to be fashioned by the prevalent ideologies of the day. For readers who are not Christians, the challenge may rather be to take more seriously than they previously have the continuing force of the impact of Christian belief and communal practice on culture, society, and politics in the modern world. My primary concern as author is simply stated. In 1990 the Canadian church historian Gavin White (1927–2016) published a short introductory book with the engaging title *How the Churches Got to Be the Way They Are*.[4] The primary focus of White's book was on the churches in Britain, though he made brief forays into the ecclesiastical history of North America, Australasia, and the Soviet Union. In contrast, this current volume aims in principle to cover the globe, with particular attention given to the transformative growth of Christianity beyond Europe and North America. Its central question, however, is much the same as the one White posed in 1990. This book is an attempt to enable serious readers—whether or not they consider themselves to be Christians—to understand how the churches of the world got to be the way they were in specific geographical locations at crucial turning points in the course of the century.

The twentieth century has suffered comparative neglect at the hands of modern Western historians of Christianity, who have, on the whole, remained more interested in the intellectual and social challenges posed to the European churches in the nineteenth century. Yet it was the twentieth century that shaped the contours of the Christian faith as it is now, a culturally plural and geographically polycentric religion clustered around a number of new metropolitan loci in the non-European world, from Seoul to São Paulo. The majority of its rapidly growing number of adherents found the post-Enlightenment questions that preoccupied the churches of the North and West to be remote from their pressing everyday concerns of life and death, sickness and healing, justice and poverty. In Islamic regions of Africa and in almost all of Asia they were also intimately concerned with the implications of living as religious minorities in a context dominated by the majority religious tradition, as chapter 8 expounds with reference to Egypt and Indonesia. Their theological priorities and ethical perspectives differed accordingly from those of Christians in the North. The twentieth century thus set the agenda for the theological and ethical issues that now constitute the fault lines dividing Christians and churches from each other—fault lines that are significantly different from those inherited from the European religious past and that still determined the denominational geography of Christianity in 1900. The twentieth century has thus made it necessary for students of ecumenism to redraw the map of Christian unity and disunity, as chapter 6 explains. This history therefore has a contemporary purpose as well a more strictly historical one. It is concerned with enabling us to understand how the churches got to be the way they are *now*. For that reason, while its formal chronological endpoint is the close of the twentieth century rather than the present day, it will from time to time take brief note of events and developments that have occurred since the turn of the twenty-first century.

The central concerns of this book have dictated its shape. It is neither a comprehensive region-by-region survey nor a straightforward chronological narrative. Rather it selects fifteen themes that are of preeminent importance for understanding the global dimensions of contemporary Christianity and analyzing the various ways in which Christians have responded to some of the most important social, cultural, and political trends of the twentieth century. Each theme is introduced and then illustrated by two geographical case studies, mostly taken from different continents. The comparatively unusual juxtaposition of some of these case studies may raise the eyebrows of regional or subject specialists. Scholars of Catholic nationalism in Poland, for example, will not be accustomed to viewing their subject alongside the phenomenon of Protestant nationalism in Korea, as chapter 2 does, and the converse will be true of scholars of Korean nationalism. Such unconventional juxtapositions are designed to illuminate by comparison and contrast, as well as to identify transnational connections that have often been overlooked. The case studies have also been selected with an eye to ensuring a reasonable measure of geographical comprehensiveness across the volume as a whole: they are intended to broaden horizons and to rescue from implied marginality some regions, such as Melanesia (chapter 3), Scandinavia (chapter 5), or the Caribbean (which receives some, albeit inadequate, attention in chapter 15), that are too often neglected by broad-brush treatments. Academic history tends to be populated by regional or national specialists, and the history of Christianity perhaps more so than some other fields of study. Although the recent growth of transnational history has stimulated a welcome broadening of scholarly horizons, and has begun to shape approaches to the modern history of popular religious movements,[5] its impact on the writing of ecclesiastical history of a more conventional kind has so far been quite limited. Nevertheless, historians working in the still emerging interdisciplinary field of "world Christianity" have begun to point the way by uncovering the transnational linkages between regional Christian movements and the polycentric nature of the structures created or facilitated by Catholic and Protestant missions from the sixteenth century onwards.[6] If this book succeeds in placing key episodes and narratives of national Christian history in the twentieth century in an illuminating transnational perspective, it will have achieved one of its goals.

The thematic approach adopted by the book may prove challenging to those readers who prefer to follow a single story from beginning to end, and it is hoped that such readers will be patient with the amount of chronological switching that this approach inevitably involves. It has also necessitated some hard choices of inclusion and correspondingly of omission. The case studies drill quite deeply into the hidden strata of the Christian movements that have been selected, and of necessity leave others that are of undoubted importance relatively untouched. In the same way, the case study approach gives prominence to some individual Christian men and women who might not find their way into a more conventionally structured world history. For example, Amir Sjarifoeddin, the Indonesian Lutheran layman and nationalist politician who appears in chapter 8, or Patricia Brennan, the Sydney evangelical Anglican who features in chapter 12 as the unlikely architect of the Australian branch of the Movement for the Ordination of Women, are unlikely to gain a mention in any other published survey of modern Christian history. Conversely, some high-profile ecclesiastical statesmen who might normally be expected to occupy center stage have only bit parts in the narrative or may not even feature at all. If popes and archbishops find themselves playing second fiddle to comparatively unknown laywomen and laymen, that is no bad thing, for this is a history of Christianity in its myriad popular embodiments, not a narrow institutional history of denominations and their higher echelons of leadership. Named Christian women feature less often in the text than they should in view of the consistent predominance of women in the membership of almost all churches in the twentieth century. Those who write global histories can do a certain amount to redress the balance of a century during most of which women were seen but not allowed to be heard in the churches of almost all Christian traditions. Thus chapter 1 highlights the somewhat surprising role of the suffragette Christabel Pankhust in promoting Adventist teaching in Britain between 1918 and 1958, while chapter 9 singles out Pilar Bellosillo, Spanish president of the World Union of Catholic Women's Organizations, who almost—but not quite—succeeded in addressing the Second Vatican Council. Chapter 13 records the leadership exercised in the early Pentecostal movement by such remarkable women as "Pandita" Ramabai Dongre, Minnie Abrams, and Aimee Semple McPherson, while chapter 15 directs attention to the extraordinary Chicago pastorate of the African American Pentecostal Elder Lucy Smith. Noteworthy though such individual examples undoubtedly are, what may be even more significant in the long term is the distinctive appeal exercised by Pentecostal forms of Christianity to millions of women whose names are not generally preserved in the historical records but who found Pentecostal teaching and practice to be a source of personal fulfillment and emancipation. More often than not the role of female Christians in the narrative remains inescapably veiled in such historical anonymity, but it must be stressed that anonymity need not imply marginality.

Historians strive to deal with the available written or oral evidence with rigor and fairness, but that does not mean that neutrality on their part is possible or even desirable. Chapter 7 devotes the most attention to historiography. It shows how historians have struggled to interpret and explain the apparent widespread failure of the Church to act Christianly in two of the greatest moral crises of the century. The chapter examines the part the churches may have played, whether wittingly or unwittingly, in supplying a sinister ideological apparatus for the implementation of genocide in Nazi Germany and Rwanda in 1994. No historian can or should write about such grave matters from a position of "neutrality." Historians of religion write about questions of ultimate concern, and their own religious commitment or lack of it will inevitably affect what they choose to write about, and the way in which they do it. This history of world Christianity is written by a British evangelical Protestant. A history of the same subject written by a Brazilian Pentecostal or one by a Lebanese Maronite Catholic would be strikingly different in both content and perspective. Good history writing should nevertheless seek to transcend the limitations of the historian's own background and ideological inclinations, even though the historian will never be wholly successful in achieving such transcendence. If this book is judged by its reviewers to be weaker in its treatment of Catholicism than of Protestantism, and weaker still in its coverage of the Orthodox churches (confined to chapters 8 and 14) and its substantial neglect of the Oriental Orthodox churches, that is precisely what one would expect, and indeed is what the author himself feels. Books of this wide range stretch authors well beyond their specialist expertise, and the stretch marks are sometimes disconcertingly obvious. The author's primary expertise lies in the modern history of Protestant missions and their varying reception by indigenous peoples, resulting in the growth of what has become known as "world Christianity." That academic background has nevertheless supplied a very useful foundation for understanding a century in which Christianity took root in the indigenous cultures of Africa, Latin America, and parts of Asia to a greater extent than in any other century.

Scholars of world Christianity, in their commendable enthusiasm to redress the Eurocentric bias of so much historical and theological writing, sometimes give the impression that the declining Christianity of Europe and North America is no longer worthy of attention, for that represents the past, whereas the booming Christianity of the Global South represents the future. That is both an overreaction to previous scholarly imbalance and a potential fallacy of overconfident prediction. World Christianity means world Christianity, and not simply the Christianity of the southern hemisphere. For that reason, this book pays more attention to the churches in Europe and North America than some colleagues who work on southern Christianity may deem to be either necessary or appropriate.

The churches of Africa, Asia, Oceania, and Latin America continue to be deeply impacted by Christian teaching that originated in the North and West—above all, but not wholly, in the United States—and the nature of that impact can be traced in some of the chapters that follow, notably in chapter 13 on Pentecostal Christianities. Furthermore, the North also has its indigenous peoples who have had their own encounters, for good or ill, with mission Christianity: chapter 11 accordingly includes a case study of the often problematic experience by the First Nations peoples of Canada of white "civilizing" Christianity communicated through the medium of Catholic and Protestant residential schools. Two chapters—4 and 5—are devoted to surveys of the classically "European" theme of secularization. Chapter 4 considers the aggressively secular anticlerical campaign conducted by the State in France and the still more explicit attack on religion itself by the Soviet State in Russia and the Ukraine. Chapter 5 engages more directly with sociological debates over secularization, specifically by examining the markedly contrasting patterns of believing and belonging exhibited in the twentieth century by the Scandinavian countries (especially Sweden) on the one hand and by the United States on the other. These two chapters do not accept the supposed inevitability of secularization as the metanarrative that integrates the entire sweep of modern global history, yet neither do they accept the converse implication beloved of some students of world Christianity that the southern hemisphere is somehow immune to the supposedly northern disease of secularization and destined for unending church growth until the eschaton. Any idea of a simple polarity between the diametrically opposite religious trajectories of North and South is becoming less and less tenable, not least because of the extent of southern and East Asian migration to Europe and North America, a theme discussed in chapter 15.

The Bible is the fountainhead of all Christian traditions, and a colorful array of characters and images drawn from both the Old and the New Testaments adorn the walls of the long corridors of Christian history, providing inspiration and models for Christian living. Yet the twentieth century may have a better claim than any other to be labeled as the century of the Bible. In the course of the century more peoples received the Scriptures in their own language than in any preceding century. As they did so, biblical narratives and the stories of their own history—in the case of African peoples, frequently painful ones of enslavement and colonization—began to interact with one another in ways that had profound implications both for their understanding of the Christian faith and for their own developing sense of nationhood. As chapter 3 notes, the acceleration of conversion to Christianity in tropical Africa in the years after the First World War is often explained by reference to the full impact of the colonial state and the opportunities for self-advancement that mission education offered in that context. Such explanations are not without their merit, although they struggle to account for the further acceleration of church growth that took place after the end of European colonial rule. In addition, they too easily miss the fact that the same period was the one in which for the first time most peoples in sub-Saharan Africa received either large portions or the whole of Christian Scripture in their own language, and consequently began to frame their own responses to the Christian message in ways that often circumvented or even contradicted missionary interpretation.[7]

Unmediated popular engagement with the biblical message may appear to be a distinctively Protestant theme, but it is worth remembering that the British and Foreign Bible Society was happy to cooperate with Orthodox and Catholic as well as Protestant churches, and that even some Catholic bishops supported modern Bible translations. Modern vernacular translations of the Bible contributed to the formation of ethnolinguistic identity and hence national consciousness, not simply in areas of Protestant predominance such as Korea or parts of tropical Africa, but also in Orthodox Serbia or Catholic Croatia, where the first vernacular bibles had been published in 1868 and 1895 respectively.[8] Furthermore, the Second Vatican Council lifted many of the traditional restraints on lay Catholic engagement with the biblical text, opening the door to new styles of popular Catholicism such as those fashioned by the Base Ecclesial Communities in Latin America. To a greater extent than any other single ecclesiastical event in the course of the century, the Council provoked an upheaval in the tectonics of Christian confessionalism that had remained more or less stable since the sixteenth century, narrowing the old fault lines between Catholic and Protestant, while pushing up new ones between contrasting styles of Roman Catholic. In so doing, the Council, for all of its hesitations and deep fissures of internal division, began to reconfigure the global topography of the Christian religion. As chapter 9 will show, it began the transformation of the Catholic Church from its inherited role as the theological cement binding together the established political order in Europe to a genuinely missionary force, rivaling evangelical Protestantism in its subversive potential to make the Christian gospel a source of liberation for the poor and marginalized in the non-European world.

The twentieth century did not quite turn out to be the century of Christian missionary triumph that the founders of the *Christian Century* fondly imagined. Statistical estimates suggest that in percentage terms Christians accounted for a slightly lower percentage of the world population in 2000 than they had at the beginning of the century: the World Christian Database compiled by the Center for the Study of Global Christianity at Gordon-Conwell Seminary computes that the percentage of the world population that was Christian fell from 34.46 percent in 1900 to 32.65 percent in 2005.[9] There was, of course, an unprecedented and sustained growth of conversion to Christianity in Africa and other parts of the non-Western world, as chapter 3 in particular narrates, but over the course of the century it failed to keep pace with the explosion of the world population. But neither did the twentieth century prove to be one in which the clinically rational armies of science and the secular state decisively routed the forces of supposedly obsolete religious "superstition," as was so confidently anticipated by progressive modernizers in Europe, the United States, and China during the first three decades of the century. On the contrary, the hundred years that followed the First World War have been marked by the obstinate survival, and indeed widespread resurgence, of religion as a resource motivating obdurate human resistance to absolute state power and action in pursuit of a range of visions of social transformation. The central role of Christianity in issuing a bold challenge to the serene faith of secular self-belief is perhaps the most important integrating narrative of this book. Where new nation-states came into being—as in sub-Saharan Africa—their geographical contours may have been the frequently illogical outcome of colonial politics, but their emerging sense of collective identity more often than not owed a great deal to the narratives and motifs of Christian Scripture. Where other states of anti-Christian inclination huffed and puffed in their frantic determination to blow the Christian house down, they ultimately failed, even in cases such as China between 1949 and 1976, where in the short term a repressive state apparatus proved able to drive the institutional Church out of sight.

The inception of the modern Protestant missionary movement in the eighteenth century and its rapid expansion during the nineteenth century, at a time when Catholic expansion was stymied by the prolonged institutional paralysis induced by the traumas of the Napoleonic era, roughly coincided with the emergence of a new and more aggressive phase of Western colonialism. Much historiography takes it for granted that the relationship between the two was more than coincidental and was a relatively simple one of cause and effect. More recent work on the nineteenth century suggests that in fact the relationship between the missionary movement and European colonialism was considerably more complex and indeed often conflicted in nature.[10] What the twentieth-century history of Christianity indicates is a growing independence of the churches in the non-Western world from their European or North American missionary origins and hence a progressive distancing of Christianity from its apparent original status as the religion of the white colonizers. By the close of the century Europe had reverted to what it had been in the first century of the Christian era—a continent that sat uneasily at the margins of Christian demography and identity, even though Europeans or those of European ancestry still retained their centuries-old hold on the production of the majority of written Christian theology. The twentieth century may not have been the Christian century that missionary strategists hoped for in 1900, but it was indeed the century in which Christianity became more truly a world religion than ever before.

CHAPTER ONE

Wars and Rumors of Wars

THE RESPONSE OF BRITISH AND AMERICAN
CHURCHES TO THE FIRST WORLD WAR

I. The Global Religious Legacy of the First World War

The First World War—or the Great War, as it was most often called until 1939—continues to dominate historical memory of the twentieth century. For some historians, the significance of the war is so momentous that the nineteenth century is granted special dispensation from the normal mathematics of time, enabling it to become "the long nineteenth century," miraculously elongated over the whole period from the French Revolution of 1789 to 1914. The outbreak of war on August 4, 1914, is thus invested with the status of the "real" beginning of the twentieth century, or even of that indefinable entity, "the modern world." Such interpretations have a long ancestry. In 1917 the Scottish Congregational theologian P. T. Forsyth (1848-1921)—the most creative theological thinker in the British Free Churches—observed that the war had revealed to humanity what it had chosen to overlook, namely the terrible reality of evil in human nature. "This discovery," he reflected, "means the real end of the Victorian age, of the comfortable, kindly, bourgeois, casual Victorian age, so credulous in its humanism."[1] Two years later, Archibald T. Robertson, a professor at the Southern Baptist Theological Seminary in Louisville, Kentucky, wrote that "The old world passed away when Belgium took her stand in front of the Kaiser's hosts. Modern history began on that date."[2]

In reality, history does not proceed according to such neat punctuation, but what is beyond dispute is the enduring imprint of the First World War on popular consciousness. In Britain, France, and Belgium, as in the

United States and some Commonwealth nations, the forms of remembrance of the wartime dead that were developed in 1918–19, and in many cases the actual date of the Armistice of November 11, 1918, continue to this day to provide the template for all national commemorations of war and its myriad victims. This war changed everything, or so it seemed in retrospect to many who survived it. Whether, as an older generation of historiography implied, the First World War can in fact be identified as the tragic watershed separating the Victorian age of faith from the increasingly secular Western world of the twentieth century is much more doubtful. This chapter suggests that the consequences of the war for patterns of Christian belief and the life of the churches were indeed great, but that they stimulated, not an immediate loss of faith, but rather the emergence and increasingly distinct self-definition of some of the most characteristic themes and divergent styles of Christianity in the modern world.

Much of the scholarship on the impact of the First World War on the churches concentrates on Britain, France, and Germany, just as the bulk of the massive literature on the war itself is preoccupied with the Western Front, to the comparative neglect of other theaters of war. The ambiguous legacy of the war to religion in Britain is indeed the subject of the second section of this chapter. But too narrow a focus must be resisted. The Protestant character of the new world order of 1919, implemented by the Presbyterian Woodrow Wilson, has tended to divert attention from the important consequences of the war for the Catholic Church. In France, Italy, and Germany, participation in the armed forces transformed the position of Catholics in society and politics, removing the stigma of antipatriotism that the Catholic communities in these countries had borne for decades. Despite the fact that Pope Benedict XV steadfastly maintained the neutrality of the papacy throughout the war, the mobilization of both Catholic clergy and lay organizations in the Italian war effort brought church and nation into a harmonious relationship for the first time since Italian unification. The moral reputation of the Church also benefited from the massive involvement of the Vatican in relief work throughout Europe, which saw more than 82 million *lire* spent on ministries to civilians and prisoners of war, bringing the papacy to the brink of bankruptcy in the process. Yet the war also unleashed the serious political and social disorder that would provoke the rise of Fascism in Italy, a trend that under Benedict's successor from 1922, Pius XI, would ultimately prove damaging to the moral stature of the papacy.[3]

On a wider canvas, the war was indeed a global cataclysm, a clash of world empires, which affected all continents to a greater or lesser extent.

Thus Australia experienced proportionately much higher casualty rates than did Britain (whose losses were also much lower than those suffered by the French, German, and Serbian armies).[4] Of all Australians who embarked for the war in Europe—and they were all volunteers—68.5 percent were either killed or wounded, compared with only 52.5 percent of all British forces. The dreadful casualties suffered by the Australian and New Zealand Army Corps (ANZAC) following the landing on Turkey's Gallipoli peninsula on April 25, 1915, gave rise a year later to the institution of Anzac Day. In Australia especially this became the focus of a variety of civil religion, enabling an increasingly unchurched population to discover sacred meaning in the annual commemoration of their war dead.[5] More than 2 million Africans served in the war, either as soldiers or porters; more than 200,000 of them died, some in action and many more from epidemic disease; almost all traveled long distances from home, in the process encountering different African peoples, varied expressions of religion, and enticing ideas of independence from the white man's rule.[6] India recruited more than 1.5 million men for the British imperial cause, more than 1 million of whom served overseas.[7]

As historians begin to explore the reasons for the takeoff of Christianity in Africa and parts of Asia in the years after 1918, they may yet discover that the implications of the conflict for the destiny of Christianity in the non-Western world were as substantial as they were for the course of church life in Western Europe. Five main implications of the war for Christianity on a world stage may be identified.

First, the war came close to destroying the spirit of Protestant internationalism that had been so powerfully symbolized and fostered by the World Missionary Conference held at Edinburgh in June 1910. As Allied forces moved swiftly to take control of German colonial possessions in Africa and the Pacific, German mission leaders confidently expected that their missions would be regarded as part of the transnational Protestant missionary enterprise, and would be permitted to carry on their work uninterrupted. These expectations were soon dashed. German missionaries, operating in the former German colonies, and in British possessions such as India, were interned or expelled. Karl Axenfeld, director of the Berlin Missionary Society, voiced the outrage felt among German mission leaders by penning at the end of August 1914 an appeal "To Evangelical [i.e., Protestant] Christians Abroad." This manifesto, signed by twenty-nine German mission leaders and theologians, deplored the abandonment of the principle of the supranationality of missions, and defended Germany's decision to go to war to thwart the "Asiatic barbarism" of Russian aggression.[8]

The reply from forty-two British church leaders, led by Archbishop Randall Davidson of Canterbury, gave no quarter in its insistence that the responsibility for the war lay with Germany, and that the British churches stood for the principles of "international good faith" that Germany had violated through its invasion of Belgium.[9] The chairman of the Edinburgh conference, the American Methodist John R. Mott, tried to mediate between these diametrically opposed standpoints. Mott's sympathies, however, were clearly with the British, and, once the United States entered the war in April 1917, his mediation collapsed. A profound alienation ensued between Anglo-American and German Protestantism that lasted throughout the 1920s, and that helps to explain the indecent enthusiasm with which some elements of the German Evangelical Church greeted the establishment of the Third Reich in 1933 as a fulfillment of the same ideals of the *Volk* as German missions had pursued in Africa and Asia.[10] More broadly, the First World War set Protestant—and even Catholic—missions in a more nationalistic mold than had been true in the past.[11] Paradoxically, Woodrow Wilson's League of Nations served not to limit nationalism but rather to disseminate the ideal of national self-determination in Asia and Africa. As chapters 2 and 8 will show, it was an ideal taken up in 1919 by Christian nationalists in such contrasting locations as Korea and Egypt.

The second legacy of the war to some extent moderated the impact of the first. Although the Treaty of Versailles expanded the world's two largest colonial empires—the British and the French—to their largest geographical extent ever, the role of humanitarianism in those empires (especially the British) became more pronounced after 1918. Under mandates from the newly established League of Nations, former German colonies in Africa and the Pacific passed into the hands of France, Britain, Australia, New Zealand, and Japan; about 1 million square miles of African or Pacific territory were thereby added to the British Empire alone.[12] Further mandates entrusted France and Britain with vast tracts of the former Ottoman Empire—in the British case, Mesopotamia (Iraq), Transjordan, and Palestine. As the next section emphasizes, British involvement in Palestine, in the wake of the Balfour Declaration of November 2, 1917, and the fall of Jerusalem to General Allenby's army on December 9, 1917, had great symbolic significance for many evangelical Protestants. The fact that this enormous increase in British colonial territory came as a trust bestowed by international authority subtly redefined the moral tone of the providentialism that had become so marked a feature of British Protestant attitudes to empire during the nineteenth century. The balance of justification of empire began to shift from the classic Victorian evangelical position that it was a divinely appointed means to the end of evangelization toward a more diffuse civilizing rhetoric shared by Anglicans and Nonconformists alike. British Christian thinkers in the 1920s portrayed their nation's empire as uniquely committed to disseminating the distinctively British values of liberty and progress toward democracy; Protestantism was still an integral part of the mix, but it was now often presented in a broader unsectarian perspective as the embodiment of British "character."[13] J. H. Oldham (1874–1969), secretary of the International Missionary Council established in 1921, and the most influential British spokesman for this view, argued in his *Christianity and the Race Problem* (1924) that the most cogent justification for the rule of "more advanced" peoples over what he termed "weaker" ones was that the former should promote the "care and advancement" of the latter in a spirit of genuine trusteeship.[14] To a postcolonial generation, Oldham's words may appear odious, but his record of fearless agitation on such issues as forced labor in Kenya suggests that his humanitarianism was authentic.[15]

More broadly, Woodrow Wilson's insistence in 1918 that the forthcoming territorial settlements must be "in the interests and for the benefit of the population concerned, and not as part of any mere adjustment or compromise of claims against rival states,"[16] reinforced the willingness of both Protestant and Catholic missionary spokesmen to hold imperial governments to their professions of beneficence toward their subject populations. Benedict XV in his apostolic letter, *Maximum Illud*, issued on November 30, 1919, expressed the hope that the Catholic missions would soon recover from the "severe wounds and losses" inflicted by the war, but also uttered grave warnings against any missionary devoting himself to "attempts to increase and exalt the prestige of the native land he once left behind him" rather than to the spread of the kingdom of God.[17] Though increasingly dependent on colonial government subsidies, both Catholic and Protestant missions invested heavily in education and medicine after 1918; in tropical Africa and the Pacific Islands, they supplied almost the entirety of the educational provision until 1945. In parts of Africa, such as northern Nigeria, such investment in the social gospel of education paradoxically may have helped to reap the substantial evangelistic harvest of church growth that marked the African mission field in the interwar period and beyond,[18] but it was also an attempt by the churches to discharge the debt of colonial welfare imposed by the Versailles settlement. The war also enabled some African church leaders and their congregations to flourish in the absence of missionary supervision, even though the missions were quick to resume the reins of control once the war had ended.[19]

Trusteeship implied a duty to disseminate the imagined benefits of Christian civilization. Yet, a third consequence of the war was the gradual erosion of credibility of the European ideal of "Christian civilization," and consequent softening of the antithesis between "Christian West" and "Non-Christian East." J. H. Oldham, when writing his editorial survey of the year 1914 for the *International Review of Missions*, resorted to the geological analogy of "some gigantic prehistoric catastrophe," twisting and breaking the rock strata, in order to convey the magnitude of the "tremendous upheaval of the war," which had opened up "a huge fault" in the apparent unity of the Christian West expressed at Edinburgh.[20] The war questioned the assumption, so foundational to the Edinburgh conference in 1910, that Christian mission could be understood as a movement from the Christian nations of the West to the non-Christian nations of the East. There is little evidence to support the case that the war produced a short-term fall in religious observance in Europe; if anything, the reverse is true. Nevertheless, the war appeared to weaken the claims of Europe to be the ideal embodiment of Christian civilization, while at the same time its imperial outcomes encouraged the growth of Christianity outside Europe.

Fourth, the war led some theological interpreters to question the more facile expressions of Christian liberalism and social optimism to which sections of the Protestant churches had succumbed since the dawn of the twentieth century. The best-known example of such a reaction is the young Swiss Reformed pastor Karl Barth (1886–1968), who responded with disgust to the uncritical endorsement of German war aims by his former theological teachers at the universities of Berlin, Tübingen, and Marburg. Under the impact of the war, Barth began to move away from his commitment to German social democracy, with its often naïve confidence in human capacity to build the kingdom of God.[21] In July 1916, when still a village pastor in Safenwil in the Aargau, he began writing his commentary on Paul's epistle to the Romans, which gradually led Barth to the conclusion that "The oracles of God are fraught with a significance wholly independent of the course of human history."[22] Without the war, it is hard to imagine Barth arriving at the position so uncompromisingly expounded in the second (1921) edition of his *Romans*, namely that God in his sovereign and incomprehensible grace stood apart from all human striving to construct a better social order.[23] The growth of neo-orthodox theology in continental Europe over the next two decades was undoubtedly related to the war's exposure of the moral bankruptcy of German Protestant liberalism. The year 1933 saw both the appearance in English translation of Barth's *Romans* and the publication of the first major English-language study of Barth's theology, John McConnachie's *The*

Barthian Theology and the Man of Today. From then on, Barth's theology began to take deep root in the Reformed soil of Scotland, most notably at New College, Edinburgh. It reached the height of its influence in the early 1950s. In the United States, and still more in England, Barthian theology took longer to establish a foothold, and the theological legacy of the war is harder to evaluate.[24] Moreover, on both sides of the Atlantic, many Protestant leaders remained quite unshaken in their commitment to the liberal ideals of Christian reasonableness and ecumenical cooperation, and in their determination that the churches together must ensure that the war would prove to be the last great blood-letting of Christendom, purging the family of nations of the evils of national antagonism. Such expectations were prevalent in the League of Nations and its Christian ecumenical counterpart, the Life and Work movement. The movement, which aimed to develop a common Christian approach to securing international peace and justice, held its inaugural conference in Stockholm in 1925 on the initiative of the Lutheran archbishop of Uppsala, Nathan Söderblom. The French Protestant pastor and leader of "Christianisme Social," Elie Gounelle, even referred at Stockholm to the League of Nations as "a milestone on the road to the Kingdom of God."[25]

Such Christian confidence about the redemptive potential of international cooperation was not universal. A fifth spiritual consequence of the war was the stimulus it imparted to forms of religion that emphasized the suprarational, and hence the limits of rational human capacity to change the world. The resurgence of spiritualism among the home population in Britain during the war in response to the shock of mass sudden bereavement, and its continuing and growing popularity throughout the 1920s and 1930s, has been fully documented by historians.[26] Less notice has been taken of the fillip the war provided to both Catholic and Protestant traditions that wished to reassert the essentially miraculous nature of Christian faith. Barth's exposition of Romans asserted: "He who says 'God', says 'miracle'."[27] The next two sections of the chapter devote particular attention to those Christians in Britain and the United States who interpreted the war as a warning to return to the "fundamentals" of divine revelation and rediscover a pristine version of Christianity that would resist the corrosive acids of modern thought and German liberalism.

II. The British Churches: The Religious Legacy of the First World War

One of the classic historical analyses of working-class church attendance in Britain, E. R. Wickham's *Church and People in an Industrial City* (1957), concluded from his study of Sheffield that the First World War had a "catastrophic" effect on the churches, with the result that in the inter-war period "religion and the churches simply dropped out of the public interest."[28] More recent scholarship has tended to conclude precisely the opposite, namely that the war was a sustainer, rather than a destroyer of religious belief, although this belief often failed to conform to Christian orthodoxy. Evidence from the trenches suggests that large numbers of troops enjoyed lusty hymn singing, were eager to take Holy Communion before "going over the top," and were regularly found praying in the face of death. Catholics valued possession of rosaries, crucifixes, or sacred medallions, while those from a Protestant background treasured Bibles or New Testaments, even if some regarded them more as talismans that would stop the bullets than as sources of scriptural wisdom.[29]

The *Army and Religion* report of 1919, compiled by the Scottish Presbyterian theologian David S. Cairns, on the basis of extensive questionnaire evidence, reported that the typical British soldier believed in God, respected the human person of Christ, and supposed that the point of the crucifixion was as an object lesson in the moral power of self-sacrifice. He had little understanding of Christian doctrine and no patience with the divisions between the denominations. The idea of salvation by death in battle for one's country was very common among the troops, and struck Cairns as "one of those points in which the religion of the trenches has rather a Moslem than a Christian colour."[30] One would not expect such unorthodox and nondogmatic religiosity—whether it can be called "Christianity" is debatable—to issue in any commitment to active church attendance once the war was over. Yet the membership of all the major Free Churches, the figures for Anglican Easter communicants, and the figures for "active" (defined as at least once a year) communicants in the Church of Scotland, all showed significant increases during the 1920s, each series peaking at some point between the middle of the decade and 1932. Thereafter the Nonconformist figures declined slowly; the communicant rates for both the Church of England and Church of Scotland also fell gradually, and indeed partially recovered in the 1950s.[31]

The First World War thus supplied plentiful evidence of the indifference of most working men to the churches as institutions. It also deprived the churches of the presence of many of the educated and professional men who made up the ranks both of their lay leadership and of the officer class, who suffered disproportionately high casualties: almost one in five of Oxford and Cambridge graduates who served in the war lost their lives.[32] It thus seems reasonable to conclude that the moderate revival in church attendance during the 1920s was largely a female phenomenon.[33] There is no doubt that the war threw British churches to an unprecedented extent on to the resources of female energy and leadership, and thus pointedly raised the question of the substantial exclusion of women from church government and the Christian ministry. Stuart Mews has rightly asserted that "The greatest single social innovation of the war was the change in the role of women."[34] It was no accident that the war years saw the first ordination of a woman within one of the Free Churches, Constance Todd, as assistant minister of King's Weigh House Congregational Church, London, in September 1917—and the first, albeit uncoordinated, demands for the admission of women to the Anglican ministry, led by the remarkable Maude Royden, who found an outlet for her call to preach by venturing outside the Church of England to serve as assistant at the City Temple, a Congregational church.

The Church of England had a long road to travel before it would be open to such demands. During the National Mission of Repentance and Hope in 1916, the leader of the Mission, Bishop Winnington-Ingram of London, initially permitted women to address mission services held in churches, provided they did not do so from the pulpit, lectern, or even the steps of the sanctuary, but the chorus of protest from Anglo-Catholic clergy was so loud that he had to back down and limit women's permission to speak to the church hall or schoolroom.[35] Nevertheless, the greatly increased dependence of the Church of England during the war on the service of women, and the admission of women (over the age of twenty-one) to the House of Commons by the Parliament (Qualification of Women) Act of 1918, made it impossible to deny them any longer a voice in the church's developing structures of self-government. In October 1918 the Committee of the Representative Church Council recommended that women be allowed to sit on parochial church councils and ruridecanal and diocesan conferences, and in December 1919 the Enabling Act enabled them to serve as representatives in the House of Laity of the new Church Assembly, ancestor of the current General Synod.[36]

The impact of the war on theology and spirituality in Britain was ambiguous. On the one hand, it strengthened the appeal to intellectuals of liberal Anglican theories of church and state that idealized the role of the Church of England as the embodiment of "national religion" and a spiritual focus for the common purpose of an embattled nation. In the years after the war moderate Anglo-Catholics or liberal Anglicans who held to this view increasingly dominated the episcopal bench and other high offices of the church.[37] Some ecumenically minded Free Churchmen, such as J. H. Shakespeare, Secretary of the Baptist Union from 1898 to 1924, espoused their own versions of this theory. In *The Churches at the*

Cross-Roads (1918) Shakespeare tried, without success, to persuade his denomination of the advantages of joining a "truly Catholic" national Protestant church founded on a functional approach to episcopacy.[38]

On the other hand, some British theologians were quick to point out the inadequacy of liberal optimism to meet the ethical challenges of the war. One such, as we have seen, was P. T. Forsyth, who in *The Justification of God*: *Lectures for War-Time on a Christian Theodicy* (1916), criticized his own Free Church tradition for having reduced the doctrine of the love of God to a thin sentimental notion that left no room for the necessity of the cross of Christ.[39] Another was the Anglo-Catholic historian and Mirfield monk, Father J. Neville Figgis (1866–1919), who prophesied that the war would bury once and for all what he dismissed as "conventional religion": the young men who survived the war would never again wish to "slake their souls' thirst with the tepid weak tea of choristers' Anglicanism."[40] But Forsyth had slipped his original moorings in theological liberalism well before the outbreak of the war, and Figgis, similarly, had levelled trenchant criticism at "the boneless Christ of the German liberals" as early as 1913.[41] In its place, Figgis and his associates espoused an idealistic and distinctively sacramental version of Christian socialism. This first gained high visibility in the Church of England with the Conference on Christian Politics, Economics and Citizenship (COPEC) held at Birmingham in 1924 under the chairmanship of William Temple, then bishop of Manchester. The war had sharpened the old question of exactly what it meant to be a Christian nation, and men such as Figgis and Temple supplied an answer that married incarnational theology with a moderately socialist form of "Christian sociology."

Forsyth and Figgis both pointed in their contrasting ways to the sense of many in the nation that the exceptional crisis of the war called for a style of Christian faith that was not afraid to speak of spiritual power in contestation with evil, and not merely of vague Christian moral ideals. The horrors of the trenches blurred the conventional boundaries between the visible and the invisible, the human and the inhuman, and above all between life and death. Those who survived were those who had returned to life from the realm of death, but who had become like machines or animals in order to do so.[42] The devil and hell—topics that had disappeared from theological discourse in large sections of the churches—returned to the text of countless sermons before the end of 1915. "We have found out Germany," pronounced Forsyth in 1917. "And we have rediscovered Satan."[43] Among the troops and at home stories began to circulate of miraculous angelic interventions on behalf of the British forces. The most famous of these—the claim that during the battle of Mons in August 1914 a host of angels appeared in the sky in support of the British army—had fictional origins in an article written for the London *Evening News*, but this did not prevent some influential Christian leaders from endorsing the claim. Alexander Boddy, vicar of All Saints', Monkwearmouth in Sunderland, who was one of the leading supporters of the early Pentecostal movement in Britain, published a tract that represented the story as historical fact.[44] The evangelical bishop of Durham, Handley Moule, also accepted the historicity of the angels of Mons, to the intense disgust of his liberal dean, Hensley Henson. When in a sermon preached in Westminster Abbey in July 1915, Henson poured cold water on the legend, he received an indignant letter from a churchwoman complaining at his "CRUELTY" toward "our dear lads" who needed all the supernatural help they could get. For Henson, the episode symbolized the lamentable drift of rational English religion during his lifetime toward either Catholic or Protestant forms of supernaturalism:

> The sentiments expressed in this anonymous lady's letter were widely distributed, and were nowhere more general than among the clergy, as well Anglican as Nonconformist. Popular Protestantism is largely "fundamentalist", and it was apparent that the crudest angelogy could find scriptural authority. All the latent fanaticisms began to emerge into a valorous publicity. "British Israelites", Adventists, Spiritualists, even Necromancers, flourished exceedingly. Among the "Anglo-Catholics" the debased sacramentalism of the Latin Church made rapid progress; and for apparent reasons, there was a ready welcome for speculations about the life after death.[45]

Henson's tone was sneering, but his perception of the popular spiritual mood was accurate enough. What he termed "the debased sacramentalism of the Latin Church"—what scholars now call "Western Catholicism"—made great strides over the next decade. The reservation of the consecrated sacrament, which the canons had recently permitted only for the purpose of taking to the house-bound sick, became so widespread as an Anglo-Catholic devotional practice in the diocese of London during the war that Bishop Winnington-Ingram eventually abandoned the attempt to regulate it on the grounds that "the tide of human grief and anxiety had been too great, the longing to get as near as possible to the Sacramental Presence of our Lord had been too urgent."[46] By 1928 26.2 percent of all parishes in the diocese were observing perpetual reservation, which to Protestant minds made the consecrated elements an object of idolatry.[47]

Another Catholic practice, the saying of prayers for the dead, which had formed no part of Anglican liturgy since the Reformation, became popular during the war even among moderate Anglo-Catholics and some Evangelicals. The Evangelical bishop Llewellyn Gwynne of Khartoum, deputy chaplain-general on the Western Front from the summer of 1915, became well known for his endorsement and use of prayers for the dead. Confronted with such widespread support for the practice, the archbishops of Canterbury and York approved an authorized Form of Prayer for the Departed in 1917, despite vigorous protests from the Evangelical bishops Chavasse of Liverpool and Knox of Manchester.[48]

The growing popularity of extreme Catholic devotional practices necessitated the ultimately abortive attempts of the Anglican authorities to revise the Book of Common Prayer in order to draw the boundaries of legality between moderate and extreme Catholic liturgical practice.[49] The double failure of the revised Book to secure a majority in the House of Commons in December 1927 and June 1928 is largely attributable to the success of Evangelical Anglicans in convincing Free Church, Scottish and Irish Presbyterian MPs that the Protestant status of the established church—and hence of the nation itself—stood in peril.[50] Such fears were stoked by the burgeoning popularity of Catholic doctrine and devotion within the Church of England at that time. The 1920s and 1930s were the heyday of Anglo-Catholicism, as shown by the remarkable attendances recorded by the series of Anglo-Catholic Congresses, of which the first was held in London in June 1920. Numbers of attenders rose steadily. In 1920 some 16,000 tickets were sold. The second conference in 1923 had an estimated 15,000 attenders; the third in 1927 recorded 23,000, and the fourth in 1930 28,873. The final Congress in 1933, celebrating the centenary of the Oxford Movement, culminated in a High Mass at London's White City stadium, which drew an estimated 45–50,000 worshippers.[51] In 1920, the queue of people waiting to get into Southwark Cathedral for the thanksgiving service on the Friday evening of the Congress snaked right across London Bridge to the Monument. One Anglo-Catholic devotee observed: "It is the first time, surely, at any rate since the Reformation, that London Bridge heard a great crowd singing to the honour of the Mother of our Lord, as the waiting multitude sang again and again, 'Hail Mary, Hail Mary, Hail Mary, full of grace.'"[52]

While the war clearly contributed to the ascendancy of Anglo-Catholicism in the interwar Church of England, it cannot of itself explain it. The addresses at the 1920 Congress made virtually no direct reference to the war, although the topics included "The Faithful Departed. With a

Short Note on Spiritualism as Seen in the Light of Catholic Philosophy," and "Saints and Angels."[53] The congresses grew more, not less, popular as the memory of the war receded. Why did Anglo-Catholicism appeal so strongly to the interwar generation? The answer may perhaps lie in its unashamed contradiction of a barren and rationalistic modernism, its romantic and sensuous evocation of an imagined medieval Christendom, and its reassurance to a grieving and anxious generation that the grace of God was so close at hand and so certain that it could be physically encountered and received in the Eucharist.

Hensley Henson in his *Retrospect of an Unimportant Life* saw the spread of "fanaticisms" in response to the war as a trend that was observable, not simply in Anglo-Catholicism, but also in evangelical Protestantism, where it took the form of Adventism, and, in its most extreme manifestation, British Israelism. For significant numbers of evangelical Protestants throughout the English-speaking world, the true center of attention in the global convulsion of the war was not the trench warfare of the Western Front, but the conflict in the Middle East, and Jerusalem in particular.[54]

Evangelical preoccupation with prophetic speculation was most quaintly illustrated through the British Israelite movement, which claimed that the Anglo-Saxon and Celtic peoples were the direct descendants of the ten lost tribes of Israel as recorded in the Old Testament. Britain and its empire—of which the United States was sometimes granted honorary membership for prophetic purposes—had been uniquely chosen by God to fulfill his saving purposes for the world. The genesis of British Israel ideas is usually traced to publications by John Wilson (1840) and Edward Hine (1869),[55] but the movement took on a new institutional lease of life in 1919, when the British–Israel–World Federation (which still exists) was formed. It held its first Congress in July 1920, which was attended by the Princess Alice, Countess of Athlone (a granddaughter of Queen Victoria), who remained a patron of the Federation until her death in 1981.[56] Another distinguished patron was W. F. Massey, prime minister of New Zealand from 1912 to 1924. An Ulster-born Presbyterian and fervent imperial enthusiast, Massey was a skeptical observer at the Versailles Conference of Woodrow Wilson's plans for international cooperation through the League of Nations.[57] British Israelism later became the preserve of a few eccentrics on the far Christian right, but in the interwar years it commanded sufficient numbers to hold its meetings in the Central Hall, Westminster.[58] Leading British Israelites during the 1920s included a number of prominent evangelicals, such as James Mountain of Tunbridge Wells, founder of the Baptist Bible Union, Dinsdale Young, a popular Methodist preacher, and George Jeffreys, architect of the Elim Pentecostal Alliance.[59] The movement drew considerable support from members of the Elim Church and from conservative Baptists: inspection of the personal libraries of deceased Baptist ministers trained at Spurgeon's College during the 1920s and 1930s revealed a surprising number of books of a British Israelite flavor.[60]

Although not insubstantial, British Israelism remained a minority pursuit even among the most conservative of evangelicals. Of wider prevalence within evangelicalism was what Henson termed "Adventism"—the belief that the Bible taught the visible return of Christ to the earth to establish his millennial reign, and that such an event could be expected in the near future. According to this "premillennial" scheme of prophecy, the biblical books of Ezekiel, Daniel, and Revelation spoke of a revival in the last days of the Roman Empire ("Babylon") under the godless rule of the Antichrist, the return of the Jews to their biblical homeland, and a final battle at Armageddon, north of Jerusalem, between a confederacy of the kings of the North and the forces of Antichrist. These momentous developments would usher in the return of Christ and the establishment of his millennial kingdom on earth. In November 1914 the declaration of war by the Ottoman Empire on the northern powers of Britain, France, and Russia accordingly struck prophetic enthusiasts both in Britain and the United States as being of portentous significance. For other interpreters, the Bolshevik Revolution pointed toward an ominous role for Soviet Russia as the final enemy of Israel. But what heightened the excitement to fever pitch was the Declaration on November 2, 1917 by the British Foreign Secretary, Arthur Balfour, that the British government viewed with favor the establishment in Palestine of a national home for the Jewish people.[61]

Especially since Lord Shaftesbury's promotion of an Anglo-Prussian bishopric of Jerusalem in the 1840s, British evangelicals had displayed a growing interest in the evangelization of the Jews and schemes for their return to the Holy Land.[62] Within days of the issue of the Balfour Declaration the Baptist ministers J. S. Harrison, Alfred Bird, and F. B. Meyer, and the Anglican clergyman E. L. Langston, had begun to plan the formation of an "Advent Testimony and Preparation Movement," "to bring home to the Christian public the significance of this remarkable edict."[63] The Movement was launched on December 13, 1917 at meetings in the Queen's Hall in London. Against the backdrop of the news of the defeat of the Ottomans by General Allenby and his triumphal entry into Jerusalem just two days before, speakers predicted that the formation of a Jewish state in Palestine was imminent.[64] During 1918 similar meetings were held in Philadelphia's Music Hall in May, New York's Carnegie Hall in November, again in London in December, and also in Australia, South Africa, and elsewhere. A common theme at these meetings was the assertion that the sudden demise of the Chinese, Ottoman, Russian, Austro-Hungarian, and German empires; the liberation of the Holy Land from Muslim rule; and, supremely, the prospect of a return of the Jews to Palestine, were all unmistakable signs that the world was entering its last days.[65] One notable recruit to the Adventist cause in Britain was the suffragette Christabel Pankhurst, whose chance reading in 1918 of Henry Grattan Guinness's *The Approaching End of the Age Viewed in the Light of History, Prophecy, and Science* (1879) convinced her that what Guinness had identified as the herald of the end—the restoration of a Jewish national state in Palestine— was about to take place. Without losing her commitment to winning the vote for women, Pankhurst devoted the rest of her life to her death in 1958 to publicizing the Adventist message.[66]

Premillennialists were divided into two camps. Historicists maintained that biblical prophecies relating to the last days should be applied to the entire history of the church. The dominant trend by the early twentieth century, however, was futurism, according to which the prophecies referred exclusively to the events immediately prior to the return of Christ. Many futurists were dispensationalists who followed John Nelson Darby, Irish pioneer of the Christian (Plymouth) Brethren movement, in believing that in response to the Jews' rejection of Jesus as the Messiah, God had suspended his historic plan for his chosen people, Israel, and turned his attention to the Christian church. However, God's purposes for Israel would be reactivated at the close of history, when all Christians would be whisked away to heaven in the "rapture," leaving God to resume his timetable with Israel during the final dispensation of history.[67] What historicists and futurists agreed on was the critical significance of any signs that the land of Israel was to be returned to Jewish hands—hence the widespread evangelical fascination with the events unfolding in Palestine from late 1917.

The Advent Testimony and Preparation Movement was intended to appeal to both historicists and futurists. It recruited 1,103 members by September 1919 (including two bishops), and by April 1922 the figure had risen to 2,222.[68] Thereafter the membership may have declined, but the significance of these eschatological expectations was broader than the relatively small size of the movement might suggest. Evangelicals who read their Bibles alongside their newspapers had no patience with modern biblical critics who denied that the Bible should be used as a magnifying glass to decipher the meaning of present-day events. They—and futurists especially—had little confidence in President Wilson's new world order or in schemes of social improvement. F. S. Webster, prebendary of St. Paul's Cathedral, told the Queen's Hall meeting in December 1917 that the war had shattered the hopes held by many before the conflict for a new era of international peace, social improvement, the substitution of cooperation for competition, and an alliance of capital and labor.[69] In point of fact, the war reinforced the determination of many in the liberal Catholic wing of the Church of England and the less conservative sections of Nonconformity that these very ideals must be energetically pursued and implemented. But the war widened the gulf in the Christian world between social and international idealists on the one hand and conservative eschatological pessimists on the other, and the fissure has proved enduring. Chapter 3 will suggest that in Africa the flowering of prophetic speculation encouraged by the war had profoundly radical implications, motivating prophet movements that challenged the established order in church and state and often spawned African Instituted Churches. In Britain and North America, by contrast, the preoccupation with prophecy led to social and political conservatism. The divergent directions taken by progressive and conservatives in interpreting the implications of the war for the churches set the stage for the acrimonious battles of the 1920s and 1930s between those who were increasingly labelled as "modernists" and "fundamentalists."[70] Although the British churches experienced their fair share of these conflicts,[71] the battles were most extensive and vigorous in the United States, and to these we will now turn.

III. Fighting for the Faith: American Fundamentalism between the Wars

In the United States, as in Britain, prophetic speculation flourished in response to the war. Timothy Weber has written, "No event in the fifty years after 1875 did more for the morale of American premillennialists than World War I."[72] This is despite the late entry of the United States into the war in April 1917, and the geographical remoteness of the theaters of war from American soil. For many American conservative Protestants, like their British counterparts, it appears that what took place in Palestine toward the end of 1917 was worthy of more concentrated spiritual reflection than the mass slaughter in Flanders or Gallipoli. The second edition of Cyrus I. Scofield's annotated reference Bible, published in 1917, popularized the view that the Gog and Magog depicted in Ezekiel 38 making war on Israel must be identified with a now communist Russia.[73] Also prominent in American evangelical minds was the sobering recollection that their enemy in 1917–18 was the same nation that had been largely responsible for unleashing modern biblical criticism on the churches. The evangelist and former professional baseball player Billy Sunday famously pronounced, "If you turn hell upside down, you will find "made in Germany" stamped on the bottom."[74] Such attacks on modern approaches to the Bible stoked the flames of existing theological controversy between liberals and conservatives, with both sides now accusing the other of lack of patriotism as well as intellectual dishonesty. Liberals maintained that premillennialists' preoccupation with the future cut the nerve of social reform and the American commitment to make the world safe for democracy. Conservatives replied by blaming German evolutionary philosophy and destructive biblical criticism for Germany's barbarism in war and its denial of civilized values.[75]

At the prophetic conference held in Philadelphia in May 1918 plans were discussed for a further conference to be held in the following year. However, later that summer two of the leaders of the prophetic movement—the Northern Baptist pastor William Bell Riley and the evangelist Reuben A. Torrey—met at Torrey's summer home in Montrose, Pennsylvania, and agreed that the 1919 conference should focus, not on prophecy as such, but rather on defending the fundamentals of the faith against the false teaching that, according to the New Testament, would proliferate in the last days. The resulting conference, held in Philadelphia from May 25 to June 1, 1919, and attended by 6,000 participants, established the World's Christian Fundamentals Association. In response to "The Great Apostasy," which they saw "spreading like a plague throughout Christendom," speakers urged a return to "the Fundamentals" of Christian doctrine.[76] Their audience knew what the fundamentals were: the inerrancy of the original manuscripts of Scripture; the virgin birth of Christ; his vicarious atonement; his bodily resurrection; and the authenticity of biblical miracles. The list had been drawn up by the General Assembly of the Presbyterian Church (U.S.A.) in 1910 in response to concerns expressed about the orthodoxy of graduates of Union Theological Seminary in New York.[77] Conservatives of all denominations had read the twelve volumes of *The Fundamentals*, a series published between 1910 and 1915 and funded by the California oil magnates Lyman and Milton Stewart. In aggregate 3 million copies of the booklets were distributed at a cost of 200,000 dollars. Not all of the sixty-four authors of *The Fundamentals* would later become associated with "fundamentalism," but all were conservative evangelicals.

The term "fundamentalist" surfaced for the first time on July 1, 1920, in an editorial by Curtis Lee Laws in the Baptist newspaper *The Watchman-Examiner*, which urged his fellow conservatives in the Northern Baptist Convention "to do battle royal for the fundamentals" against the encroachment of liberal views in their denomination.[78] Within two years of the end of the Great War, therefore, fundamentalism as a Christian phenomenon was born, bestowing on religious and political discourse a term that was destined to breach the boundaries of Christianity and ultimately attach itself to militant varieties of Islam.

What liberals now increasingly labeled as "fundamentalism" was in fact a loose coalition of conservative groups with quite divergent sets of priorities. Baptists and Presbyterians predominated. Though not all were premillennialists, apocalyptic and military language was typical of much of the movement. The founders of the World's Christian Fundamentals Association urged believers to wage their own world war, against all the "damnable heresies" that threatened to drag Christendom in the closing years of history into a morass of apostasy.[79] The Moody Bible Institute in Chicago pronounced that it was "preparing for the greatest battle, or rather war, known to ecclesiastical history."[80] The adjective "ecclesiastical" should be noted: the enemy was within the camp, and should be driven out. Those who liked to style themselves as both liberals and evangelicals slept uneasily in their beds. Among them was the Baptist minister Harry Emerson Fosdick, who by special arrangement was associate pastor of First Presbyterian Church, New York City. On May 21, 1922 he preached a sermon entitled "Shall the Fundamentalists Win?" Fosdick attacked conservative positions on the virgin birth of Christ, the substitutionary atonement, the inerrancy of the Bible, and the visible return of Christ, and accused fundamentalists of "bitter intolerance" toward those who disagreed with them on such points.[81] Clarence Macartney, pastor of Arch Street Presbyterian Church in Philadelphia, promptly answered him in a sermon entitled "Shall Unbelief Win?" Macartney alleged that Fosdick had departed from historic Christian orthodoxy, and called on the Presbytery of New York to condemn the teaching contained in Fosdick's sermon and take steps to ensure that First Presbyterian Church conformed to the doctrinal standards of the Westminster Confession of Faith.[82]

The escalating warfare between liberals and conservatives did not affect all mainline Protestant denominations equally. Indeed, it was in large part a question of two independent battles waged among Northern Presbyterians and Baptists.[83] The leading conservative protagonist among Presbyterians was John Gresham Machen (1881–1937). Though an ordained minister of the Northern Presbyterian Church and a professor at its flagship Princeton Theological Seminary, Machen's family roots were in the socially and theologically conservative soil of southern Presbyterianism. In *Christianity and Liberalism* (1923), Machen presented Christian faith as diametrically opposed to liberalism or "modernism." "Modernism" was an originally Catholic term that was taken up by liberal Protestants. In Britain liberal Anglicans had begun to call themselves "modern churchmen" or "modernists" by 1911, when the Churchmen's Union for the Advancement of Liberal Religious Thought (formed in 1898) began publication of *The Modern Churchman*.[84] In the United States in 1924 Shailer Mathews, dean of the University of Chicago's Divinity School—an institution founded by the Northern Baptists—published *The Faith of Modernism*, which championed the application of modern scientific and historic principles to theology and biblical study.[85] Machen's contention was that modernism or liberalism—he saw the two terms as essentially interchangeable—had lost all sense of the absolute otherness of God and the inherent sinfulness of humanity. The Great War, he suggested, was partly to blame, owing to its narrowing of an awareness of sin to the atrocities committed by the other side.[86] Whereas liberalism made its appeal to religious experience, true Christianity was founded on the authority of the Bible as the revealed Word of God. All other facets of Christian doctrine could be derived from that foundational principle. For Machen, the defense of Christian orthodoxy had to be conducted on the center ground of biblical truth. The enemy was not simply modernism in theology, but also the bureaucratic centralization of power in the hands of the modern state: the war, he maintained in a vein that revealed his southern ancestry, had led to a regrettable increase in the power of central government.[87]

In 1924 Machen's colleague at Princeton Theology Seminary, Charles R. Erdman, stood for the moderatorship of the General Assembly of the Presbyterian Church. Erdman's evangelical credentials were impeccable. He was a protégé of D. L. Moody, had contributed an essay to *The Fundamentals*, even called himself a fundamentalist, and was a premillennialist, though not a dispensationalist. He was, however, inclined to limit the doctrine of the inerrancy of the Bible to its testimony to the person and work of Christ. As an enthusiast for the holiness teaching of the Keswick conventions, he also emphasized the unity in Christ of all those who had a living experience of the Holy Spirit. As such, Erdman attracted support in the Assembly elections from both moderates and modernists. In the 1924 election he lost narrowly to the conservative candidate, Clarence Macartney, but in 1925 he was nominated again, and this time he won, despite a concerted campaign orchestrated by Machen branding Erdman as the candidate of "the Modernist and indifferentist party in the church."[88] In reality Erdman had the support of many orthodox evangelicals, such as Robert E. Speer, secretary of the Church's Board of Foreign Missions. Both Erdman and Speer had attended the World Missionary Conference in Edinburgh in 1910. Though of conservative inclination themselves, they shared the conviction that the purity of Presbyterian doctrine must ultimately take second place to the cause of saving the world; in their view, the Great War was an urgent summons to the churches to come together in preaching the gospel to all humanity.[89] For Machen, on the other hand, there could be no higher cause than the preservation of doctrinal purity; without that, there would ultimately be no Christian civilization.

From 1925 the gulf within the Presbyterian Church (U.S.A.) between Machen's conservatives on the one hand and moderates and modernists on the other progressively widened. The faculty at Princeton Seminary itself became dangerously divided. In 1927 the General Assembly instigated a reorganization of the seminary designed to weaken the influence of the conservatives. In 1929 Machen and three other faculty colleagues seceded from Princeton to establish their own rival seminary, Westminster Theological Seminary in Philadelphia. In 1933 Machen took the next step by organizing an Independent Board for Presbyterian Foreign Missions committed to sending out only conservative candidates. The 1934 General Assembly declared this Board to be unconstitutional, and a year later suspended Machen from its ministry. In June 1936 Machen announced the formation of a new denomination, the Presbyterian Church of America. Some other major American churches experienced similar secessions. The Northern Baptist Convention suffered splits in 1932–3 and 1947 that led to the formation, respectively, of the General Association of Regular Baptist Churches and the Conservative Baptist Association of America. Fundamentalists had set out to drive liberals from the camp, but often found that the only option open to them was to pitch their tents elsewhere. By the 1950s, American Protestantism was divided by a fault line between the "mainline" denominations and exclusively conservative or fundamentalist churches that has endured to this day. Although many evangelicals remained in mainline churches, their position became harder to sustain after the 1930s. The adjectives "liberal" and "evangelical" that men such as Fosdick and Mathews had attempted to combine were now viewed as mutually exclusive.

One important dimension of the fundamentalist movement has so far been neglected. The crusade mounted by some fundamentalists, mainly in the southern states, against the teaching of evolution in American public schools in the 1920s first imprinted on public consciousness the now widely accepted but historically inaccurate paradigm of an inevitable war between science and religion.[90] Between 1921 and 1929 thirty-seven anti-evolution resolutions were introduced in the legislatures of twenty states and the District of Columbia, and in seven states they were, for a time, successful.[91] Conservative Christian opposition to Darwin's theory of natural selection was nothing new, but many evangelical theologians had hitherto adopted a variety of means to reduce the apparent dissonance between theories of evolution and a biblical account of human origins.[92] After the war, such reconciliations became more difficult to effect, especially in parts of the country where the predominant evangelical culture was of a dispensationalist kind. A middle ground occupied by Christian evolutionists and moderate nonfundamentalist creationists did survive, even in a predominantly conservative denomination such as the Southern Baptists.[93] A synthesis between Christianity and evolution depended on belief in the providential activity of God within the natural world, moving it forward by organic process toward higher forms. Machen was one conservative who continued to hold a variant of this view despite the war. But the war had set the tide flowing in the militants' favor. The dispensationalist case that neither natural nor human history exhibited a seamless narrative of progress seemed more plausible after 1914. Dispensationalists saw little difference between the modernist creed of progress and crude Darwinian theories of the survival of the fittest. The Baptist John Roach Straton could thus insist in a series of broadcast debates with the Unitarian minister Charles Francis Potter in New York's Carnegie Hall in 1924 that there was "no such thing as so-called 'theistic' or 'Christian' evolution. Such terms are misnomers."[94]

The war supplied fresh ammunition for the conservative onslaught on evolutionism. In an address given in 1923 T. T. Martin, a leading Southern Baptist crusader against evolution, accused Germany of having gone "wild" over the pagan creed of evolution, yet claimed that "the Germans who poisoned the wells of Belgium and Northern France" during the war were "angels" compared to the textbook writers and publishers who were poisoning the minds of American children with evolutionary teaching.[95] The Presbyterian Democrat politician William Jennings Bryan became convinced by his reading in 1917–18 of Vernon Kellogg's *Headquarters Nights* (1917) and Benjamin Kidd's *The Science of Power* (1918) that German intellectuals had swallowed a sinister nationalist form of social Darwinism based on Friedrich Nietzsche's figure of the Superman and the creed of might is right. This message—which was not without evidence—Bryan rehearsed endlessly until his death in 1925, and in so doing became the best-known fundamentalist in the nation.[96] In contrast to Machen's conservative libertarianism, Bryan was a social reformer and Progressive who lent strong support to the campaign for women's suffrage that culminated in women gaining the right to vote for Congress in 1920. His example, like that of Christabel Pankhurst, suggests that fundamentalism was not at first invariably linked to opposition to "progress"; Bryan claimed that Darwinian evolution posed the greatest threat to democracy and civilized values.[97]

For Straton, Martin, Bryan, and their supporters, the campaign to prevent the teaching of evolution in public schools was not a battle between "science" and "religion," but a contest for the religious identity of the nation. Fundamentalists were wedded to a Baconian and empiricist understanding of knowledge: for them, the Bible was a storehouse of revealed facts about the world and God's relationship to it. In contrast, evolution, as Bryan claimed, was a mere theory, "guesses strung together" rather than observable fact. Hence evolution was not science at all, but rather a nihilist form of "religion" masquerading as science.[98] According to this ingenious argument, it was those who taught the atheistic propaganda of evolution in public schools who should be indicted for transgressing the constitutional prohibition on imparting religious instruction in state schools. Thus Bryan could ask a Pennsylvania audience in 1925: "Can a handful of scientists rob your children of religion and turn them out atheists?"[99] As a prosecution witness at the celebrated Scopes trial in Dayton, Tennessee, in the spring of 1925, Bryan's claim to be more scientific than the evolutionists was mercilessly exposed as a hollow one. Although the biology teacher John T. Scopes was convicted of teaching evolution in contravention of the statute recently passed by the state, the trial left an enduring impression in the public mind that fundamentalism was an anti-intellectual and reactionary movement. It would take conservative Protestantism a very long time to shake off that reputation.

IV. Divergent Christian Responses

The temptation for the historian of Christianity in the interwar years is to attribute all the dominant trends of this period to the impact of the war. In fact the war reinforced existing religious trends more than it initiated new ones. In Britain figures for church membership and attendance were in decline well in advance of 1914, and even recovered during the decade after the war. Conservative Christian responses to modern ideologies were gathering strength in both Catholic and Protestant circles in both Britain and the United States before 1914. Conversely, many Christians of more liberal temper on both sides of the Atlantic did not allow the war to dislodge their existing confidence in the possibility of a synthesis between faith and modern scientific knowledge, or (in Protestantism) in the necessity of closer ecumenical cooperation in the work of bringing the kingdom of God to fulfillment. Nevertheless, as this chapter has sought to demonstrate, the war was of far-reaching significance for the subsequent course of Christianity. The unprecedented scale and intensity of the global conflict brought the theological and strategic choices confronting Christians into starker relief. For many it reinforced the necessity of constructing a world order founded on liberal Christian principles of tolerance, love, and mutual commitment. On an international stage this response also involved commitment to a humanitarian view of empire, in which imperial governments must be held to account for their treatment of subject peoples. At national level it implied the importance of bringing the churches into closer relationship so that they could present a united Christian voice to government and society. In Britain liberal Catholics, "modern Churchmen," liberal Evangelicals, and significant numbers of Nonconformists all tended to favor such an approach. The gap between the Church of England and political Nonconformity thus narrowed. In the United States, similar perspectives shaped the mind of the Protestant "establishment" of the mainline denominations, and characterized the social gospel that flourished during the interwar period. Even the Roman Catholic Church under Benedict XV shared to some extent in this response to the war, emphasizing the priority of Christian humanitarianism toward the victims of war and yet also the importance of Catholics demonstrating good citizenship within their respective nations.

For other Christians, the war carried a very different message. For Anglo-Catholics, it was a summons to be bolder in the expression and defence of an explicitly sacramental religion that was not afraid to invoke the intercession of the Virgin Mary and the saints. For Karl Barth or P. T. Forsyth, it exposed the moral impotence of liberal Protestantism and threw Christians onto absolute dependence on divine grace. For dispensationalists, the war opened the pages of prophetic Scripture, pointing to the imminence of the last days and highlighting the vacuity of well-meaning attempts to establish a new international order. For many fundamentalists, the war afforded evidence of the fatal consequences of the national adoption of evolutionary theory. For African Christian prophets, it heralded the beginning of the end of European colonial rule.

Although the war stiffened the resolve of ecumenical enthusiasts, it thus accentuated the existing divisions within the Christian world. Mutual understanding between German and Anglo-American Protestants collapsed. The Church of England became sharply polarized over liturgical revision. Fundamentalists and modernists were provoked to bitter warfare, with lasting consequences for the geography of Protestantism, in North America as elsewhere. Evangelical and liberal versions of Protestantism were already beginning to pull apart before 1914, but after 1918 their trajectories became more radically divergent. In the Catholic Church, it gradually became plain after the accession of Pius XI in 1922 that the church was returning to a new era of militancy, in which the new pope's passionate opposition to communism tended to align the church with the authoritarian forces of Fascism, creating an identification of Catholicism with right-wing stances that would endure until the rise of theologies of liberation in the 1970s. As chapter 6 will suggest, the twentieth century has as much claim to be called the century of Christian division as the ecumenical century.

CHAPTER TWO

Holy Nations?

UNEASY MARRIAGES BETWEEN
CHRISTIANITY AND NATIONALISM

I. Christianity and the Diffusion of Nationalism

The twentieth century—and in particular the years after the First World War—saw the global diffusion of the European idea of the nation-state and the corresponding spread of mass nationalist sentiment. As Western colonial intrusion into the economies of Asia and Africa deepened, Asian and African peoples drew on a wide variety of ideas and strategies in pursuit of a goal that was increasingly defined as "national" liberation from alien rule. The increasing circulation of global print information encouraged peoples who aspired for greater autonomy to follow with close interest parallel movements in other parts of the globe. In China at the turn of the century, for example, national reformers kept their eyes on the pursuit of national freedom by such distant peoples as Egyptians, Boers in South Africa, or Poles.[1] In retrospect, and in the light of what happened in China, we tend to associate this anticolonial dynamic with a principled antagonism to all things Western and an ideological orientation to Marxism–Leninism. Hence we also tend to assume that, from the dawn of the twentieth century, nationalism and Christianity, at least in its traditional Western forms, were set on a collision course. In point of fact, at least during the first two decades of the century, nationalism was not generally aligned in opposition to Christianity, nor even to Western thought as a whole, for the simple reason that the educated elites who pioneered the first Asian and African nationalist movements were often the product of mission education and took many of their ideas from Western ideological sources. Indeed, right through the century, there remain a few striking exceptional cases of a continuing, or even growing, convergence between Christian and nationalist identities, both in Europe and beyond it. The next two sections of this chapter examine two such examples. The first, that of Korea, is largely Protestant in character; the other, Poland, is decidedly Catholic.

The Catholic Church necessarily views nationalism with some suspicion—Catholicism by definition is about universality. The first missionary encyclical to be issued by a pope in the twentieth century, *Maximum Illud*, promulgated by Benedict XV in 1919, was unambiguous in its condemnation of Catholic missionaries who appeared more eager to promote the interests of France, Belgium, or Portugal than of the Church universal. In reality, as the late Catholic historian Adrian Hastings pointed out in one of his last publications, the story of both Catholic and Protestant mission history in the 1920s and 1930s is largely one of a clash between two nationalisms: the one represented by European missionaries and tinged by white racialism, the other being the rising national consciousness of Christians in the mission fields of Asia and Africa. There were very few Catholic mission thinkers before the Second Vatican Council who followed the Belgian missionary to China, Vincent Lebbe, in acknowledging in 1917 the need for "a living, fertile, national Church" that would be "flesh of the people's flesh, blood of the people's blood, sanctified in Christo, the only Church with a hope of survival."[2] The second case study in this chapter analyzes the immense symbolic power of the Catholic Church in Poland as a church that in the twentieth century came to fulfill precisely this function, reconstructing and reinforcing Polish national identity after centuries of territorial fragmentation and alien rule. In Ireland also, Catholic allegiance and Catholic education played a crucial role in providing the cultural framework for the first successful anticolonial movement in British imperial history. Even though most of the Catholic bishops and clergy were constitutional rather than revolutionary nationalists, discouraging any resort to violence, the struggle against British rule in Ireland, culminating in the establishment of the Irish Free State in 1921, owed much to a fusion of Gaelic and Catholic values. And yet, wherever Christianity becomes "blood of the people's blood," the people's blood necessarily begins to color Christian theology, giving it a tincture that Christians from outside the nation may find unrecognizable and even unacceptable. There is a fine line between indigenous theology and ethnocentric theology, as this chapter illustrates.

As the world emerged in 1918 from the chaos of total war and the collapse of empires, the quest began to construct a new world order founded

on the principle of the political autonomy of peoples. Three subtly different versions of this prescription were on the table. The first was the radical anti-imperialism that had triumphed in the Bolshevik Revolution in
1917. V. I. Lenin proclaimed the right of nations to self-determination as a
creedal principle of the anticapitalist and anticolonial program, especially
in Asia. For much of the century, from the mid-1920s until 1989, this radical European ideology appeared to be the most resilient of the three options, as movements more or less influenced by the ideas of Karl Marx laid
claim to moral leadership of the battle against colonialism.[3]

A second option, espoused mainly by certain nationalist leaders in
Asia, was to chart an indigenous pathway toward autonomy of European
control that drew only selectively on Western political traditions. The Indian nationalist movement under the leadership of Mohandas K. Gandhi
is the most obvious example; the *Ch'ŏndo-gyo* movement in Korea is another. Although Gandhi drew some of his ideas from European sources
such as Tolstoy or Ruskin, and ultimately from the teachings of Christ,
the texture of his program for liberation was distinctively Indian. *Swaraj*
(self- or home rule), *swadeshi* (literally "belonging to one's own country"
or self-reliance) and *satyagraha* (nonviolent resistance to injustice) were
notions informed by the teaching of the Hindu Vedic tradition, especially
the *Bhagavad Gita*, on nonattachment to material things, equability, the
need for self-restraint, and the moral power of self-suffering.[4] Anticolonial
movements in other contexts copied Gandhi's example, and some of his
ideas, as the proliferation of newspapers and other printed media accelerated the flow of nationalist sentiments across regions and continents. The
first nationalist movements in southern Africa adopted the title of Congress parties in imitation of the Indian National Congress, the pioneering
nationalist party founded in 1885 and led by Gandhi from December 1920.
The Korean nationalists who in March 1919 took to the streets in opposition to Japanese colonial oppression also drew inspiration from Gandhi's
contemporaneous *satyagraha* movement of mass protest against the Government of India's extrajudicial antiterrorist measures.

In 1918–19, however, by far the most widely circulated and acclaimed
recipe for national self-government was one cooked in an American Protestant kitchen. President Woodrow Wilson's famous Fourteen Points,
presented to the US Congress in January 1918, included in the basis for
the forthcoming peace settlement the principle that in adjudicating all
colonial claims, "the interests of the populations concerned must have
equal weight with the equitable claims of the government whose title is to
be determined."[5] Contrary to what many at the time and since assumed,

Wilson had not given a blanket endorsement of all claims of ethnic groups to absolute self-determination, and in fact he only very rarely used the phrase "self-determination." What he insisted on in 1918 was rather that all citizens of a state had the right to participate in the government of whatever polity they belonged to. It was a vision, not so much of national independence, as of the interdependence of peoples.[6] For Wilson, a convinced Presbyterian and son of a southern Presbyterian minister, the ideal model of political organization was that provided by Calvin's Geneva—a city-state that sought political liberty from the surrounding tyrannical regimes through the spiritual paradox of a covenanted submission of the citizenry to divine law. For Wilson self-government was less about ethnocentrism than submission to divine order. His brainchild, the League of Nations, was conceived in quasi-theological terms as a compact of self-governing but interdependent nations binding themselves together in a solemn *covenant*—this good Reformed word was employed both in the Fourteen Points and in the League's founding "Covenant" in 1919—in order to promote the divine mission of creating world peace.[7] For Wilson a measure of self-government appealed as the best solution to the disintegration of existing imperial structures in Europe and the Middle East. In his mind it did not imply that every ethnic group living under alien rule had the right to rise up and throw off the colonial yoke altogether. However, for many aspiring politicians in Asia and Africa, this was precisely what Wilson's rhetoric implied—hence the passionate enthusiasm with which his ideas were received in 1918–19. The Indian nationalist leader B. G. Tilak sent Wilson in January 1919 a pamphlet published by the Indian Home Rule League, entitled *Self-Determination for India*, accompanied by a letter urging that the forthcoming Paris peace conference should apply to India Wilson's "principles of right and justice." Wilson gave a noncommittal reply.[8]

As it gradually became apparent to anticolonial nationalists outside Europe that Wilson had not in fact written them a blank check to be cashed in London, Paris, or Tokyo, the appeal of his Calvinist version of collective self–government waned. From this point on, nationalist movements in most of Asia took on an increasingly militant and anti-Western tone, many of them adopting communist sympathies. In sub-Saharan Africa, nationalist politics took longer to emerge, and the virtual monopoly of education enjoyed by Christian missions ensured that Christian versions of nationalism proved more resilient than they did in Asia. But even in Africa, moderate Christian nationalism often found itself, as in Nkrumah's Ghana, rivaled and sometimes trumped by harder-edged nationalisms driven by Marxist–Leninist anticolonialist principles. As the next section emphasizes, an unusual combination of circumstances was required for a synthesis of Christianity and nationalism to be sustained in any non-Western context after 1920.

II. Protestant Nationalism in Korea: Christianity, Anticolonialism, and National Identity

In almost every country in Asia from the 1920s, Christianity found itself on the wrong end of the surging national sentiment that was so marked a feature of the postwar environment. Christianity was now branded as the religion of the Western colonial oppressor, a label of opprobrium that was now applied with greater frequency to the United States and not simply to the old colonial powers of Britain and France. The United States had, after all, annexed both Hawaii and the only Christian nation in Asia, the Philippines, in 1898. In China after the New Culture and May Fourth Movements of 1915–21, Christianity was also widely branded as an archaic creed obstinately opposed to modernity and scientific progress. Asian nationalism, therefore, began to develop a marked anti-Christian character.

Korea presents the most obvious exception to the rule. This is despite the fact that in the late nineteenth century, the small Christian community—which until the 1880s meant the Catholic community—was the recipient of a form of xenophobia that was just as militant as that demonstrated during the later years of the Qing dynasty in China. The Catholic faith was uniquely represented by the *Société des Missions Étrangères de Paris*, and hence was closely associated in the mind of the authorities with the threatening naval power of France. During the Great Persecution of 1866–71, some 8,000 Catholics—about half of the Christian population—lost their lives. Until the first decade of the twentieth century, there was little indication that the fortunes of Christianity in the Korean peninsula would be significantly different from those of the Church in China. Yet from that point on, the respective trajectories of Christian history in Korea and China began to diverge. The divergence was eventually so marked that by the late 1960s, at a time when the church in China was threatened with extinction during the Cultural Revolution, some South Korean Protestants were making claims to the effect that Korea had become the most Christian nation in Asia and "one of the most successful Protestant mission fields throughout the world."[9] Such claims were statistically exaggerated and confessionally partisan—levels of Christian adherence remained much higher in the Catholic nation of the Philippines than in South Korea—but that they could be made at all is evidence of the confidence with which South Korean Protestants could now define their prominent role within the life of their nation. Korean nationalism was not purely Christian in original inspiration: the conservative *Tonghak* ("eastern learning") movement that began in the 1860s in response to the Western impact was at least as important a source. But in the course of the twentieth century, Korean nationalism and evangelical Christianity forged an increasingly stable alliance. How such an unusual alliance proved possible in an Asian nation is the theme of this section.

The appearance in Korea in the 1890s of the first signs of a convergence between Christianity and aspirations toward the formation of a modern nation-state broadly paralleled trends in the reform movement in China at the same time. John Ross (1842–1915), a remarkable Scottish missionary of the United Presbyterian Church to Manchuria, had published the Korean New Testament in 1887. It was the first Korean book to employ what from about 1912 was known as the *Han'gŭl* phonetic alphabet, hitherto a despised script dating from the early fifteenth century. The mass of the population used *Han'gŭl* rather than the Chinese characters that only the educated male Confucian elite could read. The Protestant promotion of *Han'gŭl* would prove extraordinarily significant for the future development of Korean Christian nationalism. Korean intellectuals who had been exposed to Christianity and Western learning, and especially those who had traveled to the United States, began to express dissatisfaction with the intense conservatism of a Confucian society and contrasting admiration for the modernizing political and economic reforms being taken by post-Meiji Japan, and increasingly opted to express such sentiments in print through the medium of *Han'gŭl* rather than Chinese characters.

In 1896 Dr. Sŏ Chaep'il (Suh Jae-pil, also known as Philip Jaisohn), a progressive Christian doctor who had recently returned to Korea after a long period of exile and study in the United States, established the first Korean nationalist organization, the Independence Club (*Tongnip hyŏphoe*), which espoused the aim of liberating Korea from its practical subservience to the surrounding powers of Russia, China, and Japan. The Club soon had branches around the country, many of them associated with the first Protestant churches that had been planted by American Presbyterian and Methodist missions from 1887 onwards. The Club published *The Independent* (*Tongnip sinmun*), which was printed at the Methodist mission's Trilingual Press. It was the first Korean newspaper to use *Han'gŭl* (it had three pages in Korean, and one in English). Its editor from 1898 to its final issue in 1899 was Yun Ch'iho (1864–1945), a Korean aristocrat and reformer who had become a Christian while in political exile in Shanghai and had studied in the United States. Yun had reached the conclusion that Korea would be fitted for national survival neither through "degenerate" Confucianism nor through "abstract" and "abstruse" Buddhism, but only by adopting the progressive and morally vibrant faith of Christianity. Although the government suppressed the Club in 1898, imprisoning many of its leaders, its reforming ideas gained increasing influence. Some of those imprisoned converted to Christianity while in jail. Among them was Yi Sŭngman (Syngman Rhee; 1875–1965), who was destined to become the first president of South Korea. Rhee went into academic exile in the United States, studying at George Washington University, Harvard, and finally at Princeton, where he was the first Korean to be awarded a doctorate. At Princeton he became known to Woodrow Wilson, at that time the president of the university; Wilson used to introduce him to others on campus as "the future redeemer of Korean independence."[10]

The growing appeal of Protestantism as the religion of modernization and national autonomy was reinforced by Japan's victory in the Russo-Japanese War of 1904–5 and resulting declaration in November 1905 of a Japanese protectorate over Korea. Protestant Christianity as purveyed by the American missions appeared to offer the most promising medicine for Korea's humiliation. While the Catholic Church expressed open support for the Japanese protectorate, the Protestant missions, through their consistent use of the Korean vernacular in worship and education, and their shared commitment to the "Nevius method" of reliance on indigenous agency and funding in the expansion of the church, were able to present themselves as the authentic route to the recovery of national autonomy.[11] Nevertheless, the majority of the American missionaries were politically as well as theologically conservative, and unsympathetic to any overt involvement by their converts in anti-Japanese agitation. They lent their strongest support instead to the remarkable revival movements that first surfaced in Wonsan in 1903 and culminated in the P'yŏngyang Revival of 1907, in which thousands publicly confessed their sins, engaged in protracted prayer meetings, and sought the power of the Holy Spirit. Buoyed by the Revival, Protestant church growth accelerated, especially in the northwest, where by 1909 8,000 of the 50,000 citizens of P'yŏngyang were Protestant Christians, earning the city the title of the "Jerusalem of Korea." Enthusiasm for evangelism reached new heights: in October 1909 the annual meeting of the General Council of Evangelical Missions launched a campaign entitled "A Million Souls for Christ This Year." In fact, the number of new Protestant converts won by the end of 1910 was closer to 20,000, bringing total Protestant membership to about 178,000.[12]

The 1907 Revival formed patterns of simultaneous vocal congregational prayer and enthusiastic evangelism that have been characteristic of Korean Protestantism ever since. Some commentators see the Revival as establishing a paradigm of apolitical pietistic spirituality that represented a distinct alternative to the politically engaged Protestant nationalism that surfaced in 1919.[13] Although this interpretation is not without merit, it misses the fact that the Revival meetings often had national undertones, anticipating the subsequent, though never complete, confluence of revivalist and nationalistic streams that typifies modern Korean Protestantism. Believers confessed, not simply their own personal sins, but also the national sins that had supposedly led to the calamity of Japanese annexation. Encouraged by their pun-loving missionaries, they increasingly drew a parallel between the name of the kingdom of Korea (*Chosun* or *Chosŏn*) and ancient Israel: a "chosen" nation that had turned its back on God could still expect his deliverance if it repented of its sins and earnestly sought his forgiveness.[14]

Despite such fervent prayers, the national plight of Korea worsened. On August 29, 1910 Korea was fully integrated into Japanese territory as a colony. In 1911 ninety-eight Christians, among them Yun Ch'iho, were among those accused by the Japanese of involvement in a conspiracy to assassinate the Japanese Governor-General, Terauchi Masatake. In June 1912, 105 of the accused, including Yun, were sentenced to terms of imprisonment of between five and ten years. The case went to appeal, and a new trial was ordered, which resulted in March 1913 in the acquittal of all except six of the defendants, who were sentenced to six years in prison: one of the six was Yun. Although Protestant church attendance faltered during the first decade of full colonial rule, the symbolic identification of oppressed Korea with Israel in Egyptian bondage strengthened in Korean Protestant consciousness.

When mass Korean anticolonial resistance broke surface in the March 1st Movement in 1919, Protestants played a part disproportionate to their modest numerical strength in the nation as a whole. The Movement was the product of an uneasy alliance between Protestants—Catholics largely stood aloof—and adherents of the neo-traditionalist *Ch'ŏndo-gyo* ("the Religion of the Heavenly Way") religious movement, which built on earlier *Tonghak* anti-foreign ideas. Estimates of the number of demonstrators who took to the streets in March 1919 vary between 1 and 2 million—up to 10 percent of the population.[15] Statistics of the numbers of dead and injured also differ widely, but Korean sources report 7,509 Koreans killed, 15,961 wounded, and 46,948 arrested. Japanese military police sources record a lower figure of 19,525 persons arrested by late 1919, of whom 3,371 were Protestants, who then made up little more than 1 percent of the population. It is noteworthy that Protestant women were prominent among the demonstrators, accounting for more than 65 percent of the numbers of women arrested.[16] American missionary influence, especially in the YMCA, may have played a part in sowing the seeds of national aspiration.[17] However, not all Protestants approved of the resort to direct action: Yun Ch'iho was the most prominent of those who refused to lend his support, marking a crucial transition in his political stance from principled opposition to Japanese colonial rule toward a pragmatic position that increasingly regarded Japanese rule as an unavoidable reality with which Koreans necessarily had to come to terms. Nevertheless, the Declaration of Independence issued by the Movement drew much of its inspiration from the modern Western ideals of the nation-state and self-determination enshrined in Woodrow Wilson's Fourteen Points. In April 1919 Syngman Rhee publicly read the Declaration sitting in George Washington's chair in Philadelphia's Independence Hall, an act pregnant with symbolic meaning.[18] However, once it became clear that Wilson's rhetoric of national freedom would not be translated into any sponsorship of Korean claims for independence at the Versailles Peace Conference, Rhee grew deeply disillusioned with his erstwhile Princeton hero; the view of the State Department remained that Korea was part of the Japanese empire, and it was not for the United States to interfere in Japan's sovereign affairs.[19]

In India and China such disillusionment with the Wilsonian brand of self-determination propelled the infant nationalist movements in an anti-Western direction in the 1920s. In contrast to these two countries, however, in Korea the Protestant churches had by this point made substantial progress toward a genuinely three-self church. By 1915 the Presbyterian Church of Korea already had 115 ordained national pastors, compared with only eighty-four foreign missionaries.[20] This measure of ecclesiastical autonomy helped to ensure that in Korea, unlike in China after 1919, the churches were generally regarded as friends rather than foes by the Korean nationalist movement. When the General Assembly of the Presbyterian Church convened in 1919, it found that its moderator and a large number of the leading pastors and elders were in prison. The reports from the twelve presbyteries contained detailed accounts of fatalities, casualties, and destruction of churches and schools by Japanese troops.[21] Missionary opinion, initially strongly discouraging of the resort to direct action, grew more supportive of the protestors as the scale of Japanese abuses inflicted on them became apparent. The inter-mission English-language periodical, *The Korea Mission Field*, which had initially maintained a prudent silence on all political matters,[22] from December 1919 was bold enough to publish articles that put the Japanese in a bad light. The December 1919 issue printed an address by Arthur Berry, an American missionary to Japan, as a fraternal delegate to the Federal Council of Missions in Korea, which, though it pointedly declined to endorse the demand for full Korean independence, pulled no punches in accusing the Japanese forces of "barbarous brutalities."[23] The editorial to the next issue, in January 1920, though ostensibly devoted to the theme of "Prayer and Revival," listed "deliverance from the bondage of Egypt to the freedom of Canaan" as one of the "three mightiest revivals described in the Bible,"[24] The February 1920 issue printed an account, entitled "Korean Christians faithful in adversity," written by the Presbyterian missionary Samuel A. Moffett, which described the numerous Christian political prisoners in jails throughout the country, many of them engaging regularly in Bible studies and prayer meetings.[25] Evangelical spirituality and political activism, far from being mutually exclusive, had been fused into a potent mixture. It is surely not coincidental that Protestant church membership resumed its growth after 1919: Japanese official sources record a rise in the size of the whole Christian community from 319,129 in 1918 to 372,920 in 1922.[26]

The synthesis between evangelical spirituality and political activism that was apparent in the immediate aftermath of the March 1st Movement weakened with time, especially once it became brutally clear that the Movement had failed to recruit American support in order to realize its goal of independence for Korea. From about 1928 Korean Protestantism bifurcated into two strands: one group sought practical solutions to the colonial dilemma, either by fleeing into exile in Manchuria and elsewhere, or by pursuing Christian Socialist or other social means of reform. Others—and they were probably the larger group—took refuge in specifically religious renewal, some of it of a millenarian, mystical or Pentecostal kind.[27] However, this polarization should not be overemphasized. The largest Protestant church, the Presbyterian Church, remained conservative evangelical in its majority theological alignment, equally resistant to both the social gospel and millenarian or charismatic emphases. Within this center ground, it seems likely that the essential fusion of evangelical spirituality and nationalist aspiration remained largely intact through to the end of the Japanese colonial period in 1945. The sustained Japanese campaign to compel Koreans to participate in Shintō shrine ceremonies actually cemented the fusion by placing loyalty to the Japanese emperor and loyalty to Christ at loggerheads. This was despite the fact that the Presbyterian Church in September 1938 eventually had to abandon its opposition to Christians participating in Shintō rites, following the example set by the Vatican two years earlier in accepting the tendentious Japanese claims that the ceremonies were a matter of civil allegiance, not religious worship. At ground level, however, especially in the Presbyterian heartland of the northwest, around P'yŏngyang, resistance continued. Between 1938 and 1945 the authorities closed 200 churches, and as many as fifty Christians died in prison as a result of their refusal to take part in Shintō ceremonies, thus attaining the status of Protestant martyrs.[28]

For most Korean Protestants under Japanese rule, nationalism was more about clothing ideals of national self-determination in Christian dress than about racial theory, but by the 1930s the increasingly overt racial tone of Japanese colonialism was provoking Koreans in response to highlight the ethnic subtext latent within all nationalism. They gave new emphasis to the ancient national myth of *Tan'gun*, according to which *Tan'gun*, the father of the Korean nation, was the offspring of a union between *Hwanung*, the son of the deity *Hwanin*, and the bear-woman *Ungnyŏ*. After the end of Japanese colonial rule, in the 1950s and early 1960s, some Korean theologians employed the *Tan'gun* myth as raw material for the construction of an indigenous Korean theology. Even Christians were not entirely exempt from the tendency to ground national identity in a mythological prehistory.[29]

Korean Protestantism thus entered the post-Japanese era with impeccable nationalist credentials on display, but also with a religious culture that was still primarily shaped by American conservative Protestantism—a combination of features that was without parallel anywhere in the globe. The partition of the country in December 1945 into a northern Soviet-controlled and a southern American-controlled zone disrupted this unique synthesis, for the simple reason that about 60 percent of the Christian population were located in the communist zone. For the first time northern Protestants found themselves characterized as enemies of the people and collaborators with colonialists. The disproportion in Christian concentration soon began to right itself. Between 10 and 15 percent of the population of the North migrated southwards between 1945 and 1953, attracted by the rhetoric of Christian freedom espoused by the leaders of the interim government in the South. They included more than 70,000 Christians, at least 35 percent of the Christian population of the North.[30] Most notable among these refugees was the Sinŭiju Presbyterian pastor and Christian politician, Han Kyung-chik (1902–2002), who in December 1945 founded Bethany Evangelistic Church in Seoul, a congregation that would grow with phenomenal rapidity to become Korea's first mega-church, Youngnak Presbyterian Church. The Christian migrant leaders tended to be both more conservative theologically and more militant in their anticommunism than the Christians whom they joined in the South. In the year 1950 alone, 2,000 new Protestant churches were planted in the South, 90 percent of which were the result of initiatives by northern migrants.[31]

The disastrous Korean War of 1950–3, in which 10 percent of the population may have lost their lives, and subsequent division of the country, greatly reinforced these trends. By 1953 1.5 million Koreans had migrated from North to South Korea, among them being some 80,000 Protestants and 15–20,000 Catholics.[32] Fortified by this influx, the anticommunist tone of both Protestant and Catholic rhetoric in South Korea became more strident. The churches lent their uncritical support to the authoritarian military regime of South Korea's first president, Syngman Rhee, and increasingly adopted a pro-American stance: the United States was not simply the military protector of South Korea but also, throughout the 1950s, its bank-roller, as the South Korean economy was at this stage far weaker than that of the North, where industrial production had traditionally been concentrated and where state economic planning on a Stalinist model initially bore dividends. The economic disparity between North and South was gradually reversed from the 1960s under Rhee's successor, Park Chung-hee, as South Korea underwent rapid industrialization and urbanization, while the North Korean economy labored under heavy state regulation. With urbanization came the growth of mega-churches such as Youngnak Presbyterian or the Yoido Full Gospel Church, led by Paul (later known as David) Yong-gi Cho, which had a membership of 4,000 by 1965. Protestant membership grew in apparent symbiosis with the development of the South Korean economy, reaching its peak of 8.7 million (about 20 percent of the population) in the mid-1990s. Catholic membership grew more slowly during the same period, but since then has continued apace, rising from 2.9 million in 1995 to 5.1 million in 2005, while Protestant membership stagnated and then fell.[33]

In marked contrast to the generally benign relationship between Christianity and nationalism evident in South Korea, nationalism in communist North Korea adopted a stance that was directly antagonistic to the Christian faith. Such a marked divergence in the two forms of nationalism evident in Korea after 1953 could not have been predicted earlier in the century. The North Korean state's ideology of *Chuch'e* (or *Juche*) was a new Marxist-influenced permutation of the old theme of national self-reliance and self-determination first fashioned during the March 1st movement and its parallel movements in India and China. Its primary architect, Kim Il Sung, came from a leading P'yŏngyang Presbyterian family. But, whereas in the South after 1945 Korean Christian anticolonialism switched its target from Japan to communist China and its new vassal state across the Demilitarized Zone, in the North the national tradition of anticolonialism was redirected against Japan's enemy from 1939 to 1945, the United States, and its neocolonial presence in East Asia. Those Christians who remained in North Korea paid a high penalty for their American missionary connections. Nevertheless, Protestants survived in some numbers, though precision is impossible. In 1985 a visiting WCC delegation to P'yŏngyang, once the hub of Korean Protestantism, was officially informed that there were "many" (possibly 10,000) Protestant believers in the country, plus perhaps 800 Catholics. Protestant pastors were few in number and Catholic priests nonexistent.[34]

The nexus between Protestantism, nationalism, and increasingly also, capitalism, was intrinsic to the remarkable flourishing of South Korean Protestantism up to 1995, but also helps to explain its comparative decline in momentum thereafter. With the notable exception of the *minjung* (people's) liberation movements of the 1970s and 1980s, Korean Protestant churches were not conspicuous by their stance on human rights but instead tended to regard personal conversion as the only solution to social problems. Yet they stood in danger of making Christianity syncretic with both a narrow form of Korean ethnicity and capitalism. The sophisticated programs and slick business culture of their mega-churches appealed to the upwardly mobile, but also attracted adverse publicity when abuses, normally of a financial character, came to light, as they increasingly did as churches grew larger and the association of Protestantism with prosperity grew closer. The nineteenth-century persecutions followed by the Concordat reached with the Japanese during the colonial era had left the Catholic Church disinclined to pursue active political engagement. After the partition of Korea, the Catholic Church similarly held back from a form of Christian nationalism that idealized the United States and its Protestant free enterprise culture. By the end of the century the Church was beginning to reap a harvest from its relative abstraction from politics. Many Protestant churches also kept politics at arm's length, but they were beginning to discover the perils that accompanied their own forms of compromise with the business culture of the South Korean nation.

III. Catholic Nationalism in Poland: Mary as the Queen of a Dismembered Nation

The extensive and repeatedly redefined cluster of territories that at various times has been called "Poland" has for centuries sat uneasily at the crossroads of the European continent. Its peoples, viewing themselves as belonging neither to western Europe nor to eastern Europe, but to central Europe, have tended to look both ways. Many of them have spoken Polish, which is a Slavic language, but one that uses a Latin rather than a Cyrillic script. The vast plains of Poland marked the eastern limit of the European expansion of Latin Christianity and hence form the frontier between the Catholic and the Orthodox Churches. These lands have also included substantial numbers of Slavic Christians who have owed allegiance to Rome while retaining the right to employ the liturgies of the Orthodox Church in their worship—those who used to be called "Ruthenians," but are now more frequently described as belonging to the "Greek Catholic" Church.

Just as Korea is markedly atypical in Asian history in modeling a convergence between Christianity and resistance to colonialism, so, in the history of European Christianity in the twentieth century, Poland is the great exception to the rule. Whereas in most of Europe the second half of the century witnessed a sustained erosion of popular adherence to the churches, in Poland the Roman Catholic Church continued to command the allegiance of the majority of the population throughout the century; in 1997 about 90 percent of the inhabitants described themselves as Catholic. By this date Poland was in fact a much more uniformly Catholic country than it had been as recently as 1918, when Poland first regained its independence as a sovereign state after the period of the Partitions (1795–1918). The idea that Poland has been a monochrome Catholic nation from time immemorial is a myth of twentieth-century construction: as late as 1918, as many as one-third of the population were not Catholics.[35] Woodrow Wilson's extraordinary popularity outside America in 1918–19 extended to central Europe. Polish Protestants were doubtless among those mentioned in the enthusiastic report that George Creel, chair of the United States Government's Committee on Public Information, brought to President Wilson in February 1919 at the conclusion of his recent tour of Poland and Czechoslovakia, states created by the Treaty of Versailles. Nevertheless, when Creel informed the astonished Wilson that the Poles and Czechs thought this Presbyterian president a "popular Saint" and wanted him to "reign over them," Catholic sentiment was clearly to the fore.[36]

The impression that since that era Poland has seen Catholic advance at the expense of other religious affiliations is, however, somewhat illusory. The main explanation of the change is the arbitrary slicing off of substantial chunks of the Polish state by the Treaty of Riga in 1921 and the Yalta Conference of 1945, which between them deprived the nation of many of its ethnic minorities, most of them being adherents of the Lutheran, Greek Catholic, or Orthodox churches. Poland under communist rule thus became more ethnically monochrome and more religiously Roman Catholic than it had been at any stage in its history. Although by the 1990s less than 50 percent of the population could be described as regularly practicing Catholics, this percentage was still well in excess of that recorded in other traditionally Catholic countries. A survey conducted in the early 1990s suggested that 79.2 percent of Poles were able to give an affirmative answer to the central Christian doctrinal question, "Is there a God who became Man?" compared to 67.2 percent of the population of Ireland, or a mere 21.8 percent of the population of France.[37] In Poland the industrial working class, whose increasing abstention from public Christian worship from the mid-nineteenth century onwards had caused such alarm to the European churches, largely retained their Catholic piety. Indeed, from 1989 religious devotion became a potent ingredient in the new collective power of organized labor in Poland, with far-reaching consequences for the political geography of central and Eastern Europe. In the second half of the century, while vocations to the Catholic priesthood in most of the Catholic world were in free-fall, in Poland under communist rule, they showed a steady increase: the number of priests grew from c. 10,300 in 1945 to more than 20,000 in 1982, while the number of professed religious grew even more, from 1,500 to more than 5,000.[38]

The striking abnormality of Poland's religious trajectory in the twentieth century is comprehensible only in the light of the peculiarly determinative role that the Catholic faith in general, and devotion to the Virgin Mary in particular, has occupied in the articulation and maintenance of the problematic concept of a Polish national identity. Establishing a historically stable definition of the boundaries of the Polish nation in territorial or even ethnic terms is a virtually impossible enterprise, as for much of their history, the identity of the Polish people has been interwoven with that of a miscellany of other groups—among them, Czechs, Slavs, Lithuanians, Russians, Austrians, and Germans.[39] Poland's national identity has had to be constructed and reconstructed—even invented—in response to periodic and sometimes prolonged dismemberments of Polish territory, and religious symbols or events that have been invested with deep religious significance have been quarried to supply the raw materials for the edifice. Poland constitutes the most prominent example in modern history of a variety of nationalism that has been explicitly Catholic in character. The idea of "Catholic nationalism" might appear to be a contradiction in terms, but in Poland the antimony has been held together by the figure of the Virgin Mary, the one who is revered both as the universal Mother of all the faithful and as, in a very particular sense, the Queen of the Polish nation. Of the more than 800 Catholic shrines in contemporary Poland, 700 are devoted to Mary.[40] Polish nationalism, like much other nationalism, rests on the identification and commemoration of certain episodes in the past as symbolically constitutive of the identity of the nation. Both the justification for the selection of these particular events, and the retrospective interpretation placed upon them, may be historically dubious, but their mythical power does not depend on historical accuracy. Three such episodes stand out as being particularly significant, and each has an overtly religious connotation.

The first was the baptism into the Roman Church in 966 CE of Miesko I, chief of the Slav tribe, the *Polanie* (Polanians) following his dynastic marriage the previous year to Dobrava, the daughter of Boleslav I of Bohemia. Polish Catholics remember the baptism of Miesko and his people both as the beginning of their ecclesiastical history—the ecclesiastical province of Poland was created in the year 1000, and the first Polish see established at Gniezno—and as the inception of their recorded history as a nation, for it marked the advent of literacy. In 1966, when the communist regime in Poland was at the height of its power, the nation celebrated the millennium of Miesko's baptism as the climax of a Great Millenary Novena, a nine-year period of prayer and fasting. A decade earlier, the Cardinal-Primate, Stefan Wyszyński (1901–81), had been placed under house arrest by the regime for four years from September 1953 to October 1956. Following his release, Wyszyński began planning the millennium celebrations. In 1957 he began an annual schedule of catechetical itinerations to every parish in the country, drawing vast crowds wherever he went. By 1966 every Catholic church in Poland displayed a banner proclaiming *Sacrum Poloniae Millenium* ("Poland's Sacred Millennium"), *966-1966*, and other slogans such as *Deo et Patriae, Poloniae Semper Fidelis*, or *Naród Z Kościołem* ("The Nation Is With The Church"). Even the Communist Party joined in the celebrations, reinterpreting them as the anniversary of the birth of the Polish nation. Ecclesiastics and atheist politicians alike had fused church and nation in collective memory, with scant regard for historical accuracy. [41]

The focus of attention in Wyszyński's annual schedule of nationwide itinerations was not the cardinal himself but a transported replica of the Byzantine icon of the Black Madonna that from 1382 had been housed at the fortified monastery of Jasna Góra, situated on a hill above the southern Polish city of Częstochowa. Jasna Góra is one of the most celebrated sites of Marian devotion in the country. The blackness of the Virgin's face in the icon is simply the result of smoke damage, but by becoming designated as the *Black* Madonna, the Jasna Góra image connected Polish Marian devotion to the ancient Catholic biblical exegetical tradition that saw the figure of the bride in the Song of Solomon ("Black am I and beautiful") as a type of the Virgin.[42] The exceptional symbolic power of the Jasna Góra icon derives from its association with the second episode in Polish history that has played a leading role in the construction of Polish national identity.

The fortress of Jasna Góra was one of the few strongholds to resist the invasion of the united Commonwealth of Poland–Lithuania by the Lutheran Charles X Vasa of Sweden in the 1650s. The then king of Poland and grand duke of Lithuania, John Kazimierz, attributed the successful defense of Jasna Góra in 1655 to the miraculous intervention of the Virgin Mary. In 1656, in the Catholic cathedral of Lwów, Kazimierz accordingly pledged, not merely himself, but the entire Polish nation, in a heavenly nuptial covenant to the Virgin, declaring her to be the Queen of Poland. Mary thus became both bride and mother of the nation. The ascription to the Virgin of the title of *Regina Coeli* (Queen of Heaven), and the notion that, following her bodily assumption into heaven, her Son crowned her as Queen of Heaven, was well established in Europe by the twelfth century. Kazimierz in 1656 transposed the coronation of the Virgin into a Polish nationalistic key; subsequently his proclamation became particularly associated with the icon kept at Jasna Góra, the scene of the nation's miraculous deliverance.[43] From this source there developed the ascription to Mary of the further and theologically highly dubious title of *Hetmanka*—a female commander-in-chief of the Polish armed forces who would fight for the nation against its foes, who might be brown-shirted Germans, red Russians—or even, most morally disquieting of all—Jewish interlopers within the nation.[44] The "miracle on the Vistula" in 1920, when the Poles defeated the godless Bolshevik troops, was widely attributed to the intervention of the *Hetmanka*. Conversely, the defeat of the Polish armies by Soviet and Nazi forces in the Second World War was interpreted as evidence that the Virgin had withheld her blessing on the nation on account of its spiritual unfaithfulness.[45] In 1956 Wyszyński composed an updated version of Kazimierz's national oath, pledging the Polish nation in "an eternal, maternal slavery of love" to the Virgin: at the climax of the millennium celebrations on May 3, 1966 the pledge was solemnly repeated in every parish in the country.[46] The intensity of the devotion now lavished on the Black Madonna of Jasna Góra was such that when the communist authorities "arrested" the Virgin on her journey from the Catholic University of Lublin to Warsaw, confiscating the icon, Wyszyński simply continued the procession, with no more than the empty frame of the icon attracting the veneration of the crowds; in the end, the regime was shamed into returning the replica, and the Madonna resumed her honored place in the processions.[47]

The third episode to attain particular symbolic importance in the narrative of Polish Catholic nationalism (though actually the second in chronological terms) was the murder on church premises of Stanisław, the first bishop of Kraków, by King Bolesław II the Bold in 1079. Canonized by Innocent IV in 1253, Stanisław became the patron saint of the Poles, the archetypal martyr whose experience of suffering foreshadowed the ensuing tragic history of the Polish nation. During the nineteenth century, Polish poets and intellectuals living in exile from Russian oppression in France developed the theme of Poland as a suffering Redeemer nation into a Romantic tradition of national messianism. In the Second World War the exploits of Polish aviators in the Royal Air Force and of Polish troops at Monte Cassino became part of this national mythology of redemptive suffering, as did the Warsaw Uprising by the Polish resistance against Nazi rule in 1944.

In early October 1978, within hours of receiving news of John Paul I's death after less than a month on the papal throne, another bishop of Kraków, Cardinal Karol Wojtyla (1920–2005), wrote what would prove to be his last poem, "Stanisław." Its theme conformed to this Polish messianic tradition: Poland was a land baptized in blood, "torn apart on the maps of the world," yet united in its experience of martyrdom for the sake of Christian truth.[48] Two weeks later Wojtyla was elected as Pope John Paul II, an event that evoked exuberant rejoicing throughout his native land. The first Polish pope began planning his first papal visit to Poland to coincide with the 900th anniversary of Stanisław's martyrdom on the feast day of St. Stanisław on May 8, 1979. The Polish government, under pressure from Leonid Brezhnev in Moscow to forbid any such visit, refused to allow this timing, but knew it could not resist a visit in principle. After months of negotiation, it was agreed that John Paul II would come for nine days in June rather than two days in May as originally planned. In fact the Polish episcopate astutely extended the anniversary celebrations for a month so that they culminated in the papal visit. The papal itinerary was to include Warsaw; the primatial see of Gniezno, where the relics of another martyr, St. Adalbert, the first missionary to Poland, were held; the shrine of the Black Madonna at Częstochowa; Auschwitz; and Kraków.

Few religious episodes of the twentieth century were so highly charged with political significance as John Paul II's tour of Poland from June 2 to 10, 1979. His opening address in the Cathedral of St. John in Warsaw referred to the biblically resonant remark that St. Stanisław is supposed to have made to King Bolesław, "Destroy this Church, *and Christ, over the centuries, will rebuild it.*" At Jasna Góra, which he termed "the nation's shrine," where one could hear "the echo of the life of the whole nation in the heart of its Mother and Queen," John Paul II appealed to the memory of St. Stanisław's death at the hands of arbitrary state power to enforce the lesson that the laws of the state must be subordinated to the law of God. The pope also visited another great national Marian shrine, Kalwaria Zebrzydowska, between Kraków and his birthplace of Wadowice, where as a young man he had joined 50,000 other pilgrims in the annual Marian liturgical feast of the Assumption. At Auschwitz the pope knelt in prayer in Cell 18 of Block 11, where in 1941 the Polish Franciscan friar Maksymilian Kolbe—the most assiduous proponent of militant Marianism in interwar Poland—had died a martyr's death as a voluntary substitute for another inmate condemned to death by starvation.[49] John Paul went on to celebrate Mass before a crowd of more than a million at Auschwitz II (Birkenau) concentration camp. The pilgrimage culminated with a mass on Kraków Commons attended by between 2 and 3 million people, the largest crowd in Polish history. John Paul II's sermon urged the faithful to recall "the powerful intercession of the Mother of God at Jasna Góra and at all her other shrines in Polish lands" and invoked the memory of "St. Adalbert who underwent death for Christ near the Baltic Sea" and of "St. Stanisław who fell beneath the royal sword at Skalka." The Communist Party slogan, "The Party Is for the People" was displayed throughout the country during the visit, but one such banner was doctored by the addition: ". . . but the People are for the Pope." In course of the pilgrimage, more than 13 million Poles, more than a third of the population, saw the pope in person, and almost all others saw him on television or heard him on radio.[50]

John Paul's pilgrimage to his native land in June 1979 was a watershed in the history, not simply of Poland, but also of central and Eastern Europe as a whole. It gave a repeatedly humiliated people new confidence in their national identity and solidarity in the face of a brutal communist regime. It lit a subversive fuse that burned slowly, setting off the nonviolent explosion of the Solidarity revolution in 1980, which in turn did much to provoke the collapse of communism in Europe. The alliance between the power of organized labor and the Catholic Church was not in itself new: two of the largest trade unions during the Second Republic had been professedly Christian—the Polish Employees Union and the Christian Employees Union of the Polish Republic.[51] But it is hard to conceive of the *Solidarność* (Solidarity) movement taking the course that it did without the decisive impact made by the visit of a Polish pope in 1979: one of the first acts of the striking shipyard workers in Gdansk in 1980 was to affix a Cross, an image of the Virgin, and a portrait of John Paul II to the shipyard gates. They became, as their leader Lech Wałęsa put it, *"the symbols of victory."*[52] When Wałęsa signed the agreement with the Polish government legalizing the Solidarity union in August 1980, he did so using a huge souvenir pen from the 1979 visit, bearing a picture of a smiling John Paul II.[53] When martial law was imposed on December 13, 1981, the Church responded with a massive demonstration of support for internees, prisoners, and their families. In Warsaw special masses at St. Stanisław Kostka Church conducted by Father Jerzy Popieluszko were especially important in sustaining morale. Following his murder by secret service agents in October 1984, more than 250,000 people attended his funeral, and his grave in the churchyard became an important pilgrimage site; Poland had gained another Catholic martyr. In the first partly free national elections of June 4, 1989, Solidarity gained its greatest success in the regions where Catholic parochial structures were strongest and Sunday mass attendance highest.[54] Solidarity took over the government in the summer of 1989, heralding the collapse of communist regimes throughout eastern Europe in the autumn of 1989. In 1992 the former Communist Party holiday on October 12, Polish Armed Forces Day, was abolished and transferred to August 15, which is both the Feast of the Assumption of the Virgin Mary and the anniversary of the "miracle of the Vistula" in 1920, a national deliverance that is attributed to the Black Madonna of Częstochowa.[55] The repeatedly dismembered but now newly independent nation of Poland was renewing its homage to its Virgin Queen and Mother.

IV. Christianity and Nationalism: Uneasy Bedfellows

Twentieth-century experience, no less than that of earlier centuries, suggests that nationalism and Christianity will always be uneasy bedfellows. On the one hand, Christian belief, when yoked to faith in the fatherland, has proved extraordinarily effective as a dynamo of collective resistance to colonial oppression or other forms of injustice. In Korea under Japanese rule in 1919, and in a more diffuse fashion over the whole period from 1905 to 1945, Christianity, and in particular Protestantism, functioned as the most powerful magnet drawing the educated elite and the populace together in protest against Japanese cultural hegemony. In Poland, Catholicism of a strongly Marian hue performed a similar function as a means of focusing a national identity whose definition is historically contested and as a rallying cry for resistance to Nazi or Soviet tyranny. But both examples also illustrate the morally ambiguous nature of Christian nationalism. Nationalism feeds off opposition to those who are perceived as enemies of the nation, and hence stands in perpetual tension with the injunction of Christ to love our enemies. In the near apocalyptic climate brought about by a divided Korea after 1953, the nationalist legacy shaped during the colonial period assumed a different and more obviously problematic character as many leading Protestants in South Korea increasingly gave absolute moral value to opposition to the North and lent their unqualified support to those dictatorial regimes that appeared to offer the most reliable defense against the communist threat. In Poland, the Catholic militancy encouraged by the cult of the Virgin as the Queen of the nation was always capable of degenerating into xenophobia or even racism. In the interwar period it was very widely associated with antisemitism.[56] As it entered the twenty-first century, Christianity in South Korea and Poland—not to speak of elsewhere—remained in uneasy and ultimately contradictory alliance with nationalist sentiment.

CHAPTER THREE

The Power of the Word and Prophecy

PATHWAYS OF CONVERSION IN AFRICA AND THE PACIFIC

I. The "Great Century" of Conversion to Christianity

The American Baptist historian and Yale professor Kenneth Scott La-tourette wrote a seven-volume history of the expansion of Christianity that famously denominated the nineteenth century as the "great century."[1] Undoubtedly it was the great century of the geographical extension of Christian, especially Protestant, missions from Europe and North America into Asia, Africa, and Oceania. It was not, however, a great century for the numerical expansion of the church outside of Europe and North America. With some striking exceptions, notably in Jamaica, Polynesia, Buganda, Sierra Leone, and a few parts of the Indian subcontinent, the nineteenth century did not witness major collective movements of conversion to the Christian faith. Missionaries traveled far and labored hard, but until the 1880s their numbers were few, and even then many saw no great fruit for their labors. This was especially the case in India and China, the two fields that received the vast majority of nineteenth-century missionaries.

The "great century" for the numerical expansion of Christianity has in fact been the twentieth, not the nineteenth, although that growth has not even kept pace with the explosion of the world population. It has been estimated (and accuracy is impossible) that the global Christian population grew from approximately 558,130,000 in 1900 to 2,128,937,459 in 2005. The most spectacular growth was in Africa, where it is estimated that the aggregate Christian population grew from 9,918,018 in 1900 to 437,832,263 in 2005.[2] The proliferation of movements of conversion to Christianity from the second decade of the twentieth century onwards is often related to the influence of European imperialism, and especially to the British Empire in sub-Saharan Africa. Christian missions virtually monopolized the provision of education in colonial Africa, and a high proportion of those who attended mission schools became at least nominally Christian. However, if adherence to the white man's religion had been merely an instrumental choice to achieve advancement and self-enrichment in the colonial economy, the rate of conversion to Christianity would have tailed off after decolonization. Contrary to widely held expectations in the 1960s, this did not happen: independent Africa south of the Sahara was by the end of the century much more strongly Christian than it had been on the eve of independence. Some parts of the non-Western world that were neither subject to formal colonial rule nor culturally predisposed to accept a European religion also witnessed significant movements of conversion to Christianity in the first half of the twentieth century. The most telling example is China, where, despite a deeply ingrained tradition of anti-foreignism and a singular eruption of anti-Christian violence in the Boxer Rising of 1900, the numbers of Protestant Christians grew from about 100,000 in 1900 to approaching 1 million by the Communist revolution in 1949, while the size of the Catholic community rose from about 700,000 in 1900 to approximately 3 million in 1949. The more spectacular growth experienced by the church in China after the Cultural Revolution should not be allowed to obscure the fact of significant Christian expansion before 1949. Moreover, the most substantial Christian growth in republican China was among independent churches that owed little to foreign missionary influence; by midcentury they accounted for at least 20 percent of the Chinese Protestant community.[3] Once due weight has been given to the temporary stimulus imparted by Western colonial rule, other explanations of the growth of Christianity in the twentieth-century non-Western world are called for.

The enormous increase in foreign missionary numbers from the mid-1880s undoubtedly played a part, notably in the Catholic Church, for which the twentieth century marked the culmination of recovery from the almost total collapse of its missionary institutions during the crisis of the Napoleonic era. Old orders such as the Jesuits were revived, while major new foundations such as the Missionaries of Our Lady of Africa (the White Fathers), founded by Cardinal Lavigerie of Algiers in 1868, or the Society of the Divine Word (Societas Verbi Divini or SVD), formed by

Albert Janssen at the height of Bismarck's *Kulturkampf* in 1875, extended the Catholic presence to new fields, especially in Africa, China, and New Guinea. The presence of foreign missionaries, however, is never a sufficient condition for mass conversion to Christianity, and as in post-1949 China, may not even be a necessary condition. Large-scale conversion to a new religion will take place only when the massive ruptures of customary practice intrinsic to such a change make sense within at least some of the categories of the existing world view. In the Catholic case, two interrelated features of the missions facilitated the process whereby Christianity began to "make sense." The first was the traditional Catholic emphasis on schooling. Those being educated were baptized and catechized, and the baptized community *was* the church. For some who experienced Catholic mission education, this felt like indoctrination, and that charge was sometimes justified.[4] But at their best, Catholic schools enabled pupils to discern the presence of God within the forms and artistic creations of their own culture in a way that few Protestant missions managed.

The Catholic Church before Vatican II placed a low priority on the production of vernacular scriptures: in East Africa at the end of the 1950s there were only three Catholic translations of the New Testament compared with fifty by Protestants, plus thirteen Protestant translations of the entire Bible. Yet, as a second feature, Catholics often surpassed Protestants in the production of works of linguistic and ethnological scholarship.[5] The Belgian Franciscan missionary in the Congo Placide Tempels (1906–77) was possibly the first European to claim, in his *La Philosophie Bantoue* (1945), that Africans had a coherent philosophy of their own. But this rather essentialist dissection of African mentality led him in 1953 to initiate a spiritual renewal movement for married Christians, the Jamaa (Swahili for the family) that attracted thousands of followers in Katanga and Kasai provinces. Although its mystical and charismatic character aroused fears in Rome, Jamaa has remained within the boundaries of the Catholic Church. Tempels has been termed a "white prophet" of African Christianity.[6]

If the power of the word was most often expressed in Catholicism through educational catechesis, in the Protestant case it was most evident through the impact of Bible translation. The role of the Bible societies in effecting the transformation of Christianity into a global religion is still undervalued. Societies such as the British and Foreign Bible Society (1804), the American Bible Society (1816), and, more recently, the Wycliffe Bible Translators (1942) have supplied the vernacular scriptures without which Christianity could never have taken its current shape as a multicultural religion. As a number of scholars have recently pointed out, Christianity is distinguished from Islam by its refusal to ascribe unique sacral significance to the original languages of its scriptures: the Bible, unlike the Qu'ran, does not cease to be the word of God once it is translated.[7] Like the crowds on the Day of Pentecost, those who have heard "the wonderful works of God" declared in their own tongues have been able to interpret the message within the linguistic and conceptual categories of their own culture.[8] While still being good *news*, the gospel has not been an entirely unintelligible novelty. But translating the Bible took time. It had to be preceded by learning the language from indigenous teachers, and often involved reducing that language to writing, and the compilation of dictionaries and grammars. For these reasons, a time lag of a decade or more usually elapsed between the arrival of missionaries and the production of the first portions of vernacular Scripture. Publication of properly revised entire bibles that captured native speech and idiom with sufficient accuracy to communicate to ordinary people took longer still. The earliest full Bible translations in Chinese appeared as early as 1822 and 1823, but the first complete "Union" Bible in a vernacular style of Mandarin understandable to most ordinary Chinese was not published until a century later in 1919.[9]

In much of central and West Africa the Protestant missionary era began in the 1860s or 1870s, but the process of Bible translation did not bear substantial fruit before the 1890s. The Bakongo people of the lower Congo who will feature prominently in the next section of this chapter, received their first Protestant missionaries in 1878. The British Baptist missionary, William Holman Bentley, and one of his Bakongo deacons, Nlemvo, produced the first New Testament in the Mbanza Kongo dialect of the Kikongo language, in December 1893, but the complete Kikongo Bible in the same dialect did not follow until 1916, eleven years after Bentley's death.[10] The Bakongo prophet movements that will be discussed in the next section followed within five years.

As Bible translations into a host of non-European vernacular languages multiplied in the course of the twentieth century, the Bible ceased to be a European book. Or, to be more accurate, it finally became recognized as what it always had been—a book (or library of books) rooted in the Semitic cultures of western Asia and whose central themes resonated with the everyday concerns of many "primal" peoples. For those who lived in critical proximity to disease, hunger, poverty, social dislocation, and even exile, the biblical narratives were no alien story. The Hebrew Bible and the Gospels depicted scenarios that were part of the regular experience of many non-European peoples. Furthermore, they recorded narratives of national exodus from colonial captivity and miraculous restoration to the homeland, stories of hope and healing, and evil forces vanquished. The priests and pastors who had for centuries occupied the center stage of a more static European Christianity were largely absent from such narratives. Their central figures, with the obvious exception of Christ himself, were those whom the churches, whether Catholic, Orthodox, or Protestant, had filtered out of their hearing of the biblical message. The twentieth century was the age of the evangelist and the prophet. Much of the regular growth of the churches in Africa, Asia, and Oceania in this century was the result of the unspectacular witness of indigenous leaders of minimal theological education but abundant zeal—those known in the Catholic tradition as catechists and in Protestantism as evangelists— whose only textbooks were a vernacular catechism for Catholics, New Testament or Bible for Protestants, and sometimes a hymnbook. Also crucial was the ministry of "Bible women"—women remunerated at minimal level by churches or missions to share the gospel with other women and teach them the rudiments of the faith and Christian family life.[11] But some of the most notable movements of Christian conversion owed their impetus to leaders of a more charismatic variety who appeared to combine the word of the gospel with apostolic signs and wonders.

The office of the prophet had died out in the church of the late second century, discredited by the excesses of Montanist enthusiasm. In Africa and some parts of the Pacific in the twentieth century, the often bruising encounters between the claims of Christianity and indigenous systems of spiritual power encouraged the reemergence of the prophet. Prophets were raised up at particular times, often those of great crisis or danger. The First World War and its aftermath was the most notable of these periods. Prophets called the faithful to radical repentance and faith, urging them to sever their reliance on traditional sources of spiritual protection and trust in God alone. In the context of the First World War, their message often had a radical edge that caused the colonial authorities considerable anxiety. William Wadé Harris in the Ivory Coast in 1914, John Chilembwe in Nyasaland (Malawi) in 1914–15, Garrick Braide in eastern Nigeria in 1915–16, and Simon Kimbangu in the Belgian Congo in 1920–1 all in their different ways interpreted the war as a sign that the dominance of the white man in Africa must soon come to an end.

As early as the first decade of the century, there were a few in the Western churches who partially anticipated the rediscovery of the office of the prophet with some sympathy, although they mostly imagined that it would be India rather than Africa or Oceania that first raised the issue. They were often to be found among those at the Catholic end of the Anglican spectrum who combined evangelistic enthusiasm with respect for lost medieval patterns of Christian propagation. Anglo-Catholics such as Charles Gore, E. J. Palmer, Herbert Pakenham-Walsh, and Father Walter Frere, superior of the Community of the Resurrection at Mirfield in Yorkshire, in an address to the World Missionary Conference in Edinburgh in 1910, suggested that the new apostolic age of global propagation of the faith might demand a restoration of the full range of ministries found in the New Testament.[12] They were voices crying in an ecclesiastical wilderness.

The vast majority of European Christians, whether Catholic or Protestant, whenever they encountered the "prophetic" on the mission field over the next few years, recoiled with caution or downright skepticism. But so, as will be seen, did some indigenous church leaders. As a result, movements that were not originally hostile to the mission churches frequently turned against their missionary mentors, branding them, like the disciples on the road to Emmaus, as "slow of heart to believe all that the prophets have spoken."[13] Out of such prophet movements many of the independent churches of modern Africa were born. Among the Yoruba of Nigeria, many of the Aladura or "praying" churches trace their origins to a revival that sprang up in 1930–1 under the leadership of an Anglican, Joseph Babalola (1904–59), in congregations of the Faith Tabernacle, a faith-healing church with its headquarters in Philadelphia and indirect links to the eccentric Scottish émigré and healer John Alexander Dowie (1847–1907) of Zion City, Illinois.[14] Dowie had declared himself in 1904 to be "Elijah the Prophet of the Restoration of All Things," with a divine commission to restore the church to its primitive apostolic power and purity.[15] Dowie's influence can also be identified behind the formation of the earliest "Zionist" and Apostolic churches of southern Africa among Zulus, Swazis, and in what is now Zimbabwe.[16] But prophetic styles of Christianity disseminated through print or missionary influence from North America appealed to Africans precisely because they meshed so neatly with indigenous traditions of illumination from dreams and visions. Perhaps the greatest of the Zulu prophets, Isaiah Shembe (c. 1870–1935), founder of the Nazaretha church at Ekuphakameni near Durban in 1910, was reluctant to acknowledge any major debt to missionary teaching, but he was undoubtedly influenced by Zionist and Apostolic ideas that can ultimately be traced back to Dowie. Biblical, especially Old Testament, motifs were prominent in his teaching and in the numerous hymns that he composed, which themselves became sacred texts of canonical authority.[17]

The next section examines three early twentieth-century prophets whose impact on African Christianity has been particularly widespread.

The final section of the chapter will examine some analogous conversion and revival movements in Melanesia.

II. Three West African Prophet Movements

GARRICK SOKARI BRAIDE (C. 1884–1918)

Garrick Braide was a fisherman and small trader from Bakana in Calabar, near Port Harcourt in the southeast of modern Nigeria.[18] He became an inquirer in St. Andrew's Church at Bakana, where the pastor, Moses A. Kemmer, was one of the black Sierra Leonean missionaries who made such a large contribution to the evangelization of the Niger Delta. St. Andrew's belonged to the Niger Delta Pastorate Church—a quasi-autonomous African-led Anglican church established in the wake of the notorious crisis in the Church Missionary Society (CMS) Niger mission in 1890–1 that had led to the humiliation of Samuel Adjai Crowther, the first black Anglican bishop. While still illiterate, Braide learned by rote the catechism, Lord's Prayer, Ten Commandments, and portions of scripture in the Ibo language that was used in the Niger Delta churches.

Braide soon acquired a reputation for extraordinary zeal in prayer and spirituality, sometimes spending all night in prayer in the church with his Bible and Prayer Book. Although not deemed ready for baptism until January 1910, by 1909 Braide had dedicated himself to calling his fellow-countrymen to put their faith in Christ alone rather than in traditional religious practitioners, charms, and shrines. He urged fervent prayer and abstention from alcohol. Reports began to circulate of his abilities to trounce the traditional practitioners in rain-making contests, call down divine judgment on Sabbath-breakers, and pray successfully for healing. His followers accordingly awarded him the title of "Prophet Elijah II"—a title he did not repudiate. One of those healed following Braide's prayers was Kemmer's wife, who became a strong supporter of Braide, reporting as early as September 1909 that "There has never been an instance where Garrick consented to pray for any sick person in which his prayers failed to be efficacious."[19] Kemmer made him a lay preacher and introduced him to the Yoruba assistant bishop of the Niger Delta Pastorate Church, James Johnson. Braide encouraged a more charismatic and African approach to worship, with clapping, ecstatic dancing, and the use of locally composed praise songs rather than hymns from the Anglican hymnbook. His movement drew much of its power from the fact that the first Union version of the Ibo Bible, capable of being understood by speakers of all

Ibo dialect, had been completed in 1912–13: his followers all preached from it.

Until the Christmas of 1915 Braide's prophetic ministry had the blessing of Kemmer, Johnson and the Anglican authorities: it seemed like a fulfillment of their hopes for an evangelical revival. On Christmas Eve that year a crowd of Braide's followers formed a quasi-royal entourage to present him to the bishop in Bonny for his approval, only for it to be withheld: Johnson refused to listen to them unless they described Braide as an evangelist rather than a prophet.[20] Johnson appears to have feared a challenge to the exclusively Yoruba leadership of the Delta Pastorate Church, and was anxious that Braide's movement was becoming a healing cult that could subvert Anglican order. The most senior African Anglican leader of the day had repudiated Braide's prophetic credentials, and his followers rapidly went into schism. By this point Braide was using the narrative of David handing over power to Solomon in 1 Kings 2 to teach that the world war was bringing the era of European colonial rule to an end.[21] This alarmed the colonial authorities, as did reports that his followers were looting traditional shrines and pocketing the offerings left by devotees. With the movement now beyond the control of the Anglican Church, the British colonial administrator Percy Talbot stepped in and arrested Braide. He was convicted of inciting people to commit larceny, receiving money obtained by felony, and making seditious statements "likely to incite natives of Nigeria to commit offences against Britons."[22] He was imprisoned in November 1916, released, and then rearrested. Witnesses spuriously alleged that he had claimed to be the king of the whole world before whom the King of England would have to bow the knee. On being released again early in 1918, he found himself forbidden by the chiefs of Bakana to resume his healing ministry, while many of his followers had joined the Christ Army Church, an independent church founded in Lagos in 1916 by another Sierra Leonean Anglican, S. A. Coker. Coker institutionalized Braide's movement, moderating his more radical emphases. The Christ Army Church in Nigeria today is Braide's main legacy.[23] He died in November 1918 without ever regaining his former influence.

WILLIAM WADÉ HARRIS (C. 1860–1929)

William Wadé Harris was a Glebo (or Grebo), one of the indigenous peoples of Liberia.[24] He was converted through the American Methodist Episcopal mission, but joined the Protestant Episcopal Church in 1885 after his marriage to Rose Farr, a member of that church. His call to the ministry of a prophet came suddenly and mysteriously while he was in prison in Liberia in 1910. He had been jailed by the Liberian authorities on a charge of treason: at a time of considerable political instability over the contested future of the territory, he had publicly unfurled a Union Jack in protest against the American-supported regime and allegedly poured ridicule on the Liberian flag. While in prison, Harris received during the night a vision of the angel Gabriel, telling him that God was going to anoint him as a prophet for a ministry of preaching, baptism, and the destruction of fetishes. He was to begin by burning his own fetishes: though already baptized, he, like many others, had relapsed into a measure of syncretism. Harris's ministry, which took place mainly along the shores of Liberia, the Ivory and Gold Coasts, thus began with a second conversion. He experienced a triune anointing by God, which felt to him as if water and ice were being poured on his head. The angel told him that he must abandon his European dress and reclothe himself in a kind of simple white toga, which his wife was to make for him. He was to take a long cane as a symbol of his prophetic office and begin to preach, summoning people to repent, believe in Jesus Christ, and be baptized. According to some sources, the angel led him, like the apostle Peter in Acts 12, out of prison, to begin his ministry, although he was recaptured and subsequently released.

Although Harris compared himself on occasion to Moses, Daniel, John the Baptist, or even Christ himself, his primary biblical model, as in Braide's case, was Elijah. He was an African Elijah, called to show the prophets of Baal (the traditional religious practitioners) that they were powerless in the face of God and Christ. He made repeated reference to the transfiguration narrative of Mark 9, in which Christ assured the disciples that Elijah had indeed come, or returned, as the prophet who would herald the inauguration of the final age.[25] There are also numerous traditions that suggest that Harris believed that he had the power to call down both rain in time of drought, and fire from heaven in judgment on sin, as Elijah did. The fire of judgment was a constant theme in his preaching. On one occasion in the Ivory Coast port of Grand Bassam he was horrified to find cargo boats being laden with goods on a Sunday, and prophesied that a boat would burn there the next day—which it duly did.[26]

Unlike Braide, who did not himself baptize, Harris gave a prominent place to baptism in his ministry. In marked contrast to Protestant mission practice, Harris administered baptism to all who sought it without waiting for any teaching to be given or for any evidence of understanding of Christian doctrine. He always carried with him a small bowl from which he administered baptism by making the sign of the Cross with water on the forehead of the baptized, in the name of the Father, the Son, and the Holy Ghost.[27] He also carried a dog-eared English Bible, and placed it on the head of those baptized as the final act of the sacrament. He viewed the Bible as a vehicle of spiritual power, even if the person being baptized was illiterate. Had Harris made the Bible into a new fetish, a mere repository of spiritual energy? Perhaps—yet he urged his followers to learn to read, then read the Bible, and seek out those, whether white or black, who were equipped to teach it.[28] Harris applied to his own ministry in a literal sense the commission to baptize the nations given in Matthew 28. Baptism was the sign of repentance and turning toward Christ, and he issued dire warnings of judgment for any who should revert to use of fetishes once they had been baptized. The simple symbolic power of the sacrament appears to have convinced his hearers that by turning to Christ they would be secure from all evil, secure enough to burn their fetishes without fear of the consequences. Whilst Harris did heal the sick on occasion, healing did not occupy the prominent place in his ministry that it did for Braide: baptism itself was the outward sign accompanying the word and indicating that the recipient had been sealed by the protective power of Christ.

Harris, like Braide, eventually fell afoul of the colonial authorities, though for different reasons. He proclaimed peace and nonviolence at a time when the French administration in the Ivory Coast was raising its first contingent of troops to be sent to Europe to fight in the First World War. The majority of Catholic missionaries saw his activities as a Protestant plot and were prepared to believe the worst reports about him. Perhaps the decisive factor was the numerous imitators who sprang up in Harris's wake. Some of these "false prophets" urged their followers to withhold paying taxes to the colonial government. As a result, Harris was deported from the Ivory Coast back to Liberia in December 1914.

Nevertheless, Harris was the most explicitly pro-missionary of the three prophets, and urged his thousands of converts to join whatever mission church was available. In parts of Liberia, the Ivory Coast, and the Gold Coast both the Catholic Church and the Protestant mission churches saw a great upsurge in membership as a result of his preaching. The greatest beneficiary of his ministry were the Methodists, as a result of a creative intervention by a British Methodist missionary, W. J. Platt, who arrived in the Ivory Coast in late 1923 and worked hard to ensure that the Methodist Church reaped a considerable harvest in terms of lasting church membership. By October 1926 the Methodist Church could claim some 32,000 church members on the Ivory Coast in some 160 congregations. However, in the Ivory Coast in 1931 an independent church, the *Eglise Harriste*, was established by Jonas

Ahiu, whom the aged Harris had designated as his successor by the gift of his cross and Bible. In the Gold Coast two of his disciples, Grace Thanni and John Nackabah, founded the Church of the Twelve Apostles, which is now one of the largest of the so-called "spiritual" churches in Ghana.

SIMON KIMBANGU (C. 1887–1951)

Simon Kimbangu was a member of the Baptist church at Ngombe Lutete in the Lower River region of the Belgian Congo, now the Democratic Republic of Congo. The Baptist churches among the Bakongo people who lived on both sides of the colonial frontier with the Portuguese Congo (now Angola) were planted by the (British) Baptist Missionary Society (BMS). The BMS had established their first station in Mbanza Kongo, the capital of the ancient Kongo kingdom, in 1879. Kimbangu was a baptized church member in good standing, but, unlike Garrick Braide, was not regarded by his missionary pastor as an outstanding spiritual prospect. Like Harris, he received a call to preach in a vision, in 1917 or 1918, after which he began to study under the supervision of one of the deacons at the local communion center of Massangi. The deacons' verdict, however, was that he could not "read" (learn) sufficiently well, and the Ngombe Lutete missionaries accordingly refused the request of the people in Kimbangu's village of Nkamba that it should be constituted as a church center in its own right, with Kimbangu as its evangelist. He was, however, permitted to take weekday services with the status of lay preacher. He went to Kinshasa to work for three months in Lever Brothers' palm-oil factory, and after his return in 1920 attempted once more to persuade the church that he should be recognized as an evangelist. Again he was rebuffed, and this repudiation of his sense of calling was the trigger for his commencement in March 1921 of his own ministry of preaching and healing.

On the night after his rejection, Kimbangu received a further vision in which God gave him direct authority to become an apostle. When challenged by the Baptist deacons about the source of his pretended apostleship, he referred to a blessing bestowed during his infancy on his aunt (who brought him up after the death of his parents) by the BMS missionary, G. R. R. Cameron. She had protected Cameron from attack by a hostile crowd, and in gratitude he had prayed for God's blessing upon her. This incident, which Kimbangu's aunt had related to her nephew, in retrospect acquired the status of a divine commissioning, investing Kimbangu with the apostolic authority that the missionaries were believed to possess.[29] Like Harris, he donned a simple white robe: for the Bakongo, white was the color of the ancestors. But white, for Kimbangu, as for Harris, also symbolized the new eschatological community of the redeemed, as depicted in Revelation.

The preaching ministry on which Kimbangu now embarked urged people, as Braide and Harris had done, to destroy their fetishes and make a clean break with traditional sources of religious protection. His ministry lasted only six months. Kimbangu's preaching was not explicitly anticolonial, but had apocalyptic elements that caused the Belgians concern. Like Braide in 1915–16, he preached that the present world order, with its characteristic feature of European colonial rule in Africa, was destined soon to come to an end. Expectations grew that the dead would soon be raised, authority restored to the Bakongo kingdom, and colonial rule terminated. By early June 1921 the local Belgian administrator had decided that military intervention was necessary. He sent troops to arrest Kimbangu, but the prophet managed to slip through the crowds and get away. However, in September he heard the voice of God telling him to return to his New Jerusalem of Nkamba and offer himself up to the authorities. Kimbangu was consciously reproducing in his own life the passion narrative of Jesus, and the parallels were strongly developed subsequently by his followers. He was duly arrested, and in October 1921 was sentenced to death in a farce of a trial on a charge of sedition and hostility toward whites. The BMS interceded with the Belgian King Albert, pleading for clemency, and the King commuted Kimbangu's sentence to life imprisonment. He was transported hundreds of miles away to Lubumbashi, where he spent the rest of his days in prison, dying there in October 1951.

For Kimbangu, even more than for Braide, the primary sign of his prophetic authority was his performance of healing miracles. It was this that drew the crowds from miles around: the wards of the American Baptist hospital at Mbanza Manteke rapidly emptied as relatives carried their sick to Nkamba.[30] The prophet patterned his healing ministry on the example of Christ in the gospels; for example, mixing spittle and soil to apply to the eyes of the blind. His supporters, who included all but two of the Ngombe Lutete Baptist deacons, were in no doubt that Kimbangu made the blind to see, the deaf to hear, the lame to walk, and even raised the dead. Yet missionaries of different societies, even those who visited Nkamba to see for themselves, were equally certain that no such cures had occurred.[31] One or two European observers, notably Jeanne Maquet-Tombu, the wife of a Belgian colonial official, admitted that the phenomenon could be explained only if occasional cures had indeed taken place. Conversely, a few African eyewitnesses shared the European skepticism. Budimbu, a friend of Kimbangu's affiliated to the American Baptist mission, recorded case after case of failed cures.[32]

Kimbangu, as did the host of "minor prophets" who sprang up in his wake, displayed immense respect for the Bible. Demand for Kikongo Bibles throughout the Lower Congo soared, as did attendance at prayer meetings and services in the mission churches. In response to Kimbangu's gospel preaching, polygamists sent their additional wives away and fetishes were abandoned. If the Belgian authorities had not intervened to suppress the movement, it is likely that there would have been a mass accession of converts to the Baptist mission. The enthusiasm for Kimbangu's teaching was such that the road to Nkamba became littered with discarded fetishes.[33] Yet Robert Haldane Carson Graham, a firm Ulster Protestant in charge of the BMS mission at Mbanza Kongo, spoke for his missionary colleagues in expressing perplexity that a movement apparently so committed to biblical truth could produce such spurious wonders.[34] However, the Baptist members who had joined Kimbangu believed that they were following no new teaching, but simply reproducing the faith of the Gospels they had learned from their missionary teachers. They could not understand why their mentors seemed so unimpressed. Three of them wrote from prison to G. R. R. Cameron in June 1923:

> Now that you see the answer to your prayers do not think that this is "new teaching". It is what you taught yourself. What you sewed [*sic*] has sprung up. . . . Now, Mr Cameron, do you believe what Jesus said in Mark 16:16?[35] And in Luke 9.49.[36] Are they not true? Please remember what you prayed to God for—now He has answered you, you can give thanks and rejoice for all. . . . What you taught us, it is that we believe. . . .[37]

Kimbangu's movement, like Braide's and Harris's, was not intrinsically anti-missionary. His followers turned against the BMS for two reasons. The first was the missionaries' consistent refusal to believe that he had performed miracles. The second was that the contacts they made with the Belgian authorities—with the intention of dissuading them from armed intervention—were interpreted as evidence of complicity and even betrayal. The mission thus got the blame for Kimbangu's arrest and the imprisonment of his leading followers, and received little credit for its intercession on behalf of his life. The movement was forced underground for more than three decades, though it continued to gain secret adherents in both Protestant and Catholic congregations. In 1956 it resurfaced through the formation of the *Eglise du Jesus Christ sur la Terre par le*

Prophète Simon Kimbangu. In December 1959, on the eve of Congolese independence, the Church gained legal recognition under the leadership of Kimbangu's third son Diangienda Kuntima Joseph, who had previously been a practicing Catholic. In April 1969 the Church became the first African Initiated Church to be admitted to membership of the World Council of Churches (WCC). Diangienda was keen to promote acceptance of the Church in ecumenical circles and hence downplayed the Church's less orthodox features. His elder brother, Dialungana Kiangani Salomon, cared less for ecumenical approval, and in various theological documents, such as the Kimbanguist catechism of 1957, identified his father as the Comforter or Holy Spirit of whom Christ spoke in John 14. Dialungana succeeded his brother as *Chef Spirituel* in 1992, and in 1999 adopted his own birthday as the date of the Kimbanguist Christmas. The convergence of identity between Simon Kimbangu and the Holy Spirit made possible a further step in which Dialungana, shortly before his death in 2001, declared himself to be "the Jesus Christ whom the world was looking for," fathered by the Spirit.[38] In June 2003 the new *Chef Spirituel*, Kimbangu's grandson, Simon Kimbangu Kiangani, completed the journey to heterodoxy by affirming explicitly that Simon Kimbangu *was* the Holy Spirit. Despite such heterodox statements, the Church remains in membership with the WCC. By 1995 its number of adherents in the Democratic Republic of Congo alone totaled 7.5 million.[39]

III. Conversion and Revival Movements in Melanesia

Since the 1830s European commentators have divided the islands of the Pacific into three groups: Polynesia, extending from Easter Island to Hawaii in the north and New Zealand in the southwest; Micronesia, embracing the scattered groups of small islands to the east of the Philippines; and Melanesia, which includes Fiji, New Caledonia, Vanuatu (formerly the New Hebrides), the Solomon Islands, and New Guinea (though between 1962 and 1969 the Dutch and western half of New Guinea was forcibly incorporated into the new Asian nation of Indonesia). Many of the island groups in Polynesia and Micronesia, with the addition of Fiji, had become predominantly Christian in the course of the nineteenth century. Some, such as Tonga and Fiji (Wesleyan Methodist), or Samoa, Tahiti, and the Cook Islands (London Missionary Society), were evangelized by British Nonconformist missions and became miniature Christendoms in which a particular brand of Protestant Nonconformity ironically became the religious establishment. Other islands, such as Uvea (Wallis Island), its

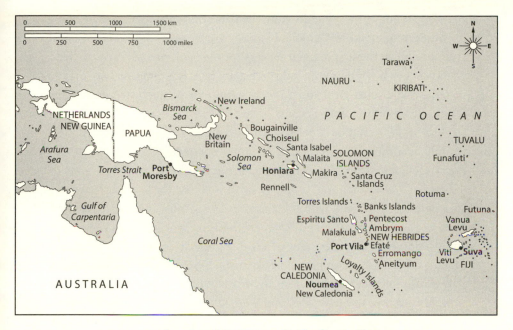

MAP 1. Melanesia and the Western Pacific after World War I

neighbor Futuna, and parts of French Polynesia, became strongholds of Catholicism, evangelized by French Marists or the Paris-based Congregation of the Sacred Hearts of Jesus and Mary (the Picpus Fathers).

In contrast, few of the peoples of Melanesia became Christian before the twentieth century. In the Solomon Islands and the New Hebrides Anglican missionary work by the Melanesian Mission had begun under the leadership of Bishop Selwyn of New Zealand as early as 1849, but the progress of conversion was generally slow, especially in Malaita, the most heavily populated of the Solomon Islands. Sustained Catholic work in the Solomon Islands dates only from 1898. In western New Guinea, Protestant (mainly Dutch) missions had been at work since 1855, but the number of converts at the dawn of the twentieth century was no more than 200.[40] In the northern (German) part of eastern New Guinea Catholic fathers from the Sacred Heart and Divine Word Missions operated from 1885 and 1896 respectively; two Lutheran missions, the Neuendettelsau Mission and the Rhenish Mission, also began work in 1886–87. In Papua, the London Missionary Society (LMS) mission along the southern coast, staffed mainly by Polynesian or Loyalty Island evangelists, had seen some success by 1900. The Catholic missions on the north coast soon began to reap a harvest from their investment in education. In the Neuendettelsau

Mission an emphasis on addressing the Christian message to entire communities, pioneered by Christian Keysser (1877–1961) between 1899 and 1921, produced the first marked success for the Lutherans.[41] Nevertheless, Melanesia as a whole remained the least Christian region of the Pacific into the mid-twentieth century. Two reasons may be suggested for the difference in the chronology of conversion.

The first is a matter of geography. The greater size of the Melanesian islands in comparison with those in Polynesia or Micronesia meant that many Melanesian peoples were not incorporated into colonial empires or spheres of Western cultural influence until well into the twentieth century. In a parallel movement with the European "scramble" for Africa, eastern New Guinea was partitioned between the European colonial powers by the Anglo-German agreement of 1886. Similarly most of the Solomon Islands became a British protectorate in 1898–99. In both cases, however, it was only in the decade before the First World War that colonial administration became effective, and even then only in the coastal areas. Not until the mid-1920s did British rule become effective throughout the Solomons, and from that point the schools run by the Melanesian Mission became a powerful instrument of Christianization.[42] In New Guinea also, there was a time lag between the formal imposition of colonial rule and its impact on the majority of the population. From 1905 British New Guinea (Papua) was administered by Australia, and in 1914 Australian administration was extended to German territory. Neither the Australians nor the Japanese who occupied the island from 1941 to 1945 succeeded in penetrating the highlands in the interior. In the remote highlands Australian control did not become effective until well after 1945. As late as the 1970s New Guinean indigenous peoples and their traditional religions were the object of research by anthropologists interested in studying peoples untouched by Western "civilization." For markedly different reasons, the Western "discovery" of the same peoples attracted the attention of evangelical and fundamentalist missions concerned to reach "unreached" peoples for Christ. In response to the pioneering journey in 1926–28 of C. Karius and I. Champion, the first white men to traverse Papua New Guinea from south to north, the Australian branch of the Unevangelized Fields Mission (UFM) began work in 1933 among the Gogodala people who occupy the region from the lower Fly River to the Aramia River.[43] From the 1950s onwards other such interdenominational "faith" missions would follow the UFM into the New Guinean interior, with remarkable results.

A second possible reason for the delay in conversion to Christianity in comparison to other Pacific island societies is the extraordinary linguistic diversity of Melanesia. Of the approximately 7,000 spoken languages in the world, nearly 1,200 are found in Melanesia.[44] With linguistic units being so small, and those who spoke these languages so often being geographically inaccessible, Melanesian languages lagged behind those elsewhere in the Pacific in the sequence of Bible translation.[45] In northern New Guinea, an obvious option was to concentrate first on Tok Pisin, a pidgin language that took shape during the nineteenth century. The Divine Word missionaries in the 1920s were the first to adopt Tok Pisin as a language of evangelization, and one of their Madang missionaries, Father Francis Mihalic, did much to standardize and legitimate Tok Pisin through a dictionary and grammar produced in 1957 and a newspaper, *Wantok*, first published in 1970.[46] Another milestone in the formalization of the language was the publication in 1963 of the four Gospels in Tok Pisin, *Gutnius Bilong Jisas Kraist*, in an ecumenical translation project initiated by the Lutherans. The New Testament followed in 1969 and the complete Bible in 1989. In the south, another pidgin language, "Police" Motu, flourished for a time before giving way to Tok Piksin. Despite the currency of pidgin languages, the Wycliffe Bible Translators and their partner organization, the Summer Institute of Linguistics, who began work in Papua New Guinea in 1957, were committed to the goal of translating scripture into Melanesian indigenous languages: by 1997 they had translated parts of the Bible into 100 languages in Papua New Guinea. The translation in 1965 of Matthew's Gospel into the language of the Binumarien people of the eastern highlands caused great excitement, for Matthew's genealogy of Jesus revealed him to be one of us, unlike many spirits who have no ancestors.[47]

In most Pacific cultures, as in sub-Saharan African and many Asian ones, human life is played out under the watchful eye of the spirits of the ancestors, the forest, the mountains, or the sea. Those who are recognized as having unusual ability to mediate between humans and the world of the spirits, and as possessing the authority to manipulate and channel their powers, have special social and ritual significance. In many Pacific societies the special charisma or power that both the spirits themselves and their human intermediaries possess is known as *mana*. In Polynesia and Micronesia *mana* was traditionally thought to reside in hereditary chiefs and their associated priestly cults. In Melanesia it has more often been associated with "big men" who have muscled their way to power. Institutionalized priesthoods were rare. Much more common were ecstatic forms of religious life that valorized the prevailing masculine warrior culture of "payback," in which the spirits of the warrior dead were invoked to protect the community from its enemies and wreak revenge upon them.[48]

Melanesian societies are now among the most heavily Christianized on the planet. The styles of church life created by this religious transformation during the twentieth century were quite diverse, but a common theme in the process was that of Christianity as a source of superior spiritual power. Melanesia had its share of prophet movements of a very similar kind to those in West Africa. From about 1920 to 1922 the so-called "Vailala Madness" among the Elema people living along the Vailala River in the Papuan Gulf, though initially welcomed by the local LMS missionary, combined charismatic phenomena with a concern to use the authority of the ancestors to protect the Elema people against the growing financial demands of the colonial administration and usher in a new era of prosperity.[49] From 1959 to 1961, in New Georgia in the western Solomons, a Methodist charismatic leader of long-standing, Silas Eto (c. 1905–84), led a secession from the Methodist Church to form a new independent church, the Christian Fellowship Church. As in the Kimbanguist church, hymns were the central feature of worship, and many spoke of Eto ("Holy Mama") as a vehicle of the Holy Spirit, or even as God himself.[50] However, in Melanesia the mainstream churches proved rather more successful than in West Africa in containing the dynamism of power-oriented Christianity within the boundaries of church order. A good example is the Anglican religious order, the Melanesian Brotherhood.

Anglicanism in Melanesia has retained the High Church tradition of Bishop Selwyn, but also exhibits an indigenous character that derives in part from the influence of the Melanesian Brotherhood. The order was formed in 1925 by a policeman in the Solomon Islands constabulary, Ini Kopuria (1900–45).[51] Kopuria was inspired by what he had heard from his missionary schoolteachers in Norfolk Island of the Franciscan order and the role of English monks such as Boniface in the evangelization of Germany. The Melanesian Brothers took annual vows of poverty, chastity, and obedience, lived in households of no more than twelve, and went out in pairs to preach the gospel. They wore the simplest of dress (a black loincloth and white sash, and on Sundays and saints' days a white loin-cloth and black sash) and each carried a walking stick that had both practical use and symbolic significance: it represented the constant presence of Christ, and could only be used or touched by the Brothers. They were widely recognized as those who possessed unique *mana*. They were invited to cleanse areas inhabited by bad spirits, and became involved in power contests with traditional practitioners, as on the atoll of Sikaiana in 1929, when the latter tried without success to implore the spirits to bring rain to dampen the Christmas feast organized by the Brothers for those who were hearing the Christian message.[52] The square in the Brothers' head-quarters at Tabalia on Guadalcanal was regarded as a site of such sanctity that it was believed that even the birds would not fly over it. Stories circulated of healings and miracles worked by Kopuria: like Moses, he was said to have dried up the Mataniko River by striking the waters with his walking stick when he and another Brother wished to cross.[53] Within ten years there were 128 Brothers working in the Solomons, New Britain, Fiji, and the New Hebrides. The expansion of the Brotherhood was halted by two reverses in the 1940s. First, Kopuria renounced his life-long vows to get married in 1940 and left the Brotherhood. Second, the Japanese occupation of the Solomon Islands from April 1942 made their itinerations impossible. After the war the Brotherhood had to be rebuilt virtually from nothing. Kopuria died of tuberculosis in 1945, but his memory remained a powerful inspiration. Following principles analogous to those pioneered by Christian Keysser in New Guinea, the Brotherhood evangelized entire village communities rather than individuals. Between 1955 and 1957, for example, they initiated the conversion of forty-five villages in New Britain and New Guinea, with an aggregate population of 9,500.[54] The spread of Anglicanism in Melanesia owes much to the Brotherhood.

The incarnational theology of Catholic Anglicanism encouraged a strongly incultured form of Christianity. Conservative evangelical missions such as the UFM required their converts to make a more radical break with traditional customs, yet were capable of finding other routes toward cultural acceptability. The UFM baptized its first converts from the Gogodala people in 1940. On the extension of the Second World War to the Pacific in December 1941, the missionaries were evacuated, leaving the church with about forty baptized members and only the Gospel of Mark in the Gogodala language. Yet by the end of the century, the Evangelical Church of Papua New Guinea (ECPNG), established by the mission in 1966, claimed the allegiance of the majority of the population of 25,000, more than 90 percent of whom were Christian. The success of the UFM has been ascribed to its ability to transpose the Gogodala's respect for big men and warriors into an evangelical key: its missionaries were tough Australian farmers and rural working men who themselves embodied masculinity, and their evangelism singled out the "big men" in the community who would be able to influence others. At a deeper cultural and conceptual level, therefore, Christianity was able to insert itself into the traditional value structure of society, rather than overturn it.[55] Nevertheless, by the mid-1970s there were signs of disillusionment with the failure of Christianity to deliver the material prosperity or "cargo" that many had anticipated. Disillusionment deepened when national independence in 1975 also failed to effect any noticeable improvement in the material prosperity of the Gogodala. Perhaps in reaction to such disappointed hopes, from 1977 revival movements emanating from the South Sea Evangelical Church in the Solomon Islands swept some of the congregations. "Revival" pitted the young who sought a Pentecostal understanding of spiritual power as signs and wonders against more conservative church leaders.[56] The publication of the Gogodala New Testament in 1981 widened the scope for religious dissent. By the late 1990s the ECPNG was facing competition from a new charismatic church, the Congregation of Evangelical Fellowship [sic], which challenged evangelical taboos on indigenous cultural practices by making dance a central feature of Christian worship.[57]

From the late 1970s—roughly simultaneous with the end of the colonial era[58]—the varied Christian monocultures of the Pacific Islands were increasingly eroded by the eruption of revival and charismatic movements that challenged the cultural conservatism of the older mission churches.[59] How these new movements should be interpreted remains a matter of debate. Are they new variations on an old primal theme, in which religion is primarily a vehicle for the acquisition of power or material "cargo"?[60] Or do they represent a second and deeper stage of conversion, in which Christianity becomes for the first time an independent variable, no longer simply an imported means to a material end, but rather the source of a new indigenized framework of meaning, the architect of a new culture? This alternative interpretation is suggested by Joel Robbins' study of the Urapmin, a minute tribal community living in the far western highlands of Papua New Guinea.[61] The Urapmin first encountered Christianity in the 1950s, when they sent some young men to contact Australian Baptist missionaries who worked among a neighboring Min group. By the late 1960s some had been converted, even without the presence of a resident missionary. But it was not clear that this first stage of the conversion process was anything more than a prudential adjustment to the growing encroachment of the Australian colonial economy. The second stage of conversion, in which the Urapmin made Christianity their own, was, Robbins suggests, the result of the same charismatic revival movements originating from the Solomon Islands that impacted the Gogadala from 1977. Rather like Kimbangu in 1921, Urapmin church leaders came to ground their spiritual authority in the direct infilling of the Spirit, rather than in delegation from missionaries, and Christianity ceased to be an alien entity.[62] Also relevant was the publication in 1969 of the New Testament into Tok Pisin, the language normally used by the Urapmin in church contexts.[63]

IV. The Ambiguous Power of the Word

This chapter has charted a number of different trajectories whereby a religion emanating from Western societies became in the course of the twentieth century a faith rooted in the soil of West African or Melanesian societies. For the first six or seven decades of the century, the Catholic and Protestant trajectories tended to diverge, though perhaps less markedly so than European church history would lead one to expect. Catholic missions before Vatican II were fearful of unleashing the vernacular Bible on the laity and relied instead on a tightly controlled network of schools to grow a Christian community from childhood upwards. Conversion came not through sudden movements of indigenous revival and initiative, but through the steady growth in the numbers of school rolls and hence of the baptized. The resulting Christian community was comparatively immune from schism, and had a strong sense of the universality of the one faith, though this was held in tandem with a greater willingness to incorporate indigenous cultural features than most Protestant missions displayed. Its weakness was its vulnerability to the charge that it was an exercise in the colonization of the mind, as well as the risk that Christian allegiance could become a mere by-product of educational aspirations.

Protestant mission schools ran a similar risk, but evangelical theologies of the word and of individual conversion ensured that Protestant missionaries were even more conscious than their Catholic counterparts of the dangers of mere head knowledge or forms of adherence to the church that appeared to lack strong personal conviction. The real point of education was that it opened the door to read the Bible for oneself, in one's own language, and thus laid the individual soul open to the regenerating power of the Spirit. Yet Protestant missionaries were well aware of the potential for aberrant interpretation and hence delayed both baptism and subsequent admission to church leadership until they could be confident that the candidate had "learned" sufficiently well. As the stories of Braide and Kimbangu illustrate, however, reading—or even simply hearing—the scriptures in one's own language was enough to permit individual and corporate appropriations of the Christian message that radically challenged European preconceptions, even if, at least originally, they could plausibly claim to be direct and literal applications of the biblical text. As vernacular translations exposed the extent to which European Christianity had denuded the biblical text of its prophetic and miraculous elements, Africans and Melanesians who had unusual charismatic gifts or *mana* sometimes assumed the mantle of the prophets and challenged their missionary mentors to join their many indigenous converts in believing their mighty works. When they did not do so, schism could result, although not invariably, as the ministry of William Wadé Harris evidences. Over time, a few independent churches, such as the Kimbanguists or Eto's Christian Fellowship Church, invested their prophet-founders with such unique revelatory significance that the doctrine of the Trinity itself had to be reinterpreted to make room for them. Many others continued to venerate their founder as one of the prophets, even as a second Elijah, but remained so strongly biblical in their essential emphases that missionary fears of heterodoxy proved exaggerated or wholly unfounded.

The parallels between African and Melanesian experience should not be pushed too far. Indigenous Christian leaders in Melanesia who displayed remarkable *mana* were less likely to be categorized as prophets than their West African counterparts, primarily because *mana* in Pacific societies was never solely linked to concepts of spirit possession. Neither, of course, were the Catholic and Protestant trajectories mutually exclusive. The Melanesian Brotherhood combined a Catholic respect for church order with an evangelical passion for preaching the word, and manifested some elements of the prophetic model of ministry: the Brothers have challenged people to give up their traditional practices. Yet Ini Kopuria never claimed to be a prophet and appears never to have contemplated schism from the Anglican Church. In the Congo the Jamaa movement remained just about obedient to Catholic authority even while incorporating charismatic and indigenous cultural dimensions in its spirituality.[64] The Second Vatican Council narrowed the gap between Catholic and Protestant missiology by its rediscovery of the apostolate of the laity and its endorsement of private Bible reading. Conversely, Protestant missions from the 1960s moderated their historic individualism as the people group missiology pioneered by Christian Keysser and Bruno Gutmann was adopted by large sections of the conservative evangelical missionary movement under the influence of Donald McGavran of Fuller Theological Seminary and his "church growth" school—a theme to which we will return in chapter 9.[65] Charismatic renewal further narrowed the gap between Protestants and Catholics, and rendered both more open to dimensions of Christian experience that were already familiar to many non-Western Christians. Christianity by the close of the century wore many faces, but insofar as a single family likeness could now be discerned, behind that likeness lay the power of the word.

CHAPTER FOUR

Making War on the Saints

THE CHURCH UNDER SIEGE IN FRANCE AND THE SOVIET UNION

I. Varieties of the Secular

The theory that the grand narrative of twentieth-century religion is one of an irreversible global process of secularization was especially cherished in the 1960s and 1970s, when the advance of the secular was all the rage. Today it looks decidedly threadbare. The manifold evidence of the continuing flourishing and political influence of religious belief in the twenty-first century has compelled the remaining defenders of secularization theory to recast their arguments. Perhaps the most articulate of those embattled defenders, the sociologist Steve Bruce, has maintained that the default setting of modernized societies is that religion should gradually lose its social significance, *"except where it finds work to do other than relating individuals to the supernatural."*[1] Such exceptional functional "work" takes the form either of cultural defense, in which religion is a useful ally for a national or ethnic identity that finds itself under threat, or of cultural transition, in which religion eases the process of transition for migrant groups in new locations. In his most recent recasting of his thesis to meet his numerous critics, Bruce has insisted that he does not regard the global march of secularization as somehow inevitable. His claim is now more modest, namely that *"if other places modernize* in ways similar to the European experience, then we can expect the nature and status of religion also to change in similar ways."*[2] Bruce further maintains that a central feature of modernization, the loss of social significance of religion through its progressive removal from the public sphere, will normally precipitate "a decline in the number of religious people and the extent to which people are religious." The end result, Bruce predicts, will be, not the triumph of atheism but the growth of religious indifference—religion will simply cease to matter.[3] Soviet Russia and France in the twentieth century provide two obvious examples of sustained campaigns by the state, supported by significant sections of popular opinion, to diminish the social significance of religion, and of Christianity in particular. They therefore enable us to measure Bruce's theory against the yardstick of historical experience.

The Union of Soviet Socialist Republics (USSR) was inaugurated in December 1922 in the wake of the October 1917 Bolshevik Revolution, and was finally dissolved in December 1991. The intervening seventy years of Soviet rule over Russia and its dependent republics represented the first sustained attempt in history to run a state—indeed an entire empire—on avowedly atheistic principles. Revolutionary France during the years of "dechristianization" in the 1790s provides a precedent of a kind, when the revolutionaries extended their hostility from the Roman Catholic Church to the Christian faith itself. But the French Revolution was never explicitly atheistic: most of its leaders were Deists, and subscribed to the cult of the Supreme Being alongside their devotion to Reason. By 1801 the anti-Christian phase of the Revolution had been terminated by Napoleon's Concordat, whereby Catholicism was recognized as "the religion of the great majority of French citizens," the state agreed to pay clergy salaries, and the head of state gained the right to nominate bishops. The Concordat lasted until 1905, when, as the culmination of a protracted culture war in the Third Republic between Catholics and anticlerical republicans for the soul of France, the Law of Separation was enacted. The Law of Separation, however, was not intended to extirpate Christianity, but only to curb the influence of the clergy and emancipate lay people from the domination of the Catholic hierarchy. The French variety of the secular—summed up in the term *laïcité*–was primarily cultural and aimed at the political limitation rather than the complete ideological elimination of religion. With its strongest champions among the bourgeoisie, it was particularly concerned to subvert the predominant influence of the religious orders on public education. Russian secularism could not at first draw on the same reservoirs of middle-class and intellectual support. As a working-class and revolutionary movement it had to be more far-reaching in its objectives and visceral in its tone than its French counterpart.

There were, nevertheless, striking parallels between the two secularist campaigns. When the Bolsheviks after 1917 began to target the church that had formed the spiritual handmaid of the Russian *ancien regime*, some church leaders drew the obvious comparison with revolutionary France. Archbishop Antonii Khraporitskii of Kharkov, when asked for comment on the Bolshevik onslaught on the Russian Orthodox Church, simply recommended his questioners to read a historical account of the attacks on the Catholic Church in France in the 1790s.[4] Both varieties of the secular objected to the hierarchicalism that was intrinsic to the Catholic and the Orthodox traditions, and instead affirmed the sovereignty of the people. Both directed their hostility toward priests and ecclesiastical property in particular. Both suspected Christians as being of dubious loyalty to the nation—though in both cases experience in the two world wars decisively refuted the allegation. Both tended to idealize the supposedly masculine values of manual labor (in the Soviet case) and critical independence of mind (in the French case). Traditional historiography, at least, has maintained that secularist campaigns appealed more to men than to women, who, it is conventionally alleged, were more likely to be "submissive" and entranced by the sentimentality of Christian devotion, such as the fervent Ultramontane Marian piety that attracted many French Catholic women from the mid-nineteenth century onwards. Such generalizations must be treated with caution. In the French case, they reflect the rationalist and misogynist prejudices of anticlerical republicans of the Third Republic, prejudices that were largely responsible for delaying the award of the franchise to women until as late as 1944.[5] In the Soviet Union similarly, atheist writers for long maintained that women, lacking in education in "scientific" principles, were peculiarly susceptible to the false emotional consolations offered by religion. While it is true that women constituted the large majority of Orthodox congregations in the Soviet Union, their predominance moderated in the 1970s and 1980s; it was also less marked in the case of Protestant churches.[6] It is also not clear that this gender imbalance was more extreme in the Soviet case than in other parts of the world.

Above all, both campaigns proved largely incapable of undermining the deep foundations of popular religiosity. They may even have had the opposite effect. Marx himself had viewed religion as an opiate that dulled the senses of the proletariat to the pain of their oppression: according to Marx, in the coming socialist society, the opiate would no longer be necessary and hence would simply disappear. Jean Jaurès, the French socialist who was one of the influences behind the separation of church and state in France in 1905, repeated Marx's view, describing Christian belief as "the old lullaby which soothed human misery."[7] The anticlerical tradition in France had its own "religion"—the confident scientific humanism of positivism, frequently given institutional expression by membership of a Masonic lodge. It postulated that if only the minds of the young could be prised from the grip of the religious orders, Catholic superstition would soon wither on the vine, and the goddess of Reason would at last reign supreme in the French republic. Although it is undoubtedly the case that many more French people were indifferent to Christianity in 2000 than was the case a century earlier, the causes of this seepage of faith appear to be only indirectly related to the anticlericalism that dominated French politics before the Second World War.

In Soviet Russia, by contrast, Lenin and Trotsky adopted a more militant antagonism to the very existence of Christianity. They castigated religion as a capitalist and reactionary force that could not be permitted to obstruct the immediate progress of the revolution, and it was not long before the Russian Orthodox Church experienced the full weight of the Soviet onslaught. However, the story of Christianity in the Soviet Union cannot be reduced to a simple narrative of the persecution of Christians by an atheistic state. There were always pragmatic voices in the Communist Party who argued that the interests of the state were better served by controlling religion than by combatting it, and for significant periods those voices prevailed. The Soviet state looked all-powerful but in reality was relatively powerless as an agent of dechristianization. While ruthlessly capable in the destruction of the formal apparatus of the national church, it had limited success in the manipulation of those sectors of religious organization that it chose to tolerate, and was utterly ineffective in its attempts to extinguish the flames of popular Christian belief.

II. The Catholic Church, the State, and
Religious Practice in Secular France

Between 1901 and 1908 the successive anticlerical governments of Pierre Waldeck-Rousseau, Émile Combes, and Georges Clemenceau systematically dismantled the connection between Church and State in France that Napoleon had restored in 1801. The law of associations of July 1, 1901 denied to the religious orders the automatic right of freedom of association; they had to seek authorization from parliament. To be a member of a nonauthorized order was illegal. A further law of July 1, 1904 made it illegal for any member of a religious order to teach in schools, though the law was widely circumvented, as many religious continued teaching in civilian dress; between 1904 and 1911 the Republic succeeded in closing only 1,843 of the 8,200 schools run by religious orders.[8] On December 9, 1905, the Law of Separation removed the clergy from the payroll of the French state and removed the legal personality of the Catholic Church. Finally, a law of April 1908 formalized the transfer of the bulk of church property into state hands. Republican France had charted a course of radical separation of church and state that would be followed by Portugal in 1910, Spain between 1931 and 1939, and even in some measure by Russia after 1917.

The 1905 Law of Separation assumed that the state had rightful ownership of churches and cathedrals built before the Concordat of 1801. Those built from private church funds since the Concordat were given outright to "*associations cultuelles*," voluntary groups of citizens to be formed in each commune, proportionate in size to the population of the commune (7 for up to 1,000 inhabitants; 15 for 1,000–20,000; 25 for those over 20,000). It was originally proposed that the *associations cultuelles* would have to pay rent to the authorities for their use of church buildings, but in the event it was agreed that they could do so without rent. The associations would be the sole legal embodiment of the church, administering its property on the same basis as would any other voluntary association.[9] An avowedly secular state was telling the Catholic Church what form its future attenuated polity should take, and it looked suspiciously like a system of congregational government by laypersons. The Law made no mention of pope, bishops, or clergy, for that would have given Catholic ecclesiology continuing legal recognition. Pope Pius X was not amused. In an encyclical of February 11, 1906, *Vehementer nos*, he denounced the system of *associations cultuelles* as an attempt by the French state to impose a constitution on the church, an entity of divine origin whose episcopal governance had apostolic authority. A second encyclical issued in August 1906, *Gravissimo officii*, solemnly forbade any Catholic from joining such associations. The church thereby repudiated the only form of legal recognition being offered by the state, and in so doing said goodbye to about half a million francs' worth of ecclesiastical property. Many French Catholics, already faced with paying for some 42,000 clergy, regretted the intransigence of the papacy, believing that some way could have been found of integrating the associations in an episcopal structure of governance. In the event, the government fell back on the pragmatic and surprisingly conservative principle of allowing parish priests to remain in *de facto* possession of their parish churches. Local mayors often permitted them to remain in their presbyteries, advancing the fiction that they were "caretakers" of the property on behalf of the state. In contrast, bishops' palaces were turned into museums or public libraries. The French Catholic Church was left in a precarious state of legal limbo that lasted till 1924, while the loss of so much of its property in 1908 would never be entirely made good.[10]

The anticlerical program of the Third Republic was designed to push the Catholic faith to the margins of national life. It had considerable success in achieving that goal. The influence of the church on public education was severely curtailed. From the teacher training colleges there emerged a new generation of teachers, especially at the primary level, whose political sympathies were socialist or even communist. The trade union representing primary school teachers, the *Syndicat national d'instituteurs*, formed in 1920, became known for its militant anticlericalism.[11] The removal of clergy from the state payroll and uncertain legal status of the church had a serious impact on recruitment to the clergy: ordinations fell from 1,733 in 1901 to 825 in 1913.[12] The numbers of young people entering religious orders also fell: the number of monks in France, which had risen from 3,000 in 1848 to 37,000 in 1901, declined to 29,500 by 1945.[13] Catholics were systematically excluded from high office in key departments of state, such as the Ministry of Education and the Council of State; very few became government ministers.[14]

Catholicism undoubtedly lost social significance in France between 1870 and 1940, but the loss was not absolute. Ordinations to the priesthood recovered substantially after the church's legal position was regularized in 1924, reaching a figure of 1,355 by 1938, and continued to rise until 1956.[15] French Catholics did not meekly accept their marginalization from the affairs of state. In an attempt to reverse the process, the *Fédération Nationale Catholique* was established in the wake of the victory of the "Cartel des Gauches" in the May 1924 general election. By September 1926 it had accumulated 1.8 million members. In Catholic strongholds such as Brittany it attracted vast numbers to its rallies calling for resistance to the pernicious influence of Freemasonry, and the restoration in France of a Christian social order.[16]

However, by the mid-1920s the ideological warfare between the Vatican and the French state was already subsiding. The First World War had begun the process by proving the national loyalty of French Catholics: many of the bishops actually took up arms in defense of their country. Furthermore, Pope Benedict XV (1914–22) was of a much more conciliatory temper than Pius X. Early in 1921 Benedict's secretary of state, Cardinal Gasparri, opened negotiations with the French government with a view to reaching the compromise that many French clergy had advocated in 1906–8, namely forming a single *association cultuelle* for each diocese to be chaired by the bishop. This was the agreement reached in 1924, after Benedict's death and replacement by Pius XI. Pius was no social democrat, but, to the dismay of conservative Catholics, he did at least in 1926 condemn the extreme reactionary organization, the *Action Française*.

The formation of diocesan associations allowed the church in France once again corporately to be the legal owner of property. Catholics hoped that the new associations would enable the church to recover some of the still unallocated property lost in 1908, but this possibility was stymied by the victory of the Left in the 1924 election. That hope would not be realized until February 1941, when the pro-clerical Vichy government of Marshall Pétain returned to the church the dwindling residue of unallocated property. Its value in real terms in 1941 was barely 1 percent of what the church had forfeited in 1908.[17] Pétain, himself only a nominal Catholic, had the enthusiastic support of the bishops, though not of all clergy or laity. He revoked the 1904 law prohibiting regular clergy from school-teaching, and in August 1941 his private office even advocated that Catholicism should be restored to its official status as "the most favored religion," since it was the religion of the majority.[18] As in the Soviet Union, the Second World War blunted the force of secularist attacks on Christianity, and in the French case the impact was enduring.

The Vichy regime brought to a close the supremacy of *laïcité* in modern French politics, though it has remained a powerful influence in national life until this day. For a brief period from the liberation of Paris in August 1944 to the spring of 1947, France even witnessed a rapprochement between progressive Catholics, socialists, and communists, forged by their collaboration in the Resistance to the Nazis. Their common ground was a simple ideal of humanity. Some Catholic workers actually joined the Communist Party as a concomitant of their trade union membership. This was true especially of members of the *Jeunesse Ouvrière Chrétienne*, a branch of the Catholic Action movement founded in 1927 that encouraged young Catholics to express their faith in their secular employment. Some worker-priests—a phenomenon that originated as a byproduct of the termination of state remuneration of the clergy—joined the unions, and a few even became members of the Communist Party. Although a Vatican decree of 1949 soon put a stop to Catholics being Communist Party members, enough of the ideological common ground from the Liberation period survived to affect the relations between church and state in postwar France.[19]

The presidency of Charles de Gaulle, who was a committed Catholic, inaugurated in 1958 a period of right-wing government that lasted until the accession of François Mitterand to the presidency in 1981. Anticlerical campaigns against Catholic influence in education continued, but with dwindling prospects of success. When the Socialist government of Mitterand's prime minister Pierre Mauroy attempted to intensify state control of the remaining large number of Catholic schools, it found to its cost that they retained considerable public support: over a million parents (many of them not practicing Catholics) took to the streets of Paris in June 1984 to defeat the proposals.[20] Although the Catholic share of national education continued to decline in the second half of the century, it remained quite substantial. In 1935 47.7 percent of secondary pupils were in private schools (almost all of them being Catholic). By 1992–93 the proportion had fallen to about 20 percent. Nevertheless, seventy years after the secularist campaigns of 1901–4, there remained more than 2 million children in Catholic schools in France.[21] Ironically, the "religion" of *laïcité* suffered its own critical reaction in the last two decades of the century. In a postmodern philosophical and increasingly pluralist religious environment, the confident scientific rationalism of the Third Republic now looked decidedly *passé*, and Catholicism could occupy a more comfortable, if still limited, space in French public life.[22]

Secularization theory, at least in the form advocated by Steve Bruce, suggests that a sustained campaign to marginalize religion from public life and institutions can normally be expected to result in a progressive attenuation of personal faith and devotional practice. The statistical data on religious observance in twentieth-century France are unusually comprehensive, thanks to the development in France of the discipline of *sociologie religieuse*. However, the conclusions of the French sociologists of religion do not offer much support to Bruce's contentions. The two pioneers of the discipline were admittedly both committed Catholics. Gabriel Le Bras (1891–1970) was a Breton scholar who had been depressed by the rapidity with which Bretons lost their Catholic devotion once they had migrated to Paris. In an article published in 1931 he made the first scholarly attempt to quantify the level of religious observance in France.[23] His collaborator Fernand Boulard (1898–1977), through his experience as a priest of a rural parish and later chaplain to the Catholic young women's organization, the *Jeunesse agricole chrétienne*, had acquired an unusually comprehensive understanding of the condition of the Catholic Church in rural France. In 1947 he used Le Bras's research to publish a map of religious practice in France that set the pattern for all subsequent academic interpretation of the subject. The work of Le Bras and Boulard also substantially influenced the small but highly significant book published in 1943 by two *abbés*, H. Godin and Y. Daniel, *La France pays de Mission?* The question posed by Godin and Daniel was answered in the affirmative: large parts of France, they warned, were now pagan territory.[24]

Although Godin and Daniel placed greatest emphasis on the damaging impact on religious practice of migration to the cities, uprooting Catholics from their historic communities of faith, the most controversial conclusion advanced by Le Bras and Boulard was that the secularist paradigm of a nationwide linear evolution toward an endpoint of a dechristianized society simply could not be supported from the statistics. Rather they emphasized the marked extent of regional variation in levels of religious observance, following patterns of cultural differentiation that had a long history, antedating not simply industrialization and modern anticlericalism but even the French Revolution. Boulard's map divided France into three categories: areas of majority religious practice, such as Brittany, the southern Massif Central, and the western Pyrenees; areas of minority religious practice but "seasonal conformity" to Catholic traditions (which formed the largest category); and mission areas that were "partially detached" from the Christian faith, where at least 20 percent of children were not baptized or being catechized, such as the Paris basin and the Limousin.[25] Levels of church attendance in Paris itself, though low, were not as low as in the hinterland. Boulard demonstrated that levels of religious adherence could vary enormously within a relatively small area: in the diocese of Chartres, only 1.5 percent of men and 15 percent of women attended Easter communion at the beginning of the twentieth century; whereas in the diocese of Nantes, only 100 miles away, 82 percent of men and 96 percent of women did so.[26]

As the data from Chartres and Nantes exemplify, Le Bras and Boulard also revealed what has since become a commonplace of scholarship, the "sexual dimorphism" of religious practice in modern France. Whether the region concerned was one of high or low levels of religious observance, the proportion of women attending mass regularly was invariably higher than that of men. Male abstention from churchgoing appears to have been related to growing antipathy to the confessional. Following a pattern that goes back to the eighteenth century, if not before, men grew resentful of priestly interrogation of their private sexual behavior, particularly of their increasing use of contraception by means of *coitus interruptus*. The church laid the blame for this "sin" exclusively on men, who responded by absenting themselves from confession, resulting in their being debarred from communion.[27] The contrasting resilience of female attendance at mass can be explained in a variety of ways. As already mentioned, older historiography postulated a supposedly natural feminine inclination toward the emotional intensity of the Marian piety that had developed in nineteenth-century France. Such a hypothesis cannot be too readily dismissed. The explosion of pilgrimages to Lourdes from the 1870s was made possible by the opening of the railway from Bourdeaux in 1866, but the overwhelmingly female composition of the pilgrims suggests that gendered dimensions of spirituality need to be given some weight in explaining the phenomenon. Thousands of laywomen and nuns carried their sick to the grotto where in 1858 a young peasant girl, Bernadette Soubirous, had seen apparitions of a female figure who claimed, mysteriously, to *be* "the Immaculate Conception." They were impelled by a devotion to the Virgin Mary and a vision of an organic and compassionate Christian society that provided a compelling alternative to the clinically scientific and inescapably masculine creed of the Third Republic. In 1908, at the height of the anticlerical campaign in France, more than 1.5 million people came to the jubilee celebrations of the apparitions. Similar numbers flocked to Lourdes in 1950 when the dogma of the Assumption of the Virgin was promulgated.[28] The cult of St. Thérèse of Lisieux, a young Carmelite nun who died of tuberculosis in 1897, also became extremely popular among women.[29] As already indicated, however, explanations that appeal to stereotypes of feminine piety can disguise secularist and misogynist assumptions: what needs emphasis is that the Catholic Church and its religious orders provided avenues for women to exercise both service and leadership in a professedly "secular" society that denied them such opportunities.[30]

The strong probability that the gap between male and female religious practice narrowed rather than widened in the first half of the century places a further question mark against secularist explanations of the sexual dimorphism of French Catholicism.[31] It was not so much that women became less religious in response to secular influence—though doubtless that was true of some—but rather the reverse: men, especially middle-class men, appear to have become somewhat less irreligious. Paris, the stronghold of the anticlerical campaign, actually witnessed a gradual rise in the figures for Easter communions and Sunday mass attendance between 1909 and 1954; the levels reached a plateau between 1954 and 1962, and began to fall only from 1962.[32] Boulard also showed that in the diocese of Chartres, another bastion of infidelity, rates of Easter communicants rose from the 1900 figures of 1.5 percent for men and 15 percent for women to 7 percent for men and 20 percent for women in 1960.[33] One of the leading historians of modern French Catholicism, Y.-M. Hilaire, has characterized the whole period from 1905 to 1960 as one of *"réveil et de militantisme,"* provoked by the crisis of the Separation and assisted by the *Union Sacrée* between Catholics and Republicans during the First World War and the reentry of many Catholics into political life during the period of Vichy and the Resistance.[34] Boulard estimated that in the late 1950s, nearly a quarter of the French population regularly attended Sunday mass, and almost a third took Easter communion. In light of such evidence, the late Maurice Larkin observed that the majority of Catholics in the mid-1950s thought that the church had actually profited from its enforced independence from state aid. The clergy had gained in self-reliance and public esteem, while lay people had had to take greater responsibility.[35] The reduction in the political power and social salience of Christianity under the Third Republic had not led to a waning of personal faith; if anything, it had inspired a modest revival.

However, the comparatively optimistic scenario painted by Boulard's statistics for the 1950s and early 1960s was not destined to last. In France, as in western Europe as a whole, the 1960s initiated a period of protracted religious crisis. Whereas in 1952, a fifth of practicing adult Catholics in France went to confession at least once a month, by 1983 the proportion had fallen to 1 percent.[36] Baptisms fell from 91 percent in 1958 to 51 percent in 1990. The proportion of marriages solemnized by the Catholic Church dropped from 79 percent in 1958 to 51 percent in 1990. The level of regular attendance at Mass began to decline from 1961, briefly stabilized between 1965 and 1968, and then plummeted from 1969 to 1975. By the end of the 1980s it had dropped further to about 10 percent.[37] Within this overall picture regional differences were still discernible, following the pattern first described by Boulard in the 1940s.[38] Nevertheless, by the end of the century, France had in large measure become what all the stridency of republican anticlerical rhetoric had earlier failed to achieve—a secular society.

Explanations of the collapse of Christian practice in France from the early 1960s cannot ignore the fact that similar trends were widely apparent elsewhere. They were, for example, evident among Catholic populations in Spain, the Netherlands, Quebec, and Australia, and also among Protestants in Britain. In France, as in Britain and probably elsewhere, evidence points to the progressive weakening of a previously robust tradition of female domestic piety as at least one crucial factor.[39] In France in 1900, women had made up as many as 70 percent of practicing Catholics. Between 1930 and 1960 the proportion was still about two-thirds. By the end of the century, however, it had dropped to about one-half, thus erasing a pattern of sexual dimorphism in French religion that went back at least as far as 1789.[40] One important influence was the decline in segregated girls' education delivered by female religious orders: as single-sex education within state schools increasingly became the norm, the differences between the religious outlooks of young men and women evaporated.[41] Developments in higher education also played their part in undermining traditional Catholic allegiance. The radical student protests of 1968—more widely supported in Paris than in any other European city—promoted an ideology of absolute individual freedom that was hard to square with traditional Catholic norms. The French Catholic student movement, the *Mission Étudiante*, declared itself in 1970 to be "an association of believers and of communities of believers, situating itself within the revolutionary current," but such revolutionary egalitarianism soon took the movement beyond the boundaries of Catholic obedience.[42]

At the heart of the cultural transitions that affected France in the 1960s was the fact that the long-standing disillusionment with Catholic teaching on sexual practice appears finally to have spread from men to women. Specifically, Pope Paul VI's unambiguous reaffirmation in *Humanae Vitae* in July 1968 of the Catholic Church's traditional opposition to all artificial forms of birth control appeared to magnify the distance of the church's teaching from the reality of sexual practice in most French marriages. The legalization of oral contraceptives in December 1967—though they did not become fully available until 1972—signified the willingness of the state to abandon Catholic moral norms in the face of accumulating evidence that they no longer commanded the support of the majority. The birth rate in France fell from 1965, even before oral contraception became available. The *Mouvement de Libération des Femmes*, founded in August 1970, set its sights on the more ambitious goal of the legalization of abortion, which was achieved in January 1975.[43]

In a society in which a rapidly rising proportion of women were in paid employment—between 1968 and 1984 the proportion rose from 36 to 45 percent—growing numbers of women found the feminist creed of the women's liberation movement more appealing than traditional Catholic devotion, with its emphasis on continual submission to the authority of men in both church and home.[44] The old revolutionary creed of the inalienable democratic rights of the male citizen had left the fabric of Catholic Christendom substantially intact in those regions of France where religious observance had for long been strong. A new revolutionary creed of a more radically individualistic character—the ideology of women's unlimited rights over their own bodies—has proved a more potent secularizing force since the 1960s.

IV. Orthodox and Protestant
Churches in the Soviet Union

Between November 1917 and August 1918 the new Bolshevik regime in Russia effected its own separation of church and state. In a decree of November 8, 1917 Lenin nationalized all private property. Further legislation in January–February 1918 separated the Russian Orthodox Church from the state and specifically deprived the church of all its property, schools, and monasteries. All religious teaching in schools, whether public or private, was banned. The Russian Orthodox Church as an institution was deprived of legal personality and the right to hold property in the future. In a close replication of the precedent set by the French Law of Separation, legal measures were put in place whereby groups of twenty or more lay believers (of whatever religious stamp) were permitted to register as religious associations and to negotiate with the local authorities for the lease without charge of church premises for "cult activities."[45] In November 1920 similar measures effected the disestablishment of the Orthodox Church in the Ukraine.[46] As in France in 1906, the state was attempting to reduce historic national churches that lay at the heart of national identity and culture to loose agglomerations of citizens' voluntary associations for religious worship, but with the significant difference that these were to be subject to ongoing close monitoring by the state authorities. However, Orthodox believers were, at least in theory, left in a stronger legal position than their French Catholic counterparts between 1906 and 1924, for the Orthodox hierarchy did not prohibit parishioners from forming the associations as Pius X had done in *Gravissimo officii*.

The regime also subverted the monopolistic authority of the Orthodox Church by nurturing a schism by "renovationist" or "red" clergy who believed that Orthodoxy and Soviet principles could be reconciled; this had its origins in the 1905 revolution, but surfaced only after 1917.[47] As in France, the religious orders came under particular attack: by 1920 673 Orthodox monasteries had been closed. As many as 12,000 lay people, several thousand clergy, and at least twenty-eight bishops, were executed. Archbishop Tikhon Belavin (1865–1925), elected in October 1917 as the first patriarch of Moscow and All Russia for 200 years, survived, but was labeled as a "bourgeois parasite" and deprived of ration cards, rendering him dependent on gifts of food from the faithful.[48] Worse was to come.

The economic chaos precipitated by the revolution and ensuing civil war led to a severe famine in 1921–2. Tikhon urged parishes to sell those church valuables not needed for sacramental purposes to raise funds for famine relief, but the state went further, confiscating sacramental vessels. There is evidence that the government used famine relief as a pretext for a campaign designed to boost its coffers. When clergy and—even more— laity vigorously resisted the confiscations of parochial property, they paid the penalty: between 1921 and 1923, 2,691 priests, 1,962 monks, 3,447 nuns, and an unknown number of laypersons were executed.[49] When Tikhon died in April 1925, the government arrested 117 of the 160 bishops in a successful attempt to prevent the canonical election of a new patriarch. The hierarchy was decimated, and leadership of the church devolved to a series of temporary administrators or *locum tenentes*. From 1936 the *locum tenens* was metropolitan Sergeii (Stragarodski), who had been compelled to issue a compliant declaration of loyalty to the government and had thereby lost a good deal of support among his people.

To the exasperation of the regime, the first phase of antireligious campaigning often appeared only to reinforce the vitality of popular piety. In the Ukraine, party officials in the mid-1920s regularly reported with dismay on outbreaks of mass religious revival in response to supposed "miracles" and icon processions. A party report in 1925 found that in the Ukraine 41 percent of those aged over 18 were active registered members of a religious group. "Sectarians"—Evangelical Christians and Baptists— showed the greatest increase, rising from 24,544 adherents in 1917 to 148,627 by 1925.[50] In the Orthodox Church, the number of clergy was actually marginally higher by 1927 than it was in 1914.[51]

The government responded to such evidence of the persistence of "Superstition" by intensifying its efforts to eliminate popular belief and curb lay activists. A propagandist group, the League of the Militant Godless, was founded in 1925, and by 1932 claimed 5.67 million members, 2 million more than the Communist Party itself.[52] As in France in the 1790s, an attempt was made to abolish Sundays: a six-day week was introduced in 1929 (with one-sixth of the population enjoying a day of rest in rotation), but had to be abandoned in 1940.[53] The rate of church closures escalated. In Moscow, for example, which in 1928 still had 500 Orthodox churches, only 87 churches remained by 1932.[54] A further phase of church closures followed in the late 1930s. Although estimates of the numbers of churches remaining by the end of that decade vary widely, archival statistics suggest that the numbers of Orthodox churches within Russia's 1936 boundaries fell from 39,930 in 1917 to 14,090 in 1936, and to 950 at most in 1940; by that date 97.6 percent of the Orthodox churches open on the eve of the Bolshevik Revolution had been closed.[55] In some parts of the Soviet empire, such as Byelorussia or certain regions of Ukraine, it was reported that no Orthodox churches at all remained open.[56] In institutional terms, the Orthodox Church appeared on the verge of extinction, yet at the level of popular devotion it was far from dead. The fewer churches there were, the more crowded and attractive they became. Figures supplied by a government source suggest that in 1944, more than 148,000 people attended Easter services in Moscow alone, with two or three times more gathering outside to participate in the Easter midnight processions.[57] Few western European cities at the time could have matched such levels of attendance.

What rescued the Russian Orthodox Church from the brink of institutional annihilation was the Soviet Union's entry into the Second World War on June 22, 1941. On that day metropolitan Sergeii issued a letter addressed "To Pastors and Parishioners of the Orthodox Church of Christ," calling on the faithful to rally to the defense of the motherland. The church did more than indulge in patriotic rhetoric: it subsequently raised funds to fund a tank column and a fighter squadron, and in all raised 300 million rubles for the war effort. Such demonstrations of the church's national loyalty tipped the balance of power in the Communist Party in favor of those elites who advocated a managerial policy toward the church. In particular, it seems to have convinced Josef Stalin himself that the support of the hierarchy was indispensable for the conflict with Nazi Germany. On September 4, 1943, the three surviving metropolitan bishops, Sergeii, Aleksii Simanski, and Nikolai Yarushevich, were summoned to a meeting with Stalin, his deputy V. M. Molotov, and a colonel in the secret police, Georgii Karpov. Stalin invited the metropolitans to raise any questions or requests that they might have. When Sergeii replied that the most urgent priority was the convening of a Holy Synod to elect a Patriarch, Stalin offered full government support. He also promised that no objection would be raised to the opening of theological courses, seminaries, and academies to replenish the thinning ranks of the clergy, and gave reassuring answers to every other concern that the metropolitans raised. Only at the conclusion of the interview did Stalin add that the government intended to create a special state office, the Council for the Affairs of the Russian Orthodox Church (hereafter CAROC), to be headed by Karpov.[58] Under the pressure of war, the Soviet state had changed tack to a policy of manipulating rather than opposing religion. For the next twenty-two years the Council would play a central but ambiguous role in managing church affairs.

The opening of secret state archives following the collapse of the Soviet Union has enabled historians to reconstruct in detail the complex and shifting relationships that linked CAROC to the Orthodox hierarchy and different elements in the regime.[59] Karpov's relationship with Sergeii, who was duly elected as patriarch just four days later, but lived only to May 1944, was distant, but he became close friends with his successor, Patriarch Aleksii I (1877–1970), exchanging birthday greetings, presents, and invitations to meals. Orthodox bishops were granted apartments, cars, and dachas, and given access to first-class medical treatment. Theological academies were opened in Moscow, Leningrad, and Kiev, and eight lower-level theological training courses were instituted.[60] The numbers of Orthodox clergy began to grow again, and churches were reopened. According to CAROC's own statistics, the total number of Orthodox churches and chapels that were open throughout the USSR rose from 9,829 in October 1943 to 14,187 in January 1948. However, only 1,270 of these were reopened as a result of permission by CAROC; 7,405 of the additional churches had been reopened by the Nazis during their occupation of Russian territory and the Soviets judged it prudent not to close them again once they had recovered the territory. Comprising 2,491 of the total were former Uniate (Eastern Catholic) churches in the Ukraine absorbed by the Russian Orthodox Church as part of a program of enforced "reunification" initiated in tsarist times and strongly supported by the Soviet government as an element in its policy of opposition to the "fascist" Vatican. Only 3.5 percent of all requests made by believers to CAROC for reopening of churches between 1944 and 1948 were granted.[61]

The appearance of renewed state benevolence to the Orthodox Church was thus more impressive than the reality. From 1948 church closures supplanted church reopenings as the dominant trend, and the numbers of Orthodox churches resumed their decline. Karpov's policy of selective toleration of the church became increasingly suspect in the Central Committee of the Communist Party, especially after Stalin's death in March 1953. In self-defense he became more blatant in his manipulation of episcopal appointments, and distanced himself from Patriarch Aleksii. The assumption of power of Nikita Khrushchev from September 1953 heralded a new militancy in antireligious policy. Although this campaign eased between 1955 and 1957, the onslaught was resumed with sustained ferocity from 1958, masterminded by the regime's chief ideologist, Mikhail Suslov. Karpov, now deemed to have been too soft on the church, was removed from the chairmanship of CAROC in February 1960. The consequences soon became apparent: the number of Orthodox churches and chapels fell from 13,008 in January 1960 to 7,873 in January 1965, and the number of monasteries declined from 63 in January 1959 to only 18 in the mid-1960s.[62]

Karpov's policy toward the Orthodox Church was based on two cognate principles. The first was the premise that religious life conducted under the leadership of bishops closely supervised by CAROC officials was less dangerous to the state than the alternative—forcing religious activity into underground channels, thereby requiring the government to adopt repressive measures that would attract international criticism. The second was that a compliant Russian Orthodox Church could be decidedly useful to the Soviet Union in its foreign policy. Although these pragmatic principles came under challenge from the strident ideological tone of Soviet religious policy from 1958, they were never completely vanquished, and experienced something of a revival under Khrushchev's successor, Leonid Brezhnev. The aspirations of the Russian Orthodox Church to establish its preeminence in the Orthodox world, presenting Moscow as "the third Rome," reinforced the endeavors of the Soviet regime to hold the vast Russian empire together.[63] The absorption of so many Uniate churches in Ukraine into the Orthodox fold was particularly welcome to Moscow.

The strategic function that a managed approach to religion could play in Soviet foreign policy is most clearly displayed in relation to the World Council of Churches. At first Russian Orthodox hierarchs had denounced the infant Council as a tool of American imperialism, but from 1955 they responded to persistent courting by WCC officials. The Russian Orthodox Church joined the WCC at the New Delhi Assembly in November–December 1961, at the very time when Khrushchev's campaign against the church was reaching its peak. The Russian delegation at New Delhi was led by archbishop Nikodim (Rotov) of Yaroslavl, then only thirty-two years old. Nikodim (1929–78) was destined, not simply for high office in the church itself, as metropolitan of Leningrad and Lagoda from 1963, but also to be the chief Russian Orthodox spokesperson in the ecumenical movement. He was elected to the Central Committee of the WCC in 1962, and from 1975 until his sudden death on a visit to the Vatican in 1978 was one of its presidents. In his memoirs, WCC general secretary Willem Visser 't Hooft passes an understated but leading comment on "how remarkably well informed" CAROC commissioners were about ecumenical affairs.[64] Later WCC general secretaries were easier game. The now accessible records of the KGB are replete with references to "agents" sent abroad to undertake "counter-revolutionary tasks" as Orthodox delegates at ecumenical meetings: in 1967 alone 122 agents were dispatched as part of religious delegations.[65] Metropolitan Nikodim, like several of his fellow bishops, was one such agent, charged with defending the religious and foreign policy of the Soviet Union against foreign criticism, and deflecting the human rights agenda within the World Council from an embarrassing preoccupation with religious liberty in Eastern Europe to a focus on combatting racism and American neo-colonialism.[66] However, being employed as an agent of the KGB did not guarantee that a bishop had the complete confidence of the authorities. Nikodim used his state-approved status to promote the interests of the Orthodox Church vigorously. When in 1974 the state Council for the Affairs of Religions drew up three categories of Orthodox bishops according to the measure of their pliability for state purposes, Nikodim appeared only in the second rank; Patriarch Pimen (1910–90), who had succeeded Aleksii I in 1971, appeared in the first category, made up of those who were not simply loyal to the state but who also did not "display any particular activeness in extending the influence of Orthodoxy among the population," even though he was not technically a KGB agent.[67] The strategy of manipulation had its limits. The decisively anti-Western orientation of the Fourth General Assembly of the WCC at Uppsala in July 1968 cannot be adequately explained as the result of KGB machinations, and the WCC could still on occasion criticize Soviet policy.[68] Moreover, the state exploitation of the Orthodox hierarchy from the late 1960s was paradoxically accompanied by growing evidence of a revival of Orthodox piety among younger people, including intellectuals, as well as increasing protests from clergy against the extent of state interference in church life.[69]

The trajectory of Soviet policy toward Protestants was broadly similar, except that the Bolsheviks were at first happy to tolerate the Protestant dissenters who had suffered significant repression under the tsarist regime—mostly "Evangelical Christians" and Baptists.[70] These baptistic groups were potential allies against Orthodox predominance and included many industrious small farmers or entrepreneurs who were economically useful to the government. Some, such as Ivan S. Prokhanov, leader of the All-Russian Union of Evangelical Christians, were committed Christian Socialists who established Christian communes. Many Evangelical Christians and Baptists initially welcomed the Soviets' separation of church and state as a vindication of their ecclesiological principles of independency. Both groups grew rapidly in the early years of communist rule, especially in the Ukraine, where they experienced annual growth rates of up to 15 percent between 1917 and 1924.[71]

The honeymoon period for Protestants under Soviet rule did not last. For them, like the Orthodox, the 1930s were a decade of severe repression. The fact that in 1929 up to three-quarters of Baptists in the USSR were to be found in the Ukraine, and mostly in the western Ukraine at that, made them an especially sensitive community for the regime. The Baptists (known as the Union of Evangelical Christians-Baptists) had some

600,000 members throughout the USSR in 1929, but their numbers fell sharply over the next decade.[72] However, from 1944 Soviet Protestantism experienced a transition from overt repression to a new era of state management that closely paralleled the Orthodox story.

Modeled on CAROC, a Council for the Affairs of Religious Cults (CARC) was established in May 1944 to supervise the state's relations to all religious communities other than the Orthodox Church. Its chairman was another KGB colonel, I. V. Polianski. On October 26, 1944 forty-five participants from both the Baptists and the All-Russian Union of Evangelical Christians met in Moscow to discuss a merger between the two groups. CARC provided transport, hotel accommodation, and food. None of the participants were mandated delegates from regional associations of either group. The meeting reached a unanimous decision to form a Union of Evangelical Christians and Baptists governed by an All-Union Council of Evangelical Christians and Baptists (AUCECB). Officials of the Baptist World Alliance—J. H. Rushbrooke in London and Walter Lewis in Washington—doubted whether the new Union represented the views of Baptists, but it was the only basis on which the state was prepared to permit Baptists and Evangelical Christians an official existence. Persuaded by the logic of survival, most Baptist and Evangelical Christian congregations affiliated to the new union.[73] In August 1945 CARC organized and funded a similar meeting in Moscow at which it was decided that all Pentecostals would join the AUCECB. Some 400 congregations representing 25,000 Pentecostals did so, but in this case the theological differences between Evangelical Christians-Baptists and Pentecostals proved more of an obstacle. By 1949 many Pentecostals had left the Union, leaving Pentecostalism in the Soviet Union largely as an underground movement: it is estimated that by 1984 there were 500,000 Pentecostals in the USSR, of whom only 55,000 were affiliated to registered churches.[74]

CARC, like CAROC under Karpov, was committed to the goal of ensuring that church life operated within the boundaries of Soviet legality. That meant obstructing the more arbitrary acts of repression of believers instigated by other elements in the state.[75] But is also demanded close regulation of communities that were highly decentralized and democratic in their church polity. CARC ensured that AUCECB was structured in a way that was amenable to central control. The key figures were "senior presbyters." The head of CARC in Ukraine proudly reported in 1947 that the new Union's structure "completely liquidates the sect's vague 'democratism' in questions of leadership," vesting power in presbyters whom CARC could "select" and "regulate."[76] AUCECB churches were also prohibited from undertaking work with children and young people; no person under the age of eighteen could be baptized; services of believer's baptism were not to take place in public; and the right to preach was strictly limited to the presbyter of a given congregation or to the elite of senior presbyters. The AUCECB leadership endorsed these restrictions as early as 1949–50, though securing their acceptance in the local churches proved difficult.[77] On an international stage, as at the Baptist World Alliance Congress in London in 1955, Yakov Zhidkov, president of the AUCECB, reassured fellow Christians that "all our churches enjoy full freedom for preaching the Gospel" and "in conducting our services we do not encounter any obstacles."[78] At best this was economical with the truth. The evidence is compelling, though not conclusive, that some internationally prominent AUCECB leaders, notably Alexei Stoian, chairman of the Union's international department from 1959 to the late 1980s, were in the employ of the KGB.[79] In 1962 the AUCECB was accepted into membership of the WCC, with the encouragement of the British Baptist leader, Ernest A. Payne, chairman of the WCC Central Committee; thereafter AUCECB delegates voted consistently with their Orthodox brethren in seeking to block any resolutions critical of the Soviet Union.[80]

The Soviet management of Baptist affairs hit the rocks in the 1960s. In the summer of 1960, the AUCECB leadership, under pressure to implement CARC policy at local church level, issued a "New Statute" and accompanying secret "Instructional Letter" to senior presbyters that tightened the noose further. The minimum age for baptism was raised to thirty, and all evangelistic activity was forbidden. The New Statute proved deeply unpopular in the churches. A dissident *initsiativniki* (Initiative) group emerged in May 1961, demanding an extraordinary all-union congress to elect a new set of leaders uncompromised by the state.[81] In the event CARC allowed a congress to be held in October 1963, but on terms dictated by the AUCECB leadership; only modest changes were made to the New Statute. Nonetheless, by September 1965 the dissident group had evolved into a major schism, forming the Council of Evangelical Christian Baptists (CECB). This signal defeat for government religious policy prompted the dissolution in December 1965 of CAROC and CARC and their replacement by a single body, the Council for the Affairs of Religions, led until 1984 by the hardline successor to Karpov as leader of CAROC, Vladimir Kureodov. Prominent CECB leaders such as Georgi Vins were imprisoned, attracting damaging publicity in the West. During the 1970s Christian opinion in the West increasingly bought the CECB message that the "true" church in the Soviet Union was a persecuted one, even though European Baptist leaders continued to maintain close relationships with the AUCECB.[82] The hard work of the state in cultivating selected Orthodox and AUCECB leaders had been in vain. Eventually the regime had to travel full circle by encouraging CECB congregations to register and thus submit to a degree of state control; many other Baptist congregations emerged from 1976 that chose to remain autonomous of either group.[83] In the three years up to 1991 the AUCECB claimed to have doubled their membership, restoring the size of the community to its 1929 level of 600,000; the total number of Baptist adherents may have been more than 3 million.[84]

The final years of the Soviet era were marked by widespread evidence of religious revival. The celebration of the millennium of Russian Christianity in June 1988 received extensive coverage in the press, and encouraged a resurgence of Orthodox nationalist piety. In the Ukraine an autocephalous Orthodox Church reemerged in 1989, refusing allegiance to the Moscow Patriarchate. In the Ukraine especially, but also in other parts of the Soviet Union, the fragmentary evidence available from the last two decades of Soviet rule points toward a revival of religious commitment among the young. Under the impact of modernization and globalization, the pseudo-eschatology of communism itself became desacralized, and as it lost its appeal, interest in Christianity revived, contributing to *perestroika* and the collapse of Soviet power.[85] Although Orthodox churchgoing may not have recovered its pre-1917 levels, the conclusion must be, as one scholar observed in 1988, that "the end result of all the propaganda work of the Soviet atheistic establishment is nil practically, especially if we remember that the decline of religious belief in the West over these last seventy years, although unaided by any organized and institutional atheistic establishments, has been much more dramatic."[86] If Russia and its former satellite states today are any less Christian than they were before 1917, the cause is more likely to be related to globalizing forces disseminating Western cultural indifference to religion than to earlier communist efforts to eliminate it.

IV. The Impotence of the Secular State

France and the Soviet Union constitute the two most prominent European examples of a concerted campaign by twentieth-century states to reduce or even eliminate the social influence and political role of Christianity, especially as represented by the national church. In the further reaches of the Soviet empire in Eastern and central Europe, Communist Party aims were similar, though in some countries—such as Poland—their implementation was highly problematic. Although obviously differing in the extent of their antagonism to religion itself, the two case studies reveal the capacity of the modern state, if it so chooses, to marginalize Christianity from the mainstream of public life and destroy much of the institutional and economic infrastructure of historic national churches. Yet both examples equally suggest that such measures of "official" secularization turned out to be comparatively impotent in subverting popular Christian belief and practice.

In France levels of Catholic practice showed a limited recovery in the wake of the anticlerical legislation of the first decade of the twentieth century. Ironically they began to decline only during the later years of conservative and pro-Catholic Gaullist government. The more catastrophic decline in observance from the end of the 1960s may have borne some relation to the weakening ecclesiastical hold on the education of girls, but the most severe restrictions in the influence of the religious orders had come earlier in the century, without immediate effect on levels of Christian observance. France since the late 1960s has indeed demonstrated the triumph of religious indifference rather than of atheism, but this outcome cannot be convincingly related to the state's protracted and quite successful efforts to reduce the social significance of Christianity. Rather it was the product of a profound and chronologically quite specific cultural revolution that transformed popular, and especially female, attitudes to gender roles and sexual behavior, leaving the church isolated and beleaguered.

In the Soviet Union, the repeated alternation of state religious policy between bouts of severe repression and phases of controlled toleration indicates the chronic inability of the communist regime to identify a consistently effective strategy for the eradication of popular religion. Although we do not have the benefit in the Soviet case of the systematic statistical analyses of religious practice produced by the French exponents of *sociologie religieuese*, the exhaustive and now accessible records of the CAROC and CARC reveal a picture of continued religious vitality in the face of formidable obstacles erected by the state. Soviet atheism proved adept at dividing Christian believers between those who were prepared to cede autonomy of ecclesiastical governance for the sake of a limited toleration and those who resisted all compromise with the government, but it was quite unable to extinguish the sources of popular Christian devotion. Steve Bruce's first special case of the defense of threatened national identity could perhaps be invoked to help explain the resilience of religion in republics such as Ukraine or Georgia that had been forcibly absorbed within the Russian empire, but it is much less applicable to Russia itself, where the Soviet regime itself adopted and exploited Russian nationalist aspirations. His second special case, namely where religion is functionally useful in easing transitions of migrant populations to new contexts, is clearly inapplicable to religion in the Soviet Union. Both France and the Soviet Union, therefore, suggest that the churches ultimately have more to fear from cultural than political varieties of the secular.

CHAPTER FIVE

Contrasting Patterns of Belonging and Believing

SCANDINAVIA AND THE UNITED STATES

I. Who Is the Exceptional Case?

Historians of religion are increasingly forming the conclusion that the blanket sociological term "secularization" covers a variety of distinct and potentially quite divergent or asynchronous processes of religious change. One of the surest guides to this difficult terrain, Hugh McLeod, has identified no fewer than six different spheres in which secularizing tendencies may be apparent: individual belief; formal religious practice; the place of religion in public institutions; the prominence of religion in public debate; the significance of religion as an aspect of group identity; and the relationship of religion with popular culture.[1] The studies of France and the Soviet Union in the previous chapter have suggested that trends in belief, popular religious practice, and the relationship of religion to popular culture may be largely independent of, and strongly resistant to, efforts by the state to marginalize or eliminate religion from the public sphere. The present chapter analyzes the strikingly divergent trajectories of Christian belief and practice in two cases of a very different kind from those examined in the previous chapter. In the first, Scandinavia, with a particular focus on Sweden, the state for most of the century maintained its traditional support for an established church. In the second, the United States, the state scrupulously maintained its traditional postrevolutionary distance from any religious institution, creating a "free market" of voluntary religious practice that proved highly favorable to the flourishing of evangelical varieties of Christianity, to such an extent that, paradoxically, these attained a greater leverage on national politics than did any form of Christianity in twentieth-century Europe.

Scandinavia[2] is frequently cited as the most extreme regional example of the secularization of formerly Christian countries, and as confirmation of the generalization that northern Protestant Europe has been more vulnerable to secularizing trends than southern Catholic Europe. Yet the Nordic region retains some of the highest levels of formal religious adherence of any part of the Christian world. The British sociologist of religion, Grace Davie, has popularized the thesis that modern western European religiosity is characterized by "believing without belonging." The phrase formed the subtitle to the original 1994 edition of her major study, *Religion in Britain since 1945*.[3] It disappeared from the title of the second edition, published in 2015, in which the author confessed to having from the outset entertained some misgivings about the phrase on the grounds that it too easily separated two aspects of religious identification that are necessarily interconnected.[4] Nevertheless, Davie's essential thesis remains that European religion can be broadly described as exhibiting continuing high levels of personal religious belief in combination with falling levels of church membership or active participation in religious worship. Christians in western Europe since the early twentieth century, she maintains, have increasingly expressed their religious faith vicariously, depending on religious professionals to maintain the formal structures of religion so that they remain available to the majority of the population for emergency use in times of either national or personal crisis. European secularity, far from being a template of modernity that the rest of the world is destined sooner or later to follow, should be understood as exceptional, a special case, and indeed something of a mirage, for underneath the surface appearance of a population disenchanted with the churches lies a residual deep adherence to at least some aspects of Christian belief.[5] Her thesis reflects her own experience of the Church of England, and carries some plausibility in relation to Britain as a whole. It becomes much more tenuous when applied beyond Britain. Is there really such a thing as "European religion"? Scandinavia presents an obvious problem for Davie's argument, as she has occasionally acknowledged.[6] The next section will suggest that Christianity in the Nordic region in the twentieth century was characterized, not by "believing without belonging," but more by "belonging without believing."[7]

Much of the academic warfare over the theory of secularization within the sociological fraternity has been waged between those, such as Grace Davie and David Martin, who have presented Europe—or, more precisely,

Western Europe—as the special case that requires explanation, and those, such as Steve Bruce or the late Bryan Wilson, who have continued to hold that Europe exemplifies the secularized default setting to which the modern (or at least, modernized) world is generally heading, albeit at different speeds. For the latter group, the special case that demands explanation is not Europe, but the United States, where modernization and high levels of Christian belief and practice have appeared to coexist quite happily.

The second case study selected for this chapter is therefore Christianity in the postwar United States. Particular attention will be devoted to the waning of the "mainline" Catholic and Protestant denominations, the converse growth—at least until the 1970s—of diverse forms of evangelical Protestantism, and yet the subtle processes of intellectual accommodation to contemporary cultural and social norms that can be observed even within this Christian constituency during the final decades of the twentieth century. For devotees of secularization and their unlikely bedfellows, Christians of deeply conservative inclination, these processes of creeping accommodation provide irrefutable evidence that the acids of secular modernity are steadily corroding even a nation with high levels of participation in churchgoing, eating away at authentic Christian faith from within the structures of formal church affiliation. For other commentators with a more cross-cultural perspective, such accommodations are simply examples of what churches have always done for the sake of their mission— namely, to negotiate tactical compromises with the surrounding culture and its prevailing mores. For a third group of American sociologists of religion, led by Rodney Stark and Roger Finke, the distinctiveness of the modern American religious experience consists in the unusual degree of success achieved by conservative American churches in supplying religious products tailored to the demands of the contemporary market, thus enabling religious consumers to make "rational choices." This "supply-side" paradigm correlates American religious "success" with the existence of a competitive free market. Conversely, European religious "failure" is explained in terms of the lingering baneful influence of a monopolistic approach to religion inherited from medieval Christendom, which encourages "laziness" and complacency among clergy and laity.[8]

The academic debates over whether the world is or is not becoming more secular have been conducted primarily between scholars operating within the Western academy. Whether it is Europe or the United States that constitutes the "special case," the horizons of the debate have therefore been fixed mostly on the Western world. There are some notable exceptions. The distinguished British sociologist of religion David Martin, who first entered the field through the publication in 1978 of his *A General Theory of Secularization*,[9] began in 1986 to investigate the explosion of Pentecostal styles of Christianity in Latin America, and subsequently extended his research on Pentecostalism to other parts of the globe. The result was to compel Martin to undertake a substantial revision of his original theory. He now conceived secularization, not as a once-for-all unilateral process, but rather as a series of recoils or reactions to successive pushes of Christianization, which he described as salients of faith driven into the territory of the secular from different angles, and each paying a characteristic cost that affects the distinctive character of the recoil. Each salient then undergoes a partial collapse into some version of what he called "nature" or pre-Christian forms of understanding the world.[10] Secularization thus ceases to be the master narrative of humanist eschatology, and becomes simply a particular type of social or intellectual reaction, apparent at certain times and in certain locations in response to movements of religious advance or renewal. José Casanova, an American sociologist of religion who also has urged the importance of adopting a global perspective on the theme of secularization, has reached the similar conclusion that secularization can no longer be understood as one universal teleology; instead he proposes the model of multiple processes of differentiation and interconnection between the religious and the secular, shaped by the great variety of ways in which societies of differing religious traditions have come to terms with modernity. According to Casanova, sociologists of religion should abandon their obsession with the supposed universal decline of religion, and instead investigate the changing forms of individual, group, and societal expressions of religion provoked by the impact of modernity and globalization.[11]

Such sociological reassessments of a now largely discredited grand narrative are welcome, but serious consideration of the possibility that embryonic secularizing tendencies may nonetheless be identified in specific non-Western societies of a predominantly Christian character remains rare. Scholars of world Christianity, in an understandable reaction to the narrow and frequently secular preoccupations of Western academics, tend to present the recent story of Christianity in the majority world as one of unsullied growth, vibrancy, and creativity, thus relegating all narratives of declension, stagnation, or nominal religious adherence to the backward-facing Christianity of the West. Such rose-tinted portraits do no service to the serious challenges that regularly confront the churches in Africa, Asia, or Latin America, and conceal the forms of "recoil" that by the 1990s were already apparent in some countries or regions where the Christian presence was old and influential enough to provoke dissident reactions.

In many places, of course, these reactions took a religious rather than a secular form, through adherence to dissenting expressions of Christianity that offered highly participatory and more culturally relevant alternatives to long-established Christian traditions. Chapter 13 will explore the attraction of Pentecostal varieties of Christianity as rivals to the historic Catholic or Protestant churches, especially in Latin America and Africa. In South Africa, the mainline Protestant churches ceased to grow relative to population among white, colored (mixed-race) and Indian people as early as 1960, and from the early 1980s their absolute membership numbers were in decline. By the 1990s the Catholic Church was going the same way. Among the white population of South Africa, the later decades of the century witnessed a similar trend of recession from active churchgoing to that evidenced in Europe, although the downward trend began from a much higher level and was less severe. Among the black population, however, the decline in the older denominations was more than offset by the rising popularity of African Instituted Churches (AICs), while Pentecostal and new evangelical churches showed growth among all ethnic groups.[12]

In South Korea, a century of spectacular Protestant church growth began to slow from the mid-1980s and came to an end about 1995. The smaller Catholic population, by contrast, continued to grow throughout the 1990s, but at a lower rate than hitherto. While the younger generation grew increasingly distrustful of the Protestant churches' preoccupation with size, status, and material prosperity, the Catholic Church profited from a reputation for financial probity, commitment to human rights, and a more sensitive approach to evangelism. The rapid modernization and urbanization of South Korea from the 1960s had an effect similar to that of the Industrial Revolution in Britain, stimulating the growth of voluntaryist evangelical Christianity, but in the longer term, as in Europe, it expanded social and economic inequality with consequences that proved less favorable to the continued flourishing of the churches.[13] In Polynesia and Melanesia, churches of Congregational, Methodist, Anglican, Lutheran, and Catholic traditions were by the late twentieth century facing stiff challenges from Seventh-Day Adventists, Mormons, and Pentecostals. In Papua New Guinea the Adventists formed the fourth largest church by the end of the century. In Tahiti the Mormons grew from 2,000 in 1962 to 12,000 in 1992, about 8.5 percent of the population.[14]

In some non-Western contexts, therefore, the recoil from a historically predominant Christian tradition apparent by the later decades of the twentieth century bears some similarity to trends observable in the West. The major difference, of course, is that the recoil has more often found an outlet in adhesion to alternative forms of institutional Christianity than in abstention from any church affiliation, even though the "institutional" Christianity has often been of a highly fluid and populist variety. The closer non-Western societies have come to a European model of monopoly by a single Christian tradition—and only a few have done so—the more vulnerable they have been to forms of reaction that bear some of the marks of what is often labeled "secularization." In the Pacific Islands, many of which had become Protestant theocracies in the course of the nineteenth century, the communal role of the historic churches was eroding by the 1990s.[15] Similarly in the predominantly Christian states of northeast India, whose hill peoples converted *en masse* to Presbyterian or Baptist forms of Christianity from the mid-nineteenth century onwards, the quasi-monopolistic position of the Presbyterian or Baptist churches in the different states came under increasing challenge in the later decades of the twentieth century from Catholics, Adventists, Pentecostals, and a variety of sects or cults. In Mizoram, for example, although the 2001 Census suggested that 87 percent of the population remained Christian, the complexion of Mizo Christianity by this date showed evidence of considerable heterogeneity as well as some abstention from active churchgoing of those who self-identified as Christian.[16]

The encroachment of Christian pluralism and even of nominal adherence to long-established churches in the non-Western world does not, however, imply that Asia, Africa, and Latin America will eventually fall into line behind Europe and North America as arenas of radical secularity. Rather it is to endorse the suggestions of Martin and Casanova that particular configurations of religious monopoly are likely in conditions of globalization to provoke marked dissenting reactions, many of which may take religious forms, such as Pentecostalism, while others may lead their adherents beyond the boundaries of organized church life.

II. Scandinavia: Belonging without Much Believing

Historians of popular religion in modern Europe have paid surprisingly little attention to Scandinavia. Hugh McLeod's *Secularisation in Western Europe* is based on analyses of Britain, France, and Germany, and makes no mention of Scandinavia.[17] A more recent collection of authoritative historical essays on *Secularization and Religious Innovation in the North Atlantic World*, edited by David Hempton and Hugh McLeod, is again strangely silent on Scandinavia, with only occasional and brief exceptions, mostly in relation to the strength of Pentecostalism in Sweden.[18] Sociologists have paid the region rather more attention, although it is still striking that Steve Bruce's edited volume bringing sociologists and historians together to debate the topic of secularization has no entry for any Scandinavian country in its index.[19] Yet surveys of religious participation in Europe conducted during the last three decades of the twentieth century consistently placed the Scandinavian countries toward the bottom of the table, with none recording more than 7 percent of the population claiming to attend religious services at least once a week.[20] The European Values Study undertaken by the University of Tilburg showing frequency of church attendance in western Europe in 1999–2000 indicated considerably lower average rates of weekly church attendance: 3.8 percent in Sweden, 3.2 percent in Iceland, and only 2.7 percent in Denmark, as compared with a European average of 20.5 percent.[21] Statistics that rely on self-reporting are notoriously unreliable, and different surveys from the same period produced discrepant data,[22] but there is no doubt that by the last three decades of the century—and, as we shall argue, probably long before that—regular church attendance in much of Scandinavia was the lowest in Protestant Europe, with France being the only Catholic nation recording broadly comparable levels of religious participation.

However, these abnormally low rates of church attendance were combined with exceptionally high levels of membership of the national Lutheran churches, even though these levels were declining by the end of the century. In Denmark in 1994 87 percent of the population belonged to the Lutheran Church and 80 percent of the nation's children were baptized into it.[23] Sweden has a smaller proportion of the population in membership with the Lutheran Church than any other Scandinavian country, but the figure in 2003 was still as high as 80 percent, with the church baptizing 70 percent of infants, solemnizing 58 percent of weddings, and conducting 87 percent of funerals. Unusually, in Sweden membership of the national church does not exclude membership of a free church: dual membership remains common.[24] Although the stark disjunction between mass church membership and low regular attendance was a little less marked in Norway, and rather less so in Finland, where attendance rates were significantly higher, the overall picture is clear—by the end of the twentieth century the great majority of Scandinavians chose not to opt out of membership of their historic national churches, and depended on them for the performance of rites of passage. Yet very few thought it important to attend regularly.

Whether this pattern can accurately be described as "belonging without believing" is more debatable.[25] The European Values Study indicated that in 1999–2000 a small majority of Swedes (53.4 percent), and larger majorities of Danes (68.9 percent), Finns (82.5 percent), and Icelanders (84.4 percent) continued to profess belief in God; a separate survey in 1995 recorded a middling figure of 65 percent for Norway, despite the fact that the country has had a large and active humanist association.[26] However, the European Values Study in 1990 reported that only 15 percent of the Swedish population professed to believe in a *personal* God.[27] Hence while theistic belief of a kind survived in the Nordic countries, despite the widespread collapse in active engagement with the churches, it appears in many cases to have been a highly privatized and amorphous variety of religious belief. Another survey conducted in the mid-1990s that asked respondents in Scandinavia whether they regarded themselves as "a confessing Christian," "a Christian in your own way," or "not a Christian," found that more than half of all respondents placed themselves in the second category, ranging from 53 percent in Iceland to 76 percent in Finland.[28] More recent research in Sweden has found that only 16.6 percent of those who self-identify with the Church of Sweden would call themselves *at best* "somewhat religious," as opposed to "extremely non-religious, very non-religious, somewhat non-religious, or neither religious nor non-religious."[29] By the end of the century, Scandinavians had retained considerable loyalty to their national Lutheran churches and a residual attachment to Christianity, but for many there was not much content left to their believing—Christianity had become a form of what Zuckerman has termed "cultural religion."[30] The question for the historian is how recently this pattern of belonging without much believing emerged, and how it is to be explained.

The previous chapter pointed to the conclusion reached by Hugh McLeod and Callum Brown that the crucial decade for the collapse of regular Christian practice in a number of different countries—France, Spain, the Netherlands, Canada, Australia, and Britain among them—was the 1960s. In the Nordic region, however, the evidence points in a very different direction. Statistical data on levels of church attendance before the 1960s is fragmentary, but what there is suggests that the low levels of religious participation recorded later in the century were not so new. Clergy returns for Denmark, even excluding the metropolis of Copenhagen, where levels of church attendance were known to be exceptionally low, recorded that only about 8 percent of Danes attended Lutheran churches on "an average Sunday" in the 1930s, falling to 6 percent in the

1940s, 5 percent in the 1950s, and 4 percent in the 1960s. The further decline apparent in the remainder of the century was simply a continuation of an established trend. Statistics from other Scandinavian countries paint a similar picture. In Sweden in 1927 it is estimated that only 5.6 percent attended a Lutheran church on a normal Sunday; by the 1950s it was under 3 percent. In Norway (which only became independent from the Swedish crown in 1905) an estimate of 3.4 percent of the population was recorded as early as 1938. In Finland rates were below 3 percent by the late 1950s.[31] These figures apply only to the Lutheran Church; aggregate attendance at all churches was obviously rather higher, particularly in Sweden, where evangelical free churches such as the Baptists and the Pentecostals accounted for a higher proportion of the total churchgoing population than in other Scandinavian countries. Yet in Stockholm in 1952 regular attenders at *any* church made up as little as 1 percent of the city's population.[32] Again, the evidence suggests a long-term decline in overall church attendance extending over a long period, rather than any sudden collapse in the 1960s.

Recent scholarship, which is most extensive for Sweden, is tending to the view that the origins of this decline predate the twentieth century. In the rapidly urbanizing central region of Sweden in 1890, only 5 percent of the population was estimated to attend communion at least once a month.[33] In Denmark the Lutheran Church, just like the Church of England, was slow to adjust its parochial structure to the realities of rapid urbanization. Copenhagen had only two more full-time Lutheran ministers in 1890 than it had in 1800, despite the massive expansion of the city since the 1870s. The establishment of the Copenhagen Church Fund in 1896 resulted in the building of 50 new parish churches, and a consequent reduction of the mean size of parish from 20,000 parishioners in 1880 to 11,000 in 1911, but the damage had been done.[34] Nevertheless, urbanization in itself cannot be held responsible for the low rates of religious participation in modern Scandinavia, for there is ample evidence from both nineteenth-century Europe and twentieth-century Latin America (and elsewhere) that rural–urban migration may lead to an increase rather than a decline in religious practice, depending on the capacity of churches to respond to the challenges of the urban environment. Parishes in rural Sweden and Norway were vast in geographical extent, leaving many parishioners many miles away from their parish church. Until 1860 regular attendance at the parish church was legally obligatory on all Swedish citizens other than the Sami (Lapps), with the requirement varying according to residence: those who lived within 10 kilometers of a church had to attend weekly;

those between 10 and 30 kilometers, in alternate weeks; those further away, every third Sunday. In northern coastal regions of Sweden, "church towns" were constructed to provide lodging to enable distant parishioners to fulfill their compulsory attendance requirements. Similarly in Norway as late as the mid-twentieth century it could be said that for many of the rural population churchgoing was "a summer excursion." Going to church required time, effort, and money.[35]

Although Scandinavian rates of church attendance fell steadily throughout the twentieth century, the likelihood, therefore, is that they did so from levels that were already exceptionally depressed. The course of what is now identified as "secularization" thus stretches back to the period of state religious compulsion before the mid-nineteenth century, leaving the historian with the unanswerable question of how low levels of participation would have been during this period if there had been no legal requirement to attend church. There is a strong argument that historians should look further back still. In the sixteenth century, the progress of Protestant belief among the Scandinavian population was extremely slow, particularly in Norway and in Sweden, where the Reformation was a political process closely associated with Sweden's emancipation from Danish rule and the establishment of a Swedish monarchy under Gustav Vasa. If English Puritanism can be understood as a movement to complete the work of a top-down Reformation by achieving the conversion of the ordinary people to Protestant faith, the implications of Scandinavia's lack of a Puritan movement may have been long-lasting. Taking a still longer historical perspective, it should be noted that some northern parts of Scandinavia did not become Christian until as late as the thirteenth century; indeed, the conversion of the Sami was not anything like complete until the eighteenth century. The history of Scandinavian Christianity may in fact be a religious exemplification of the brutal dictum of business employment—"last in, first out." In light of the fact that both the initial conversion of Scandinavia from the tenth century and its Lutheran Reformation in the sixteenth century were top-down processes initiated by the monarchy, Zuckerman has even raised the serious possibility that the majority of Danes and Swedes *never* became Christians at a level more profound than that of formal collective adherence.[36]

Scandinavia did experience its own movements of lay Protestant renewal emanating from Pietist, Moravian, or Methodist sources, but not before the end of the eighteenth century. They were especially strong in Norway, under the leadership of Hans Nielsen Hauge (1771–1824). In response to the growing influence of these evangelical revival movements, religious dissent was legalized in Norway in 1845, and in Denmark in 1849. In Finland and Sweden the pietist movements in the Lutheran Church were firmly suppressed, and driven out into autonomous Free Churches. Despite the accumulating evidence of religious dissent, Sweden maintained the fiction of the coextensiveness of church and state for longer than Norway or Denmark. In Finland some Protestant Nonconformist churches were tolerated from 1889. Following Finland's declaration of national independence from Russia in 1917, the Evangelical Lutheran Church in 1919 was relegated to the unusual status of being one (albeit much the larger) of two national churches, alongside the Orthodox Church. Complete religious liberty in Finland was granted in 1922. In Sweden legal penalties for nonattendance were lifted in 1860, when the Decree on Foreign Religious Adherents also gave Swedes the limited right to leave the Lutheran Church of which they were members by birth (not baptism) in order to join certain Christian bodies approved by the Crown. However, full religious freedom was not granted until the Religious Liberty Act of 1951, while the Church of Sweden's criterion of membership by birth rather than baptism survived until as late as 1996. Until 1991 the church had responsibility for the registration of births, marriages, and deaths, and even for the provision of some data to the tax authorities.[37] As the public face of Scandinavian Protestantism became more and more secular, it is worthy of note that in parts of the Nordic region, especially in Sweden, the Roman Catholic Church experienced modest growth during the century from its previous position of extreme marginality.[38]

The extent and timescale of religious pluralization thus varied significantly from one Scandinavian country to another, and so did the degree to which the constitutional mechanisms governing the relations of church and state were readjusted in response. The Evangelical Lutheran Church in Finland gained substantial autonomy through a Church Assembly as early as 1870. In Iceland the Evangelical Lutheran Church gained its Church Assembly and other democratic institutions in the late 1950s[39]; by 1998 the Church Assembly had been granted virtually complete legislative powers for the church. The Swedish Lutheran tradition was more High Church in character than anywhere else in Scandinavia. Its bishops and theologians often looked with some admiration at the Oxford Movement and its legacy to the Church of England. Hence in Sweden aspirations toward self-government sat in somewhat uneasy relationship with a desire to maintain exclusive recognition of the Lutheran Church as the spiritual face of the nation. The distinctive form of self-government that emerged reflected the very literal sense in which the Church of Sweden regarded itself as a folk church (*folkkyrka*) open to all Swedes, virtually irrespective of their level of religious belief. During the final two decades of the century, the church was progressively set free from state control, but it had no desire to distance itself from the politics of the nation. Hence when a General Assembly was established in 1982, all 251 members were to be elected indirectly through parish councils. There were no reserved places for either bishops or clergy, and more than 85 percent of the seats could be apportioned to those wearing a political party label. In 1999 even responsibility for theological matters was removed from the bishops and vested in the General Assembly. Full disestablishment came in January 2000. Bishops, formerly appointed by the Crown, were to be popularly elected.[40] Despite its high churchmanship, therefore, the Church of Sweden has espoused a strongly laicized and politicized version of ecclesiastical autonomy. On the eve of disestablishment, one Polish-Swedish journalist wryly observed that "The new Swedish church is a unique contribution to the history of religion: the world's first religious association where bishops are denied the right to vote in matters of faith and where the meaning of Christianity is established by political parties."[41] In Norway disestablishment came later, in 2012.

In Denmark the concept of a folk church had rather different associations than in Sweden, owing in part to the influential legacy of Nikolaj Grundtvig (1783–1872), the Lutheran pastor, politician, and philosopher. Grundtvig united revivalism with Nordic mythical romanticism and nationalism, and in Denmark the idea of the folk church has had particularly strong sentimental and nationalist associations as a result. Lacking the High Church Lutheran emphasis of Sweden, Denmark has maintained the historic model of a State-controlled established church through to the present day. Elected parish councils were instituted in 1912, which select the parish priest and together elect the diocesan bishop, but there is no national synod or assembly. The Danish Lutheran Church remains as the Church of England was before the Enabling Act of 1919—directly subservient to the Crown in parliament. The politically appointed Minister for the Church is its highest administrative authority under the monarch. Although the possibility of the separation of church and state was first mooted in the Danish parliament in 1982, the once anticlerical Social Democratic Party defended the continuance of parliamentary control over the church as a natural expression of the integral relationship between the people's church and the nation. The church retains its role as the registration authority for births and deaths, and is the burial authority for the state. Although the payment of tithes was abolished in 1903, the church receives a large income from the payment of church tax plus a substantial supplement from the national budget.[42] The Danish Lutheran Church is in effect an integral part of the state welfare system in a social democratic society. It has survived largely intact the major readjustments of church–state relationship in twentieth-century Europe and remains the most striking example of Protestant Constantinianism.

David Martin proposed in his *A General Theory of Secularization* that the combination of minimal religious pluralism with low levels of religious practice has pushed the Lutheran national church in each Scandinavian country further toward "generalized historical nostalgia" and "into the role of a social service station."[43] Peter Berger, Grace Davie, and Effie Focas have suggested that the Scandinavian countries represent "the remnants and mutations of an old story of Christian Europe and of Christian European nations."[44] In fact, they may be remnants and mutations of a still older story of pagan Europe. The narrative of Scandinavian Christianity is as much one of long-term failure in Christianization as one of twentieth-century secularization. Just as religious historians of modern France have concluded that the roots of the extreme secularity of some regions of modern France are to be found in persistent traditions of abstention from religious practice that antedate the Industrial Revolution, so it seems probable that the exceptional religious patterns of much of the Nordic region have a long historical ancestry. They should not be interpreted, therefore, as the typical European default setting to which the continent as a whole—let alone the rest of the world—is destined sooner or later to conform.

In a number of ways the Scandinavian Lutheran pattern was unique. The Lutheran conception of the function of national churches encouraged the maintenance of low levels of regular religious participation. Yet the very emphasis on their national function also paved the way during the twentieth century for the assimilation of the Lutheran churches into the welfare apparatus of modern social democracies. Whereas in Catholic Europe the Church had to contend with radical anticlericalism, in northern Protestant Europe the Social Democratic parties were not so much anticlerical as antireligious, which sounds more thoroughly atheistic but in practice left ample room for manipulation of the precise role of the churches.[45] In the long run, Social Democrats succeeded in Scandinavia in co-opting the churches into their program of social reform, stripping them of as much distinctive religious content as possible. In Sweden and Denmark they were the dominant political party for much of the century; in the former they won between 40 and 55 percent of the vote in all general elections from 1930 to 1990, and wielded a persistent secularizing influence on the teaching of religion in secondary schools. In Sweden (and probably also in Denmark) the phenomenon is now quite common of those who describe themselves as Christian—in that they gladly self-identify with the Lutheran Church—but as not believing in God.[46] Belonging without much believing has become the norm.

III. The United States: Changing Patterns of Belonging and Believing

To those accustomed to European rates of religious practice, the United States in the mid-twentieth century looked like a society characterized by an unusually high measure both of the formal recognition of Christianity and of regular adherence to it. In 1956 the US Congress adopted "In God We Trust" as the official motto of the nation. From then on, the motto appeared on all newly minted United States coins; banknotes followed suit a year later. Despite rising levels of urbanization, about 60 percent of the American population in the late 1950s professed membership of a Christian church, and surveys indicated that about half of the population (49 percent in 1958) claimed to attend church at least once a week, even though actual performance in modern American church going has persistently lagged somewhat behind the claims of survey respondents.[47]

For some denominations the postwar years were a period of remarkable expansion. The largest Protestant denomination, the Methodist Church (formed by the union in 1939 of the northern and southern branches of the Methodist Episcopal Church), saw its membership increase more rapidly between 1944 and 1947 than at any time since 1925, to a figure of about 8 million. The second largest, the Southern Baptist Convention, acquired nearly 300,000 new members in the four years after the end of the war, raising its membership to more than 6 million; between 1946 and 1949 the Convention constructed 500 new churches at a cost of $97 million and extended its denominational reach far beyond its southern heartlands.[48] The Catholic community in the United States doubled in the twenty years between 1940 and 1963, from 21 to 43.8 million members, and over half of this increase took place during the period from 1954 to 1963.[49] Although much of the growth was accounted for by mass immigration, notably of Hispanics, Filipinos, Italians, and Portuguese, these were years of rising self-confidence for the American Catholic community. The election of the first Catholic president, John F. Kennedy, in November 1960 appeared to symbolize the arrival on the American political stage of a once-despised and marginal Christian communion. Catholics, along with Jews, now joined Protestants as the constituents of an expanded American "civil religion" of a vaguely Judeo-Christian kind. Cardinal Francis Spellman, archbishop of New York from 1937 right through to 1967, was the close associate of a series of American presidents and an influential spokesman for the anticommunist preoccupations of large sections of the nation during the Cold War; he lent his public backing to the dubious campaigns of the Wisconsin Catholic senator Joseph R. McCarthy to root out suspected communists from their hiding places in national life. On the Protestant side, the Southern Baptist evangelist from Charlotte, North Carolina, Billy Graham (1918–2018), first won the respect of church leaders from a wide theological and denominational spectrum in 1957, during his eight-week crusade at Madison Square Garden in New York. At first no less of an anticommunist than Spellman, Graham's reputation and political influence grew, symbolizing the expanding cultural role and increasing political respectability of southerners in national affairs. In addition to his global evangelistic ministry, he became the spiritual confidant of a string of American presidents from Eisenhower to George W. Bush, eventually assuming the unofficial mantle, in the words of President George Bush senior, of "America's pastor."[50]

The churches' unalloyed good fortunes in the 1950s did not last. The 1960s were a cultural and religious watershed in the United States, just as they were in Europe, but the outcomes were rather different. Self-reported regular church attendance peaked at 49 percent of the population in 1958 and then declined before stabilizing at a level of about 40 percent during the 1970s. Aggregate church membership relative to population reached a plateau in the 1960s, and fell for the first time in the century in the following decade.[51] This was against a backcloth of steadily rising population: the national population grew by 19.0 percent per annum in the 1950s, 13.3 percent in the 1960s, and 11.5 percent in the 1970s.[52] By the 1960s, the signs were unmistakable of a progressive seepage away from Christian commitment among young people who had been exposed to the expanding and increasingly secular world of American higher education. Regular church attendance fell by 11 percent among college-educated persons between 1958 and 1968, but only by 5 percent among those who had not been to college.[53] Both Catholics and mainline Protestants felt the chill from the new ideological climate. Polls conducted by Gallup and the National Opinion Research Center suggest that the proportion of the Catholic population attending mass regularly fell from about three-quarters in the late 1950s to only half in 1975.[54] The same period also witnessed a dramatic collapse in the number of Catholic vocations. The numbers of Catholic seminarians fell from 48,992 in 1964 to 13,226 in 1980. The total of Catholic sisters, who formed the mainstay of Catholic charitable institutions, dropped from 181,421 in 1965 to 126,517 in 1980; the much smaller number of religious brothers also fell from 12,539 in 1965 to 8,563 in 1980.[55] The mainline Protestant denominations, including the Presbyterians, Methodists, Episcopalians, Lutherans, American Baptists, and United Church of Christ, after nearly doubling their aggregate membership between the 1930s and the 1960s, similarly began a period of membership decline that has continued and accelerated to this present day; absolute numbers peaked in the late 1960s, but relative to population mainline strength was in decline from the beginning of the decade.[56] The 1960s were the decade of avowedly secular and liberationist theologies that sought to realign Christian doctrine with the human-centered radical ideologies of the day, but such accommodations appeared only to accelerate the processes of decline.[57] In these sectors of American Christianity, therefore, the last four decades of the century witnessed a very similar story of retreat from active church membership to that seen in most of Europe. By 2001, the percentage of Americans who claimed to have "no religion" was, at 14 percent, close to the European average.[58]

Decline in both the Catholic and Protestant mainline was, however, largely, and perhaps even entirely, offset by absolute growth in conservative Protestant denominations, and increasingly also by the proliferation of new church networks, many of them the product of the charismatic renewal movements that will be surveyed in chapter 15. Gaustad and Barlow's *New Historical Atlas of Religion in America* suggests (contrary to most authorities) that, after significant decline during the 1960s and 1970s, aggregate church membership in relation to national population may have risen during the 1980s and 1990s, climbing back above the 60 percent level.[59] In a population whose numbers were being constantly swelled by immigration, not all conservative denominations succeeded in increasing their share of the national population in the second half of the century, but the absolute numbers were impressive. The Southern Baptist Convention gained more than 2 million new members between 1970 and 1985, in so doing supplanting the United Methodist Church (formed in 1968 by a merger between the Methodist Church and the Evangelical Brethren Church) as the largest Protestant denomination in the country.[60] The National Association of Evangelicals (NAE) was a federation of mainly small conservative denominations that was formed in Chicago in May 1943 to unite conservative Protestants who identified neither with the mainline Federal Council of Churches (FCC) nor with the militant separatism of hard-core fundamentalists. Its initial appeal was to small church groupings that sought strength in wider association. In 1946 its twenty-two member denominations had an average membership of only 45,000 each, whereas the twenty-five denominations comprising the FCC averaged about 1 million members each. However, by the 1970s, the aggregate membership of the NAE had risen to 3.5 million.[61]

Other groups that proved largely impervious to the secularizing trends of the 1960s and beyond included the Pentecostals and the African American denominations. Counting Pentecostals is notoriously difficult. A sample survey of 4,001 adult Americans conducted in 1992 produced an estimate of as many as 9 million Pentecostals in the country as a whole, and at least as many again charismatics, many of whom would have been members of historic denominations. By the end of the century the two largest Pentecostal denominations, the Church of God in Christ (an African American church) and the Assemblies of God, claimed membership of 5.5 million and 2.5 million respectively.[62] Scholars of American Christianity still devote surprisingly little attention to the other major African American bodies such as the National Baptist Convention of America, the National Baptist Convention of the USA, the Progressive National Baptist Convention, the African Methodist Episcopal Church, and the African Methodist Episcopal Zion Church, but these denominations were among the largest in the country. Unlike the mainline white denominations, they have not always kept full membership or attendance statistics, but it is estimated that in 1979 as many as 61 percent of the African American population—who represented a large proportion of the nation's poor, especially in the inner cities—remained members of Protestant or Catholic churches. The black Baptist churches had an estimated aggregate membership of more than 8 million, the black Methodist churches of 2.8 million, while the Church of God in Christ at that stage had 3 million members, compared with the 5.5 million claimed twenty years later.[63] Even allowing for the fact that a fair proportion of these African American Christians may have been somewhat nominal in their church commitment, these figures present a striking contrast with the large-scale abstention of the European working classes from the churches in the twentieth century. The more recent growth of Pentecostal churches among the mushrooming Hispanic population of America's cities reinforces this general point. American cities continue to present compelling evidence of the capacity of popular Protestantism, especially of a Pentecostal variety, to survive and even grow in the modern urban environment.

The tenacity of American conservative Protestantism in continuing to flourish in the most economically advanced modern society on the planet has occupied the attention of both the defenders and the critics of secularization theory. The latter make their appeal to the obvious evidence of the harmonious coexistence of extensive urbanization, unprecedented technological sophistication, and unusually high levels of religious participation. The case of the former remains substantially the same as that expressed by Bryan R. Wilson in 1966: "Whereas in England secularization has been seen in the abandonment of the Churches—as in other European countries—in America it has been seen in the absorption of the Churches by the society, and their loss of distinctive religious content."[64] Hence Steve Bruce explains the growth of conservative Christianity in postwar American society by reference to the success of evangelical churches in reinventing their historic message as a recipe for individual fulfillment and personal growth. Many late twentieth-century Americans were preoccupied with cosseting their own inner well-being and enhancing their outer material prosperity, and evangelical churches offered a commodified religious package neatly tailored to these demands of the popular market.[65] As the American cultural and religious historian R. Laurence Moore put it, they became masters in the art of "selling God."[66] According to this interpretation, both liberal and conservative sectors of American Christianity accommodated themselves to what they judged to be the predominant cultural mood of the age. The mainline denominations estimated the prevailing sentiment to be one of radical humanism and commitment to human rights, whereas conservatives judged the public preference to be for free market forms of highly individualized programs for self-betterment. Quite simply, the liberals got it wrong and the conservatives got it right. The "baby-boomer" generation that grew to maturity in the 1960s and 1970s turned inwards in its spiritual preoccupations, and "born-again" Christianity trimmed its sails to make the most of the prevailing wind. This style of inward-looking evangelical spirituality extended its reach well beyond the conservative Protestant churches. One sociologist of American religion has estimated that in the late 1980s and 1990s 25 percent of the "born-again" Christian community comprised Catholics, and another 20 percent were affiliated to mainline denominations.[67]

The most successful example of this conservative repackaging of the Christian gospel was the popular evangelistic tool, the Four Spiritual Laws, devised by the California-based campus evangelist Bill Bright in 1957. Rather than beginning his gospel presentation as evangelicals have conventionally done, with human sinfulness, Bright selected as the opening question that evangelists should address to their hearers, "Has it ever occurred to you . . . that God has a wonderful plan for your life?" The assertion that "God loves you and has a wonderful plan for your life" became the first of "The Four Spiritual Laws," which Bright's organization, Campus Crusade for Christ, marketed as a booklet throughout the United States and increasingly far beyond its borders. The bad news of God's judgment on human sin slipped down the *ordo salutis* to become the second spiritual law; the atoning work of Christ on the Cross was the third, and the need for a personal response of faith in order to find salvation the fourth.[68] The extent of Bright's innovation can be exaggerated. His emphasis on the highly specific nature of God's supposed plan for each individual life was much indebted to the teaching of the Director of Education in the church in which he was converted, First Presbyterian Church in Hollywood, Los Angeles, Henrietta Mears (1890–1963), whose influence extended nationally through the publishing company she founded in 1933, Gospel Light Publications.[69] But Bright both symbolized and helped to effect the shift in postwar American evangelicalism from a confidence in the supposed providential destiny of the United States as the redeemer nation toward a narrower focus on the well-being of the individual and the Christian family—providence was increasingly personalized.[70]

In her book *Material Christianity* (1995) Colleen McDannell has vividly illustrated the progress of "commodified evangelicalism" in the modern United States by charting the expansion of popular Christian retailing. In 1965 the Christian Booksellers Association had some 725 stores in the United States. By 1984 there were 3,200. By 1995 the total number of Christian bookstores, both members of the Association and others, was estimated at more than 7,000. Their best-selling books were either those that pandered to the continuing popular absorption with prophetic subjects—notably Hal Lindsey's *The Late Great Planet Earth* (1970)—or those that focused on family and marriage issues, such as Marabel Morgan's *Total Woman: How to Make Your Marriage Come Alive* (1973), which by 1975 was selling between 10,000 and 20,000 copies a week. The Jesus Movement of the 1970s supplied a new impetus to the Christian retail industry, so that Christian bookstores sold an expanding range, including gospel music and branded Christian merchandise, such as t-shirts bearing the intriguing message that "In Case of Rapture, This T-Shirt Will Be Empty." As a growing proportion of American evangelicals chose to home-school their children, some sections of the evangelical community began to wall themselves off from what they perceived to be a dissolute and godless society, creating a parallel Christian universe free of contaminating secular influence; in some parts of the country, there were even Christian Yellow Pages directories that listed only certified Christian suppliers.[71] As David Hempton has emphasized, the United States should be understood as a patchwork of distinct religious subcultures; those that were closest to the centers of political liberalism and intellectual sophistication on the East Coast tended to be predominantly secular; those that were most remote from such centers were the heartlands of conservative Protestantism.[72] By the end of the century, the United States had developed its own version of what has become known in Dutch history as "pillarization"—the vertical differentiation of society and its institutions into quite distinct traditions of belief, though in this case the differentiation was not between Catholic and Protestant so much as between "born-again" and "non-born-again."

The United States is the clearest exemplification in the modern world of the chameleon-like capacity of Christianity—and especially its evangelical forms—to adapt itself to the assumptions and cultural patterns of a free market society. However, the commodification of religion was a phenomenon that was neither peculiarly Protestant nor even confined to the advanced capitalism of the late twentieth century. Catholic Christianity, with its predilection for the visual image, has for long been rather more inclined than word-centered Protestantism to mass-produce religious bric-a-brac for the consumption of faithful pilgrims to holy places, and most of McDannell's book is in fact concerned with the material culture of American Catholicism. Furthermore, as she shows, the evangelical merchandise of the late twentieth century can be traced back at least as far as the 1880s, when the Holiness devotee Daniel S. Warner established the Gospel Trumpet Company, to publish, not simply his newspaper *The Gospel Trumpet*, but also Christian stationery, bookmarks, postcards, and other items. The company eventually became Warner Press, one of the largest publishers of religious merchandise in the country.[73]

Any religion that attracts its adherents on the basis of voluntary free association, as American Protestantism has done from its beginnings, is always liable to the temptation to go overboard in its self-presentation, so that winsome preaching becomes mere performance and Christian literature intended to be accessible to the ordinary reader degenerates into religious pulp fiction. But it is important not to confuse such recurrent tendencies of voluntaryist Protestantism to over-accommodate itself to the ethos of its context with evidence of the supposed universal and irreversible march of a secularizing process that will lead to the eventual marginalization of religion. In *Selling God,* R. Laurence Moore issues a salutary warning against the common assumption that the current American form of religious secularity will prove to have a special capacity to undermine religion. Churches are always partly secular institutions, simply because they seek to persuade the world of their message. He writes:

> The particular form of worldliness that churches in the United States have exhibited by entering the marketplace of culture has only displaced earlier forms of church worldliness: direct political involvement in the domestic and foreign policy of states, conspicuous displays of non-bourgeois pomp and wealth, and heavy investment in the higher forms of philosophical and scientific knowledge.[74]

Nevertheless, Moore, a confessed secularist, makes the telling point that the extent of Christian accommodation with current popular culture in the United States denudes churches of their transformative and prophetic power.[75] The growing realization of this cultural and philosophical weakness in American Christianity prompted both Catholic and Protestant intellectuals in the last three decades of the century to seek to develop a more robust Christian worldview capable of interrogating the secular premises of the surrounding culture. For some, such as the Catholic thinker, Michael Novak (1933–2017), the rediscovery of a distinctively Catholic perspective on the world led in the direction of an angular neo-conservatism. Novak reacted to his first-hand experience of the extremes of student radicalism at Stanford University and the State University of New York in the 1960s by recasting his entire philosophical system in a conservative mold. In his view, a liberal white Anglo-Saxon Protestant "superculture" dominated television, the universities, and the press, which only a traditional Catholic view of revelation could successfully challenge. He repudiated his erstwhile opposition to the Vietnam War and fell out of sympathy even with most of the progressive developments in the Catholic Church in the wake of Vatican II.[76] There were Protestant parallels to Novak, such as the evangelical philosopher Francis Schaeffer (1912–84). A former missionary to Western Europe on behalf of the fundamentalist Carl McIntyre's International Association of Christian Churches, Schaeffer published a series of semipopular books between 1968 and his death in 1984 that were designed to challenge the hold of Enlightenment rationalism on Western culture. He was one of the first evangelicals to call attention to the environmental crisis, and also urged the evangelical constituency to adopt a simple lifestyle. Latterly, however, he became associated with creationism and neo-conservative politics generally.[77]

While Novak and Schaeffer represent divergent Catholic and evangelical Protestant responses to secularity, what may prove more significant in the long run was the strengthening tendency for conservative intellectuals from Catholic and Protestant backgrounds to make common cause in the defense of the relevance of Christian orthodoxy within the "naked public square" from which religious beliefs and values had been excluded by a dogmatic secularism.[78] The author of *The Naked Public Square*, published in 1984, was the Lutheran minister Richard J. Neuhaus, who later (in 1990) converted from Lutheranism to Catholicism. In 1985 he joined forces with the evangelical Republican Charles Colson who, before his conversion to evangelical faith, was notorious for his role in the Watergate scandal, to form "Evangelicals and Catholics Together." The alliance produced a declaration in 1994 calling for evangelicals and Catholics to collaborate in the public defense and propagation of historic Christianity in the coming third millennium.[79] From the mid-1970s onwards a remarkable succession of leading evangelical scholars such as the philosopher Alvin Plantinga, the historians George Marsden, Nathan Hatch, and Mark Noll, and the sociologist Christian Smith made their way to join the faculty of the University of Notre Dame, the traditional headquarters of Marian devotion and Lourdes piety in the United States.[80] More generally, a growing number of thinking evangelicals sought to achieve some form of "convergence" of evangelical theology with sacramental ecclesiastical traditions and became attracted to denominations that emphasized their historic ancestry in the church of apostolic times. Some, such as Wheaton College professor and Reformed Presbyterian minister, Robert E. Webber, joined the Protestant Episcopal Church (in 1972). Others, such as Webber's close associate, the Gordon College professor Thomas Howard, ended up in the Catholic Church (in 1985). Others again, such as the former Campus Crusade evangelist, Peter Gillquist (1938–2012), accompanied by 1,700 of his evangelical associates, formed themselves into a New Covenant Apostolic Order in an endeavor to restore visible continuity with apostolic tradition. In 1987 the Order assumed the name "Antiochian Evangelical Orthodox Mission" and became an affiliate of the Antiochian Orthodox Church. In 1995 the Mission became fully integrated within the Antiochian Orthodox Church.[81]

Such trajectories—along with others that took some evangelicals on a quite different spiritual journey into a form of postmodern experientialism that began to style itself as "postevangelicalism"—supply telling evidence that by the end of the century, American evangelicalism was facing something of a crisis of coherence and authority.[82] But they can also be taken as evidence that the defenders of religion in the United States were not going to succumb meekly to secularizing forces but rather to mount various, if divergent forms of counterattack. If secularization is properly to be understood as a recoil mechanism against particular phases of monopolistic religious ascendancy, then it generates its own recoil reactions, some more successful than others. The evangelical revival movements of the late eighteenth and early nineteenth centuries can in fact be understood as among the most successful of such counterattacks, for they led to the substantial spiritual renewal of much of Protestant Europe as well as laying the foundations for a Protestant America. One leading commentator on modern American religion, the Christian sociologist James Davison Hunter, has lamented the fact that, for all their talk about the recovery of a Christian world view, evangelicals have failed to shift the hold of secularity on the American universities and media, leaving Christian culture in the United States marginalized from the centers of power, even if still largely supported.[83] Hunter may be right, but there is no sign that Christianity itself is destined to wither on the American vine. The churches in twentieth-century America reacted in various and complex ways to the challenges of modernity. The most successful turned the freedom of the religious market and the individualistic mood of the age to their own advantage, yet at the same time the blatant nature of some of their adaptations prompted others to mount counteroffensives against the encroachments of secularism on American intellectual life, including the life of the churches themselves. The American case points toward the paradox that societies may in fact be deeply religious and profoundly secular at the same time.

IV. Marriages of the Religious and the Secular

At the beginning of this chapter reference was made to Hugh McLeod's list of six possible spheres in which tendencies to secularization may be evident: individual belief; formal religious practice; the place of religion in public institutions; the prominence of religion in public debate; the significance of religion as an aspect of group identity; and the relationship of religion with popular culture. The evidence from the twentieth-century history of Christianity surveyed in this chapter confirms McLeod's view that there is no necessary or straightforward relationship between all six. Some of them have indeed frequently belonged together. The rise or fall of individual belief has found an understandable reflection in rates of religious practice, though the correspondence between the two may not be exact. All Scandinavian countries in the twentieth century experienced a decline in regular church attendance that appears to have been consistent throughout the century, and that may have begun as soon as religious compulsion was lifted in the nineteenth century. This protracted decline mirrored the slow waning of orthodox Christian belief, but this was not a decline from a previous golden age of faith; rather there seems every likelihood that the adherence of many Scandinavian people to Christian faith had been quite tenuous ever since the region was first evangelized. Yet the Scandinavian countries also illustrate in a pointed way the possibility that in certain conditions stable patterns of religious belonging can exist almost independently of personal religious belief. They exemplify the fact that churches, if they attain the status of public institutions that express a people's sense of collective identity, can retain the formal loyalty and quite strong cultural allegiance of the majority of the population even in the substantial absence of personal Christian belief. The twentieth-century history of Sweden, Denmark, and Iceland, and to a lesser extent, of Norway and Finland is thus one of increasingly unbelieving societies that nonetheless retained a consistent, highly visible and legally protected place for the national church.

The United States in the twentieth century was by some criteria a more "secular" nation than Sweden or Denmark. The American state from its inception has, of course, refused to give any religious body privileged status before the law. In consequence religion in the United States has always been divorced from the apparatus of government and public institutions to a much greater extent than in the Scandinavian nations, and in the course of the twentieth century that divorce became more absolute in certain spheres, notably in the universities, public education, and the media. Many Christians reacted to such "secularizing" trends by withdrawing from large sectors of public life into their own "pillarized" alternative structures. In the experience of most Christians by the end of the century, church and nation were much further apart in the United States than they were in Sweden or Denmark. Yet at another level, the adherence of the great majority of Americans to a broad Judeo-Christian civil religion strengthened in the course of the century. Furthermore, the churches as a whole steadily increased their collective market share during the first half of the century, and, after two lean decades in the 1960s and 1970s, regained much of their former position in the 1980s and 1990s, thanks to the success of the more conservative churches. They did so at a price of substantial accommodation to the individualism and self-preoccupation that characterized popular American culture in this period. Christianity made its peace with popular culture. From one standpoint that could be viewed as an antisecularizing trend, preserving the ability of the churches to command widespread allegiance. From another, as Wilson and Bruce have argued, it can be understood as a form of cultural secularization, and one that provoked valiant attempts by both Catholic and Protestant intellectuals to push the boundaries back and reclaim the intellectual high ground of the nation for Christianity. However, if it was "secularization," it was only one more phase in the continual ebb and flow between church and culture that marks all Christian history. In other sectors of the nation's life, as chapter 15 will explore, migrant populations were bringing forms of Christian life nurtured in Latin America, Asia, and Africa into the heart of American religious life. In so doing they eroded some elements of American civil religion, while at the same time greatly enhancing the visibility of churches in many American cities. The United States remains both a secular and a Christian nation.

CHAPTER SIX

Is Christ Divided?

THE ECUMENICAL MOVEMENT
AND ITS CONVERSE

I. Was the Twentieth Century the Ecumenical Century?

The twentieth century has sometimes been denominated by historians of Christianity as "the ecumenical century."[1] Narratives of the ecumenical movement typically begin with the World Missionary Conference, held in Edinburgh in June 1910, which assembled some 1,215 Protestant delegates from various parts of the globe to devise a more effective common strategy for the evangelization of the world. Viewed with the benefit of hindsight, the Edinburgh conference has been widely identified as the birthplace of the formal ecumenical movement. Without it, there would be no World Council of Churches. Yet, as will be shown in the text that follows, serious attempts to bridge divisions between Protestant Christians were already under way in India and China before 1910. Furthermore, the World Missionary Conference was precisely that—a gathering of mission executives and missionaries (plus a small number of national church leaders from Asia) convened to consider questions of missionary policy. Delegates represented missionary agencies rather than churches, and discussion of questions of doctrine and church order was forbidden, in deference to the Church of England, whose endorsement would not have been given if the conference had been expected to discuss matters of faith and order with Nonconformists.[2]

There were no Catholics or Orthodox present at Edinburgh, though an unofficial message of greeting was read from one liberal-minded Italian bishop, Geremia Bonomelli of Cremona. Bonomelli (1831–1914) was a friend of a young priest, Angelo Roncalli, and had suggested to Roncalli in June 1908 that the time might be ripe for the summons of "a great ecumenical council." Bonomelli was using the word "ecumenical" in its original Greek sense of "pertaining to the whole household of humanity"—he was suggesting a successor to the Vatican Council of 1869–70, not an assembly of Catholics and Protestants together.[3] Similarly, the World Missionary Conference was originally entitled "The Third Ecumenical Missionary Conference" (previous ones had been held in London in 1888 and New York in 1900), to signal that it would include the whole human race in its scope. But the word was acquiring a more specific church-related meaning. Hence in September 1908 the original title was dropped in order to avoid misunderstanding arising from the fact that "the word "ecumenical" has acquired a technical meaning": the organizers sensed that no event that excluded the Catholic and the Orthodox had an unquestioned right to the title.[4] Half a century later, Angelo Roncalli was elected as Pope John XXIII, and almost immediately, on January 25, 1959, announced that he was summoning an "Ecumenical Council." The Second Vatican Council that assembled in Rome on October 11, 1962 was "ecumenical" only in the original formal sense that had survived within Catholic usage. Chapter 9 will indicate how nevertheless, rather like Edinburgh 1910, it too was to prove of immense significance for relations between Christian churches.

The World Missionary Conference in 1910 was thus not an ecumenical conference in the modern sense. Nevertheless, participation in the event left many with a deep conviction that the greatest obstacle to the world mission of the church was its manifold divisions. One such was Charles H. Brent (1862–1929), American Episcopal missionary bishop of the Philippines. It had made him, he testified, into "an apostle of church unity."[5] The Philippines were the most Catholic country in Asia, and hence raised acute questions for Episcopalians about the legitimacy of missionary efforts by other churches, and whether some measure of cooperation with the Catholic Church was called for. The Convention of the Protestant Episcopal Church in Cincinnati in October 1910 adopted Brent's idea of summoning a world conference in which representatives "of all Christian communions throughout the world" would discuss these matters of Faith and Order. That expansive vision was never fully realized. The first Faith and Order conference at Lausanne in 1927 included delegates from several Orthodox Churches, but the Catholic Church declined to participate in the Faith and Order movement.

The Edinburgh conference also imparted new momentum to efforts at practical cooperation between Protestant missions. These were formalized by the creation in 1921 of the International Missionary Council, but, well before this, missionaries in the field had formed regional associations that in some cases went beyond mere cooperation. In the summer of 1913 Anglican missionaries of the CMS met with Presbyterian, Methodist, Quaker, and Africa Inland Mission colleagues at Kikuyu in British East Africa (modern Kenya). The bishops of Mombasa and Uganda took a full part in the meeting, which proposed a federation between the participating missions and even limited intercommunion between their respective churches.[6] To the consternation of Frank Weston, the Anglo-Catholic bishop of Zanzibar, the Kikuyu gathering ended with a joint communion service, held in the Church of Scotland church, and presided over by the bishop of Mombasa. Weston subsequently indicted the two participating bishops to the archbishop of Canterbury for propagating heresy and schism. Randall Davidson, the archbishop of Canterbury, declined to condemn the united communion service, yet made it clear that it must not happen again. Nevertheless, the years that followed saw various initiatives to tackle the divisive questions of Faith and Order that had been excluded from the agenda at Edinburgh. In the United States, Congregationalists and Episcopalians engaged in a series of discussions on Faith and Order that culminated in a concordat in 1919.

In Britain similar discussions between Anglican and Free Church representatives took place from 1914. The General Secretary of the Baptist Union, J. H. Shakespeare, caused a stir in his own denomination in 1918 by publishing a book that advocated reunion of the Free Churches with the Church of England on the basis of a constitutional episcopate.[7] As a culmination of these initiatives, the Lambeth Conference of Anglican bishops in July 1920 issued an "Appeal to all Christian People," drafted by the archbishop of York, Cosmo Lang, and a small group of bishops, of whom Brent was one.[8] The Appeal invited all Christians to accept that the episcopate was not merely "the best instrument for maintaining the unity and continuity of the Church" but "the one means" for ensuring a ministry that all could recognize as possessing the commission of Christ and the authority of the whole body of Christ.[9] The Free Churches gave a guarded welcome to the Appeal, but stressed that their acceptance of episcopal order would depend on two conditions: first, that no particular *theory* of episcopacy would be required; and second, that no disowning of the spiritual validity of their previous non-episcopal ministries must be implied.[10] The second of these two conditions, along with the implication that in future all ordinations must be at the hands of bishops, would prove the rock on which ecumenical negotiations in Britain involving the Church of England and the Free Churches would repeatedly founder, whereas in India the ecumenical vessel managed, not without difficulty, to steer a course around it.

Although the Lambeth Appeal was framed with relations with the English Free Churches particularly in mind, it was explicitly addressed to "*all* Christian people." The archbishop of Canterbury, Randall Davidson, had the Appeal translated into Latin and sent it to Pope Benedict XV. In December 1921 a leading lay Anglo-Catholic, Viscount Halifax, used the Appeal as a basis for initiating a series of confidential and originally unofficial meetings at Malines in Belgium with Catholic figures led by the archbishop, Cardinal Mercier. The ultimate end in view was nothing less than to ascertain whether terms could be agreed for the reunion of the Anglican Communion with Rome. From November 1922 these discussions had the blessing of Pope Pius XI. Although the discussants were never representative enough of their respective churches for there to be any prospect of success, the fact that they took place at all is further evidence that as early as the 1920s there were some whose thinking about church unity extended beyond the frontiers of Protestantism.[11] Talks also took place from 1919 to 1922 between Anglican representatives and a delegation from the Eastern Orthodox Church that led to a declaration by the Holy Synod of Constantinople that it accepted the validity of Anglican orders.[12]

The momentum achieved by these ecumenical discussions in the early 1920s was not sustained. More significant for the future was the series of global Protestant conferences that assembled in the interwar years and which were marked by the increasingly assertive presence of representatives of the so-called "younger" churches, especially in Asia. Whereas at Edinburgh in 1910 the twenty non-Westerners made up a mere 1.65 percent of the 1,215 delegates, by the International Missionary Council meeting at Tambaram near Madras in 1938, 182 representatives of the younger churches accounted for 39.82 percent of the total.[13] In his enthronement sermon as archbishop of Canterbury in April 1942, William Temple referred to "the great world-fellowship" of Christians that had arisen in every nation as "the great new fact of our era."[14] At a time when the world was torn asunder by war, it was not entirely fanciful to imagine that the brightest hope for the unity of humanity lay in the strengthening ties binding Christians together across the continents. The inauguration of the World Council of Churches at Amsterdam in August 1948, coming soon the formation of the United Nations in October 1945, raised hopes of a new era of international harmony and cooperation.

Not all Christians, however, welcomed the formation of the WCC. Carl McIntyre (1906–2002), founder of a small American fundamentalist denomination, the Bible Presbyterian Church, had in 1941 formed the American Council of Christian Churches as a fundamentalist alternative to the mainline Federal Council of Churches. In August 1948, at the same time as the inaugural assembly of the WCC, McIntyre brazenly selected Amsterdam as the location for the founding meeting of his International Council of Christian Churches (the implication was that the member churches of the WCC were not Christian). His militantly separatist organization remained small, but a greater concern for the WCC was that most Pentecostal churches and conservative evangelical denominations in the United States hung back from joining, fearful that the WCC was liberal and weak in its commitment to biblical authority.

More serious still for the comprehensiveness of the Council were the anxieties of the Eastern Orthodox. There were only two sizable Orthodox delegations at Amsterdam—those of the Ecumenical Patriarchate of Constantinople and the Greek Orthodox Church. The Orthodox remained on the fringe of the ecumenical movement throughout the 1950s, partly because of the political realities of the Cold War, and partly for theological reasons. The WCC had inherited a minimalist doctrinal basis from the Faith and Order movement that affirmed belief in "Jesus Christ as God and Saviour" but little else. The first general secretary of the WCC, the Dutchman W. A. Visser 't Hooft, responded to those concerns. During a visit to Leningrad (St. Petersburg) in 1959, he scribbled a new and explicitly Trinitarian basis on the back of a hotel breakfast menu. After slight revision, this became the basis of the WCC at its third assembly at New Delhi in 1961: "the World Council of Churches is a fellowship of Churches which confess the Lord Jesus Christ as God and Saviour according to the Scriptures and therefore seek to fulfil together their common calling to the glory of the one God, Father, Son, and Holy Spirit."[15] The new basis encouraged the Orthodox Churches in Soviet Russia, Rumania, Bulgaria, and Poland to join the Council. It also resulted in the first two applications from membership from Pentecostal churches. However, most conservative evangelical churches remained wary of the WCC. As will be seen in chapters 7 and 8, from the mid-1960s the theological divergence between ecumenical and evangelical Christianity was to widen.

For some twenty-five years after the formation of the WCC it appeared that structural reunions of major Protestant traditions were destined to dominate the Protestant ecclesiastical landscape in the second half of the twentieth century. Some trans-confessional unions of Protestant churches had already taken place during the interwar period in China, the Philippines, Guatemala, Puerto Rico, Siam (Thailand), and Canada.[16] The

United Church of Canada, formed in 1925, combined mainly Methodist, Congregational, and Presbyterian traditions. Eight major unions followed after 1945: the Church of South India (1947), the United Church of Christ in the Philippines (1948), the United Church of Zambia (1965), the United Church of Jamaica and Grand Cayman (1965), the Church of North India and the Church of Pakistan (both formed in 1970 through a common negotiating process), the United Reformed Church [in Great Britain] (1972), and the Uniting Church in Australia (1977). As such unions became more numerous, leaders of other churches set targets for achieving their own unions: the years 1980 or 2000 were the most commonly adopted. One of the earliest examples of such a target comes from Sri Lanka (Ceylon) in 1932, when a conference of Christian teachers at Trinity College, Kandy made three predictions regarding the condition of the nation in the year 2000: first, that Ceylon would have gained independence from British rule; second, that Buddhism would have consolidated its ascendancy over the island; and, third, that the churches would by then have accepted that Christian unity was essential.[17] The first two predictions proved spot on; the third off target. Tamil Anglicans in Jaffna diocese joined the Church of South India (CSI) in 1947, but two attempts to form a united "Church of Lanka" failed in 1972 and 1975.[18]

The period from the 1960s to the early 1980s was marked by conspicuous failures as well as some notable successes of church union. Other examples of the collapse of union schemes during these decades included Nigeria (1965), Ghana (1983),[19] and in Britain two successive rejections by the Church of England of a scheme of reunion with the Methodist Church (1969 and 1972). The Methodists voted in favor of this scheme, but determined opposition by conservative Anglo-Catholics twice proved sufficient to wreck it; in July 1969 the scheme obtained only 69 percent support in the Church Assembly, when 75 percent was required; in May 1972 in the newly formed General Synod, the majority in favor fell to below 66 percent, dealing a death-blow to the scheme. As in almost every case where union between an episcopal and a non-episcopal church was in prospect, the stumbling block was the mechanism devised for the unification of the two sets of ministries. A central service of reconciliation was envisaged, in which representative Methodist ministers would kneel before the archbishop of Canterbury and receive the laying on of hands with a prayer that each "according to his need" might receive the Holy Spirit for the work that lay before them; similarly, the archbishop and bishops would receive the laying on of hands with a similar, but not identical, prayer from Methodist ministers. The plan admitted that the success of this proposal depended on a mutual acceptance that there would be contradictory inter-pretations of what this rite meant.[20] For Anglo-Catholics, it was an act of ordination, admitting Methodists into the apostolic priesthood. For Meth-odists and Anglican evangelicals, it was merely an act of commissioning to a new sphere of pastoral ministry. Archbishop Michael Ramsey was comfortable with the ambiguity, believing that he would be asking God to give Methodist ministers whatever grace they might need for the exercise of their future apostolic ministry; exactly what that spiritual deficit was, he did not claim to know. Others, including his predecessor at Canterbury, Geoffrey Fisher, thought such a procedure would be "open double deal-ing."[21] The success or failure of church unity negotiations in this period could turn on the willingness of different parties to tolerate such studied ambiguity of language. By 1980 the search for institutional unity had run out of steam. The emerging postmodern cultural climate bred skepticism toward preoccupation with structures and institutions.[22] No significant church unions were formed in the remainder of the century.[23]

II. Church Union and Disunion in the Indian Subcontinent

Christians, and especially Protestants, formed a tiny minority of the vast population of India. The impulse to draw together in their witness came primarily from the logic of their context, and antedated the Edinburgh conference. Thus in 1908 the Congregational churches planted by the Lon-don Missionary Society (LMS) and the American Board of Commissioners for Foreign Missions (ABCFM) united with Presbyterian churches planted by the Reformed Church in America and the Free Church of Scotland to form the South India United Church (SIUC). Congregational and Presby-terian churches had different systems of church government, but shared a broadly similar theology. However, some missionaries and Indian church leaders were beginning to think in more ambitious terms. Traveling back to India together in 1910, three of the Edinburgh delegates conferred on what immediate steps could be taken toward a church union in India that would bridge the wider gap between the Anglican Church and the Free Churches. One was the young Anglican clergyman V. S. Azariah (1874–1945), founder of India's first two indigenous missionary societies, the In-dian Missionary Society of Tinnevelly in 1903 and the National Missionary Society in 1905. In 1912 Azariah would be appointed bishop of Dornakal, the first indigenous Anglican bishop anywhere in Asia. A second was an American Congregational missionary, J. P. Jones. The third was another

American Congregationalist, the YMCA evangelist George Sherwood Eddy (1871–1963). Eddy believed that "the great, tolerant East"—by which he meant India in particular—held out the best prospect for healing the centuries-old rift between the episcopal and non-episcopal churches, and that the way to do this was through a purified "constitutional" episcopacy modeled on the patristic church. The coming united church in India would necessarily have bishops, but they would be bishops shorn of any connection with the British state and in harmony with what Eddy vaguely termed "the genius of the Orient." Rural India was accustomed to a consensual form of government in which the princely authority of the *rajah* was counterbalanced by the collective voice of the *panchayat* (the village council of elders); "constitutional" episcopacy would be patterned on the same model.[24] He accordingly convened a three-day unofficial meeting between representatives of the Anglican Church and the SIUC held, probably toward the end of 1910, at the residence of the bishop of Madras, Henry Whitehead.[25]

The majority of those present at the Madras meeting were missionaries, but three Indians attended: Azariah; his close associate in the National Missionary Society of India K. T. Paul (1876–1931), who was also prominent in both the SIUC and the YMCA in India, of which he in 1916 became the first National General Secretary; and J. P. Cotelingam, another lay leader in the SIUC. Both Paul and Cotelingam had marked sympathies with the burgeoning Indian nationalist movement. Paul became one of Gandhi's strongest Christian supporters and one of two Christian representatives in the Round Table conferences on constitutional reform in India. Cotelingam had addressed the inaugural assembly of the SIUC in 1908 on the politically sensitive topic of "swadeshi and the South India United Church."[26] *Swadeshi* (self-reliance) was a slogan that had come to the fore in the Indian nationalist movement since 1905 and was destined to become the basis for a demand for full Indian independence. The early Indian advocates of church union, and not a few of their missionary supporters, saw the goal of creating a self-governing Indian national church as a corollary of the developing movement to establish one self-governing Indian nation.

Although the Madras meeting in 1910 had no immediate structural consequences, Christian leaders in India took careful note of the attempts in East Africa, England, and the United States to effect a rapprochement between the episcopal and non-episcopal streams of the Protestant tradition. In May 1919 Bishop Azariah was the prime mover behind a conference on church union held at Tranquebar, site of the first Protestant mission in India begun in 1706. The conference issued a statement that became known as the Tranquebar Manifesto. It was largely the handiwork of Sherwood Eddy, who was visiting India again that year and was one of only two Westerners present. The Manifesto suggested that any union between the Anglican Church and the SIUC should be on the basis of the "Lambeth Quadrilateral"—four points, devised by a New England Episcopal clergyman, William Reed Huntington, and subsequently adopted by the Lambeth Conference of 1888 as the only basis on which Anglicans could contemplate reunion:

1. The Holy Scriptures of the Old and New Testaments, as containing all things necessary to salvation
2. The Apostles' Creed and the Nicene Creed
3. The two Sacraments ordained by Christ Himself—Baptism and the Lord's Supper
4. The Historic Episcopate, locally adapted

The Manifesto adopted the Quadrilateral *verbatim* and similarly reproduced Huntington's principle that acceptance of the *fact* of the historic episcopate did not imply acceptance of any particular *theory* of episcopacy.[27] South Indian Presbyterians and Congregationalists were being invited to accept a modified form of episcopal government, but without any compulsion to accept Anglo-Catholic theories of apostolic succession. The proposed united church would combine congregational, Presbyterian and episcopal elements in what was termed an "episcopresbygationalist" hybrid. Furthermore, in June 1919 Eddy met with Metropolitan Titus II Mar Thoma of the Mar Thoma Church—a reformed branch of the ancient East Syrian Church—and obtained his agreement to submit the proposal for a united church to his Synod.[28] Eddy was ecstatic, writing home that there was now a prospect of uniting

> the three great divisions of the Christian Church, the Western Church, the Eastern Church, and the Free Protestant Churches. . . . If this union is formed it will be the first time in four hundred years since the Reformation that the great division between the Episcopal and non-Episcopal Churches has been united. It will be the first time in nine centuries, since the division between the Eastern and the Western Church, that these two branches of the Church have ever come together.[29]

Eddy's rhetoric outstripped reality. The Mar Thoma Church represented only one branch of the Syrian Orthodox Church, and in the event did not participate in the protracted negotiations for a united Church of South India that followed. Similarly, representatives of the Lutheran tradition that had brought Protestant Christianity to India in 1706 would take no part in the negotiations. Neither, of course, did the Catholic Church. Even in a nation such as India where Christians were a small minority, the dream of a single Christian church has proved remarkably elusive.

Although the Tranquebar conference was attended mainly by Indian ministers, its most tangible outcome, the Manifesto, had impeccably Western origins. Eddy's advocacy of a functional view of episcopacy and his endorsement of the Lambeth Quadrilateral were borrowed from his friend, the New England Congregationalist Newman Smyth, himself a friend of Huntington's. Cynical observers could be forgiven for deducing that South India was being used as a remote laboratory in which to test potentially explosive Western formulae for ecclesiastical reunion. This impression was reinforced by the congruence between the Tranquebar Manifesto and the Lambeth Appeal that followed in 1920. K. T. Paul responded to the Appeal with a series of three acerbic articles in the YMCA periodical *The Young Men of India*. Although Paul was prepared to give a muted welcome to evidence of growing Anglican openness to other churches, he saw the Appeal's insistence on episcopacy as typical of the West's preoccupation with institutional forms and inimical to India's emphasis on the life of the spirit. A culturally appropriate form of church organization for India would, Paul argued, largely abandon the concept of a full-time professional ministry and give priority to the autonomy of the local congregation, discussing its own affairs on the model of the *panchayat*; if it had bishops at all, their role would not be administrative—they would be chosen on the basis of exceptional spiritual giftedness.[30] Whereas Eddy regarded Indians as too "depressed" and "ignorant" to handle the democracy of congregational government,[31] here was the premier Christian spokesman for Indian nationalism arguing precisely the opposite: "Episcopacy," insisted Paul, "is likely to be for a long time a perplexity to the Indian mind."[32]

K. T. Paul represented an Indian view rather than *the* Indian view. Once he had become a bishop, V. S. Azariah proved unbending in his advocacy of episcopacy and his opposition to attempts by LMS missionaries in the late 1930s to include provision for lay presidency at the communion table within the scheme for a united church. The weight of Indian opinion, even within the SIUC, took Azariah's side of the argument in maintaining that the "Indian temperament" would find it "most sacrilegious" to permit anyone to celebrate a sacred rite who had not been solemnly set apart for that purpose.[33] Yet Indian Christian opinion was never united in support of the union proposals. Supporters and opponents alike appealed to the Indian penchant for the inner spirit rather than the outward forms of religion; as evidenced by the contrary claims of Eddy and Paul, invocations of the religious mind of India could work in either direction.

A. J. Appasamy, a gifted Indian theologian who in 1950 would be appointed bishop in the CSI, published in 1930 his *Church Union: An Indian View*, which used the Hindu tradition of *bhakti* (devotion) to argue in favor of the scheme; since dogma was ultimately secondary to devotion, all should be able to unite in common worship. In the same year his *Manifesto on Church Union* in support of the scheme was signed by nearly 200 Indian church leaders.[34] Nonetheless, some politically articulate Indian Christians remained unconvinced. A group of radical Christian thinkers in Madras, formed in 1913 under the title of the *Christo Samaj* (Christ society), had mounted consistent attacks on the union scheme through a newspaper, *The Christian Patriot*. In terms similar to those used by Paul, the *Christo Samaj* castigated the union proposals as an attempt to form a national church on a Western pattern, "which will for ever be a handicap to the development of Christianity on Indian lines."[35] On the eve of the International Missionary Council conference at Tambaram in 1938, the leading figures associated with this group published a series of essays, *Rethinking Christianity in India*. One chapter was devoted to attacks on the union scheme by three leading laymen in the SIUC. The longest contribution was by D. M. Devasahayam, a Nagercoil tea planter who had studied theology at Serampore College and was an inveterate opponent of anything that smacked of sacerdotal power. His article assembled a collection of Indian voices against the union proposals. One of those cited was an Evangelical Anglican participant in the 1919 Tranquebar meeting, the Revd S. G. Maduram, who had subsequently turned against the scheme, warning that "The one terrible result to South India if this union were to take place— may God Almighty forbid it!—will be to kill evangelicalism in our land."[36] Like K. T. Paul before him, Devasahayam argued that the scheme contradicted "the religious genius of India": it stood for organization rather than spiritual simplicity, and represented the triumph of Catholic over liberal Protestant principles. The other two contributors—P. Chenchiah and V. Chakkarai—were both lawyers. They regarded the proposed united church as an attempt to impose "a Western solution of Western controversies on the Eastern mind,"[37] or, as Chenchiah playfully put it:

> It appears to a convert indescribably funny that anybody should entertain the idea that by knocking together the Church of England, the

Church of Scotland, Swedish and Lutheran and American churches, an Indian Church would be produced. But for the fact that the religious man rarely has any sense of humour, the scheme would never have survived the mirth it provokes. It is a capital joke.[38]

Capital joke or not, enough members of the Anglican Church, SIUC, and the South India Province of the Methodist Church (the product of British Wesleyan Methodist missions who joined the negotiations in 1925) supported church union for the negotiating churches to persist in trying to overcome the obstacles placed in its path. Chief among these was the apparent incompatibility between the insistence of Catholic Anglicans that episcopacy (and hence episcopal ordination of ministers) was of the *essence* of the church and the equally emphatic refusal of ministers in the non-Anglican churches to accept reordination at the hands of a bishop, which would have implied that their previous ministries were invalid. The compromise reached was that while all new ministers in the united church would receive ordination at the hands of a bishop, for an interim period of thirty years after the formation of the new church, all existing ministers ordained in the amalgamating churches would be recognized, whether or not they had been episcopally ordained.

The Methodist Provincial Synod was the first to approve the South India proposals in January 1943. In February 1944 the General Council of the [Anglican] Church of India, Burma, and Ceylon gave its qualified approval, by a decisive majority in the House of Laity, but more narrowly in the Houses of Clergy and Bishops. The SIUC General Assembly overwhelmingly approved the scheme in September 1946, by 103 votes to 10. Devasahayam maintained his opposition to the end, but now found himself in a small minority.[39] Even so, the North Tamil district of the SIUC failed to give the scheme the necessary two-thirds majority, and stayed out of the CSI, though it subsequently (in 1950) joined. More seriously, until the eleventh hour the birth of the CSI was placed in jeopardy by the anxiety of the Church of India, Burma, and Ceylon to ensure that no former Anglican congregation should be required to accept a minister who had not been episcopally ordained. The scheme was rescued by an ingenious statement drafted in 1946 by the bishop of Madras, A. M. Hollis, which affirmed that no presbyter in the United Church would exercise his ministry in a congregation who conscientiously objected to his ministrations, but equally that no member of the church would be at liberty to object conscientiously to the ministrations of any presbyter ordained within the church. This apparent contradiction was intended to give former

Anglicans the right to exclude non-episcopally ordained ministers from their parishes while assuring former non-Anglicans that in principle the right of their ministers to operate within the church as a whole could not be impugned.[40] Hollis's verbal dexterity proved just enough to keep the principal parties in India on board, but securing the endorsement of the Anglican Communion as a whole proved infinitely more difficult.

In England Anglican supporters and opponents of the scheme had conducted a fierce debate ever since 1942 and this continued after the official inauguration of the CSI on September 27, 1947. Of the fourteen diocesan bishops, only six were Indians. Eight were British, of whom seven were Anglicans (the eighth was the English Presbyterian, Lesslie Newbigin). About half of the new church's million communicants were former Anglicans, and Anglo-Catholics spoke as if they had become apostates. The Society for the Propagation of the Gospel (SPG) accordingly discontinued its grants to the three of the four Anglican dioceses that had joined the CSI and were previously in receipt of its support. However, 30,000 Anglicans in the Nandyal archdeaconry of Dornakal diocese voted to stay out of the CSI and maintain their links with the SPG; as so often, church union provoked a new schism by diehard traditionalists.[41] The 1948 Lambeth Conference declined to give rights of intercommunion between the CSI and Anglican churches. Full intercommunion between the CSI and Anglican churches was not established until 1998. Although some supporters hailed the inauguration of the CSI as an event that might prove of "even greater significance than the political freedom of India," won just six weeks previously on August 15, 1947,[42] the adult membership of the CSI by 1995 accounted for only 4.5 percent of the estimated Christian population of India.[43] Indian Catholics and Syrian Orthodox, of course, remained separate.

In North India the process of church union attracted less controversy than in the South. This was perhaps surprising, since the Anglican tradition in the North was more uniformly High Church than in the South, and also because the negotiations in the North, unlike those in the South, included Baptists, thus making baptism an issue in a way it was not in the CSI discussions. The explanation for the lower level of polemics directed against the North India plans is partly that they came to fruition later, after the storm raised by the CSI had blown itself out and in an era when enthusiasm for church reunion was at its peak; and partly because a different solution was adopted to the problem of unification of ministries.

As in the South, the process in North India began with the formation of a united church by two denominations formerly separated mainly by church government rather than by theology: Presbyterian and

Congregational churches united in 1924 to form the United Church of Northern India. This church invited others to consider the possibility of a wider union, and discussions began in 1929. A first edition of a plan of church union in North India and Pakistan appeared in 1951.[44] From 1954 these discussions included representatives of the Baptist churches of North India, Bengal, and Orissa (Odisha) planted by the [British] Baptist Missionary Society. In contrast to the South India scheme, the North India proposals adopted the principle that the unification of ministries must follow, rather than precede, the formation of a united church. The first act of the new church would be an act of unification of ministries in which the bishops and representative presbyters would lay hands on each other, praying for the bestowal of whatever grace each might need for their new commission. Surprisingly, in the fourth and final edition of the plan Baptists accepted an Anglican request that the original statement that this rite was "not ordination or re-ordination" should be deleted. Both infant and believer's baptism would be practiced. The main difficulty lay with the potential case of a member of the Christian community who had been baptized as an infant who might subsequently request baptism as an adult believer. Baptists wished to allow for such an exceptional case on grounds of liberty of conscience; Anglicans were adamant that no such act of "re-baptism" could be permitted. In the end the question was left open for the new church to resolve.[45]

The Church of North India (CNI) was constituted at Nagpur on November 29, 1970. It was the first church union to bring those practicing both modes of baptism together in one church. However, a substantial proportion of the Baptist community in Bengal and northwest India stayed out of the united church. The Church of Pakistan was formed at the same time, comprising Anglicans, Methodists, Lutherans, and Presbyterians affiliated to the Church of Scotland mission. However, Protestant unity was again incomplete: the American-originated United Presbyterian Church declined to join. The much smaller Church of Bangladesh (uniting the Anglican Church and churches planted by the Presbyterian Church of England) followed in 1971.[46] A Joint Council of the CNI, CSI, and Mar Thoma Church was formed in 1978 as the "visible organ" of their common witness; it was renamed in 2002 as the Communion of Churches in India.[47]

III. Christian Unity and Disunity in Republican and Communist China

In China, even more clearly than in India, the quest for a visible expression of Christian unity began several years before the ripples emanating from the 1910 conference lapped the shores of Asia. A meeting of the Peking Missionary Association in November 1902 appointed a committee to consider progress toward church union in China, initially on a federal basis. It sent letters to all Protestant missionaries in China inviting their opinion on the desirability of federation: at least 90 percent responded in the affirmative. The Centenary Missionary Conference held in Shanghai in April–May 1907 to commemorate 100 years of Protestant work in China recommended the formation of a federal union under the title "the Christian Federation of China."[48] Such moves were missionary rather than indigenous initiatives, but Chinese Christians were taking their own steps toward unity, inspired by more overtly patriotic ideals. In 1902 Yu Guozhen, a Shanghai pastor, formed a Chinese Christian Union that aimed to "connect Chinese Christians to be a union, to promote self-propagation in China, with the heart of loving the country and its people." In 1906 Yu formed a federation of independent congregations in Shanghai bearing the title "The Chinese Jesus Independent Church." By 1909, the aggregate membership was more than 10,000 and a General Assembly was formed in 1910.[49] In February that year a young Beijing assistant pastor, Cheng Jingyi (1881–1939), was invited to contribute an article to the missionary journal *The Chinese Recorder* on "What federation can accomplish for the Chinese Church." Cheng, who from 1906 to 1908 had studied in Glasgow at the interdenominational Bible Training Institute, wrote about the creation of a "union Chinese church where denominationalism will be out of the question."[50] When in June he electrified the Edinburgh conference with his striking assertion that "speaking plainly we hope to see, in the near future, a united Christian Church without any denominational distinctions," he was not speaking from impulse but expressing a view widely held among Chinese Protestants.[51]

In the heady atmosphere created by the 1911 Republican Revolution, the vision of creating one national Protestant Church within a broadly Christian republic did not seem far-fetched. At a national Christian conference held in Shanghai in 1913 under the presidency of John R. Mott (who had chaired the Edinburgh conference), a resolution was passed recommending that all Protestant churches should adopt a common title of "Zhonghua Jidu Jiaohui" (The Chinese Christian Church or the Church of Christ in China); the conference also established a China branch of the Edinburgh Continuation Committee, of which Cheng Jingyi became joint secretary. In May 1922 the China Continuation Committee convened a National Christian Conference in Shanghai. Unlike previous conferences, Chinese formed a slight majority of the delegates (564 out of 1,050)—it was the first assembly that could plausibly claim to be representative of the Chinese Protestant community. The conference report, in a section drafted by a commission chaired by Cheng Jingyi, deplored the importation to China of Western denominational divisions and expressed the longing of Chinese Christians for "a speedy realization of corporate unity" that would fulfill the prayer of Christ for his disciples.[52] The conference established the National Christian Council of China to forward the cause of Protestant unity; in 1924 Cheng became its first full-time secretary. In 1927 the vision outlined in his Edinburgh speech was partially realized through the formation of the Church of Christ in China, a federation of sixteen denominational groups, mostly Presbyterian, Congregational, and Baptist; Cheng was appointed as its first moderator, and from 1934 served as its general secretary until his death in 1939. The Church adopted a simple Doctrinal Bond of Union affirming the Lordship of Christ, the supreme authority of the Scriptures, and the Apostles' Creed as "expressing the fundamental doctrines of our common evangelical faith." It declined to adopt a full creed on the grounds that any creed constructed at that time "would bear unduly the stamp of the churches of the West."[53]

The quest for a united Protestant church in China made appeal to central theological convictions. But it had also been initiated in the closing years of the Qing dynasty when educated Chinese were beginning to think of themselves not just as subjects of a dynastic empire but as citizens of a proud nation that demanded their loyalty.[54] From 1911 until 1919 the respective demands of Christian discipleship and patriotism seemed to be reasonably convergent, but after that date China was plunged into a whirlpool of ideological turbulence and political chaos. The Chinese churches found themselves on the receiving end of a new and aggressive brand of nationalism, frequently linked to a Marxist–Leninist dogma that derided Christianity as unscientific and premodern, and Western missions as imperialistic. Christian schools and colleges were denounced as instruments of indoctrination owing to their compulsory Christian religious instruction. 1927, the year of formation of the Church of Christ in China, was also the year in which the anti-Christian movement reached its climax. Some missionaries were killed, and most of those who worked in inland China were withdrawn; some 2,000 returned home, while others fled to European enclaves on the coast. It was the beginning of the end of the missionary era in China.[55]

In this unstable climate, Christian unity seemed more desirable yet more elusive than ever. The most politically committed Protestants, especially those prominent in the YMCA movement, such as Wu Yaozong (Y. T. Wu; 1893–1979), gravitated toward the left wing of the Nationalist

Guomindang or even to the Chinese Communist Party (CCP), formed in 1921. Conservatives narrowed their focus on evangelism, while fears of rampant theological modernism placed all ecumenical ventures in question. The Bible Union of China was formed in 1920 with the aim of extirpating liberalism from the China mission force and the Christian colleges; by 1923 it had the allegiance of some 30 percent of all Protestant missionaries.[56] In 1926 the largest mission in China, the interdenominational China Inland Mission (CIM), withdrew from the National Christian Council. The Church of Christ in China was denounced as "a theological jellyfish," lacking doctrinal backbone, and in 1929 an alternative and fundamentalist League of Christian Churches was formed. By 1932 it had more than half as many communicant members as the Church of Christ in China.[57] Moreover, by the 1940s up to a quarter of all Chinese Protestants belonged to networks of independent churches such as the Jesus Family, the True Jesus Church, or the Little Flock that had no relationship to foreign missions or ecumenical structures.[58] Following the Japanese invasion of 1937, the country split into three sectors: Japanese-controlled north China; "Free China" in the west remained in the hands of Chiang Kai-shek's Guomindang government, while the CCP steadily expanded their grip on the countryside from an original base in northern Shaanxi. By 1945 it was clear that the post-1911 dream that a united Protestant Church might provide the ideological foundation of a new China had evaporated. China was turning to a new savior from chaos and disintegration.

The communist regime that came to power in 1949 had as its priority the creation of a New People's China free of external control by capitalist forces. The churches would be tolerated provided they did not infringe the absolute priority of patriotism. Initially it appeared that this could be achieved principally by the severing of ties with Western missions. For the missions the period from 1949 to 1951 was a harrowing one involving much self-examination—had they brought this catastrophe upon themselves?[59]—and considerable disagreement over whether the interests of the Chinese churches required missionaries to be withdrawn immediately or encouraged to stay as long as possible. In the CIM, which worked exclusively in China, and where authority had traditionally flowed downward from the man at the top, these tensions were so severe that the General Director, Bishop Frank Houghton, was forced to resign in December 1951.[60] By that date most Protestant missionaries had departed from mainland China—they jumped before they were pushed.

For Chinese Christians the choices were even harder. Following the outbreak of the Korean War in June 1950, in which American and other

United Nations troops supported the South and Chinese armies the North, the CCP hardened its resolve to purge religious bodies of all imperialist influence. In October 1950 the National Christian Council endorsed the Christian Manifesto, a document drawn up following a series of meetings between Protestant leaders and CCP officials led by Zhou Enlai. It committed the churches to move immediately to full implementation of the long-standing but unrealized missionary goal of the "Three-Selves"—self-government, self-support, and self-propagation (the Church of Christ in China, for example, had been self-governing and self-propagating, but far from self-supporting).[61] More controversially, it also required them to support the government in its program to oppose "imperialism, feudalism, and bureaucratic capitalism." Considerable pressure was applied on ministers and laity to sign the Manifesto. A final total of 417,389 signatures were claimed, over half the total membership of the Protestant churches. Those who signed believed that they were defending the church against the charge that Christianity was an imperialist and anti-patriotic force.[62] Those who refused stood alongside the pioneers of the Confessing Church in Germany in the 1930s in believing that no government has the right to demand the ultimate allegiance that Christians owe to Christ alone. Many of them became objects of denunciation campaigns in 1951-2 and some were imprisoned, including Ni Tosheng (Watchman Nee; 1903–72), leader of the Little Flock movement, and Wang Mingdao (1900–91), a highly influential preacher and pastor of the Beijing Christian Tabernacle.

The contrasting responses of signatories and nonsignatories heralded the fissure that opened up between the Three-Self Patriotic Movement (TSPM), formally organized in April 1951 by Wu Yaozong and others who supported the regime, and Christians who sought to maintain church life independently of all state control.[63] The fissure corresponded broadly, but not entirely, with the earlier division between church leaders who had identified with the National Christian Council and those had either withdrawn from it or had never been members. However, supporters of the TSPM included some theological conservatives such as Cheng Chonggui (Marcus Chen), president of Chongqing Theological Seminary and a close associate of Bishop Houghton of the CIM.[64] The TSPM represented ecumenism by government diktat: the state hoped to achieve by close regulation what decades of intra-Protestant discussions had failed to do—the creation of one non-denominational Chinese church. In fact this contravention of one of the three selves—self-government—proved unable to eliminate dissenting congregations that were in reality, rather than name, "three-self" churches and would by the end of the century eclipse the TSPM church in size.[65]

So far this chapter has made no mention of the Catholic tradition. The Catholic community in China was two centuries older than any Protestant community and in 1949 was more than three times as large, with 3 million communicants. Until the communist era the Catholic Church in China was, of course, a single institution, united by its apostolic ties to its head in Rome. It was precisely that overt dependence on a foreign authority, who was himself sovereign of a distant state, which made the Catholic Church more threatening than the Protestant churches to the communist regime. European politics between the wars inclined the papacy to a fiercely anticommunist stance. In his encyclical *Divini Redemptoris* (1937), Pius XI had condemned communism as "intrinsically hostile to religion in any form whatever." His successor, Pius XII, appeared no less opposed to communism. In 1949 he issued a general excommunication of all militant communists. Furthermore, Catholic missions were even more dependent than Protestant ones on foreign manpower. Although Pius XI had consecrated the first six indigenous bishops in 1926, French and American missionaries still dominated the priesthood.

From November 1950 Catholic equivalents to the Christian Manifesto were circulated in various Chinese cities, calling on patriotic Catholics to sever their ties with the Vatican, but understandably these attracted relatively few signatures. It was clear that the creation of a Three-Self patriotic movement would be far more difficult among Catholics than among Protestants. The CCP focused its most determined efforts to divide the Catholic community on the city of Shanghai, whose 110,000 Catholics represented nearly 2 percent of the city's population. Shanghai was a center of Marian devotion, and in May 1947 a crowd of 60,000 had attended a mass at the Marian shrine at Sheshan in the suburbs, at which the Virgin was crowned "Queen of China."[66] Many young Catholics in the city were devoted members of the Legion of Mary, a lay sodality established in Ireland in 1921, and introduced to China by Irish Columban missionaries in 1937. The promulgation of a set of Regulations for the Suppression of Counterrevolutionaries on February 20, 1951 led to mass arrests of Catholics in Beijing, Tianjin and Shanghai. In Shanghai alone at least 1,000 executions were reported. The *Liberation Daily* began attacking the Legion of Mary as "truly an earthly army, hiding under the cloak of religion, which swears loyalty to serve the reactionary cause of the imperialists."[67] In November 1951 a Chinese Jesuit priest with a Sorbonne doctorate, Beda Chang, died in police custody in Shanghai and was immediately hailed as a martyr. Some 2,500 students attended his funeral, and the requiem masses said for him were so crowded that the authorities forbade any more. The faithful began to expect miracles from the martyr, and the bishop of Shanghai, Ignatius Gong Pinmei (1901–2000), was warned by the police that he would be held personally responsible for any miracles performed by the deceased![68]

Unlike the Protestants, most Catholic priests, determined to maintain eucharistic ministry to their flocks, remained in China until expelled. By February 1953 all but 100 of the 2,500 foreign priests resident in China in 1949 had been expelled; seventy-five of the hundred were in Shanghai.[69] As Chinese were hurriedly ordained to the priesthood, it paradoxically became more difficult for the authorities to brand the church as a foreign institution. The primary obstacle in the way of creating a patriotic Catholic church was the incompatibility between the concept of a self-governing national church and Catholic teaching. In December 1954 Pius XII published an encyclical, *Ad Sinarum Gentem*, that left Chinese Catholics in no doubt of his opposition to Three-Self principles: "they seek . . . to establish finally among you a 'national' church, which could no longer be Catholic because it would be the negation of that universality or rather 'catholicity' by which the society truly founded by Jesus Christ is above all nations and embraces them one and all."[70] Nevertheless, from 1954 the unity of the church began to splinter under the intense governmental pressure. The head of the Jesuit mission, Fernand Lacrelle, had cracked under interrogation and signed a confession attacking Bishop Gong as an imperialist, and implicating others. This was taped and played endlessly to others in prison. On September 8, 1955 Bishop Gong was arrested along with a number of priests and some 300 lay Catholics. At last resistance began to crumble, though it was the summer of 1957 before the Chinese Catholic Patriotic Association (CCPA) was formed under the leadership of twelve bishops and seventy priests; in Shanghai, where resistance had been fiercest, the CCPA was not organized and a compliant bishop installed until April 1960. Pius XII condemned the consecration of CCPA bishops as "criminal and sacrilegious" and many laity stayed away from masses celebrated by CCPA priests in protest: abstention from mass paradoxically became an index of Catholic fidelity.[71] Bishop Gong was sentenced to life imprisonment in March 1960 and remained behind bars until 1985. The day after he was sentenced, the American Maryknoll Father, James Walsh, the last remaining foreign missionary in China, was tried and convicted of espionage.

During the Cultural Revolution all public worship ceased. As religious life slowly reemerged from the late 1970s, it was clear that for both Catholic and Protestant communities the fundamental division between registered and unregistered churches would remain. This was despite the fact that the government now encouraged as many religious believers as possible to affiliate to officially sanctioned institutions in order to minimize underground religious activity. The former Anglican bishop, K. H. Ting (Ding Guangxun; 1915–2012), who had succeeded his mentor, Wu Yaozong, in 1979 as head of the TSPM, presided in 1980 over the formation of a new parallel body to the TSPM, the China Christian Council (CCC). While the TSPM would continue to represent the Protestant church to government, the CCC was to attend to the pastoral needs of Christians; its professed aim was "to unite all Protestant Christians" in furthering the cause of a self-governing, self-supporting and self-propagating church. Ting encouraged house meetings and was even successful in persuading some evangelical leaders to join the TSPM.[72] In reality, however, the distinction between the TSPM and the CCC appeared academic when Ting remained head of both until his retirement in 1996. In a parallel development, the head of the "Patriotic" Catholic Church, Louis Jin Luxian, who was released from prison in 1979, sought to maintain the fiction of unity by claiming that there was only one Catholic Church in China, supervised by the CCPA, but with its own Catholic Bishops' Conference, also formed in 1980.[73] If anything, the gulf between the official and underground churches widened after the Cultural Revolution. In the Protestant case, this was owing to the enormous expansion, especially in rural areas, of forms of charismatic, often apocalyptic Christianity more closely attuned to the traditions of Chinese folk religion than to the more formal Western liturgical style of the TSPM churches.[74] In the Catholic case, the impact of the Second Vatican Council was partly responsible. In an irony that was presumably lost on the state bureaucracy, it was the CCPA Church, disconnected from the Vatican, which continued for a time to use the Tridentine Latin mass, whereas the underground church, supposedly representing the "imperial" interests of the Vatican, began to adopt Chinese liturgy in accordance with the Vatican II reforms.[75] In both cases, the communist state had strangely ended up endorsing the more foreign of the two faces of Protestant and Catholic Christianity in China.

Nevertheless, by the 1990s there were some signs of rapprochement in both Catholic and Protestant churches, a process that has become more marked since the turn of the century. As it became evident that substantial numbers of the Catholic faithful were in CCPA churches, the Vatican softened its stance. To the dismay of ultra-loyalists in the underground church, John Paul II showed himself ready to reach agreement with the CCPA on the election of new bishops, a trend that Benedict XVI continued.[76]

Bishop Ting cultivated the friendship of some Western evangelicals such as Richard Mouw, president of Fuller Theological Seminary, though this may have been a ploy to influence intransigent evangelicals in China.[77] More significant was the fact that in the cities Chinese Christians could often be found attending both TSPM and unregistered churches, following a pattern of religious eclecticism that had also become common in the Western world. By the year 2000 China was still some way from having a united Catholic Church, and further still from having a united Protestant one. Nevertheless, the simple polarities of earlier decades were blurring.

IV. The Failure and Success of the Ecumenical Movement

The English Methodist historian John Kent once acerbically described the ecumenical movement as "the great ecclesiastical failure of our time."[78] If the yardstick is the number of separate Christian denominations in 2000 as compared with the number that existed a century earlier, he was almost certainly correct: in institutional terms the global Church was far more disunited in 2000 than in 1900, and included a host of new evangelical or Pentecostal denominations and networks that did not exist in 1900. Although some major church unions had been formed in the course of the century, such unions paradoxically added to, rather than reduced, the sum total of denominations in a particular country. In the United States especially, the controversies between modernists and fundamentalists between the world wars split some historic denominations—notably the Presbyterians and Baptists—and it was not uncommon for the conservative secessions to suffer subsequent divisions of their own.

The twentieth century has decisively given the lie to the fond supposition that denominationalism is a peculiarly Western religious disease. In Korea, for example, a single Presbyterian Church of Korea was established in 1907, served by four different missions (Northern Presbyterian, Southern Presbyterian, Canadian Presbyterian, and Australian Presbyterian); yet in the 1950s a process of continuous division started, which by the year 2011 had resulted in no less than 215 separate Presbyterian denominations in South Korea.[79] In India, despite the formation of the two united churches, the rapid multiplication of Pentecostal churches since the late 1940s has made the face of Indian Protestantism more, rather than less, diverse than it was in 1900. In Africa, the proliferation of African instituted and Pentecostal churches has again rendered the Christian landscape infinitely more diverse than it was in 1900. Parts of the globe in which historic churches once wielded a virtual monopoly, such as the Catholic Church in Latin America or the Orthodox Church in eastern Europe in the latter, were by the end of the century hotly contested territory between the historic church and more recent Pentecostal and evangelical arrivals. By the 1990s the issue of homosexuality and its acceptability within the ordained ministry had emerged as a new source of Christian disunity, threatening splits within confessional families, notably the Anglican Communion, which within a few years would lead to the creation of new conservative denominations such as the Anglican Church in North America (formed in 2008).

To this extent, the ecumenical movement looks like a signal failure. And yet it is also the case that in 2000 "denominationalism" was much weaker, at least in the Western world, than it had been 100 years previously. Among younger people especially, denominational loyalties were often tenuous, eroded by their experience of non-denominational evangelical Christianity in universities or simply by the accelerated geographical mobility of modern urban society. The same anti-institutional cultural influences in Western societies that punctured enthusiasm for structural church unions after about 1980 also made younger generations of Christians much more open than their forebears to united fellowship, worship, and mission with those of different denominational backgrounds. Even the historic three-way division between Orthodox, Catholic, and Protestant began to look less watertight as new spiritual currents unleashed by Vatican II and charismatic renewal flowed across the historic confessional boundaries. Ironically, by the close of the century, passionate long-term commitment to the propagation of a particular denomination or network of churches was more often to be found in the non-Western world than in Europe or North America. For good or ill, denominationalism was not dead, but in its non-Western contexts it was being reshaped into a more active, forward-looking, and missionary-minded mentality.

CHAPTER SEVEN

The Voice of Your Brother's Blood[*]

CHRISTIANITY, ETHNIC HATRED, AND
GENOCIDE IN NAZI GERMANY AND RWANDA

I. Theories of Race and Vocabularies
of Ethnic Hostility

What was arguably novel about the twentieth-century phase in the long history of the brutality that human beings have periodically shown to each other was the ideological prominence that was repeatedly given to the spurious idea of "race" as a legitimating basis for systematic violence. The approximately 6 million Jews who were slaughtered in the Holocaust or Shoah, and the 800,000 to 1 million Tutsi and Hutu who were killed in Rwanda in 1994, died because they belonged to an ethnic category whose very existence was deemed to threaten the health and even survival of the nation to which they belonged. It should be said at once that those who pursued extermination on such a scale also included among their victims those whose threatening "otherness" was not racial in character, such as homosexuals or the disabled in Nazi Germany, or those Hutu in Rwanda who were seen by their fellow Hutu as dangerous compromisers with Tutsi designs. Neither was ethnicity a dominating factor in every genocide of the century—it was not, for example, the *primary* motivation of either Stalin's notorious purges of actual or suspected political opponents during the 1930s or the murderous campaigns waged by the Khmer Rouge against all opponents of their communist regime in Cambodia between 1975 and 1979. It must also be emphasized that religious antagonism was

---

[*] "The voice of your brother's blood is crying to me from the ground." (Genesis 4:10).

inextricably entangled with ethnic hatred in some of the genocidal acts of the twentieth century, such as the massacre and forced starvation of possibly 1 million or more Armenian Christians by the Ottoman Turks in 1915–16, or the Bosnian crisis of the early 1990s, in which Serbian Orthodox Christians targeted Bosnian Muslims. The Armenian massacres are generally ranked as the first genocide of the century; they were also the first of several occasions in the century on which the inability or unwillingness of governments in the supposedly Christian West to take action against the perpetrators of genocide in inconvenient parts of the globe came under the spotlight. American missionaries who had been driven out of Turkey urged the administration of Woodrow Wilson to intervene on behalf of the Armenian Christians, and the American ambassador to the Ottoman Empire, Henry Morgenthau, did his best, but the American government was unwilling to jeopardize its then neutral status in the First World War. Britain, on the other hand, was at war with Turkey; although the British press did much to publicize the Armenian atrocities, the foreign secretary, Edward Grey, expressed caution about some of the reports; in wartime conditions, action in a humanitarian cause took second place behind strategic priorities.[1] Racial hatred does not in itself provide a total explanation of what took place in Turkey in 1915–16, or in Germany under the Nazis, or in Rwanda in 1994. To suggest that it does so would itself give to the category of race a legitimacy that it does not deserve. But the fact remains that ideas of racial difference played a more prominent part in the history of collective human violence than in previous centuries. It is also undeniable that the churches in many cases proved receptive to such ideas to an extent that poses uncomfortable questions for Christian theology.

The unprecedented dimensions that acts of ethnic violence acquired in the modern world made necessary the formulation of a new vocabulary of ethnic hostility. Hatred of the Jews as "Christ-killers" had been endemic in European history for centuries, but the attempt to define the "Jewish race" in terms of a specific biological identity was a creation of late nineteenth-century pseudo-science that became an almost unquestioned axiom in the early twentieth century. The term "anti-Semitism" (now more often spelled as antisemitism), denoting an antagonism to Jews that was specifically racial and not merely religious in nature, entered popular currency from the late nineteenth century. It was probably first employed in Berlin in September 1879, when the German journalist Wilhelm Marr and others formed the Anti-Semitic League.[2] The term "racialism," meaning belief in the innate superiority of a particular racial group, first appeared in the English language in 1907, according to *The Oxford English Dictionary*.[3]

The ideological category of "racialism" would eventually be supplanted by the harder-edged term "racism," which emerged three decades later when the validity of racial classifications of humanity first came under serious question in response to the explicit policies of racial engineering adopted by the Nazi regime. The word "racism" was coined in about 1933–34 by the sexologist Magnus Hirschfeld, a German Jewish exile from that regime, in a work entitled *Rassismus* (Racism), that sought to uncover the racial theory of eugenics underpinning the "race war" on which the Nazis had embarked. The term thus originally possessed a narrow scientific meaning that it has since lost. Hirschfeld's work was published posthumously in London in English translation in 1938.[4] Later still, in the wake of the Nazi Holocaust, the hybrid term "genocide"—meaning the systematic killing of peoples—made its first appearance. The neologism was invented by Raphael Lemkin, a Polish Jew and lawyer, in a massive legal tome published in 1944, *Axis Rule in Occupied Europe*.[5] Lemkin had been deeply affected as a young man by hearing of the Armenian atrocities, and as early as 1933, had tried without success to secure the agreement of the League of Nations to outlaw crimes against large collectivities of people and their cultures—what he then termed respectively crimes of "barbarity" and of "vandalism." When the Germans occupied Poland in September 1939, Lemkin fled the country and eventually made his home in the United States. He was appointed as legal advisor to the United States Chief Prosecutor at the Nuremberg Tribunal in 1945, and was largely responsible for the drafting of the 1948 Convention on the Prevention and Punishment of the Crime of Genocide and its subsequent ratification by the United Nations in 1951.[6]

Attempts to describe the variety of humankind as made up of separate races on the basis of physical type were, of course, nothing new, going back at least as far as the eighteenth century. The deepening European commercial and imperial penetration of the tropical world from the sixteenth century, and supremely the transatlantic slave trade, played major roles in reinforcing stereotypes of different racial identities and convictions of the supposed superiority of the white race. Increased European exposure to human diversity in imperial contexts encouraged the construction of philosophical edifices designed to provide an intellectual safe house for European treatment of other peoples. Although the majority of thinkers in the age of Enlightenment stressed the common biological origins and hence the fundamental unity of humankind, other strands of the Enlightenment, represented in France by Voltaire or in Scotland by David Hume and Lord Kames, gave more or less consistent endorsement to polygenist theories of human origins that proved fertile soil for the growth of racial ideology.[7] However, it was only in the course of the nineteenth century that the concept of race became a category of supposedly *scientific* classification and knowledge, progressively fortified in its intellectual respectability by the new professional status that science gradually acquired during the century. The idea of race also underwent substantial reconstruction as the previous notion of a single European or "Caucasian" race was modified by the impact of new and often fragile European nationalisms.[8] As a result, the categories of "race" and "nation" were now frequently blurred. Those who had been stigmatized as racially "other" now found themselves increasingly branded as threats to the unity and identity of the nation. In German Protestant thought especially, shaped as it was by the continuing legacy of Johann Gottfried von Herder's Romantic view of peoples as each possessing their own distinctive corporate personality or animating spirit (*Volksgeist*), nationalist sentiment and racial theory often fused to form an explosive mixture.

The systematic violence inflicted on Jews in Nazi Germany or on Tutsis in Rwanda in 1994 was not the result of instinctive mob passion alone—though that was certainly not absent from either case. Rather it was the outworking in a particular political context of a set of myths of racial differentiation. Intellectuals invested these myths with the status of "moral" principles, and in nations shaped by the Christian tradition it was not surprising that they were quite frequently buttressed with arguments of an explicitly theological character. To some extent at least, it can be claimed that both sets of racial violence drew on a common reservoir of ideological resources: the influence of late nineteenth-century racial theory can be traced in the ethnic politics of twentieth-century Rwanda as well as, more obviously, in the course of German history after 1918. Neither the gift of intelligence nor the possession of advanced educational qualifications proved an effective inoculation against infection by racial hatred directed against Jews in Germany or Tutsi in Rwanda: some of the key architects of the Rwandan genocide had received a sophisticated Western higher education at the Sorbonne in Paris. Nor, it must be said, did the profession of Christian belief or even the acquisition of an ostensibly high level of theological scholarship provide an effective firewall against the virus of ethnic hostility. For Christians, what is doubly disturbing about the unprecedented scale and rate of ethnic killing in these two cases is the seeming impotence of their faith to resist the destructive power of racial hatred. The two holocausts—in Nazi Germany and in Rwanda—that formed the dreadful culmination to the case studies selected in this chapter both tell a depressing story of widespread, though never total, capitulation by churches and Christian leaders to the insidious attractions of racial ideology, and of the habitual silence or inaction of many Christians in the face of observed atrocities. These failures were apparent both at a popular and at an intellectual level. Both Germany in the 1930s-1940s and Rwanda in the 1990s had extremely high levels of formal Christian affiliation, even if, in most German cities, rates of regular church attendance were far lower.

In Rwanda, some 90 percent of the population were baptized members of either the Roman Catholic Church or a number of smaller Protestant churches. More than 90 percent of Rwanda's Catholics attended mass at Easter in 1955, and by the early 1990s Catholics accounted for 63 percent of the population.[9] One recent historian of the response of the Rwandan Anglican Church to genocide has suggested that the question of why it was possible for such slaughter to take place in a Christian country is not the most useful question to ask, and that we should think instead of Christianity as a reservoir of ideas and symbols which can be used to support a wide variety of actions.[10] That is not a conclusion that most Christians can easily accept, for it suggests that any idea that Christianity offers a distinctive moral dynamic to society as a whole is unfounded. What may be more illuminating for Christians is to ask how it was that the churches in the twentieth century so often came to baptize racial ideologies with the holy water of theological approval.

It is easy to assume that the weight of Christian teaching will always fall on the unity of humanity and therefore in opposition to any emphasis on the distinctiveness of each of its supposed component races. In fact this was not so during the late nineteenth and early twentieth centuries. During the Victorian period, racial patterns of thought became increasingly common, if divergent in the direction to which they were put, and Christian theology reflected the trend. The dominant tradition of biblical criticism in nineteenth-century Europe, as represented by the Tübingen school, had disseminated the notion that the religion proclaimed by Jesus was a uniquely spiritual and ethical creed starkly opposed to the degenerate "oriental" legalism of Palestinian Judaism. The French orientalist and former Catholic seminarian Ernest Renan, whose radical *Life of Jesus* was published in 1863, similarly depicted Jesus as a Galilean whose religion of love enabled him to overcome his Jewishness and oppose "that obstinate Judaism, which, founded by the Pharisees, and fixed by the Talmud, has traversed the Middle Ages, and come down to us."[11] European biblical scholars, like other intellectuals, were commonly reared on an educational diet of the Greek and Roman classics, and hence were inclined to minimize the Jewish, and maximize the Greek elements of the New Testament. German high culture in particular was fascinated by the legacy of ancient Greece, though parallel trends can be observed in Britain. The Cambridge classical historian T. R. Glover, a devout if liberal Baptist, made his academic reputation in 1909 with a book, *The Conflict of Religions in the Early Roman Empire*, which argued that Jesus had set religion free from the primitive tribalism of ritual and taboo that characterized not simply the pagan cults but even Judaism itself. Glover made Jesus into a classical hero of the human spirit whose teaching had "nothing local or racial about it," but such language itself carried antisemitic overtones.[12]

Racial discourse was endemic in early twentieth-century Christian Europe, but it was not necessarily illiberal. At both the Pan-Anglican Congress held in London in 1908 and the World Missionary Conference held in Edinburgh in 1910 leading churchmen endorsed the notion that mankind was made up of various races, each of which had its own distinct characteristics and ideals. The most progressive theorists who spoke at these assemblies, such as A. G. Fraser, Anglican missionary principal of Trinity College, Kandy, Ceylon, at the 1908 congress—or Charles Gore, Anglo-Catholic bishop of Birmingham, at the 1910 conference—urged that Christian missions should study and respect these racial characteristics, reflecting them in their patterns of church worship and governance, and even, within limits, in their theological formulations. Just as Christianity had become "Greek to the Greeks, and Teutonic to the Teutons," so, Fraser urged, it should become "Indian to the Indians."[13] Such statements represented the first flowering of theological approval of what would now be termed cultural diversity: in an age when the anthropological notion of plural cultures was still in its infancy, "race" was the category that enabled Christianity to begin to come to terms with the legitimacy of substantial cultural diversity within the Church. But Christian endorsement of the notion of race was fraught with ambiguity from the outset. In the year following the Edinburgh conference, the First Universal Races Congress took place in the University of London. Alfred Caldecott, professor of moral philosophy at King's College London (an Anglican-founded institution), addressing the congress on "The Influence of Missions," referred with approval to the statements made at the 1908 and 1910 conferences on Christianity and race, and urged that "Religion"—and Christianity was evidently uppermost in his mind—must pay respect to the scientifically proven idea of "Race":

It must welcome the results of Anthropologists in ascertaining differential race-characters and race-capacities, and leave large freedom for the influence of these in the ethical and social systems for which Religion will contribute principles and provide sanctions. In short, the *Vocation* of Nations and of Races must be accepted.[14]

It was but a short step from affirming the different characteristics and providential vocation of various races to prescribing their different moral and intellectual capacities. The two case studies that follow provide ample evidence of the deleterious consequences that could follow from an insistence that Christianity must conform its teaching to the supposedly assured results of anthropological science on the subject of race.

II. Race and Religion in Nazi Germany

No chapter in the history of the twentieth century has attracted a greater volume of academic and indeed popular writing than Nazi Germany. Within that very extensive field of scholarship, the role played by Christianity and the churches remains one of the most sharply contested areas of debate. An older generation of historians tended to portray Nazism as a form of neo-paganism or pseudo-religion grounded in Teutonic and Nordic mythology, and hence as intrinsically hostile to Christian belief. Nazi ideology, they suggested, functioned as a secular substitute to fill the vacuum left by the collapse of liberal Christianity in the wake of the First World War.[15] Protestant accounts often highlighted and applauded as "heroic" the principled resistance to Hitler of Dietrich Bonhoeffer (1906–45) and some other leaders of the Confessing Church that was established by the famous Barmen Declaration of May 1934. This was drawn up by the great Swiss Reformed theologian Karl Barth (1886–1968), and promulgated in prophetic denunciation of the attempt of the Nazi state to dictate terms to the Evangelical Church.[16] Despite the heretical aberrations of the minority German Christian movement, the resulting narrative was one that reassuringly placed Christianity and Nazism in fundamental opposition to each other.

Historical reality, however, was considerably more ambiguous, as scholars were coming to realize. At first critical attention was confined mainly to the Roman Catholic Church. Historians of the papacy began to ask awkward questions about how much Pius XII knew about the "final solution" to the Jewish problem, and when. Why had the pope obstinately maintained silence throughout most of 1942 when the news of the systematic extermination of both Jews and Poles began to leak out to the world, and when at last he did say something in his Christmas broadcast on December 24, 1942, why did he refrain from mentioning either the Nazi regime or its Jewish and Polish victims by name?[17] And why, in October 1943, when the Nazis deported the Jewish population of Rome itself, many of them being dispatched to the gas chambers of Auschwitz and Birkenau, did "Hitler's pope" still refrain from public censure, limiting himself to private representations to the German ambassador to the Vatican?[18] Attempts have been made to defend the Vatican on the grounds that the Catholic Church must remain neutral in wartime, that quiet diplomacy was more likely to benefit the Jews than outright condemnation of Nazi policies, and that its networks of information were much less reliable than might be supposed.[19] While Pius was not devoid of compassion for the Jews, the evidence is unambiguous that both during the Second World War and during the Cold War that followed it (he lived until 1958), his chief concern was to combat the menace of atheistic Soviet communism. Pius XII for long clung to the hope that a strong Germany could be preserved as a bulwark against Soviet Russia. The flood of scholarly writing both for and against Pius has continued with no sign of abatement.[20]

Other recent research has uncovered the role played by the Roman Catholic Church in Germany itself in the origins of National Socialism. Derek Hastings, in *Catholicism and the Roots of Nazism: Religious Identity and National Socialism* (2010), has directed attention to the roots of the *Nationalsozialistische Deutsche Arbeiterpartei* (NSDAP) in the Catholic community in Munich in the years after 1918. The origins of the ideal of "Positive Christianity" espoused by the early NDSAP can be found in the constituency of Reform Catholicism that developed in Bavaria inspired by the ideas of Ignaz von Döllinger and in reaction to the prevalence of "ultramontanism" (extreme devotion to the pope "over the Alps") within the Catholic Church after the definition of papal infallibility at the First Vatican Council in 1870. By "Positive Christianity" Reform Catholics meant a distinctively Germanic style of being Catholic that contrasted with the "effeminate" and Italianiate religious culture of the ultramontanes; it implied a positive attitude toward modern German theological scholarship, an emphasis on true piety rather than "political Catholicism," and a willingness to explore common ground between Catholics and Protestants in uniting all Germans across lines of class and confessional division under the banner of a single German and Christian national identity. While it is true that after 1933 the Nazi movement became increasingly antagonistic to the Catholic Church, practicing Catholics and Catholic teaching contributed much more to the formative years of the movement than has hitherto been realized.[21]

Despite this initial historiographical concentration on the stance of the papacy, other strands of scholarship have increasingly uncovered the disturbing extent to which German Protestantism made its peace with Nazism. First, even the Confessing section of the German Evangelical Church was not to remain unscathed from the increasingly critical historical scrutiny of Christian reaction to the Nazi atrocities. In 1970 Wolfgang Gerlach completed a doctoral thesis at the University of Hamburg on the Confessing Church and the persecution of the Jews, but it was not published in German until 1987, and did not appear in English translation until 2000. Gerlach noted the prevalence of racial language in the Protestant press in the 1920s, and cited an Easter address to the pastors of Berlin-Brandenburg in 1928 by Otto Dibelius (1880–1967), later a prominent figure in the Confessing Church and the best-known German Protestant leader of the postwar era, in which Dibelius had applauded the motivation of the *völkisch* movement, proudly declared himself an anti-Semite, and pronounced it undeniable that "Judaism plays a leading role in all the corruptive phenomena of modern civilization."[22] Gerlach's book went on to make clear that Bonhoeffer was quite atypical of the Confessing Church leadership in the consistency of his support for the Jews. Even the splendid theological affirmations of the Barmen Declaration said nothing explicit about the notorious "Aryan paragraph" which extended to Christian ministers the ban on employment as civil servants of all those of Jewish ancestry: the Declaration alluded in general terms to "strange propositions" that threatened the theological integrity of the church, but did not address the Jewish question.[23] Despite the fact that it was precisely the introduction of the paragraph that had triggered the formation of Martin Niemöller's Pastors' Emergency League in October 1933, the Barmen synod was anxious to unite the entire Evangelical Church against the German Christian heresy and appeared willing to pay as the price for such unity the maintenance of silence on the crucial question of whether non-Aryan Christians had a legitimate place within the church.[24]

A second strand of scholarship has indicated the extent to which the widening experience of German Protestant overseas missions supplied the raw materials for constructing a theology of the *Volk*. German missionaries, influenced by Romantic ideas of how the character of every *Volk* was shaped by its distinctive ethnic ancestry (*Blut*) and immediate physical environment (*Boden*), were quicker than their Anglo-American counterparts to become disillusioned with approaches to evangelization that too obviously conformed to European cultural assumptions. Some mission theorists were not afraid to transfer these ideas to the domestic context.

Siegfried Knak, director of the Berlin Mission, welcomed the advent of the Third Reich as an endorsement of the *völkisch* principles learned by German missions overseas. A more notorious example was Jakob Wilhelm Hauer, a missionary with the Basel Mission in South India and subsequently professor of Indology and Comparative Religion at Tübingen, who took the notion of the missionary duty to respect distinctive national cultures to its logical extreme by positing the idea of a distinctive German national religion: his neo-pagan "German Faith" movement, formed in July 1933, was essentially anti-Christian and never attracted large support, but it was indicative of the way in which misconceived missionary anthropology could stoke the fires of racialism.[25]

A third body of historiography has presented accumulating evidence that antisemitic patterns of thought were deeply embedded in German religious and intellectual life long before the Nazis came to power. In 1985 Robert P. Ericksen's study of three leading German Christian academics— the New Testament scholar Gerhard Kittel, the theologian Paul Althaus, and the Kierkegaard scholar Emanuel Hirsch—showed that some of the country's most respected Protestant intellectuals became devoted supporters of Hitler. Kittel (1888–1948) was the founder, and editor of the first four volumes of the *Theologisches Wörterbuch zum Neuen Testament* (*TWNT*), published from 1933 to 1945. In its final ten-volume form the *TWNT* remains to this day the most authoritative dictionary on the New Testament. Kittel joined the NSDAP in May 1933, viewing the Nazi movement as "a *völkisch* renewal movement on a Christian, moral foundation." In a public lecture in his own university of Tübingen in June 1933 Kittel considered four possible solutions to the Jewish problem, and appeared to reject the option of extermination only on the grounds that it would be unworkable.[26] In October 1937, at the invitation of the New Testament scholar Edwyn Hoskyns, he famously delivered two lectures in the University of Cambridge, creating a stir by wearing his Nazi party membership badge.[27] Althaus, in a fashion typical of German Romanticism, saw in the Nazi creed a commendable affirmation of the divinely ordained institutions of family, *Volk*, and race. Hirsch similarly regarded Nazi values as a proper response to the fragmentation and individualism of modern society. Similarly disturbing conclusions have been reached about arguably the most influential figure in twentieth-century European philosophy, Martin Heidegger (1889–1976), who had an ambiguous relationship to the Catholic Church in which he had been reared. Heidegger welcomed the Nazi regime as one that would heal the German *Volk* and restore its rightful status as the heir to the glories of ancient Greece; he never retracted his support of Hitler throughout the Nazi years.[28] None of these figures can be categorized as either essentially evil or intellectually vacuous: they were highly intelligent men whose reactions to the social chaos apparently threatening modern European civilization led them to condone solutions that those in other contexts have no difficulty in recognizing as evil.[29]

Such reactions were not confined to intellectuals. Richard Steigmann-Gall's *The Holy Reich: Nazi Conceptions of Christianity, 1919–1945* (2003) argued that many within the Nazi movement saw themselves as Christians, and traced some of the principal tenets of Nazi ideology to sources within liberal German Protestantism. He drew attention to the extended celebrations of the 450th anniversary of Martin Luther's birth on November 10, 1933, only a few months after the Nazi seizure of power. Leading Nazis enthusiastically patronized the celebrations as an opportunity to extol the greatness of the German *Volk* and some did not hesitate to present Hitler as Luther's true heir. Steigmann-Gall drew the uncomfortable conclusion for Christians that it would not do to label the numerous Nazis who designated themselves as Christian as not "real Christians" and suggested that "Christianity . . . may be the source of some of the dangers it abhors."[30] His analysis reinforced the case that to uncover the roots of the virulent German antisemitism that came to the surface in the 1930s and 1940s, historical inquiry had to extend backwards over several decades into circles that had previously commanded the reverence of the academic community. He pointed out that the celebrated historian of early Christianity Adolf von Harnack (1851–1930), was a friend and admirer of the English apostle of Aryan race theory, Houston Stewart Chamberlain, who became a naturalized German citizen and whose influential ideas were taken up by Alfred Rosenberg and by Hitler in *Mein Kampf*. In his barely disguised hostility to the Old Testament, von Harnack followed the second-century Christian leader Marcion: in his liberal Protestant schema, the Old Testament represented "Jewish carnal law" and as such was ethically inferior to the New Testament message of the love of God.[31]

At the heart of the intellectual program of Christian antisemitism in Nazi Germany was a systematic endeavor to dissociate the figure of Jesus from Judaism. The ostensibly absurd idea that Jesus cannot have been a Jew was first articulated in the late 1870s by the German orientalist and biblical scholar Paul de Lagarde, and then given fuller exposition by Houston Chamberlain in 1899 in *The Foundations of the Nineteenth Century*, a book that sold 60,000 copies over the next decade.[32] Theories designed to prove that Jesus, as a native of "Galilee of the Gentiles," must in fact have been an Aryan, most probably the descendant of Assyrian colonization of

the region, did not seem as ludicrous in the first half of the twentieth century as they do now. In such an intellectual climate the claims of biblical
scholars in Nazi Germany that the apparent Jewishness of Christian doctrine derived, not from Jesus, an Aryan Galilean, but from a distortion of
his teaching by the Jew Paul, did not appear so eccentric, even to scholars
outside Germany.

A fourth body of historical scholarship has accentuated the disturbing implications for Christians of the story of the German churches under
Nazi rule. Three books within this category were especially significant.
First, Doris L. Bergen's *Twisted Cross: The German Christian Movement
in the Third Reich* (1996), although pointing out that the movement commanded the allegiance of less than 2 percent of the Protestant population
(about 600,000 people), emphasized how much the German Christians
had in common with other German Protestants, and identified many who
held senior leadership positions within the German Evangelical Church.[33]

A second publication in 1996, Daniel Jonah Goldhagen's *Hitler's Willing Executioners: Ordinary Germans and the Holocaust*, attracted a great
deal of controversy through its contention that the Holocaust could not be
understood merely as the work of a comparatively small group of crazed
ideologues but on the contrary involved the willing cooperation of multiple actors, ordinary Germans who staffed the concentration camps and
manned the police battalions charged with slaughtering Jews. Hence, according to Goldhagen, the Nazi genocide could be explained only as the
consequence of an endemic and quite irrational antisemitism that had permeated German society since the late nineteenth century and which was
rooted in a broader and older tradition of European hostility to Jewish people. This ingrained European antisemitism, Goldhagen maintained in one
of his looser passages, was "a corollary of Christianity" and could be traced
back all the way to the Gospel of John.[34] However, his account ultimately
placed more weight on the contradictory argument that in Germany the
power of a uniquely Germanic *völkisch* ideology so overwhelmed Christian
notions of the universality of humanity that as early as the last four decades of the nineteenth century the physical extermination of the Jews was
being regularly advocated by German antisemitic writers as the solution
to "the Jewish problem."[35] This poisonous climate of Christian hostility to
the Jews explains why even the leaders of the Christian resistance to Hitler
did not dissent from the fundamental premise that the Jewish "race" posed
a problem to the stability and unity of the German nation: a document
prepared on Bonhoeffer's initiative in early 1943 by the "Freiburg Circle"
of leading Protestant theologians and intellectuals included an appendix

entitled "Proposals for a solution to the Jewish problem in Germany" that envisaged a future for Germany in which it might be possible to concede full rights to Jews only because their numbers would have been so drastically reduced by the Nazis.[36]

A third noteworthy book, by an American Jewish scholar, Susannah Heschel, has revealed the extraordinary lengths to which biblical scholars in Nazi Germany went in order to de-Judaize not simply Jesus, but the Bible and Christianity itself. The main focus of Heschel's research was the Institute for the Study and Eradication of Jewish Influence on German Church Life, opened at Eisenach in Thuringia in May 1939.[37] The Institute published its radically de-Judaized version of the synoptic gospels, *The Message of God*, in 1940; all references to Jesus as the fulfillment of Jewish messianic expectations were removed from the biblical text, and excerpts from the gospels were rearranged in order to present him more as a conquering Teutonic hero than as a suffering victim. It was followed in 1941 by a hymnbook from which most references to the Old Testament, and Hebrew terms such as "Hallelujah" or "Amen," had been expunged. The Institute can be presented as a gross infringement of scholarly integrity that could have found a place only in Nazi Germany, and some of its supposed scholars were men of scant intellectual caliber.

Heschel's research, like that of Ericksen, raises questions about the vulnerability of supposedly objective "scientific" scholarship in the field of religion to prevailing political and ideological winds. The Institute's Academic Director until March 1943 was Professor Walter Grundmann of the University of Jena. Grundmann (1906–76) was a serious New Testament scholar who had been a research student of Kittel's and had assisted him in the preparation of the *TWNT*: he contributed twenty-two articles to the first four volumes which tended to highlight Greek and Roman backgrounds to biblical words rather than Jewish ones.[38] Grundmann's monograph, *Jesus der Galiläer und das Judentum* (1940) built on currently accepted New Testament scholarship by Walter Bauer, Wilhelm Bousset and Ernst Lohmeyer to argue that the eschatology of Jesus was of a distinctively Galilean variety focused on the supposedly Hellenistic idea of the Son of Man rather than on the Jewish concept of the messiah. Yet he also used the more obviously dubious theories of Emanuel Hirsch to present Jesus as being of Gentile parentage and as implacably opposed to the "tribal" and "degenerate" beliefs of Judaism. It is deeply ironic that biblical scholars in Nazi Germany, as elsewhere, should condemn first-century Judaism for racial exclusivity and xenophobia. It is also salutary to note that Grundmann remained active in biblical scholarship after the war and was allowed to remain as a founding member of the respected international Society for New Testament Studies until his death in 1974.[39]

Intellectuals such as Grundmann who attempted to reengineer the Bible and Christian doctrine to fit the contours of Nazi ideology were not in fact close to the levers of power or in any way the ideological drivers of the "final solution." To their intense frustration, the love affair of leading German Christians with Nazism was largely unrequited. To that extent, the traditional depiction of the Nazi regime as a neo-pagan entity at best cynically indifferent to Christianity and at worst openly hostile to it remains intact. Nevertheless, the extent of liberal Protestant ideological approximation to Nazi views of race and the *Volk* goes a long way to explain why the Protestant churches proved so unwilling to attempt open resistance to the hellish strategies that led to Auschwitz, Belsen, and Treblinka. In the case of the Roman Catholic Church, the evidence points not so much to the influence of antisemitism or racial theory on Catholic responses to the Holocaust—though that cannot be discounted—as to the morally paralyzing effect of the Vatican's fear of communism. Both racial theory and anticommunism would also play their part in the story of the Catholic Church's role in ethnic conflict in Rwanda.

III. The Church and Ethnic Conflict in Rwanda

The escalating violence inflicted by the Hutu majority on the Tutsi minority population of Rwanda made its first limited appearance in November 1959 and reached its horrific culmination in the full-scale genocide of April to July 1994. In the eyes of the world press the genocide was a sinister upsurge of the primeval "tribal" Africa. In point of fact, however, the categories of Hutu and Tutsi did not conform even to the somewhat artificial notions of what constituted a "tribe" that European observers of African societies had constructed during the colonial era. Hutu and Tutsi people spoke the same language of Kinyarwanda, shared the same cultural practices, lived side-by-side in the same villages under the authority of the same chiefs, and on occasion intermarried. Some differentiation was observable in terms of economic activity and social status. Most Hutu were poor peasant cultivators, while a much higher percentage of Tutsi owned the land and cattle that formed the main source of wealth in traditional African societies—the facts that the majority of Tutsi also were poor peasant farmers, and that Hutu who acquired sufficient cattle to become wealthy could become "Tutsified," rarely attracted comment. The Tutsi had for long monopolized the office of chief. Under colonial rule—German from 1897–98 and Belgian from 1916—they comprised the overwhelming majority of the elite that controlled the apparatus of the state. European observers also thought they could discern—and to a limited extent they were correct—a physiognomic difference between Hutu and Tutsi. Hutu were typified as being characteristically "Bantu" or Negroid in appearance, dark in complexion and stocky in stature; Tutsi were seen as lighter in complexion, tall and slender, exhibiting the distinguishing features of a natural aristocracy, and more akin to the pastoralists of Ethiopia. Colonial ethnography speculated that the Tutsis had migrated to Rwanda from Ethiopia or Egypt (some said even from Tibet) and had subjugated the aboriginal Hutu. Late Victorian anthropological theorists such as T. H. Huxley and the Irishman A. H. Keane who held to the idea of a superior "Caucasian" race had also posited the existence of a half-white "Melanochroid" branch of this race whose descendants could still be found in the highlands of East Africa.[40] The continuing popularity of such racial theories in the early twentieth century enabled European observers of Rwandan society to identify the Tutsi as distant cousins of Indo-Europeans—in effect as "black Aryans." They were not explicitly described as such, but rather as "Hamitic" people, whose supposed derivation from the sons of Ham, son of Noah, was, as in African American racial theory, a badge of nobility, not of servility, as in Afrikaner discourse in South Africa. They were viewed as the feudal lords of Rwanda, with the Hutu being type-cast as their natural serfs.[41]

The prevalent tendency of scholarship since Rwandan independence in 1962 has been to portray the so-called tribal division between Hutu and Tutsi as to a greater or lesser extent a colonialist fiction encouraged by Catholic racial theory that subsequently became a ghastly reality.[42] Some accounts have tried to pin responsibility for the events of 1994 on the colonial dissemination of the same German *Rassenkunde* (racial theory) that gave rise to the Nazi Holocaust, thus implying a picture of precolonial intercommunal harmony unspoilt by the ethnic divisions brought by European rule.[43] In fact German administrators were too few in number (there were only five in 1913)[44] to wield such an ideological influence; more numerous were the Catholic missionaries, most of whom were French. Although the precise original meaning of the labels of Hutu and Tutsi remains a mystery, it now seems clear that hard-edged ethnic politics in Rwanda began to emerge as early as the 1860s, during the reign of the Tutsi king Rwabugiri, when the originally flexible classifications of Hutu and Tutsi became rigidified.[45] But if the Germans did not invent the ethnic division between Hutu and Tutsi, the Belgians certainly widened it by

their consistent cultivation of the Tutsi elite as their principal collaborators in the system of indirect rule. As elsewhere in Africa, colonial regimes
did not "invent" tribal identities, but there is no doubt that their policies
of political subjugation, fiscal administration, and education hardened
boundaries that had previously been porous and indeterminate.

Throughout Africa, Christian missions played a crucial part in this
process of the construction of harder versions of ethnicity. Bible translation and the lexicographical tools on which it depended gave African vernacular languages the solidity of written grammatical form, and imparted
a consciousness of distinct nationhood to clusters of peoples, such as the
Yoruba, who had previously shared little more than their language.[46] In
Rwanda, however, with its single national language and absence of region-
ally defined ethnicities, the impact of missions was rather different. The
Society of Missionaries of Africa founded by Cardinal Lavigerie of Algiers
in 1868—popularly known as the White Fathers—sent their first mission
party to the royal court of Rwanda in 1900. The progress of conversion
was initially slow, at least in comparison with the neighboring kingdom of
Buganda, but from the 1920s, as it became clear that Belgian rule was here
to stay, the Catholic community grew exponentially: the number of cat-
echumens grew from 5,000 in 1922 to 20,000 in 1927 and 100,000 in 1931.
By 1939 there were 300,000 baptized Catholics; by 1950 there were almost
400,000. The bulk of the early converts were Tutsi, many of them chiefs and
other members of the ruling elites, and in 1943 the king, Mwami Mutara,
was baptized.[47] Protestant churches also saw growth, particularly after the
outbreak of revival phenomena at the Evangelical Anglican Ruanda Mission's station of Gahini in December 1933, giving birth to an increasingly
indigenous movement of spiritual renewal that eventually spread throughout East Africa. Its adherents were known in Rwanda as the *Abarokore*
("saved ones") and beyond it under the Luganda name of the *Balokole*.[48]

The White Fathers formed a natural alliance with the Catholic Tutsi
elites. Some missionaries undoubtedly accepted the racial mythology of
the Tutsi as being of superior Hamitic stock, and passed it on to their
Tutsi protégés, such as Fr. Alexis Kagame, a Tutsi of the royal line who
studied for his doctorate in Rome and published an influential history of
Rwanda that employed the Hamitic hypothesis to reinforce Tutsi claims
to pre-eminence.[49] For others, the decisive factor was not racial theory but
simply their instinctive preference for political leaders who looked likely
to deliver a Catholic vision of a Christian kingdom founded on a close
partnership between church and state.[50] During the 1950s, the delivery of
this vision became both more urgent and more problematic. In the context

of the Cold War, the gathering momentum of anticolonial forces first in Asia and then in Africa, and, after the Cuban revolution of 1959, the threat of Marxist revolution in Latin America, Catholic fears of spreading communist influence in Africa intensified. These fears appeared to be given substance in 1954–5 when demands grew, supported both by the Belgian government and by Tutsi politicians, for a secular system of education in place of the existing virtual monopoly of education wielded by the Catholic Church. At the same time, Hutu political consciousness was stirring as the Hutu flocked to the church schools to reduce the educational deficit between themselves and the Tutsi; the Hutu majority of the population was by now reflected in the church. A new generation of younger missionary priests arrived from Europe, influenced by the social democracy tradition inaugurated by Leo XIII's 1891 encyclical *Rerum Novarum*. Both theological conviction and anticommunist political prudence inclined them to side with the oppressed Hutu rather than with the Tutsi elites. The same impulses and strategic considerations that led in Latin America to the growth of liberation theology led a growing proportion of Catholic clergy in Rwanda to take the preferential option for the poor.

As Rwandans took their first steps toward political mobilization in a context of heightening ethnic tension, unanimity of stance on the part of the Rwandan church could no longer be guaranteed. The Swiss White Father, André Perraudin (1914–2003), from 1952 rector of the country's influential major seminary at Nyakibanda, vicar apostolic of Kabgayi from 1956, and archbishop of Kigali from 1959 to 1976, did not instinctively view Rwandan ecclesiastical politics in ethnic terms. He saw his priorities as being the protection of Christian civilization in Rwanda, the combating of forms of nationalism that seemed likely to lead to secular or even communist outcomes, and the maintenance of the unity of the church—a very similar agenda to that which shaped Pius XII's stance toward the Nazi regime in the 1940s. Yet from November 1959 the logic of those priorities increasingly propelled Perraudin to oppose the main political organ of Tutsi opinion, the *Union National Rwandaise* (UNAR), which had adopted a strongly anticlerical and secularist tone, and by default to align himself with Hutu political aspirations as represented by the Parmehutu political party. In contrast, the first Rwandan national to be elevated to the episcopate, Aloys Bigirumwami (1904–86), vicar apostolic and then bishop of Nyundo from 1952 to 1974, regarded Perraudin's increasing alignment with the cause of Hutu emancipation as a dangerous contribution to raising the temperature of ethnic tension. Bigirumwami was of mixed descent, but was officially categorized as Tutsi.

In November 1959 Hutu militias attacked Tutsi in a number of localities. Although the death toll was only in the hundreds, thousands of Tutsi fled into exile into Uganda and the Belgian Congo. The response of the Belgian military resident, Colonel Guy Logiest, a devout Catholic, was to set in motion what amounted to a Hutu revolution whereby Tutsi elites were removed from their monopoly of chiefly office and replaced by Hutu politicians. In the name of democracy and national security, the distribution of political power was abruptly reversed, and Archbishop Perraudin was perceived as being fully supportive of the reversal. The revolution reached its climax in January 1961 with the abolition of the monarchy and the installation of a Hutu Catholic journalist-turned politician, Grégoire Kayibanda, as president. When Belgium granted Rwanda its independence on July 1, 1962, a Parmehutu government was formed in close alliance with the Catholic Church. Perraudin's warnings of the danger of "communism" represented by the UNAR grew more insistent, yet he remained largely silent about the more insidious threat of an ethnic politics as represented by Parmehutu. Bishop Bigirumwami, on the other hand, grew increasingly alarmed at the church's close identification with the Parmehutu government, but kept his misgivings largely to himself.[51]

From 1962 to 1994 the dominant note of Rwandan politics was the mutual hostility between the Parmehutu government and Tutsi supporters of the UNAR, who from their exile in Burundi, Tanzania, Uganda, or the Congo mounted regular armed attacks on the country. From 1986 the most powerful of these exiled military forces was the Tutsi-dominated Rwandese Patriotic Front (RPF), formed from the remnants of Yoweri Museveni's National Resistance Army in Uganda. In such a context, government propaganda was able to characterize the Tutsi as external threats to the peace and stability of the country. Such stigmatization first bore genocidal fruit at the end of 1963, when Hutu militias massacred thousands of Tutsi. Thousands more joined the exodus across the frontiers, thus compounding the problem that Tutsi could easily be branded as enemies of the state. Under Perraudin's leadership, the Catholic authorities condemned the violence, but somehow contrived to identify external UNAR "terrorists" rather than Hutu militias inside the country as the chief culprits. Sporadic killings took place during this period, especially from February to April 1973. Neighboring Burundi also experienced its own genocide in 1972, when Tutsi troops killed more than 200,000 Hutu; many others fled north into Rwanda, exacerbating ethnic tensions there.

The genocide that erupted in Rwanda between April and July 1994 was thus the culmination of three decades of mounting ethnic hostility in which the government-controlled media increasingly depicted the RPF—and, by extension, their Tutsi supporters–as *inyenzi* (cockroaches). Hutu were urged to prepare themselves for a Tutsi attack and to hunt down and kill the *inyenzi*. In this way the Hutu majority became convinced that all Tutsi were potentially rebels and enemies of the state: to take violent action against these alien elements was necessary to *preserve* the state from an imminent genocide supposedly being planned by the Tutsi.

The characterization of a substantial minority group as vermin that threatened the survival of the nation bore close similarities to the nature of antisemitic invective in Germany earlier in the century. It was a stance directly contrary to any Christian understanding of humanity, yet during this period the alignment between the churches and the Hutu government that disseminated such rhetoric grew ever closer. Perraudin's successor as Catholic archbishop of Kigali from 1976, Vincent Nsengiyumva, was a Hutu who identified himself unequivocally with the government, becoming personal confessor to Madame Habyarimana, wife of the second president of Rwanda, and a member of the central committee of the single national political party, the *Mouvement Révolutionnaire National pour le Développement* (MRND), which President Habyarimana had founded in 1975. Even the Protestant churches shared to some degree in this process of ethnic realignment. The Ruanda Mission always remained strongly pro-monarchist and deeply sympathetic to Tutsi assumptions of national leadership, but by the late 1970s all of the Anglican bishops were Hutu; the first indigenous Anglican bishop, Adonia Sebununguri, bishop of Kigali since 1965, was a strong supporter of the Habyarimana government.[52]

On April 6, 1994 President Habyarimana was flying back from a regional summit in Dar-es-Salaam, where he had capitulated to pressure to implement an agreement to implement genuine power sharing with the Tutsi. As his jet (a present from President François Mitterand of France, who was closely implicated in his regime) came in to land at Kigali airport, two rockets were fired, bringing the plane down. Habyarimana and also the president of Burundi were killed. Who fired the rockets is not known. The "official" view is that the perpetrators were Hutu extremists who were not prepared to share power with the Tutsi, but there is compelling evidence pointing toward the involvement of the RPF under the command of Paul Kagame, who became president of Rwanda in July 1994. Within one hour of the plane coming down, the killings had begun—a sure sign that what ensued was premeditated. At first, most of the victims were leaders of the Hutu opposition, those who stood in the way of the implementation of genocide. But soon the violence turned against the Tutsi. By the afternoon of the 7th the massacres had spread beyond the capital.

In the course of the genocide itself, church premises became one of the primary killing grounds, precisely because it was remembered that in the earlier outbreaks of violence in 1963–64 and 1973 they had provided a secure place of sanctuary. In 1994, such hopes of sanctuary proved hollow: in the grounds of one single parish, Kabgayi, as many as 65–75,000 Tutsi were slaughtered.[53] In all it is estimated that between 810,000 and 850,000 Rwandans—about 11 percent of the population—lost their lives between April and July 1994. The distribution of the fatalities between Tutsi and Hutu, and the primary responsibility for the genocide, remain matters of contestation. The daily killing rate was at least five times as high as that in the Nazi concentration camps. Another 30 percent of the population were forced into exile. In a few cases, clergy were actively involved in the killing, having persuaded themselves that they were defending their flocks against the "enemies" who threatened them. In others, both clergy and laity risked their lives by sheltering Tutsi in their homes; this was particularly true of Protestants involved in the *Abarokore* movement, which had generally valued the trans-ethnic spiritual fellowship of the revived more highly than Christian political involvement.[54] Yet at Gahini, birthplace of the East African Revival, three out of the four Anglican clergy in 1994 swallowed the dominant ideology, legitimating the murder of Tutsi by appeal to Old Testament precedents such as Samson's slaughter of the Philistines.[55] Genocide in the Christian nation of Rwanda was justified as an act of self-defense, a just war waged against those who had been made into external enemies of the nation.

IV. Christian Prophecy and Its Failures

Christians often look for inspiration for their guidance in political behavior to the Hebrew prophets, who fearlessly declared the word of the Lord to king and nation, often at risk to their own lives. The hopeful expectation is that the churches should display similar theological fidelity and moral courage, but it tends to be forgotten that the Old Testament prophets were often isolated and deeply unpopular figures. Effective prophetic speech depends on a paradoxical balance between maintaining access to the sources of political power and preserving sufficient distance from those sources to enable moral independence to be safeguarded. Both the case studies discussed in this chapter, not to speak of many other historical examples, suggest that, wherever churches have become large and influential human institutions, they tend to prioritize the maintenance of political access over the safeguarding of moral independence. "One of the Rwandan church's greatest sins," reflects the Catholic historian J. J. Carney, "has been the general failure of church leaders to maintain prophetic distance from state leaders."[56] However, it equally has to be said that neither does the opposite ecclesiastical temptation to withdraw into a quietist model of isolation from political involvement guarantee the preservation of theological integrity. The Free Churches in Nazi Germany—a group frequently omitted from consideration in discussion of this topic—were small in number and politically insignificant. Their responses to Hitler's regime were varied, but substantial numbers of Baptists and Methodists were closer in sympathy to the German Christians than to the Confessing Church; indeed many gladly endorsed the sentiment that "National Socialism has kindly let us do as we like because we stay away from politics."[57] Similarly in Rwanda the evangelical adherents of the Abarokore movement, despite their absorption with the egalitarian message of the unity in Christ of all the "saved," and their safe distance from the structures of power, were not conspicuous by public opposition to the genocide; their courage, though often evident, was displayed more at the level of individual acts of heroic rescue or shelter.[58]

The appropriate judgment on the role of the churches in both Germany and Rwanda is not that they directly inspired the actions of those who instigated genocide, but rather that they made the latter's commands to take immoral and violent action "comprehensible and tolerable."[59] Current Christian political theology, passionate as it is about the pursuit of justice, is inclined to criticize the churches of earlier generations for inadequate commitment to the cause of justice. Although such charges may have their place, the examples of Nazi Germany and Rwanda both highlight the extent to which in times of crisis Christian perceptions of where the path of justice lies are liable to be blown off course by the prevailing winds of ethnic sentiment and ideology. Perverse as it may seem, measures against the Jews in the 1930s were justified on the basis of removing distress from the poor oppressed people of Germany. More blatantly still, in Rwanda, observes Carney, "liberationist rhetoric precipitated some of the worst violence in Rwanda's postcolonial history."[60] Ethnic conflicts usually turn on mutually contradictory perceptions of what is just, and a Christian political theology that simply appeals for justice is unlikely to attain adequate moral independence from the competing rhetorical platforms. The late Catholic historian and theologian Adrian Hastings commented in 1993 in the context of the Bosnian genocide, but also with earlier German examples in mind, that "Without a very strong sense of the power of sin, of evil in the world, it is impossible to formulate a theology of politics or of history, or to defend the ground out of which effective prophecy can come."[61] That awareness of sinfulness ought to lead Christians, not in the first instance to censure the behavior of others, but to continual self-criticism and repentance. Carney admits at the end of his study of the Rwandan Catholic Church to a sense of frustration that Archbishop Per-raudin, who from his retirement in Switzerland learned of the catastrophe that had engulfed the country to which he had devoted so much of his life, never expressed regret for any action or stance of his that might in any way have contributed to the disaster.[62] Christianity proclaims a gospel of redemption from sin, but what Christians find hardest of all is to recognize the extent to which evil can infect even the company of the redeemed.

CHAPTER EIGHT

Aliens in a Strange Land?[*]

LIVING IN AN ISLAMIC CONTEXT
IN EGYPT AND INDONESIA

I. Christianity and Religious Plurality

For the Western churches in the modern period the issue of Christianity's relationship to religious plurality was until the late twentieth century primarily a missionary question—a challenging reality that the tiny minority of Christians whose missionary or imperial vocations had led them to live overseas could not escape, but which was comfortably distant from the experience of those who resided within the boundaries of Western Christendom.[1] For the historic Christian churches of the Middle East, on the other hand, the challenge of living as Christian communities within the context of an Islamic empire or state has been a continual reality ever since the Arab conquest of the seventh century. It is only since the 1960s that the explosion of intercontinental migration to the affluent West has forced religious plurality back onto the agenda of the Western churches as entire religious communities, although even then their experience remained very different from that of their fellow religionists in minority situations. What is new about the modern situation is not the fact of religious plurality, but the extent of awareness and debate of the issue among Western Christians.[2] It is a measure of how introverted Christianity in its European form had become, and how insulated from the religious experience of the rest of humanity, that Western commentators in the 1990s could still refer to the fact that we *now* live in a religiously plural world as if that had not always been the case.

---

[*] "I have been an alien in a strange land." (Exodus 18:3).

Surveys of the historical relationship between Christianity and other faiths often suggest that through a process of theological enlightenment the churches in the modern period have moved from crusade to cooperation, from diatribe to dialogue. For liberal-minded Western Christians this is a fundamentally attractive thesis: who would not wish to assert that we have left bigotry and antagonism behind, and moved on to stances of mutual respect and tolerance? For obvious reasons, this trajectory is most marked in studies of Christian–Muslim relations, overshadowed as they are by the legacy of the Crusades. The temptation is to write history from a didactic stance for the sake of promoting harmonious intercommunal relations in the contemporary world. Hugh Goddard's history of Christian–Muslim relations acknowledges that some in both the Christian and the Muslim communities, "perhaps even an increasing proportion of the membership of both communities, see the relationship as being intrinsically and essentially an adversarial one," but suggests that "history itself points to the existence of a more positive irenical way of thinking among both Muslims and Christians at certain stages of their history."[3] It is noteworthy that Goddard's account of the nineteenth and twentieth centuries focuses on attempts by academic theologians to define Christian–Muslim relations in more harmonious terms, rather than on intercommunal relations. Sidney Griffith's account of Oriental Christian theological writing in the Islamic world between the eighth and the thirteenth centuries provides a good example of the more amicable relationships to which Goddard refers: Christian theology during this early Islamic period was shaped by the priorities of maintaining intercommunal harmony and hence assumed an Arabic cultural idiom. Griffith has expressed the hope that his historical research may provide resources for Western Christians faced with the challenge of learning to live with Muslims on their own doorstep.[4]

However laudable this aspiration may be, historians of Christian–Muslim relations should be alert to the danger of trawling the oceans of history in order to catch in their nets only those examples of mutual toleration that will be most morally edifying for the present. What Herbert Butterfield labeled "the Whig interpretation of history" in relation to the progress of religious liberty within Christian Europe is still alive and well, but is now evident in the wider field of the history of interreligious relations.[5] It is a poignant irony that the ultimate origins of Pakistan's notorious anti-blasphemy laws, which have inflicted considerable suffering on Christians in Pakistan, can be traced to provisions in the Indian penal code of 1860, drafted in 1837 by the archetypal Whig, Lord Macaulay, out of concern to protect the sensibilities of all faith communities in

British India. Although the laws in their current and specifically Islamic form date from the early 1980s, they owe their genesis to the Utilitarian principle that the state should not permit the giving of any public offence to any religious community, or the holding to public ridicule of any institution or symbol of religious worship, a principle rooted in the concern of the British Raj to maintain harmonious intercommunal relationships.[6]

The first case study of Christian–Muslim relations selected for analysis in this chapter focuses on Egypt, which in the first part of the twentieth century was the intellectual and publishing hub of the Muslim world, and hence was regarded by Western Christians as the key to its regeneration by the Christian gospel and "modern" ideas of reform.[7] Egypt was also the home of Africa's oldest church, the Coptic Orthodox Church. Until about the ninth century, the Copts formed the majority community. They have had slowly to come to terms with their attenuated and increasingly vulnerable status as a statistical minority, even if they still decline to accept the implication of marginality by ranking themselves among the "religious minorities" of the Middle East. They would rightly dissent from the title of this chapter. Far from regarding themselves as "aliens in a strange land," Coptic Christians regard themselves as *the* true Egyptians, descended from the Pharaohs and of one blood with the steady stream of their fellow countrymen who over the centuries have abandoned their Christian heritage and conformed to the increasingly dominant Islamic identity.[8]

The second case study examines a younger Christian community within a younger nation, that of the church in Indonesia. Only 20 percent of the world's Muslims live in the Middle East, compared with about 60 percent in the Asia-Pacific region. In 2000 the vast and ethnically diverse archipelago of Indonesia had an estimated Muslim population of 167 million, larger than any other nation, but also had a Christian population nearly twice the size of that of South Korea (25 million as compared with 14 million).[9] Christians in some parts of Indonesia form a large majority of the regional or "Outer Island" population. Interreligious relations also involve Hindu and Buddhist communities as well as Christian and Muslim ones. The new nation of Indonesia was constructed between 1945 and 1950 from the disparate components of the Dutch colonial empire in the East Indies. It remained in a real sense an empire, but one ruled from Jakarta. For much of its short history, the primary question has been, not how Islamic the state should be, but just how viable and permanent this new nation would prove to be.

In the Egyptian case there was never any serious possibility of the dismemberment of the nation on religious lines. The challenge for the churches was starker and simpler: in both the colonial and post-independence eras the state appeared to privilege Muslims over Christians. In all Islamic contexts British colonial governments, while prepared to treat missionaries with courtesy and even with favor, took a skeptical line toward native converts from the majority religious community, who were frequently regarded as opportunists and cultural deviants.[10] The British government of Egypt in 1913 instituted a register for recording "the names of those who change their religion in Egypt," but the decree, in conformity with long-established Islamic precedent, made provision only for those who wished to embrace Islam.[11] The decree exemplifies the stark asymmetry of the official British approach to religious conversion in Muslim majority states: whereas conversion *to* Islam was something to be carefully monitored, conversion *from* Islam was simply not contemplated as a possibility. Protestant missions were in no doubt that this disjunction mirrored *shari'a* law, and in 1921 tried to persuade the Foreign Office to ensure that the new constitution of Egypt contained specific legal protection for converts.[12] But in Egypt, the Sudan, or northern Nigeria, for the colonial administration to lend open support to converts from Islam risked upsetting the delicate political equilibrium on which indirect rule depended. Hence converts or potential converts were left exposed to the hostility of their families and local communities, with no support from the colonial state. The British Empire at its peak in the late 1920s ruled over more than 100 million of the world's 233 million Muslims—many more than did the French or Dutch colonial empires. To Samuel Zwemer, the American Protestant missionary publicist who became known as "the Apostle to Islam," as to many other Christian observers, it seemed to be more of an Islamic empire than a Christian one; the British crown, observed Zwemer in 1929, claimed to be the Defender of the Faith, but in its imperial capacity it was defending the wrong variety of faith.[13]

The Egyptian case study also highlights the dissonance between the post-Enlightenment political philosophy of individual rights and freedom of religion that undergirds Western academic discourse on the subject of interreligious relations and the markedly different concept of religious toleration that prevails in Muslim majority states. Those whose views of religion and the state have been fashioned by the European prescription of a religiously tolerant or even indifferent state as the solution to wars of religion accept the more or less substantial relegation of religion to the private sphere as a necessary price to pay for religious harmony and the freedom of the individual. Modern Islamic political theory, on the other hand, has a view of religious toleration shaped by the *dhimma* system of the Islamic empire, instituted by the Pact of 'Umar, generally attributed to 'Umar II in the eighth century.[14] Those who were "people of the book" (*ahl al-kitab*), neither Muslims nor unbelievers (*kuffār*) but believers in the one God, that is Jews and Christians, could expect communal protection from the Islamic state on condition that they accepted its fundamental rationale, paid their *jizya* taxes in lieu of military service, and respected both the dictates of *sharī'a* law and the religious sensitivities of Muslims. In its most developed institutionalized form in the later Ottoman Empire, the toleration of *dhimmīs* thus implied, not the separation of religion from the state, but the state's agreement to grant conditional acceptance to *millats*—officially recognized and self-governing religio-political communities comprising a particular minority group—who did not share its religious values but who agreed to abide by its authority. From the early nineteenth century onwards, however, as the Ottoman Empire entered its long decline, Eastern Christians came under the growing influence of Western ideas of religious toleration, shaped by the Enlightenment and French and American Revolutions. As a result, they were emboldened to claim something quite different from the corporate status of *dhimmis*—namely, the status of individual *citizens* of a religiously neutral or "secular" state, with all that implied in terms of a theory of individual human rights entirely independent of religious commitment.

By the mid-nineteenth century, the increasingly fissiparous Ottoman state was not unresponsive to the cohesive potential of these ideas: the *tanzimat* (reform) process manifested in the *Hatt-ı Şerif* decrees of 1839 and the more radical *Hatt-ı Hümayûn* decrees of 1856 proclaimed such a separation of Ottoman citizenship from religious identity.[15] For many Muslim subjects of the empire, however, this revolutionary principle of political organization destabilized the covenantal character of the *dhimma* system, just as for many conservative Anglicans in the 1830s it appeared to threaten the very foundations of Christian political order.[16] It thus provoked in reaction more frequent and blatant instances of anti-Christian violence than were ever known during the centuries of Ottoman rule—most notably in the Balkans, Anatolia, and Syria.[17] The demise of the Ottoman Empire after the First World War left the Western idea of the nation-state as the only obvious political option on the table, but it was rarely obvious either what the boundaries of the nations should be or that new national identities would obliterate older religious ones. "The principle of nationality has come to rule," reflected the American missionary scholar, Duncan Black Macdonald, in his editorial on the demise of the Ottoman Empire in the *Moslem World* in January 1919: "Pan-Islam has now no meaning but one of sentiment and religion."[18] The course of Christian–Muslim relations in the Islamic world in the twentieth century is largely the story of the very uneven progress made by Western and "modern" notions of citizenship in eroding older Islamic concepts of the limited toleration that could be granted to *millat* communities.[19]

II. Coptic Christianity in Egypt

The Coptic community in Egypt has experienced a steady decline in numbers over many centuries. Since the mid-twentieth century a major contributor to that numerical decline has been the process of emigration, especially to the United States. But in a longer perspective the predominant cause has been conversion to Islam, a process that is still continuing. It is estimated that by 2010 some 10–15,000 Copts were converting to Islam annually.[20] There have been a mere handful of converts in the other direction. In the early twentieth century the few Muslim converts to Christianity that there were often found themselves shunned by the Coptic Orthodox Church or being shunted on hurriedly to one of the Protestant churches; the Coptic Church, like other ancient minority churches elsewhere, has tended to fear the convert as an infiltrator of the Christian community and a potential cause of trouble.[21] It has for long been a church in survival mode. The preference of the Coptic Orthodox Church for communal survival over evangelistic expansion branded it in the eyes of many Protestant missionaries as an institution almost as spiritually moribund as Islam itself: one American missionary at the end of the nineteenth century even likened the Church in its unreformed state to a mummified body taken out of the tombs.[22] Nevertheless, they hoped for a biblically-inspired reformation of this ancient church, and used their influence to promote its renewal. The CMS had begun work in Egypt in 1825, and after an interval from 1865 to 1882, had resumed its activities on a more substantial basis after the British occupation. From 1906 onwards it took the view that it was no part of its commission to seek the conversion of Copts to Anglicanism. CMS missionaries such as W. H. Temple Gairdner now cultivated the friendship of those in the Coptic Church who appeared committed to its reformation, and encouraged them in their efforts.[23] While the reformation for which missionaries longed tarried, they saw it as their duty to lead the way by directing evangelistic endeavors toward the Muslim population. Yet they were consistently frustrated by the fact that, to employ Samuel Zwemer's graphic image, "the doors of this vast temple reared by the Arabian Prophet swing only inward, not outward."[24] Zwemer, who served in Egypt from 1913 to 1929, was the most prolific exponent of the typical Protestant view that Islam was a dying religion of ritual and tradition, a stagnant creed that would be unable to withstand the inevitable onset of modernity.[25]

Zwemer's United Presbyterian Church of North America mission that had labored in Egypt since 1854 had won few converts from Islam; the great majority of the adherents of the Coptic Evangelical Church planted by the Presbyterians were in fact Copts from Upper Egypt.[26] Missions frequently laid the blame for the paucity of conversions at the feet of the British government. Even before he began work in Egypt, Zwemer had imbibed the prevailing evangelical view that the professed religious neutrality of the British colonial administration was a sham; as late as 1929, he endorsed the verdict of an experienced Sudan missionary that "The only real props of Islam left are the Christian powers who, for political purposes, are keeping from decent burial what might still infect a considerable portion of humanity, and keep salvation—that is soul-health—from reaching the soul-sick millions of our fellow-men, for whom Christ died."[27]

If colonial policy was intended to keep Christians and Muslims safely apart, the nationalist reaction against British rule proved capable of bringing them together. Christian–Muslim relations in the first decade of the century were at a low ebb, reaching their nadir in April 1910 with the assassination by a Muslim extremist of the first Coptic Prime Minister, Boutros Ghali Pasha. Yet the period from about 1911 to the foundation in 1928 by Hasan al-Banna of the Islamist group, the Muslim Brotherhood, has been described as the golden age of Christian–Muslim cooperation in Egypt in the common cause of a nationalist movement whose goal was the creation of a secular Arab state.[28] March 1919 marked the outbreak of a tumultuous and often violent revolution against British control. American and British missionaries feared for their lives, but the revolution was not fundamentally anti-Christian. Missionary sources focused on the disorder, while ignoring the part played by Copts in the revolution.[29] In Cairo Copts and Muslims, women as well as men, marched together to the mosque at the heart of the world's oldest university, al-Azhar, in protest against the British dispatch into exile of four leaders of the nationalist party, the Wafd. The chief mufti, Sheikh Muhammad Bakhit, paid a friendly visit to the Coptic patriarch; Muslims spoke on the subject of national independence in Coptic churches; attendance by Muslims at Christian services increased; while for fifty-nine consecutive days in March and April 1919, a Coptic priest, Malti Sergius, addressed Muslim congregations from the al-Azhar pulpit—the first Christian ever to be granted that privilege.[30]

The American evangelist George Sherwood Eddy conducted campaigns in Cairo, Tanta, and Assiut in October 1920. In Tanta, which he described as "the most bigotted [sic] Muhammedan centre in Egypt," he attracted a thousand hearers a night, among them Muslims who listened as quietly as the Christians, even when Eddy spoke at length, in unashamed contravention of the Qur'an, of the death of Christ. In Assiut, Muslims "almost fought to get copies of the Gospels," and signed cards pledging that they would read them.[31] In 1923 one American Presbyterian missionary even reported that a Muslim sheikh had been hurt by being refused the elements at a communion service which he had taken, asking: "Why not let me have a share in your blessing? Are we not all one now?"[32] In 1924 Copts won a considerable number of seats for the Wafd in the first parliamentary election held under the 1922 constitution, which gave Egypt limited independence under British suzerainty. The emblem of the nationalist Wafd party displayed the cross interlinked with the crescent—a political symbol that would be unthinkable in the Islamized Arab world of the postcolonial era.

The interreligious cooperation that characterized this phase of the nationalist movement was not generally extended to Christians associated with Western missions and was short lived. It failed to survive the decline of the Wafd in the 1930s and the growth of more overtly Islamist styles of nationalism in a fully independent Egypt after the revolution of 1952. Nasser's pan-Arabist regime of the Free Officers which ruled Egypt from 1952 to 1970 was officially secular. Nasser nearly lost his life to an assassin from the Muslim Brotherhood in 1954, and hence found it prudent to cultivate good relations with Pope Kyrillos VI. He therefore authorized the building of a new cathedral in the Abbassiyah district of Cairo, and promised the patriarch that licenses for the building of twenty-five new churches would be issued annually.[33] However, the humiliating defeat of Egypt at the hands of Israel in the Six Days' War of 1967 strengthened the hands of the Islamists. In practice the Nasser years witnessed the steady erosion of the influence of Copts in national life and of the interreligious nationalism that had characterized the period from 1919 to the 1930s.

Even while it lasted, Coptic–Muslim collaboration in the nationalist cause was largely confined to the Egyptian political elite and was not a reliable indicator of intercommunal relations among the populace at large. The most lasting contribution of Western Protestant missions to Egyptian Christianity in the twentieth century lay, not in the denominational churches that they planted, but in the fillip they often unwittingly gave to the renewal and modernization of the Orthodox tradition. In the course of the century, the reformation for which they had prayed did, to an extent, come to pass. The laity increasingly found a voice and an opening for ecclesiastical influence through the institution in 1874 of the Coptic communal council, the *Majlis al-Milli*, which owed a debt to the Presbyterian model set by the Coptic Evangelical Church.[34] As an elected body it posed a challenge to the existing control of Coptic affairs by the patriarch and bishops. The previously low standard of education of Coptic priests was gradually raised following the foundation of a Coptic seminary in 1893. The face of lay piety and Christian education was gradually transformed by the institution of the Sunday school. Habīb Girgīs, professor of theology and subsequently for many years principal in the Coptic seminary, opened the first Sunday school in the Fagella district of Cairo in 1908; from 1918 he organized Sunday schools on a national basis.[35]

Its middle-class lay promoters regarded the Sunday school movement as a revival of the catechetical methods of the church in third-century Alexandria, but its genesis owed more to contemporary American Protestant example than to patristic precedent.[36] The Sunday schools (which now mostly meet on Fridays) were concerned to renew Coptic tradition through a revival of the Coptic language and ancient hymnody, yet they also fostered a new puritan style of lay spirituality, more biblically based, and more strident in its demands for reform and in its articulation of Coptic interests. The parallel with radical Puritanism is implicit in the pages of one of the most illuminating academic analyses of the Coptic revival, written by a secular Muslim woman, S. S. Hasan. Hasan's book, *Christians versus Muslims in Modern Egypt*, acknowledges her debt to her teacher in political science at Harvard, Michael Walzer, and makes several allusions to his study of Puritan politics, *The Revolution of the Saints*, published in 1965.[37] In contrast to early modern England, however, in modern Muslim-majority Egypt direct evangelization of the unchurched population was almost unthinkable; in the Egyptian revolution of the saints, the only hope for church renewal lay in the religious socialization of the young in the Christian community.[38] By 1950 it is estimated that 85,000 young Copts were graduating annually from the Sunday schools.[39] One of the leaders of the Sunday school movement in the Shubra suburb of Cairo, and the chief editor of the movement's national magazine from 1947 to 1950, was Nazir Gayed, who later became a monk, Father Anthony, and in 1971 was elected as Pope Shenouda III.[40] Protestant precedent also lay behind the adoption by the Coptic clergy from the 1940s of the practice of preaching sermons at the mass, while the practice of catechizing the young was borrowed from the French Catholic missions introduced during the Napoleonic period.

Nazir Gayed's personal progression from Sunday school organizer to monk to patriarch points to another important ingredient of the Coptic revival that owed less to Western missions than it did to the symbolic power of the ancient tradition of desert monasticism. The same educated laymen, many of them university graduates, who were the architects of the Sunday school movement also pioneered the monastic revival under Kyrillos VI (1959–71). Decaying monasteries were rebuilt, new ones founded, and the number of monks grew from 200 in 1971 to at least 1,200 in 2001; many were university graduates. Parties of the faithful, including schoolchildren, were bussed into the desert for short visits to give them a taste of the religious life, to inspect relics and ancient manuscripts, and to learn about the lives of the saints.[41] The desert monks became invested with almost angelic significance as those who mediate between the heavenly realm and the temporal sphere in which the faithful endure oppression.[42] The monastic revival played a crucial role in validating the suffering of the Copts at the hands of militant Islam through encouraging remembrance of the saints and martyrs of early Christian history. The Coptic community dates its solar calendar from the beginning of the age of the martyrs on the original "9/11," September 11, 284 AD in the Gregorian calendar, the date of the accession of the emperor Diocletian.[43] Those who have lost their property or their lives to militant Islamists can be joined to the company of martyrs killed under Diocletian, and can take their place among the perfect symbolic number of 144,000 martyred saints mentioned in the book of Revelation—a figure that in Coptic tradition is said also to represent both the number of children murdered by Herod in Bethlehem, and the number of martyrs under Diocletian.[44]

Under Anwar Sadat's presidency from 1970 to 1981 Christian–Muslim relations deteriorated markedly. Sadat cultivated the image of a devoutly Muslim president, and relied increasingly on Islamist support, even though he always fell short of the expectations of the militants. Episodes of sectarian violence multiplied, and Sadat did little other than issue vague pleas for intercommunal reconciliation. Shenouda increasingly saw his role as one of mobilizing Copts to defend the secular character of the Egyptian state, and in 1977 convened a Coptic Conference to demand freedom of worship and government protection against Islamic attacks.[45] Shenouda was also determined not to allow his people to play their allotted role within Sadat's grand design to normalize relations between Israel and Egypt following the Camp David agreement of 1978. While Sadat looked to Copts to satisfy the desire of the Israeli government to see Egyptian tourists flocking to Israel, Pope Shenouda, in a striking reversal of crusading precedent, banned Christians from participating in pilgrimages to Jerusalem until such time as the holy city was again under Arab control, and promised not to enter the holy city until he could do so walking hand in hand with the Palestinian leader, Yasser Arafat. Any Copt who persisted in such pilgrimages was threatened with excommunication.[46]

In 1980 Shenouda took the dramatic step of cancelling the public celebrations of Easter, in which state representatives had traditionally played a part, and withdrew in protest with his bishops into the seclusion of a remote monastery. Sadat retaliated the following year by sending Shenouda into internment in the desert monastery of Bishoi, and appointing a five-man panel of bishops to run the church in his absence—an extraordinary Islamic example of high-handed erastianism. Sadat knew, however, that he could count on some influential Christian supporters. Shenouda's high-profile tactics and dictatorial style, while they had the endorsement of the young and many of the middle classes, caused anxiety among the Coptic aristocracy and among the episcopate, some of whom feared that politics were supplanting spirituality, and preferred quiet diplomacy as a way of defending Christian interests.[47] The five bishops co-opted by Sadat seemed happy to play his game, while the more pietistic segment of the Coptic community, led by the abbot of the great monastery of St. Macarius, Father Matta El Meskeen (renowned internationally as "Father Matthew the Poor"), "stood firmly on the touchline"; so, it must be said, did the global ecumenical community.[48] In January 1983 the archbishop of Canterbury, Robert Runcie, sent the bishop of London, Graham Leonard, to investigate the Egyptian church struggle; Leonard met both Shenouda and one of the five, Bishop Athanasius, but advised against siding openly with Shenouda.[49] The only consistent and vocal international support Shenouda received was from the American Coptic Association, formed in 1974 by the growing Coptic émigré community in the United States to report on human rights abuses in Egypt.[50] The pope remained in detention for 1,213 days, being released in January 1985 by President Hosni Mubarak only on three conditions: that he avoided political statements, returned regularly to his desert residence, and should never be present in Cairo on a Friday for fear of inflaming Muslim opinion.[51]

The final period of Shenouda's long patriarchate from his reinstatement in 1985 until his death in March 2012 was marked by a quieter tone. Once freed from his long incarceration, Shenouda appeared to abandon political confrontation for conciliation of the Mubarak regime, and repeatedly urged cooperation with Muslims. The government nominated Shenouda for the UNESCO–Madanjeet Singh Prize for the Promotion of

Tolerance and Non-Violence in 2000. He appeared on public platforms alongside the grand mufti, Dr. Muhammad Sayed Tantawi. Such high-profile collaboration was intended to demonstrate that Copts had a recognized place alongside Muslims in Egyptian national life; it was, in effect, a reversion to the communal politics of the Ottoman *millat*. Once again, however, it did not signify that at the local level, Christian–Muslim relations were any more amicable.[52] The vessel of the modern Egyptian state had taken another tack in its zigzagging course, sometimes choosing to run with the prevailing winds of Islamic militancy, at other times attempting to make headway against them; Shenouda had simply adjusted his own tiller accordingly. By the final decade of the century it seemed to increasing numbers of Copts that the only lasting solution to their minority status was to emigrate, notably to the United States; the time may come when the Coptic Church is to be found more on American soil than on Egyptian.

III. The Church in Indonesia

Even though Indonesia boasts the largest Muslim population of any nation, it witnessed, in marked contrast to Egypt, a steady growth in the size of the Christian community in the course of the twentieth century. The Roman Catholic community grew from only 26,000 in 1900 to 500,000 in 1940, and to 6 million in 2003. The numbers of indigenous Protestants rose from 285,000 in 1900 to 1.7 million in 1940, and to perhaps 16 million in 2003. What is more, it is estimated that 1 million of the new Christians converted in the course of the century were of a Muslim rather than a traditional religious background.[53] Whereas Protestant church growth took place without any substantial increase in missionary numbers, Catholic growth was related to a large and sustained expansion in the numbers of missionaries sent by male and female religious orders to Indonesia. Missionaries of the Sacred Heart, Capuchins, and members of the Society of the Divine Word increasingly took the place of the Jesuits who had pioneered Catholic evangelization in the Dutch East Indies; many were involved in education, which became the main Catholic weapon in the race with Islam for the conversion of traditional religionists.[54]

There was no direct correlation between the progress of conversion and the extension of colonial authority from Java and Sumatra to other parts of the archipelago—a process of subjugation that continued after independence, as Indonesia annexed Netherlands New Guinea (West Papua) between 1962 and 1969. In Batakland and Halmahera mass conversions preceded subjugation to colonial rule. In Karo, Sumba, and Torajaland in South Sulawesi mass movements followed national independence. In Flores, the educational missions of the Society of the Divine Word saw steady success after the Dutch assigned them the territory as part of a colonial strategy of pacification in 1913: 90 percent of the population are now Catholic. In West Papua conversion of the highland Dani, a Melanesian people, began in the early 1960s when the Dutch had barely established control of the region, and accelerated under the equally alien rule of Jakarta.[55] Nevertheless, it is clear that the Dutch took an instrumental view of conversion to Christianity: in areas that were already Islamized, it was strongly discouraged, just as it was under British rule in Africa; by contrast, in the outlying areas not yet subject to full colonial control the Dutch actively supported missions, viewing their provision of education and health services as useful tools in the incorporation of these marginal societies within the administrative structures of colonial rule. The same was true of the government of independent Indonesia, especially under the "New Order" regime of Suharto from 1966 to 1998: mission-led development and modernization programs were a useful antidote to the appeal of radical Islam to tribal peoples, binding them to a very distant central government and the national economy.[56]

The Dutch colonial view of missionary activity as useful only when it served the interests of the state was shared by the colonial established Protestant church, the *Indische Kerk* (or Protestant Church of the Netherlands Indies), which had its own missionary work in outlying regions such as the southern Moluccas, but showed no signs of wishing to evangelize the predominantly Muslim Sundanese or Javanese who formed the heart of the Dutch empire. Hendrik Kraemer, missionary with the Dutch Bible Society in Indonesia from 1922 to 1935, and the most influential Dutch missionary theorist of the twentieth century, commented in 1933 that such political opportunism had brought fatal consequences for the cause of the gospel in Java.[57] Kraemer took a dim view of the *Indische Kerk*, believing it to be so thoroughly permeated by the centralist bureaucratic mindset of the colonial government and so indifferent to the propagation of the faith for its own sake that it did not warrant being called a church at all.[58] The Protestant missionary societies and Catholic religious orders that conducted the bulk of missionary activity were in theory independent of the state, yet in practice heavily dependent on state subsidies for their educational and medical work in the "Outer Islands": in Torajaland, for example, up to half of the missions' income came from government sources.[59] The public face of Indonesian Christianity in the

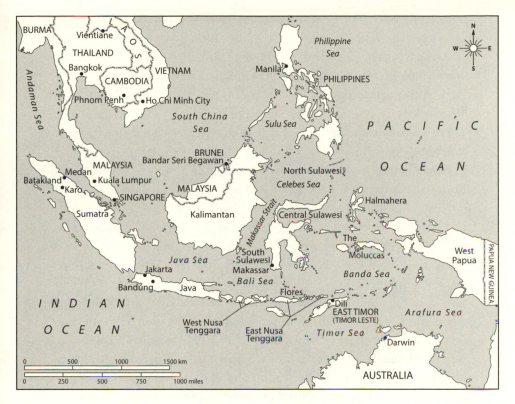

MAP 2. Indonesia in the late twentieth century

first half of the twentieth century was overwhelmingly a Dutch one, in both the Catholic and Protestant Churches. The first Indonesian Catholic priest was ordained in 1926, and the first bishop in 1940, yet at that date only sixteen of the 570 priests were Indonesians. As late as 1979, only 42 percent of the priests were Indonesian nationals.[60] Protestants were little better. When visiting the Dutch East Indies, both John Mott (in 1926) and William Paton, secretary of the International Missionary Council (in 1936) commented on the slow progress made by the Protestant missions in developing indigenous leadership.[61]

As elsewhere in the missionary movement, the progress toward indigenization that was belatedly made in the interwar period made a virtue out of necessity. One of the largest Protestant agencies, the *Rheinische Missionsgesellschaft* (Rhenish Mission Society), which worked among the Batak people of northern Sumatra, was hit hard by the First World War and its economic aftermath in Germany. Although the society had been deeply influenced by the German Romantic ideal of founding a *Volkskirche*—a church that would reflect the customs and corporate personality (*Geist*) of an entire people—its devolution of power in May 1930 to an autonomous Batak church, the Huria Kristen Batak Protestan (HKBP), was precipitated by the widening gulf between a growing church and an attenuating financial base in Germany. Hendrik Kraemer reported later the same year that "Notwithstanding the name of People's Church (*Huria Kristen Batak*) there is no people's church yet in actual reality. There is a people among whom Europeans are carrying out church activities, but there is no spiritual community borne by the people and rooted in their relationships."[62] Nevertheless, the HKBP grew to be the largest Protestant church in the country. More generally, all missions found their government subsidies severely cut after the financial crash of 1929. Dutch Protestant missions soon followed the Rhenish Society's example in establishing autonomous churches during the 1930s, though missionaries in many cases still occupied senior leadership positions. When the Japanese occupied Indonesia in 1942, almost all expatriate missionaries were interned. In the younger churches in the east and in many parts of Sulawesi, where missionaries had been in sole control, a few evangelists in these regions were hurriedly ordained on the eve of the Japanese takeover and were given charge of mission funds. The Japanese imposed ecumenical organization, requiring all Protestant churches to join regional Councils of Churches in north and central Sulawesi, south Sulawesi, Kalimantan, and the Moluccas, thus extending to Indonesia a Protestant ecumenism that was already a feature of missionary policy in the Netherlands—the Netherlands Missionary Council (Nederlandse Zendingsraad) had been established in 1929. An attempt to include the Roman Catholic Church in the Councils of Churches failed. Although these Councils collapsed after the war, the foundations had been laid for Indonesian ecumenism.[63]

In view of the role of the *Indische Kerk* as the religious arm of empire and of the financial dependence of even the voluntary mission agencies on the colonial state, it is not surprising that the anticolonial movement that developed in the early twentieth century drew much of its religious dynamic from Islam. The Indonesian nationalist movement dates from the foundation in Java in 1911 of the first nationalist political party, Sarekat Islam. The movement rapidly attracted a mass following, and branches were formed throughout Indonesia. In the wake of the Bolshevik Revolution, Marxist ideology became increasingly influential within the nationalist movement, leading to a split in 1921 between Sarekat Islam and the newly formed Indonesian Communist Party, *Partai Komunis Indonesia* (PKI). From now on, the Islamist and the Marxist routes toward Indonesian nationhood increasingly diverged. Given the options available, many

Christian sympathizers with the nationalist cause gravitated toward the Communist Party. Most Indonesian Christians before the 1940s had little exposure toward Islam; even in Java, where the Muslim presence was largest, many Christians lived in Christian villages.[64] The most prominent of these Christian sympathizers with communism was a member of the HKBP named Amir Sjarifoeddin.

Amir Sjarifoeddin (1907–48) came from the Islamized coastal city of Medan in north Sumatra.[65] His mother was a Muslim and his father, a senior civil servant in the colonial administration, was a convert to Islam from nominal Christianity. After high school in the Netherlands, Amir studied at the Law College in Batavia (Jakarta), where he joined the inter-ethnic, secular nationalist Indonesian Students Association. At law school he was exposed to the revolutionary idea that a future independent nation would take the form, not, as had previously been supposed, of a federation of all the different ethnic groups within the Indonesian archipelago, but rather, as expressed in a slogan coined by his fellow law student Muhammad Yamin, of "one state, Indonesia, one nation, Indonesia, and one language, Indonesian." A single national youth organization, Indonesia Moeda, was formed, and Amir became treasurer of its organizing committee. Simultaneously with his adoption of nationalist politics, however, Amir had become a Christian through the influence of one of his law professors, J. M. J. Schepper, who had been raised in Amsterdam within the Exclusive Brethren, but whose evangelicalism was now of a broader kind. From 1918 to 1922 Schepper served as one of the two Protestant missionary consuls in Batavia, fulfilling a key role as intermediary between the colonial government and the missions. By the early 1930s Schepper was deploying his Christian convictions and eminence as a jurist to interrogate the colonial government's repression of the nationalist movement. His grand house in Batavia became the meeting place of the infant Indonesian *Christen Studenten Vereiniging* (Student Christian Movement or SCM), where students gathered to discuss Rudolf Otto's *The Idea of the Holy*, the German Confessing Church theologian Hanns Lilje, and Karl Barth; on occasion the topics ranged wider still to include Gandhi, Tagore, C. F. Andrews, and the Japanese theologian Toyohiko Kagawa.[66]

Amir was baptized into the HKBP in 1931. His mother, horrified at such apostasy, committed suicide. Amir became a leader, not simply in the Indonesian SCM, but on a broader stage in the developing Indonesian nationalist movement, eventually becoming recognized as third in line behind Sukarno and Mohammad Hatta; another of his SCM contemporaries, Johannes Leimena, also attained eminence in the nationalist movement, becoming deputy prime minister under Sukarno. Amir's fiery oratory within the Gabungan Politik Indonesia (the Federation of Indonesian Political Parties, formed in 1939), made a deep impression on the young T. B. Simatupang, of whom I shall say more later.[67] He was imprisoned owing to his subversive activities against the Japanese authorities, and allegedly was sentenced to death by a Japanese military tribunal, only being saved by the intervention of Sukarno and Hatta.[68]

Following the Indonesian declaration of independence made two days after the Japanese surrender in August 1945, Amir was released from prison and given a seat in the first independent cabinet, serving first as minister of information, and then as minister of defence, and after July 1947 also as prime minister. As minister of defence, he coordinated the armed forces of the infant Indonesian republic in the war of independence, in which Muslims and Christians fought side by side against the Dutch. He remained a leading figure in church circles, and was originally selected as one of the Indonesian representatives at the inaugural assembly of the World Council of Churches due to convene in Amsterdam on August 22, 1948. Why he was not in fact selected is unclear, but on August 31, to the shock of some of his fellow Christians, Amir announced that he had been a communist ever since 1935. When his colleagues in the Council of Churches called him in to explain his profession of communism, he informed them that he was a genuine Christian who loved truth, and that there was truth in communism. Perhaps they should not have been surprised. Amir's first four children, all girls, had been given biblical names, but his fifth child, a son, born in April that year, had been named Tito, after the Yugoslavian partisan.[69] Amir did not live to see the Dutch recognize the sovereignty of Indonesia on December 27, 1949. After his announcement that he was a communist, he became involved in the Madiun revolt, an abortive leftist rebellion against the provisional Republican government. He was captured by Republican troops and executed in Jakarta along with other leaders of the PKI on 19 December 1948.[70]

Amir Sjarifoeddin's ideological pilgrimage toward revolutionary Marxism perplexed even politically sympathetic Christians who knew him well, such as T. B. Simutapang.[71] But in the final years of Dutch rule he was not alone among Indonesian Christian intellectuals in finding in the pages of the New Testament a blueprint for the organization of a new independent nation on communist principles. Indonesian communism before 1945 was a loosely organized movement with no strong ties to Moscow. Sjarifoeddin's significance for our purposes is as a graphic illustration of how for much of the twentieth century, in Indonesia to an even greater extent than in Egypt, anticolonial nationalism relativized the religious divide between Christianity and Islam. Indeed, what Christianity and Islam had in common—monotheism—became the first of the "five principles" or *Pancasila* first enunciated by Sukarno in June 1945 as an ideological basis for a state that would be both secular and theistic. In their final form the *Pancasila* comprised belief in one supreme God; a just and civilized humanity; the unity of the Indonesian nation; representative democracy through consensus; and social welfare for all.[72] In a religious, ethnic, and geographical context far more diverse than in Egypt, some of the Islamic majority, especially its predominant Javanese adherents, were willing to concede a basis for the state that many Muslims regarded as thoroughly secular. Muslims tried hard in 1945 to add to the first principle—belief in one God—the seven words [in Indonesian] "with the obligation for adherents of Islam to carry out the Islamic law," but finally had to drop this insistence when it became clear that there was a danger that the Christian parts of eastern Indonesia would secede in protest.[73]

Many Christians in Muslim-dominated Java and Sumatra were understandably supportive of *Pancasila* and of Sukarno's regime. One of Sukarno's closest supporters was Amir's one-time young admirer, T. B. Simatupang (1920–90), who came from a devout second-generation Protestant family in Tapunuli, North Sumatra.[74] Trained at the Royal Dutch Military Academy at Bandung, he rose rapidly through the ranks and after the nationalist proclamation of independence became the chief military strategist planning the contest with the better equipped Dutch forces. He also had to put down the Madiun revolt in which Sjarifoeddin played such a prominent role. From 1950 to 1953 he was deputy chief of staff and then, at the age of only twenty-nine, chief of staff in the Republic's armed forces. After falling out with Sukarno, he was removed from office in 1953, and thereafter developed a new career as a lay theologian and ecumenist. He was a well-known figure in the Christian Conference of Asia and in the World Council of Churches, of which he served as one of the six presidents, representing Asia, from 1975 to 1983. Simatupang became the best-known Christian spokesperson for Christian–Muslim relations in Indonesia, and the most articulate Christian supporter of *Pancasila*. His early interest in the writings of Marx left him with an abiding enthusiasm for the concept of revolution, but in his case revolutionary fervor was moderated by his more recent reading in development studies and theology, especially in the social ethics of Reinhold Niebuhr. "What gave me much new passion," he records, "was that in the perspective of Christian faith the problems of freedom, justice and humanity suddenly came to be seen through more realistic glasses

although with a vision that was more hopeful."[75] As interpreted by Simatupang, the Indonesian revolution had entered a second phase in which
Pancasila was best expressed through the creed of national development.

The relative harmony enjoyed by Christians and Muslims under Sukarno was not, however, destined to last under the "New Order" regime
of President Suharto from 1967 to 1998. Suharto deployed religion as a
weapon in his drive to purge the country of communism. Islam, Protestantism, Catholicism, Hinduism, and Buddhism were now declared to be
the five recognized religions that constituted the Indonesian nation. As in
communist China, Protestantism and Catholicism were regarded as separate religions, while, following Dutch colonial precedent, traditional religionists were regarded as "people who do not yet have a religion."[76] Soon
after General Suharto's effective assumption of power from President Sukarno in March 1966, in a move designed to flush out communists, affiliation to one of these five religions was declared obligatory on all citizens.
Up to half a million communist sympathizers were killed by Suharto's
army. It was no coincidence that the Javanese churches received a flood
of converts from traditional religion between 1965 and 1971. Avery Willis, the American Southern Baptist missionary who chronicled this movement, was in no doubt that the decree requiring adherence to one of the
five religions was the primary cause of these conversions, though he did
not scruple to entitle his account of the movement *Indonesian Revival:
Why Two Million Came to Christ*: God could work even through political
expediency to draw people to Christ.[77]

Muslims initially welcomed the state's campaign against atheistic communism, and expected to obtain a dominant position in Suharto's New
Order regime, but their expectations were rapidly disappointed. Tensions
between Christians and Muslims intensified in consequence, culminating
in a riot at Makassar on October 1, 1967, when a crowd of Muslim youths
destroyed fourteen church buildings, three schools, a monastery, the office
of the Catholic student organization, and injured some Christian youth.[78]
In response to these escalating tensions, the government convened an interreligious consultation in Jakarta on November 30, 1967, followed by
similar regional meetings. The consultation failed because the Christians
refused the Muslim proposal that each community should not make the
other the target of proselytism. Simatupang argued strongly that both
Christians and Muslims were bound by their scriptures to propagate their
faith, and appealed to the Universal Declaration of Human Rights. A more
problematic consequence of the Makassar riot was that the government
began (in an echo of Egyptian precedent) to regulate the building of places

of worship, thus limiting for the first time the freedom of Christians to construct churches in Muslim areas. Buoyed by reports of the Indonesian "revival," evangelical and Pentecostal mission agencies had poured into Indonesia after 1966, each constructing their own church buildings. Muslims often felt encircled and threatened, as there was usually only one mosque per neighborhood.[79] It is estimated that the average annual number of attacks on Christians rose from zero in the period from 1945 to 1955, to 0.2 in 1955–65, 4.6 in 1965–74, 8.9 in 1975–84, 13.2 from 1985 to 1994, and 52.5 from 1995 to 1997.[80] The deterioration in Christian–Muslim relations compelled the World Council of Churches to abandon its plans to hold its fifth assembly, due to take place in 1975, in Jakarta, and relocate the event to Nairobi.[81]

The Indonesian tradition of a tolerant and inclusive form of Islam was thus weakening well before the end of Suharto's authoritarian regime in 1998. Nevertheless, the collapse of the Indonesian economy and ensuing fall of the Suharto government precipitated a new upsurge of intercommunal violence, notably in west and central Kalimantan, west and east Nusa Tenggara, central Sulawesi, and the Moluccas. The worsening situation owed a good deal to the growing influence of militant Salafist varieties of Islam, especially among university students, and also to rumors of an international Zionist–Christian conspiracy to destroy Muslim hegemony in Indonesia, coordinated by the American government of George W. Bush. Although there were still influential liberal intellectuals within the Islamic community, particularly in the Islamic state universities, by the close of the century the prospects for a revival of the Indonesian pattern of Christian–Muslim harmonious coexistence were not good.[82]

IV. The Politics of Christian Survival

Both of the case studies we have examined exemplify the fact that for Christians living as a minority community within an Islamic environment the story of Muslim–Christian relations in the twentieth century cannot be told as if it were a single narrative of two religious communities learning through a process of theological enlightenment to accept each other and live together. Both examples suggest that if there is any discernible common trend over the century, it is in the opposite direction, involving a regression from some measure of Christian–Muslim collaboration in the anticolonial cause in the first half of the century to intensifying religious rivalry and antagonism in the post-colonial era. Furthermore, both in Egypt and in Indonesia, the responses of Christians to Islam have been shaped less by principled theological reflection than by the day-to-day demands imposed by the state—which itself has had to determine and periodically adjust its stance toward Muslim demands for the conformity of the legal system to Islamic norms. The juxtaposition of the two case studies highlights the role played by geography and demography. In Indonesia, Christians have constituted majority or near-majority elements of particular regions within a geographically dispersed nation, and they have been able to use the threat of secession to block attempts at Islamization of the state. In Egypt, in contrast, the regional concentration and numerical weight of Christians has been less marked, and their capacity to resist Muslim absolutism has been correspondingly reduced.

Throughout the twentieth century the unchanging dictates of survival were more powerful than theological principle in determining the stance of Christian communities toward majority Muslim populations, whether the state was in some degree part of the British Empire, as was the case in Egypt from 1882 to 1922; or within the Dutch colonial empire, as in Indonesia until 1949; or an apparently liberal constitutional democracy, as in Egypt from 1923 to 1952 and Indonesia during the 1950s; or an increasingly Islamist regime, as in Indonesia from 1960 and Egypt from 1970. The deterioration in Christian–Muslim relations evident in both Egypt and Indonesia from the 1990s owed much to the growing appeal of Salafist or Wahhabist varieties of militant Islam, but the fact of their rising popularity itself requires explanation. Islamic militancy arises when Muslims feel under threat, either from a morally dissolute Western secularism, or from a revival of the crusading spirit in the supposedly Christian West. Crusading rhetoric, whether deployed by American presidents or by evangelical missions whenever they are oblivious to the consequences of uncoordinated and unreflective evangelistic campaigns for the viability of their own work, engenders heightened Islamic absolutism in response. However, it would be a theologically cheap solution to suggest that the only ways forward for Christians in Islamic environments are either to revert to spiritual introversion, as in the unreformed Coptic Church of the early twentieth century, or to choose indefinite exile in the West, as more and more Christians from the Middle East have found themselves compelled to do in recent decades.[83] The challenge for Christianity in the Islamic world is to find ways of embodying the universal compulsion of the gospel that evoke the spirit of Christ rather than the memory of a powerful Christendom.

CHAPTER NINE

That the World May Believe

CHRISTIAN MISSION TO THE MODERN WORLD

I. From "Making Jesus King" to the Missio Dei

Christianity is a missionary religion. It has at its heart beliefs about the unique redeeming significance for all humans of the life and work of Jesus Christ. The New Testament defines the person of Christ in terms that make it theologically inconsistent to limit the relevance of his claims to those inhabiting any particular segment of the globe or period of history—though it has to be said that the church has an impressive track record of such inconsistency. The nineteenth century, however, was one in which first the Protestant churches and then the Roman Catholic Church devoted themselves with increasing enthusiasm to the task of spreading the gospel to the non-Christian world. Catholics, of course, had made the running in missionary expansion ever since the sixteenth century, but in the nineteenth it was Protestants who seized the initiative while the Catholic Church gradually recovered from the disruption of the French Revolution and its legacy. In the course of the nineteenth century, the support of "foreign" or "overseas" missions became established as an integral part of Protestant church life in Europe and North America. The material and human resources devoted by the Western churches to the task of world mission continued to increase until the early 1920s, when intensifying theological controversies between fundamentalists and modernists combined with tightening economic constraints to erode the enterprise. From that point on, the priority of overseas missions began to slip down the agendas of the historic churches of the Western world, though in aggregate terms such decline was more than counterbalanced by the rise of new mission endeavors mounted by conservative evangelical, fundamentalist, and Pentecostal churches, and, toward the end of the century, by African, Asian, and Latin American churches.

Perhaps the most powerful generator of enthusiasm for foreign missions among North American and British Protestants in the first two to three decades of the twentieth century was the Student Volunteer Movement for Foreign Missions. In the whole period from its formation in 1886 until 1945, the movement recruited 20,745 university students (mostly from the United States, Canada, and Britain) for overseas missionary service by urging them to sign a solemn pledge affirming, "It is my solemn purpose, if God permit, to become a foreign missionary." The rallying cry of the Student Volunteer Movement was the stirring appeal to eager Christian young people to "Make Jesus King!" by taking the gospel to those who had not heard it.[1] It was good rhetoric but bad theology, making the Lordship of Christ dependent on human endeavor.

The conviction that the person and work of Jesus Christ have such an authoritative significance for all humanity that Christians have felt compelled to seek to realize the kingship or lordship of Christ over all peoples through their conversion to Christianity has been labeled "Christocentric universalism." The term was coined in 1991 by the incoming General Secretary of the World Council of Churches, Konrad Raiser (b. 1938), in his book *Ecumenism in Transition: A Paradigm Shift in the Ecumenical Movement?* Raiser, a German Lutheran, employed the term in a less than fully approving sense to describe the theological outlook that characterized the World Missionary Conference held at Edinburgh in 1910 and the Protestant ecumenical movement organized in its wake, leading to the formation of the World Council of Churches in 1948. Mainstream Protestant missions had not been at all indifferent to human need or the demands of justice, but their humanitarian activities had been framed within an overarching commitment to the ultimate goal of seeking the conversion of those of other faiths to Christianity. In Raiser's view—and he was not alone in that view—such deeply held theological convictions about the need to "make Jesus king" through the global diffusion of the gospel had slid all too easily into specious cultural and political assumptions about the justified global dominance of Western power. They had also gone hand in hand with a dismissive attitude toward other religions. In the modern world in which the acceptance of religious plurality is the necessary precondition for global harmony, Raiser therefore saw the need for a radical modification to this Christocentric universalism, a modification so fundamental that it could be described as a "paradigm shift," a notion drawn from Thomas S. Kuhn's best-selling work in the philosophy of science, *The Structure of Scientific Revolutions* (1962).[2] Raiser believed that a social and nonhierarchical doctrine of the Trinity grounded in the theology of the Greek Fathers provided the necessary resources for such a paradigm shift in the Christian understanding of mission. He identified the fourth WCC Assembly held at Uppsala in 1968 as the crucial watershed between the "Christocentric universalism" of the early ecumenical movement and the emergence of a more "trinitarian" or inclusive approach that was "open to humankind and to the creation as a whole by the action of the Spirit," although in point of fact this new secular theological paradigm can be traced back at least as far as a conference in Strasbourg in 1960 of the World Student Christian Federation.[3]

In the new ecumenical missionary paradigm that first attracted widespread notice at Uppsala, the focus was not on inducing non-Christian peoples to accept the lordship of Christ but rather on Christians learning to discern the signs of the liberating and restorative movement of the Holy Spirit, manifesting the love of God to all humankind. Since the Spirit blew wherever she willed, such signs could in principle be found anywhere; the love of the Father for all humans was evidenced through the liberating and humanizing work of the Spirit. However, the latter was no longer thought to be sequentially connected to the explicit confession of Jesus Christ as Lord and Savior. The central theological motif of the new paradigm was the *missio Dei*: mission was being wrestled out of the grasp of Western evangelizing agencies and reconceptualized as an activity of God that was in principle prior to and even independent of the agendas of the churches. The term *missio Dei* had been coined as early as 1934 by Karl Hartenstein, director of the Basel Mission, in an article for a mission magazine surveying the financial crisis currently afflicting German missions and reminding his anxious readers that mission ultimately depended not on human activity but on the sending purpose of God.[4] The concept of *missio Dei* first attained prominence in Protestant ecumenical circles at the Willingen conference of the International Missionary Council in 1952, but it attained its distinctively secular flavor only in the course of the 1960s, culminating in 1967 in a WCC study on the "Missionary Structure of the Congregation" that reached the conclusion that "the old sequence of God–Church–World" was untrue to the biblical witness and needed to be replaced by a new sequence of "God–World–Church" that prioritized the autonomous humanizing and liberating action of God in a world afflicted by oppression and injustice. In this new sequence, Western missions were no more than "transitory forms of obedience to the *missio Dei*," while the church itself was relegated to the status of "a segment of the world, a *postscript* . . . added to the world for the purpose of pointing to and celebrating both Christ's presence and God's ultimate redemption of the whole world."[5]

Raiser's claim that the new liberationist theology of mission was more robustly trinitarian than the implicit Christomonism that it sought to replace was directly challenged in 1994 by the former Presbyterian missionary and bishop in the Church of South India, Lesslie Newbigin (1909–98), who had himself been prominent in the ecumenical movement as the last general secretary of the International Missionary Council from 1959 to 1961 and from 1961 to 1965 as the first director of the WCC's Division of World Mission and Evangelism. In a well-known book review and exchange of articles in the *International Bulletin of Missionary Research* Newbigin employed Reformed theology to pose telling questions against Raiser's endorsement of a mission paradigm that appeared to separate the activity of the Spirit from the work of Christ.[6] Nevertheless, Raiser's critique of "Christocentric universalism" had some historical validity. Both Protestant and Catholic mission theology in the nineteenth and earlier twentieth century had derived the origin of Christian mission narrowly from the parting command of Christ to his disciples, or what evangelical Protestants in the course of the nineteenth century began to term the "Great Commission"; by the early twentieth century they had come to associate this phrase almost exclusively with Matthew 28:18–20.[7] They had also tended to define the goal of mission as the universal confession of Christ as Lord, with comparatively little attention being paid either to the hidden agency of the Spirit or to the achievement of the Father's redemptive purpose, extending to the renewal of all creation. If Christian mission was reduced to what Western Christians could do to "make Jesus King," the planting of churches and educational institutions closely patterned on Western models, funded by Western money, and controlled by Western personnel, inevitably took center stage.

This tendency was all-pervasive throughout the missionary movement in the first half of the twentieth century. It is often perceived to be an epiphenomenon of colonialism, but it had relatively little to do with the possession of formal empire. Missionaries from the United States, a country that liked to think of itself as opposed to colonies on principle, displayed these traits more than most. This was true above all in China, which was both the lynchpin of American Far Eastern policy and the nation that attracted more American Catholic and Protestant missionaries than any other field in the interwar period: in 1942 there were 652 Catholic missionary personnel serving in China, compared with 329 in Oceania, the second-ranking field; for Protestants, the equivalent figures (for 1935–6) were 2,785 in China and 2,006 in India, the second most popular Protestant field.[8] Missionaries from Norway, Sweden, or Switzerland, which were unambiguously non-imperial nations, may have been less susceptible to overtly colonialist sentiments, but they were certainly not immune to the temptations of power and prejudice that assailed all white Europeans in an African or Asian context. From its eighteenth-century origins the Protestant missionary movement had been rooted in an evangelical transnationalism that was never wholly extinguished, even amidst the international conflicts and high colonialism of the twentieth century. American missionaries could be fervent advocates of British colonial rule in Africa. British missionaries could be highly critical of the pragmatic reality of British imperial policy, particularly in areas of Islamic predominance, such as northern Nigeria, where the structures of indirect rule required the cultivation of the goodwill of Muslim authorities. Passionate advocacy of the theological rationale for empire and indignant criticism of the way in which it worked in practice were in fact two sides of the same coin. The complexity of the relationship among Christian ideals, cultural imperialism, and specifically national identities is well illustrated by German Protestant missions in the interwar period. They were well ahead of the game in their perception of the need to plant *Volkskirche*—people's churches—each of them grounded in the local soil of an Asian or African culture, and yet their openness to the concept of ethnically based churches also left them more vulnerable than most to nationalistic and even racist distortions of the faith.[9]

As noted in chapter 3, in the second half of the nineteenth century, the Roman Catholic Church gradually recovered its overseas missionary impetus. New streams of Marian devotion and ultramontane fervor gave birth to a cluster of new missionary orders. In the early decades of the twentieth century, some of these new orders experienced phenomenal growth. The Society of the Divine Word (SVD), was founded in 1875 by a priest from the Rhineland, Arnold Janssen, against the backcloth of Bismarck's *Kulturkampf* against the German Catholic Church. Although most of its missionary force was German, it always drew from a wider international constituency, including Americans and, in the second half of the twentieth century, increasingly large numbers of Filipinos and others from Southeast Asia. Between 1920 and 1932 alone, the total of SVD missionaries grew from 1,783 to 3,782.[10]

Nevertheless, although some of the new orders such as the SVD were transnational in character almost from the beginning, Catholic missionaries as a whole were no less liable—they may even have been *more* liable—to succumb to national loyalties than Protestant ones. One of the most farsighted missionary documents of the century was Benedict XV's 1919 encyclical, *Maximum Illud*, which roundly criticized missionary publications that exalted the nation of the writer more than the kingdom of God. The main target of the encyclical was Catholic missions in China, where, ever since 1858, all Catholic missionaries of whatever nationality carried French passports and came under the protection of the French government. Benedict held out a clear vision of the urgent need to indigenize the priesthood, above all in China; it was a message that the SVD in particular proved reluctant to implement.[11] Although only France was in the premier league of colonial powers, both Portugal and Belgium had substantial African empires, while Italy and Spain belonged to the lower imperial divisions. The universality of a Catholic understanding of the faith could easily fall prey to national ambition. The Catholic bishop of Saigon declared in 1908 that missionaries in Saigon "only have one desire: to serve the influence and interests of France to the best of their abilities."[12] Catholic missionaries were fiercely loyal to their own religious order, and French missionaries gave peculiar loyalty to French religious orders.

The older international orders such as the Dominicans or the Jesuits were divided into national provinces, each of which had exclusive responsibility for a particular foreign mission.[13] Catholic theology traditionally identified the mystical Body of Christ exclusively with the sacred hierarchical institution of the Roman Catholic Church, and hence employed the language of "the missions" to refer to the organized endeavors of the Church under the direction of the Vatican's Sacred Congregation for the Propagation of the Faith (*Propaganda Fide*) to baptize and catechize the inhabitants of the "mission territories." The United States itself remained classified as one of those mission territories until 1908, and was thus a late starter as a Catholic sending nation. In practice it often fell to Catholic missionaries from one European country to bring the inhabitants of a particular territory within the fold of salvation, resulting in a pattern of territorial evangelization by nationally homogeneous ecclesiastical units that was more unusual, though not unknown, in Protestant missions. In Catholic thought before the Second Vatican Council, evangelization was most often conceived as the planting of the sacramental presence of the Catholic Church as an institution, incorporating those of other faiths in the body of Christ, and leading eventually to the establishment of the full Catholic hierarchy.

Evangelization leading to formal incorporation in the Roman Catholic Church was the dominant strand of Catholic mission, but not the only one. No less than their Protestant counterparts, Catholic missions had a noble record of sacrificial humanitarian activity and of campaigning against abuses such as the slave trade. The most celebrated personification of this tradition in the twentieth century was the Albanian nun from Skopje in modern Macedonia, Agnes Gonxha Bojaxhiu—better known as Mother Teresa (1910–97). Sent to Bengal in 1931 by the Sisters of the Institute of the Blessed Virgin Mary (the Loreto Sisters), Mother Teresa's long ministry among the poor of Kolkata's slums drew inspiration from classic Ignatian spirituality and the mystical devotion of the late nineteenth-century French Carmelite, St. Thérèse of Lisieux. The new religious order she founded in 1950, the Missionaries of Charity, became renowned as a form of Catholic mission characterized by pure Christian compassion and a determination to find Christ's presence even in the lives of the poorest and most dejected. By the late 1960s this diminutive nun had acquired a global reputation as an instantly recognizable icon of disinterested humanitarian service, revered by those of all faiths and none. She had her uses to the Vatican as a shining exemplar of Christian identification with the poor who had nothing to do with liberation theology, and was beatified by John Paul II in 2003 and canonized by Pope Francis in September 2016.[14]

Despite their general lack of a strong ecclesiology, conservative Protestants rivaled Rome with their own brand of ecclesiocentrism. The polarizing effect of the fundamentalist controversies of the 1920s and 1930s was to make them wary of the "Social Gospel" and as a result to insist on a narrow definition of Christian mission as an almost entirely future-oriented commission to change the eternal destiny of individual human beings. It was, quite simply, they liked to say, a rescue enterprise to depopulate hell and make heaven as crowded as possible. They also, especially in the United States even to this day, continued to employ the language of "missions" in the plural to describe a clearly delineated sector of church activities aimed at the conversion of non-Christians overseas, but in the Protestant case these were increasingly conducted by numerous voluntary and often nondenominational agencies rather than by ecclesial bodies. With the agencies of mission often bearing no formal relationship to the churches from which the missionaries came, the perennial temptation for evangelical Protestants was to reduce the biblical idea of salvation, not in this case to sacramental incorporation into the one institutional body of Christ, but instead to a willingness by individuals to subscribe to formulaic distillations of the Christian message that qualified one for admission into the visible but anonymous company of the statistical elect.

The most widely used of such evangelistic formulae, "The Four Spiritual Laws" written in 1959 by the American Presbyterian Bill Bright, the founder of Campus Crusade for Christ and published as a booklet from 1965, defined the nature of salvation in highly individualistic terms as the individual's acceptance of God's offer through faith in Christ of "a wonderful plan for your life."[15] However, large sections of the North American evangelical constituency counterbalanced this individualism with an increasing fascination with the phenomenon of "people movements" of group or mass conversion that first attracted serious attention in India in the 1930s.[16] Counting converts—using the new computer technology to plot the progress of people movements and, crucially, to alert mission strategists to where they might appear next—became the specialty of the highly influential church growth school associated with the Institute of Church Growth founded in 1961 by the former Disciples of Christ missionary to India Donald A. McGavran (1897–1990), and located from 1965 at Fuller Theological Seminary at Pasadena, California. Church growth theory was premised on the straightforward empirical observation that conversions were more numerous when no cultural frontiers had to be crossed, and thus discovered that it had some retrospective affinity with the German Romantic *Volkskirche* missiology of the interwar period. The classic work by the German missionary to northern New Guinea and one-time Nazi sympathizer Christian Keysser, *Eine Papuagemeinde* (1929), was republished in English by McGavran in 1980 under the title *A People Reborn;* McGavran's foreword makes clear that he became aware of Keysser's work in about 1958, three years after the publication of his pioneering work of church growth theory, *The Bridges of God.*[17] Conservative Protestant approaches to mission could thus combine an individualistic understanding of salvation with their own forms of preoccupation with the growth of the visible church, and with a greater awareness of cultural difference than they are often given credit for; indeed, church growth theory is open to precisely the opposite accusation, namely that, like German *völkisch* theory before it, it absolutizes and essentializes culture.

The next two sections of the chapter will examine how the Catholic and Protestant churches respectively reconceived their theologies of mission in the final four decades of the century. Particular attention will be devoted to the Second Vatican Council of 1962–65, the Uppsala assembly of the WCC in 1968, and the Lausanne Congress for World Evangelization convened by the Billy Graham Evangelistic Association in 1974. It was not accidental that this process of fundamental revision was concentrated on the 1960s and 1970s, decades that witnessed the rapid dismantling of the Western colonial empires, the emergence of the "Third World" as an ideological bloc, and the highly charged political atmosphere of the Cold War between the Soviet Union and the West. Neither the Catholic nor the Protestant missionary movements were the offspring of colonialism, but both regularly employed the language of global Christian dominion and both tried to use colonial governments to forward their evangelistic objectives. It was thus inevitable that the anticolonial invective of these decades should not leave the churches' overseas missionary activities unscathed. These years were also an era of social and intellectual ferment in European societies. Movements of revolutionary protest against established institutions and their perceived role in the perpetuation of structural injustice and international capitalism swept through university campuses. The historic churches and their governing hierarchies were often caught in the gunfire. Their formulation of their role in the world and even of their message itself could not be unaffected.

II. Reconceiving the Catholic Church and Its Mission: The Second Vatican Council, 1962–65

On January 25, 1959, within three months of his election as pope, John XXIII announced that he planned to convoke not simply a diocesan synod for the Vatican City but also an Ecumenical Council for the entire Catholic Church. This announcement by Angelo Roncalli aroused both surprise and euphoria among the faithful. The First Vatican Council of 1869–70 had so exalted the status of the papacy, whose *ex cathedra* pronouncements on faith and morals it declared to be infallible, that some imagined that there was no longer any place for General Councils of the church. Pope John XXIII's announcement referred to the need "to define clearly and distinguish between what is sacred principle and eternal gospel and what belongs rather to the changing times."[18] Roncalli's vision was one of *aggiornamento*—a renewal that was an updating or modernization. It was an explicitly missionary vision: the pope envisaged the impending Council as "a new Pentecost" that would equip the church for a new mission to the modern world.[19] His first encyclical issued in June 1959 also spoke openly of his hopes that the Council would promote a process of ecumenical convergence—that it would be such "a spectacle of truth, unity, and love that when seen by those separated from this Apostolic See will be for them a gentle invitation to seek and enter into that unity for which Jesus Christ prayed so ardently to his heavenly Father."[20] Such statements of intent alarmed conservatives within the curia and more widely within the church, and the protracted process of preparing the agenda for the

Council through its "ante-preparatory" and then preparatory phases was characterized by running battles between the old guard in the curia and those who shared John XXIII's hopes for *aggiornamento*.

In a radio broadcast on September 11, 1962, a month before the Council opened, the pope reiterated his insistence that its primary purpose was evangelization. He urged that in the light of the challenges being presented by "the underdeveloped countries," the Council must present the church "as it is and wishes to be, as the Church of all, and particularly as the Church of the poor."[21] The Council met in four separate sessions, extending from October 1962 to December 1965. The much-loved John XXIII presided only over the first session, which concluded on December 8, 1962. He was already a sick man, and died of cancer on June 3, 1963. The remaining three sessions of the Council were presided over by Paul VI, Giovanni Montini, archbishop of Milan and the first cardinal appointed by John XXIII. Though he lacked the personal charisma of his predecessor, and was instinctively more of a conservative, Paul VI maintained the reforming momentum initiated by John XXIII, and made the College of Cardinals more representative of the church worldwide, thus breaking the stranglehold exercised by the Italian bishops over elections to the papacy.

The First Vatican Council had attempted to shore up the Catholic Church as an embattled institution encircled by the incoming political and intellectual tide of the modern world. Its primary defensive strategy was to assert the unique character of the Roman Church as a sacred monarchy in which unchallengeable divine authority flowed downwards from the pope as the Vicar of Christ, through the bishops as the pope's representatives to the priesthood, and eventually to the faithful. This heavily institutional and hierarchical view of the Catholic Church still had its staunch defenders at Vatican II, and is reflected in sections of the Council's decrees. But throughout the course of the Council this understanding of the church was repeatedly subverted by an alternative, more collegial and confident vision of the church as the missionary people of God, a transnational fellowship of the faithful called in their entirety to take the gospel into the world under the leadership of the bishops as the descendants of the apostles. The two visions were divergent, if not incompatible. The presence of these two competing ecclesiologies within the Vatican II documents is in no small part responsible for the battle for the heart of the Catholic Church that has been waged ever since.

Thus the proposed text of *Lumen Gentium*, the dogmatic constitution on the Church adopted in the third session of the Council, delighted progressives in article 21 of its third chapter by deriving not simply the right to teach but crucially also the governmental powers of a bishop directly from his episcopal consecration rather than by delegation from the pope's supreme jurisdictional authority.[22] Paul VI received two separate representations from conservatives, expressing grave concern that Chapter III as it stood would make the church no longer monarchical and reduce the pope to a mere *primus inter pares*. They secured some concessions and a note of clarification from a pope who was anxious to retain the support of the minority of traditionalist bishops.[23] In its final form the constitution in articles 22 and 25 emphasized that the college of bishops had no authority unless it were exercised in relation to their head in the papacy, and reaffirmed the Vatican I statements that the pope had "full, supreme and universal power over the whole Church" which he can "always exercise unhindered," and that he did not require the consent of the bishops for his *ex cathedra* definitions to be infallible.[24] Catholic commentators tend to highlight the "revolutionary" nature of article 21, and quietly downplay the more conservative tenor of articles 22 and 25.[25]

Vatican II gave unprecedented emphasis to the place of the laity in the church, yet it was, of course, a council made up of more than 2,500 male and celibate bishops. There was a small group of eight male lay "auditors" whose name indicated their limited function. In the third session their number was increased to twenty-one, and eight women religious and seven single laywomen were invited to join them; in the fourth session one married couple joined the auditors. In a vain attempt to segregate them from the fathers who congregated during the coffee breaks at two bars known as the Bar-Abbas and the Bar-Jonah, the women were given their own coffee bar that was soon dubbed the Bar-Nun. The auditors were not permitted to speak in the council debates, but in October 1964 a request was received from the Commission on the lay apostolate that a layman should be allowed to speak, and a British lay Catholic, Patrick Keegan, was then permitted to speak in English on the subject, though only after the formal discussion had been concluded. The auditors then made a further request that in the debate on *Gaudium et Spes* (on the Church in the World), that permission be given for a Spanish woman Pilar Bellosillo (1913–2003), president of the World Union of Catholic Women's Organizations, to address the Council on the role of the laity in tackling the problem of world poverty. The Council moderators discussed the request, appealed to the Pauline text "Let the women keep silence in the churches," and refused; a lay Argentine male spoke instead. Not until the third session of the Council were women even admitted to the public masses that accompanied the Council. Cardinal Suenens of Belgium (1904–96), one of the most influential progressive voices in the Council, commented acerbically during the second session, "Women, if I am not mistaken, make up one half of humanity." Despite such pleas, on the place of women in the church the Council remained obstinately conservative.[26]

Probably the most obvious transformation made by the Council to the public face of Catholicism was the encouragement given for the first time to celebrate the mass in the vernacular. The issue of language arose first in relation to the conduct of the Council's own business. This had to be conducted entirely in Latin, with no simultaneous translation allowed, to the dismay of many of the bishops from outside Europe, who hesitated to speak and struggled to follow the flow of debate. The use of Latin was also objectionable to the bishops of the Eastern Catholic churches, particularly the Melkite bishops of Syria and Lebanon, who had never regarded themselves as part of Latin Christendom. To those outside western Europe, the continuing use of Latin seemed to symbolize the anachronistic dependence of the Catholic Church on a medieval European and originally Roman culture[27]; to many others influenced by the twentieth-century liturgical renewal movement, especially German-speaking Catholics, it was equally unacceptable. Traditionalists maintained that only the common use of Latin in the liturgy could adequately express the unity of the church across all nations and cultures, that it alone had the precision to convey the subtleties of Christian dogma, and that adoption of the vernacular would lead to doctrinal confusion. On this issue John XXIII initially appeared to be on the side of the conservatives; he justified the compulsion to use Latin in the Council on the grounds that it was the language of unity, and before the Council opened had defended the use of Latin in the liturgy on a similar basis.[28] Nevertheless, the first schema to be considered and adopted by the Council was that on the sacred liturgy.

In its final form, promulgated by Paul VI on December 4, 1963, the schema faced both ways. Its crucial article 47 began by reiterating that "the use of the Latin language is to be preserved in the Latin rites," yet immediately went on to declare that the bishops' conferences in different nations had the right to decide whether, and to what extent, the vernacular should be used in the liturgy, subject only to the "confirmation" of the Holy See.[29] The dam had been breached. No longer would the liturgy of the Catholic Church automatically be unintelligible to the majority of the faithful. The consequences for the inculturation of Catholicism in the southern hemisphere were incalculable.

The Catholic Church had stood apart from, and maintained general hostility to, the twentieth-century ecumenical movement that had developed out of practical cooperation between Protestant missions. Vatican II marked the beginning of the end of such isolationism. In June 1960 John XXIII established the Secretariat for Christian Unity as one of the commissions that would prepare the way for the Council; it would outlive the Council, being renamed in 1988 as the Pontifical Council for Christian Unity. He also soon made it clear that observers from other Christian communions would be welcome at the Council. The principle of ecumenical reciprocity implied that the conventional ban on Catholics attending assemblies of the World Council of Churches had been lifted, and five Catholic observers duly took part at the New Delhi Assembly in November–December 1961. At the first session of the Vatican Council forty-six observers from other churches were in attendance. By the fourth session there were 106 non-Catholics present. Over the whole life of the Council, 192 non-Catholics attended, either as observers or guests. They represented every major Christian communion except for the Baptists (the Baptist World Alliance declined the Vatican's invitation to send delegates). In the third session there was even an Assemblies of God pastor, the South African David du Plessis, the only Pentecostal leader who was then prepared to participate in global ecumenical assemblies. The French Dominican priest Yves Congar (1905–95), who probably wielded more influence than anyone else behind the scenes on the wording of the Council's decrees, commented that the presence of non-Catholics at the Council symbolically marked "the end of the Counter-Reformation."[30]

That Vatican II should modify the previous Catholic position on the status of other churches was not a foregone conclusion. The preparation of the schema on the Church was dogged by running battles between progressives, led by the Secretariat for Christian Unity, and the conservative rear guard, who controlled the Council's Theological Commission. In the first session of the Council the conservatives, led by the Dutch bishop Sebastian Tromp, succeeded in producing a text of the schema that asserted unambiguously that the church founded by Christ simply *is* the Roman Catholic Church. In contrast, the final text of *Lumen Gentium* as adopted in the third session, affirmed that the one Church of Christ *"subsists in"* the Catholic Church governed by the successor of St Peter. This minor adjustment in wording left the door open—even if only by an inch—to the recognition that other churches might indeed be reckoned as *churches*, part of the Body of Christ.[31] The following article spoke of the church as a messianic people whose goal was the extension of the kingdom of God inaugurated by the coming of Christ and to be perfected at the end of time. Church and kingdom were being distinguished in a way not seen in Catholic history since the early middle ages.[32] These were significant concessions, yet at other points in the Council the ecumenical observers found themselves dismayed by the reassertion of traditional Roman positions. The Decree on Ecumenism, for example, had until an eleventh-hour intervention by Paul VI, stated boldly that the "separated brethren" "at the prompting of the Holy Spirit . . . *find* God in the Holy Scriptures"; after the pope's intervention the text read: "While invoking the Holy Spirit, they *seek* in these very scriptures God as He speaks to them in Christ."[33] Non-Catholic Christians had been reduced by papal fiat from finders to seekers. Such interventions by Paul VI perplexed and depressed the ecumenical observers, leading them to speculate that he may have fallen into the clutches of the old guard opposed to change. In reality, Paul was less of a traditionalist than a conciliator, anxious above all to keep the church united.[34]

Most of the Council's decrees left the Catholic Church poised on the cusp between traditional and "progressive" stances. The progressive majority among the fathers won enough battles for subsequent liberal Catholics to be able to find plausible endorsement of their aspirations in the Council's statements, though the decrees do not always bear the full weight of reformist interpretation that later generations of liberal Catholics wish to place on them. Equally, however, the conservative minority succeeded in inserting enough of their traditional formulae in the texts for the outcome of later battles to be far from certain. These ambiguities are nowhere better illustrated than in what the Council had to say—in reality not that much—about other religions. *Nostra Aetate*, the Declaration on the Relationship of the Church to Non-Christian Religions, was at 1,117 words the shortest of the Council's sixteen decrees. Its primary concern was to redefine the church's problematic relationship to the Jews, by affirming Christian indebtedness to the Jewish tradition, and deploring antisemitism "at any time and from any source," though it stopped short of expressing any apology for the church's own part in that sorry history.[35] One article in the decree was specifically devoted to Islam, and Hinduism and Buddhism each received a few lines in the second article of the decree. More generally, the Declaration made the unquantifiable statement that the church "rejects nothing of what is true and holy" in other religions, which were said often to "reflect a ray of that Truth which enlightens all men."[36] Such Johannine language about Christ as the light who enlightens all humanity was scattered throughout the Council decrees, but the extent to which such enlightenment had salvific value was far from clear. *Ad Gentes*, the decree on the church's missionary activity, was couched in more robustly conservative terms, though it did urge the duty of missionaries to uncover the "seeds of the Word" that "lie hidden" in the national and religious traditions of all peoples, a task which called for "sincere and patient dialogue."[37] Perhaps most significantly, *Lumen Gentium* article 16 held out the possibility of salvation for "those who do not know the Gospel of Christ or His Church" yet who sincerely seek God and to do his will, according to the dictates of their conscience.[38]

Whether such fragmentary hints and qualified statements amount, as one recent theological commentator has claimed, to a coherent and radical doctrinal thesis of "Jesus Christ and the Holy Spirit being actively present everywhere to enlighten and save all people" is more debatable.[39] A Council that held out only tentative hopes that members of other Christian communions might be counted as members of the one salvific body of Christ is unlikely to have intended to convey the message that the Holy Spirit was *ordinarily* at work in all other religions, outside the boundaries of *any* church, bringing their adherents to universal salvation.

On the theology of salvation, as on ecclesiology, the Second Vatican Council was thus less radical than some subsequent commentators have chosen to imagine. Where it was undoubtedly revolutionary, however, was in the last and longest of its decrees, on the Church in the Modern World. *Gaudium et Spes* abandoned almost entirely the Vatican I mentality of a church under siege from the world, and spoke instead in terms of a common humanity that possessed rights deriving from the status of all human beings as those made in the image of God. The Catholic Church, which ever since the French Revolution had regarded human rights as a godless notion hostile to Christian dogma, was now prepared to assert that the human person has universal rights which are "inviolable" because they stem from the "sublime dignity" originally given to humans in the divine created order and now restored in Christ, the perfect new man.[40] The gospel proclaims "the freedom of the sons of God," and "rejects all bondage resulting from sin." By virtue of the gospel entrusted to her, therefore, the church is committed to the promotion of the common good of the social order, a common good that is built on justice, and to the proclamation of the rights of man.[41] Although *Gaudium et Spes* did not use all the language that would shortly become typical of theologies of liberation, here, in the Vatican itself, were laid out the essential theological resources on which such theologies could subsequently draw.[42] Perhaps the greatest significance of the Second Vatican Council was that it marked the point at which the Roman Catholic Church, the seeming archetype of ecclesiastical conservatism, began to take sympathetic note of the concerns for justice and liberation that were being voiced by educated opinion in the non-Western world. In this respect, a broad parallelism can be discerned between Vatican II and the two very different Protestant assemblies that followed it, at Uppsala in 1968 and Lausanne in 1974.

III. Reconceiving Protestant Missions: The Uppsala Assembly of 1968 and the Lausanne Congress of 1974

Protestant missionary thought since the mid-nineteenth century had enshrined as the supreme goal of the missionary enterprise the planting of "native" churches that would be self-governing, financially self-sustaining, and self-propagating—the famous "Three-Self" theory that had been most fully articulated by the Evangelical Anglican Henry Venn and the American Congregationalist Rufus Anderson. Such an objective was in principle radical in its commitment to the creation of churches in the non-Western world that would be free of Western control, though it has to be said that until the era of decolonization that followed the Second World War, Western missions were better at enunciating the theory than they were at implementing it in practice. During the 1950s and 1960s, as Protestant missions scrambled to effect full devolution to indigenous churches, first in Asia and then in Africa, before the privileged position the missions had enjoyed under the colonial regimes was swept away by the tidal surges of decolonization, the status of the church as the central goal of mission ironically came under increasing theological question.

The most influential source of criticism of "church-centric" mission was a Dutch missiologist named Johannes (Hans) C. Hoekendijk (1912–75). The child of missionary parents serving in western Java, Hoekendijk himself spent a period as a missionary in Indonesia before becoming secretary, first of the Netherlands Missionary Council (1947–49) and then of the Department of Evangelism of the World Council of Churches (1949–53). He then held academic posts at the University of Utrecht from 1953 to 1965 and subsequently at Union Theological Seminary in New York, where he remained until his death.[43] Hoekendijk took a radically eschatological view both of the church and of mission itself. His doctoral dissertation on "Church and *Volk* in German missiology" (1948) was deeply critical of German mission theorists' elevation of the Romantic idea of the *Volk* into a pseudo-theological category. The concept of "church" could not be identified with any natural form but should rather be understood functionally and eschatologically, as simply a means to the end of the establishment of God's saving kingdom in the world. Hoekendijk first elaborated these ideas publicly in a paper, entitled "The Church in missionary thinking"

prepared for the International Missionary Council's conference at Willingen in Germany in 1952, but they did not secure general acceptance
among the delegates. The church, he maintained, was "an illegitimate centre" for mission, and any mission strategy premised on the centrality of the
church was "bound to go astray."[44] However, by 1960 the currents of progressive theological thought were flowing in a direction more sympathetic
to Hoekendijk's secular approach to mission. At the World Student Christian Federation conference held in Strasbourg in July Hoekendijk received
an enthusiastic reception when he described the coming of Christ as a
secular event, "an event in the world and for the world," and hence Christianity itself as "a secular movement" dedicated to the goal of restoring
human beings "to normal human manhood."[45] Hoekendijk was a decisive
influence on the two study groups, one European and one North American, that produced the 1967 WCC report on the "Missionary Structure of
the Congregation," *The Church for Others*, cited in the first section of this
chapter. The report roundly repudiated any idea of proselytization, which
it saw as "the very opposite of mission." Instead "the world must be allowed to provide the agenda for the churches." Even Christian worship was
described as "not something that happens between the Church and God,
but between the world and God, the Church serving as the instrument."[46]

This radical secularization of the idea of Christian mission reached its
apogee at the Fourth Assembly of the World Council of Churches at Uppsala in July 1968. Norman Goodall, the English Congregationalist who
edited the Assembly's report, commented that "It was not only recognized
that—as it was often expressed—the world was writing the agenda for the
meeting; the right of the world to do this was largely taken for granted." The
most obvious feature of the Assembly to Goodall was its preoccupation—
"at times, almost, its obsession—with the revolutionary ferment of our
time" whose political and ideological upheavals "broke in again and again
with the effect of a thunder-clap and lightning-flash." Another commentator, the American Lutheran Arne Sovik, referred to the clash in the assembly between "the restrictive and limited definition of mission as the
proclamation of the saving word of Christ's redemption" and "the modern
and still not well-defined concept of mission as 'discovering God's action in
the world'."[47] Uppsala divided the Protestant community as never before.
Lesslie Newbigin, Bishop of Madras in the Church of South India since
1965, who had himself been deeply involved in the ecumenical movement
as general secretary of the International Missionary Council and then as
director of the WCC's Division of World Mission and Evangelism, was not
unsympathetic to an emphasis on the secular, having himself published in

1966 a series of lectures entitled *Honest Religion for Secular Man*.[48] Yet he found the 1968 assembly a "shattering" and disillusioning experience. The evident polarization between a social radicalism that appeared to be divorced from the love of God and an evangelical pietism that seemed complacent about the demands of justice alarmed Newbigin, who in the wake of Uppsala began to move toward an emphasis on the need to interrogate the assumptions of post-Enlightenment Western secularity on the basis of the distinctive principles of the Christian gospel.[49]

The Uppsala assembly had more than rhetorical significance. In the following year the executive committee of the WCC, resolved, under the leadership of its moderator M. M. Thomas (1916–96), a leading Indian theologian from the Mar Thoma Church, to set up a Programme to Combat Racism (PCR). As chapter 11 will make clear, the creation of the PCR was a sign that the urgent issues of racial justice raised by the civil rights movement in the United States were now being applied on a global stage. Most controversially, the PCR gave a series of modest grants to armed liberation movements seeking to overthrow the minority white regimes in South Africa, Namibia, and Zimbabwe (Rhodesia) and the Portuguese colonial governments in Angola and Mozambique. Although the grants specified that the money was not to be used for military purposes, the PCR attracted a great deal of criticism from individual Christians and churches who felt it morally inappropriate for the World Council to endorse armed resistance movements. Individual critics included Michael Ramsey, the archbishop of Canterbury, who consistently maintained that the guerrilla movements were insufficiently organized and responsible to meet the necessarily strict ethical criteria for a just rebellion against tyrannical power.[50] Ecclesiastical opposition came from, among others, the Salvation Army, a founding member of the World Council, which in 1978 suspended, and in 1981 finally withdrew, its membership in protest.

Many conservative Christians in the northern hemisphere regarded the PCR as evidence that the WCC had departed from Christian orthodoxy and fatally succumbed to the political pressures of the secular and anticolonial age. For Billy Graham, who was by now the acknowledged figurehead of the world evangelical movement, the Uppsala assembly and the PCR pointed to the sorry fact that "There is a vacuum developing in the world church. Radical theology has had its heyday." In response, between December 1971 and March 1972 Graham and his aides in the Billy Graham Evangelistic Association formulated initial plans for a world congress dedicated to the promotion of Christian mission in the traditional evangelistic sense, a congress in which "every participant must be totally and thoroughly evangelical" and at least half should be under the age of forty.[51] The resulting International Congress on Evangelization, which in July 1974 assembled a total of 2,473 evangelical Protestants in Lausanne, Switzerland, would, however, reveal that even conservative evangelicals were not exempt from the impact of the social and political ferment that in different ways had shaped the agenda both at Vatican II and at Uppsala in 1968. One thousand of the delegates at the Lausanne Congress were from the "majority world." Three of these southern hemisphere voices exercised an influence on the gathering out of all proportion to their numbers. All three were Baptists, of the same denominational affiliation as Graham himself, though of a markedly different stamp. The first two of the three had also been deeply involved in evangelical ministry among university students in Latin America, and as such had witnessed at first hand the magnetic attraction that Marxist ideology then exerted on educated youth in a continent marked by enormous disparities of wealth between rich and poor and the general impotence of liberal capitalist strategies of "development" to solve the problem.

The first was C. René Padilla, who was born in Ecuador in 1932 but lived in Argentina. He contributed one of eleven precirculated papers on the topic "Evangelism and the World," and followed it up with an address on the same topic. His paper insisted that the gospel has cosmic as well as personal dimensions, and openly attacked American forms of "culture Christianity" that reduced the Christian message to a form of cheap grace, a marketed product guaranteeing the consumer "the highest values— *success* in life and personal *happiness* now and forever." He criticized the strategists of the church growth movement for treating the task of world evangelization as a mere mathematical calculation of how to "produce the greatest number of Christians at the least possible cost in the shortest possible time," employing the new technological wizardry of computers to solve the problem.[52] Padilla's paper caused "a minor sensation" and was attacked as a "caricature." The address that followed, pointedly delivered in Spanish rather than English (and simultaneously translated), continued on the same theme, and "really set the congress alight," attracting the warmest applause of any speaker so far.[53] In response to those who had questioned why he had attacked the identification of the gospel with the American way of life but not with other cultures, Padilla replied that because of the predominant role of the United States both in world affairs and in missionary endeavor, "this particular form of Christianity, as no other today, has a powerful influence far beyond the borders of that nation." Still more fundamentally, Padilla answered the charge that he was

confusing evangelism with political action by insisting that "the imperative of the evangelical ethic forms an indissoluble whole with the indicative of the Gospel."[54]

The second majority world contribution to attract particular comment
was by a Peruvian, Samuel Escobar, who, like Padilla, had extensive experience of evangelism among university students. Escobar's precirculated
paper on "Evangelism and man's search for freedom, justice and fulfil-
ment" warned against the danger of making Christianity the official ideology of the West in the same way as communism had become the official ideology of the Eastern bloc. Like Padilla, Escobar also identified the
temptation currently facing evangelicalism as one of withdrawal from the
ethical demands of a discipleship lived out in active engagement with a
social context in which injustice was rife.[55] In his Congress address, Escobar boldly took the text dear to liberation theologians, the "Nazareth
manifesto" of Luke 4: 18–19, and insisted that it could not be spiritual-
ized in a world where millions were poor, broken-hearted, captive, blind,
and bruised. While he emphasized that the freedom of which the gospel
speaks is not simply freedom from human masters, he went on to argue
that "the heart which has been made free with the freedom of Christ cannot be indifferent to the human longings for deliverance from economic,
political, or social oppression." He pointed out that many of the countries
that had succumbed to a violent revolution conducted on Marxist principles were those where Christianity had allowed itself to be identified with
the interests of the ruling class.[56] The British Anglican leader John R. W.
Stott (1921–2011), whose exceptional stature in the evangelical world owed
much to his global ministry among university students through the Inter-
Varsity movement, later described Escobar's address as having "put the cat
among the pigeons."[57]

The third radical voice from Latin America audible at Lausanne was
that of Orlando Costas (1942–87), a Puerto Rican aged only thirty-two. In
one of two papers prepared for the Congress, Costas rendered the message of Padilla and Escobar still more explicit by arguing that the "Great
Commission" had an inescapably structural dimension: to evangelize "in-
depth" meant bringing the gospel to bear, not simply on individuals, but
on the unjust socioeconomic structures of the present age. In language
whose radical connotations may have escaped many of his readers, Costas also borrowed the term, coined by the Brazilian educationalist Paulo
Freire in his classic work *Pedagogy of the Oppressed*, to describe the process of *conscientization* which had to take place if ordinary Christian believers were to be mobilized to apply the gospel to all areas of their lives.[58]

Not being a platform speaker, Costas was less visible at Lausanne than Padilla or Escobar, yet it is significant that the American evangelical theologian Carl Henry, writing in *Christianity Today*, identified him as the leader of the most radical group among the Latin American evangelicals at the congress, distinguished by his accusation that "American evangelical missionary support is tainted by links to imperialistic culture and vested economic interests."[59]

The concerns voiced by Padilla, Escobar, and Costas, were shared in large measure by the Theology and Radical Discipleship group, an informal group whose fringe meetings attracted more than 500 participants, mainly of the younger generation. It represented both the new Latin American evangelicals and some more radical evangelicals in the North. It succeeded in obtaining significant amendments to the Congress statement that became known as the Lausanne Covenant, which was in most respects a resounding reaffirmation of the traditional understanding of Christian mission as the call to conversion to Christ. Before the final version of the Covenant appeared, the Theology and Radical Discipleship Group circulated an alternative statement of its own, "A Response to Lausanne," affirming the cosmic scope of redemption and repudiating any attempt "to drive a wedge between evangelism and social action" as "demonic."[60] John Stott, who was responsible for the final drafts of the Covenant, incorporated key phrases from the Response in the Covenant, notably the potentially radical emphasis that "those who proclaim the cross must be continually marked by the cross." Stott also promoted the section on Christian social responsibility from paragraph 7 to paragraph 5, and significantly strengthened in its phrasing. Despite being instinctively a social conservative from a highly privileged English social and educational background (Rugby School and Trinity College, Cambridge),[61] Stott, more than any other leading figure at Lausanne, took up the concerns of those who spoke for evangelicals in the majority world. As an impeccably orthodox conservative evangelical himself, he was nevertheless able to interpret these concerns sympathetically to those, in the United States in particular, who were instinctively fearful that the new radical evangelicalism was simply a reincarnation of the old "social gospel" which they believed had led inexorably to what they felt was the spiritual bankruptcy of the WCC. There is little doubt that Stott's own capacity to endorse the concerns of the southern evangelicals was enhanced by the fact that the two leading spokesmen—Padilla and Escobar—were trusted leaders in the evangelical student movements which were so close to his own heart.

IV. Mission in a Postcolonial Age

Although the strongly evangelistic understanding of Christian mission exemplified in the Lausanne Covenant stands in marked contrast with the
predominantly secular emphasis of the Uppsala Assembly of 1968, the divergence would have been more striking still if it had not been for the three
voices from Latin America and the wider body of opinion represented by
the Theology and Radical Discipleship Group. Uppsala 1968 revealed the
significant—though far from complete—extent to which the predominantly secular understanding of mission pioneered by Hans Hoekendijk
had captured the allegiance of ecumenically-minded Protestants in an age
of mounting hostility to Western colonialism and multiplying episodes of
student revolt on university campuses. To a greater or lesser extent, varying according to the theological inclinations of successive WCC General
Secretaries, that understanding of the mission of the Church has remained
orthodoxy within the World Council of Churches ever since. Vatican II in
1962–5 and the Lausanne Congress in 1974 equally laid bare the theological bifurcation between conservatives and progressives that had simultaneously opened up among both Roman Catholics and evangelical Protestants. Nevertheless, both the Catholic and evangelical constituencies
retained to the close of the century a much stronger commitment to the
extension of the institutional church as the divinely appointed vehicle of
salvation than did more liberal Protestants, who tended to go with the flow
of the passionate hostility to established institutions that marked so many
new cultural movements in the late 1960s and 1970s. Yet both the Catholic Church and large sections of the evangelical movement also began to
display unmistakable signs that they too had taken note of the mood of
the age.

In the context of the revolutionary anticolonial and antiestablishment
sentiment of the 1960s and 1970s the "secular" issues of justice and liberation had forced their way to the top of the agenda of Christian theologies
of mission to an extent that was unprecedented in Christian history. Previously unquestioned aspects of theological tradition, whether Catholic or
evangelical Protestant, came under increasing critical scrutiny as a result.
As they did so, the theological gulf between conservative and liberal ecumenical approaches to Christian mission that had opened up in the 1960s
began gradually to narrow. By the end of the century, at least some liberal
Christians in the West, confronted with the stark evidence of plummeting
membership rolls and a critical paucity of recruits to the ordained ministry, were once again rather more ready to accept that evangelism must

form at least part of the core of the mission of the church. Equally, a growing proportion of theologically conservative Catholics and Protestants no
longer needed convincing that the gospel of the kingdom of God which
Jesus came to proclaim must include an insistence on the social values of
the kingdom, and hence on the priority of justice. Christian mission would
never be quite the same again.

CHAPTER TEN

Good News to the Poor?

THEOLOGIES OF LIBERATION IN LATIN AMERICA AND PALESTINE

I. The Priority of Praxis

Liberation theology was one of the stranger stepchildren of the Cold War. Ever since the genesis of the modern political terminology of "Left" and "Right" during the French Revolution, the churches, and the Roman Catholic Church above all, had more often been found on the Right than on the Left of the political spectrum. Ideologies that vested sovereignty in the populace challenged Christian claims that sovereignty belonged to God alone and descended through his appointed representatives in church and state. The concept of the citizen as the holder of inalienable human rights, among them the right to hold monarchs and other holders of power to account, subverted traditional Christian assumptions of the subject who owed absolute obedience to constituted authority. As the new notions of popular sovereignty transmuted in the course of the nineteenth century into the harder-edged class-based politics of socialism, the choices confronting the churches became more momentous. Independent-minded Christians in France, Germany, Britain and the United States took up the idea of "social Christianity" as a moderate Christian variant of socialism quite widely in the later nineteenth century. In much of Catholic Europe, notably in Italy, lay Catholics organized themselves under the banner of "Catholic Action" in a variety of confraternities and associations designed to reinforce Catholic loyalties among the working classes and young people. Nevertheless, among those who held ecclesiastical power, the predominant view of socialism itself remained a hostile one. The infamous

Syllabus of Errors of 1864, in which Pope Pius IX assembled a gloomy compendium of previous papal pronouncements against the characteristic errors of the modern age, ranked socialism and communism alongside "secret societies," "biblical societies" and "clerico-liberal societies" as "pests," forms of ideological vermin that ought to be exterminated from the dark corners of Christendom. In the new European political landscape fashioned by the First World War and its aftermath, the political alignments of the papacy for the next half-century were dictated above all by persistent anxieties about the threat posed to Christianity by communism.

At first sight, therefore, it might seem surprising that it was in the 1960s and 1970s, at the height of the Cold War between the communist East and the capitalist West, that a movement should arise within Christian theology whose chief concern was to align the historic institutions of the churches unambiguously and radically with the poor and oppressed. Liberation theology drew, albeit very selectively, from Marxist ideology to construct an approach to Christianity that turned on their head many previous assumptions about what Christian theology was. Instead of defining theology as the ordered pursuit of understanding the eternal being and salvific activity of God, theologies of liberation prioritized first committed action and then empirical reflection in response to the condition of impoverished human beings in their particular social and political contexts. In a shift that turned on its head the materialist critique of religion offered by the nineteenth-century thinker Ludwig Feuerbach, theology was decisively reoriented toward anthropology—the study of God could best be pursued through the study of man. Instead of beginning with the revelatory authority of sacred text or ecclesiastical tradition, theological activity now took its starting point from observed social realities within the historical process. "Praxis" was the new absolute to which theology must respond. In the much-cited words from the opening of Gustavo Gutiérrez's ground-breaking work, *A Theology of Liberation*: "Theology is reflection, a critical attitude. Theology follows; it is the second step. What Hegel used to say about philosophy can likewise be applied to theology: it rises only at sundown."[1]

In the new liberationist order of salvation, therefore, social context was logically prior to sacred text. The present human condition was necessarily prior to the wisdom of Christian tradition, which was relevant only to the extent that it illuminated that human condition. The very notion of Christian salvation was re-defined. Instead of being conceived as redemption through the saving work of Christ from the power and eternal consequences of humanity's sinful rebellion against God, salvation was increasingly understood in this-worldly terms: salvation for the oppressed could come only through their self-conscious participation in the historical process of liberation, the struggle to create a just society and a new humanity.

Forged within the crucible of a postwar Latin America marked by mushrooming urban slums, brutal military juntas and mass student protests, liberation theology established a new model of doing theology that was subsequently taken up and amended by contextual theologians elsewhere, notably in Africa, Asia, and Palestine. In 1977 Juan Luis Segundo (1925–96), the Uruguayan Jesuit who ranks second only to Gutiérrez among the Catholic architects of liberation theology, was able to claim that the new direction taken by the theology of liberation in Latin America was "irreversible."[2] By the late 1980s the essence of the model had become so widely adopted that supporters of the movement were emboldened to claim that the theological agenda had been changed irrevocably, for all time. Over a period of five weeks in the summer of 1989, a group of more than 100 theologians from all continents gathered at the New York headquarters of the Catholic Foreign Mission Society of America (better known as the Maryknoll Fathers and Sisters) for an extended Summer Institute of Justice and Peace convened in honor of the recognized father of liberation theology, the Peruvian Dominican priest, Gustavo Gutiérrez (1928–). They were simultaneously marking his sixtieth birthday, the thirtieth anniversary of his ordination to the priesthood, and the fifteenth anniversary of the publication by the Maryknoll press, Orbis Books, of the English translation of Gutiérrez's *A Theology of Liberation*, first published in Spanish in Lima in 1971 under the title *Teología de la Liberacíon: Perspectivas*.

The introduction to the collected papers presented during this celebration, written by Otto Maduro, a Venezuelan-born scholar at Drew University, even went so far as to assert that liberation theologies were becoming "the point of reference for all other discourse about God and religion."[3] Ironically the autumn of 1989 would witness a series of popular revolutions in Eastern Europe that terminated the communist regimes of Poland, Hungary, East Germany, Bulgaria, Czechoslovakia, and Romania, and formed the writing on the wall for the survival of the Soviet Union, which finally broke up in December 1991. In academic circles theologies of liberation would comfortably survive the fact that the masses of Eastern Europe had so widely repudiated Marxist philosophy as the source of their subjugation to totalitarian governments, but in the post-1989 ideological climate such theologies would never again carry quite the same instantaneous and near-universal moral authority. As the Cold War came to an end, the star of liberation theology waned, increasingly eclipsed by neo-Pentecostal theologies of the Spirit that took a very different route to the goal of salvation for the poor. This chapter seeks to explain why it was that liberation theology was born and able to flourish very widely in the apparently uncongenial environment of the Cold War. The answer is fourfold.

First, the theological architects of liberation were able to draw on wider trends in social and political theology observable from the late 1960s. Chief among these were the progressive strands of Catholic social teaching emanating from Vatican II and the pontificate of Paul VI. Of the 2,778 fathers invited to the first session of the Council, 601 (21.6 percent) came from Latin America, which was second only to Western Europe in the size of its delegation. In aggregate, bishops from dioceses in Africa, Asia, Latin America, the Arab world, or Oceania accounted for no less than 45.8 percent of the total.[4] Although their presence made a significant contribution to the strength of "liberal" opinion apparent at the Council, relatively few of them were indigenes, and the principal drivers of ecclesiastical reform at the Council were Europeans.

The experience of attending Vatican II had a far greater formative impact on indigenous bishops from Latin America, Asia, or Africa than their presence had on the outcomes of the Council. The sources of the new model of theology were not, however, confined to the Catholic tradition. Latin American liberation theologians drew heavily on European political theologies of hope, secularity, and humanization, which were the products of self-critical Christian contemplation on the apparent impotence of the churches to resist the secularization of northern European societies. Some of these were Catholic—for example, Johann Baptist Metz's (b. 1928) *Theology of the World*, published in English translation in 1969.[5] But perhaps the most important was Protestant, namely the Lutheran theologian Jürgen Moltmann's (b. 1926) *Theology of Hope*, published in English translation in 1967.[6] To this extent liberation theology was a creative reworking in a southern hemisphere context of a set of ideas crafted in the north. The context in which much liberation theology was written was indeed one of extreme urban impoverishment: Gutiérrez wrote most of his work from his home in Rimac, a slum area of Lima. It is often claimed that liberation theology is "not primarily academic discourse" but a genuinely church-generated theology.[7] It is portrayed as a home-spun method of action and reflection manufactured, not in a university lecture hall, but in the Base Ecclesial Communities (CEBs), the lay-led groups of reflection on the contemporary meaning of biblical texts which by the 1980s could be found in myriad locations in the back streets of the burgeoning cities

of Latin America. In reality, however, liberation theology was most enthusiastically taken up by expatriate missionary priests and by a select group
of European-trained theological advisers to the Latin American bishops.[8]
Their thinking was shaped by the enforced missionary exodus from China
after 1949, an experience that carried the unmistakable message that the
church could no longer afford to be perceived as the inveterate enemy of
socialism. The CEBs were not so much the cradle of liberation theology
as neighborhood workshops in which the urban poor were handed hermeneutical tools originally fashioned in Europe to guide their reflection
from the scriptures on the God who takes the side of the enslaved and oppressed. The most important of these hermeneutical tools was the idea of
"conscientization," a concept developed by the Brazilian lawyer and pedagogical theorist Paulo Freire, using ideas whose roots go back to Gramsci,
Marx, and ultimately to Kant.[9]

The second key factor is that one geotectonic upheaval in Latin American politics—the Cuban revolution that reached its climax with the overthrow of Fulgencio Batista by Fidel Castro in January 1959—sent shock
waves reverberating throughout the Catholic world. They reached the
doors of the Vatican itself, and then bounced back from Rome in new
papal strategies of anticommunism designed to stiffen the wavering religious allegiance of the Latin American poor. Once on the ground in contexts such as Brazil or Peru, these responsive strategies often passed out of
Vatican control and proved capable of leading the Latin American Catholic
Church in surprising directions. Fear of communism inspired Christians
to identify themselves with the cause of the poor, and with time such radical identification engendered forms of Christian social theory that often
struck conservatives as being not so very different from communism itself.

Third, the idea of liberation took its material shape from the growing disillusionment that set in during the 1950s and 1960s with the optimistic postwar economic theories of development prescribed by northern
economists as the solution to the needs of impoverished Latin American
and African countries seeking to achieve economic takeoff into "modernization." In Latin America especially, the rapid proliferation and expansion of cities—those defining symbols of modernity—seemed to make the
poor poorer rather than richer. For the inhabitants of the favelas of São
Paulo, liberal capitalism, far from offering the solution to the impoverishment of the global south, thus appeared as a means of deepening its
dependence on the north. In response economists such as the American
Marxist Paul A. Baran and the German-American Andre Gunder Frank
constructed what became known as "dependency theory." The attraction

of dependency theory was that it seemed to make sense of the experience of continuing and deepening impoverishment. It portrayed the glittering promise of modernization and development as a gigantic hoax inflicted on the peoples of the southern hemisphere by those who controlled the levers of global economic power, an insubstantial mirage designed by the rich nations of the north to mesmerize southern economies and keep them wandering in a trackless desert of structural injustice.

In intellectual terms, liberation theology was dependency theory translated into Christian theological categories, but with the crucial addition of a promised way out of the cycle of dependence. *"Dependence and liberation,"* affirmed Gutiérrez, "are correlative terms. An analysis of the situation of dependence leads one to attempt to escape from it."[10] Liberation theologians, just like dependency theorists, paid homage to Karl Marx in their social analysis while studiously ignoring those fundamental aspects of Marx's philosophy of history that offered the poor little hope in societies that had more in common with European feudalism or mid-twentieth century China than with the industrial conurbations of nineteenth-century Britain or Germany. Marx—and, still more, Lenin—believed the global proliferation through imperialism of bourgeois industrial capitalism to be the indispensable precondition for the creation of the revolutionary proletariat and introduction of the socialist utopia. In contrast, liberation theology followed dependency theory in attempting to short-circuit altogether the capitalist stage of historical development.[11] The intellectual guru of the Cuban revolution, the Argentinian Che Guevara, looked for inspiration not to Marx but to Mao Tse-Tung and the vision of an agrarian peasant revolution. Gutiérrez led liberation theology down a somewhat similar path, but offered a distinctive roadmap of the route away from dependency that combined a selective reading of the Bible with reliance on Freire's notion of "conscientization."[12] The Latin American poor, whether rural peasants or urban migrant workers, once made critically aware of their oppressed condition, and enabled to interpret it in the light of their reading of the biblical accounts of Yahweh's liberation of the oppressed, could become the authors of their own deliverance. They would become the instruments of God's salvation and the creators of a new humanity. Whatever this was, it was not Marxism. Whether it was Christianity, the reader must judge.

The fourth and last answer to the question of why liberation theologies emerged when they did relates to the prominent role played by students in most of the radical protest and countercultural movements of the 1960s and 1970s. In many contexts, but possibly to a greater extent in Latin America than anywhere else, universities in the 1960s and 1970s underwent extraordinarily rapid expansion, creating a new population of politically literate and ideologically idealistic young people. In 1965 the student population in Mexico City was higher than 65,000, and in Buenos Aires higher than 70,000, more than twice the size of the University of California, Berkeley, the campus that became globally renowned for the student revolt that extended from September 1964 to January 1965.[13] Especially in countries whose intellectual culture was shaped by the majority Catholic tradition, the universities became the primary ideological battleground between Christianity and Marxism, and many of those with personal experience of student ministries, whether Catholic priests, Protestant pastors, or missionaries, became the chief architects of theologies of liberation. Juan Luis Segundo claimed that the foundations of theologies of liberation were being laid in Latin American universities at least ten years before the publication of Gutiérrez's *A Theology of Liberation*.[14]

Postwar Latin America was the original furnace in which liberation theology was forged, but the hermeneutical shape that emerged from the furnace did not necessarily fit other contexts in which Christians had cause to reflect deeply on issues of justice and freedom. The second case study in the final section of the chapter accordingly examines the markedly different contours that a Christian theology of liberation assumed in the context of Palestine after the creation of the state of Israel in 1948, and more especially after the further loss of Palestinian territory effected by the Six-Day War of June 1967. In this setting, the oppressed were defined, not by class but by the simple fact of nationhood, and the central biblical motif selected by Latin American liberation theology—the exodus from Egyptian slavery—proved singularly unappealing. Whereas Latin American liberation theologians interpreted the Old Testament motif of the Promised Land as a utopian metaphor beckoning the poor to seize their place in history and throw off their bonds, for Palestinian Christians the Promised Land was itself a symbol of oppression, a sinister theological device employed by Jews and their numerous Christian Zionist supporters in the West to deny Palestinians their right to remain in possession of their ancestral homeland. Works by Palestinian theologians of liberation did not receive the same level of global scholarly attention as those written by their Latin American counterparts. Palestinian theologies of liberation remained firmly rooted in the experience of Palestinian Christian communities. For this reason, whereas the next section of the chapter focuses quite narrowly on the origins and evolution of what became the central hermeneutical motif of Latin American texts of liberation theology, the third section has a broader and more communal emphasis, situating Palestinian liberation theology in the distinctive context of the Palestinian people after 1948.

II. The Origins of Latin American Liberation Theology

Liberation theology in Latin America is widely assumed to be an originally Catholic movement with only occasional and largely derivative Protestant expressions. Thus *The Cambridge Companion to Liberation Theology*, a volume of more than 300 pages, contains in its index just one reference to a Latin American Protestant—the Argentinian Methodist José Miguez Bonino (1924–2012).[15] No mention can be found in the *Companion* of the Brazilian Presbyterian Rubem A. Alves (1933–2014), who deserves to be remembered, if not as the father of liberation theology, at least as one of its most important precursors. Neither is Alves mentioned in the three volumes of Mario Aguilar's *The History and Politics of Latin American Theology*, even though Aguilar properly devotes sustained attention to three Protestant theologians of liberation—Bonino, the Mexican Presbyterian Elsa Tamez (1950–), and the Argentinian Methodist Marcella Althaus-Reid (1952–2009).[16] Another standard survey of the movement, David Tombs' *Latin American Liberation Theology*, makes passing mention of Alves, but sees him as a product of a supposedly separate Protestant "theology of revolution."[17] In fact Latin American liberation theology was, almost from the outset, a movement formed by a confluence of diverse streams, not all of which had Catholic origins. The Catholic currents flowed principally from the springs of Vatican II and the political theology of Johann Baptist Metz. Among the Protestant sources of the movement were the World Council of Churches and its growing preoccupation in the 1960s with ideas of humanization, expounded in the previous chapter. The crucial mediators of such ideas to the Latin American context were M. Richard (Dick) Shaull (1919–2002), a Presbyterian missionary in Brazil before becoming Henry Winters Luce Professor of Ecumenics at Princeton Theological Seminary, and his Princeton doctoral student, Rubem Alves.

The World Council of Churches had sponsored a series of study conferences between 1955 and 1965 on Christian responsibility in the face of the rapid social, economic, and political changes currently taking place in Asia, Africa, and Latin America. In Latin America the first of these consultations was held at Huampaní in Peru in July 1961. At this meeting Dick Shaull and José Miguez Bonino were the prime movers in the formation of a group entitled *Iglesia y Sociedad en América Latina* (ISAL).[18]

Under their leadership ISAL developed a radical Christian perspective on the intensifying debate over development and underdevelopment in Latin America. Shaull is sometimes dismissed as having formulated in response a theology of revolution that would have no enduring influence in comparison with liberation theology, and his name appears only rarely in histories of liberation theology.[19] Yet his influence on Alves's pioneering Princeton Theological Seminary dissertation (1968) on "Toward a Theology of Liberation" is clear. He also coauthored with Gutiérrez a volume on *Liberation and Change* in 1977.[20] Dick Shaull has a strong claim to be remembered as one of the architects of liberation theology.[21]

Rubem Alves's doctoral dissertation was published in 1969 as *A Theology of Human Hope*, which was the title preferred by his publishers.[22] In fact, many, though not all, of the central emphases of applied liberation theology are to be found in Alves's work. He quoted both the anticolonial classic by the Martinican Frantz Fanon, *The Wretched of the Earth* (first published in English in 1963), and Paulo Freire's first book, *Educação como Prática de Liberdade* (Education as the Practice of Freedom; 1967) on the need for the oppressed of the Third World to become conscious of their oppression and make their own history.[23] He cited Paul VI's encyclical *Populorum Progressio* on the importance of man becoming "author of his own advancement" and invoked Feuerbach in support of the contention that "The beginning, middle, and end of God's activity is the liberation of man."[24] Of particular importance for the future of liberation theology is the fact that Alves also referred to the exodus as the paradigmatic act through which God forcibly revealed his liberating nature to Israel, a point which he drew from the American Presbyterian biblical archaeologist G. Ernest Wright (1909–74) and the German Lutheran Old Testament scholar Gerhard von Rad (1901–71). Wright's description of the exodus as "the central or focal point in Israelite history and faith" and his contention that God was known to Israel through objective historical acts, not mystical experience, was given particular emphasis by Alves, and was destined to become the keystone of liberationist exegesis.[25] If any of the essential ingredients of liberation theology were missing from Alves's recipe, the most obvious of these was theoretical reflection on the nature of theology itself and its necessarily dependent relationship to the praxis of the historical context.

Gustavo Gutiérrez had already begun to construct the framework of his theology of liberation before Rubem Alves's thesis was published. Gutiérrez's paper "Toward a Theology of Liberation," delivered at a conference in Chimbote, an impoverished fishing port in Peru, in July 1968, contained a number of the essential lineaments of his *A Theology of Liberation* that would be published three years later, including the crucial methodological affirmation of the priority of committed existential action over theological reflection. The paper drew from both *Gaudium et Spes* and, to a much greater extent, *Populorum Progressio*. *Gaudium et Spes* was invoked in support of the assertion that all activity by humans to better the circumstances of their lives was in accord with the will of God. More controversially, Paul VI's innocuous statement in *Populorum Progressio* that "In the design of God, all human beings are called upon to develop and fulfil themselves, for every life is a vocation" was interpreted as a revolutionary theological claim about the meaning of salvation:

> what is done for the love of God, but everything which contributes to growth in humanity, as *Populorum Progressio* says, everything which makes a person more human and contributes to human liberation, contains the value of salvation and communion with the Lord. In other words, and this vocabulary is new in the church, integral development is salvation.[26]

What was radical about Gutiérrez's Chimbote paper was precisely its boldness in offering an interpretation of a papal encyclical that took Paul VI's references to the desirability of the "integral development" of humanity, redefined them as meaning "the creation of a just and fraternal society," and then claimed papal authority for the theologically subversive conclusion that integral development simply *was* salvation. In other respects what Gutiérrez presented at Chimbote was unremarkable. There was precious little Marxist social analysis in the paper; Marx was cited at the end about the collusion of Christianity with the dominating class, but was immediately trumped by a citation from Isaiah 65, expounding the biblical vision of the kingdom of God in which there would be no more weeping or human distress. Neither was there any mention of Paulo Freire's theory of conscientization, probably for the simple reason that Gutiérrez was not yet familiar with it. Freire's *Educação como Prática de Liberdade* would be published in Spanish translation in both Montevideo and Santiago in 1969, but Gutiérrez as yet showed no awareness of the original work.[27] Freire's *Pedagogy of the Oppressed* was not published in New York until 1970. Also significant is the omission from the Chimbote paper of any reference to the biblical narrative of the exodus of Israel from Egypt: its primary biblical foundations were rather those used by many earlier generations of Christian advocates of social action, namely, the gospel texts of Luke 4 (Jesus' sermon at Nazareth proclaiming that he had been appointed to preach good news to the poor and release to the captives) and Matthew 25 (the parable of the sheep and the goats in which the nature of human response to the poor and needy is said to be the index of response to Christ himself).[28] At this stage the exodus is conspicuous by its absence from Gutiérrez's understanding of God's mission to the poor, in contrast, for example, with the prominent historical role it had consistently played in the theological reflection of the Christian slave communities of North America, as notably expressed in the African American ("Negro") spirituals.[29] It contrasts also with the use made of the motif from the earliest days of black theology in the United States, a movement whose genesis lies with the Black Power movement and its preoccupation with the issue of race; it was at first wholly autonomous of Latin American liberation theology. When James H. Cone (b. 1938) published his *A Black Theology of Liberation* in 1970, he was, he recalls, "completely unaware of the beginnings of liberation theology in the Third World, especially in Latin America." Cone, unlike Gutiérrez in 1968, made repeated reference in his book to the exodus as a "revelation-liberation" granted to oppressed peoples. Like Alves, Cone referred to G. Ernest Wright as the source of his emphasis that God disclosed himself through saving events.[30]

Within a month of the Chimbote conference, on August 26, 1968, the Second General Conference of Latin American Bishops assembled at Medellín in Colombia. Pope Paul VI delivered the opening address. The Medellín conference marked the point at which the progressive theological reorientation achieved by the Vatican Council succeeded in capturing—at least for a time—the allegiance of the Latin American hierarchy. It took place against the backcloth of the explosion during the spring and summer of 1968 of frequently violent student protests and countercultural agitation in many European and North American cities. In such a context, even theological conservatives judged a degree of commitment to social justice to be prudent. The agenda for the conference had been prepared in a series of six preparatory consultations held from June 1966 to August 1968, in which Gutiérrez had played a dominant role. Medellín, like Vatican II itself, spoke with more than one voice, but those documents of the conference dealing with the themes of justice, peace, and poverty were written by Gutiérrez and other leading advocates of a radical social Catholicism, such as the Brazilian Helder Cámara, archbishop of Recife and Olinda, who was a close friend of Paul VI.[31] They endorsed in unambiguous terms the aspirations of Latin American people for "authentic liberation" and "growth in humanity," and included repeated citations from both *Gaudium et Spes* and *Populorum Progressio*. Passing allusion was made to the biblical exodus as a manifestation of God's purpose to move all people toward "more human" conditions, but the exodus was not the primary biblical reference point of the documents: the gospels and the vision of the new humanity in Christ expounded in the Pauline epistles were much more central.[32]

Just over a year afterwards, in November 1969, the Catholic and Protestant streams feeding the reservoir of liberation theology first began to intermingle, when Gutiérrez attended an ecumenical consultation in Cartigny, Switzerland, convened by SODEPAX, the Committee on Society, Development, and Peace jointly sponsored by the World Council of Churches and the Pontifical Commission Justice and Peace. The twenty-eight participants included such names as Jürgen Moltmann; the Sri Lankan Catholic theologian Tissa Balasuriya; the South Indian Protestant theologian Stanley J. Samartha; Father George Khodr, later metropolitan of the Antiochene Orthodox Church of Lebanon; and the Ghanaian Catholic priest Peter Sarpong (later archbishop of Kumasi). Gutiérrez claims that it was only on the transatlantic flight to Switzerland that he made his famous decision to abandon the assignment that he had been given for one of the seven working papers—"The meaning of development"—and deliver instead a revision of his Chimbote paper under the title "Notes on a theology of liberation."[33] Rubem Alves, by now Professor of Theology at the University of Campinas in Brazil and Study Secretary of ISAL, was also a presenter at the consultation, on the topic "Theology and the liberation of man." Gutiérrez and Alves had never met before.

Gutiérrez's lengthy working paper was subsequently published in the report of the consultation formally under the original title "The meaning of development" but with "Notes on a theology of liberation" as the subtitle (or real title) in brackets.[34] A footnote in his Cartigny paper marks the first brief and understated appearance in his writings of any reference to Paulo Freire's theory of conscientization, a topic that received some attention at Cartigny and would receive much fuller mention in *A Theology of Liberation*.[35] The paper was mainly devoted to expounding the case that liberation was theologically a more satisfactory concept than development, but included a brief biblical section on "liberation and salvation." This followed his Chimbote paper in giving priority to an exposition of the themes of creation and new creation. Only one mention was made (in the next section on "eschatology and politics") of the significance of the exodus as an event that "expresses very well the situation of the Christian community within history"; as before, the biblical foundations of Gutiérrez's understanding of liberation were not the exodus but the prophets (especially Isaiah), the Psalms and the gospels.[36] In contrast, Alves's paper stated unambiguously that "The Exodus is the primary fact" whose meaning for those who participated in it was "liberation from bondage, liberation for the future, liberation for life"; its lasting meaning was that it was about "the liberation of man." Immediately prior to these statements Alves had asserted that "truth is derived from praxis" and "truth is act," contentions that his footnotes show were drawn directly from G. Ernest Wright's *God Who Acts*, with a secondary reference to Moltmann's *Theology of Hope*.[37]

By the appearance of *Teología de la Liberacíon* in 1971, Gutiérrez had shifted his biblical focus quite markedly from the position expounded in his Chimbote and Cartigny papers. Among the welter of biblical texts cited in the second and more exegetical half of the book, Luke 4 strangely did not appear at all. Matthew 25, on the other hand, retained its centrality in Gutiérrez's exposition of his central theological point that love for God could be expressed only through love of one's neighbor.[38] What was now given even greater emphasis in Gutiérrez's biblical theology was the status of the exodus as a theological event that was uniquely revelatory of the sort of God that Yahweh was and of his purpose for humanity: "The exodus experience," he now asserted in an echo of Alves's Cartigny paper, "is paradigmatic."[39] Gutiérrez cited various texts from Second Isaiah and the Psalms in which the exodus from Egypt is described in terms that compare the event to the original creation of the world, to such an extent that the original act of creation and the subsequent act of redemption are almost fused to become one single demonstration of God's creative and liberative power. His point was that the divine act of liberation from Egyptian slavery was a creative act, a "political action . . . the creation of a new order."[40] The exodus was now defined as the archetype of the creation of the new humanity.

The evidence is compelling that this new exegetical element in Gutiérrez's liberation theology derived primarily from Alves. The understanding of creation as God's first salvific work was already present in "Notes on a theology of liberation," but it was not therein related to the exodus, but rather to the Psalms, the prologue to the Fourth Gospel and the Pauline epistles.[41] The footnotes to chapter 9 in *A Theology of Liberation* suggest that Gutiérrez had been reading extensively in Old Testament theology, especially the writings of Gerhard von Rad, but crucially also they contain an acknowledgment by Gutiérrez of his specific indebtedness to Rubem Alves's *A Theology of Human Hope* (published soon after the Cartigny consultation) for his understanding of the exodus as "a historical-salvific fact which structures the faith of Israel."[42] *A Theology of Liberation* contains three references to Alves's book; the last two commended his critique of Jürgen Moltmann's concept of hope as being implicitly docetic, as tending to remove the object of human hope from the sphere of history; but this first reference to Alves's view of the exodus, although tucked away in a footnote, may be the most significant.[43] It is theoretically possible that between the Cartigny meeting and the publication of his book in 1971 Gutiérrez arrived at this expanded view of the significance of the exodus simply on the basis of his own biblical reflection. However, his published acknowledgment to Alves, the fact of their mutually fruitful encounter in Switzerland in November 1969, and the comparison of their respective working papers at Cartigny, point unmistakably toward the conclusion that the roots of this emphasis were in fact Protestant ones, going back via Alves and his mentor Shaull to the biblical theology of the Presbyterian G. Ernest Wright and the Lutheran Gerhard von Rad.[44]

Gutiérrez's consequent elevation of the exodus to the most potent symbol of God's self-revelation and saving activity soon became almost a defining tenet of Latin American liberationist orthodoxy. The Argentinian Old Testament scholar J. Severino Croatto (1930–2004) developed the motif into a fundamental hermeneutical principle of scriptural interpretation in his work *Liberación y libertad: Pautas hermenéuticas* (1973), which appeared in English translation in 1981 as *Exodus: A Hermeneutics of Freedom*. Croatto described the exodus as "not an event solely for the Hebrews but rather the manifestation of a liberative plan of God for all peoples," a historical process that was not yet concluded.[45] Croatto's work was cited repeatedly by the American political philosopher Michael Walzer in his book *Exodus and Revolution* (1985), which sought to give a political history of the interpretation of the exodus in the Western world.[46] By 1977 Juan Luis Segundo could observe that "liberation theology is known to have a preference and a partiality for the Old Testament in general, and for the Exodus event in particular." Segundo, it should be noted, was not entirely content with this scriptural reductionism, branding it as naive.[47] Furthermore, the exodus received only one passing mention in the 160-page document on "Evangelization in Latin America's Present and Future" issued by the Third General Conference of Latin American Bishops held in Puebla, Mexico, in January–February 1979, an event that both opponents and supporters of liberation theology hailed as a victory for their side. Although the Conference repeated Catholic orthodoxy in warning that the social analysis of Marxism could not, as liberation theologians maintained, be separated from its essentially atheistic ideology, it called for the whole church to be converted to "a preferential option for the poor." However, the biblical basis for this call was found, not in the Old Testament, but in the Magnificat and the ministry of Jesus.[48]

Nevertheless, it was not long before the identification of liberation theology with a hermeneutical focus on the exodus soon became incontestable in the eyes of its increasingly vocal critics in the Vatican. In March 1984 Joseph Ratzinger, prefect of the Congregation for the Doctrine of the Faith (and from 2005 to 2013 Pope Benedict XVI) published a grave warning against the dangers of the new theology, noting that it transformed the exodus into "a central image of the history of salvation," the paschal mystery of the death and resurrection of Christ into a revolutionary symbol, and the eucharist into a liberation feast.[49] The Congregation for the Doctrine of the Faith's first official statement on liberation theology followed in August 1984. It illustrated its central charge that theologies of liberation were engaging in "an essentially political rereading of the scriptures" by referring first to the "major importance given to the exodus event inasmuch as it is a liberation from political servitude"; the second example given was the interpretation of the Magnificat.[50] A rather more balanced document issued by the Congregation in March 1986 acknowledged that the exodus event was "major and fundamental" with a meaning that was "both religious and political," but still warned against any isolation of the political aspect of the event for its own sake, implying that this was precisely the charge of which liberation theology was guilty.[51]

Despite the very mixed reception given to them by the Vatican, by the late 1980s theologies of liberation were firmly established as the predominant mode of discourse on church and society in both Catholic and mainline Protestant circles. In the course of the 1970s the number of base communities throughout the continent had reached almost 200,000.[52] Liberation theology had produced its own saints and martyrs—most notably archbishop Oscar Romero of El Salvador, assassinated in March 1980, and the Jesuit theologian, Ignacio Ellacuría, murdered by the Salvadorian army on 16 November 1989 together with five other members of his Jesuit community. Theologies of liberation had spread from the Americas to Asia and Africa and to other contexts in which questions of social and political justice were high on the agenda of the churches. Some of the agents of transmission were among the twenty-eight present at Cartigny, including Balasuriya and Samartha. In the process of transmission, theologies of liberation necessarily assumed new and multiple shapes. As the next section of this chapter shows, in the Palestinian context, the liberationist biblical motif of the exodus that had come to be regarded as a central feature of the Latin American theological agenda proved wholly incapable of such international transmission.

III. Palestine: Searching for Liberation without Exodus

Although Christianity in Palestine has a very long history, liberation theology as a self-conscious movement came late to Palestine. The first significant book to advocate a Palestinian theology of liberation was by the Palestinian Anglican priest Naim Stifan Ateek (b. 1937), *Justice and Only Justice: A Palestinian Theology of Liberation*, published by Orbis Books in 1989. The back cover described the book "as the very first of its kind" and Ateek prefaced his chapter on "The Bible and liberation: a Palestinian perspective" by asserting that "nothing of this kind has been done before."[53] The foreword, by the prominent Catholic feminist theologian Rosemary Radford Ruether, asserted that the advent of a Palestinian liberation theology called "for a profound paradigm shift" in the way in which much liberation theology had been done. Use of the Exodus motif, she confidently proclaimed, had been "unquestioned" in liberation theology, but for Palestinians "The Jewish exodus from oppression in Europe is the rationale for their conquest" while the biblically rooted Jewish claim to the Promised Land was the exact source of Palestinian dispossession from their own land. "Jewish redemption," observed Ruether bluntly, "is Palestinian oppression."[54]

In *Justice and Only Justice* Ateek informed his readers that the problem for Palestinian Christians was in fact wider than the exodus narrative and its sequel conquest narrative in the book of Joshua—the difficulty lay with the Old Testament itself and its unashamed exaltation of the God of Israel. Before the creation of the state of Israel in 1948, Palestinian Christians had regarded the Old Testament as an essential part of Christian Scripture, witnessing to Jesus as the Christ. But since 1948 the political capital which both Christian and Jewish Zionist interpreters had made of the Old Testament had made it "almost repugnant to Palestinian Christians," with the result that it had fallen into general disuse among both clergy and laity.[55] Ateek's book was an attempt to reclaim at least some of the Old Testament for Palestinian Christian use, highlighting its emphasis on the sole divine ownership of the land and on the imperative of justice for all who lived on the land. He thus favored the prophetic tradition of the Hebrew Bible, while effectively dismissing the exclusive nationalism that appears to characterize much of Joshua, Judges, the books of Samuel and Kings; a third tradition, that of the Torah, giving rise to rabbinic Judaism, he interpreted as being about the regulation of the behavior of Jews toward other peoples according to principles of justice. In later publications Ateek would commend the writer of the book of Jonah as "an archetypal Palestinian liberation theologian" and celebrate it as "the greatest book in the Old Testament" on account of its message of radical opposition to a narrow Jewish nationalism.[56] *Justice and Only Justice* made little or no mention of Latin American liberation theologians, and referred to Marxism only to dismiss any accusation that his own theology of liberation owed anything to Marx—it was, he claimed, "firmly based on the Bible."[57] Here was a radically different form of liberation theology, in both ideological tone and biblical focus. It also differed, as we shall see, in its intellectual origins and primary inspiration.

As a child of 11 in 1948 Naim Ateek had experienced first-hand the grim reality of dispossession following the establishment of the state of Israel. It is estimated that at least 35 percent of the Palestinian Christian population—some 50–60,000 people—became refugees as a result of the 1948–9 war; within the space of a few months, the proportion of the population of Palestine that was Christian fell from 8 to as little as 2.8 percent.[58] Ateek's family were compelled to leave their home in Beisan, 20 miles south of Galilee, and relocate to Nazareth, where they lived under military law as second-class citizens of the new Jewish state. His father, originally from an Orthodox background, had become an Anglican lay reader of evangelical inclination through contact with missionaries of the Church Missionary Society (CMS). Like many other Palestinians who sought higher educational opportunities denied to them in their own country after 1948, Naim left for the United States in 1959, and began to study for the Anglican priesthood, taking degrees from Hardin–Simmons University in Abilene, Texas, and the Church Divinity School of the Pacific, in Berkeley, California. In 1985 he secured a doctorate from San Francisco Theological Seminary, a Presbyterian institution with a very strong tradition of commitment to racial justice and political action. *Justice and Only Justice* is the published version of that doctoral dissertation. Ateek's theology of liberation, like Palestinian Christian theology as a whole, thus owed more to liberationist theological traditions originating in the United States than to those shaped in Latin America.[59] Ironically, it was a Jewish American scholar, Marc H. Ellis, who persuaded the initially hesitant editorial director at Orbis Books that this was a work that deserved to be published.[60] Ateek served as an Episcopal priest in Nazareth, Haifa, and other towns in the West Bank and in Jerusalem, before becoming canon in charge and eventually rector of the Arabic congregation at St. George's Cathedral Church in East Jerusalem. In 1989, at the height of the Palestinian intifada of 1987–91, he convened a committee of ten theologians and lay people to discuss the construction of a specifically Palestinian theology of liberation. The group decided to organize an international conference. This took place in March 1990 at the Tantur Ecumenical Institute located between Jerusalem and Bethlehem. Invitations were sent to liberation theologians across the world to attend, but it is significant that the majority of those who came were from North America; no Latin American liberation theologian attended. The proceedings were published in a book titled *Faith and the Intifada*.[61] The conference led by late 1993 to the formal establishment of *Sabeel* (Arabic for "river," "channel," or "spring"), the Ecumenical Liberation Theology Centre in Jerusalem. *Sabeel* has ever since been the primary hub of Palestinian liberation theology.

In February 1998 *Sabeel* held its third conference at Bethlehem University in the West Bank. The keynote speaker before a packed audience (with hundreds more watching on closed-circuit television) was none other than Edward W. Said (1935–2003), the leading Palestinian intellectual and postcolonial theorist. Said is not generally remembered for his sympathy for Christianity, but his address went out of its way to express admiration for Naim Ateek; Said, who was already suffering from the cancer that killed him, confessed that it was only because of Ateek that he had taken the trouble to attend. Said spoke of his own Christian roots, how he had been baptized in St. George's, Jerusalem, and educated for a time at its accompanying boarding school. Ateek, Said whimsically asserted, "represents what has so often been left out of Christianity, namely Christianity: dedication, the total absence of any egotistical, or personal kind of arrogance of any kind."[62]

Said's Christian background is sometimes forgotten. His autobiography recalls his great-grandfather, Yousif Badr, who was the first native evangelical minister in Lebanon; his mother's father, who was minister of Nazareth Baptist Church; his aunt Nabia, who had worked with the CMS among Palestinian refugees in Egypt after 1948, and to whom Edward gave the credit for his passionate commitment to the cause of Palestinian refugees; and the very close connections that all of his family had with the YMCA in Jerusalem. Said's school education was strongly Christian: his secondary education was spent mainly at the Cairo School for American Children, but he also studied at St. George's in Jerusalem, and finally for a year at Mount Hermon School in Massachusetts, founded by the

American evangelist D. L. Moody. What he unkindly termed the "dreadful, pietistic, non-denominational" religion of Mount Hermon School seems to have inoculated Said against the Christian faith, but he retained warm memories of his teachers in Cairo and Jerusalem. Catechism classes at All Saints' Anglican Cathedral in Cairo left him with an enduring, if mainly literary, affection for the Book of Common Prayer and John's Gospel. His senior Arabic teacher at St. George's was Khalil Beidas (1874–1949), his father's cousin, who had studied in Russia as a ward of the Russian Orthodox Church and had imbibed ideas from nineteenth-century Russian cultural nationalists such as Dostoyevsky, Gorky, and Tolstoy. Beidas was a key figure in the intellectual construction of a Palestinian national identity during the 1920s and 1930s.[63] The Palestinian Lutheran theologian Mitri Raheb (b. 1962) has even portrayed Said's life in biblical categories, marked by a Christ-like escape into the safety of Egypt after 1948 and by deep Hebraic-style reflection on the meaning of history from his "Babylonian" exile in the United States, leading to the publication of the postcolonial classic *Orientalism* in 1978.[64] Such analogies may appear fanciful, but there is no doubt that Said derived his Palestinian nationalism from Christian sources, and in that he was not unique.

Throughout the twentieth century Palestinian Christians were a diminishing minority in a nation that was itself being eroded by a protracted exodus. By 1995 they accounted for no more than 2 percent of the Palestinian population of the West Bank and Gaza.[65] In the early years of the century migration was primarily an economic process, driven by the lure of economic opportunity in the Western world, especially in the Promised Land of the United States. After 1948 the exodus was as much a movement of refugees as of economic migrants. About 83 percent of the small Palestinian Christian community in 1995 was Greek Orthodox or Roman Catholic. Protestants accounted for only a small proportion: in Jerusalem, where their numbers were probably greatest, the proportion was less than 8 percent.[66] Yet the role of Protestants, and especially of Anglicans, in the construction of Palestinian Christian theology down to the present day has been seminal. The primary reason for that disproportionate influence may be the unusual contribution that was made by Protestant educational institutions to the nurturing of an urban Palestinian elite.

From the early days of the British Mandate over Palestine, established by the League of Nations in 1922, Protestant schools proved attractive, not simply to Christian Palestinian families, but also to Muslim ones. Some of the products of such schools in British-mandated Palestine and throughout Ottoman Syria became the architects of a free Arabic press and of the embryonic Arab nationalist movement.[67] About 20 percent of the delegates to the First Palestinian Congress in January 1919, and about half of the delegates from Jerusalem—which formed the hub of emergent Palestinian nationalism—were Christians.[68] Of particular importance was the cluster of Anglican educational institutions associated with St. George's Cathedral Church in Jerusalem. Originally established by the Jerusalem and the East Mission, the St. George's schools and colleges for men and women became during the Mandate period a cooperative venture involving the Jerusalem and the East Mission, the CMS, the Church of Scotland mission, and the Church's Mission to the Jews.[69]

Anglicans had first become involved in Palestine in the early 1840s as a result of Lord Shaftesbury's evangelical Zionist vision of the return of the Jews to their homeland in order to play their divinely appointed strategic role in salvation history.[70] In the period of the Mandate, however, both the CMS and the Anglican bishop of Jerusalem redefined Anglican missionary objectives. The original goal of converting Jews to Christianity receded, and in its place Anglicans sought to promote the harmonious coexistence of Jews, Muslims, and Christians within Palestine. The influx of Jewish settlers from the 1920s and growth of Zionism seemed to place that objective—as also the existing Christian preeminence in government employment—in peril. In response Anglicans increasingly threw their weight behind the developing Arab nationalist movement, which at that stage was a mainly secular rather than a predominantly Muslim force.[71] Edward Said's story is only one prominent example of how Christianity helped to forge Palestinian nationalism. The Palestine Liberation Organisation, established in 1964, had a strong Christian leadership base in its early years. George Habash, chairman of the radical leftist Popular Front for the Liberation of Palestine and Nayef Hawatmeh, at one time chair of the Democratic Front for the Liberation of Palestine, were both members of the Greek Orthodox Church.[72]

Palestinian liberation theology grew from the soil of this preexisting Christian Palestinian nationalism. The scale of the refugee problem created by the 1948–49 war had the effect of drawing Palestinian Christians into both Catholic and Protestant international networks, forging links which in time would connect the Palestinian churches to theologies of liberation in other parts of the world. The Catholic Church took the lead in relief efforts. Coordinated by the Pontifical Mission to Palestine, established in June 1949, Catholic agencies gave vast sums to the Palestinian cause: The American National Catholic Welfare Conference supplied 1.3 million US dollars between the summer of 1948 and February 1950, while

Catholics in other parts of the world gave a further $5 million. Protestant agencies such as the American Church World Service, the YMCA, YWCA, and the WCC's Department of Interchurch Aid and Service to Refugees, also contributed substantial, though somewhat smaller, amounts.[73] As was often the case in the postwar era, Christian involvement in relief to refugees proved to be a bridge by which churches and mission agencies broadened their understanding of the nature of Christian mission.

The Six-Day War of 1967 was the watershed separating the period of Christian involvement in a secular Palestinian Arab nationalist movement from a new era in which a harder-edged Palestinian theology of liberation would gradually take root. Within ten days of the end of the war, on June 18, a group of mainly Catholic Middle Eastern theologians who had gathered in Beirut issued a statement that in effect denied the right of Israel to exist as a nation: the divine vocation of Israel, they proclaimed, was to be a witness to all the nations, not to be itself a nation; the nation of Israel was a racist state born out of violence.[74] One of those theologians was the Antiochene Orthodox Lebanese priest George Khodr (b. 1923), who two years later would be one of those present at the Cartigny consultation alongside Gutiérrez. More broadly, the humiliation experienced by the Arab world at its astonishingly rapid defeat by the state of Israel spelt the effective end of secular Arab nationalism; the future throughout the Middle East lay with increasingly radical Muslim brands of Arab nationalism.

Christians throughout the Middle East now found themselves isolated, and in response strengthened their ecumenical connections. The "Near East Council of Churches," formed by Protestant missions in 1956, was in 1974 expanded to include Orthodox and Oriental Orthodox churches in the new Middle East Council of Churches. The Roman Catholic Church and other Catholic churches joined the Council in 1989–90, and in 1995 the Assyrian Church of the East joined the Council.[75] Influenced by the priority given by the Second Vatican Council to the development of dialogical relationships with those of other faiths, the Palestinian Catholic churches in 1982 established the Al-Liqa (meaning "encounter") Centre for Religious and Heritage Studies in the Holy Land under the directorship of a Melkite Catholic from Galilee, Dr Geries Sa'ed Khoury (1952–2016).[76] Originally part of the Tantur Ecumenical Institute founded by Pope Paul VI in 1972, the Al-Liqa Centre was in 1987 made into a fully autonomous center located in Beit Sahour near Jerusalem in order to clarify its distinctive focus on Muslim–Christian dialogue. Whereas Naim Ateek's Sabeel Centre has been outward-facing to the world Christian community, seeking to present the Palestinian cause before Christians in the West,

Al-Liqa has been more concerned to develop a sense of common purpose among all Palestinians, whether Christian or Muslim. Sa-ed Khoury, who was a distinguished scholar of medieval Arabic philology, was not unsympathetic to liberation theology, but chose instead to speak of a historic tradition of Christian theology in Palestine stretching back to medieval times.[77] Another theologian involved in the Al-Liqa Centre, the Catholic Dr Rafiq Khoury, has similarly preferred to style his work as being in "contextual theology" rather than liberation theology: what distinguishes Christianity in the Middle East, he has argued, has been its centuries-old experience of living within an Islamic context. The same preference has been expressed more recently by Mitri Raheb. The term "liberation theology" in Palestine appears to define Christian theology in relation to the primary source of oppression, namely Israel, whereas for Geries Khoury, Rafiq Khoury, and Mitri Raheb, the priority has been to develop a Palestinian theology that takes seriously both the subject status of the Palestinian nation and the Islamic environment within which Christian life and worship have to be expressed.

IV. The God Who Acts

There is liberation theology and there are theologies of liberation. The controversial prominence that Latin American liberation theologians achieved in the Catholic world from the early 1970s ensured that the singular term "liberation theology" acquired an automatic and apparently lasting association with Latin America. Contrary to what many commentators have assumed, however, that dominant expression of liberation theology was not originally premised on the centrality of the biblical motif of the exodus as the paradigmatic self-revelation of God as the one who acts in deliverance of the oppressed. Latin American Catholic liberation theology acquired its identification with the exodus motif only after Gutiérrez's *A Theology of Liberation* became known in the English-speaking world after 1973. The sources of the new hermeneutical emphasis were Protestant ones, which is not surprising in view of the long history of Protestant exegesis of the exodus as an archetype of the deliverance of God's people from bondage, a history that can be traced back to John Calvin, as John Coffey has demonstrated.[78] In Gutiérrez's case, the debt to the Reformed tradition appears to have been quite specific: the channel was the Brazilian Presbyterian Rubem Alves. Behind Alves's *A Theology of Human Hope* lay the tradition of biblical theology, and its emphasis on God who acts in history, especially as articulated by G. Ernest Wright.

The theologies of liberation that emerged in other parts of the world from the 1970s onwards had varying relationships to Latin American liberation theology and its most distinctive hermeneutical characteristic. Allan Boesak (b. 1946), for example, one of the most able exponents of South African black theology, frequently employed the motif of the exodus and made regular allusions to Latin American theologians, but entered into much more explicit dialogue with the black theology of the United States.[79] Black theology had its own independent lineage of appeal to the exodus, grounded in the historic spirituality and hymnody of the American slave population, but it is interesting that its most notable pioneer, James Cone, also acknowledged his dependence on G. E. Wright. Gina Lende and Samuel Kuruvilla have suggested that Palestinian theologians of liberation expressed their indebtedness to their Latin American predecessors, but the evidence of anything more than nominal influence is slight.[80] Naim Ateek, the Palestinian theologian who has been most eager to appropriate the term "liberation theology" has been one of the most robust in his repudiation of the exodus motif. The sources of his theology are to be found in North rather than Latin America. The one figure to appear in both case studies in this chapter, George Khodr, contributed to the Beirut memorandum of 1967 over two years before he met Gutiérrez and Alves at Cartigny. Palestinian theologians, while they have framed their theologies within the context of a Zionist state which has deprived them of their land, owed more to the early twentieth-century tradition of Christian Arab nationalism and to much older traditions of Christian theology constructed within an Islamic environment than they did to influences from Latin America.

CHAPTER ELEVEN

Doing Justice in South Africa and Canada

THE HUMAN RIGHTS AGENDA, RACE, AND INDIGENOUS PEOPLES

I. The Churches and Human Rights Ideology

Human rights discourse was more prominent in the second half of the twentieth century than in any preceding period, not excepting the era of the American and French Revolutions in the late eighteenth century. In the decades after 1945 the passion expended on the articulation and defense of human rights often acquired an intensity that was comparable to the fervor traditionally evoked by religious convictions. The proponents of human rights came from both the left and the right of the political spectrum. They included in their number many who saw human rights as a profoundly Christian concept, but especially from the 1960s onwards, these were joined by others who viewed Christianity as an inherently oppressive ideology subversive of the very notion of human rights. Just as, in the late eighteenth century, the revolutionary idea of "the rights of man" elicited widely divergent responses from the churches, so, in the late twentieth century, the new global creed of human rights stood in an ambiguous relationship to Christian belief. This chapter considers the impact on the churches of the human rights agenda in its application to issues of racial justice and the treatment of indigenous peoples. Chapter 12 will examine the equally far-reaching ramifications for Christian belief and practice of the application of human rights ideology to questions of gender and sexuality.

Most discussions of human rights discourse in the second half of the twentieth century begin with the aftermath of the Second World War and the Holocaust, and consequent adoption of the Universal Declaration of Human Rights at the Third General Assembly of the United Nations in Paris in December 1948. However, it is not always recognized how deeply the text of the Declaration was affected by Christian concerns, many of which antedated the war. Although the first draft of the text was the work of a Canadian lawyer of secularist convictions, John P. Humphrey, the Declaration in its final form owed a great deal to distinctively Christian emphases. In particular, it was indebted to the Protestant ecumenical movement that had increasingly taken institutional form in the wake of the World Missionary Conference held in Edinburgh in 1910, culminating in the formation of the World Council of Churches in Amsterdam in August 1948. One of the key constitutive bodies of the embryonic United Nations organization, the Commission on Human Rights, established in the spring of 1946, was chaired by Eleanor Roosevelt, a committed Episcopalian. She was responsible for incorporating in the preamble to the Declaration the Four Freedoms that her late husband, President Franklin D. Roosevelt, had enunciated in his State of the Union address of January 6, 1941: freedom of speech, freedom of worship, freedom from want, and freedom from fear.[1] The first two of these were principles that had been dear to the heart of Protestants from the sixteenth century onwards, often forming the indispensable basis of their right to exist under the authority of Catholic states.

Ecumenical leaders, influenced by concerns arising from mission field experience in Asia and Latin America, were, however, determined that the Declaration should go further still, incorporating a full statement of freedom of religion, including the increasingly contested right to convert to another religion. While Eleanor Roosevelt played her part, the practical securing of this objective at the Paris conference was the joint achievement of an American Lutheran minister and a Lebanese Greek Orthodox layman. The American Lutheran minister was Dr. O. Frederick Nolde (1899–1972), director of the Commission of the Churches on International Affairs, a body established by an ecumenical conference at Girton College, Cambridge, in August 1946. The Commission was given consultative status on the Commission on Human Rights and at the Paris conference, where Nolde labored incessantly to defend the freedom to convert against pressure from representatives of majority religious populations. The Lebanese layman was the philosopher and diplomat, Charles Malik (1906–87), chairman of the Third Committee at the Paris conference that had formal responsibility for the text of the Declaration. Malik, an Orthodox Christian of exceptionally broad ecumenical sympathies, was influenced both by the American Protestant missionary tradition of the American University in Beirut, where he had studied, and by the ideas of the neo-Thomist philosopher, Jacques Maritain, for whom the inviolable rights of the human person derived from natural law. To Nolde and Malik belongs much of the credit for the unambiguous text of Article 18 of the Declaration, affirming, in the face of substantial Muslim opposition, that "Everyone has the right to freedom of thought, conscience and religion; this right includes freedom to change his religion or belief, and freedom, either alone or in community with others and in public or private, to manifest his religion or belief in teaching, practice, worship and observance."[2]

Throughout the 1950s, and well into the 1960s, the affirmation and defense of human rights followed the trajectory laid down by the Universal Declaration: human rights were a charter for individual freedom of conscience, and a standard to hold governments to account for their treatment of dissenters. They were not yet a general platform for liberation movements. Although decolonization was in the air, there was no automatic association between the defense of human rights and opposition to colonial rule. The author of the preamble to the United Nations Charter of 1945, affirming faith in "the equal rights of men and women and of nations large and small," was none other than Jan Smuts, then prime minister of South Africa, and a defender of white supremacy, though not of the policy of apartheid that would be introduced by the National Party in 1948.[3] Indeed, in the polarized ideological climate of the Cold War, the defence of human rights, and specifically of freedom of religious conscience and association, became central to the campaigns of Christian conservatives against communism. Cases such as the internment and trial of Cardinal Jósef Mindszenty (1892–1975), the fearless Primate of Hungary, attracted much publicity and indignation on both sides of the Atlantic. Mindszenty was arrested by the communist authorities in December 1948 because of his public opposition to the nationalization of Catholic schools, and in February 1949 was convicted of treason. He remained in prison until the Hungarian uprising of October–November 1956, when, after a brief period of freedom, he took refuge in the American embassy in Budapest. There he remained until he went into exile in Vienna in 1971.[4] The Catholic Church, once an inveterate opponent of human rights as a godless libertarian ideology, had become a firm supporter of a creed that seemed integral to its survival under totalitarian communist regimes. Influenced by Maritain's natural law defense, Western European Catholic thinkers and politicians were instrumental in securing the European Convention on Human Rights (1950) and the consequent establishment of the European Court of Human Rights (1959).[5]

In the course of the 1960s and 1970s human rights discourse acquired a sharper edge. Alongside its older Cold War use as a weapon against communist totalitarianism there developed a radical human rights tradition that addressed the condition of oppressed groups and spoke the language of liberation. This alternative human rights tradition confronted the churches with a choice—either to realign themselves with the demands for liberation, or to pay the price for their apparent collusion with the status quo.

The churches first faced this stark choice in relation to the civil rights movement in the United States. It was not initially apparent that this would be the case. Eleanor Roosevelt was a consistent and not always popular supporter of African American rights.[6] The Federal Council of Churches (FCC; formed in 1908) had established a Department of Race Relations as early as 1921, and sponsored an annual Race Relations Sunday in the churches. Its successor from 1950, the National Council of Churches (NCC), continued the department, now named the Department of Racial and Cultural Relations. But both the FCC and the NCC pursued a gradualist and primarily educational approach to racial issues in the tradition of the Social Gospel movement; reform rather than revolution was the watchword.

From the early 1960s the tone of the NCC's racial policy altered. This was in part due to the advent of a new and more radical generation of leadership in the NCC influenced by the more secular theologies of that decade. More fundamentally, it was a reflection of the quickening of pace in the civil rights movement itself initiated by Martin Luther King's instigation on April 3, 1963, of a campaign to desegregate the public institutions of Birmingham, Alabama, leading to his imprisonment. When publicly criticized by seven religious leaders for his "unwise" identification with the civil protests, King in response wrote on April 16, 1963, a 7,000-word letter from Birmingham City Jail, urging the churches to meet the challenge of the hour and identify themselves unequivocally with the struggle for justice in the American South.[7] The letter was widely published in the Christian and secular press. In May 1963 the United Presbyterian Church set up a Commission on Race. The NCC itself followed in June, establishing a Commission on Religion and Race; the United Church of Christ set up its own Commission a month later.[8] The Protestant mainline churches had belatedly begun to grasp the urgency of the civil rights agenda. The assassination of Martin Luther King on April 4, 1968, accentuated its gravity.

Within twelve months the churches would find themselves the direct objects of attack from radical African American opinion.

In April 1969 the National Black Economic Development Conference was held at Wayne State University in Detroit, sponsored by the NCC and the Interreligious Foundation for Community Organization, a body set up in New York in May 1967 by Protestants, Catholics, and Jews. The Detroit meeting made the Conference a permanent body, the Black Economic Development Conference (BEDC). The most sensational moment of the meeting was when James Forman (1928–2005), former executive secretary and now director of international affairs of the civil rights group, the Student Nonviolent Coordinating Committee (SNCC), read to the conference a "Black Manifesto." This made sweeping criticisms in revolutionary Marxist language of "the racist white Christian church," and called for churches and synagogues to pay $500 million in reparations to the black community. "We are no longer afraid," it asserted, "to demand our full rights as a people in this decadent society." It expressed the hope that churches and synagogues would see fit to meet its "demands" (a word that appeared thirty-one times), but warned that, if they did not, "then we declare war and are prepared to fight by all means necessary."[9] Forman was not the first to call for reparations to the black community—Martin Luther King's proposed "Economic Bill of Rights for the Disadvantaged" in 1967 had called for massive federal and church investment to redress the impoverishment of African Americans—but Forman's tone and methods were unprecedented.

Over the next few months, Forman took the Manifesto directly to most of the mainline denominations. The most famous of these encounters took place on Sunday May 4, 1969, at the "Cathedral of Protestantism," the imposing Riverside Church on the Upper West Side of Manhattan.[10] Ignoring the pleas of the senior minister, Ernest Campbell, Forman interrupted the Sunday morning service to read the Manifesto, and to demand that Riverside give him unrestricted use of the church's radio station and hand over 60 percent of its annual income from church stock, property, and real estate. The ministers and a sizeable proportion of the congregation walked out, but about 500 of the congregation remained to hear the Manifesto. By the end of May Forman had placed his demands before the United Church of Christ; the United Presbyterian Church, USA; the Lutheran Church in America; the American Baptist Convention; officials of the United Methodist Church; and the presiding bishop of the Episcopal Church. An attempt to confront the Catholic archbishop of New York failed.[11]

Forman's appeal at Riverside Church was made in the context of a protracted series of student demonstrations on race issues at nearby Columbia

University. Eight days after Forman's intervention at Riverside, students occupied Union Theological Seminary (located between Columbia University and Riverside Church), demanding that the trustees support the Manifesto, give $100,000 of the seminary's budget for the following year to the BEDC, and raise $1 million for the SNCC. The trustees declined to place any funds under Forman's control, but voted to raise $100,000 for black development, invest $500,000 of the endowment in black enterprises, and try to raise $1 million for projects to be operated in Harlem under seminary enterprises. From May 14 Forman and his supporters occupied parts of the Interchurch Center or "God-box," the office block across the street from Riverside Church that housed both the NCC and key departments of the United Presbyterian and United Methodist churches; on June 9 many of the 2,200 staff employed in the Center went on strike throughout the premises in solidarity with Forman.[12]

The extreme language of the Manifesto drew widespread criticism, and a Gallup Poll taken in May 1969 found that 90 percent of respondents, and even 52 percent of black respondents, opposed the demand for reparations.[13] Nevertheless, most of the mainline churches, led by Riverside Church itself, supported reparations in principle and practice. The American Baptists, United Methodists, United Church of Christ, Episcopalians, United Presbyterians, and Disciples of Christ all donated large sums, amounting to millions of dollars, not to Forman himself, but to projects for African American welfare. The NCC supported these donations, and proposed a massive social investment scheme to the tune of tens of millions of dollars to be used by a black-controlled foundation for the development of minority communities. This never got off the ground.[14] The General Assembly of the NCC, held in Detroit from November 30 to December 5, 1969, revealed how deeply unpopular the reparations were, even in mainline circles. Significantly, the first African American to be nominated for the presidency of the NCC, Albert Cleage, a Detroit pastor, was defeated by the first woman to be elected, Cynthia Wedel. The rights agenda had been extended from race to gender, and on this occasion race lost the contest. The rapid decline of churches' giving to the NCC from 1969, as also of the membership of its affiliated denominations, may not be unrelated to their espousal of a cause that even in "liberal" churches appealed to denominational hierarchies far more than to those in the pews.[15] Despite its mixed reception within the United States, the Manifesto helped to establish the struggle against racism on an international stage, which was precisely Forman's brief in the SNCC.

Martin Luther King had been invited to preach at the opening service of the Uppsala Assembly of the World Council of Churches in July 1968;

after his assassination, the writer James Baldwin, the son of a Baptist minister, took his place. The Assembly instructed the WCC to take active steps to combat racism. A consultation on racism scheduled for May 19–24, 1969, in Notting Hill, a multiracial area of London, was charged with implementing the Uppsala assembly's commitment. One of the speakers was to be Eduardo Mondlane, a product of the Swiss Presbyterian mission in Mozambique and founding president of FRELIMO, the Mozambique Liberation Front, but only three days after receiving his invitation to speak, he was assassinated in Dar es Salaam. The acting president of the African National Congress (ANC), Oliver Tambo, who was a practicing Anglican, took his place. Tambo spoke repudiating the charge of the South African government that ANC leaders were terrorists, but the most dramatic moment of the consultation came at the end, when five young blacks, most of them Americans drawn from the SNCC, seized the microphone and read a "Declaration of Revolution." The Declaration concluded with a demand that by 11 am the following morning the WCC pledge itself to make reparations of £60 million—Forman's campaign had crossed the Atlantic and forged a connection with the anti-apartheid movement.[16] No such pledge was forthcoming. Nevertheless, with the strong support of the WCC general secretary Eugene Carson Blake, the meeting formulated a response that committed the WCC to a seven-point plan of action. Point 3 expressed support for the principle of reparations. Point 4 committed the World Council to establish a unit "to deal with the eradication of racism." Point 6 made specific reference to southern Africa. Point 7 declared "That all else failing, the Church and churches support resistance movements, including revolutions, which are aimed at the elimination of political or economic tyranny which makes racism possible."[17]

The WCC had embarked on the most hotly debated undertaking in its history. The Programme to Combat Racism (PCR) was formally launched in 1970. Although the WCC Central Committee rejected the principle of reparations, it created a Special Fund to support organizations working for the liberation of oppressed people. Initial grants of $200,000 were made to nineteen organizations. By the end of 1974 grants amounting to more than $1 million had been awarded from the Fund.[18]

II. Apartheid and the Churches

Delegates attended the Notting Hill consultation from many different parts of the globe, and its concerns covered racial and indigenous issues in all continents. Participants included Cath Walker, an aboriginal Australian woman, and Hector Martinez, a Peruvian Indian anthropologist.

Nonetheless, southern Africa, and South Africa in particular, were the most prominent objects of the PCR in the first twenty-five years of its history. Others present at Notting Hill included such strong supporters of African interests as the New Zealander Garfield Todd, who was a former Churches of Christ missionary and prime minister of Rhodesia from 1953 to 1958, and Michael Scott, a former Anglican missionary to South Africa who had in the 1940s helped to organize a nonparty group called the Campaign for Right and Justice before being expelled from the country in 1950. The first speaker at Notting Hill was Scott's close associate, Trevor Huddleston (1913–98), who at the end of 1955 had also been forced to leave South Africa, though in his case he was recalled by his religious order, the Community of the Resurrection, before he was pushed out by the government. Huddleston, author of a fearless exposé of life in the Johannesburg slum of Sophiatown, *Naught for Your Comfort*,[19] served as bishop of Masasi in Tanzania from 1960 to 1968 before being appointed bishop of Stepney in the east end of London.[20]

With Canon John Collins of St. Paul's Cathedral, Scott and Huddleston were the prime movers in the early British campaign against apartheid. Collins first became involved in South African affairs as early as 1952. In 1956, in response to the arrest for treason of Nelson Mandela and 155 others, he set up the Defence and Aid Fund for Southern Africa, a forerunner of the Anti-Apartheid Movement formed in 1960.[21] Collins is also of note as one of the founders in February 1958 of the Campaign for Nuclear Disarmament. Scott and Huddleston—and to a lesser extent Collins—were Anglo-Catholics, heirs to the Victorian Christian Socialist tradition that emphasized the radical implications of the incarnation of Christ, which gave sacramental value to the material world. Another controversial adherent of that tradition who soon became a thorn in the side of the South African government was Ambrose Reeves (1899–1980), bishop of Johannesburg from 1949 to 1960. Through a letter to the *Rand Daily Mail* and a subsequent book, *Shooting at Sharpeville*, Reeves publicized the truth behind the Sharpeville massacre on March 21, 1960, when, in a mass demonstration against the pass laws, which required Africans always to carry a pass legitimating their presence in "white" areas, 69 Africans were shot dead (mostly in the back) by the South African police, and 186 wounded.[22] The government responded in September 1960 by deporting Reeves: he was the first Anglican cleric to face such a sanction. Later, in 1985, Desmond Tutu, then secretary-general of the South African Council of Churches (SACC), would be appointed as the first black bishop of Johannesburg. As spokesman for the SACC, then as bishop of

Johannesburg from 1985 to 1986, and finally as archbishop of Cape Town until 1996, Tutu maintained and extended the tradition pioneered by Scott, Huddleston, and Reeves. After the coming of majority rule he was appointed chairman of South Africa's Truth and Reconciliation Commission, established in 1995 to promote national reconciliation and healing of the deep wounds inflicted by apartheid.

The prophetic stance of these Anglican leaders gives the lie to any suggestion that the English-speaking churches were uniformly supine in the face of the systematic injustice that was apartheid. Their theology of the kingdom of God propelled them into confrontation with a state dedicated to the preservation of racial hierarchy. Nonetheless, it would be equally misleading to imply that such figures as Reeves or Tutu carried the majority of their church constituency with them in their opposition to the white regime. Reeves, for example, in July 1960 came under intense pressure to resign from white clergy of his diocese who complained in the wake of the Sharpeville massacre that he had devoted too much time to "extra-ecclesiastical affairs." Geoffrey Clayton, metropolitan of the Church of the Province of Southern Africa (now the Anglican Church of Southern Africa) from 1948 to 1957, regarded Scott, Reeves, and Huddleston as misguided extremists.[23] In the twenty-five years between Reeves's deportation and Tutu's accession to the see of Johannesburg, the church, while maintaining a stance of theoretical opposition to apartheid, reached a measure of accommodation to the apartheid regime.

Although the majority of the members of the mission-founded Anglophone churches were black, these churches were incapable on their own of making an effective challenge to government policy. Ultimately a successful Christian challenge to apartheid would have to originate from two sources. First, it would require at least some support within the community that exercised power, which meant from the Dutch Reformed churches of the Afrikaner people (who made up approximately 60 percent of the minority white population), especially the *Volkskerk*, the *Nederduitse Gereformeerde Kerk* (NGK). Second, it would require mass support from a wider cross section of the churches that represented the majority black African population. We will consider these two constituencies in turn.

Contrary to popular belief, the Dutch Reformed churches were not the originators of segregationist policy in South Africa earlier in the century. Rather that unhappy distinction belongs to English-speaking paternalist moderates. During the 1920s the question of African education—how far it should aim at equipping Africans for full assimilation as equals in white society, and how far it should be adapted to the subordinate roles that blacks played in the economy—became of central importance in South African politics. Christian theorists of African education—among them Charles T. Loram, Chief Inspector of Native Education in Natal,[24] and Edgar H. Brookes, author of the influential *The History of Native Policy in South Africa* (1924), saw the partial territorial segregation of races as a realistic compromise, a halfway house between what they held to be the unachievable goal of full racial assimilation and the unacceptable exploitation of blacks by unenlightened settlers, especially in the Transvaal. This was a position that at a church-sponsored conference on Native Affairs in September 1923 received the substantial endorsement of Zaccheus Richard Mahabane, a spokesman for the ANC.[25] Loram and Brookes were liberals at heart, and were among the founders of the South African Institute of Race Relations in 1929. Loram had served on both the Phelps–Stokes Commissions on African education in 1920–21 and 1924. Brookes in 1930 publicly recanted his earlier advocacy of separate racial development and became a close friend of the celebrated anti-apartheid writer Alan Paton.[26]

Over the next few years various mission thinkers in the Dutch Reformed churches articulated a more absolute and highly theorized doctrine of separate development. Their leading mission scholar, Professor Johannes du Plessis, expounded a paternalistic view of the missionary responsibility of the DRC, in which the church, empowered by its synodical structure, had a key national role to play in advancing the welfare of the African population. In 1931 the NGK synod in the Orange Free State added a more explicitly territorial dimension, explaining that the missionary objective must be to enable Africans to live "on their own terrain, separated and apart," forming their own *christenvolk* [Christian people]. In 1935 the Federal Council of the NGK committed the Church to a policy of assisting the "Native and the Coloured [mixed-race] to develop into self-respecting Christian nations." In the 1940s these ideas assumed a more explicitly neo-Calvinist character, deriving in part from the ideas of the Dutch statesman and Calvinist theologian, Abraham Kuyper (1837–1920). Pseudo-scientific or Germanic notions of race played little or no part in Kuyper's ideas. Nevertheless, the principle that God in his sovereignty had separated nations into their allotted spheres within which their distinctive cultures could flourish became one of the ideological foundations of the policy of "apartheid" implemented by the National Party after 1948.[27]

Since Dutch Reformed mission theology was so instrumental in the construction of the ideology of apartheid, it might seem logical to assume that there would be little challenge from within the DRC to the operation of apartheid by the South African government. This would be a false assumption. Theorists develop idealistic visions of the political systems they propose; politicians, if they adopt such visions, do so for reasons that may be quite distinct; and it may not be long before the theorists protest at what has happened to their vision. This divergence first became apparent in December 1960, when eighty delegates from ten different South African churches gathered in the Johannesburg suburb of Cottesloe for a consultation sponsored by the WCC to investigate the crisis provoked by the Sharpeville killings. Among them were delegates from the Transvaal and Cape NGK, and also a delegation from the politically ultraconservative Transvaal-based *Nederduitsch Hervormde Kerk* (NHK). There were eighteen black delegates. With the exception of the NHK delegation, all participants agreed a Statement that was openly critical of some aspects of the way in which apartheid policy was being implemented. It included a paragraph that subverted the foundational assumptions of government "Bantu" policy, but was in fact borrowed, with small but significant amendments, from a memorandum issued by the NGK itself:

> It is our conviction that the right to own land wherever he is domiciled, and to participate in the government of his country, is part of the dignity of the adult man, and for this reason a policy which permanently denies to non-White people the right of collaboration in the government of the country of which they are citizens cannot be justified.[28]

It was not surprising that the Cottesloe Statement was soon attacked by several Afrikaans newspapers and by Prime Minister Hendrik Verwoerd, and was eventually repudiated by the NGK Synods of both the Transvaal and the Cape. A consultation that appeared initially to have bridged the racial and ecclesiastical divide in South Africa ended by widening it, for both the Transvaal and the Cape NGK churches soon withdrew from membership of the WCC, entering an international ecclesiastical isolation that would endure until after the coming of majority rule. Cottesloe revealed that there were some in the NGK for whom "apartheid" was an admissible system only if it could be shown to be a genuine attempt at the protection of African interests. One such participant at Cottesloe was the acting moderator of the Transvaal NGK Synod, Dr. Beyers Naudé.

Beyers Naudé (1915–2004) was a member of the Afrikaner nationalist secret society, the Broederbond, and came from impeccable Dutch Reformed stock.[29] Yet, in the wake of his own church's repudiation of the Cottesloe Statement, Naudé came to the view that as a political system apartheid did not, and could not correspond to the vision of appropriate cultural autonomy for the different peoples of South Africa that Reformed theology had outlined. He resigned from the Broederbond in March 1963. In the following September he established the Christian Institute of Southern Africa (CI), an interdenominational group concerned to promote reconciliation. The NGK responded by depriving him of his status as an ordained minister. He launched a journal, *Pro Veritate*, and began to forge a broad-based Christian alliance in opposition to the regime, inspired by the model of the Confessing Church in Germany. By 1972 the Christian Institute was forming connections with the black liberation movements funded by the PCR, and Naudé came under increasing government scrutiny. He was summoned to testify before the Schlebusch Commission, appointed by the government to investigate the Institute and other bodies that had become prominent in the struggle against apartheid. Naudé declined to appear, protesting that the Commission lacked impartiality and was illegally holding its sessions in secret. Certain unnamed theologians gave evidence to the Commission. Its report, published in November 1974, was an extraordinary piece of work for a secular body composed of members of parliament. It devoted a whole chapter to an exposition of "Black Theology" and its links to the Black Power movement in the United States, describing Black Theology as a synthesis between the American Social Gospel and communism. The report catalogued the links of the CI to the WCC, which was castigated for having succumbed to the heresy of "horizontalism" articulated by political theologians such as Johannes Baptist Metz and Richard Shaull. The report concluded that certain activities of the Institute constituted "a danger to the State."[30]

Naudé, along with others who had similarly refused to appear before the Commission, was put on trial. His trial in the Pretoria Regional Court in November 1973 attracted enormous international interest. The Anglican archbishop of Wales, Dr. Gwilym Williams, attended on behalf of the British Council of Churches. Professor A. N. Allott, representing the International Committee of Jurists, described the mood in the crowded courtroom "as akin to the joyful spirit of the Early Christians before a public interrogation."[31] The court found Naudé guilty, and imposed a nominal fine of 50 rand or a jail sentence of one month, plus a further suspended sentence of three months. He elected to go to prison, but was soon released after a friend paid his fine. More serious was the action of the government in response to the report of the Schlebusch Commission: the CI was declared to be an "affected organization," meaning that it could no longer receive the substantial overseas funding on which it had depended. The end came in October 1977, in the wake of the protests against the death in custody on September 12 of the black activist Steve Biko: the CI and a number of other anti-apartheid organizations were banned. Naudé himself was one of a number of CI activists to be "banned"—a form of house arrest. From this point the Christian campaign against apartheid passed increasingly into black hands, although Naudé's role in the struggle was not yet over: on his unbanning in 1985 he succeeded Desmond Tutu as general secretary of the SACC. On his death in September 2004, this former member of the Broederbond was given the honor of a state funeral, with Tutu preaching the sermon.

We now turn to the question of how the wider community of the black Christian population became mobilized in active opposition to apartheid. Many of the black Christians who now came to the fore in the anti-apartheid movement came from a theological tradition that differed markedly from either the Anglo-Catholic sacramentalism of Ambrose Reeves or the Reformed vision of Beyers Naudé. The evangelical student movement in South African universities dates from 1895, when at a conference at Stellenbosch University chaired by the influential Dutch Reformed evangelical, Andrew Murray Jr., the Students' Christian Association (SCA) was formed. Unlike other branches of the student Christian movement represented by the World's Student Christian Federation (WSCF), the South African branch remained conservative evangelical in theology. In January 1965 conservative Afrikaners succeeded in dismembering the SCA on racial lines into four separate movements representing respectively Afrikaners, English-speaking whites, coloreds (mixed-race), and blacks. In protest against this dismemberment, a group of more radical Anglicans within the movement joined forces with like-minded Catholics in 1967 to form a new multiracial University Christian Movement (UCM), which adopted an explicit liberation theology stance. Its members included the Anglicans Steve Biko and Barney Pityana. Though it lasted only until 1972 before being suppressed by the government, the UCM gave birth in July 1968 to the South African Students' Organisation (SASO), led by Biko, which was a primary influence shaping the Black Consciousness movement of the 1970s—a movement that was closely related to the growth of a self-consciously Black Theology in South Africa.[32]

The UCM thus played a short-lived but strategic role in mobilizing radical opinion in the black universities and seminaries. But perhaps more significant still was the evangelical black body formed as a result of the dismemberment of the SCA in 1965. It took the title of the Students' Christian Movement (SCM), though its theological stance remained much closer to that of the International Fellowship of Evangelical Students

(IFES) than to that of the SCM in Britain. Indeed, when the Students' Christian Movement and the Students' Christian Association reunited in 1997 after the end of apartheid, the resulting united body, the Students' Christian Organization, affiliated to IFES rather than to the World's Student Christian Federation (WSCF). Unlike the UCM, the South African SCM worked, not simply in the three university colleges designated by the government for the black population—at Fort Hare in the Cape, Ngoye in Zululand, and Turfloop in the northern Transvaal—but crucially also in the black high schools, where it had contact with up to 100,000 students by the early 1980s.[33]

In 1972 a young Pentecostal enrolled to study mathematics and physical sciences in what was now "The University of the North" at Turfloop. Frank Chikane (b. 1951) had been involved in the SCM as a pupil at Orlando High School in Soweto, but on arrival at Turfloop discovered that the student body had banned the SCM on the grounds that its conservative theology aligned it with the white oppressor. SCM meetings thus took place unofficially and furtively, frequently off campus. However, in the election of the new committee for the 1972–3 academic year, a new chairman was elected. Cyril Ramaphosa (b. 1952) had been chairman of the SCM in his high school, Mphaphuli High School in Sibasa. A law student at the University of the North from early 1972, he proceeded to restructure the SCM and incorporate an explicit repudiation of apartheid into its doctrinal basis. The SCM now became an accepted feature of the student community at the University of the North and a significant political force in the channeling of black student sentiment.[34] Chikane was elected a member of the SCM national executive and chairperson of the SCM's Evangelistic Fellowship (mission department). At the 1974 national SCM conference at Moriya in Lesotho in June Ramaphosa first came into contact with Caesar Molebatsi (b. 1949), leader of Youth Alive, an evangelistic movement that worked in the Soweto high schools. Molebatsi, whom Chikane knew from his high school days, had just returned from four years of study at Northeastern Bible College in New Jersey. When a government informer was discovered among those present, it took an impassioned exposition by Molebatsi of the implications of the cross of Christ as taught in John's Gospel to persuade the radicals present that he should not be lynched.[35] Ramaphosa and Molebatsi became firm friends, and Ramaphosa soon became chairman of the Board of Youth Alive. Chikane, Ramaphosa, and Molebatsi began to collaborate closely, both in SCM evangelistic missions in the black universities and in Youth Alive evangelistic campaigns in Soweto. However, such evangelistic encounters with young people increasingly compelled them to seek to relate evangelical Christianity to the rising tide of black consciousness.

At various discipleship courses or national evangelical intervarsity conferences held between 1973 and 1976, some of which were joint events with the SCA, SCM delegates gave vent to their mounting sense of grievance and frustration at the seeming indifference of the SCA to issues of racial justice. The 1976 SCM conference held at Cyara in the Hekpoor Valley in July, unanimously issued a public declaration that owed some of its theological formulations to the Lausanne Covenant of 1974 and yet indicted apartheid as "unchristian, anti-God, demonic and anti-man."[36] Ramaphosa, by now national chairman of the SCM,[37] suffered two extended periods of imprisonment at the hands of the government between September 1974 and February 1977. In December 1982 he became the founding general secretary of the National Union of Mineworkers, which played a pivotal role in the defense of the rights of black labor; in July 1991, he was elected secretary-general of the ANC. His future career would be played out mainly in the political area; his connections with organized Christianity weakened over the years.[38]

Frank Chikane, on leaving university, taught for a short while at Naledi High School in Soweto, the school where in June 1976 the Soweto school uprising began, marking a milestone in the history of anti-apartheid mobilization. On behalf of the SCM he conducted devotional meetings in schools in Soweto and elsewhere, but increasingly found it impossible to separate evangelism from politics. At the same time he was studying by correspondence to enter the ministry of his Pentecostal church, the Apostolic Faith Mission, and became involved with the evangelistic crusades of the German Pentecostal evangelist Reinhard Bonnke. Ordained in 1980, Chikane soon found himself in trouble with the Apostolic Faith Mission on account of his "political" activities; in October 1981 his ministerial recognition was withdrawn. Chikane refused to resign his church membership or transfer to an AIC, maintaining that he remained committed to its evangelical stance and Pentecostal understanding of spiritual experience.[39] In any case the AICs were, with some exceptions, not distinguished by overt commitment to agitate against the government. In September 1982 Chikane was appointed coordinator (later general secretary) of the Institute of Contextual Theology (ICT) a body founded in Johannesburg in 1981. The ICT became the midwife of the famous Kairos Document issued in September 1985.[40] Its principal authors were Chikane and a Dominican priest, Albert Nolan, who was a committed supporter of liberation theology. The Kairos Document urged that now was the critical moment or *kairos* for the South African churches to take urgent and radical steps to secure justice. It appealed to South African Christians to adopt a truly prophetic theology of action for regime change, arguing that the South African government had lost all moral legitimacy. It therefore concluded that it was "the *moral duty* of all who are oppressed to resist oppression and to struggle for liberation and justice."[41] In July 1987 Chikane succeeded Beyers Naudé as general secretary of the SACC. Like Ramaphosa (later deputy president under Jacob Zuma), he was appointed to high office in majority-ruled South Africa, eventually becoming director-general in the office of President Thabo Mbeki.

The end of apartheid in May 1994 was not the work of Christians alone, or even primarily. Arguably it was the result of a prudential calculation by the regime that South African whites stood a better chance of maintaining their standard of living under a majority rule produced by negotiation than in a country that was descending into violent chaos. But in a country with one of the highest rates of church going in the world,[42] it was inevitable that the churches would exert unusual influence, one way or the other, on the process of political change. Moreover, in a church context in which many of the missionary influences on African Christians were of a decidedly evangelical character, it is hardly surprising that evangelical Christians were prominent, not simply in the theoretical construction of apartheid, but also in its subversion. The radicalization of the SCM from 1972 was a response to the mood its evangelists had encountered in the black universities and high schools. Nevertheless, the SCM appears to have been more than a simple barometer of the changing ideological climate. Its nationwide network of university and high school groups became a crucible for the emergence in the black townships of a new style of Christianity that combined evangelical faith with an increasingly radical political commitment to the restoration of the rights of the black population. With the UCM forcibly removed from the stage in 1972, the evangelical liberationists of the SCM played a more strategic role in the demolition of apartheid than is generally acknowledged. When as a young student myself I attended the annual conference of the SCM held at Turfloop in the summer of 1975 as one of an uncomfortable handful of whites among several hundred black participants, what took my breath away was the extent and depth of the political resentment apparent among the evangelical teachers who ran the SCM groups in the township high schools and comprised the majority of the delegates. I was therefore not surprised when in June 1976 the Soweto uprising began among high school students: it was, "in part a rebellion organized by Christians."[43]

In South Africa in the 1920s and 1930s advocates of the Social Gospel had taken the first cautious steps in Christian thinking about race problems. Liberal Christian theorists such as C. T. Loram and E. H. Brookes initially saw the partial segregation of South Africa's black indigenous peoples as the best way to achieve their protection from white exploitation. They also advocated forms of Christian education "adapted" to African needs as the means to promote their advancement in "civilization," while disagreeing with other missionary theorists, mainly from the European continent, who held to a more absolute form of differentiated education premised on the use of the Bantu vernaculars.[44] After the Bantu Education Act of 1953, which removed black education from Christian missionary control, this Social Gospel or liberal tradition largely disappeared from the educational sphere. [45] When the apartheid system reached the peak of its oppressive force in the 1970s, it was the township high schools and the campuses of the new black universities that became the arena within which the spiritual and ultimately political evangelists of the SCM could articulate the ethical demands of the Christian gospel.

III. The Canadian Churches and the Residential Schools

The same Social Gospel tradition that was influential in South Africa between the world wars shaped Christian approaches to the "advancement" of the indigenous peoples in Canada, but in "native education" there it survived unchallenged for longer—at least until 1969—only for its eventual collapse in the face of human rights ideology to be all the more traumatic for the churches.

Although less widely publicized internationally than the South African case, the Canadian residential (boarding) schools constitute another example of the ambiguous role played by the churches in the treatment of indigenous peoples by white settler populations. The great expansion in the churches' educational work on the "Indian" reserves (mostly located in western Canada) came in the 1880s and 1890s, in the wake of the Davin Report on Industrial Schools for Indians and Half-Breeds of 1879, which made Indian education a government priority and increased the federal funding available to the churches and Christian mission agencies. The schools were of three kinds: mission-operated day schools situated in Indian communities on the reserves; the residential schools, located either on or close to the reserves; and industrial or trade schools in the larger urban centers. The day schools were always more numerous than the residential schools, though they have been largely ignored in historical discussion. The residential schools were originally all established and operated by the churches, but were supervised and funded by the federal government on a per capita basis. In 1902 there were 221 day schools, 40 residential schools, and 22 industrial schools. 100 were Catholic (by far the largest number being run by the French congregation, the Oblates of Mary Immaculate), 87 were Anglican, 41 Methodist, 14 Presbyterian, and 41 non-denominational.[46] Throughout the century, Catholic institutions accounted for about 60 percent of the residential schools; the Anglican Church was the second largest operator, followed (after its formation in June 1925) by the United Church, a union of Methodists and Congregationalists with the majority of Presbyterian churches.

At their peak from the late 1920s to the late 1940s, the residential schools never numbered more than eighty institutions throughout Canada. Estimates of the proportion of First Nations children educated in the residential schools vary; the schools probably never housed more than one-third of all First Nations and Inuit children of school age, though in 1948 they still accounted for an estimated 60 percent of all First Nations children who actually attended school.[47] From 1948, and especially after the Indian Act of 1951, the Department of Indian Affairs adopted a policy of integrating Indian children wherever possible with other children, and hence began closing the residential schools. In 1969 the Department terminated the partnership with the churches and assumed direct management of the remaining seventy-two schools. Increasingly the residential schools became venues for the education of orphans and children from broken or isolated homes. The last residential schools closed in 1986.

So far as the federal government was concerned, the residential schools were an essential plank in its program to "assimilate" or absorb aboriginal peoples within the Dominion of Canada. Whereas the demography of South Africa made the prospect of the full assimilation of indigenous peoples threatening to the ruling white minority, in Canada the state espoused the assimilation of the much smaller First Nations population as a prudential route to their absorption. Education, pronounced the Minister of Indian Affairs in 1908, would "elevate the Indian from his condition of savagery" and make "him a self-supporting member of the State, and eventually a citizen in good standing."[48] Residential education, it was believed, offered a controlled environment that would transform wandering tribal populations into economically productive members of settled communities, willing and able to play their subordinate part in the construction of a white-led (and predominantly Protestant) Canada. The vast open spaces of the Canadian prairies were viewed as a blank page on which Anglo-Saxon Protestants could write their script for a new imperial nation that would be pro-British, Christian, and civilized.[49] Training in useful trades and agriculture would wean First Nations people off their dependence on hunting and fishing, and promote stable and self-sustaining communities, while Christian teaching would inculcate the moral values and responsibilities of citizenship. Instruction in the English (or in Francophone Canada French) language was integral to the policy of assimilation; hence the Department of Indian Affairs as early as the 1880s attempted to prohibit the use of Indian languages in the schools, not simply in the classroom, but also outside it.

The entire program depended on persuading aboriginal parents to send their children to school. Although the system of per capita grants introduced in 1893 supplied the churches with incentives to maximize their enrolment, both government and churches encountered widespread parental reluctance to send their children to a school that was often far distant from their settlements. This was an indication, not necessarily of the poor quality of the education, but more likely of the indispensable role of children in the indigenous domestic economy. One Anglican school principal in Saskatchewan commented in 1906:

> [The] teacher or missionary is entirely powerless in the matter of persuading or forcing the parents to send their children to school. . . . Indians either simply laugh or point blank refuse, or in some cases take the children away, or coax them to run away after they have been in school for some time, and all efforts to get them back are utterly futile.[50]

In 1920 the government responded by making education compulsory between the ages of seven and fifteen, and gave authority to truancy officers to enter Indian homes and fine parents who were keeping their children from school. In 1930 the period during which attendance was normally compulsory was extended to the age of sixteen, and in 1933 officers of the Royal Canadian Mounted Police were appointed to act as truancy officers.[51] Such measures of enforcement had mixed success, and are not without parallel in many other modern societies. Nonetheless, they have given rise to the now widely disseminated picture of First Nations children being "interned" against their will in the residential schools. This vision of enforced cultural assimilation supplied the motive power of the residential school system, at least until 1948, when Canada began to move toward a more nuanced policy of "integration" that allowed a continuing place for aboriginal cultures within the life of the nation. As in South Africa, the churches responded with varying degrees of enthusiasm to different aspects of the assimilative vision. The concern to promote sustainable agriculture instead of reliance on hunting and fishing had the enthusiastic support of almost all Catholics and Protestants, and finds parallels in countless other missionary contexts, not to speak of present-day environmentalism.[52]

In contrast, the predominantly Protestant and Anglophone character of the assimilation policy was less welcome to the Oblates of Mary and their female collaborators, the Sisters of Charity of Montréal, or "Grey Nuns." As a Francophone religious congregation identified with Canada's Catholic minority, the Oblates had every reason to resist the drive toward Anglicization.[53] Originally they were strongly committed to learning Indian languages and to their use in education, but over time the weight of government influence greatly weakened this commitment.[54] The main concern of the Oblates was a characteristically Catholic one—namely, to secure a distinctively Catholic approach to education that kept both Protestant and secular influence at bay. Sometimes that concern dovetailed with government Indian education policy, but often it did not. The Oblates regarded the Department of Indian Affairs as deplorably pro-Protestant,[55] yet supported the introduction of compulsory education in 1920, seeing it as an opportunity to extend Catholic influence. By 1946 an Oblate Commission on Indian Work was able to make the smug declaration: "The present system of education approved by the Dominion Government and set up by the Indian Affairs Department is satisfactory to us, and no change whatever is desired or will be accepted by us."[56] Hence, when, two years later, major change did come, in the form of a government commitment to move First Nations children increasingly to integrated day schools, the resistance from the Oblates was determined, except in those areas where there were Catholic day schools to which Catholic children could be sent. Father A. Renaud, Director General of the Oblates, argued that Catholic residential schools in fact afforded more opportunities for a Christian education that was sensitive to aboriginal culture than did religiously mixed day schools. Significantly, many aboriginal Catholic parents shared his resistance. The Indian Catholic League, formed in Alberta in 1954, increasingly championed their interests. A conference in January 1960 on Indian high school education in the Prairie provinces heard evidence from the Catholic Church that "at recent meetings held in the West a number of Indians had expressed a strong objection to sending their children to non-Indian schools" because their "children did not feel at ease among non-Indians."[57]

Thus the policy of racial and educational segregation embodied in the residential schools for a time attracted significant indigenous support, at least among the Catholic constituency to which the majority of residential schools were affiliated. However, from the 1960s onwards, public support for the residential schools waned rapidly; from the late 1980s, the close Catholic association with the schools became toxic in the light of revelations of sexual abuse. The Oblates paid a high price for their tenacious adherence to the principle of the residential school long after other churches and the government had abandoned it.[58]

The case of the second largest provider of the residential schools—the Anglican Church—points to two further conclusions. The Anglican case suggests, first, that the accusation that the schools mounted a linguistic assault on indigenous cultures has only limited veracity. Anglican work among the indigenous communities of western Canada was pioneered by the Church Missionary Society (CMS), whose policy, influenced by the legacy of the great Victorian missionary strategist Henry Venn, was strongly supportive of the use of vernacular languages as a necessary foundation for the building of an indigenous church. In the nineteenth century Anglican missions, like the Catholic ones, were a significant force for the preservation of Indian languages, even though the chiefs were often keen for their people to learn English. However, the formation in 1893 of the general synod of the Church of England in Canada prompted the CMS to plan to devolve its Canada missions to the Church in Canada; in 1902 the Missionary Society of the Church of England in Canada (MSCC) was formed, and the CMS announced its intention of withdrawing its support of the Indian missions within ten years.[59] Historians suggest that the gradual transfer of responsibility to the MSCC rendered the Anglican missions more inclined to accept the Department of Native Affairs' opposition to the use of Indian languages in the schools.[60] Nevertheless, the weight of oral evidence from both former staff and former pupils of the Anglican schools suggests that even in the final decades of the schools' history, there were significant numbers of schools in which use of Indian languages was encouraged outside of the classroom and whose principals had learned Cree or other aboriginal languages. Missionaries produced probably the majority of the published grammars of the Cree language—hardly what one would expect of those committed to cultural genocide. The use of English in the classroom was a pedagogical necessity in schools where pupils came from different language groups, in addition to being a government requirement. The charge of cultural genocide via a systematic assault on Indian languages may be justified in relation to government policy, but at least in the Anglican residential schools, many teaching staff regarded English instruction as an addition to, rather than a replacement for, the vernaculars.[61]

The progressive transfer of the Anglican schools from the CMS to the MSCC after 1902 had a further significance, which leads to a second conclusion, namely that some Christians from an early date were well aware of the failings of the schools. The officials of the new Canadian missionary society, anxious about their ability to shoulder the financial burden of the Indian missions, began to view them with a critical eye. This was especially true of a leading Toronto lawyer, Samuel Hume Blake.[62] Blake was a firm conservative evangelical and enthusiast for missions overseas. Appointed chairman of a committee appointed by the MSCC to investigate its Indian missions, he soon formed the view that the total cost of supporting the Anglican schools work would consume all the resources of the MSCC, leaving nothing for its foreign mission (in Japan). More broadly, he succeeded in 1907 in persuading the government to appoint an interdenominational (though exclusively Protestant) Advisory Board of Indian Education, which began to make radical recommendations for the reform of the Indian school system.

Blake found ample support for his case in the findings of a damning report on the Indian Schools of Manitoba and the North West Territories submitted to the government in June 1907 by Dr. Peter H. Bryce, the Chief Medical Officer for the Departments of the Interior and Indian Affairs. Bryce, a Presbyterian of strong Social Gospel convictions, included in his report the shocking revelation that 24 percent of all Indian students of the residential schools in these provinces had died in, or shortly after leaving the schools, mostly as a result of tuberculosis, which was endemic throughout the reserves, but obviously spread like wildfire in the closed quarters of a boarding school. The government refused to publish the main recommendations of his report, which called for expensive improvements to sanitary conditions and greater government control of the schools system, but they were widely leaked to the press.[63] Blake began to collaborate with Bryce, using his evidence as ammunition in a 1908 pamphlet *Don't You Hear the Red Man Calling?* which published the results of the Advisory Board's inquiry. Blake lambasted the residential schools as fatally unhealthy, inefficient, and unnecessary: like many later critics, he highlighted the deleterious effect of the per capita grant in encouraging competition between the denominations to "lure" children into the overcrowded schools.[64] Under the influence of Blake's pamphlet, the MSCC committed itself to the goal of the full secularization of Indian education, and both the Methodists and the Presbyterians lent their support to the call for increased government funding.

Blake's call for the secularization of the Indian schools soon foundered on the rocks of principled Catholic opposition and government concerns for economy. The Methodists and Presbyterians hesitated to support full secularization. Even the MSCC, under pressure from the bishops and many of the missionaries involved, in October 1910 reversed Blake's policy and authorized a special grant of 10,000 Canadian dollars in support of the residential schools. In November 1910 representatives of the churches signed a new agreement with the government, by which industrial schools would gradually be phased out and residential schools reduced in number but given substantially higher funding.[65] Bryce returned to the fray after his enforced retirement from government service, publishing a hard-hitting pamphlet in 1922, *The Story of a National Crime: An Appeal for Justice to the Indians of Canada.*[66]

The exposés by Bryce and Blake of the chronic underfunding of the residential schools failed to produce fundamental reform, even though the level of federal funding was raised by the 1910 settlement. Although motivated as much by the concerns of the Toronto Anglican establishment for financial prudence as by humanitarian concern for First Nations people, Blake's outspoken criticisms of the schools anticipated those that have been made in more recent years. The campaigns waged by Bryce and Blake constitute evidence that some Christians were aware of the grave deficiencies of the schools from an early stage in their history and attempted to do something about them. Sadly they remained minority voices.

The Social Gospel principles shaping Bryce's concern to reform the physical environment of the residential schools were widely shared by the Methodists, Presbyterians, and Congregationalists who formed the United Church in Canada in 1925. The Social Gospel, however, did not necessarily lead Christians to perceive the residential schools as intrinsically unjust. As in South Africa in the 1920s and 1930s, it often seems instead to have intensified their determination to place indigenous people within a physical and educational environment believed to be conducive to their moral improvement and progress in civilization. One of Charles Loram's final contributions before his death in 1940 was to convene a joint conference on "The North American Indian Today" organized by the University of Toronto and Yale University, where he was Sterling Professor of Education from 1931. The premise of the conference, in Loram's words, was that "the only question" was the rate at which "Indian" culture "should be eliminated or superseded or changed"; the role of progressive Christian schooling was to prepare the Indians "for their inevitable acculturation."[67] John Webster Grant's conclusion is apposite, if unwelcome to modern ears: "To an extent that is seldom recognized, the assault on Indian culture bemoaned by social activists today was led by social activists of an earlier era."[68] By the 1930s similar motives were widely discernible among the Catholic missionaries, who were increasingly influenced by the social reformist ideas of *Rerum Novarum* (1894) and Pius XI's *Quadragesimo Anno* (1931).[69] As recently as 1955 the Committee on Missionary Education of the United Church could publish a review of the Church's Indian missions that included the following assessment of its educational work:

> In the annals of a primitive race no greater inspirational story can be told than that of the influence of education on the Canadian Indian people, progressing to the high standard of attainment of the present day. It is a story of release from primitive superstition; of the reclamation of a completely primitive race exposed to the impact of a modern civilization with all its appalling vices and complex contradictions; of the dissipation of deeply-rooted prejudices engendered by shameful exploitation. It is a fascinating story.[70]

Yet within fifteen years, an article published in the magazine of the United Church could refer to the attempt to use education to conform indigenous peoples to the aggressive economic practices of white Canadian culture as akin to "feeding them into a new kind of cultural gas chamber."[71] From the self-satisfied tone of the 1955 survey, the United Church moved steadily toward a position of public declaration of shame for its work among indigenous communities: in August 1986 the Moderator of the Church issued a formal "Apology to First Nations" for the Church's "cultural imperialism."[72] Similar public apologies followed from the Catholic Bishops Conference in March 1991, the congregation of the Oblates in July 1991, the Anglican Church in August 1993, and the small Presbyterian Church in October 1994. The difference between the United Church apology of 1986 and its successors was that the former was generalized and made no mention of residential schools, whereas the others focused specifically on the schools. The reason for the difference was almost certainly the impact of the disclosure in October 1990 by Phil Fontaine, grand chief of the Assembly of Manitoba Chiefs, of his abuse by Oblate clergy while a pupil at Fort Alexander School in Manitoba.[73] Fontaine's disclosure triggered many similar revelations; in their wake came a flood of lawsuits from former pupils demanding substantial reparations for the multiple forms of abuse they claimed to have experienced in the residential schools. The toxic demand that James Forman had first laid at the door of the American mainline churches in 1969 now hit the Canadian churches, with consequences that were even more serious. The cost of these lawsuits took the Anglican Church in Canada to the brink of bankruptcy, and forced the closure of one Anglican diocese, the diocese of Cariboo, at the end of 2001. The scale of litigation compelled the federal government to intervene to negotiate a settlement.

On May 10, 2006 the government of Canada announced the Indian Residential Schools Settlement Agreement, a legally binding agreement concluded between the government, the largest Canadian churches,[74] and the Assembly of First Nations. The Agreement, which came into effect in September 2007, provided for the payment of compensation to members of the First Nations who had been pupils in residential schools controlled by the government. Under the terms of the Agreement, any former residential school student was entitled to a payment of 10,000 Canadian dollars in respect of their first year in such a school, and a further 3,000 dollars for each subsequent year. In addition, provision was made for judicial assessment of claims of specific physical, sexual, or emotional abuse made by former pupils. By September 30, 2012, the deadline set for the submission of claims under the Agreement, average payments to claimants were running at 28,000 dollars, and an aggregate of 1.6 million in reparations had been paid out; the final total is likely to be as high as 3.5 million.[75]

Alongside this legal process, Canada has followed South African precedent in establishing in 2009 its own Truth and Reconciliation Commission. The Commission has no judicial function or powers to summon witnesses. Former staff members of the schools have generally declined to appear, thus effectively nullifying the goal of "reconciliation" and indeed placing in jeopardy the Commission's parallel goal of establishing the "truth."[76] The Commission has instead organized public events at local, regional and national levels at which "survivors" of the residential schools have shared testimony of their traumatic experiences of abuse and cultural oppression. The repeated use of the term "survivor" consciously evokes memories of the Nazi Holocaust; other terms now regularly employed refer to the former pupils' "internment" in the schools or to their experience of "cultural genocide."[77] The language employed in the residential schools debate has been extreme, for the passions it has evoked have run deep.

IV. From Civilization to Human Rights

Whatever the true balance is in the history of the residential schools between Christian altruism and abuse or cultural oppression—which is almost impossible to determine in the current highly charged political atmosphere—what has to be explained is the relative speed with which Canadian churches from the late 1960s substituted a rights-oriented narrative of culpability in cultural genocide for the older Social Gospel narrative of reforming and equipping indigenous people through Christian civilization. Theological radicalization, especially within the United Church, played its part: the 1960s witnessed the substantial disintegration of the liberal evangelicalism that had marked the church since its formation.[78] The decade also witnessed the beginnings of a growing divergence between the Christian histories of Canada and the United States, in which Canada, hitherto decidedly the more religious of the two nations, embarked on a pathway of self-conscious multiculturalism and top-down secularization.[79] The implication of the residential schools in the spate of sexual abuse scandals that afflicted the Catholic Church in North America, Britain, and Ireland from the late 1980s was also a factor. The most powerful influence, however, was the progressive erosion of the transformative social ideals of Christian civilization that had hitherto shaping Christian attitudes toward indigenous peoples by a postcolonial ideology of indigenism.

The American civil rights movement did not simply give rise to the WCC Programme to Combat Racism, and impact the growth of black consciousness in South Africa—it also profoundly affected attitudes to indigenous peoples north of the border. Canadian First Nations organizations were among those who received grants from the PCR in the early 1970s.[80] The demand for substantial reparations from the Canadian churches for abuses inflicted by the residential schools followed the precedent set by James Forman, and achieved a degree of success far greater than that seen in the United States, with consequences that were little short of disastrous for some of the Canadian churches. Unlike South African blacks, however, First Nations people did not want "integration"— for that seemed only one degree better than the "assimilation" associated with the residential schools. Neither did they agitate for political independence—for that was beyond the reach of political possibility for a small minority population. Whereas in South Africa the Christian affiliation of the black majority fused with liberationism to propel the country to majority rule, in Canada indigenous spokespersons set their sights on the only postcolonial goal within reach—the preservation of First Nations cultural indigeneity and the reaffirmation of Native American spirituality. Christian missions thus became the primary object of aboriginal and (even more) of media criticism, both for their educational policy and for their alleged complicity in the alienation of aboriginal lands. As white

Canadians increasingly tormented themselves with guilt for their treatment of indigenous peoples, residential schools—and the churches that had operated them—became the obvious scapegoat.[81] While in South Africa Christian influence in the black schools and universities proved to be a strategic resource for radicalization and eventual liberation, in Canada the role of the churches in indigenous education has exposed them to the full force of the postcolonial reaction.

CHAPTER TWELVE

A Noise of War in the Camp[*]

HUMAN RIGHTS, GENDER, AND SEXUALITY

I. Egalitarianism and Christian Tradition

For many centuries the majority of Christians had been taught that a hierarchical and hence unequal social order bore the unmistakable stamp of divine approval. That assumption first came under serious challenge from ideas of individual human rights during the age of the Enlightenment in the eighteenth century. With varying degrees of enthusiasm, and at speeds that ranged from a snail's pace to a canter, different sectors of Christendom began to find their way toward theological endorsement of the originally highly contentious notion that the individual human being possessed inalienable natural rights. In this "modern" view, such rights bestowed on the human person a status of fundamental equality with other human beings and hence became the basis for democratic political principles and campaigns for the freedom of the oppressed. However, during the eighteenth and nineteenth centuries the notion was almost entirely restricted to males (and not even to them universally) in its practical application.[1] It was only in the course of the twentieth century that rights ideology crossed the gender divide, giving rise to the women's suffrage movement and the substantial erosion of previously unquestioned assumptions about the God-given roles and hierarchical relationship of the sexes. The extent of this erosion was much greater in the West than in the non-Western world, creating marked divergences between "modern" and many traditional cultures in

---

[*] "There is a noise of war in the camp" (Exodus 32:17).

their estimations of the appropriate roles of women and men in family, society, and politics.

From the second decade of the century in North America and Europe inherited Christian convictions about the theological and ethical legitimacy of restricting ordained leadership in the churches to men began to be questioned. In Protestant and Anglican churches, these convictions were slowly and unevenly abandoned as the century proceeded. Until the 1970s, the ordination of women remained highly unusual, permitted in theory and sporadically practiced by a few denominations, but only very rarely leading to a woman being in sole pastoral charge of a congregation. From the 1970s, in response to the growing influence of the women's liberation movement, campaigns for the admission of women to the ministry or priesthood gathered momentum. For the many who supported their admission, the issue was one of fundamental human equality and hence also of Christian justice; for them, the denial of a natural human right in the name of God was a theological monstrosity, a blasphemy. For their opponents, on the other hand, the demand for women clergy was a spineless capitulation to secular pressure; for them also, it was a theological monstrosity, but of a different kind, because they believed that it contravened apostolic Christian tradition—an argument advanced mostly by those of more Catholic sympathies—or the allegedly clear teaching of the Bible about the divinely ordained "headship" of men—an argument beloved of some conservative evangelicals. The resulting arguments within the churches were thus impassioned. Women were to be found on both sides of the contest.

The first case study in this chapter will examine the debate in one particular church, the Anglican Church in Australia, where the weight of conservative opinion, particularly in the diocese of Sydney, succeeded in delaying the ordination of women in the priesthood until 1992, and even then reserving to individual dioceses the right to choose not to do so. Nevertheless, by the close of the century, the ordained ministry of women had become the norm in Protestant and Anglican churches throughout Europe, North America, and Australasia, and was increasingly common, although far from universal, in Asia, Africa, and Latin America. In the Roman Catholic and Orthodox communions, of course, women remained excluded from the priesthood. The contrast is striking between the eventual Protestant-Anglican consensus in favor of the ordination of women, and the continuing weight of opinion against it among Catholics (though that was beginning to weaken in some parts of the church) and the Orthodox (where opposition remained virtually unanimous). The explanation of the contrast lies in the divergence of Protestant traditions from both Western and Eastern medieval precedent in their assessment of the relationship of church order to "the faith once delivered to the saints." For most Protestants, the way in which a church orders its ministry and worship is, to a greater or lesser extent, a "thing indifferent," a matter to be determined on grounds of what leads most effectively to the growth and nurture of the body of believers, and on which there is legitimate room for disagreement. For Catholics (at least until Vatican II), and even more for Orthodox, the historic ministry of bishops, priests, and deacons is of the essence of the church, an integral part of the timeless deposit of the faith, and hence not amenable to modification in response to cultural change.

The late twentieth century witnessed two momentous sea changes in popular understanding of human rights. First, as expounded in the previous chapter, in the course of the 1960s and 1970s human rights discourse became more closely associated than hitherto with the Left. This liberationist understanding of human rights first surfaced in the American civil rights movement, closely followed by the feminist movement. Second, the locus of rights discourse began to shift from the civil to the personal sphere. From the eighteenth century to the mid-twentieth century, human rights had to do with the place of the individual in society and his or her relationship to the state; they sought to protect political freedoms against authoritarian intervention. However, from the early 1960s in North America and Western Europe the idea of human rights became conjoined with a particular understanding of the source of personal fulfillment. According to this way of thinking, human beings did not simply have a natural right to be free from all types of economic or political oppression—they also were believed to have a right to maximize their personal happiness and satisfaction through the discovery and untrammelled expression of their essential identity or selfhood. The predominant cultures in the Western world in the later twentieth century were more radically subjective in character than their predecessors, encouraging individuals to pursue their own fulfillment through the location of their particular inner "self," if necessary at the expense of conformity to established social norms. Such subjectivity was most controversially expressed in the area of human sexuality. What is authentic to my individual identity and demonstrably fulfilling for me, increasingly became a self-validating axiom of human behavior, limited only by the principle that the pursuit of such personal satisfaction should not be at the expense of the personal well-being of others, particularly of those who were young or vulnerable. As the third section of the chapter indicates, the idea that most people have by nature a fixed sexual orientation, either heterosexual or homosexual, was a relatively novel and still professionally contested one as recently as the 1970s, yet by the end of the century it had become in most Western cultures an established "scientific" truth defining who we are.[2]

This individualized approach to sexual morality and identity posed a mounting challenge to the traditional ethical teaching of the churches. Advances in medicine and human psychology both made possible and accelerated the shifts in cultural mood. Beginning in the late nineteenth century in Germany and Britain, human sexual behavior became the object of serious scientific study through a discipline sometimes known as "sexology." Freudian psychology drew attention to the centrality of sexual impulses to human consciousness and emotional well-being. As scientific discussion of sex became increasingly open, some significant movement on the part of some denominations on certain issues of sexual ethics is discernible even in the first half of the century. The traditional teaching of the churches that sex was validated by its procreative function within the divine institution of marriage, and that, even within marriage, any artificial restriction on that function was inadmissible, now looked dangerously remote from the experience of many people. In the Anglican communion, for example, the Lambeth Conference moved from "an emphatic warning against the use of unnatural means for the avoidance of conception" in 1920 to a more open, though still cautious attitude to the use of such methods only ten years later at the 1930 Conference.[3] However, the decisive change in Christian attitudes to birth control came in the wake of the development of the oral contraceptive pill in the late 1950s. In the United States the pill was approved for use as a regular method of birth control in 1960; it is estimated that by 1965 6.5 million American women were on the pill.[4] Many of those women were churchgoers, either Protestant or Catholic. As discussed in chapter 4, Pope Paul VI's uncompromising repudiation of birth control in *Humanae Vitae* in July 1968 was profoundly disillusioning to many lay Catholics, and was almost certainly a major contributor from the late 1960s onwards to the growing exodus of women from the Catholic Church in countries such as France; the United States was not exempt from the trend.

These far-reaching shifts in popular attitudes to sexual ethics were rooted in modern urban and individualistic cultures in the Western world, and hence it was the churches of Europe and North America that were the first to have to respond to them. But as a result of the large-scale missionary expansion initiated in the previous century, the historic denominations born in European Christendom had given birth to global Christian communions representing churches from many different cultural contexts.

Anglicans, Presbyterians, Congregationalists, Methodists, Baptists, and Lutherans all formed global denominational fellowships at some point between 1867 (the first Lambeth Conference) and 1947 (the formation of the Lutheran World Federation).[5] The weight of numbers in these global communions lay increasingly with the newer churches of "the Global South," where the predominant understanding of gender roles and sexual ethics remained more conservative. As a result, by the final decade of the century some of these global denominational forums had become the arena for heated debate between conservatives and liberals. The arguments at the 1998 Lambeth Conference constitute the best-known example, but there are others. Some commentators have interpreted these clashes as evidence of a global Christian "culture war" between northern liberals and southern conservatives,[6] but the reality was more complex. As the chapter emphasizes, there were many northern conservatives, as well as some southern liberals. Churches or individuals could be "liberal" on an issue such as the ordination of women and "conservative" on homosexuality. The reverse was much less common, though not unknown among Anglo-Catholics. It is also the case that the nature of the global denominational polity of a particular Christian communion influenced the extent to which northern churches felt constrained by the majority view of their fellow believers in the south. In so far as a global culture war in Christianity over sexuality was apparent by the end of the century, it cannot be portrayed in simple terms as a clash of civilizations between north and south.

II. The Ordination of Women in Australian Anglicanism

One of the poignant ironies of modern ecclesiastical history is that the same global Christian communion that has attracted most public attention on account of the serious fractures provoked by the American Episcopal Church's eventual full acceptance of gay clergy also includes within its ranks—at the opposite end of its broad theological spectrum—the most striking Protestant example anywhere in the globe of a sustained rearguard action against the ordination of women. It needs to be emphasized at the outset that evangelicals of a conservative or even fundamentalist stamp have not been universally opposed to the public ministry of women: recent work on fundamentalism in the interwar period has indeed drawn attention to some of the surprising ways in which fundamentalism and feminism could converge.[7] Nevertheless, the Reformed strand of the evangelical tradition has been conspicuous by its principled opposition to the exercise of pastoral leadership or teaching authority by women, and it is that strand that is the subject of this case study.

Anglicanism in Australia, like the nation itself, has in the course of the twentieth century progressively severed its historic constitutional links with its British parent. In 1962 the "dioceses of the Church of England in Australia and Tasmania" attained legislative autonomy under the name of "the Church of England in Australia," and in 1981 the church changed its name to "the Anglican Church of Australia." In November 1992 the Anglican Church of Australia, faced with irreconcilable differences of view between its dioceses on the issue, voted to allow each diocese to determine its own policy on the ordination of women to the diaconate and priesthood. By the end of 1999 women accounted for 11 percent of all Australian Anglican clergy, including 156 deacons and 244 priests. Yet by far the largest diocese—Sydney—continued, alongside four other dioceses, to refuse to admit women to the priesthood, or to permit women deacons to be in pastoral charge of a congregation, while in two of the newer dioceses—Ballarat and The Murray—even the diaconate remained closed to them.[8] How was such an outcome—so unrepresentative of Protestant history as a whole in the late twentieth century—possible?

Australia's early colonial history continued to affect its cultural and religious attitudes well into the last century. One aspect of this legacy was the simple fact that Australia was not one colony, but six separate and partly self-governing colonies. The different colonies acquired their own religious complexions associated with the varying national origins within Britain of the predominant groups of settlers. The oldest Anglican dioceses differed markedly in churchmanship, nurtured by their own theological colleges, and continued to cherish their autonomy of each other long after the Commonwealth of Australia was formed on January 1, 1901. Although a General Synod was established as early as 1872, national Anglican administrative structures remained embryonic as late as the 1960s.[9]

A second aspect of the colonial legacy was that Australian religious history in the twentieth century, to a greater extent than in any other part of the British Empire, was shaped by the distinctive sectarian religious politics of Ireland. About a quarter of all convicts transported to Australia up to 1868 came from Ireland, one-third of Australian Catholics in the mid-1880s were Irish-born, and until the 1930s more than half of all Australian Catholic clergy were Irish.[10] In response to the Irish Catholic predominance, Australian Protestantism assumed a fervently pro-British and militantly anti-Catholic hue, especially in Sydney, where the Catholic preponderance was most pronounced. As a convict settlement, Sydney had developed a reputation as a hedonistic "sin city," and its churches have tended to be markedly conservative in reaction to this. The Anglican diocese of Sydney had a strong evangelical tradition that stretched back to its first colonial chaplains, Richard Johnson and Samuel Marsden.[11] It was possibly the only Anglican diocese in the world where the contest between conservative and liberal evangelicals, which first surfaced in the University of Cambridge in 1910 through the secession of the Cambridge Inter-Collegiate Christian Union (CICCU) from the Student Christian Movement (SCM) in protest at the latter's openness to modernist theology,[12] was decisively settled in favor of the conservatives. The Anglican Church League, formed in Sydney in 1909 as an anti-ritualist pressure group, came increasingly under conservative control. In 1933 it succeeded in securing the election as archbishop of Sydney of Howard W. K. Mowll (1890–1958), the missionary bishop of West China, in preference to the liberal evangelical candidate, Joseph Hunkin, archdeacon of Coventry. Mowll had been the president of the CICCU in 1911–12; though no fundamentalist, he set about making the diocese of Sydney a stronghold for evangelicalism of a decidedly conservative stamp.

In November 1935 Mowll gained a stalwart ally through his appointment as principal of the diocesan theological college, Moore College, of T. C. Hammond (1877–1961), formerly superintendent of the Irish Church Missions in Dublin, an agency intended to win Irish Catholics to evangelical Protestantism.[13] Hammond transformed Moore College from an institution of liberal evangelical sympathies into a bastion of theological conservatism. In 1938 he came to Mowll's rescue when a group of fifty dissident Sydney clergy presented the archbishop with a memorial complaining that he was in danger of reducing the diocese "to a monochrome" in which all the key posts were being allocated to conservative evangelicals. On Mowll's behalf, Hammond penned an uncompromising response in which the archbishop sent each of the signatories a questionnaire demanding factual substantiation of their charges. This robust response served only to alienate his critics further.[14] Mowll softened with age, and as primate of Australia from November 1947 to his death in October 1958 played an important part in revising the constitution of the General Synod in a direction acceptable to non-evangelicals.[15] Nevertheless, by the end of the 1930s, Mowll had established the character of Sydney diocese as a place in which only conservative evangelicals could feel fully at home. Other Australian dioceses had moved in a contrary direction, some becoming havens of Anglo-Catholicism, while others, such as Melbourne, retained a clear evangelical stamp, but of a less militant kind. The stage was thus set for a radically divergent set of reactions to the issue of the ordination of women when it came to the head of the Anglican agenda from the late 1960s.

The thin end of the wedge for the campaign to open the Anglican priesthood to women was the ambiguity surrounding the Anglican Order of Deaconess. Inspired by German Lutheran precedent, the office of the deaconess had become common in late Victorian England, but its canonical status remained unclear. The Lambeth Conference of 1920 sought to regularize the position by ruling that "The Order of Deaconess is for women the one and only Order of the Ministry which has the stamp of Apostolic approval, and is for women the only Order of Ministry which we can recommend that our Branch of the Catholic Church should recognize and use." The Conference laid down a procedure for the making of Deaconesses that sounded remarkably like ordination to the diaconate, to include prayer by the bishop, laying on of his hands, a formula giving authority to execute the office of a deaconess in the Church of God, and the delivery of a New Testament to the candidate.[16] In fact, both Canterbury and York provinces still refused to allow deaconesses to preach or pray in ordinary services or to allow them to read morning or evening prayer. The 1930 Lambeth Conference attempted to clarify the matter, but only muddied the waters further. It ruled that the Order of Deaconess was an order *sui generis*, not to be equated with the diaconate. The phrase "which has the stamp of Apostolic approval" was removed, as was the provision for the bishop to hand the candidate a New Testament. Yet it confirmed that deaconesses were to be formally ordained. Women were to be "ordained," but not to the apostolic threefold ministry as traditionally understood by Anglicans.[17]

Deaconesses became an important feature of Anglican church life in Australia, as also in the Methodist and Presbyterian churches.[18] Gippsland in Australia was one of the few dioceses that after the 1920 Lambeth Conference treated deaconesses as being in full Holy Orders as female deacons.[19] Anglican deaconesses were also prominent in the work of the Bush Church Aid Society, formed by Sydney evangelicals in 1920 to take the gospel into the outback. Archbishop Mowll valued their ministry, but only on strict conditions. He allowed Sydney deaconesses to attend the conferences of the All Australian Fellowship of Deaconesses (established in 1940) only once the conference had agreed not to make any decisions affecting deaconesses without the approval of the bishops.[20]

The first woman to be ordained to the Anglican priesthood was a Chinese deaconess, Florence Li Tim Oi (1907–92), in 1944. Bishop R. O. Hall of Hong Kong, constrained by the emergency conditions of the Japanese occupation of Hong Kong, agreed to ordain Li Tim Oi so that she could administer the sacraments in the parish in Macao for which she found herself solely responsible. Hall had obtained the private approval of the archbishop of Canterbury, William Temple, though after the event (and Temple's death) a handwritten letter arrived from Canterbury, written by Temple but signed by Archbishop Cyril Garbett of York, apparently repudiating the emergency measure; Li Tim Oi was forced to withdraw from exercising her priestly ministry.[21] Hall's action seems not to have attracted much notice in Australia. The key that unlocked the wider Anglican debate on the ordination of women was the Lambeth Conference in 1968. The Conference resolution on the question was conservative, expressing the opinion that the theological arguments for and against the ordination of women were currently "inconclusive." Nevertheless, every national or regional church or province was requested to consider the question of women's ordination and report its findings to the Anglican Consultative Council, which would hold its first meeting at Limuru in Kenya in 1971. Furthermore, one of the two section reports submitted to the Conference, on Renewal of the Church in Ministry, found "no conclusive theological reasons for withholding ordination to the priesthood from women as such." The report also called for canonical provision to be made for deaconesses to be included in the order of deacons.[22] Over the next decade women were ordained to the Anglican priesthood in Canada (1976), the Protestant Episcopal Church in the United States of America, popularly known as the ECUSA (1976), and New Zealand (1977). The Church of England moved more slowly, agreeing in principle in July 1985 to allow women to be ordained as deacons, and in February 1987 giving the green light for the preparation of legislation that might eventually permit women to be ordained to the priesthood. In Australia, by contrast, the Lambeth resolutions met with a decidedly cautious response.

In 1969 the General Synod of the Church of England in Australia duly considered the Lambeth resolutions. It repudiated the declaration that deaconesses belonged to the order of deacons, and instead recommended that its Commission on Doctrine study the question of the ordination of women. In 1976, the Commission's report on *The Ministry of Women* concluded, with one dissentient, that theological objections did not constitute a valid barrier to the ordination of women as either priests or bishops. The 1977 General Synod endorsed the Commission's report, though only by 107 votes to 72. However, the constitution of the church required that for a major constitutional change such as this, the support of all five metropolitan sees and a majority of the dioceses was required. For fifteen years an alliance of Sydney evangelicals and Anglo-Catholics from rural dioceses combined to block the measure.[23]

Leading Sydney evangelicals opposed the ordination of women on the grounds that the exercise by women of leadership in the church would constitute an infringement of the unchanging order of creation. Subordination was intrinsic to the way in which God had structured the world. Even the Trinity itself, they maintained, exemplified the principle, for the Son was subordinated to the authority of the Father. In theory the divinely intended subordination of women to men extended to the whole of creation, and hence to society and politics, though for obvious reasons conservatives increasingly tended to restrict the application of the doctrine to the domestic and ecclesiastical spheres.[24] The subordination argument was widely employed by conservative Protestants in other contexts, but it acquired a particular cultural resonance in societies such as Australia and the United States that placed a premium on masculinity: if men were required to submit to female leadership in the church, it was feared that their masculinity would be in peril.[25]

The most influential exponent of the order of creation view—and the sole dissentient from the 1976 Commission on Doctrine report—was Canon David Broughton Knox (1916–94), principal of Moore Theological College from 1959 to 1985. Knox's father was an Ulsterman, and Knox imbibed from his father a fierce Protestant loyalty to Puritan theology that ultimately transcended his allegiance to Anglicanism. Knox's ecclesiology was more congregational than Anglican, for he contended (as Baptists and Congregationalists have always maintained) that in the New Testament the *ekklesia* (church) is a term used in reference either to the church universal or to the local congregation, but never to any intermediate regional or national body.[26] Through his long tenure at Moore College, Knox wove the distinctive confessional texture of modern Sydney Anglicanism, patterning it according to his pronounced Reformed sympathies in theology. He was brother-in-law to Marcus Loane, archbishop of Sydney from 1966 to 1982. Loane's successor as archbishop from 1982 to 1993, Donald W. B. Robinson, had served under Knox as vice principal of Moore College. Knox was succeeded as principal of Moore College by his gifted disciple, Peter Jensen, who would later (from 2001 to 2013) serve as archbishop of Sydney.

Knox's influence was thus extensive and enduring. Nevertheless, he did not speak for all Australian evangelicals on this issue. In Melbourne diocese, the New Testament scholar Leon Morris, as principal of Ridley College from 1964 to 1979, exemplified a conservative evangelical tradition of a rather different kind, focused more on the atonement than on the doctrine of revelation; for Morris, the cross of Christ, rather than a particular understanding of divine revelation through verbal propositions, lay at the heart of the Christian gospel.[27] Melbourne evangelicals generally backed the ordination of women. Even in Sydney diocese, there were vocal evangelical supporters of the cause. The chief architect of the Australian branch of the Movement for the Ordination of Women—first established in Britain in 1979, and formed in Melbourne diocese in 1983—was Dr. Patricia Brennan, a Sydney evangelical and former medical missionary in West Africa with the theologically conservative Sudan Interior Mission. However, sympathetic evangelicals became uneasy with Brennan's increasingly radical identification of the Movement with international feminism, and as a result formed the group Men, Women, and God to argue the case for ordination on biblical grounds.[28]

There were also in Australia, as in Britain, committed Anglo-Catholic opponents of the ordination of women. When the first three Anglican women deacons in Western Australia were ordained at St. George's Cathedral on Perth in March 1986, the dean of Perth, David Robarts, declined the archbishop's invitation to lead the ordination retreat and preach at the ordination, on the grounds that "no guarantee could be given as to the possibility of the women concerned not proceeding to Priesthood in the future if legislation to do so were enacted"; Robarts received considerable public and media criticism for his stance.[29] Evangelical and Anglo-Catholic conservatives were prepared to make common cause on the question, despite their major theological differences. The traditionalist Association for the Apostolic Ministry, formed in 1985, was an international body whose co-chairmen were Donald Robinson, archbishop of Sydney, and Graham Leonard, the Anglo-Catholic bishop of London. The Association had an Australian branch from March 1989, of which Robinson was one of the four presidents; within six months it had recruited 2,000 members, including fourteen bishops. Robinson's own opposition to the ordination of women depended on an essentially Catholic appeal to the authority of primitive apostolic tradition.[30]

By the end of 1991 Australian supporters of the ordination of women were becoming increasingly impatient with the blocking tactics being employed by traditionalists. Two bishops announced that they intended to proceed unilaterally with ordinations of women to the priesthood. Both faced legal challenges in the Australian courts. The first such challenge, to the plans of Bishop Owen Dowling of Canberra and Goulburn to ordain eleven women as priests on February 2, 1992, was successful. But the second, to the intention of Archbishop Peter Carnley of Perth to ordain ten women in his diocese to the priesthood on March 7, failed. The Perth ordinations went ahead, and the Anglican Church in Australia now appeared to stand on the brink of schism.[31] On April 18 reports appeared in the *Sydney Morning Herald* alleging that a Sydney clergyman and vice president of the Anglican Church League, Bruce Ballantine-Jones, was proposing that the Sydney diocese withdraw from the Anglican Church on the grounds that the ordination of women priests symbolized a more general "drift away from biblical authority" within the church. The prospect of the secession of a diocese that accounted for approximately half of Australian Anglicans and contributed up to 70 percent of its income was an extremely serious one.[32]

On November 11, 1992 the Church of England's General Synod finally voted to ordain women to the priesthood by the required two-thirds majorities; the vote was 75 percent in the House of Bishops, 70.5 percent in the House of Clergy, and 67.3 percent in the House of Laity.[33] Ten days later the precedent set by the mother church in England combined with the mounting pressure from other Australian dioceses to produce the compromise reached by the General Synod in Australia: by the narrowest of margins (two votes), the Synod agreed to allow those dioceses that so wished to ordain women to the priesthood.[34] This radical extension of the diocesan autonomy that had always characterized the Australian church proved enough to retain evangelical opponents within the Anglican fold; it was, after all, congruent with the quasi-congregational ecclesiology of D. B. Knox. Formal schism had been avoided by resort to federal diversity. Anglo-Catholic ecclesiology was much less accommodating to a development that conservative Anglo-Catholics frequently chose to interpret as a dismemberment of the one apostolic ministry. Even before the 1992 vote, Albert Haley, a traditionalist Brisbane vicar, had formed the Diocese of Australia in the Anglican Catholic Church; by 1992 this had split into two rival jurisdictions, each claiming to represent the "Anglican Catholic Church in Australia."[35] Several of the most prominent Australian Anglo-Catholic opponents of women's ordination—among them David Robarts—would eventually take up the opportunity to enter the Catholic Church provided by Pope Benedict XVI in his creation in June 2012 of a "Personal Ordinariate of Our Lady of the Southern Cross" for Anglicans who wished to enter into full communion with the Catholic Church.[36]

III. Debates over Gay Rights in the American Churches

The question of how the churches should respond to the affirmation of gay and lesbian identity and sexuality is now the most divisive bone of contention in the world Christian community. For centuries the issue had been

entirely absent from the agenda of theological argument. The first signs
of its emergence became apparent in the United States in the late 1960s,
and it was in the United States that Christian debates over homosexuality first became headline news. For that reason, this section will focus on
the origins and course of the debate over homosexuality in the American
churches. The debate was focused on the rights and identity of gay and
lesbian people: the extension of the gay rights campaign to bisexual and
transgender people (producing the acronym LGBT) was largely a post-
2000 development, although the first organizations representing the interests of bisexual and transgender people appeared in the 1990s.

There is ample historical evidence that homosexual practice, and (less
frequently) long-term homosexual relationships, have been features of
many human societies down the centuries. However, the term "homosexuality" is a modern invention, being coined in 1868 by the Hungarian
advocate of the decriminalization of homosexual activity, Karoly Maria
Kertbeny. Until that date, male homosexual behavior was generally labeled as "sodomy," a term deriving from the biblical account in Genesis
19. Sodomy was a particular sexual act, usually defined as the anal penetration of one male by another. Although there is evidence of small gay
subcultures in the largest European cities (Amsterdam, Paris, and London) as early as the late seventeenth century, there was no concept of fixed
homosexual orientation or identity. The term "lesbian" dates from the rise
of the feminist movement in the late nineteenth century, prior to which
there is slender evidence for the existence of self-identifying female gay
communities. Before the mid-twentieth century those who engaged in
same-sex relations were generally understood to do so as a result of their
free choice, not out of compulsion from their nature, and such relations
were rarely thought to exclude engagement in heterosexual relations as
well. The most common pattern of same-sex relationships was either that
of a transient adolescent passion or one in which a socially dominant and
usually older partner exploited a socially subordinate and younger partner
(often a pupil or household servant) for their own pleasure.[37]

From the mid-nineteenth century recognizable homosexual communities began to emerge in certain urban locations in the United States as in
Europe. The earliest and most significant of these appeared in San Francisco in the wake of the gold rush of 1848–49, where an abnormal society of
prospectors for gold developed, comprising more than 90 percent males.
Later in the century, seamen and then bohemian literary figures added
to the human mix. In this atypical environment, a distinct homosexual
subculture took shape in the young city. After the repeal of prohibition

in 1933, the subculture became more visible, manifested through the opening of gay bars and the emergence of recognizably gay districts of the city, notably Castro. The gay population grew substantially at the end of the Second World War, when many American ex-servicemen who had found in military life exposure to and opportunity for homosexual experience, settled there. By 1964 *LIFE* magazine could describe San Francisco as "the gay capital" of America.[38] Its gay residents developed their own code phrase for mutual recognition, "Are you a friend of Dorothy?" taken from the 1939 Metro-Goldwyn-Mayer film, *The Wizard of Oz*. The teenage star of the movie, Judy Garland, unwittingly became a gay icon, because Dorothy, whom she played, was fully accepting of personal difference. As Les Wright has written, "San Francisco became the land of Oz, the Technicolor world over the rainbow where gays would finally find a home." Dorothy's hit song, "Somewhere over the Rainbow," is the probable origin of the adoption in 1978 of the now universal rainbow flag, designed by the San Francisco artist, Gilbert Baker, as a symbol of gay identity.[39] The city was also the location for the formation in October 1955 of the nation's first lesbian society, the Daughters of Bilitis; it was also a stronghold of the first homosexual society, the Mattachine Society, founded in Los Angeles in November 1950. In the late 1960s—especially in the celebrated "Summer of Love" in 1967—San Francisco became the center of emerging hippie culture, a site of uninhibited experimentation with rock music, drugs, and sex. The presiding guru of this countercultural revolution was the openly gay beat poet Allen Ginsberg. By 1978 it is estimated that 150,000 out of the 750,000 population of San Francisco self-identified as gay.[40]

Other American cities—notably Los Angeles, New York, and Chicago—saw the development of smaller but still sizeable gay communities in the postwar period. Such communities both nurtured and drew confidence from the liberating notion that homosexuality was neither a psychopathological condition (as medical orthodoxy maintained into the early 1970s), nor an eccentric lifestyle choice, but a natural orientation of a significant proportion of the population. Gay theorists believed they had found support for this conviction in the best-selling Kinsey reports—*Sexual Behavior in the Human Male* (1948) and *Sexual Behavior in the Human Female* (1953), which were widely described as proving that the extent of homosexual proclivity in the population was as high as 10 percent, much higher than hitherto believed.[41] In fact, Alfred Kinsey's research pointed in precisely the opposite direction, for he sought only to measure varieties of sexual activity, and was profoundly skeptical of the concept of innate homosexual identity. He classified humans on a seven-point scale, ranging from wholly heterosexual to wholly homosexual, insisted that it made no sense to attempt to establish what proportion of the population was heterosexual and what proportion homosexual, and bluntly concluded "that one is not warranted in recognizing merely two types of individuals, heterosexual and homosexual."[42] Nevertheless, professional medical evaluation of homosexuality began to change in the two decades after the publication of Kinsey's reports. In December 1973 the board of trustees of the American Psychiatric Association—representing the psychiatric profession that gay activists had previously regarded as the enemy on account of its adherence to a pathological interpretation of homosexuality—voted to remove homosexuality from its Diagnostic and Statistical Manual of Psychiatric Disorders. The decision was challenged by a dissident group of members, but was upheld in a referendum of all members in 1974 by the relatively modest majority of 58 to 37 percent. Even in supposedly liberal Sweden, homosexuality was classified as an illness until as late as 1979.[43]

San Francisco provided the first signs of a specifically Christian response to the developing gay movement in the United States in December 1964, when a small group of the city's ministers combined with representatives of the gay community to form the Council on Religion and Homosexuality. The intention of the Council was simply to promote empathetic dialogue between the churches and the San Francisco gay community, but the Council soon acquired a more campaigning tone after the police forced their way into the New Year's Eve Ball organized by the Council, arresting four persons on charges of obstructing an officer. The case, which led to not-guilty verdicts, attracted great publicity to the cause of gay rights in the city. Similar councils were formed in Dallas, Los Angeles, Washington, Seattle, and elsewhere.[44] With the exception of Illinois, which had decriminalized homosexuality in 1961, homosexual acts were still illegal in all American states at the time. Heavy-handed police action such as that which broke up the San Francisco Ball probably did more than anything else to transform the embryonic networks of gay consciousness into a major civil rights campaign. The most notorious example was the police raid in June 1969 on the Stonewall Inn, a well-known gay bar in Greenwich Village in New York, which provoked riots that many historians identify as the genesis of the American gay activist movement and hence the beginning of the international gay rights movement.

In October 1968 Troy Perry (b. 1940), a former Pentecostal pastor in the Church of God of Prophecy who had recently "come out" as gay, advertised in the Los Angeles *Advocate* for those interested in forming a "Metropolitan Community Church" to come to his home in the city. In his inaugural sermon Perry told the twelve people who turned up that "we were not a gay church; we were a Christian church," but one in which gays were welcome. The congregation grew rapidly, necessitating successive moves to the Embassy Auditorium and then the Encore Theater. Finally in late 1970 the congregation purchased an old church building at Union and 22nd Streets in Los Angeles.[45] The Metropolitan Community Church (MCC) soon established branches in San Francisco and other American cities, and later overseas. By October 1972 the Los Angeles congregation had grown to more than 800, making it the third largest church in the city. Research on the early San Francisco congregation found that the bulk of MCC members were from conservative church backgrounds: about 40 percent were former Catholics, and another 40 percent came from fundamentalist churches. Sunday worship followed a monthly cycle, with a Pentecostal-style service on the first Sunday of the month, the second being Baptist in style; the third more formal on an Episcopalian pattern; the fourth more Catholic; and any fifth Sundays in the month taking an experimental form. It is estimated that women accounted for less than 10 percent of the new denomination, a sign that lesbian Christians did not feel comfortable in a male homosexual worshipping environment.[46]

The MCC provided a spiritual home for gay Christians from predominantly conservative backgrounds. Although it received criticism in the conservative Christian press for encouraging hitherto celibate homosexuals to give physical expression to their sexual orientation,[47] its separateness from the mainstream of church life largely insulated it from the heat of theological argument. In some mainline Protestant denominations, attitudes toward homosexuality were beginning to change, but only very patchily. The first ordination of a known gay person to the ministry of an American denomination took place on November 11, 1970, when William Reagan Johnson was ordained to the Northern California conference of the mainly liberal United Church of Christ.[48] In the Catholic Church, the Augustinian priest Pat Nidorf formed the first support organization for gay people in San Diego in early 1969: "Dignity" developed into a network of local chapters for gay Catholics, and held its inaugural national convention in Los Angeles in September 1973. Dignity adopted a Statement of Position and Purpose that drew on published articles by the Jesuit theologian John J. McNeill to claim that "homosexuality is a natural variation on the use of sex. It implies no sickness or immorality"; McNeill had argued that in certain circumstances stable homosexual relationships ought to be accepted as a lesser evil than promiscuity.[49] The attitude of the Catholic hierarchy was, however, extremely hesitant, and Dignity was compelled to rely on lay leadership. In the autumn of 1986 the Congregation for the Doctrine of the Faith issued a *Letter to all Catholic Bishops on the Pastoral Care of Homosexual Persons*, under the signature of Joseph Ratzinger. The Letter reaffirmed Catholic teaching on the unacceptability of homogenital acts and in effect debarred Dignity chapters from meeting on church premises. Individual voices in the Catholic Church called from time to time for a reevaluation of the church's traditional teaching on homosexuality, and by the late 1980 surveys suggested that a substantial minority of American Catholics dissented from the church's official teaching on homosexuality, but the Catholic understanding of the role of the magisterium allowed little room for maneuver on the question.[50]

The stance of the Protestant Episcopal Church in the United States of America (known increasingly as the ECUSA and from 2006 simply as "the Episcopal Church") was not at first markedly different from that of the Catholic Church. In 1967 the General Convention of the ECUSA called for a serious ethical study of homosexuality, but nothing was done. In 1974 the first issue of a newsletter entitled *Integrity: Gay Episcopalian Forum* was published; the appearance of the newsletter prompted the formation of local Integrity chapters, which soon constituted a national network, somewhat similar to the Catholic Dignity, known as Integrity.[51] The watershed in Episcopal attitudes to gay issues came in January 1977—just four months after the General Convention voted by narrow majorities to permit women to be ordained as priests—when Paul Moore (1919–2003) the bishop of New York, stirred up a national furor by ordaining the deacon Ellen Barrett (b. 1946) to the priesthood. Barrett had made no secret of her lesbianism, but what set the flames truly alight was the publication of an article in *Time* magazine, entitled "The Lesbian Priest," which reported Barrett as saying that her relationship with her lesbian lover "is what feeds the strength and compassion I bring to the ministry."[52] Moore maintained that the question of whether Barrett was a practicing lesbian was not, and should not have been, any concern of his committee that decided to ordain her; conservative Episcopalians, by contrast, thought that this was precisely the question on which her ordination should have turned. Moore's autobiography, published two years later, made explicit his view that committed same-sex relationships were morally acceptable.[53]

The controversy provoked by Barrett's ordination led to a ruling of the House of Bishops in October 1977 that "pending further enquiry no bishop should ordain a homosexual person." Opinion in the Episcopal Church was deeply divided. At the 1979 General Convention, a confusing series of divergent resolutions appeared to leave individual bishops and diocesan committees to exercise their discretion in determining whether or not to ordain homosexuals, advising them to "focus care and discernment upon individuals, and not upon categories."[54] The ECUSA in the late 1970s was by no means uniformly wedded to the "liberal" position on homosexuality with which it has subsequently become identified in the fractured politics of global Anglicanism. Even Jack Shelby Spong (b. 1931), bishop of Newark from 1979, who would soon become notorious in conservative eyes for his advocacy of radical positions on questions of both Christian doctrine and sexuality, testified in a book published in 1988 that ten years previously he would have been "shocked and aghast at the things I am writing at this moment" in support of the church giving its blessing to same-sex unions; he confessed that even five years ago he still "had to be pushed to take an inclusive position" on homosexuality.[55]

As liberal Christian intellectuals such as Spong redefined their position on human sexuality during the 1980s, the gay issue became a major line of division, not simply between liberals and conservatives within the ECUSA, but increasingly also within the Anglican communion as a whole. The backcloth to the early debates on the question was the disastrous spread of the HIV–AIDS pandemic through the United States and elsewhere, which some conservatives interpreted as the judgment of God upon homosexual behavior; the first five American deaths from AIDS were recorded in June 1981, and by early 1986 30,000 victims had been recorded.[56] In Newark diocese, a task force established by Bishop Spong published in 1987 a report on "Changing Patterns of Sexuality and Family Life." The report recommended that all sexual relationships, whether heterosexual or homosexual, should be assessed according to the extent to which they reflected the values of the realm of God. In response, conservatives, fearing that the Newark report would be adopted by the denomination as a whole, formed in 1988 a body called "Episcopalians United," with the aim of opposing the ordination of practicing homosexuals, the normalization of homosexual relationships, and also the imminent prospect of women bishops—the Episcopal Church would consecrate its first woman bishop, Barbara Harris (b. 1930), in Boston in February 1989.[57] She was the first female bishop in the Anglican communion, and was, in addition, an African American. In 1996 the church withdrew its ban on the ordination of practicing homosexuals. In June 2003, amidst great controversy, the church elected its first openly gay bishop, Gene Robinson, as bishop of New Hampshire.

The Episcopal Church had moved further and faster than any other American denomination in abandoning the historic Christian position on homosexuality. Such realignment did not go unchallenged, for, by the late 1980s, conservative evangelicalism, once a negligible force within the Episcopal Church, was increasingly influential. Trinity Episcopal School for Ministry, the evangelical seminary founded in 1976 in Ambridge, Pennsylvania, was training a growing proportion of Episcopal clergy, and evangelical Episcopalians grew in confidence as a result of their participation in the global network, the Evangelical Fellowship in the Anglican Communion, established by John R. W. Stott in 1958. During the 1990s evangelical Episcopalians utilized such networks to mobilize conservative opinion in other parts of the Anglican communion, especially in West and East Africa and Singapore, to resist the global influence of liberal voices within the Episcopal Church, and in particular the campaign to bestow moral legitimacy on stable same-sex unions. The unity of the Anglican communion thus began to fragment under the stress of two contradictory globalizing forces. This polarization first became fully apparent at the Lambeth Conference in 1998, when Tanzanian archbishop Donald Mtetemela led bishops from the Global South in amending a middle-of-the-road resolution so that it declared all homosexual practice incompatible with Scripture and opposed the blessing of same-sex unions and the ordination of those in such unions.[58]

Some recent scholars have gone so far as to claim that the various global conservative networks established by Stott and his disciples were primarily responsible for reenacting the sectional civil war between American liberals and conservatives on a global Anglican stage, leading southern Anglicans to dance to a reactionary tune composed in a northern secular society.[59] Such a view overestimates the capacity—and probably also the willingness—of Stott to orchestrate African and Asian Anglican opinion, and is in danger of denying autonomy to the ethical stances of southern conservatives. Furthermore, in an attempt to find a nonracist explanation of the obstinate resistance of southern Christians to the adoption of progressive ethical positions by northern liberals, this interpretation invokes an organizational narrative that was distinctive to Anglicanism. Yet this same pattern of resistance to northern Protestant liberalism was also apparent in other global Christian communions. It was also evident in Afro-American and diasporic Korean Presbyterian churches in the United States, which in November 1992 were instrumental (along with the Orthodox churches) in blocking the application of the Universal Fellowship of Metropolitan Community Churches to be given observer status on the National Council of Churches.[60] Miranda Hassett's observation that "African Christians' responses to homosexuality are not dictated by northerners, but reflect African contexts and concerns" is both apposite and more generally applicable to churches of non-Western origins.[61]

Trends in the Methodist and Presbyterian churches in the United States, though they differed from the Episcopal case in some essential respects, point toward the same conclusion. The United Methodist Church (UMC; formed in 1968), the largest mainline Protestant church in the United States, and the second largest Protestant body after the Southern Baptist Convention, is a theologically mixed denomination embracing a substantial liberal constituency, as well as many conservatives. Yet, to the intense dismay of Methodist gay activists, the United Methodist Book of Discipline retained from the 1970s to the end of the century (and beyond) a statement condemning homosexuality as "incompatible with Christian teaching," a prohibition of noncelibate gays and lesbians from ordination, and a ban on ministers conducting same-sex commitment ceremonies.[62] This was despite the fact that a denominational committee of inquiry requested the 1992 General Conference to replace the language condemning homosexual practice with a simple acknowledgment that "the church has been unable to arrive at a common mind on the compatibility of homosexual practice with Christian faith." At the 1996 General Conference fifteen bishops similarly declared their disagreement with the church's stance on homosexuality. The most concerted attempt to persuade the UMC to abandon its opposition to homosexual practice was made at the 2000 General Conference. The attempt failed, by a majority of two to one, defeated by an alliance between conservative American Methodists and the great majority of delegates from the African, Asian, and Latin American Methodist churches planted by American Methodist missions. Few of these churches owed anything to the British evangelical networks associated with John Stott. But, in contrast to the devolved national polities of the Anglican communion, these churches retained voting rights within the councils of the American mother church, and hence were able to challenge the predominantly liberal tendencies of the UMC denominational hierarchy. Nearly all the spokespersons for the African, Asian, and Latin American Methodist churches testified that for them the retention of the homosexuality prohibitions was a matter of fundamental principle on which the holiness and spiritual integrity of their churches in their national contexts depended.[63]

However, the United Methodist case should not be taken as evidence that the debate on homosexuality has uniformly juxtaposed northern liberalism and southern conservatism. The United Methodist Church occupies a moderate rather than a uniformly liberal position, and in these debates the concerns of southern hemisphere Methodists drew significant support from conservative American Methodists uneasy with the progressive leanings of their denominational leadership.

The Presbyterian Church (U.S.A.), generally known as PCUSA, is also, like the United Methodist Church, a mainline denomination whose leadership and scholarly elites tend to be more liberal than many of its members, who are predominantly white, middle class, and heterosexual. The PCUSA was the product of a merger in 1983 between the United Presbyterian Church in the United States of America (representing northern Presbyterians) and the Presbyterian Church in the United States (representing southern Presbyterians). Both antecedent churches had passed resolutions, in 1978 and 1979 respectively, debarring self-affirming and practicing homosexuals from ordination. In the case of the United Presbyterian Church, the resolution was the denomination's eventual response to the candidacy for ministry of an openly gay person, Bill Silver, in New York in 1975. As in the UMC, gay activists campaigned from the mid-1970s on behalf of gay rights in the Presbyterian churches: a Chicago Presbyterian minister, David Sindt, founded the caucus Presbyterians for Gay and Lesbian Concerns in 1974.[64] In response to the increasing prominence of the gay issue, the PCUSA in June 1987 commissioned a study group on human sexuality. Its report, *Presbyterians and Human Sexuality*, presented to the General Assembly in June 1991, proposed an ethic for all sexual relationships, whether inside or outside marriage, that appealed to the priority of seeking justice and love, without any reference to sexual orientation. The situational and liberationist basis of the report proved too radical for the Assembly, which declined to endorse the report, and reaffirmed the 1978 and 1979 resolutions debarring homosexuals from church leadership.[65] The PCUSA did not open its ordained ministry to practicing homosexuals until 2011, a step that led to the secession of a number of conservative churches to form a new denomination known as "ECO: the Covenant Order of Evangelical Presbyterians."

A similar picture emerges from the Evangelical Lutheran Church of America, where a study group's report on sexuality advocating liberalization of the church's position was overwhelmingly rejected by the denomination as a whole in 1993.[66] Taking a broad view of American Christianity as a whole, what is striking is how limited was the distance traveled by most denominations on this issue before 2000, and of how unrepresentative was the Episcopal Church in reversing its previous opposition to the ordination of practicing homosexuals in 1996. No other major mainline American denomination altered its principled stance on either the definition of marriage or the ordination of practicing homosexuals before the end of the century. Interpretations that treat the arguments within global

Anglicanism as emblematic of a generic culture war between northern and southern Christianity are, therefore, bound to be wide of the mark, though they may have gained a little more plausibility in the twenty-first century. The Episcopal Church, shaped by an ecclesiological tradition that gave bishops both a distinctive leading role and considerable latitude in the determination of Christian teaching, was more prone to accommodation to intellectual trends in the surrounding culture than was either the Catholic Church, with its centralized magisterium, or those American churches rooted in a democratic and originally evangelical tradition, where the greater role in church governance allotted to lay opinion imposed, at least for a time, a brake on the inclinations of many theologians and denominational leaders to redefine Christian stances on sexuality.

IV. Christian Culture Wars

The two controversial questions surveyed in this chapter intersected in complex ways. The great majority of supporters of the admission of gay people to the Christian ministry also supported the ordination of women; for them, both issues turned on an acceptance of the absolute authority of the human rights of the individual and a corresponding willingness to conclude that historic Christian tradition on both issues must simply be repudiated as mistaken. Conversely, the most stalwart opponents of women's ordained ministry in Australia were united in their resistance to campaigns on behalf of gay clergy or the blessing of same-sex unions. In their view, both the ordination of women and the reevaluation of Christian attitudes to homosexuality represented a capitulation of the church to modern secular and liberal values, and an abandonment of the divine order of creation as revealed in the Bible.

Yet there was no exact parallelism between the two debates. The Australian and American examples both suggest that, at least in the Protestant churches, a substantial body of Christian opinion in the last thirty years of the century wished to draw a sharp distinction between the two moral issues. Those Australian evangelical Anglicans in the diocese of Melbourne and elsewhere who supported the campaign for the ordination of women took a conservative line on homosexuality. The Uniting Church of Australia, formed in June 1977 by a union of Congregationalists, Methodists and (some) Presbyterians, ordained women from its inception. However, attempts by the denominational leadership to open its ministry to those in same-sex relationships met with stout resistance from more conservative elements within the lay membership, including those from the aboriginal and islander churches represented by the Uniting Aboriginal and Islander Church Congress. As in the Anglican communion and the United Methodist Church, those from a non-European ethnic background proved generally unsympathetic to the legitimization of homosexual relationships. Not until 2003 did the Uniting Church secure passage, in the face of considerable opposition, of a resolution giving individual presbyteries the right to decide whether or not to accept as candidates for ordination persons in a committed same-sex relationship.[67] Similarly, the many lay people in the ECUSA, UMC, and PCUSA who found themselves unable to endorse the growing enthusiasm of their denominational leadership for the ordination of homosexual clergy were, with few exceptions, supportive of the admission of women into the ordained ministry of their respective denominations. The "culture wars" over gender and sexuality in late twentieth-century Christianity overlapped to a significant extent, but they were never identical and did not conform to a simple geographical or cultural polarity between north and south.

CHAPTER THIRTEEN

The Spirit and the spirits

GLOBAL PENTECOSTAL CHRISTIANITIES

I. The New Pentecost

The twentieth century was the century in which the Holy Spirit attained a prominence in Christian experience and theological reflection not seen since the days of the Montanists of the late second century. By the year 2000, multiple forms of Pentecostal or charismatic Christianity constituted the most vibrant features of the Christian landscape in Latin America and Africa, as well as in many parts of Asia, Oceania, and eastern Europe. Chapter 15 will take note of how migrant populations in the northern hemisphere, especially Hispanics and Afro-Caribbeans in the United States, and West Africans in European cities, transmitted southern Pentecostalism to the North. In addition, from the 1960s through to the 1990s widespread movements of "charismatic renewal" in both Catholic and Protestant churches drew from older Pentecostal sources to disseminate experience and theological understanding of the more spectacular gifts of the Spirit—speaking in tongues, healing, and intuitive "words of knowledge" or declarative prophecies. In Protestantism, the charismatic movement began among Episcopalians and Lutherans in California in 1959–60, and from there spread eastwards in the United States, across the Atlantic, especially to evangelicals in the Church of England, and further afield to South Africa, Australasia, and Singapore.[1] In the Catholic Church, charismatic renewal originated at Duquesne University in Pittsburgh in 1967. It was soon transmitted to other university campuses and Catholic parishes via an expanding network of prayer groups, many of which included some Protestants; by 1977 there were some 2,500 of them in the

United States, with an aggregate membership of 110,402.[2] The movement could appeal for support to the Second Vatican Council, with its emphases on liturgical reform and the bestowal of spiritual gifts on the laity to equip them for mission.[3] As in Protestantism, charismatic renewal movements became global in extent, transforming the character of popular Catholicism in some countries, such as the Philippines and Brazil. The movements were plural in genesis: the El Shaddai movement in the Philippines, for example, traces its origins not to the Catholic charismatic renewal in the United States, but to a nondenominational Christian radio program in Manila begun by a Catholic layman, Mike Velarde, in 1983. By the 1990s, the El Shaddai movement, which has close links to the prosperity gospel, had between 9 and 11 million adherents in the Philippines.[4]

As a result of charismatic renewal, patterns of worship in large sections of the church in the closing decades of the century became less obviously liturgical and more closely aligned to late modern cultural forms, with an emphasis that paradoxically combined individual freedom of expression with a focus on what was often known as "body ministry"—the reinforcement of the corporate identity of those renewed by the Spirit. The emphasis of charismatics and Pentecostals on the availability of the power of the Holy Spirit to all Christians, irrespective of education, social class, or gender, narrowed the status gap that the historic churches had created between clergy and laity. Women found Pentecostal forms of Christianity to be particularly liberating: a 1936 census in the United States found that women accounted for 65 percent of the membership of eleven Pentecostal churches, compared with 56 percent for all denominations.[5] By the end of the century Pentecostal Christianities—whether in charismatic form within the historic churches or in a host of autonomous Pentecostal churches—were highly visible in almost every part of the Christian world. The main emphasis of this chapter is on Pentecostals rather than charismatics, though no absolute differentiation between the two movements is sustainable.

Throughout the first half of the century, scholars had taken little notice of the growing religious phenomenon that had gradually acquired the label of "Pentecostalism." In academic circles Pentecostals were viewed as Christians of feeble brain whose highly enthusiastic and experiential brand of spirituality was scarcely worthy of serious study. However, in November 1952 Lesslie Newbigin, Bishop of Madras in the newly formed Church of South India, delivered a series of lectures at Trinity College, the Church of Scotland institution in Glasgow, under the title *The Household of God*. In his Kerr lectures Newbigin reflected on the developing ecumenical movement in which he was intimately involved, and in so doing drew attention to the existence of a third stream of Christian tradition in addition to the more familiar Catholic and Protestant traditions whose interrelations formed the substance of most ecumenical debate. This stream he labeled "The Community of the Holy Spirit" or simply "Pentecostal." Newbigin observed that Catholics defined the church in terms of a structure that claimed to be in line of succession from the apostles of the first century, while Protestants defined it in terms of the fidelity of its message to the teaching of the apostles. In contrast to both traditions, Pentecostal Christians defined the church in terms of "the experienced power and presence of the Holy Spirit today." For them, without such a tangible reality of spiritual power, there was no church. Hence, whereas they shared with Protestants a tendency to downplay visible order and structure, they were closer to Catholics in their insistence that new life in Christ involved a real ontological change, a translation into a divine society of transcendent spiritual power.[6] In Latin America Pentecostals are termed *evangélicos* alongside other Protestants. Nevertheless, the extraordinary success of Pentecostal Christianities can be understood only once it is grasped that they represent a recovery of liminal and suprarational dimensions of popular religious experience that the sixteenth-century Reformers had sought to erase from the Christian landscape.

It took some time for Newbigin's call for serious study of the Pentecostal tradition to be widely heeded. The father of modern scholarship on Pentecostalism was the Swiss theologian, Walter J. Hollenweger (1927–2016), originally a Pentecostal himself, who in 1966 produced a massive ten-volume doctoral dissertation at the University of Zurich entitled *Handbuch der Pfingstbewegung*. The core of this work found its way into print in English in 1972 as *The Pentecostals*,[7] while as Professor of Mission at the University of Birmingham from 1971 to 1989 Hollenweger pioneered the scholarly analysis of the movement. By the end of the century, scholarly literature on Pentecostalism and its charismatic offspring in the historic denominations was expanding rapidly. As the movement gathered pace in the southern hemisphere, anthropologists, sociologists, and scholars of religion rapidly swamped the still modest numbers of theologians who were prepared to follow Hollenweger into Pentecostal territory. The social scientific analysis of Pentecostal Christianities now represents the most prominent growth industry in the study of contemporary global Christianity, eclipsing by far the number of recent publications on theologies of liberation.

Historical writing on Pentecostal Christianity—especially that emanating from a white American Pentecostal stable—for long adhered to a theory of American monogenesis that privileged the Azusa Street revival which surfaced in Los Angeles in April 1906 as the "origin" or epicenter of Pentecostalism. The appearance in William James Seymour's Apostolic Faith Mission located at 312 Azusa Street of glossolalia (speaking or singing in tongues), being "slain in the Spirit," miraculous healings and ecstatic worship, soon attracted attention from other parts of the United States and from far beyond it. Evangelical tourists, most of them white, flocked to Los Angeles to witness phenomena that originally were mostly evident among those who, like Seymour (1870–1922), were African American. As these visitors returned home, and aided by the international circulation of Seymour's periodical, *The Apostolic Faith*, the message and increasingly the experience of Pentecost radiated in ever-widening circles to other continents. Spiritual tourism was soon reinforced by active missionary propagation. With surprising rapidity, Pentecostal missionaries—most of them, for obvious economic reasons, being whites—were soon dispatched, both from Los Angeles and from other nodes of the extending network (especially Oslo and Stockholm) to South and West Africa, India, China, and elsewhere. Although few Christians from the historic denominations took much notice of the phenomenon, a new pattern of Christian experience was being woven that was destined to become more and more prominent as the century proceeded.

The first Pentecostals believed that they were living in the last days, and had an urgent commission to spread the gospel while there was still time. To speed them on their way, they believed that the Spirit had endowed them with the convenient facility to speak in identifiable foreign languages without having to learn them. This supposed replication of the missionary gift bestowed on the apostles on the Day of Pentecost—known technically as xenolalia—followed teaching that Seymour had imbibed from Charles Fox Parham (1873–1929). Parham was a white Holiness teacher whose Bible School at Topeka in Kansas had witnessed the first claimed outbreak of xenolalia on the first day of the new century, January 1, 1901, initiated by a student, Agnes Ozman, who spoke repeatedly in what Parham claimed to be "the Chinese language."[8] Seymour had studied briefly under Parham in 1905 in Houston, where Parham had founded another Bible School. However, once Pentecostal missionaries arrived on the field, they soon discovered that the gift of tongues was not what they had supposed. With a few possible exceptions, notably the case of George and Sophia Hansen, who, according to various witnesses, regularly spoke in Mandarin in Shanghai between 1908 and 1916, Pentecostal tongues-speaking proved unintelligible to indigenous hearers.[9] In consequence, as early as the end of 1907, the gift was being redefined as the ability to speak in an unknown spiritual language that needed the assistance of those with the gift of interpretation, as expounded by the apostle Paul in I Corinthians 12.

The Azusa Street revival was undoubtedly one of the most inspirational sources of the global Pentecostal movement, but it was not the sole origin. Neither was it in its early phases a white-dominated movement. On the contrary Charles Parham, who held views of racist tendency and was an exponent of the British Israelite theory, visited Azusa Street in the autumn of 1906 to see the ministry of his erstwhile pupil Seymour and was horrified at the "Africanisms" he witnessed; he wrote later of his disgust as seeing white people imitate "the unintelligent crude negroism of the Southland."[10] Transatlantic Africans whose spirituality had been forged in the furnace of plantation slavery had for decades found styles of worship that privileged charismatic gifts and ecstatic infilling by the Spirit to be both natural and liberating. Thus African Baptist churches in Jamaica and Trinidad in the early nineteenth century displayed at least some of the features that would later become associated with Pentecostalism, thereby creating considerable difficulties for their British Baptist missionaries.[11] Pentecostalism in the United States drew deeply from African religious sources but for a time succeeded in holding whites and blacks together in a single movement. However, racial tensions within the movement mounted, and in the 1920s and 1930s two of the largest American Pentecostal bodies fragmented on racial lines: the Pentecostal Assemblies of the World split in 1924 into separate white and black denominations, while most of the white members of the Church of God in Christ left to join the Assemblies of God or other white-dominated bodies.[12]

Such modes of worship were not, however, peculiar to people of African descent. Tongues, prophecies, and healings had marked Edward Irving's ministry in Church of Scotland congregations in Glasgow and London in the 1830s. In South India outbreaks of charismatic phenomena had surfaced in the 1860s and 1870s associated with the Tamil evangelist John Christian Arulappan or his disciples. From the Welsh Revival of 1904–5 currents of spiritual renewal flowed in many directions. Welsh Calvinistic Methodist missionaries channeled them to the Khasi hills of northeast India. In western India the learned Brahman female convert Ramabai Dongre (1858–1922)—known by the honorific titles of "Pandita" (female pandit) and "Sarasvati" (after the Hindu goddess of knowledge)— dispatched her daughter Manoramabai and the American Methodist Episcopal missionary Minnie Abrams to Wales to report on the Revival. Their return to Ramabai's "Mukti" (Salvation) mission at Kedgaon near

Pune provoked a Pentecostal-style outbreak from July 1905 that attracted almost as much international attention as Azusa Street. In Los Angeles itself, the English pastor of the First Baptist Church, Joseph Smale, visited Wales during the Revival, and on his return to Los Angeles commenced revival meetings of his own that preceded those at Azusa Street. Minnie Abrams wrote a booklet, *The Baptism of the Holy Ghost and Fire*, describing the Mukti revival and sent a copy to her former classmate in Bible School, May Louise Hoover, who, with her husband, Willis, was a Methodist missionary in Valparaiso, Chile. Its second edition, published later in 1906, included a discussion of the restoration of the spiritual gift of speaking in tongues, and was the first appearance in print of a Pentecostal understanding of the baptism in the Spirit. Through reading the booklet and correspondence with Abrams, the Methodist churches in Valparaiso and Santiago began in 1907 to experience a Pentecostal revival. This proved impossible to contain within the Methodist Episcopal structure, and in 1909 the Hoovers became the founders of the first Pentecostal church in Latin America, the *Iglesia Metodista Pentecostal*.[13] Chile thus became joined to western India and Wales in a transnational web of spiritual revitalization. Mexicans also were involved in the Azusa Street revival, and before long several had spread the Pentecostal experience to northern Mexico and Central America. The third section of this chapter examines how Latin America, and in particular, Brazil, became part of that web.

Pentecostal Christianity is thus not a single ecclesial tradition deriving from a single source, let alone a denomination. Rather it is a way or style of being Christian that has plural origins and multiple institutional expressions. Scholars struggle to construct a watertight definition of such a polycentric and amorphous religious phenomenon. One recent authority has proposed the inclusive definition: "'Pentecostalism' includes all those movements and churches where the emphasis is on an ecstatic *experience of the Spirit* and a tangible *practice of spiritual gifts*."[14] In any case, the label "Pentecostal" was not at first owned by all strands of this emerging movement, and the concept of "Pentecostalism" was later still. According to *The Oxford English Dictionary*, the first appearance of the term "Pentecostalism" was not until 1927, when the *New York Times* reported the resignation of five deacons of Calvary Baptist Church, New York City, in protest against the encouragement by the pastor, the fundamentalist champion John Roach Straton, of "manifestations of a nature commonly associated with Pentecostalism."[15] However, the Baptist deacons' protest, coupled with the misspelling "Pentacostalism" that appears in the article subheading, constitute evidence that the term was gradually forcing its way into American religious vocabulary by that date. The most common self-designation used by Pentecostals in the two decades of the century was rather that they belonged to "the Apostolic Faith." They believed that they were witnessing a revival of pristine Christianity in its apostolic power, baptizing or immersing believers in the Holy Spirit. A growing number of them believed that the gift of tongues was either the normal or even the necessary outward evidence of being baptized by the Holy Spirit, but there were strands of the apostolic movement that did not even practice glossolalia.

The most influential "apostolic" in global terms predated the Pentecostal movement as strictly defined and appears never to have spoken in tongues: he was the eccentric Scottish emigré whom we introduced in chapter 3, John Alexander Dowie, founder of the Christian (Catholic) Apostolic Church in Chicago and subsequently theocratic ruler of the millenarian community of Zion City, Illinois. While no single person can be identified as the fountainhead of African Pentecostalism, Dowie's direct or indirect influence is of exceptional significance.

From the 1890s until 1906 John Alexander Dowie distributed internationally—including to Africa—a periodical, *Leaves of Healing*. Its articles and illustrations depicting abandoned surgical appliances triumphantly displayed as trophies of divine victory over Satan spread the message that in the last days the power of the Spirit was available to heal the sick without any recourse to biomedicine. Another American holiness periodical, *Sword of the Spirit*, published from May 1901 by Faith Tabernacle, the Philadelphia offshoot of the Christian (Catholic) Apostolic Church, circulated widely in West Africa from about 1917, and soon led to the formation of Faith Tabernacle churches, especially on the Gold Coast (Ghana).[16] Some of the Pentecostal missionaries who mediated the experience of Azusa Street to Africa after 1906 had also been leading members of Dowie's Zion City community. Among them were two couples included in a missionary party that arrived in Cape Town in May 1908—John and Jennie Lake and Thomas and Charlotte Hezmalhalch. They planted a church at Doornfontein in the suburbs of Johannesburg and then took over a city-center congregation in Bree Street affiliated to Dowie's church, which led in September 1908 to the inception of the Apostolic Faith Mission in South Africa. The first black Zionist church in South Africa, planted at Wakkerstroom in the Transvaal in 1903–4 by a former Dutch Reformed minister, Pieter le Roux, also owed its inspiration to Dowie's teaching, mediated through *Leaves of Healing* and Dowie's emissary to South Africa, Daniel Bryant. Like its American counterpart, the Apostolic movement in South Africa was originally interracial but from 1915 the black and white strands followed divergent trajectories. The black strands became the Zionist churches of South Africa, while the whites remained within the Apostolic Faith Mission, which developed into the largest Pentecostal denomination in South Africa, and was the church into which Frank Chikane was ordained in 1980.[17]

II. Pentecostal Christianities in Ghana

Whereas the genesis of Pentecostal Christianities in southern Africa owed a large debt to Dowie and his periodical, on the Gold Coast, as also in Nigeria, it was the *Sword of the Spirit* rather than *Leaves of Healing* that made the greater long-term impact.[18] The influence of these two magazines was one reason why in Africa the predominant emphasis of Pentecostal Christianity was not on the gift of tongues but on the power to heal the sick. Another and more substantial reason was the context in which the holiness and Pentecostal movements spread in Africa in the years after the First World War. The global influenza epidemic of 1918–19 hit the continent particularly hard. In South Africa at least 300,000 died. In the British colony of the Gold Coast some 100,000 people, about 4 percent of the population, died between October and December 1918. In Nigeria conservative estimates reported 450,000 dead out of a population of 18 million.[19] This was not the end of West Africa's postwar troubles. The cocoa market on which the economy of the Gold Coast depended collapsed in 1918–19, leading to widespread economic hardship. In 1925–26 Lagos suffered devastating smallpox epidemics. In this tragic environment, the efficacy of both traditional sources of spiritual protection and the new and still fragile European biomedicine came into question. Conversely, both the Faith Tabernacle movement and the Spiritual churches of West Africa that promised immediate healing and total security for the future to those who submitted themselves to the power of Christ, exerted a powerful appeal. In Ghana these Spiritual churches were known as the *Sunsum sorè* (Spirit worshipping) churches. They included such churches as the Musama Disco Christian Church and the Twelve Apostles Church. In Nigeria, where they were known as Aladura or "praying" churches, they originated, not in the immediate wake of the influenza epidemic, but a decade later, from 1930. Nevertheless, Aladura leaders in their subsequent teaching about the folly of reliance on European medicine pointedly recalled the impotence of the colonial medical service to stem the advance of smallpox in Lagos in 1925–26.[20]

Exorcism—the deliverance of disturbed persons from the oppression of indwelling spirits—was a feature of many strands of the Apostolic movement from the beginning. If sickness was fundamentally, as Dowie and his disciples taught, the "foul offspring of its father, Satan, and its mother Sin," then the atoning work of Christ included delivering the sinner from sickness as the work of the devil.[21] Hence the work of healing in the power of the Spirit involved a contestation with evil spiritual power. Healing was likely to involve a measure of deliverance, and deliverance certainly could be expected to bring healing. However, the great majority of Pentecostals taught that, although truly "born-again" and Spirit-baptized Christians may still be subject to attack and affliction by demonic forces, they could not become possessed or indwelt by demons, for their bodies were the temple of the Holy Spirit and hence in principle inviolable. The largest white American Pentecostal denomination, the Assemblies of God, formed in 1914, was consistent in its explicit teaching that born-again believers cannot be demon possessed.[22]

This fundamental ambiguity in the structure of Apostolic doctrine on sickness and spiritual contestation was destined to carry exceptionally far-reaching consequences on the African continent. In Africa, the prophet movements of the first half of the century practiced exorcism, but they generally did so as an accompaniment of the initial work of evangelization. The first-hand accounts of William Wadé Harris's ministry on the Gold and Ivory Coasts by Joseph Casely Hayford and the French colonial administrator Paul Marty both make it clear that for Harris the expulsion of evil powers from the souls and bodies of his hearers was a regular part of the evangelistic commission, frequently seen as a necessary prelude to the act of baptism. Although Harris appears not to have used the term "exorcism," the crucial symbolic role played in his baptisms by requiring the convert to touch the physical objects of the Bible and Cross suggest that he was making explicit appeal to the power of Christ to vanquish and decisively expel evil forces from the person concerned.[23] The remarkable success of Harris, as also of Garrick Braide and later Joseph Babalola in Nigeria and Simon Kimbangu in the Belgian Congo,[24] in inducing people to do what European missionaries had repeatedly tried and conspicuously failed to persuade them to do—that is, destroy or abandon their "fetishes"—is explicable only if their hearers were convinced that in submitting themselves to the lordship of Christ they would find a more secure and lasting protection against evil forces than indigenous rituals or charms could supply. If they had been led to believe that even after repentance and baptism they could still be subject to being taking over by the evil powers whom the missionaries described as the devil and his minions, then they surely would not have taken the dramatic step demanded by the prophets of a total rupture with indigenous sources of spiritual protection. Thus Joseph Babalola's evangelistic and baptismal preaching urged his hearers to burn their traditional objects of spiritual power and entrust themselves to the all-surpassing power of God alone; at the Ekiti town of Efon, Babalola deliberately selected a site traditionally associated with evil spirits to make a bonfire of the "juju." The power of the name of Jesus of which the leaders of the Aladura churches frequently spoke was, as the former Faith Tabernacle member and Lagos Aladura pastor David Odubanjo wrote in his diary on March 5, 1950, a power that "heals, saves, *protects*, provides . . ."[25]

For much of the colonial period both the "spiritual" churches arising from the prophet movements, and the Apostolic or Pentecostal churches that traced their origins to the Faith Tabernacle movement—and the two categories overlapped—were successful in persuading significant numbers of Nigerians and Ghanaians that there was indeed sufficient protection in the name of Jesus to make a repudiation of indigenous sources of spiritual power acceptable. As early as 1926 Faith Tabernacle alone had at least 177 branches in Ghana with an estimated aggregate membership of 4,425 and a further 46 branches with 920 members in Nigeria. From these roots three of the main branches of contemporary Ghanaian Pentecostalism grew—the Ghana Apostolic Church (known from 1962 as the Church of Pentecost), the Apostolic Church of Ghana, and the Christ Apostolic Church. All three of them were associated with the ministry of the onetime Presbyterian Peter Anim (1890–1984), whose introduction to Apostolic Christianity in the early 1920s came through reading *Sword of the Spirit*. Similarly in Nigeria the Assemblies of God, Apostolic Church, and Christ Apostolic Church, all trace their origins to leaders schooled in the Faith Tabernacle movement. Adam Mohr has estimated that by 2010 in Nigeria and Ghana together, the churches that trace their history to Faith Tabernacle had an aggregate membership of between 8 and 15 million.[26]

However, there were two closely related challenges confronting this style of Pentecostal Christianity in the African context. The first was the apparent incompatibility between the theological presumption that sickness must in some sense be the product of evil powers and the observable fact that adherents of the new churches still fell ill and died. Was the protection afforded by the name of Jesus quite so lasting after all? The churches that derived from the prophet movements softened the problem to some extent by being more or less open to the use of traditional herbal medicines. Wadé Harris counseled his converts to use herbal remedies, and so did most of the *Sunsum sorè* churches in Ghana.[27] As time went on, the Spiritual churches also tended to make greater ritual space for the use of sacred objects that could serve as a focus of the believer's trust in the protective power of Christ—such as candles, holy water, crosses, or incense. They thus exposed themselves to the criticism from Pentecostal purists that they had reinvented the traditionalist's fetish in Christian guise; by gravitating back to the dependence of indigenous religionists on material objects of power, they were thus readmitting the devil by the back door. True Pentecostals set the Apostolic churches on a different and more radical course, distancing themselves both from the Spirituals' use of sacred objects and from the readiness of their missionary teachers to use biomedicine when push came to shove.[28] Thus the Christ Apostolic Churches in Ghana and Nigeria were established in 1939 and 1941 respectively as a result of African disillusionment with the teaching of the British missionaries in the Apostolic Church that use of European medicine was not incompatible with reliance on the Holy Spirit.[29]

The second challenge faced by African Pentecostal Christianity stemmed from the fact that Protestant missions, with few exceptions, had made theological sense of the ever-present African spirit world by interpreting it as the dark realm of Satan and his minions. Birgit Meyer has shown with reference to the Ewe of Ghana how missionaries, in this instance German Pietist missionaries from the Bremen Mission, "diabolized" African indigenous religion and in so doing unwittingly gave the figure of the devil a prominence that he does not possess in the Bible itself. The Evangelical Presbyterian Church of Ghana that resulted from the work of the Bremen Mission, and similarly the Presbyterian Church of Ghana planted by the Basel Mission, were left with a problematic legacy. Their members had been taught that the entire spirit world was under the control of the Evil One, but had been given apparently ineffective protective mechanisms to counter his devices. The growing incorporation of Ghana into a modern capitalist economy between 1918 and the 1950s augmented rather than lessened popular beliefs in witchcraft, stoking fears that demons were to blame for the misfortunes that afflicted individuals exposed to the fluctuations in the cocoa trade.[30] In such an environment, the younger generation of Christians left the mainline denominations in droves for Pentecostal alternatives. The Presbyterian Church of Ghana was the first of these to embark in response on its own ministries of healing and deliverance, and as a result succeeded in stemming the exodus by the late 1980s.[31] At the same time, the *Sunsum sorè* churches also went into decline, perhaps because their dependence on the ritualized charisma of their founding prophets lost its appeal with the passing of the years; the Pentecostal churches with their more democratic emphasis on the availability of the power of the Spirit to all were now a more attractive option.[32] By the end of the century, in Ghana as in many other parts of Africa, a broadly Pentecostal style of Christianity had become the default setting to which even the historic mission churches, Catholic as well as Protestant, began to conform.

The success of the Pentecostal option did not, however, eliminate the second challenge identified above, namely the question of whether God or the devil occupied the center of the theological universe. African Pentecostals had repudiated both mission Christianity, with its biblically orthodox but apparently unconvincing assurances that the power of Christ was all that was needed, and the willingness of the Spiritual churches to find some room for ritual objects and traditional medicine in their therapeutic universe. They were bold enough to claim that those who by sole reliance on the Bible surrendered themselves wholly to the power of the Spirit could be sure of the full blessing of God in all areas of their lives. This claim became increasingly hard to sustain. By the 1980s it was apparent that decolonization in West Africa had failed to deliver the increase in general prosperity that had been anticipated. In Ghana living standards actually declined in the wake of independence in 1957. Whereas in 1957 per capita annual income in Ghana was comparable to that in Hong Kong, Singapore, Malaysia, or South Korea, at about $400 per annum, by 2000 per capita income in Ghana had fallen to between $360 and $390, in comparison with the phenomenal increases in prosperity recorded by these Asian economies, where per capita income by the end of the century was between $18,000 and $32,000.[33] Ghana's plight became especially critical in the 1980s, under the double burden of the structural adjustment programs imposed by the International Monetary Fund and the self-serving regime of Jerry Rawlings.

It is not fortuitous that the same decade of the 1980s was one in which African Pentecostals turned in growing numbers to new transnational sources for a twofold answer to the seeming contradiction between what their theology promised and what the currently depressing economic realities allowed. The two dimensions of this answer—the American prosperity or "Word of Faith" gospel and an emphasis on deliverance ministry—have been interpreted, either as two distinct but overlapping categories of neo-Pentecostal response,[34] or as a sequence in which the failure of the first to deliver led logically to the latter,[35] but in Africa the extent of overlapping between the two is so substantial that absolute differentiation is problematic. Much greater scholarly attention has been devoted to the former strand, the influence of the prosperity gospel that emerged in the United States from a variety of non-Pentecostal and Pentecostal sources—including the "positive confession" teaching of the Baptist pastor E. W. Kenyon (1867–1948), the influential book, *The Power of Positive Thinking*, published in 1952 by a New York pastor in the Reformed Church of America Norman Vincent Peale (1898–1993), and the emphasis on "seed faith" and "abundant life" of the Pentecostal (later Methodist) preacher Oral Roberts (1918–2009).[36] Roberts exercised enormous influence in West Africa through his publications, weekly television broadcasts, and evangelistic campaigns, such as a visit to Ghana in 1988. His disciples in West Africa included the Nigerian Benson Idahosa (1938–98) and the Ghanaian Nicholas Duncan-Williams (b. 1957).[37]

The prosperity gospel appeared to offer to Ghanaians the hope of escape from poverty by the dedicated pursuit of spiritual obedience and faithfulness in financial giving to God. It did not always disappoint, not least because Pentecostals have stressed the importance of hard work, moral integrity, and the avoidance of expenditure on drink. Nevertheless, in the context of a chronically dysfunctional economy such as that of Ghana, the recipe offered by American prosperity gospel advocates was insufficient. A further dimension was required, one that addressed directly the underlying causes of the country's problems. For some West African Pentecostals, the solution lay in a fusion of Pentecostal and liberation theologies. Notable among them was the Ghanaian founder of the International Central Gospel Church, Mensa Otabil (1959–), who combined a Pentecostal theology of blessing with a prophetic stance on issues of justice and a firm belief in Africans' capacity to throw off the legacy of centuries of exploitation.[38] For many other African Christians, however, a distinct strand of the transnational charismatic movement that also became prominent in the 1980s offered a more persuasive answer. This strand took a different route toward the goal of abundant life by identifying and confronting the spiritual blockages to God's blessing. Its emphasis that Christians should be continually vigilant in seeking expulsion of evil powers from their own lives as well as from the life of their nation resonated strongly with the long-standing concerns of African Christians, and by the end of the century had become as prominent a feature of the African religious landscape as its close partner, the prosperity gospel.

Pentecostal deliverance ministry in modern Africa, like the prosperity gospel, both coheres with indigenous understandings of the reality of the spirit world and owes a major debt to external influences. Its rapid diffusion in the 1980s and 1990s was again assisted by technological innovation—in air travel, television and video communication, and above all by the invention in 1962 of the compact audiocassette tape, a medium that enabled the global circulation at very low cost of recorded messages by popular Christian preachers. The most influential disseminator of deliverance teaching in Africa and elsewhere was Derek Prince (1915–2003). A prolific writer, he had published more than forty books by 1984.[39] Through an American daily radio program broadcast internationally in thirteen languages, and an international cassette and book ministry established in late 1983, Prince became a figure of international significance.[40] His visit to Ghana in 1987 was instrumental in securing widespread acceptance for deliverance ministry at a time when it was still controversial even within Pentecostal circles in Ghana.[41] Opoku Onyinah describes Prince as "the 'mentor' of this kind of ministry in Ghana."[42] He was particularly influential both on Paul Owusu Tabiri, founder of Bethel Prayer Ministry International and a leading figure in developing Ghana's highly popular "prayer camps" (specializing in spiritual warfare) in the early 1990s, and on Aaron Vuha of the Evangelical Presbyterian Church.[43] His influence extended beyond Protestant circles and reached all continents. Roman Catholics who acknowledged a specific debt to his teaching included: the Nigerian priest and popular author, Stephen Uche Njoku; the controversial archbishop of Lusaka from 1969 to 1983, Emmanuel Milingo; and the American exponent of divine healing, Francis MacNutt.[44] Some of the most globally popular charismatic authors on deliverance ministry traced their understanding of demonization and its remedy in greater or lesser measure to Prince—among them, Southern Baptists Frank and Ida Hammond; the New Zealand Anglican Bill Subritzky; and the British founder of Ellel Ministries, Peter Horrobin.[45]

Derek Prince, though he resided in the United States (latterly in Florida) from 1963, was a Briton. Educated at Eton College and King's College, Cambridge, he was elected a Fellow of King's in March 1940. His Fellowship dissertation, on "The Evolution of Plato's Philosophical Method," was a discussion of Plato's analysis and use of Socrates' philosophical method from the perspective of the philosophy of language, as understood by "the Cambridge School" of modern philosophy, and in particular by Ludwig Wittgenstein, who taught Prince.[46] At the time Prince was not an evangelical Christian—he was converted and baptized in the Spirit through contact with the Assemblies of God a year later. But Plato's philosophy, and especially Socrates' insistence in the *Phaedo* that all material things were transitory, left an enduring imprint on this young Cambridge philosopher.[47] Prince's popular writings on deliverance reproduce the language of Plato's *Phaedo* almost verbatim:

> The things that belong to the visible realm are transitory and impermanent. It is only in the invisible realm that we can find true and abiding reality. It is in this realm, too, that we discover the forces which will ultimately shape our destiny, even in the visible realm.[48]

Prince's message that the world of contesting spiritual powers was not simply to be taken seriously, but was in fact *more* real than the transitory world of material suffering and poverty, exerted peculiar fascination in Africa. Furthermore, he departed decisively from the tradition of both Western Pentecostalism and of the prophet movements of the earlier twentieth century in his explicit teaching that even Spirit-filled Christians could be not simply afflicted, but even possessed by demons. If such as Harris or Babalola had been mistaken in their assumption that "once protected, always protected," then might that not explain why even fervent Christians were falling into sickness and failing to escape from poverty? According to Prince, from the invisible realm of spiritual reality both blessings and curses flowed down the bloodline from up to four generations back, conveying good (evidenced in prosperity) or ill (manifested in poverty or hereditary sickness), a claim that meshed closely with African beliefs about the ancestors. Though Prince claimed to derive his teaching on ancestral blessings and curses from biblical sources, such as Deuteronomy 28, Plato's influence may again be evident here: Plato shared with much Greek thought a belief in the polluting capacity of ancestral curses, and in his *Phaedrus* refers to families "afflicted by horrendous illnesses and sufferings as a result of guilt incurred some time in the distant past."[49] For Plato, however, daemons were not the villains of the piece, but rather intermediary spiritual beings that usefully protected the gods from polluting contact with matter. Prince, by contrast, followed Tertullian in assimilating the whole assembly of ancestral and other spirits into the Pauline concept of evil principalities and powers.[50]

Prince's teaching appealed to many Christians in Ghana—and elsewhere in West Africa—as a total explanation for their continuing predicament in the final years of the century. Whether it offered them a lasting solution is another question. In practice, an approach that urged Christians to be constantly on the hunt for inherited malevolent influences that might account for their problems inculcated not trust in the power of Christ, but enduring fear and mutual suspicion. Nevertheless, by the end of the century, substantial sections of African Christianity had espoused a version of Pentecostalism that reordered the entire architecture of Christian doctrine around the motif of spiritual warfare.

III. Pentecostalism in Brazil

As noted in section I of this chapter, Chile and Mexico were the first Latin American countries to be touched by the new style of apostolic and Spirit-centered Christianity that surfaced at Azusa Street and a number of other locations in the first decade of the twentieth century. By 1909–10, sporadic outbreaks of similar phenomena were evident in Central America, Argentina, and Brazil. Other parts of the continent were affected much more slowly: Pentecostalism did not reach Venezuela and Peru until 1919, Uruguay until 1935, and Ecuador did not have a Pentecostal church before 1956. In aggressively secular Uruguay, the Protestant percentage of the population rose only marginally from 1.6 percent in 1908 to 1.9 percent in 1980.[51] Relative to population, Mexico, despite being affected at an early date by Pentecostal influence, remained quite stony soil for Pentecostals, as for other Protestants, perhaps because of the resilience of popular Catholicism focused on devotion to Our Lady of Guadalupe. Nonetheless, by the end of the century, Mexico's estimated 7 million Protestants (out of a population of 99 million) were mostly Pentecostal, and in absolute terms represented the second largest Protestant population on the continent behind Brazil.[52] The Pentecostal penetration of Latin America during the twentieth century was thus uneven and initially quite limited, and those countries where it first made noticeable headway—Brazil and, to a lesser degree, Chile—dominate the scholarly literature on the subject. However, as late as 1980, Pentecostals accounted for only about 3 percent of the population of Brazil. It was only from the 1960s that Pentecostals began to make substantial inroads in the second half of the century into the ostensible Roman Catholic hegemony of the continent.

The less spectacular yet still substantial growth achieved in some areas by non-Pentecostal Protestants, specifically by Baptists in Brazil, has been almost entirely ignored, or even denied, in the scholarship. Latin American Baptists, who numbered only about 250,000 in 1965, had grown to nearly 1.4 million by the mid-1990s, 1.1 million of whom were to be found in Brazil.[53] It is estimated that as late as 1980, non-Pentecostal Protestants accounted for more than half of the Brazilian Protestant population; it was only in the last two decades of the century that Pentecostals attained majority status among Brazilian Protestants, accounting for perhaps two-thirds by the year 2000. Census records indicate that the number of

Brazilian Pentecostals more than doubled in the course of the 1990s.[54] By 2000 all Protestants probably accounted for between 9 and 10 percent of the total population of Latin America. In Brazil census figures for 2000 indicated that Protestants formed 15.5 percent of the population, 10.4 percent of them being Pentecostals.[55]

In the south of Brazil and Argentina, the early history of Pentecostalism is closely associated with the course of immigration from southern Europe. In 1910 Luigi Francescon (1866–1964), an Italian emigrant to Chicago, established Brazil's oldest Pentecostal church in São Paulo, which had an Italian immigrant population of over one million. Converted to Protestantism in 1891 by a group of Italian Waldensians in Chicago, Francescon became a Pentecostal in August 1907 through contact with William H. Durham's North Avenue Mission in the city. He then established Italian-American Pentecostal churches in Chicago, Los Angeles, Philadelphia, and St. Louis before visiting Argentina in October 1909. There, with Giácomo Lombardi and Lucía Menna, he founded the *Iglesia Asamblea Cristiana* among the Italian community in Buenos Aires, the first Argentinian Pentecostal church. Finally in 1910 he came to São Paulo, where he planted the *Congregacioni Cristiani*. The denomination remained entirely Italian-speaking until 1935, when it began to hold Portuguese-medium services in order to reach native Brazilians; eventually it became known by its Portuguese name of the *Congregação Cristã*.[56] The church grew mainly in rural and small-town settings in the state of São Paulo, where it remained the largest Pentecostal denomination at the end of the century.

In the less economically developed north of Brazil, Pentecostalism had quite separate origins, following the arrival in November 1910 in Belém, capital of the Amazonian state of Pará, of two Swedish Baptists, Gunnar Vingren and Daniel Berg. Vingren was a graduate of the University of Chicago Divinity School (a Baptist-founded institution) and pastor of a Swedish Baptist church in South Bend, Indiana; Berg was a foundry man who had previously resided in Chicago. Led to Brazil by a word of prophecy that they should go to "Pará," a place they had never heard of, they initially joined the local Baptist church. Excommunicated from the Baptist church in June 1911 on account of their divisive teaching of baptism in the Spirit, they established their own Pentecostal congregation in Belém under the name of the Apostolic Faith Mission. In 1918 they registered their expanding network of assemblies under the title of the *Assembléia de Deus*. These churches had no formal links to the Assemblies of God in the United States—their international connections were mainly with the large and internationally influential Filadelfia Church in Stockholm, led by another former Swedish Baptist, Petrus Lewi Pethrus. Belém , with its damp equatorial climate, was notorious for the incidence of malaria, yellow fever, cholera, and other diseases, and in this context the emphasis of the *Assembléia de Deus* on healing proved a powerful attraction.[57]

The *Congregação Cristã* and the *Assembléia de Deus*, which Paul Freston has identified as comprising the "first wave" of the Brazilian Pentecostal movement, developed into two of the largest Pentecostal churches in Brazil.[58] By the mid-1980s the *Assembléia de Deus* alone claimed 13 million baptized members; although this is almost certainly an inflated estimate, it compares favorably with the 5 million or so adult Brazilians involved in the Catholic Base Ecclesial Communities (CEBs) at that time.[59] The church had expanded from its original base in the north and northeast to every state of the country. Although both these Pentecostal denominations planted many congregations in São Paulo, they also attracted strong support in rural and small-town environments, thus contradicting the stereotype that Latin American Pentecostalism is an exclusively urban phenomenon. Although many commentators have linked the postwar progress of Pentecostalism with the rapid urbanization of the continent from the 1950s onwards, suggesting that Pentecostalism may be a form of Christianity uniquely attractive to migrants who are encountering urban modernity for the first time, such explanations now appear less compelling. In Brazil rates of Pentecostal growth toward the end of the century continued to increase in a society that was already predominantly urbanized, with falling rates of rural–urban migration.[60] Pentecostal expansion also took place against the backcloth of Brazil's series of repressive military regimes between 1964 and 1985; Pentecostal leaders mostly supported these regimes and generally stood back from Christian attempts to defend human rights in Brazil.

The second wave of Brazilian Pentecostalism, beginning in the 1950s, was by contrast an almost exclusively urban phenomenon. Freston has identified four denominations within this second wave. The *Igreja do Evangelho Quadrangular* (Four-Square Gospel Church) was an offspring of the International Church of the Foursquare Gospel, founded in 1927 by the Canadian-born evangelist Aimee Semple McPherson (1890–1944). The Foursquare Gospel proclaimed Jesus as Savior, Baptizer with the Holy Spirit, Physician and Healer, and Coming King. As befits a church that can trace its foundation to a woman, 35 percent of its Brazilian pastors by 1995 were women.[61] The other three denominations all had indigenous Brazilian origins: *A Igreja Evangélica Pentecostal O Brasil Para Criso* (Brazil for Christ, 1955); *A Igreja Pentecostal Deus é Amor* (God Is Love, 1962);

and *Casa da Benção* (House of Blessing, 1964). These churches were more closely attuned to the cultural preferences of urban populations, making greater use of modern media, especially radio broadcasts. Brazil for Christ, founded by Manoel de Mello, was one of the first Pentecostal churches to join the World Council of Churches (in 1969), though it rescinded its membership following Mello's death in 1990.[62]

It is the "third-wave" churches originating from the late 1970s that have made the greatest contribution to the explosion of Pentecostal Christianity in modern Brazil. The largest and most prominent of these third-wave churches is *Igreja Universal do Reino de Deus* (IURD, or Universal Church of the Kingdom of God), founded in 1977 by Edir Macedo and his brother-in-law Romildo Soares. Other churches of this generation include *Comunidade Evangélica* (1976); *Renascer em Cristo* (1986), and *Igreja Internacional da Graça de Deus*, a secession from the IURD in 1980 led by Soares. Macedo, born in 1945 into a Catholic home in Rio de Janeiro, was an official in the state lottery. His first Protestant affiliation was to the *Igreja da Nova Vida*, a lower-middle-class Pentecostal church planted in Rio in 1960 by a Canadian former Assemblies of God missionary. His passion to reach the urban poor led to a split with the pastor. Macedo and his supporters then joined the *Casa da Benção* church, into which two of them were ordained. In 1975 Macedo was set apart by pastors from the *Casa da Benção* for his own ministry in a district of Rio, and the IURD was born. By 1995 it had a membership of at least one and a half million, mainly in the big-city environments of Rio, São Paulo, and Salvador (Bahia). It was the fourth-largest Brazilian Protestant church with estimates of its membership by the end of the decade varying between 2.1 and 4 million in 2,014 churches, though there is evidence that since then its membership has seen a measure of decline.[63] In 1989 Macedo bought up Brazil's oldest but ailing television network, the *Rede Record de Televisão*, and transformed it into the second largest in the country. By the close of the century Macedo's church also owned thirty radio stations and a newspaper. It had become a major force in national politics, securing in 1998 the election of fifteen of its members as deputies to the federal congress and a further twenty-six as deputies to state assemblies. Furthermore, in the course of the 1990s the IURD established itself as a major player in transnational Christian missions, planting churches in at least 52 countries by late 1998; these included Portugal, with 62 churches, and South Africa, with 115 churches. Bishop Macedo would later earn the dubious accolade of being the richest pastor in the world, a billionaire with a reputed net worth of 1.1 billion dollars by 2013.[64]

Like their West African counterparts, this third generation of "neo-Pentecostal" churches have enthusiastically adopted televangelism and proclaimed the prosperity message of the Word of Faith. Like them also, they have given particular emphasis to deliverance ministry from malevolent spiritual forces. Whereas the first Brazilian Pentecostal churches sought to win adherents from Catholicism by emphasizing the spiritually democratic gifts of tongues and prophecies, the third-wave churches have identified their chief competitors as the Afro-Brazilian spiritist religions, particularly *umbanda*, and hence have brought spiritual confrontation with demons to the foreground of their activities. As in West Africa, the panoply of spirits associated with the indigenous religious context have been interpreted as emissaries of Satan, "multiple disguises of a single demonic force."[65] IURD congregations have a service of *libertação* (exorcism) every Friday: the liberation is both of individuals from the devils possessing them, but also of the evil spirits themselves from the bodies that imprison them. These services became so popular that they set a precedent for other Pentecostal churches to follow: even the *Assembléia de Deus*, which traditionally had kept deliverance ministry at arm's length, adopted the practice of Friday exorcism services in 1988.[66] As in Ghana or Nigeria, deliverance has encompassed liberation from a wide range of social and political evils as well as more personal problems—prostitution, unemployment, corruption, inflation, violence, and especially the betrayal or abuse of women.

Like some of the latest generation of African Pentecostal churches, the new Brazilian Pentecostals have also modified the traditional Protestant reliance on the word alone by the increasing use of material objects invested with symbolic power in the battle with demons, such as holy water, oil, sand or ashes.[67] In IURD services, the Bible itself has become a ritual object of sacramental power in the battle against the demons. It is still formally invested with supreme authority, but comparatively little attention is paid to the reading or exposition of the text. While Vatican II and the Base Ecclesial Community (CEB) movement rendered Brazilian Catholicism in the later years of the century more recognizably "Protestant" in its emphasis on preaching and encouragement to the faithful to read the Scriptures for themselves, some major sections of Brazilian Pentecostalism reverted to a traditionally "Catholic" reliance on ritual power, and effectively marginalized the historic Reformed emphasis on the written word. As in West Africa, there has also been a tendency to magnify the authority of the pastor as the Spirit-filled "big man" and restrict the role of the congregation in decision-making—an ironic counter movement to the spiritual egalitarianism intrinsic to the early Pentecostal movement.[68]

One of the most commonly repeated dicta on Christianity in modern Latin America pithily reflects that "liberation theology opted for the poor, and the poor opted for Pentecostalism."[69] Scholars of the movement, especially those who concentrated on churches that originated in the first wave of Brazilian Pentecostalism, have been in no doubt that this was a creed tailor-made for the poor and disenfranchised. Researchers in Rio de Janeiro in 1988 discovered that in the impoverished *favelas* to the west of the city the proportion of *evangélicos* to the overall population was three times greater than in the affluent suburbs to the south, such as Copacabana.[70]

In Brazil, as elsewhere on the continent, the Pentecostal message proved to have a particular attraction to working-class women. Although the Foursquare Gospel Church has been atypical of the movement as a whole in allowing women to be pastors, more than 60 percent of Latin American Pentecostals are women. Testimonies from Pentecostal women reveal that their faith has proved to be a source of empowerment for women in the home, emasculating the Latin American sexist ideology of *machismo*, reaffirming familial values of marital fidelity and mutuality, and redeploying meager household resources from expenditure on drink and tobacco for the man into food and clothing for the family.[71] For the poor in Latin America, as in so much of the developing world, religion is about utilizing all available spiritual resources to meet the pressing everyday needs of survival, and engaging in contractual relationships with the spiritual patrons who appear to promise the desired benefits. Popular Catholicism sought such resources through the heavenly intercession of the Virgin Mary and the saints, who were expected to work miracles of grace on behalf of the faithful in response to their devotion. The devotees of *umbanda*—many of them formally "Catholic"—resorted to intermediaries with the spirit world in search of similar intervention. Pentecostals may appear to be little different in that they also sought miraculous spiritual aid to combat sickness, poverty, and evil. But the Pentecostal explosion cannot be explained simply by drawing an analogy with existing popular religiosity. The decisive added value that Pentecostal faith brought was its promise of a decisive personal transformation through the regenerating power of the Holy Spirit. The characteristic evangelical emphasis on the conversion of the individual had no parallel in either traditional Catholicism or *umbanda*. The promise of spiritual power here and now, and hence of a decisive rupture with the past that did not depend on any political transformation of the social environment, ultimately explains why so many of the Latin American poor from the late twentieth century onwards have preferred Pentecostalism over liberationist solutions to their predicament.[72]

These Pentecostal solutions, however, did not necessarily imply severance from the Catholic past. Just as the Presbyterian Church in Ghana from the 1960s sought a measure of accommodation with Pentecostal styles of worship and spirituality, so the Catholic Church in Latin America began in the 1970s to experiment in a modest and guarded fashion with charismatic renewal. In Brazil, where Pentecostalism was highly visible in the media, the Catholic charismatic renewal movement made substantial headway. The number of charismatic Catholics in Brazil grew from an estimated 10,000 in 1976 to at least 6 million by 1994, some 4 percent of the Brazilian population, as opposed to Pentecostals' 10 percent.[73] By this time, they were probably more than twice as numerous as members of the CEBs in Brazil, which continued to be stronger in rural areas than in the cities, where 70 percent of the population lived. Catholic charismatics had also come to dominate the airwaves of Brazil's 181 Catholic radio stations. The realization had dawned among the Catholic hierarchy that the most effective and ecclesiastically acceptable way of exercising a preferential option for the poor was by a "preferential option for the Spirit."[74] By the close of the century the numbers of charismatic Catholics may have been as high as 33–35 million in Brazil, 73–75 million in Latin America as a whole, and perhaps 119 million worldwide.[75] Pentecostal or charismatic Catholics undoubtedly accounted for a much higher proportion of the Latin American Pentecostal movement than is often acknowledged. Catholic charismatics easily outnumbered Protestant Pentecostals in some Latin American nations—such as Colombia and Mexico–and probably had achieved a modest lead in the continent as a whole (75 million as opposed to 66 million). The religious demography of Latin America remains an extremely inexact science. Some estimates for Brazil suggest that Protestant Pentecostals in 2000 totaled as many as 41 million, as opposed to 33–35 million Catholic charismatics; in contrast, official census figures recorded only 18 million Brazilians as being members of Pentecostal churches in 2000.[76]

IV. The Religious Chameleon

The global Pentecostal movement throughout the twentieth century drew its most numerous adherents from the ranks of the poor, in a variety of urban and rural contexts. But as the century proceeded, it became apparent that this was not a faith for the poor alone, but rather a religious chameleon that had an extraordinary capacity to adapt itself to a wide range of social and economic contexts and ecclesiastical traditions. Pentecostalism has found a home amidst prosperous business families in Seoul

or Singapore as well as among the *favela* dwellers of São Paulo or the
Dalits of South India. The respective histories of Pentecostal culture in
Ghana and Brazil both reveal a gradual but incomplete shift in style from
the modest aspirations to social respectability and economic improvement
characteristic of the Apostolic churches in Ghana or the *Assembléia de
Deus* in Brazil to the sophisticated middle-class materiality and exhibi-
tionist style typical of modern Ghanaian neo-Pentecostal churches or of
the third-wave metropolitan churches in Brazil. The dominant cultural
tone of those neo-Pentecostal churches that have espoused the gospel of
prosperity is set, not by the very poor, but by the upwardly mobile, those
with middle-sized pockets but larger ambitions. Freston describes the
ethos of the IURD as "a religious version of the yuppie ethic, of rapid enrichment through daring risks."[77] Nevertheless, the poor continued to provide the bulk of its actual membership, at least in Rio de Janeiro, through
to the end of the century: a 1996 survey indicated that the economic and
educational levels of IURD members were significantly lower than for the
Protestant population as a whole.[78]

The increasingly prevalent emphasis on spiritual warfare was another
feature of the shift in cultural mood. Both African and Latin American
Pentecostal churches of the first three-quarters of the century offered the
poor the blessings of healing and a public voice through the democratic
charismata of speaking in tongues and prophecies. In contrast, the new
churches that became prominent in both continents from the 1980s prioritized the employment of deliverance to identify and remove the supposedly spiritual obstacles that stood in the way of the full physical and
economic well-being of their members. For many—though not for all—in
these churches Pentecostal Christianity was in danger of becoming a form
of theology of liberation focused almost entirely on the individual and unashamedly yoked to the ideology of capitalism.

The Presbyterian Church of Ghana may have been ahead of the game
in its dawning realization from the 1960s that it faced the choice between
a degree of accommodation with Pentecostalism and continued decline
into extinction, but increasingly other mainline churches throughout the
African continent either consciously reached the same conclusion about
the nature of the religious market or found themselves pulled against their
better judgment in the same direction. By the end of the century it was
clear that "Pentecostalism" in both Africa and Latin America—and indeed
in other continents as well—was not so much a single movement as a style
of following and worshipping Christ that exerted a compulsive appeal
across the boundaries of historic Christian traditions, and was capable of

blurring the historic boundary in European Christendom between Catholic and Protestant. However, to end the story at the turn of the century, as the formal boundaries of this book require us to do, may lead to premature conclusions. The undoubted fact that the late twentieth century witnessed a remarkable global expansion of Pentecostal styles of Christianity is not in itself a guarantee that such forms of Christianity will remain dominant throughout the twenty-first century, let alone beyond it, though they are clearly likely to remain highly influential for the foreseeable future. In Brazil, for example, the remarkable Pentecostal growth of the 1990s has not been sustained into the present century. There have been signs of a seepage from Pentecostal to historic Protestant churches, which grew more rapidly than Pentecostal churches in the first year of the new century, particularly in the major conurbations in the southeast of the country.[79]

CHAPTER FOURTEEN

The Eastern Orthodox Church
and the Modern World

I. The Westward Diffusion of Eastern
Orthodoxy in the Twentieth Century

History is all about change, and the writing of history seeks to explain processes of change. Of the main strands of Christianity, Eastern Orthodoxy is the most resistant to change and the most reluctant to admit that patterns of Christian worship, let alone Christian belief, ought to display any variation in response to shifts in the cultural and political climate. The Orthodox Church views itself as the divinely appointed witness to the unbroken "Tradition" of primitive apostolic Christianity. Through its divine liturgy it unites the faithful in mystical communion with the holy fellowship of saints and martyrs extending backwards through the centuries of Christian history and forwards into the heavenly company of the redeemed. The church is the visible embodiment of heaven on earth.

Protestant and Catholic history since the eighteenth century has substantially been a narrative of either positive or negative responses to the challenges to ecclesiastical authority presented by modernity—both those intellectual challenges created by the Enlightenment and modern scientific knowledge, and the social or institutional challenges posed by the emergence of democratic politics and an urban industrial society. In comparison with the Protestant or Catholic churches, the Orthodox Church has appeared relatively untroubled by either of these sets of questions. It has seen comparatively little need to adjust the presentation of the faith to the presuppositions of the Age of Reason. Although Orthodoxy made its own responses to the European Enlightenment and its secular ideological offspring, they were not generally of a kind that demanded extensive theological restatement. The Greek Orthodox Church, for example, never had to face the sustained anticlerical onslaught that assailed Catholicism in France or Italy, and was largely successful in harnessing the potentially threatening new power of nationalism to loyalty to Orthodox tradition.[1] Moreover, in contrast to western Europe, many of the Orthodox heartlands in Russia, the Balkans, and West Asia were for a long period substantially unaffected by the severe challenges posed to organized religion by the development of urban industrial society.

Yet, the apparent inference that the Orthodox Church, by its unyielding adherence to Tradition, somehow stands outside of, and impervious to, history and its processes of constant change would be a demonstrably false one. The missionary expansion of Orthodoxy, such as the work of Cyril and Methodius among the Slavs in the ninth century, brought with it inevitable liturgical change and the dynamism of the vernacular. Nevertheless, until the twentieth century, Orthodox Christianity was, by and large, eastern Christianity, being largely confined to its historic territories in the Balkans, Slav and Russian lands, the Middle East, South India, Egypt, and Ethiopia, with outposts in Japan and Alaska. Most Catholic or Protestant Christians in the West knew very little about Orthodox Christians, and vice versa. In Britain, for example, there were at the beginning of the twentieth century only five Orthodox congregations: four churches serving the Greek immigrant communities in London, Manchester, Liverpool, and Cardiff, plus the chapel at the Russian Embassy in London, which was itself closed in 1917. Yet by 1998 there were 209 Orthodox congregations in Britain, served by nearly 200 clergy.[2]

In the course of the twentieth century, the position of the Orthodox and Oriental Orthodox Churches weakened markedly, and apparently irreversibly, in some of their historic strongholds, such as Egypt and Palestine, while in most of eastern Europe Orthodoxy came under severe ideological pressure from communist regimes between 1917 and 1989, only to emerge into the post-Soviet era remarkably intact. However, perhaps the most striking feature of Orthodox history during the century is the extent of the global diffusion—yet at the same time tendency to ethnic fragmentation—of Orthodox Christianity. By the close of the century there were more than 3 million Orthodox Christians in North America, who were subject to at least fifteen different ecclesiastical jurisdictions.[3] The primary reason for such geographical and institutional diffusion was the intercontinental migration of diverse Orthodox populations from various parts of eastern and central Europe, but an important secondary reason was the growing appeal that Orthodoxy exerted on Christians who for one reason or another had become dissatisfied with their former Protestant or Catholic allegiance. By the 1990s the Orthodox Church was one of the very few churches in western Europe or North America that was displaying steady growth, as a result of both immigration and conversion.[4] The Orthodox tradition also possessed a distinctive appeal to some African Americans and African Christians, in that it represented an apostolic form of Christianity with primitive African roots that antedated white racism and colonialism. The third section of this chapter will accordingly trace some of the trajectories of expansion of Orthodox Christianity in twentieth-century Africa. These trajectories, though they followed pathways very different from modern western strands of mission Christianity, adhered to the Christology of the Council of Chalcedon in AD 453 and were very largely independent of the ancient Oriental Orthodox traditions of Egypt, Ethiopia, and Syria, with their "Miaphysite" understanding (holding to the one nature—*mia physis*) of Christ.

For the Orthodox, perhaps more than for other Christians, the twentieth century was a century of immense institutional disruption and consequently also of radical diversification of the sociopolitical and geographical environments in which the Orthodox Church found itself. Paradoxically it was this very process of disruption that did much to transform the Orthodox Church into a truly global Christian communion. The First World War played its part by placing many Russian Orthodox Christians in German prisoner of war camps, often in close proximity to French or British prisoners, who were thus able to observe their distinctive habits of prayer. Of the 2.4 million prisoners of war taken by Germany by 1918, more than 1.4 million were Russian, and on the Western Front they were often housed in labor camps alongside British and French captives.[5] We will note the possible significance of such exposure for one such French prisoner of war in the text that follows. But the more far-reaching of these sources of disruption was the October 1917 Revolution in Russia.

As recounted in chapter 4, the Bolshevik Revolution deprived the Orthodox Church in Russia of its legal personality, right to own property, role in public education, and perhaps most spiritually damaging of all, extensive monastic life. Yet the Revolution, by provoking large-scale Russian emigration to western Europe and the United States, did more than any other event to commend Orthodox spirituality to Western Christians. Over one million Russians, among them most of the Church's theologians and intellectuals, fled to the West after 1917.[6] The most influential émigré community formed in Paris in the course of the 1920s. Several thousand strong, it included some outstanding thinkers, such as the former Marxists Sergei Bulgakov and Nikolai Berdyaev, who became key channels for mediating Russian Orthodox intellectual influence to the West. In particular the characteristic emphasis of Orthodox ecclesiology on *sobornost* (a Russian term meaning the fellowship of the many in the one) affected a number of young French Catholic theologians, such as Yves Congar, who was to become perhaps the most powerful advocate of a more conciliar understanding of Roman Catholicism at the Second Vatican Council.[7]

Another young Russian lay refugee, Nicolas Zernov (1898–1980), at that time secretary of the "Russian Student Christian Movement in Exile" in Paris, was a prime mover in the organization of two Student Christian Movement conferences in St. Albans, England, in January 1927 and December 1927–January 1928 that brought together Orthodox and mainly Anglican young people to discuss matters of shared theological concern. The second and larger of these two conferences bore lasting fruit through the formation of the Fellowship of St. Alban and St. Sergius to promote continued spiritual exchange between the Orthodox and Anglican traditions. The Fellowship played an important wider role in furthering the revival of the mystical tradition in English Christianity. The revival was associated particularly with the Anglo-Catholic Evelyn Underhill (1875–1941), who joined the Fellowship in 1935, first attended its annual conference in 1937 and made an immediate impression on Bulgakov and Zernov as a woman of exceptional spiritual wisdom.[8] Zernov served as secretary of the Fellowship from 1934 to 1947. In the 1940s he was instrumental in encouraging the British and Foreign Bible Society to produce the first Russian Bible translation to appear since the Bolshevik Revolution.[9]

In 1947 Zernov became the first Spalding Lecturer in Eastern Orthodox Culture in the University of Oxford, a post he held until 1966.[10] Zernov used his position in Oxford to travel widely, commending the Orthodox tradition through lectures in many parts of the world, including North America, India, Australia, and the South Pacific.[11] In his writings Zernov hinted at the overruling hand of providence in the apparent disaster of the Russian Revolution. The events of 1917 had proved highly strategic in scattering the Russian Orthodox intelligentsia throughout the globe and at the same time encouraging a marked spiritual renewal in the church, an awakening that was in part the result of being liberated from its previous subservience to the tsarist state. This enforced diaspora forged new ecumenical links between the Russian church and Western Christians, especially Protestants. It was Russian exiles who, beginning at the Stockholm Conference of the Life and Work movement in 1925, led the generally hesitant Orthodox churches into participation in the ecumenical movement.[12] The story of Orthodox involvement in the ecumenical movement has been far from smooth, but without the Russian Revolution, there might have been no story to tell.

Hesychasm refers to the originally monastic Orthodox mystical tradition of the silent meditative repetition of prayer. The archetypal expression of hesychast spirituality was the late sixth- or seventh-century prayer rooted in the traditions of Egyptian desert monasticism known as the "Jesus Prayer." This involved the unceasing and silent repetition of the formula "Jesus Christ, Son of God, have mercy on me" (sometimes the phrase "a sinner" is added). The Jesus Prayer began to be transmitted from Russia to the West in the years after the Russian Revolution. If united with the right inner devotion of the heart, such continual invocation of the all-powerful name of Jesus is believed to be uniquely powerful in the life of the believer, transforming surrounding material realities into transparent sacraments of the presence of God. The Jesus Prayer had been widely used in the Russian Orthodox Church and in eastern Europe since the publication in 1793 of the *Dobrotolubie,* a translation by the Moldavian monk Paissy Velichkovsky of the *Philokalia* (the classic anthology of hesychast spiritual texts) into Church Slavonic. Its growing popularity among the laity was enhanced by the widespread distribution from 1884 of a book entitled *Sincere Tales of a Pilgrim to His Spiritual Father*, generally known in English as *The Way of a Pilgrim*, which described the instruction given to a wandering Russian pilgrim by a monastic *staretz* (spiritual elder) that he should repeat the Prayer at first 3,000 times a day, then 6,000, and finally 12,000 times.[13] Translations of *The Way of a Pilgrim* into English, French, and German did much to popularize the Jesus Prayer in western Europe and North America in the interwar period. Increasingly the Prayer became used in Catholic and even some Protestant circles as well as in Orthodoxy.[14] From the early 1960s the Jesus Prayer was promoted in India by a group of Catholics concerned to promote a radical synthesis between Christian mysticism and Hindu *bhakti* devotion, led by the Swiss ambassador to India, Jacques-Albert Cuttat, and including the Benedictine monks, the Frenchman Henri Le Saux (Abhishiktananda) and the Englishman Bede Griffiths. Cuttat, Le Saux, and Griffiths were not afraid to underline the apparent parallels between the Prayer and the mantras of Hindu devotional practice.[15]

Another French Benedictine, Louis (Lev) Gillet (1893–1980), became one of the most influential contributors to wider Christian knowledge of the Jesus Prayer through the wide circulation of his publications issued, after his conversion to Orthodoxy, under the pseudonym of "A Monk of the Eastern Church." His own spiritual pilgrimage took him from Catholicism through the Eastern Catholic (or Uniate) Church to Orthodoxy. While a member of the French Benedictine community of St. Michael's Abbey in Farnborough, Hampshire, Gillet was deeply impressed when Andrew Szeptycky, Metropolitan of the Uniate Church in Galicia in western Ukraine, visited the monastery; as a result, Gillet traveled in 1924 to Lvov, where he was professed a monk and ordained deacon and priest by Metropolitan Andrew. It is possible that Gillet had become familiar with the Jesus Prayer during the First World War when living alongside Russian Orthodox Christians during a two-year sojourn in a German prisoner of war camp at Altdamm, though his period in the Galician monastery from 1924 seems the more likely source.[16] Further contact with Russian refugees in Nice, and his dismay at Pius XI's scornful repudiation of the ecumenical movement in his encyclical *Mortalium Annos* (January 1928), led him to take the next step of adherence to the Orthodox Church.

Archimandrite Lev Gillet, as he was now known, spent ten years ministering to the Francophone Orthodox congregation in Paris, before moving to Britain in 1937. He became warden of a hostel in the East End of London for young Jews and Jewish Christians fleeing Nazi persecution, and from 1940 to 1942 taught at Woodbrooke, a Quaker institution in the Selly Oak Colleges in Birmingham. He then served as chaplain to the London headquarters of the Fellowship of St. Alban and St. Sergius.[17] In London in August 1946 Gillet hosted three visitors from the Antiochian Orthodox Church, on their way to attend the summer conference of the Fellowship of St. Alban and St. Sergius; one of the three was George Khodr, later metropolitan of the church and liberation theologian, whom we encountered in chapter 10.[18] This was the beginning of a relationship with Lebanon that led Gillet to pay several visits to the country between 1948 and 1975. He exercised particular influence on the youth movement of the Antiochian Orthodox Church. This branch of Orthodoxy in the 1980s and 1990s proved particularly receptive to inquirers from evangelical and charismatic backgrounds in the United States and Britain, leading to some high-profile conversions.[19] Gillet's style of Orthodoxy was unusually evangelical and ecumenical in tone: in London he formed close links with Catholics, Anglicans, French Protestants, Pentecostals, and Quakers. His classic work on the Jesus Prayer first appeared in French in a series of articles from 1947 to 1952 in *Irénikon*, the periodical of the Benedictine monastery of Chevetogne in Belgium, an ecumenically minded house founded in 1925 with which Gillet became closely associated. For many years it has uniquely and simultaneously practiced both the Latin and Byzantine liturgical rites in two adjacent churches within the one monastic community. The first four chapters of Gillet's book were published in book form in 1951, and the first English translation appeared in 1967.[20]

The impact of the First World War closely followed by the enforced exodus of Orthodox Christians from Russia after 1917 were not the only examples of how political hardship advanced the global dissemination of Orthodox Christianity. Later in the century, the growing exodus of Orthodox and Oriental Orthodox Christians from deteriorating political contexts in Egypt and other parts of the Middle East added further elements to the diversifying ecclesiastical mix in the West, especially in the United States. The consolidation in western Europe and North America of distinct émigré Orthodox communities, each with their respective ethnic churches—not simply Russian, but also Greek, Antiochian, Belarusian, Bulgarian, Coptic, Romanian, Serbian, and Ukrainian—gave a new and radical twist to the complex relationship between Christian universality and national identity that has characterized the Orthodox Church in the modern world. The Russian Orthodox community in the United States itself became split into four rival jurisdictions, whose origins can be traced to the complex ecclesiastical politics of the church in exile after 1920.[21] As the Orthodox tradition in its various national and ecclesiastical forms engrafted itself into the ethnically and culturally pluralistic environments of western European and American cities, it encountered delicate issues of church relationships—both internally with other Orthodox churches and externally with Catholic and Protestant churches—that had never arisen in quite the same way in the Orthodox homelands.

A second and scarcely less momentous cause of the realignment of Orthodox Christianity in the twentieth century was the collapse of the Ottoman Empire in the wake of the First World War. The Orthodox Church in the Ottoman Empire from 1453 had a clearly subordinate yet uniquely privileged position. In return for submission to the principle of Islamic rule, the Ecumenical Patriarch in Constantinople was recognized as the "exarch," the civil as well as ecclesiastical head of the *Rum* (or Roman) people, the largest of the non-Muslim *millet* communities in the empire. He symbolized, and presided over the spiritual unity of all the Christian peoples of the Balkans, including those belonging to the other three ancient patriarchates of Alexandria, Antioch, and Jerusalem, and his exalted office still reflected something of the fading glory of the ancient Christian emperors of Byzantium. Until the early nineteenth century, such pan-Christian identity was virtually untouched by the corrosive acids of nationalist sentiment. The subjects of the Ottoman Empire were peoples who were loosely defined either as "Greek" (i.e., Orthodox of various ethnicities), or as "Latin" (Roman Catholics of various ethnicities), or as "Turk" (Muslims of various ethnicities, including Albanian or Bosnian).[22] But from the early 1820s burgeoning movements of romantic nationalism in Greece and the Balkans increasingly subverted these universal religious loyalties with sectional nationalist ones, a process that led to the establishment of autocephalous national Orthodox churches in Serbia in 1832, Greece in 1833, and the Bulgarian Exarchate in 1871–72. Such nationalizing trends met with initial resistance from the Ecumenical Patriarch. As a result the Orthodox Church of Greece remained uncanonical—formally out of relationship with Constantinople—from 1833 to 1850; the same was true for the Orthodox Church in the Bulgarian Exarchate (a more extensive territory than modern Bulgaria), which remained in a state of schism for even longer, from 1872 to 1945. In Greece and Serbia especially, the Orthodox populations increasingly began to equate adherence to the historic Orthodox faith with fidelity to the new national allegiance, with lasting consequences that proved deleterious both for Orthodox unity and for relationships with other religious communities, especially Muslim ones. The upsurge of national sentiment also culminated in the replacement of the last Ottoman sultan, Mehmed VI, by a secular Turkish state in November 1922. The next section of this chapter will therefore explore the major implications for Orthodox Christianity of the progressive replacement of Ottoman rule by modern nation-states, with particular relation to Greece and Turkey.

II. Orthodoxy in Greece and Turkey: Ethnic Cleansing, Nationalism, and the Holy Mountain of Athos

Greece won her independence from the Ottoman Empire between 1821 and 1830, but only a minority of Greek-speaking peoples was included in the kingdom of Greece, which included only the least economically developed south of the country. As late as 1910, of the estimated 7 million Greeks living around the shores of the Aegean Sea, only 37 percent lived in the Greek state. The fervent aspiration of Greek nationalists after 1830 was therefore to "liberate" the majority of Hellenes who continued to live under Ottoman rule and to extend the Greek state to include all such populations in a re-creation of the Byzantine Empire. This "Megali Idea" (Big Idea) seemed to find promise of fulfillment in the Treaty of Sèvres, signed with Turkey on August 10, 1920, which recognized Greek sovereignty

MAP 3. Greece and Turkey after World War I

over the Balkan Islands acquired during the Balkan Wars and over virtually the whole of western and eastern Thrace, and held out the alluring prospect that within five years the ancient Christian city of Smyrna and its Anatolian hinterland would become Greek territory as well.[23] The Treaty, however, soon proved to be a dead letter, and these dreams of a new Byzantium rapidly evaporated in the national catastrophe of the Greek-Turkish War of 1922, in which the Greek army was routed in Anatolia. Large parts of Smyrna—mainly its Greek and Armenian quarters—were burned to the ground. Fire and massacre between them resulted in the loss of up to 30,000 Christian lives. On September 9 the Metropolitan of Smyrna, Chrysostomos Kalafatis, was arrested by the Turks, handed over to a lynch mob, tortured, and killed in full view of onlooking French troops; in 1993 the Holy Synod of the Church of Greece declared him to be a saint and martyr.[24] Many of those who died were Armenians, for whom the episode formed the final chapter in the sequence of genocidal horrors that began in 1894 and peaked with the massacres of 1915–16. An exodus of more than 1 million Anatolian and Turkish-speaking Greek Christians now began across the Aegean to northern Greece. The Treaty of Lausanne of July 1923 deprived Greece of almost all the territory that she had gained as a result of the Treaty of Sèvres and confirmed the terms of a separate convention negotiated in January 1923. In an extraordinary instrument of double ethnic or religious cleansing, fully supported by the Great Powers, the fleeing Turkish nationals of the Greek Orthodox faith were to be exchanged for all Muslims living in Greece (with the exception of the Muslim community of western Thrace, who were allowed to stay as a trade-off for allowing some 100,000 Greeks to stay in Istanbul). The expulsions were compulsory for those who had not already fled, but seem to have attracted very little humanitarian protest in the West at the time. Some 380,000 Greek Muslims were accordingly exchanged for 1.1 million Turkish Christians. If refugees from Russia and Bulgaria are included, the total number of Christian refugees entering Greece, whose existing population was no more than 4.5 million, amounted to nearly 1.3 million.[25]

As a result of this state-imposed exchange of populations, in the western half of Greek Macedonia during the 1920s the majority faith changed from Muslim to Christian, while the predominant language paradoxically ceased to be Greek and became Turkish.[26] Conversely, the distinguished Christian tradition of Asia Minor, which had existed unbroken since New Testament times, was brought to an abrupt and almost complete termination. Over the whole turbulent period from the outbreak of the First World War in 1914 to 1923, it is estimated that 3.5 million Greek Orthodox, Armenian Apostolic, or Assyrian Christians were killed by the successive regimes of the Young Turks or Mustafa Kemal.[27] Within the space of a few years in the 1920s, the proportion of the population of Turkey that was non-Muslim (in effect, Christian) fell from 20 percent to 2.5 percent.[28] Even the surviving Orthodox population of Istanbul provided for by the 1923 convention declined steadily from the 1923 level of 100,000 to only 2,000–3,000 by the year 2000.[29] By the close of the century the once-mighty Ecumenical Patriarch of Constantinople, though he continued to be generally recognized as the spiritual head of the entire Orthodox communion, presided over a tiny domestic flock. Furthermore, the Patriarch is required by Turkish law to be a male Turkish citizen, and hence has to be elected from the dwindling company of Orthodox clergy left in the country.

The only conceivable justification that might be advanced for the brutal exchange of populations that was enforced in 1922 is the retrospective and pragmatic one that it resulted in two religiously homogeneous and hence moderately stable nation-states in Greece and Turkey.[30] However, the twin enormities of enforced migration and genocide ensured that from the early 1920s onwards the Aegean Sea appeared to define the boundary between Christian and Islamic territory far more sharply than ever before. Notions of a stark juxtaposition between supposedly Christian Europe and Islamic West Asia paradoxically thus assumed a new plausibility in political geography at the very time that most of Europe was entering a period of deep recession from active Christian commitment from which it has yet to emerge. For the Orthodox of Asia Minor in 1922, as for the Armenian Christians before them in 1915–16, and for a whole succession of Orthodox and Oriental Orthodox Christians later in the century, exodus to the West appeared to be the only alternative to extinction.

A further implication of the 1922 exchange of populations was the marked reinforcement of the Orthodox identity of the modern Greek state. The first three constitutions of independent Greece, drawn up between 1822 and 1827, had drawn no clear distinction between the notion of a Greek citizen and a Greek Orthodox citizen,[31] and during the remainder of the nineteenth century the concept of *Ellinochristianismos* (Hellenistic Christianity) crystallized as a means of expressing the growing convergence of Orthodox and Greek national identities.[32] Nonetheless, the kingdom of Greece until the late 1920s adopted a remarkably tolerant attitude to both Catholic and Protestant missionary efforts. The monthly review of the French Assumptionist congregation, the *Echos d'Orient*, commented regularly on the tolerance that the Greek government and even the Orthodox Church displayed toward the activities of its missionaries. In 1923 the Assumptionists reported that the government was so eager to court external aid in responding to the refugee crisis that it had confiscated Orthodox monastic property and given it to American Protestant missionaries so that they could open an orphanage.[33] But such openness was not destined to last. The medium- to long-term legacy of the events of 1922 was of a very different kind.

In 1918 the Orthodox Church of Greece ran no charitable or educational institutions. But in 1923 Athens gained a new modernizing metropolitan and subsequent archbishop, Chrysostomos Papadoulous, who as the former director of the Holy Cross Academy of the Orthodox Patriarchate of Jerusalem from 1899 to 1909 had established Orthodox charitable institutions in an endeavor to inoculate his Arabic-speaking flock against the attraction of Catholic and Protestant schools, hospitals, and orphanages. Chrysostomos, realizing that a similar context of religious competition now obtained in Greece, led the Orthodox Church into active participation in "secular" charitable and educational work for the first time. By 1936 it had opened two orphanages and two hostels for young girls in the Athens region and many more in provincial towns. One hundred and fifty parish offices of relief for the poor had been established. Chrysostomos also promoted the growth of Orthodox Sunday schools, the first of which had been opened in 1920. By 1936 there were more than 300 such schools. At the same time Chrysostomos lobbied the Greek government to ban foreign Catholic or Protestant schools, not on the grounds that they were heterodox, but on the grounds that they were allegedly promoting the political interests of foreign powers, such as France or Italy, or that schools run by Jehovah's Witnesses or Seventh-Day Adventists were antipatriotic, since their adherents refused to serve in the military or carry arms. The liberal governments of the Second Hellenic Republic (1924–35) responded positively to such overtures, believing that reinforcing the dominance of the Orthodox Church was the most effective way to promote Greek nationality. They passed a series of measures against religious minorities, such as Uniate Catholics and Jehovah's Witnesses, and passed a law seriously restricting the freedom of operation of foreign schools. At the same time as the Orthodox Church of Greece on a global ecumenical stage was participating in the Life and Work movement, at home it was working hard to strengthen the nexus between Greek national identity and loyalty to Orthodoxy. By the end of Chrysostomos's archiepiscopate, in 1936, the fusion between the two was largely complete.[34]

The last government census to record religious affiliation, conducted in 1951, recorded that 96.7 percent of Greeks considered themselves to be members of the Orthodox Church. More recent unofficial statistical surveys suggested that such high levels of affiliation to the Orthodox Church continued at least to 1990. Weekly church attendance was less impressive, although for much of the century it remained at a higher level than was usual for Europe. Abstention from public worship was especially marked in Athens, where newspaper polls recorded that the proportion of the population claiming to attend church every Sunday fell from 31 percent in 1963 to only 9 percent in 1980.[35] Furthermore, the fusion of political and religious identity at an ideological level did not imply that working relationships between the church and Greek governments, especially those that were democratic, were always harmonious. Archbishop Chrysostomos fought hard but not wholly successfully in 1927 to resist the attempt of the government to confiscate some of its landed property in order to resettle the Asia Minor refugees. In 1981 the entry of Greece into the European

Community (now Union) led to a series of clashes between church and state over the ensuing decades over various measures required for Greece to conform to the liberal and secular ethos of Western Europe. Despite escalating tensions between church and state, Greece remained to the end of the century a formally Christian country, which, more than any other modern nation-state, came close to replicating on a smaller scale the Byzantine Empire's union of political and ecclesiastical authority.

Distant echoes of the ancient Byzantine Empire continued to reverberate through Greek Christian history in the twentieth century, and nowhere were they more audible than in the monastic cloisters of Mount Athos. In the twentieth century there were twenty "ruling monasteries"—seventeen Greek, one Russian, one Serbian, and one Bulgarian—plus a number of *sketes* (smaller dependent houses).[36] Located on a remote rocky peninsula in the northern Aegean, and currently accessible only by sea, Mount Athos has been the site of Christian eremitical and monastic life since the ninth century. During the Byzantine period it acquired its status as the most widely revered of a series of monastic holy mountains located within the empire. It was the only one of these holy mountains to maintain its monastic communities intact throughout the turmoil of the Crusades, the five centuries of Ottoman rule, and the two world wars of the twentieth century: as such it became a powerful symbol of enduring Greek identity. Its unique status as a self-governing theocratic republic—whose monks acknowledged no earthly sovereign other than the Mother of God—developed during the Byzantine period, and was respected by the Ottomans, in return for an annual payment. It came under the ecclesiastical jurisdiction of the ecumenical patriarch, though even his powers to interfere were strictly limited.

In 1912 Mount Athos became Greek territory for the first time after the cession by the Ottoman Empire of substantial parts of Macedonia to the kingdom of Greece as a result of the Balkan Wars. The Treaty of Sèvres of 1920 recognized Greece's sovereignty over Athos, but with a clause that protected the rights of the non-Greek monastic communities. Greece undertook to prepare a new Charter for Mount Athos, which was approved by the elected monastic parliament—the Holy Synod or Community—in 1924 and ratified by the Greek state in 1926. The Charter declared Mount Athos to be a self-governing part of the Greek state, and subject to the spiritual jurisdiction of the Ecumenical Patriarchate in Constantinople rather than to the archbishop of Athens and All Greece. Its unique governmental status was confirmed in 1952 by Article 103 of the Greek Constitution, which vests government of the territory in the Holy Community, acting in concert with a representative of the Greek state.[37] The Final Act of Agreement concluding Greece's entry to the European Community in 1981 also recognized the special status of Mount Athos.[38] Nevertheless, the holy mountain did have to cede something of its historic autonomy to the pragmatic demands of the modern Greek state: as a response to the refugee crisis of 1922 the government expropriated all landed property, including monastic lands; as a result Mount Athos lost some land on its northern boundary that was confiscated to resettle some of the Asia Minor refugees in the new village of Ouranoupoli.[39]

One visitor to Mount Athos in 1928 described it as the "station of a faith where all the years have stopped."[40] More powerfully than anywhere else in the Orthodox world, the mountain symbolizes the Orthodox aspiration to transcend linear time by immersing the faithful in a cyclical liturgical observance that anticipates the ceaseless worship of heaven. The Holy Community dissented from archbishop Chrysostomos's modernizing decision in 1923–4 to enact the new Gregorian-style calendar within the Greek Church, and continued—along with a substantial number of other Orthodox Christians—to use the Julian calendar. However, in the eyes of many non-Orthodox observers, the monks are not simply thirteen days behind the rest of the world, but several centuries behind, for Mount Athos remains to this day a sacred space from which all women are excluded by the terms of the *ávaton*, or ban on women. All females, whether women, farm or domestic animals—an honorable exception is made for cats—are forbidden to enter the mountain. Before 1924 this prohibition had simply been taken for granted. All the cultivated land on Mount Athos was owned by all-male monastic communities, so that the Mount was, in effect, a single monastery with the same right to exclude members of the opposite sex as any other monastic community possessed. The 1924 Charter simply formalized the position by prescribing that any woman who set foot on Mount Athos would be subject to deportation. After a number of high-profile violations, including one that attracted the attention of the *New York Times*,[41] the penalty was raised in 1953 to an automatic prison sentence of between two and twelve months. This legislation remains in force today, despite a number of attempts in the European Parliament to compel the Greek government to rescind it.[42] The *ávaton* is defended both pragmatically—the presence of women, it is said, would distract the monks from their prayers—and theologically, by appeal to Mariology. The holy mountain is portrayed as the Garden of the *Panagia* (the All-Holy), a new Eden dedicated to the Mother of God. Mary is the Protector both of the mountain and of the Greek nation itself. Her mystical presence in this earthly paradise is deemed to be sufficiently representative of the place of godly women in the paradise to come. Many Greek Orthodox women have accordingly proudly defended the *ávaton* as an integral element of Greek identity, and have resisted the feminist movement and demands for the ordination of women as a distinctively Western and secular agenda.[43]

Yet Mount Athos, like Orthodoxy as a whole, has not been impervious to historical circumstance. As a community that is biologically incapable of reproducing itself, it has been necessarily dependent on recruitment from other parts of the Orthodox world. The various traumas that afflicted the Orthodox Church in the first half of the century thus exacted their toll. Athos was an indirect casualty of the Russian Revolution. The Soviets made it extremely difficult for monks to leave Russia, and the nationalist Greek government was for its part reluctant to admit Russian monks to Athos. In 1903, of the 7,432 monks on the mountain, as many as 3,496 or 47 percent, were Russians. By 1965 there were just 62 Russians, accounting for 4.2 percent of a total monastic community that now numbered only 1,491. The aggregate monastic community reached its low point of 1,145 in 1971.[44] Since then, there has been a steady, if unspectacular growth in numbers. By 2000 the total monastic community had reached 1,674.[45] The revival was rooted in a renewal of spirituality that began in the hermitages and cells located at the southern tip of the peninsula, the so-called "desert of Athos." Here a few exceptional individuals recovered and embodied the hesychast tradition at its most profound, with particular emphasis on the Jesus Prayer. With time their influence extended to the monasteries on the mountain and ultimately much further afield, contributing to the global Orthodox revival. Two names stand out, one of them Russian, the other Greek.

Archimandrite Sophrony (Sergei) Sakharov (1896–1993) was a gifted artist who left Soviet Russia in 1921 and eventually made his home among the Russian Orthodox émigré community in Paris in the 1920s, where he studied for a time under Bulkakov and Berdyaev as one of the first students of the St. Sergius Orthodox Theological Institute, founded in 1925. On arrival on Mount Athos in 1926 he entered the great Russian monastery of St. Panteleimon on the west coast of Athos, where he was ordained to the diaconate and became a disciple of the barely literate Russian monk, Simeon Antonov, St. Silouan of Athos, who was himself a renowned teacher of the Jesus Prayer. After the death of his spiritual master in 1938, Sophrony fulfilled his instructions by becoming a hermit in the desert of Athos. During the war years he became a spiritual father to many monks on the mountain. In 1947 he left Mount Athos to return to France, where he worked on a life of St. Silouan, editing his works for publication, and on ascetical theology more generally. In 1958 he founded the monastery of St. John the Baptist at Tolleshunt Knights near Maldon in Essex, whose liturgy included the repetition for some four hours a day of the Jesus Prayer. He spent the rest of his life there, and made the monastery into one of the most dynamic centers of Orthodox spirituality in Britain.[46]

A second figure of comparable significance was Francis Kottis, generally known as Elder Joseph the Hesychast (1897/8–1959), a hermit who gathered a small band of brothers around him in settlements in the southwest of Athos, first in caves at Little St. Anne from 1938, and then from 1951 nearer the sea at New Skete. His teaching was based on the Pauline injunction to "Pray without ceasing," and the repetition of the Jesus Prayer, of which he became an enthusiastic advocate. His disciples were directly responsible for the spiritual revival of six of the principal monasteries on the mountain. One of them, Archimandrite Aimilianos Vafeidis, abbot of Simonopetra from 1974 to 2000, achieved international renown as an exponent of the Jesus Prayer. The Simonopetra monastery became visually recognizable to many through photographs of its uniquely dramatic location perched on top of a cliff-face. It also became widely known in the 1990s through its choir, who contributed largely to the global revival in popularity of Byzantine chant, through recordings on cassette and CD.[47] Another of Joseph's disciples, Elder Ephraim, became abbot of the Philotheou monastery on Mount Athos and went on to establish seventeen hesychast monasteries in the United States.[48]

The apparently isolated and enclosed mountain community of Mount Athos thus played an unexpectedly large role in the global dissemination of the hesychast tradition. The holy mountain became the hub from which Orthodox spirituality radiated to large sections of the Christian world during the second half of the twentieth century.

III. New Strands of Orthodoxy in Twentieth-Century Africa

The role played by Mount Athos in the global revival and renewal of Orthodoxy is typical of the central significance of monasticism in much Orthodox history. In contrast, monasteries scarcely feature in the story of the transmission of Orthodoxy in modern Africa beyond its traditional Oriental Orthodox strongholds in Egypt and Ethiopia.[49] The Orthodox Church spread in twentieth-century Africa, not because of its historic association with monasticism, but rather because of its complete lack of association with the Western European colonial powers whose Christian representatives dominated the missionary movement to Africa.

The story begins with the origins of the "Ethiopian" movement in South Africa in the 1890s. Ethiopianism was a protest movement among black South African Christians whose patience had run out with the obstinate reluctance of white missionaries to devolve power and responsibility to African ministers. The various Ethiopian churches formed by the seceders were animated by the example of Ethiopia as a surviving ancient African Christian state with its own autonomous Oriental Orthodox church, and more broadly by the Old Testament picture of "Ethiopia" as the land given by God to the sons of Ham. For the Old Testament writers the Hebrew term Cush, rendered in the Septuagint and most subsequent translations as "Ethiopia"—the land of the black-faced people—was a vast territory beyond Egypt destined by divine promise one day to stretch out its hands in supplication to the God of Israel (Psalm 68: 31). For the first, explicitly Christian, articulators of pan-African ideals, such as Henry McNeal Turner of the African Methodist Episcopal Church in the United States or Edward Wilmot Blyden, black Presbyterian missionary to Liberia, "Ethiopia" stood for the sovereign purpose of God to emancipate the entire African race, both those still living on African soil and the recently enslaved sons of Africa in America.

The first African Orthodox Church to be founded in modern times was established in New York City in September 1921 by George Alexander McGuire (1866–1934). McGuire, born in Antigua, grew up as an Anglican, but had spells with the Moravians in the Virgin Islands and the African Methodist Episcopal Church in the United States before returning to his Anglican roots. In 1920 he was appointed Chaplain-General to Marcus Garvey's Universal Negro Improvement Association (UNIA), which also invested him with the grand title of "Titular Archbishop of Ethiopia." The church he founded in New York was originally named the "Independent Episcopal Church of Ethiopia," but soon adopted the title "African Orthodox Church" (AOC). McGuire was anxious to portray his movement, not as a schismatic body, but as an autocephalous black church firmly located within the tradition of ancient Christianity. McGuire therefore tried to gain affiliation to one of the historic Orthodox Churches, despite the fact that, with the significant exception of the omission of the *filioque* clause from the creed, the church followed Western Catholic rather than Orthodox liturgical patterns.[50] His initial overtures in the direction of the Russian Orthodox Church of America led nowhere, so in Chicago on September 28, 1921 he had to make do with consecration as bishop by the Frenchman Joseph

René Vilatte, who was head of a schismatic body known as the American Catholic Church. Vilatte's links to Orthodoxy were tenuous. In June 1892 he had received consecration by a dissident Catholic bishop in Ceylon who had himself been consecrated by the Jacobite bishop of Kottayam in Malabar, but the Syrian Jacobite Patriarchate of Antioch subsequently declared Vilatte's episcopal orders to be invalid.[51] Three months after his consecration by Vilatte, McGuire gained an audience with Patriarch Meletios of Constantinople when he visited New York. Meletios did not rebuff him, but neither did he give the AOC the full recognition it desired. By October 1924 the church had elected McGuire as Patriarch Alexander I. Over the next few years his church attracted some 20,000 African American members, many of them former Episcopalians. Its greatest strength was on the eastern seaboard of the United States, but congregations also developed elsewhere in the Americas in Nova Scotia, Cuba, Nicaragua, and the Bahamas, and, crucially, in South Africa and Uganda.[52] In the long term, the spread of the AOC to Africa was to prove its most significant feature, and to that we now turn.

In 1924 McGuire was approached by Daniel William Alexander (1883–1969), a South African of mixed black African and Martiniquean parentage who had left the Anglican Church in 1908 to join the Ethiopian movement, at first becoming affiliated to the Ethiopian Catholic Church in Zion and then to a group known simply as "The African Church." Alexander had read about the AOC in the UNIA newspaper *The Negro World*, and as Vicar-General of the Diocese of the Cape of Good Hope of the African Church wrote to McGuire seeking authorization to turn his diocese into a South African branch of the AOC. McGuire duly appointed him as Vicar Apostolic in South Africa for the purpose of establishing "an independent and local branch of the Holy African Orthodox Church." In January 1925 the inaugural Synod of the African Orthodox Church in South Africa assembled to confirm affiliation to the AOC in the United States, ratified the election of Alexander as bishop, and conferred upon him the title of archbishop-elect of the AOC Province of Africa; Alexander was not actually consecrated until September 1927 on a visit to the United States. The AOC grew rapidly in urban areas in both the Cape Province and the Transvaal. By 1927 it had 1,403 members in fifteen congregations and had ordained seven priests and two deacons. The AOC was now divided into an American and an African Province, each with its own presiding archbishop—McGuire and Alexander respectively. In 1929 Alexander opened the Seminary of St. Augustine of Hippo in the Kimberley suburb of Beaconsfield, and proscribed a three-year course of training for ordination. In the same year the African United Church, an African Instituted Church founded in 1912 by Joel Davids, affiliated to the AOC, bringing an additional 1,000 members into the African Orthodox fold. The Church also began that year publication of its own newspaper, the *African Orthodox Churchman*.[53] In 1941 the AOC succeeded in gaining official recognition from the government of South Africa, one of only eight out of 800 African Instituted Churches to do so before 1948. During the 1930s the church extended its activities into Southern Rhodesia (now Zimbabwe), establishing congregations in Bulawayo.[54] The most significant expansion of the AOC in Africa, however, came through its extension first into Uganda and then into Kenya.

In April 1925 a Muganda Anglican Christian, Reuben Ssebanja Ssedima Mukasa—later known as Reuben Spartas—wrote to McGuire seeking spiritual instruction and more information about the AOC. Spartas (c. 1899–1982) was a convert of the Church Missionary Society and educated at the prestigious King's College Budo, near Kampala. He also had come across the *The Negro World* newspaper and had heard of the formation of the AOC in America. Spartas did not receive McGuire's reply until 1928, in which McGuire informed him of the consecration of Alexander and inquired whether he was still interested in the AOC. Spartas immediately replied that he was, whereupon McGuire put him in contact with Alexander, who appointed him as a lay reader under his supervision. On January 6, 1929 Spartas announced that he had left the Anglican Church to form "the African Orthodox Church—a church established for all right-thinking Africans, men who wish to be free in their own house, not always being thought of as boys." In August 1931 Alexander arrived in Uganda and on Trinity Sunday, May 22, 1932, he ordained Spartas, and a fellow Muganda, Obadiah Basajjakitalo, as priests in the AOC; two other prominent members of the CMS Buganda mission, Yosiah Mukasa and Simeon Pasha, were ordained as deacons the previous day. Spartas was appointed as Vicar General in the Uganda diocese of the AOC, which by now boasted some 1,500 adherents in seven congregations.[55] Spartas was a fervent African nationalist—and as such was imprisoned by the British between 1949 and 1957—but had also become convinced that the Anglican Church was not the true church. He wrote to Archbishop Cosmo Lang of Canterbury in 1933 informing him, "I had discovered that the Orthodox faith was the indisputable faith and far more true and original than the Anglican."[56]

Until this point, Spartas's church was Orthodox in name but was more Anglican than Orthodox in liturgical character. However, before Alexander left Uganda in 1932, a Greek employee of the Ugandan Public Works

Department, named Vlachos, invited him to baptize his children. Observing that the archbishop did not use the Greek rite of baptism, Vlachos advised Spartas to write to Nicodemus Sarikas, a Greek Orthodox priest in Moshi in Tanganyika (modern Tanzania). Ordained in 1907 as the first Greek Orthodox priest in South Africa, Sarikas had moved in 1911 to Moshi, where he worked as a farmer in addition to ministering to the scattered Greek community in the country. In response to the overture from Spartas, Sarikas visited Kampala, and persuaded Spartas to break relations with Archbishop Alexander and instead seek recognition from Meletios II, the Greek Orthodox Patriarch of Alexandria. Sarikas himself wrote to Meletios, asking him to take Spartas's church under his wing. In February 1934 a reply arrived from Meletios, sending some books on Orthodoxy, which were then translated into Luganda. Spartas then renamed his church as "The African Greek Orthodox Church." Meletios, however, wished to maintain good relations with the Anglican Church, and wrote to Cyril Stuart, Anglican bishop of Uganda, who in his reply pointed out that Spartas and his church were schismatics, a point that Meletios had not previously realized. At first Meletios urged Spartas to rejoin the Anglican Church, but Spartas would not be rebuffed and continued to seek recognition from the Greek Church of Alexandria.[57]

The Orthodox Church in Kenya, like that in Uganda, originated in schism from Protestant mission churches. The circumcision controversy in Kikuyuland that broke surface in 1929 resulted in the formation of two associations of independent schools—the Kikuyu Independent Schools Association (KISA) and the Kikuyu Karing'a Education Association—in protest against the insistence of the Church of Scotland mission that its female pupils should not undergo the rite of female circumcision. The independent schools became venues for worship on Sundays, attended by those who had left the mission churches as a result of the circumcision crisis; they were in effect an African Independent Church in embryo. On his way back to South Africa from Uganda in 1932, Daniel Alexander met James Beutah, a prominent figure in the KISA, and informed him about the AOC. In 1935 the president of KISA wrote to Alexander inviting him to return to Kenya with a view to incorporating the adherents of KISA into the AOC. Following consultation with Metropolitan Isidore, head of the recently established Greek Orthodox archdiocese of Johannesburg and Pretoria, Alexander agreed, and visited Kenya for a second time between November 1935 and July 1937. He founded a seminary for the AOC, located initially at Gituamba and later at Dagoretti, and on June 27, 1937, ordained three of its first students. He also introduced elements of

McGuire's distinctive version of the liturgy, which was translated into the Gikuyu language in 1936, though much of the Anglican liturgy remained. This marked the inception of the African Orthodox Church in Kenya.[58]

Within months of Alexander's departure, the AOC in Kenya split into two factions—the Karing'a African Orthodox Church and the African Independent Pentecostal Church. The former grew rapidly under the leadership of Arthur Gatung'u Gathuna, one of the three ordained by Alexander in 1937. By 1944 it had a membership of 20,000 and extended beyond Gikuyu territory into western Kenya. In 1938 Reuben Spartas visited Kenya and became concerned at the lack of theological training of the leaders of the young church. He and Gathuna formed plans for four students to be sent for training, initially under Spartas in Uganda, and then at a Greek Orthodox seminary that had been established in Arusha, Tanganyika. The plan was that ultimately they should be sent to Greece for further studies. In the event, the four never got further than Uganda. However, Gathuna had realized, like Spartas in Uganda, that the African "Orthodox" Church was only tenuously connected with the ancient Orthodox Church and he too began to look to the Greek Ortho- dox Patriarch of Alexandria to rectify its dubious canonical status. In 1942 Patriarch Christophorus II of Alexandria responded to the overtures from Uganda and Kenya by dispatching a personal envoy, Metropolitan Nico- laos of Axum, to East Africa. The success of his visit encouraged Spartas and Gathuna to declare the adherence of their respective churches to the Patriarch of Alexandria. Gathuna renamed his church, following Spartas's example, as the African Greek Orthodox Church. Following a sympathetic report by Metropolitan Nicolaos to the Patriarch and Holy Synod in Al- exandria, Spartas then visited Alexandria in 1946 and gained the full rec- ognition of Patriarch Christophorus II for the African Greek Orthodox Church. Spartas was appointed as Vicar for the whole of East Africa, with Gathuna as his deputy in Kenya.[59]

The African Greek Orthodox Church in Kenya grew rapidly imme- diately after the Second World War, attaining an active membership of 30,000 by 1953. The church forged close connections with Jomo Ken- yatta's Kenya African Union in promoting the interests of the Gikuyu people; party meetings were often held in its school compounds, and Or- thodox church services included prayers for national *uhuru* (freedom). In October 1952 the British colonial government declared a State of Emer- gency in response to the threat, whether real or imagined, of the Mau- Mau insurgency. During the Emergency the colonial government closed more than 300 independent schools as supposed sites of anticolonial subversion, Orthodox churches themselves were placed under lock and key throughout Gikuyuland, and a number of Orthodox clergy, including Gathuna, were incarcerated in concentration camps. Some Orthodox believers continued to worship in secret; others joined the mission church, particularly the Catholic Church, which was seen to be more distant than the Protestant churches from the colonial regime. The ban on the Orthodox Church was not lifted until 1960 and Gathuna was not released until early 1961. The rebuilding of the church after the years of colonial repression was not a straightforward matter. Influenced by events in Uganda, where Spartas was battling against efforts by some Greeks to incorporate his church within the Greek Orthodox Church, Gathuna registered the reestablished Kenyan church in May 1965 under the new name of the "African Orthodox Church of Kenya." Relationships between the church and the Patriarch of Alexandria were fraught with difficulty, leading in 1979 to a split between two factions of the church, one continuing in obedience to the Patriarch, and the other, led by Gathuna until his death in 1987, placing itself under the authority of St. Gregory Palamas Monastery in Etna, California.[60] Nevertheless, the Orthodox Church in Kenya continued to grow. Aggregate membership of the two groups in Kenya by the end of the century is estimated at 580,000, though the church itself claimed membership of over one and half million; in Uganda, by contrast, membership in 2000 stood at only 26,000.[61]

From the early 1980s the African Orthodox Church also extended its reach from its main centers in South Africa and Kenya into other parts of the continent, such as northwestern Tanzania, and parts of central and West Africa.[62] By the end of the century, ten Orthodox missionary dioceses covered sub-Saharan Africa under the jurisdiction of the Greek Orthodox Patriarch of Alexandria.[63] Thus Orthodox Christianity in Africa had become much more widely diffused and more variegated in ecclesiastical complexion than it had been in 1900. The ancient Oriental Orthodox churches of Egypt and Ethiopia, and the Greek Orthodox tradition of the patriarchate of Alexandria, were no longer the only expressions of Orthodox Christianity on the continent.

IV. Tradition and Change in the Orthodox World

The Orthodox Church, perhaps more clearly than any other Christian tradition, set its face against the claims of totalizing ideologies and nation-states in the twentieth century to command the ultimate allegiance of citizens. It paid a high price for such resistance, most obviously so in the

Soviet Union, but also in some other contexts that are too often forgotten. In the aftermath of the Greek-Turkish War of 1922 Turkish-speaking Greek Orthodox believers in Anatolia found that their religious identity had deprived them of their homes and historic place of residence, forcing them into exile across the Aegean Sea. African Orthodox adherents in Kenya between 1952 and 1960 discovered that the British colonial state had little patience with Christians who chose a church that combined a radical commitment to the principle of African leadership in church and state with conservative fidelity to ancient apostolic tradition. Yet out of the crucible of such harrowing experiences, the Orthodox family of churches discovered new constituencies of support, attracting former Catholics, Anglicans and evangelical Protestants, as well as some who had never been Christian. In so doing, it found itself, albeit with frequent reservations, participating in the Protestant-dominated ecumenical movement. Those who fled from the Bolsheviks disseminated Orthodox spirituality and devotional practice—especially the Jesus Prayer—in the West. The apparently grave decline of the Orthodox monastic tradition precipitated by state repression in Soviet Russia compelled the dwindling numbers of monks on Mount Athos to return to the roots of the hesychast spiritual tradition, and in so doing gave birth to a revival of Orthodox prayer and monastic life that spread far beyond the rocky peninsula of Mount Athos to western Europe, North America, and elsewhere. In Kenya, the African Orthodox Church rose from the verge of extinction in the 1950s to become one of the most vibrant forms of African Christianity, one that was clearly distinct from the mission Christianity of the colonial era and aspired to be in demonstrable continuity with the African church of the patristic age.

This chapter, no less than any of the others, has been unashamedly selective. Had it focused on the Ethiopian Orthodox Church, whose worship is still conducted in the ancient Semitic language of Ge'ez, it might have given greater visibility to the impression that Orthodox styles of Christianity in the modern world have remained largely insulated from the impact of modern ideologies and political structures, surviving embodiments of ancient Christianity. The case studies chosen have instead revealed some of the most striking ambiguities of Orthodoxy's encounter with modernity. A Christian tradition that proclaims the indissoluble divinely instituted unity of the church over time and space has proven to be the chosen vehicle of distinctively modern nationalist aspirations in contexts such as Greece or Kenya. It has also been problematically divided in its pluriform institutional expressions in the Orthodox diaspora in North America and western Europe, compelling the Orthodox in recent times to attempt their own internal ventures at ecumenical reconciliation. Perhaps most intriguing of all, the example of the African Orthodox Church shows how a church that was founded with only the shakiest of connections to historic Orthodoxy, ended up by being accepted within the Orthodox fold.

CHAPTER FIFTEEN

Migrant Churches

I. Migration and the Making of World Christianity

The mid-nineteenth century initiated a period in world history that is still ongoing in which large numbers of people traveled vast distances, often across the seas, to escape from war, famine, ethnic cleansing, or religious persecution, or in pursuit of new economic or educational opportunities. The transatlantic migrations are the best known, but diverse movements of peoples within Asia to destinations such as Manchuria or southeast Asia were comparable in size and impact. In terms of global aggregates, these mass migration flows reached their peak in the 1920s.[1] Over the remainder of the twentieth century, migration flows continued, but following a more selective pattern. The dominant trajectories were those that took migrants from the Caribbean, Latin America, Asia, and parts of the Middle East to cities in North America or Europe. The United States was by far the largest national receiver of these migrants. These migratory trajectories became channels of transmission of southern or eastern styles of Christianity to urban locations in the northern and western hemispheres, so that Latino/a, Chinese, Korean, and—rather later—African churches became for the first time highly visible elements enriching the tapestry of Christian life in North America and Europe. Some of these transmitted Christianities were very ancient—such as the Assyrian Church of the East. The patriarchal see of the Church of the East was even relocated from Teheran to Chicago after the Iran–Iraq war of 1980–88. By the end of the century the Church of the East had 100,000 adherents resident in the United States and a further 20,000 in Canada. In contrast, its numbers in its original West Asian heartlands were sadly depleted: perhaps 85,000 in Iraq, 20,000 in Iran, and 25,000 in Syria, while in the Hakkari region, along the present-day border between Turkey and Iraq, the church had been virtually eliminated after the First World War.[2]

Other varieties of migrant Christianity were of much more recent origin. Those that have attracted most contemporary scholarly interest were Pentecostal in character. These include the older black Pentecostal churches that were established in Britain in the decade or so after the arrival in Britain in June 1948 of the *Empire Windrush*, the first immigrant ship that transported 492 settlers from Jamaica. From the 1980s onwards, on both sides of the Atlantic, they also included African neo-Pentecostal churches, mostly of Nigerian or Ghanaian provenance. The Nigerian-originated Redeemed Christian Church of God planted its first congregation in Britain in 1985, and by the end of the century its British membership may have exceeded 50,000.[3] The church arrived in the United States rather later, planting its first congregation on Roosevelt Island in New York City in 1995.[4] The rapid growth of West African neo-Pentecostal churches in European and American cities since the 1980s has been the subject of a host of recent sociological studies concerned to elucidate the leading role of these churches in the fashioning and sustaining of corporate identities within African migrant communities. African neo-Pentecostal churches in Europe have also captured the attention of missiologists as an example of the process of "reverse mission" from south to north, because of their frequently employed rhetoric that appeals to their divine calling to evangelize the new "dark continent" of Europe. From the perspective of the history of the twentieth century as a whole, however, two rather different points need to be emphasized.

The first is that for most of the twentieth century migration from Africa to the northern hemisphere was insignificant in statistical terms in comparison with the scale of other migration flows. On an international stage, the largest flows of population included migration from the Caribbean to the United States and later to Britain, migration from Latin America and Mexico to the United States, and migration from mainland China to southeast Asia and beyond. By 1980 some 21.8 million Chinese were living in diaspora, the majority in Malaysia, the Philippines, Australia, or North America; by 1990, the figure was 30.7 million; furthermore, these large numbers exclude the substantial proximate Chinese diaspora to Hong Kong and Taiwan.[5] Throughout the century the vast bulk of overseas black immigration to the United States—much of it being to New York City—was from the Caribbean rather than from Africa. In the first great wave of black immigration to the United States, between 1911 and 1924, 82 percent of the approximately 40,000 overseas black immigrants who settled in New York City were from the English-speaking Caribbean. Approximately half of them were Jamaicans, who, as subjects of a British colony, qualified for the generous national quota allocated by American immigration policy to Britain, as also to other nations in northern and western Europe. After the Emergency Quota Act of 1921, and still more the Immigration Act of 1924, American immigration policy was much more restrictive, effectively closing the United States to immigrants from the Caribbean, as also from Asia and Africa; non-European countries were now restricted to only 2 percent of visas for entry to the United States. But in the last three decades of the century, after the Hart–Celler Immigration and Nationality Act of 1965 had again relaxed immigration controls, immigrants from Eastern Europe, Asia, Latin America, and the Caribbean poured into the United States in unprecedented numbers. They included more than half a million more Jamaicans, although their numbers were now eclipsed by immigrants from the Dominican Republic, Guyana, and Mexico.[6]

In contrast, until the 1980s, most African migration to the north was of a temporary and selective nature, being for educational purposes. Until decolonization in the 1960s, most African students chose to pursue their overseas higher education in universities located in the former colonial power—hence mainly in Britain or France. In 1960, only 0.4 percent of the foreign-born population of the United States were of African birth.[7] Only in the last two decades of the century, under the combined impact of the dislocation of African economies aggravated by the structural adjustment programs of the World Bank and International Monetary Fund and of devastating civil wars in such countries as Liberia (1989–97 and 1999–2003) and Sierra Leone (1991–2000), did migration from Africa to both continental Europe and the United States become more substantial in scale and diverse in destination.[8]

For most of the century, therefore, African churches in Europe or the United States were very few in number, and small in size. The Ghanaian businessman Thomas Brem Wilson (1865–1929) established the first black-led Pentecostal church in Britain, Bethel Chapel in Camberwell, south London, as early as 1908. However, by the 1920s its services, by now held in the neighboring district of Peckham, attracted no more than about 150 people, only some of whom were African.[9] It remained an isolated and somewhat exotic feature of the British religious landscape. In North America, very few specifically African congregations date from before the 1980s, with the exception of a handful of Ethiopian and Coptic congregations; the first Ethiopian Orthodox parish was established in New York City in 1959, and the first Coptic Orthodox parish in Toronto in 1965.[10] Even after the Hart–Celler Immigration and Nationality Act of 1965, African immigration to the United States lagged far behind that from the Caribbean, Latin America, and Asia—in the last case originating especially from China, the Chinese Asian diaspora, Korea, and the Philippines. Africa did not figure at all in the top ten regions of origin of immigrants to New York City between 1990 and 2000, whereas 33 percent (265,046 people) came from Latin America and the Caribbean, and a further 5 percent from Mexico; the former Soviet states accounted for 11 percent, China for 9.5 percent, and the Indian subcontinent for 7.1 percent. Of the 265,046 from Latin America and the Caribbean, no fewer than 91,265 came from the Dominican Republic alone; Guyana accounted for 32,545 and Jamaica for 30,315. Only in the final years of the century did the inflow of Africans to the United States become a flood: more than half a million African migrants gained legal and permanent entry to the country between 1996 and 2005.[11]

The second salient feature of the twentieth-century migrations that requires emphasis for our purposes relates to the religious composition of the migrant populations. Of those that were Christian, very few were originally Pentecostal, though rather more became so in their new locations. Many of those who migrated to the United States in the twentieth century were Catholic, from a large variety of ethnic and linguistic backgrounds, transforming the American Catholic Church into the most ethnically diverse national ecclesial body in the world. In the archdiocese of San Francisco, one in every four Catholics by the end of the century was Filipino.[12] After the Second Vatican Council, such ethnic diversity was reflected in the liturgy: by the year 2012, it is estimated that within the Catholic archdiocese of Los Angeles alone, the Eucharist was being celebrated in forty-two different languages.[13]

Among Protestant churches, some of the largest migratory flows involved Baptists and Methodists. Within the United States itself a movement now styled as the Great Migration saw some 400,000 African Americans leave the southern states to settle in northern cities between 1915 and 1919 alone, the largest number doing so within the Harlem district of New York City. The flow of migrants from the American South continued at a lower level in the late 1920s and 1930s, and then accelerated again during the 1940s.[14] As a result, the dominant Baptist and Methodist forms of black Christianity that had emerged in the American South during the nineteenth century were successfully transmitted to the North, with the result that the majority of the African American congregations that mushroomed in northern American cities belonged to these denominations.

As the next section will emphasize, these black migrant congregations have a strong claim to be denominated as the first megachurches of the modern world. The later, and smaller, Caribbean exodus to Britain followed a rather different pattern of religious affiliation. Among Caribbean immigrants to Britain in the 1950s and 1960s, Baptists and Methodists again predominated, but in this case the denominational affiliation of the migrants largely failed to survive the double shock inflicted by the racial prejudice and alien spiritual environment that they frequently encountered in British congregations. As a result, for many West Indian migrants to Britain, the experience of migration became more than a geographical relocation—it also involved a significant denominational reorientation to black Pentecostal churches that in theological and cultural terms were closer to the Baptist and Methodist churches in the Caribbean than were the churches of these denominations that they encountered in Britain. Such reorientation was also true of some Caribbean migrants to the United States, but to a much lesser extent, for there they could join African American Baptist, African Methodist Episcopal,[15] or African Methodist Episcopal Zion[16] churches that exhibited many of the same charismatic features with which they had been familiar in the West Indies.

Of the ethnic Chinese who migrated to North America, Europe, and Australia, relatively few of those who had come from mainland China were already Christian on arrival. In the first two decades of the century, when the migration of skilled and professional Chinese people to the United States was relatively uncontrolled, the Christian population of China was still small. Over the second half of the century, church growth in mainland China became much more significant, but for political reasons large-scale emigration was not possible, at least until after the Cultural Revolution of 1966 to 1976. The much larger numbers of ethnic Chinese who migrated from Hong Kong, Taiwan, and Southeast Asia in the second half of the century included a higher proportion of Christians, as the migrants were drawn mostly from the more affluent sectors of society, from whom the majority of converts to Christian missions had been drawn.[17] Many of these migrant Chinese Christians came from Methodist, Presbyterian, Baptist, or Anglican backgrounds, but in their new locations they most often did not join churches affiliated to these mainline denominations but instead formed distinct Chinese congregations, usually of a nondenominational and strongly evangelical character. Section III of this chapter underlines the importance of these new and theologically conservative Chinese diaspora churches as active agents of evangelism among their overseas communities, especially in North America. As in the case of

Caribbean Christian migration to Britain, migration of Christians from Asia thus involved some redefinition of Christian identity. In the Chinese case, however, the main reason for this was linguistic and cultural rather than theological—finding a congregation in which Cantonese (or, later, Mandarin) was the familiar language of both worship and Christian fellowship became a higher priority than finding one affiliated to the same denomination as that to which migrants had belonged in Asia.

Chinese immigrants also proved peculiarly receptive to the Christian gospel. By the end of the century, in some American cities such as Los Angeles or Chicago as many as 32 percent of the Chinese population were Christian, most of them first-generation Christians, and many of whom had been converted since arrival in the country. This contrasts both with the percentage of Chinese immigrants who self-identified as Buddhist— only 20 percent—and with the percentage of the population of mainland China who were Christian—no more than 5 percent.[18] A similar pattern is observable among Taiwanese immigrants to the United States. Whereas only about 3.9 percent of the population of Taiwan in the 1990s self-identified as Christian, about 25 percent of Taiwanese Americans did so. Leaders of the American Taiwanese Christian community reported that between 50 and 70 percent of their congregations had become Christians since their arrival in the United States.[19]

The Korean migrant experience in the later part of the century was broadly comparable. Korean migrants, like their Chinese counterparts, came from the more prosperous sectors of South Korean urban society that were disproportionately Christian. It is estimated that about half of Korean migrants to the United States were Christians when they arrived, and about half of the remainder became Christians subsequent to their arrival in the country. By the end of the century in the United States— whose Korean population grew from only 70,000 in 1970 to about 1.1. million in 2000—55 percent of Korean migrants were affiliated to Protestant churches and 20 percent to the Roman Catholic Church, whereas in South Korea itself the comparable figures were only 18 percent and 7 percent respectively.[20] In the Korean case, however, the majority of these ethnic migrant churches retained the Presbyterian or Methodist affiliation that dominated Protestantism in the country of origin, although there were also a growing number of Korean American congregations that were formally interdenominational or Pentecostal in character. On a much smaller scale, a similar pattern may have applied to Japanese migrants. Whereas Christians in Japan remained only a small percentage of the population at the end of the century—perhaps 3.6 percent—in the United States they accounted for as many as 43 percent of the Japanese immigrant population.[21]

Migrant churches in the twentieth century were thus by no means all Pentecostal—indeed the majority were not. Nevertheless, the large influx to American cities of Hispanics from the Caribbean and Mexico brought with it the distinctive religious flavour of those regions, resulting not only in a large accession of Latinos-Latinas to Catholic parishes in the United States but increasingly also in an explosion of Spanish-speaking Pentecostal congregations. Furthermore, American Latino/a Catholicism in the second half of the century diversified in two important respects. First, the original predominance of Mexicans and Puerto Ricans increasingly gave way to a much more plural population, drawn from a wide range of countries in both the Caribbean and South America. In the half-century since the Cuban Revolution of 1959 that brought Fidel Castro to power, more than 1 million Cubans fled to the United States, the vast majority of them being Catholic. An even larger American Hispanic Catholic population by the end of the century was Dominican. Under the dictatorial rule of President Rafael Leónidas Trujillo from 1930 to 1961, little emigration was possible, but following his assassination in 1961, the floodgates were opened. By 1990 there were 700,000 Dominicans in New York City alone, rivaling Puerto Ricans as the largest Hispanic element in the city's population.[22] Second, Hispanic Catholics were no longer so heavily concentrated in New York, the Southwest, and a number of urban locations in the Midwest; instead, they were increasingly to be found throughout the country, from the eastern seaboard to the Pacific coast, and from Florida to Alaska.[23]

The large majority of such Hispanics in the United States continued to self-identify as Catholics throughout the century, but Pentecostals were steadily eroding this Catholic predominance by the end of the century, especially among the younger generation of migrants. One reason for this—though probably not the main one—may have been the paucity of vocations to the priesthood among the Hispanic population. By 2012 no less than 35 percent of the American Catholic population was of Hispanic origin, but only 6 percent of American Catholic priests and fewer than 10 percent of active bishops were Hispanics. Nevertheless, the growing Hispanic influence on the American Catholic Church was of major significance in reshaping the character of American Catholic life and devotion in the later years of the century. It was one reason for the growing sensitivity of American Catholics to the issues raised by Latin American theologies of liberation. It also led to a more public and widely supported place in American Catholic life for Marian devotion, although sometimes at the cost of ethnic tensions within the Catholic community. As the Mexican population of New York tripled during the 1990s, Our Lady of Mercy parish in the Bronx erected an outdoor shrine to Our Lady of Guadalupe, causing existing Puerto Rican parishioners sarcastically to ask the priest whether he was going to rename the parish as the Virgin of Guadalupe.[24]

II. The Black Exodus from the American South and Jamaica

The first great migrant churches of modern times were the product of the "Great Migration" of African American populations from the American South to northern cities such as New York, Chicago, Detroit, Cleveland, and Philadelphia. The imagery of the biblical exodus was repeatedly invoked by those who traveled north; they felt they were escaping from the Egypt of racial oppression in the southern states for the Promised Land of the North.[25] As the southern migrants clustered in particular neighborhood enclaves, and discovered that their new urban environment was sadly no freer of racial prejudice than the erstwhile slave society they had left behind, they found church life to be their main source of support and community. The poorest among them sometimes found the existing African American churches too formal, or afflicted by their own internal hierarchies of economic status or even skin color. In response they tended to found informal house churches or "storefront" congregations, in which vacant shop premises were converted into simple church buildings. Most of these congregations replicated the Holiness and revivalistic characteristics of southern black religion, and thus reintroduced to northern cities an exuberant style of popular evangelicalism that had fallen out of favor in the late nineteenth century. Although in Chicago at least, large numbers of the storefront churches were Baptist, as many again were affiliated to various Holiness denominations. Over time many storefronts developed into full-blown Pentecostal churches; in this way much of modern black American Pentecostalism took shape.[26]

Some of the key actors in this process were women. One of the most notable was Elder Lucy Smith (1875–1952), founder of the All Nations Pentecostal Church, whose congregation was composed almost entirely of women. Though, as its name implies, it was explicitly multiracial in intent, its membership was predominantly black. Arriving in Chicago from Georgia in 1910, Smith worshipped for a time at Olivet and Ebenezer Baptist Churches, before joining the Stone Church, a mainly white Pentecostal congregation, where she began to discover her own gifts of healing. In 1916 she began a prayer and healing meeting in her own home that developed within ten years into an independent Pentecostal church with its own building. It was the first major church in Chicago to have a black woman pastor and an almost exclusively female leadership team. By the 1930s All Nations Pentecostal Church was said to have had some 5,000 members and broadcast its own radio program, *The Glorious Church of the Air*: Smith was the first black Chicago preacher to broadcast worship live on the radio. Her funeral in 1952 was claimed as the largest in Chicago's black history, with more than 100,000 mourners thronging the streets.[27] Another notable African American woman pastor was Mary G. Evans, a former minister in the African Methodist Episcopal Church who became the second pastor of Chicago's interdenominational Cosmopolitan Community Church in 1931. Though much quieter and more formal in liturgical style than Smith, Evans developed a faith healing ministry of her own. Both Smith and Evans were actively involved in debt reduction programs and other aspects of social ministry on behalf of their members.[28]

Despite the undoubted significance of such new African American Pentecostal churches, of no less importance for the African American community as a whole was the foundation and rapid expansion of numerous black congregations affiliated to the older Baptist, and, to a lesser extent, African Methodist Episcopal and African Methodist Episcopal Zion denominations. In Detroit, the number of African American churches grew from six in 1910 to sixty in 1923. In Chicago, by 1927 there were fifty-five African American Baptist churches with an aggregate membership of nearly 66,000, thereby raising Baptists to second behind Roman Catholics in the table of the city's largest denominations. In Cleveland, Baptists had by 1921 become the largest denomination, with an aggregate membership of 14,000, or 64 percent of the city's 22,000 black church members. The Baptists capitalized on the Great Migration more successfully than any other denomination, perhaps because of the flexibility afforded by their independent polity.[29] Their most important black churches became the largest Christian congregations in twentieth-century America. Whereas most commentators date the rise of the megachurch as a phenomenon from the 1970s,[30] these massive African American migrant churches had become a salient feature of the American religious scene several decades earlier.

In Chicago, the historic Olivet Baptist Church, founded in 1850, actively promoted the Great Migration by providing black Baptists from the South with employment referrals, housing assistance, and health and day nursery services. The Bethlehem Baptist Association, based at the church, advertised its services in the Chicago *Defender*—the largest-circulation black newspaper in the country—as an employment and accommodation agency for those planning to travel, or newly arrived from the South.[31] This broad mission strategy paid dividends. Between 1916 and 1919 alone, Olivet added more than 5,000 new members to its membership roll. By the mid-1920s its estimated membership had grown to between 11,000 and 14,000, making it reputedly the largest Protestant church in the world. By the 1930s Olivet's membership had reached its peak of 20,000.[32] Its pastors wielded extraordinary influence. Dr. Lacey Kirk Williams (1871– 1940), pastor from 1915 to 1940, was active in national Republican politics. Though progressive on issues of race and the rights of black labor, he was a social conservative and a strong advocate of the temperance movement.[33] He was president of his denomination, the National Baptist Convention, from 1922 until his death in a plane crash in 1940. Joseph H. Jackson (1900–91), pastor from 1941 to 1990, was a commanding and instinctively conservative figure who wielded supreme control over the National Baptist Convention as its president from 1953 to 1982. With a membership at that time of 6 million, it was the largest black organization in the world. Although originally a supporter of Martin Luther King's campaign for civil rights, by the early 1960s Jackson had become a strong opponent of any form of direct action or civil disobedience in pursuit of civil rights.[34]

In New York City, Abyssinian Baptist Church in Manhattan under the pastorate of Adam Clayton Powell, Sr., had 3,487 members by 1918, making it the second largest black Baptist congregation in the country after Olivet. The church became still larger and more politically influential after its move to Harlem in June 1923. The prophetic quality of its socially engaged and Christocentric preaching made a deep and transformative impression on Dietrich Bonhoeffer, who taught a Sunday-School class and women's Bible study group at Abyssinian while studying at Union Theological Seminary in 1930–31. There is little doubt that his exposure at Abyssinian to black Christian resistance to racism helped lead Bonhoeffer to the subsequent conclusion that fidelity to Christ demanded similarly fearless opposition to the Nazi synthesis of race, religion, and nationalism.[35] By 1937, when Powell handed the pastorate over to his son, Adam Clayton Powell Jr. (1908–72), the Abyssinian congregation had grown to more than 7,000 members. Both father and son were prominent figures in politics: Adam Clayton Powell Jr., served for fourteen terms in the House of Representatives and, in contrast to Jackson, was an ardent advocate of Black Power. Abyssinian Baptist continued into the 1990s to attract congregations of several thousand.[36] However, in the second half of the century, as the more affluent sectors of the New York black population moved out of Harlem into Brooklyn and other districts, Abyssinian found itself over-taken in size by the Concord Baptist Church of Christ in Stuyvesant. Under the remarkable ministry of Gardner Calvin Taylor (1918–2015) from 1948 to 1990, the membership grew from 5,000 to 14,000, making the church the largest congregation in New York City and probably surpassing even Chicago's Olivet Baptist Church, which was now in gradual numerical decline. Taylor was a close associate of Martin Luther King, and co-founder in 1961 of the Progressive National Baptist Convention, a body that seceded from Jackson's National Baptist Convention to promote a more active engagement of black Baptists with the civil rights movement. Yet he was never an advocate of the "social gospel" alone, combining a passion for social justice with a theological stance that was essentially evangelical. Called "the pulpit king" by *Christianity Today* magazine in 1995, Taylor was a master of oratory in the African American style, with an extraordinary vocal range and an exceptional ability to convey the drama of biblical narrative.[37]

The churches thus played a crucial role in the Great Migration that transformed the demography of the United States during the twentieth century. Although migrants from the American South to northern cities did not cross a national frontier, they faced many of the same challenges of cultural dislocation and racial hostility as did international migrants. The churches they joined or formed on arrival in the northern states provided both spiritual and material support, and in many cases became the loci of political mobilization on behalf of African American civil rights. The fact that cities such as Chicago or New York had such large and vibrant black Christian communities had a further significance. When the first Jamaican and other Caribbean migrants arrived in these locations, they encountered a growing number of existing black churches that, although not identical in character with their own homeland churches, were not markedly alien to them in cultural or theological orientation. Hence, in marked contrast to the experience of Caribbean immigrants to Britain in the 1950s and 1960s, there were features in the host religious environment in the United States that frequently made integration easier rather than more difficult.

Jamaican migration to the United States came in two distinct waves. The first began soon after 1900, peaked about 1920, and was brought to an end by the Immigration Act of 1924. About 50,000 Jamaicans settled in the United States in this period, mainly in Harlem and the Bedford–Stuyvesant district of Brooklyn in New York City. Residing alongside African Americans, many Caribbeans were quite happy to join the existing African American churches—mostly Baptist, African Methodist Episcopal, African Methodist Episcopal Zion, or Episcopal—that flourished in Harlem. Other

Caribbean immigrants established their own churches. George Alexander McGuire's idiosyncratic African Orthodox Church discussed in the previous chapter was one such. Another was the Harlem Community Church (later known as the Harlem Unitarian Church), founded in 1921 by the Jamaican Unitarian minister and one-time Episcopalian, Egbert Ethelred Brown (1875–1956); Brown became a prominent figure in politics in both New York and his native Jamaica, where, as one of the founders of the Jamaica Progressive League, he campaigned for independence from Britain.[38]

Rather more typical was Harlem's first Moravian church, Beth-Tphillah, established on West 134th Street in 1908 by Charles Douglas Martin (1873–1942), a native of St Kitts, who on his ordination in 1912 became the first black Moravian minister in the United States. His church membership was mainly Caribbean, but he also developed close ties with the African American community. In 1917, Martin joined the African American activist W. E. B. Du Bois in leading a Silent Protest Parade along Fifth Avenue, in which 15,000 black New Yorkers voiced their protest against the rising tide of racial violence in a muffled-drum march. When Martin opened a new Moravian church at 124–26 West 136th Street in 1921, many leaders of Harlem's African American congregations attended in support.[39] In a context in which class rather than ethnicity was the main line of division within the black community, the creation of separate Caribbean churches did not often appear to be necessary. These early Caribbean immigrants to New York tended to maintain their distinct identity by other cultural means, such as playing cricket or attending the coronation ball for King George VI in 1937—more than 5,000 Jamaicans attended the event.[40]

The second and larger wave of Jamaican migration to the United States was precipitated by the Hart–Celler Act of 1965. The number of officially documented Jamaican immigrants in New York City rose from 11,000 in 1960 to at least 113,000 in 1990. Between 1982 and 1989 alone, more than 70,000 settled in the city. If undocumented immigrants were included, the total would be far higher. This second wave of Jamaican immigrants to New York tended to settle in their own ethnic enclaves that had developed in the Brooklyn, Crown Heights, and Flatbush areas of the city, partly as a result of a process of gentrification, whereby the more affluent Jamaicans increasingly moved out of Harlem. By 1980 more than 50 percent of New York's West Indian population lived in Brooklyn, while less than 8 percent lived in Manhattan (including Harlem).[41] While some of the older Jamaicans continued to commute into Harlem to attend the historic African American congregations there, the trend was now for younger Jamaicans to cluster in churches in Brooklyn, Crown Heights, and Flatbush.[42] Some of these churches continued to be those of the historic denominations, such as St Mark's Episcopal Church in Crown Heights, where the influx of well-to-do Jamaicans reversed the decline in membership, at one stage making St. Mark's into one of the largest Episcopal congregations in the city, with a membership of at least 1,000.[43] But an increasing number of these new Jamaican-majority congregations were Pentecostal, such as the Latter Rain Ministries church in Brownsville, Brooklyn, founded in 1971, or Beulah Church of God, that developed out of a Sunday School ministry in Flatlands, Brooklyn, in December 1988.[44] Increasingly Caribbean Christianity in New York City took on a Pentecostal complexion as the century drew to a close, though never to the same extent as in London or the West Midlands of Britain.

In apparent contradiction of the stereotype that Caribbean Christianity and Pentecostalism are somehow inseparable, in Jamaica Pentecostalism had in fact made only halting progress in the first half of the century. Many Jamaican Protestants seemed quite content to combine membership of the historic mission churches—especially Baptist, Methodist, Moravian, and Anglican—with informal participation in popular revivalist cults that had strong charismatic or even spiritist elements closely related to the West African cosmologies of the slave population. The roots of such dual belonging are to be found in the early nineteenth-century Caribbean, where from 1814 onwards, British Nonconformist missionary Christianity, particularly Baptist and Methodist, was overlaid on an existing tradition of popular revivalism that had been imported to the slave population from the southern United States. In its exuberant style of worship and suprarational understanding of the activity of the Holy Spirit this tradition bore many similarities with what would later be termed Pentecostalism.[45] The existence of this quasi-Pentecostal substratum to Christian life in the West Indies goes a long way to explain why the formally Pentecostal churches were so slow to make inroads there, but also why Caribbean Christian migrants to Britain found the formal character of church life there spiritually sterile and increasingly looked to black Pentecostal churches to supply the deficit.

Thus in Jamaica in 1935 the New Testament Church of God (the Jamaican affiliate of the American Pentecostal denomination the Church of God) had fifty-two congregations, but with an average of only thirty members each. In 1943 only 3 percent of the Jamaican population claimed affiliation with a Pentecostal church, compared with 82 percent who belonged to a mainline denomination.[46] Yet within about a year of the arrival of the *Windrush* at Tilbury Dock in June 1948 the first West Indian Pentecostal congregation had emerged in Brixton, south London, first fruits of a Christian movement that was destined to become the typical religious expression of the African Caribbean community in Britain. By 1957 the Brixton congregation had formed an affiliation to C. H. Mason's Church of God in Christ, based in Cleveland, Tennessee. The Church of God in Christ was, alongside the Assemblies of God, one of the two largest American Pentecostal denominations. Unlike the Assemblies of God, it was predominantly black in its membership. The Brixton congregation adopted the name "Calvary Church of God in Christ."[47]

More extensive in its diffusion in Britain was the New Testament Church of God, whose first congregation owed its genesis in Wolverhampton in 1953 to Dr. Oliver A. Lyseight (1919–2006). Lyseight was reared as a Methodist in Hanover parish in Jamaica, but while still in Jamaica transferred his allegiance in 1939 to the New Testament Church of God, pastoring a church in St. Ann's parish before working in the United States during the Second World War for the War Food Administration. On arrival in England in 1951, he was unable to locate a nearby Pentecostal fellowship, so joined a Methodist church in Wolverhampton. Following a change in the pastoral leadership of the church, he experienced some racial hostility and left to begin a prayer group for like-minded Jamaicans that met first in a home and then in a local YMCA meeting hall. In 1955 they became affiliated to the Church of God, another American Pentecostal denomination, also based in Cleveland; the British arm of the denomination followed the Jamaican in adding the words "New Testament" to the church's title.[48] By 1957 seven such embryonic black fellowships—of a broadly Pentecostal character—had been formed in the West Midlands and in London. Lyseight was appointed national overseer with responsibility for the churches in the West Midlands and London area, now twelve in number, with 373 members in aggregate. By 1967 there were sixty-five congregations. By 1998 the New Testament Church of God had 102 congregations with an aggregate church membership of 6,504. If there is one generally recognized founding father of black Pentecostalism in Britain, it is Lyseight.[49] To a much greater extent than in the United States, black Christianity in Britain had become predominantly Pentecostal in character.

III. Chinese Migrant Churches:
Trans-Pacific Connections

Mass Chinese migration to the United States dates from the late 1840s, when the Californian Gold Rush first lured Chinese labourers across the Pacific Ocean. The first Chinese church in the United States was established in 1853 with the support of the American Presbyterian Board of Foreign Missions.[50] For a long time, Chinese migration to America was almost entirely a male phenomenon. As late as 1910, females accounted for only 6.5 percent of the Chinese American population. The first two decades of the century in fact saw a marked decline in the size of the Chinese American community, as a result of a series of stringent exclusion laws designed to restrict Chinese immigration. The number of Chinese in the United States fell from 107,488 in 1890 to 61,639 in 1920.[51] Although only about 4,000 of them were Christians, churches and Christian agencies located in American Chinatowns played an important role in this period in promoting the social welfare and aspirations of the more educated sections of the Chinese community. By 1931 there were forty-four Chinese churches in the country,[52] in addition to several YMCA and YWCA branches dedicated to serving the Chinese community. The second and third decades of the century marked the heyday of the influence of the YMCA in China itself, and in the ethnic enclaves of the American Chinatowns both the YMCA and the YWCA exercised a similarly wide range of social and cultural functions in the name of Christ. The first Chinatown YMCA was opened in San Francisco in 1912, and it was closely followed by others in New York City (1916), Oakland (1921), and Seattle (1923). The gradual rectification of the gender imbalance in the Chinese American community also prompted the formation of several YWCA branches located in Chinatowns. The San Francisco Chinatown YWCA opened in 1916 and by 1920 had a membership of 500.[53] As in China itself, the YMCA and YWCA promoted a liberal and modernizing brand of social Christianity that exerted a compelling appeal in the wake of the Republican Revolution but would struggle to survive in the increasingly wintry political climate created for Christianity in China by the Anti-Christian Movement from 1922.

The influence of churches within the relatively small and geographically confined Chinese American community remained marginal throughout the first half of the century. Hence a 1953 survey commissioned by the National Council of Churches of Christ in the United States estimated that there were between 7,500 and 7,700 Chinese Protestant Christians located in a total of sixty-six churches throughout the United States, thirty-three of them located in Pacific Coast cities.[54] With the exception of Hawaii, which had four large and self-supporting Chinese churches, the congregations were small. Most were externally funded mission churches, which initially had been run and supported by the mainline denominations' foreign mission boards, before being handed over to home mission boards during the 1920s. The survey report asserted, "Chinese Americans today are on the threshold of entering the mainstream of American social life. At the end of their American Experience is assimilation." With the gradual disappearance of the Chinatowns, it predicted that the younger generation of Chinese Christians would probably abandon Chinese churches and seek integration in mainstream congregations.[55] In a close parallel to the stance taken by the Canadian Protestant churches to First Nations people in the same period (see chapter 11), the missiological orthodoxy of the Protestant mainline in mid-century held that full assimilation of Asian minorities into the melange of the United States population was not simply inevitable but also to be welcomed as the only lasting solution to white racism. Hence the Methodist Church dissolved its Oriental Provisional Conference (comprising Chinese, Filipino, and Korean congregations) in 1956, and similarly its Pacific Japanese Provisional Conference in 1964. The member congregations of these Asian bodies were simply reassigned to the regional conferences of the denomination. Similarly, the American Baptists did not replace Dr. Charles Shepherd, Superintendent of Asian American Baptist ministries, when he retired in 1956. Chinese American churches, it was widely assumed, would soon be all but extinct. The leaders of these churches, however, did not take such pessimism lying down. In response to the National Council of Churches of Christ report in 1955, they formed a National Conference of Chinese Christian Churches (CONFAB) to press the continuing needs of the Chinese churches on the mainline denominations. Speakers at CONFAB meetings appealed to the same theological principles of the validity of non-Western indigenous expressions of Christianity that mainline foreign mission boards were now enthusiastically adopting to argue that, in the American context, no less than in Asia, there was a proper and continuing place for diverse ethnic and cultural forms of the faith.[56]

In the course of the 1960s and 1970s the American mainline churches— just like the Canadian churches in relation to First Nations people (see chapter 11)—eventually abandoned their commitment to racial assimilation. However, the future of ethnic Chinese churches in the United States lay not with the mainline mission churches located in the Chinatowns, but with new urban or suburban congregations that displayed a very different theological character and a more varied pattern of location. By 1979, fourteen years after the Hart–Celler Act, and just three years after the end of the Cultural Revolution, there were 366 Chinese churches in the United States. By the mid-1990s there were at least 697, and possibly as many as 785 Chinese American Christian congregations. In North America as a whole the total may have been as high as 1,100.[57] Very few of these churches belonged to the mainline denominations. Most were either independent nondenominational evangelical churches or were affiliated to conservative denominations, such as the Southern Baptist Convention. By 1982 there were at least 140 Chinese Baptist churches located in more than 25 American states, western Canada, and Puerto Rico; most had been planted since 1970. Ethnic Baptist congregations also developed rapidly among Korean, Japanese, Laotian, Cambodian, Vietnamese, and Filipino immigrant populations.[58]

The vast majority of the new Chinese churches that made their appearance in the United States from the 1970s onwards were of conservative evangelical theological complexion. This trend paralleled developments in the Chinese diaspora more generally, and indeed in China itself. The increasingly broad social gospel disseminated by the mainline Protestant mission boards in the early decades of the century had become closely associated with the modernizing religious nationalism of Chiang-Kai-shek's Guomindang regime. As disillusionment with that regime spread, and even more after its defeat by the Chinese Communist party, Chinese liberal Protestantism rapidly lost its attraction, both within mainland China and among the Chinese diaspora. The populist and revivalist varieties of evangelical Protestantism that had mushroomed in China in the interwar period, largely unnoticed by the foreign mission boards, became increasingly influential in the Chinese diaspora, especially after 1949. A number of highly gifted Chinese evangelists began to focus their attention on the Chinese diaspora as the constituency that offered the best prospects for achieving their ultimate goal of winning China for Christ.[59] Just as the Bolshevik Revolution of 1917 proved the means of disseminating the Russian Orthodox tradition in the West, the successive disruptions of the Sino-Japanese War of 1937 to 1945 and the Communist revolution in China in 1949 had the effect of propagating the distinctively charismatic style of popular Protestant revivalism that developed in mainland China in the 1930s, first among the Chinese diaspora in Southeast Asia, and then across the Pacific Ocean to North America. In this way Chinese evangelical churches eventually became one of the most salient features of urban religion in North America and elsewhere.

Of particular significance in this respect was the Bethel Worldwide Evangelistic Band, an offshoot of the Bethel Mission in Shanghai, an independent holiness mission founded in 1920 by two women, Dr. Shi Meiyu (1873–1954) and Jennie Hughes, a Methodist Episcopal educational missionary.[60] Shi Meiyu, also known as Mary Stone, was not simply one of the first two Chinese women to receive an American M.D. degree, from the University of Michigan, but also the first woman in central China to be ordained as a Christian minister.[61] Between 1931 and 1935 the Bethel Mission sent out a group of five young Chinese evangelists on a tour of 133 Chinese cities in which they conducted almost 3,400 revival meetings.

The most dynamic of these evangelists—and the most controversial on account of his abrasive polemics against all forms of theological liberalism—was Song Shangjie (better known as John Sung), who died in 1944. From 1935 Sung extended his evangelistic and healing ministry to the overseas Chinese in the Philippines, Singapore, Malaya, Borneo, the Dutch East Indies, Thailand, Vietnam, and Japanese-controlled Taiwan.[62] However, it was the organizer of the Band, Ji Zhiwen (Andrew Gih, 1901–85) who was destined to wield an even more lasting influence among the Chinese diaspora.[63] In 1947 he created his own missionary organization, Evangelize China Fellowship, which initially comprised a Mandarin-speaking church and orphanage in Shanghai. After Shanghai fell to the Communists, Ji Zhiwen moved his base to Hong Kong, convinced that God had told him "to choose some base for training the soldiers of Christ to attack China with the gospel and win the battle for the Lord."[64] With this aggressive strategy in mind, he began to coordinate evangelistic work among overseas Chinese, first from Hong Kong, then from 1951 from Singapore, and eventually from Monterey Park, California. Two later members of the Bethel Band also became pastors of leading Chinese churches in the United States. In 1961 Torrey Shih (1920–84) founded the Overseas Chinese Mission in New York's Chinatown, which became the largest Chinese congregation on the East Coast. Philip Yung Lee (1911–93), who first came to the States to further his education as a musician, pastored the Chinese Presbyterian Church (later known as the True Light Presbyterian Church) in Los Angeles in the 1940s and the Chinese Christian Union Church in Chicago in the 1950s. Both churches had mainline origins, but became increasingly evangelical.[65]

The pattern of ministry among Chinese Americans that Ji Ziwhen pioneered was adopted by others. Moses Chow, formerly a pastor of Chinese congregations in Indonesia (1949–56) and Japan (1959–61), became in 1962 the first pastor of the Chinese Christian Church of Greater Washington. With Theodore Choy he also founded in 1963 Ambassadors for Christ, an organization dedicated to the evangelization of the rapidly growing number of Chinese students on American university campuses. In 1968 Chow resigned his Washington pastorate to devote himself full-time to this student ministry, which began to develop into a broader resource and networking agency for Chinese congregations.[66] Another highly influential

Chinese American pastor, Thomas Wang (1925–), developed a nationwide and international ministry from the base of his church in Detroit, which he established in October 1961. Wang's main emphasis was on the production of Christian literature aimed at the Chinese diaspora. Beginning with an English-language magazine, *Chinese Christians Today*, he soon replaced this with the Chinese-language *Chinese Christian Monthly* and an English-language newsletter, *Challenger*. Wang's Chinese Christian Mission became, with Ambassadors for Christ, one of the two largest Chinese para-church organizations in North America; it also established branches in Taipei (November 1961), Hong Kong (1965), the Philippines (1970), Singapore (1977), Vancouver (1981), Macau (1993), and Australia (1993).[67] Chinese American evangelicals also began forming their own national networks. The First North American Congress of Chinese Evangelicals met in December 1972, and three further congresses were held in 1974, 1978, and 1980 before the network was integrated in a worldwide body, the Chinese Coordination Centre of World Evangelism.[68] However, the achievement of national unity among the expanding number of Chinese American evangelicals proved elusive. Chinese evangelical churches in North America reflected their origins in the sharp fundamentalist-modernist controversies that characterized Chinese Christianity during the interwar period in their obdurate separatism and their general reluctance to apply the gospel to social and political questions.[69] Nevertheless, in contrast to the pessimistic outlook adopted by the National Council of Churches of Christ report in 1955, Chinese American church life by the later years of the century was spiritually vibrant, strongly missionary-minded, and a prominent feature of the religious landscape of many North American cities.

IV. Migration and the Reshaping of Christianity in the West

The scale of immigration to North America and Europe since the Second World War is widely cited as one of the reasons for the substantial weakening or even total disappearance of the predominantly Christian character of North American and European societies during the second half of the century. Diana L. Eck has argued that in the United States the marked extension of ethnic and hence religious diversity through immigration has exposed the internal contradictions of the ideal of a Christian America, and compelled Americans to confront for the first time the complex issues raised by radical interreligious plurality.[70] On one level, this is self-evidently true. Most cities in North America and Europe in 2000 contained far more Muslims, Hindus, Sikhs, Buddhists, and even—in the American case—Jews, than they did in 1945, and in some urban districts non-Christian religious worship had become the majority form of religious practice. Globalization undoubtedly made a significant contribution to the progressive dissolution of Western Christendom. The twentieth century was the century in which extensive religious plurality first became an inescapable feature of the urban social and cultural environment in almost every continent, including Europe and the eastern seaboard of North America, the heartlands of the old Christendom. Yet it is also the case that the great migration movements of the century both diversified and even strengthened the Christian presence in northern-hemisphere societies. In American cities especially, but also in London, Amsterdam, Hamburg, Paris and Kiev—to name but a few of the most obvious European examples—the advent of migrant churches from Asia, Africa, Latin America, and the Caribbean transformed the Christian landscape, adding Oriental Orthodox and multiple new styles of Catholic, evangelical and Pentecostal spirituality or worship to the existing denominational mix. In Europe at least, their increasingly visible and at times audible presence in the urban environment rescued Christian practice from relegation to the status of the marginal pursuit of a small and ageing minority of the population.

Migration thus brought to Europe and North America not simply marked interreligious plurality but also greatly enhanced Christian denominational and cultural diversity, with a new infusion of spiritual vitality and missionary confidence. Migrant groups entering Europe and North America were on the whole not just more strongly Christian in religious complexion than the societies they had left behind but also—in many cases—rapidly became more emphatically Christian through conversion than the predominantly secular host societies that had received them. This was most strikingly the case among migrants to the West from East Asia— not a part of the globe that is generally associated with strong Christian influence. Although migrant churches had very limited impact outside their own ethnic constituency, it remains the case that, without such migration flows, the process of recession from Christianity in northern societies over the last century would have been far more marked, not less so.[71]

Conclusion

WERE THE HOPES of those who in 1900 confidently retitled *The Christian Oracle* as *The Christian Century* realized over the next hundred years? This book has suggested that the answer to that question is not a straightforward one. The twentieth century was indeed a period of extraordinary and sustained Christian growth in sub-Saharan Africa and parts of Asia. Yet it also witnessed a serious recession from Christian faith in most of Europe, Australasia, and parts of North America, the continuance and even intensification of serious obstacles to the progress of Christianity in the Islamic world and in most of India, and an accelerating and tragic exodus of Christians from those parts of West Asia and the Middle East that had once constituted the heartlands of Christianity. In Latin America and, to a lesser extent in Oceania, the story was different again: a story of the transformation of territories that were already formally Christian as monopolies of particular churches into areas of contestation between older and newer (specifically Pentecostal) strands of Christian expression.

Most recent accounts describe the century as one in which the locus of Christianity shifted decisively southward and eastward, a judgment that rests mainly—though by no means entirely—on the remarkable Christian success story of Africa and the no less spectacular progress of Christianity in China since the Cultural Revolution. As chapter 15 has emphasized, that valid characterization needs to be qualified by the recognition that the century also witnessed both voluntary and enforced flows of Christians northwards and westwards, infusing European and North American church life with elements drawn both from the ancient Orthodox churches of the Middle East and from the new churches—many but by no means all of them Pentecostal—of Latin America and the Caribbean, East Asia, and Africa.

As a century that was grotesquely scarred by two catastrophic global wars involving conflict between nations, most of which were professedly

Christian, the twentieth century failed to live up to its billing as a century in which Christian ethics were supposed to triumph. In religious history, as in other areas of twentieth-century history, it is tempting to treat the First World War as the cataclysm that uprooted everything and deposited new strata of religious unbelief or belief that would shape the contours of the decades that followed. Chapter 1 has suggested that such an interpretation would be a distortion. The war did not create a wholly new religious landscape. Rather it accentuated existing embryonic trends and widened emerging divisions. In the Church of England it amplified the voice of those women who were no longer prepared to accept exclusion from church leadership and government. It turned some erstwhile enthusiasts for collaborative social Christianity—such as Karl Barth—into uncompromising advocates of the uniqueness of the Christian revelation; yet numerous other liberals and modernists simply became more convinced than ever of the need for Christianity to become a creed of social reform and international cooperation. In contrast to their redoubled enthusiasm for a modernized Christianity, the war heightened the diverse forms of an already resurgent supernaturalism, whether Anglo-Catholic, evangelical, Pentecostal, or spiritualist. The supposed identification of the military aggressor with the nation that had given birth to higher biblical criticism supplied a particular fillip to the more strident forms of American conservative religion that would become known as fundamentalism. The war thus widened the incipient parting of the ways between conservative and liberal forms of Protestantism with consequences for the global architecture of Protestantism that have lasted to the present day.

In the wake of the First World War, the churches and key leaders of the emerging ecumenical movement lent their support to Woodrow Wilson's idea of a covenanted league of self-governing nation-states as the basis of a postwar and postimperial world order. They expected that under missionary tutelage the burgeoning force of nationalism in Asia and the Middle East could be harnessed for the benefit of the so-called "younger" churches, bringing forward the prospect of a Christian Asia. However, the rapid disillusionment with the failure of Wilson's idea to deliver what it appeared to promise set the nationalist movements in Asia and Egypt on a collision course with Western mission agencies and the emerging national churches. Christianity could still draw tangible advantage from nationalism in those rare instances where it was able to present itself as an anticolonial force, as in Korea, or, in Europe, as a means of focusing ancient loyalties and sacralizing mythical identities, as in Poland. Nationalism usually requires a mythological narrative of ethnic history to support its political aspirations. In the Polish case, Mariology fulfilled that function: Mary became the supernatural protector and almost the female embodiment of a constructed Polish national identity. Korean nationalism depended not on Catholic traditions but Protestant ones, which are instinctively antimythological, but even in this case some Korean theologians made use of the ancient national myth of *Tan'gun* to buttress their opposition to Japanese colonial rule.

Whether or not it can be accurately deemed to be "the Christian century," the twentieth century can properly be denominated as the great century of conversion to Christianity. It was necessarily, therefore, a period that also witnessed a radical pluralization of popular understandings of Christianity as the word of the gospel took flesh in innumerable cultural forms in non-Western societies. The resulting multiple incarnations of the faith rarely conformed to the post-Enlightenment framework of modern Western Christianity. This pluralization was perhaps most evident among Protestants; for them, it was most obviously theologically problematic in view of their historic confidence in the perspicacity of the scriptures. The nature of the problem first became apparent in movements such as Simon Kimbangu's prophet movement in the Lower Congo, which took the biblicism of an evangelical Baptist missionary tradition and put it to uses that seemed distinctly unorthodox to the British Baptist missionaries.[1] The Bible, newly available in vernacular translation to a host of non-European peoples, was the most powerful agent in the conversion process, but the rediscovery of the biblical figure of the prophet was an outcome that the Bible and missionary societies had not anticipated. Prophet figures arose to lead indigenous revival and renewal movements, sometimes within only a few decades of the arrival of missionary Christianity. Outbreaks of "revival" such as the *Balokole* movement in East Africa challenged existing churchgoers with the question of whether they were truly "saved," and in so doing disrupted existing ecclesial categories of belonging and leadership as well as accepted norms of social order and decency.[2] As Joel Robbins has argued, what missionaries termed "revivals" can be understood as indigenous missionary movements, agents of a deeper and more culturally authentic conversion, but they could equally lead to theological destinations that placed the unity of the faith under increasing strain.[3]

The indispensable but ambiguous process of the vernacularization of Christianity was most obviously apparent in Protestant circles, but it also profoundly affected Catholic and even Orthodox traditions. Although much slower than the Protestant churches to lend its full weight to the campaign for Bible translation, the Roman Catholic Church nevertheless reaped the harvest of the nineteenth-century revival of Marian spirituality and overseas missionary organization. The twentieth century thus became the second golden age of Catholic missionary expansion, rivaling the sixteenth in its significance for the global and cultural reach of Catholicism. The cultural and theological implications of that expansion first began to become apparent at the Second Vatican Council. *Gaudium et Spes* revealed how the papacy, despite the instinctive conservatism of the Vatican as an institution, was beginning to respond to Catholic voices from the Global South by reversing its traditional opposition to human rights ideology. Chapter 14 has shown how even the Orthodox Church experienced intensified pressures toward cultural diversification as a result of its missionary expansion and the adhesion of new African communities of faith, some of which were of very mixed ecclesiastical ancestry.

The twentieth century has also supplied revealing laboratory case studies of how the churches as institutions and popular Christian belief may fare in the face of sustained campaigns by hostile states to reduce the social significance and power either of Christianity itself (the Soviet case) or of the clergy (the French case). The history of the Soviet Union suggests that even modern totalitarian governments are far more limited in their capacity to eliminate or reshape popular belief than they imagine. The communist state mounted a sustained attempt to subvert and infiltrate the leadership of both the Orthodox Church and Protestant Dissent; while formally successful in recruiting religious leaders from both constituencies to serve its purposes, ultimately such endeavors ended in signal failure to weaken the ecclesiastical institutions themselves. This book adds to the evidence that popular indifference is a more potent enemy of faith than state-sponsored militant atheism.

An older generation of social science was inclined to label the twentieth century as "the secular century," yet, even in the northern hemisphere, no single global narrative of secularization is evident across the century as a whole. Radically divergent patterns of believing and belonging were discernible, even within Europe itself. Differentials in religiosity between the genders were almost universal. Distinct and long-established regional religious cultures within nation-states continued to produce divergent regional patterns of both Christian practice and religious indifference. The spectrum from a residual or virtual monopolistic Christendom on the one extreme to a wholly free religious market on the other can be observed not simply by contrasting Scandinavia with the United States, but also beyond the West: the northeast Indian states or the Polynesian islands present examples of young but already eroding monopolistic

Christendoms, while most of sub-Saharan Africa conforms more closely to a free-market model of religious competition. However, globalization, modern media, and modern ideologies of religious toleration have tended increasingly to shift all regions toward the free market model. Evangelical forms of Christianity—already shown by North American experience to be peculiarly well adapted to free market conditions—have accordingly proliferated.

In many parts of Western Christendom the "decade of the secular"—the 1960s—proved to be the great watershed between the age of faith and the age of religious indifference, but it was not universally so. In Scandinavia, the patterns of religion and irreligion are much older. In the United States, the depressive impact of the 1960s on levels of mainline church attendance was more than offset by the growth of evangelicalism among whites outside of the eastern seaboard, and by the continued vibrancy of African American churches. The growth of conservative evangelicalism in the postwar United States can be understood as a form of religious pillarization, with the result that American society by the end of the century could paradoxically appear to be at one and the same time visibly religious and highly secular.

The twentieth century was indeed the "ecumenical century" at the level of formal institutions. It witnessed not only the formation of the World Council of Churches and its associated bodies, and the creation of some major church unions outside Europe, but also within Europe and North America a general and apparently irreversible decline in Christians' traditional loyalty to their various denominations. But it was also the century of bewildering ecclesiastical diversification and fragmentation, both within northern Christendom and beyond it. Again, the general trend toward the erosion of religious monopolies is noted. China is the most telling example of how traditional Western denominational identities, with the important exception of the Protestant–Catholic divide, have been successfully expunged, thus realizing an aspiration powerfully expressed by Cheng Jingyi in his famous address to the World Missionary Conference in 1910. Yet new lines of division have taken their place, determined partly by political judgments and partly by the legacy of the fundamentalist–modernist debates of the interwar period.

Ecumenism sought to bring Christians together, but it was often played out against the backcloth of a world in which ethnic and racial divisions between different sections of humanity were becoming sharper and more absolute. Chapter 7 has explored how the churches responded (or failed to respond) to the challenge posed to Christian ethics by the ascendancy for much of the century of the spurious concept of race, which was often allied with nationalism. Much Christian theology and biblical scholarship in the earlier part of the century reconceived Jesus in an Aryanized and Hellenized image, while some strands of German missiology cloaked what was little more than sanctified racism under the guise of authentic inculturation. Hostility to both communism and individualism led the Catholic Church to form accommodations with fascist regimes and induced moral paralysis in the Vatican in response to the Holocaust; much of the Evangelical Church in Germany displayed a parallel failure of theological integrity. Later, similar sentiments aligned much of the Catholic hierarchy in Rwanda with forms of ethnic politics that absolutized and racialized what was essentially a difference of class or status rather than ethnicity. Compromise in varying measure with genocide was again the eventual outcome. In both cases Christian thinkers had failed to provide robust opposition to fundamentally anti-Christian ideologies, and had reaped the harvest of their timidity.

By the close of the twentieth century, perhaps the most pressing issue on the agenda of Christian theology was how to encourage Christians to pursue and develop a more irenic approach toward those of other faiths— and Islam above all—in the interests of intercommunal harmony and world peace. But the overriding moral imperative of this didactic purpose has tended to obscure the uncomfortable fact that the general trend of Christian–Muslim relations over the course of the century has been in the other direction. Christians and Muslims who collaborated quite widely in the cause of anticolonial nationalism during the first half of the century found themselves from the 1960s onwards engaged in intensifying competition for control of independent nation-states, as Christian advocacy of the idea of a secular and religiously plural state came into conflict with the absolutist demands of shar'ia law. In contexts such as Egypt or Indonesia the idealistic prescriptions of liberal-minded Western theologians could thus appear at odds with the increasingly problematic lived experience of Christian communities.

Perhaps the most far-reaching theological reorientation evident in the course of the century has been in the realm of Christian mission. At the start of the century both Catholic and Protestant missionary thought was almost unanimous in identifying the pursuit of conversion to Christianity as the central missionary goal of the church, though ironically both Catholics and Protestants had left the actual discharge of missionary responsibility largely to ancillary nonecclesial agencies—to Catholic missionary orders or Protestant voluntary missionary societies. By the end of the century, both Catholics and Protestants were no longer so united in their conviction that seeking the conversion of adherents of other religions to Christ constituted the essence of the missionary task. At the same time, both now placed greater theological emphasis on the essentially missional nature of the church itself than they had done previously. In the case of the Roman Catholic Church, this redefinition initiated at Vatican II signaled a fundamental though still incomplete shift in the understanding of the church, from a conception of the church as a hierarchical institution toward a more dynamic view of the church as a community of disciples called to corporate engagement in the missionary task. Such rethinking of the meaning of mission immersed both Catholics and Protestants in lively argument between conservatives and progressives or radicals about the relative priority of seeking conversion and seeking justice in Christian mission. Both Christian traditions experienced contentious polarization over this issue from the 1960s to the 1980s, but an observable degree of rapprochement thereafter.

The later decades of the century thus witnessed impassioned contestation over the Christian understanding of salvation itself. In part this was because of the prominence that the idea of human rights assumed in the postwar world, and the increasing success of theorists on the political left in wresting ideological control of the notion of human rights from the grip of the conservative opponents of communist totalitarianism. The global reach of modern media also made the widespread infringement by modern nation-states of human rights more highly visible than ever before. Decolonization imparted a sense of shared identity and purpose to the nations of the "Third World" and focused the attention of their most creative thinkers on the structural economic issues of dependency and liberation. As a result, the restoration of fundamental human freedoms and dignities to politically oppressed indigenous peoples or impoverished populations attained a more prominent position within the Christian *ordo salutis* than in any previous century. Theologies of liberation assembled their intellectual armory from various sources, Protestant as well as Catholic, Marxist as well as Christian. Where they addressed issues of racial injustice, as in South Africa, or national subjugation, as in Palestine, the civil rights and Black Theology movements in the United States seemed more relevant sources of inspiration than the Latin American fathers of the theology of liberation, whose horizons were set by the primarily economic agendas of dependency theorists. But theologies of liberation, notwithstanding their diversity of source and agenda, all redrew the contours of Christian doctrine to a greater or lesser extent. Salvation became more about the restoration of a lost humanity in this life and less about receiving the divine gift of the life that is to come. Latin American liberation theology in particular invested the poor with the sacred calling of being the primary architects of theological construction. In theory theologians were left with a secondary role as those who took the blueprints of basic theological reflection on praxis and suffering drawn by the communities of the poor and used them to erect new edifices of practical Christian doctrine. In practice, academic theologians retained a more determinative role in shaping the architecture of the new political theologies than they were prepared to admit.

All theologies of liberation called into question the optimistic remedies of Christian civilization and humanitarian improvement that had impelled much of previous Christian missionary engagement with indigenous peoples from the nineteenth century onwards. In South Africa the moral enormity of the apartheid system eventually convinced even the evangelical sectors of black Christian leadership from the mid-1970s that reform and reconciliation were not enough. Their conclusion that a more radical form of prophetic engagement with the oppressive power of the state was imperative proved a turning point in the campaign against apartheid. In Canada in much the same period, both the Catholic and the Protestant churches found themselves rewriting the narrative of their own educational missions among First Nations peoples. The demands of justice to indigenous peoples now appeared so preeminent that previous generations of Christian altruistic effort among First Nations children were now regarded, not simply as misguided acts of charity, but even as acts of intrinsic exploitation that required nothing less than a public apology.

Human rights ideology proved its emancipatory value not simply to Christian defense of the oppressed in colonial or postcolonial situations, but perhaps even more to the women who in virtually every Christian denomination formed the majority of worshippers while being almost entirely excluded from the leadership of congregational worship and church life. The campaign for the ordination of women, which first appeared on the agenda of the churches in Britain and some other Western countries during the First World War, received its second and decisive fillip as a consequence of the growing impact of the feminist movement on the European and American churches from the 1960s onwards. Not all Christians, however, welcomed the extension of rights language to questions of ministerial order, for in their minds such questions were of the immutable essence of the faith. The Orthodox, Roman Catholics, Anglo-Catholics, and some evangelicals of various denominations denied that women had a right to exercise priestly or ministerial roles. Such functions, they firmly believed, were prohibited to them by the divine order of creation, as mediated either through apostolic tradition or through biblical teaching, or both. For the majority of Anglican evangelicals in Sydney diocese—and for significant numbers in many other dioceses throughout the Anglican communion—the issue became a symbolic one. Opposing the campaign for the ordination of women became a marker of fidelity to scriptural authority and of willingness to resist the insidious march of secularization.

In the course of the last four decades of the century it became steadily more apparent that the clash between invocation of human rights and the appeal to unchanging Christian conceptions of divinely revealed truth touched not simply on the ecclesiological issues of church leadership, but, still more fundamentally, on theological anthropology—the Christian understanding of the identity of human beings. At first the question of how the churches should respond to the gathering campaign for the rights of gay and lesbian people was overshadowed in Christian circles by the various denominational debates over the ordination of women. From the 1980s onwards, the issue of whether practicing gay and lesbian people should be ordained to the Christian ministry came increasingly to the fore, sharply dividing a growing number of Protestant denominations and global communions. The Roman Catholic and Orthodox Churches remained virtually solid in their official opposition to any change in the traditional Christian moral position, though dissenters could be found, especially among Roman Catholics. While "liberal" stances on the issue were more common in the North than in the South, and "conservative" stances commanded a more decisive majority in the South than in the North, the argument did not fall neatly along geographical lines. By the end of the century, the stage was set for a series of ecclesiastical conflicts to be waged across the Protestant world that would prove to be even more extensive than—and just as vituperative as—the fundamentalist-modernist battles of the interwar years. As the supposed "Christian century" drew to a close, the Protestant global community looked even less of a united family than it had done in 1900.

Undoubtedly the most striking single contrast between the face of the world church in 1900 and that of the world church in 2000 is the salience and near ubiquity of Pentecostal styles of Christianity by the end of the century—forms of Christian expression that in 1900 were still uncommon and deemed to be at best eccentric and at worst heretical. The explosion during the twentieth century of what has come to be known as Pentecostalism presents those who seek a balanced appraisal of contemporary world Christianity with a dilemma. Should the widespread recovery of the pneumatological dimensions of Christian faith and experience after so many centuries of neglect be warmly welcomed? The majority of Christians would agree that undoubtedly it should. Should it be recognized that Pentecostal Christianity has proved eminently capable of reaching the parts of humanity that Christianity in its highly conceptual Western post-Enlightenment form has struggled to reach? Again, the consensus is that undoubtedly it should. Yet what is termed "Pentecostalism" embraces such a broad spectrum of particular embodiments of Spirit-focused Christianity that a single verdict seems impossible. In some of its manifestations that have become increasingly prominent since the 1980s, the fabric of Christian doctrine and spirituality has been so fundamentally redesigned in the interests of the pursuit of individual material prosperity that the question becomes whether Christianity has converted indigenous religionists or whether indigenous religious and cultural perspectives—whether these be African, Asian, Latin American, or even white North American—have succeeded in converting Christianity. The Christian history of the twenty-first century may provide us with the answer. If the gravest challenge faced by Christianity in the twentieth century was the repeated subversion of Christian ethics by a series of tragic compromises between Christianity and ideologies of racial supremacy, the most serious challenge confronting the religion in the twenty-first century looks likely to be the preparedness of some sections of the church in both northern and southern hemispheres to accommodate the faith to ideologies of individual enrichment.

Introduction

1. *Il Fermo Proposito: Encyclical of Pope Pius X on Catholic Action in Italy Addressed to the Bishops of Italy*, 1905, paragraph 4, http://www.vatican.va/holy_father/pius_x/encyclicals/documents/hf_p-x_enc_11061905_il-fermo-proposito_en.html (Accessed March 24, 2017).

2. Ibid., paragraphs 4–5.

3. Richard Wightman Fox, *Reinhold Niebuhr: A Biography* (Ithaca, NY, and London: Cornell University Press, 1996), 212–14; see Reinhold Niebuhr, *The Nature and Destiny of Man: A Christian Interpretation*, 2 vols. (New York: Scribner's and Sons, 1941, 1943).

4. Gavin White, *How the Churches Got to Be the Way They Are* (London and Philadelphia: SCM Press and Trinity Press International, 1990).

5. See, for example, Tony Ballantyne, "The Persistence of the Gods: Religion in the Modern World," in *World Histories from Below: Disruption and Dissent*, eds. Antoinette Burton and Tony Ballantyne, (London: Bloomsbury Academic, 2016), 137–67.

6. Klaus Koschorke and Adrian Hermann, eds., *Polycentric Structures in the History of World Christianity/Polyzentrische Strukturen in der Geschichte des Weltchristentums* (Wiesbaden: Harrasowitz Verlag, 2014).

7. Brian Stanley, "Twentieth-Century World Christianity: A Perspective from the History of Missions," in *Christianity Reborn: The Global Expansion of Evangelicalism in the Twentieth Century*, ed. Donald M. Lewis (Grand Rapids, MI: Eerdmans, 2004), 63–64.

8. Stephen K. Batalden, Kathleen Cann, and John Dean, eds., *Sowing the Word: The Cultural Impact of the British and Foreign Bible Society* (Sheffield: Phoenix Press, 2004), 263–67.

9. Todd M. Johnson and Gina A. Zurlo, eds. *World Christian Database,* table on "Global Religion over Time" (Leiden: E. J. Brill), http://www.worldchristiandatabase.org/wcd/ (Accessed February 27, 2017).

10. See especially Andrew N. Porter, *Religion Versus Empire? British Protestant Missionaries and Overseas Expansion, 1700–1914* (Manchester: Manchester University Press, 2004); Brian Stanley, *The Bible and the Flag: Protestant Missions and British Imperialism in the Nineteenth and Twentieth Centuries* (Leicester: Apollos, 1990).

Chapter 1. Wars and Rumors of Wars

1. P. T. Forsyth, *Lectures on the Church and the Sacraments* (London: Longmans, Green & Co., 1917), 34.

2. A. T. Robertson, *The New Citizenship: The Christian Facing a New World Order* (New York: Fleming H. Revell, 1919), 8; cited in James J. Thompson, *Tried by Fire:*

Southern Baptists and the Religious Controversies of the 1920s (Macon, GA: Mercer University Press, 1982), 6.

3. Nicholas Atkin and Frank Tallett, *Priests, Prelates and People: A History of European Catholicism since 1750* (London and New York: I. B. Tauris, 2003), 196–203; John F. Pollard, *The Unknown Pope: Benedict XV (1914–1922) and the Pursuit of Peace*, rev. ed. (repr. 2000; London: Geoffrey Chapman, 1999), 112–16, 162–65.

4. Michael Snape, "Civilians, Soldiers, and Perceptions of the Afterlife in Britain during the First World War," in *The Church, the Afterlife and the Fate of the Soul, Studies in Church History*, vol. 45, eds. Peter Clarke and Tony Claydon (Woodbridge: The Boydell Press for the Ecclesiastical History Society, 2009), 372.

5. K. S. Inglis, *Sacred Places: War Memorials in the Australian Landscape* (Carlton South: Melbourne University Press, 1998), 76, 83–4, 92, 458–71.

6. Hew Strachan, *The First World War*, vol. 1: *To Arms* (Oxford: Oxford University Press, 2001), 497–99.

7. A. S. Kanya-Forstner, "The War, Imperialism, and Decolonization," in *The Great War and the Twentieth Century*, eds. Jay Winter, Geoffrey Parker, and Mary R. Habeck (New Haven, CT: Yale University Press, 2000), 247.

8. For a full treatment see R. V. Pierard, "John R. Mott and the Rift in the Ecumenical Movement during World War I," *Journal of Ecumenical Studies* 23, no. 4 (1986): 601–20.

9. G. K. A. Bell, *Randall Davidson: Archbishop of Canterbury*, 2nd ed. (London: Oxford University Press, 1938), 741–43.

10. See chapter 7.

11. For nationalistic tendencies in Catholic missions in the twentieth century, see Adrian Hastings, "The Clash Between Nationalism and Universalism in Twentieth-Century Christianity," in *Missions, Nationalism, and the End of Empire*, ed. Brian Stanley (Grand Rapids, MI: Eerdmans, 2003), 15–33.

12. Kanya-Forstner, "The War, Imperialism, and Decolonization," 245.

13. Matthew Grimley, "The Religion of Englishness: Puritanism, Providentialism, and 'National Character', 1918–1945," *Journal of British Studies* 46, no. 4 (2007): 898–99.

14. Oldham did also concede the legitimacy of an economic argument for empire in terms of the world's need for raw materials from the tropical countries, but the main thrust of his book is that such a motivation was unacceptable if not controlled by humanitarian ideals of trusteeship: J. H. Oldham, *Christianity and the Race Problem* (London: Student Christian Movement, 1924), 97–101.

15. See Keith Clements, *Faith on the Frontier: A Life of J. H. Oldham* (Edinburgh: T. & T. Clark, 1998), chapter 10.

16. Kanya-Forstner, "The War, Imperialism, and Decolonization," 238.

17. *Maximum Illud: On the Propagation of the Faith throughout the World* (1919), paragraphs 19 and 41, at http://data.over-blog-kiwi.com/0/51/25/32/201309/ob _74799f42d52fa3a430ded78eef31e7c4_maximum-illud-en.pdf (Accessed March 10, 2017).

18. Andrew Barnes, *Making Headway: The Introduction of Western Civilization in Colonial Northern Nigeria* (Rochester, NY: University of Rochester Press, 2009), 181–9, 270; and Stanley, "Twentieth-Century World Christianity," 52–83.

19. Louise M. Pirouet, "East African Christians and World War I," *Journal of African History* 19, no. 1 (1978): 117–30.

20. "A Missionary Survey of the Year 1914," *International Review of Missions* 4, no. 1 (1915): 3, 60–1, 65.

21. Eberhard Busch, *Karl Barth: His Life from Letters and Autobiographical Texts*, English translation (London: SCM Press, 1976), 81–92.

22. Karl Barth, *The Epistle to the Romans*, trans. from the 6th edition by Edwyn C. Hoskyns (London: Oxford University Press, 1933), 81.

23. Busch, *Karl Barth*, 117–25.

24. D. Densil Morgan, *Barth Reception in Britain* (London: T. & T. Clark, 2010), 2–3, 43–47, 163, 220–24, 245; John McConnachie, *The Barthian Theology and the Man of Today* (London: Hodder & Stoughton, 1933).

25. W. A. Visser 't Hooft, *Memoirs* (London: SCM Press, 1973), 25–26, 29.

26. David Cannadine, "War and Death, Grief and Mourning in Modern Britain," in *Mirrors of Mortality: Studies in the Social History of Death*, ed. Joachim Whaley (London: Europa Publications, 1981), 227–30; Jenny Hazelgrove, *Spiritualism and British Society between the Wars* (Manchester: Manchester University Press, 2000); Snape, "Civilians, Soldiers, and Perceptions of the Afterlife," 371–403; Jay Winter, *Sites of Memory: Sites of Mourning: The Great War in European Cultural History* (Cambridge: Cambridge University Press, 1998), 54–77.

27. Barth, *The Epistle to the Romans*, 120.

28. E. R. Wickham, *Church and People in an Industrial City* (London: Lutterworth Press, 1957), 206, 210.

29. Michael Snape, *God and the British Soldier: Religion and the British Army in the First and Second World Wars* (London: Routledge, 2005).

30. Committee of Enquiry on the Army and Religion, *The Army and Religion: An Enquiry and its Bearing upon the Religious Life of the Nation. With a Preface by the Bishop of Winchester* (London: Macmillan & Co., Ltd., 1919), 19; see also 42–4, 51, 55, 62–3, 209, 214. Snape, "Civilians, Soldiers, and Perceptions of the Afterlife," 396, dismisses Cairns's statement as unrepresentative of the theology preached by the army chaplains, but the evidence of its popularity among the ranks is strong.

31. Robert Currie, Alan Gilbert, and Lee Horsley, *Churches and Churchgoers: Patterns of Church Growth in the British Isles since 1700* (Oxford: Clarendon Press, 1977), 33, 143–4, 164; Grimley, "The Religion of Englishness," 886–87.

32. J. M. Winter, *The Great War and the British People*, 2nd ed. (Basingstoke: Palgrave Macmillan, 2003), 94–95.

33. This conclusion is broadly congruent with the arguments of Callum Brown, *The Death of Christian Britain: Understanding Secularisation 1800–2000* (London: Routledge, 2001), although Brown does not specifically advance this suggestion.

34. Stuart Paul Mews, "Religion and English Society in the First World War," PhD thesis, University of Cambridge, 1974, 237.

35. Ibid., 236–37.

36. Brian D. Heeney, *The Women's Movement in the Church of England, 1850–1950* (Oxford: Clarendon Press, 1988), 110–11.

37. Matthew Grimley, *Citizenship, Community, and the Church of England: Liberal Anglican Theories of the State between the Wars* (Oxford; Clarendon Press, 2004),

chapters 1–2; John Maiden, *National Religion and the Prayer Book Controversy, 1927–1928* (Woodbridge: Boydell Press, 2009), 8–9.

38. J. H. Shakespeare, *The Churches at the Cross-Roads* (London: Williams & Norgate, 1918), 58; see Ian M. Randall, *The English Baptists of the Twentieth Century* (Didcot: The Baptist Historical Society, 2005), chapter 3; Peter Shepherd, *The Making of a Modern Denomination: John Howard Shakespeare and the English Baptists, 1898–1924* (Carlisle: The Paternoster Press, 2001).

39. P. T. Forsyth, *The Justification of God: Lectures for War-Time on a Christian Theodicy* (London: Duckworth & Co., 1916), 84. There is a large literature on Forsyth, but see especially: John H. Rodgers, *The Theology of P. T. Forsyth: The Cross of Christ and the Revelation of God* (London: Independent Press, 1965), 1–24; and Stephen Sykes, "P. T. Forsyth on the Church," in *Justice the True and Only Mercy: Essays on the Life and Theology of Peter Taylor Forsyth*, ed. Trevor Hart (Edinburgh: T. & T. Clark, 1995), 1–15.

40. John Nevillle Figgis, *Hopes for English Religion* (London: Longman, Green & Co., 1919), 105–6; cited in Alan Wilkinson, *The Church of England and the First World War* (London: SPCK, 1978), 249.

41. On Figgis see *ODNB* and Grimley, *Citizenship, Community, and the Church of England*, 70–72.

42. Eric J. Leed, *No Man's Land: Combat & Identity in World War I* (Cambridge: Cambridge University Press, 1979), 21.

43. Forsyth, *The Church and the Sacraments*, 34; see Mews, "Religion and English Society in the First World War," 74–76.

44. Alexander A. Boddy, *The Real Angels of Mons* (1915), cited in Wilkinson, *The Church of England and the First World War*, 194–95.

45. Hensley Henson, *Retrospect of an Unimportant Life*, 3 vols. (London: Oxford University Press, 1942–1950), 1:181.

46. Bell, *Davidson*, 812.

47. Maiden, *National Religion and the Prayer Book Controversy*, 32.

48. Bell, *Davidson*, 828–30; Snape, "Civilians, Soldiers, and Perceptions of the Afterlife," 391, 397.

49. Maiden, *National Religion and the Prayer Book Controversy*, 11–13.

50. Ibid., passim.

51. Precise numbers are impossible to determine. Compare W. S. F. Pickering, *Anglo-Catholicism: A Study in Religious Ambiguity*, rev. ed. (London: SPCK, 1991), 56, and John Gunstone, *Lift High the Cross: Anglo-Catholics and the Congress Movement* (Norwich: Canterbury Press, 2010), 9, 126–27, 198, 253, 268, 337.

52. H. A. Wilson, *Received With Thanks of P. E. Tindall, M. E. Atlay, Frank Weston, Richard Wilson, H. F. B. Mackay, H. A. Pollock* (London and Oxford: A. R. Mowbray, 1940), 88–89.

53. *Report of the First Anglo-Catholic Congress London, 1920* (London: SPCK, 1920), 143–54 and 155–60.

54. For an Australian example see L. Sale-Harrison, *The Remarkable Jew: His Wonderful Future. God's Great Timepiece*, 7th ed. (Harrisburg, PA: Evangelical Press, 1928), 4; cited in Crawford Gribben, *Evangelical Millennialism in the Trans-Atlantic World, 1500–2000* (Basingstoke: Palgrave Macmillan, 2011), 103.

55. John Wilson, *Our Israelitish Origin: Lectures on Ancient Israel and the Israelitish Origin of the Modern Nations of Europe* (London: G. J. Stevenson, 1869); see John Wilson, "British Israelism: The Ideological Restraints on Sect Organisation," in *Patterns of Sectarianism: Organisation and Ideology in Social and Religious Movements*, ed. B. R. Wilson (London: Heinemann, 1967), 345–76.

56. "The British-Israel-World-Federation: Our History," http://www.britishisrael .co.uk/history.php (Accessed March 10, 2017).

57. *The Dictionary of New Zealand Biography*, vol. 2: *1870–1900* (Wellington: Bridget Williams Books and the Department of Internal Affairs, 1993), 316–19; W. J. Gardner, *William Massey* (Wellington: A. H. and A. W. Reed, 1969), 22–23.

58. Harold Murray, *Dinsdale Young the Preacher: An Intimate Sketch of Dr Dinsdale T. Young* (London: Marshall, Morgan & Scott, n.d. [1938]), 105.

59. David Bebbington, "Baptists and Fundamentalism in Inter-War Britain," in *Evangelicalism and Fundamentalism in the United Kingdom in the Twentieth Century*, eds. David Bebbington and David Ceri Jones (Oxford: Oxford University Press, 2013), 109; William K. Kay, "Pentecostalism and Fundamentalism," in the same volume, 314–15.

60. For Elim see Bryan R. Wilson, *Sects and Society: A Sociological Study of Three Religious Groups in Britain* (London: Heinemann, 1961), 46–47, 51–56. The statement about conservative Baptists is based on personal observation by the author while on the staff of Spurgeon's College during the 1980s.

61. For a British reaction to the Ottoman entry into the war see the newspaper edited by Alexander Boddy, *Confidence* (February 1915), 26, cited in Gavin Wakefield, *The First Pentecostal Anglican: The Life and Legacy of Alexander Boddy* (Cambridge: Grove Books, 2001), 20. For the United States see Timothy P. Weber, *Living in the Shadow of the Second Coming: American Premillennialism, 1875–1982*, rev. ed. (Chicago: University of Chicago Press, 1987), 105–15; and Gribben, *Evangelical Millennialism in the Trans-Atlantic World*, 103.

62. Donald M. Lewis, *The Origins of Christian Zionism: Lord Shaftesbury and Evangelical Support for a Jewish Homeland* (Cambridge: Cambridge University Press, 2010).

63. W. Y. Fullerton, *F. B. Meyer: A Biography* (London: Marshall, Morgan & Scott, n.d.), 158; Randall, *English Baptists*, 102.

64. A. C. Dixon and others, *Advent Testimony Addresses: Delivered at the Meetings at Queen's Hall, London, W.C., December 13th, 1917: Authorised Report* (London: Chas. J. Thynne, 1918), 67.

65. A. H. Burton and others, *Further Advent Testimony Addresses: Meetings at Queen's Hall and All Souls' Church, Langham Place, December 4th, 1918: Authorised Report* (London: Chas. J. Thynne, 1919), 70, 72–3, 89, 100, 104–5; Donald W. Dayton, ed., *The Prophecy Conference Movement*, vol. 4 (New York: Garland, 1988); Ernest R. Sandeen, *The Roots of Fundamentalism: British and American Millenarianism 1800–1930* (Chicago: University of Chicago Press, 1970), 233–35.

66. Timothy Larsen, *Christabel Pankhurst: Fundamentalism and Feminism in Coalition* (Woodbridge: The Boydell Press, 2002), 21–22, 36–37, and passim.

67. For a helpful summary of the two schools of premillennial prophecy see Weber, *Living in the Shadow of the Second Coming*, 13–24.

68. D. W. Bebbington, *Evangelicalism in Britain: A History from the 1730s to the 1980s* (London: Unwin Hyman, 1989), 223–24.

69. Dixon and others, *Advent Testimony Addresses*, 86–87.

70. Bebbington, *Evangelicalism in Modern Britain*, 194; idem, "The Advent Hope in British Evangelicalism since 1800," *Scottish Journal of Religious Studies* 9, no. 2 (1988): 110.

71. D. W. Bebbington, "Martyrs for the Truth: Fundamentalism in Britain," in Diana Wood, ed., *Martyrs and Martyrologies. Studies in Church History*, vol. 30 (Oxford: Blackwell Publishers for the Ecclesiastical History Society, 1993), 417–51; Bebbington and Jones, *Evangelicalism and Fundamentalism in the United Kingdom in the Twentieth Century*, passim.

72. Weber, *Living in the Shadow of the Second Coming*, 105.

73. Gribben, *Evangelical Millennialism*, 103; Nicholas M. Railton, "God and Magog: The History of a Symbol," *Evangelical Quarterly* 75, no. 1 (2003): 41.

74. George M. Marsden, *Fundamentalism and American Culture: The Shaping of Twentieth-Century Evangelicalism* (New York: Oxford University Press, 1980), 142.

75. Ibid., 145–49, 161.

76. *God Hath Spoken* (Philadelphia: Bible Conference Committee, 1919), 7, cited in Sandeen, *Roots of Fundamentalism*, 243, and Marsden, *Fundamentalism and American Culture*, 158.

77. Marsden, *Fundamentalism and American Culture*, 117.

78. Ibid., 159; Martin E. Marty, *Modern American Religion*, vol. 2: *The Noise of Conflict 1919–1941* (Chicago: University of Chicago Press, 1991), 160; Sandeen, *Roots of Fundamentalism*, 188–207, 246.

79. Marty, *Modern American Religion*, vol. 2, 184.

80. Cited in James R. Moore, *The Post-Darwinian Controversies: A Study of the Protestant Struggle to Come to Terms with Darwin in Great Britain and America 1870–1900* (Cambridge: Cambridge University Press, 1979), 74.

81. Harry Emerson Fosdick, *Shall the Fundamentalists Win? A Sermon Preached at the First Presbyterian Church, New York, May 21, 1922* (New York, 1922).

82. Clarence E. Macartney, "Shall Unbelief Win? An Answer to Dr Fosdick," *The Presbyterian* 92 (July 13, 1922), cited in Marsden, *Fundamentalism in American Culture*, 173.

83. For a stimulating revision of the standard historiography on fundamentalism see Michael S. Hamilton, "The Interdenominational Evangelicalism of D. L. Moody and the Problem of Fundamentalism," in *American Evangelicalism: George Marsden and the State of American Religious History*, ed. Darren Dochuk, Thomas S. Kidd, and Kurt W. Peterson (Notre Dame, IN: University of Notre Dame Press, 2014), 230–80.

84. Keith W. Clements, *Lovers of Discord: Twentieth-Century Theological Controversies in England* (London: SPCK, 1988), 86.

85. Shailer Mathews, *The Faith of Modernism* (New York: Macmillan, 1924).

86. J. Gresham Machen, *Christianity and Liberalism* (New York: Macmillan, 1923), 64–65.

87. Bradley J. Longfield, *The Presbyterian Controversy: Fundamentalists, Modernists, and Moderates* (New York: Oxford University Press, 1991), 50–51.

88. Longfield, *The Presbyterian Controversy*, 149.

89. Ibid., 228; John F. Piper, Jr., *Robert E. Speer: Prophet of the American Church* (Louisville, KY: Geneva Press, 2000), 296–301, 360–61, 395–96.

90. Hamilton, "The Interdenominational Evangelicalism of D. L. Moody and the Problem of Fundamentalism," 247–58, has highlighted the extent of abstention of many northern conservatives from the anti-evolution crusade.

91. Moore, *The Post-Darwinian Controversies*, 75.

92. David N. Livingstone, *Darwin's Forgotten Defenders: The Encounter between Evangelical Theology and Evolutionary Thought* (Grand Rapids, MI: Eerdmans, 1987); Moore, *The Post-Darwinian Controversies*, passim.

93. See Thompson, *Tried by Fire*, 112–25.

94. John Roach Straton, *Evolution versus Creation: Second in the Series of Fundamentalist-Modernist Debates* (Nashville, TN: Sunday School Board: Southern Baptist Convention, 1924), 34; cited in Michael Lienesch, *In the Beginning: Fundamentalism, the Scopes Trial, and the Making of the Antievolution Movement* (Chapel Hill: University of North Carolina Press, 2007), 86–87.

95. T. T. Martin, *Evolution or Christ? Christ or Hell?* (n.p., n.d. [1923]), 26, 33, http://moses.law.umn.edu/darrow/documents/T_T_Martin_Evolution_or_Christ .pdf (Accessed October 10, 2017). Cited in Thompson, *Tried by Fire*, 68; see also T. T. Martin, *Hell and the High Schools: Christ or Evolution, Which?* (Kansas City: Western Baptist Publishing Co., 1923), 10, 72, cited in Ronald L. Numbers, *The Creationists: The Evolution of Scientific Creationism* (Berkeley and Los Angeles: University of California Press, 1993), 46–47.

96. Longfield, *The Presbyterian Controversy*, 55, 68; Marsden, *Fundamentalism in American Culture*, 169; Marty, *Modern American Religion*, vol. 2,191. See Vernon L. Kellogg, *Headquarters Nights: A Record of Conversations and Experiences at the Headquarters of the German Army in France and Belgium* (Boston: The Atlantic Monthly Press, 1917); and Benjamin Kidd, *The Science of Power* (London: Methuen, 1918).

97. Lawrence W. Levine, *Defender of the Faith. William Jennings Bryan: The Last Decade 1915–1925*, 2nd ed. (New York: Oxford University Press, 1968), 262–63; Lienesch, *In the Beginning*, 87; Longfield, *The Presbyterian Controversy*, 67.

98. Paolo E. Coletta, *William Jennings Bryan III. Political Puritan 1915–1925* (Lincoln: University of Nebraska Press, 1969), 212.

99. Cited in Lienesch, *In the Beginning*, 111.

Chapter 2. Holy Nations?

1. Rebecca E. Karl, *Staging the World: Chinese Nationalism at the Turn of the Twentieth Century* (Durham, NC: Duke University Press, 2002).

2. Hastings, "The Clash of Nationalism and Universalism in Twentieth-Century Missionary Christianity," in Stanley, ed., *Missions, Nationalism, and the End of Empire*, 21.

3. V. I. Lenin, "The Socialist Revolution and the Right of Nations to Self-Determination" (1916), in his *Collected Works*, 45 vols. (Moscow: Progress, 1960–70), vol. 22, 143–56; cited in Erez Manela, *The Wilsonian Moment: Self-Determination*

and the International Origins of Anticolonial Nationalism (New York: Oxford University Press, 2007), 37.

4. Judith M. Brown, *Gandhi: Prisoner of Hope* (New Haven, CT: Yale University Press, 1989), 67, 77, 80–84, 116.

5. Point V in Wilson's Fourteen Points, available at http://avalon.law.yale.edu /20th_century/wilson14.asp (Accessed December 20, 2016).

6. Trygve Throntveit, "The Fable of the Fourteen Points: Woodrow Wilson and National Self-Determination," *Diplomatic History* 35, no. 3 (2011): 445–481.

7. Malcolm D. Magee, *What the World Should Be: Woodrow Wilson and the Crafting of a Faith-Based Foreign Policy* (Waco, TX: Baylor University Press, 2008), 14–17, 33.

8. Manela, *The Wilsonian Moment*, 163–66.

9. Harold S. Hong, "Introduction," in *Korea Struggles for Christ: Memorial Symposium for the Eightieth Anniversary of Protestantism in Korea*, ed. Harold S. Hong, Won Yong Ji, and Chung Choon Kim (Seoul: Christian Literature Society of Korea, 1966), 5.

10. Manela, *The Wilsonian Moment*, 201.

11. Sebastian C. H. and Kirsteen Kim, *A History of Korean Christianity* (Cambridge: Cambridge University Press, 2015), 90–92. The Nevius method of developing a self-governing, self-propagating and self-supporting indigenous church was promulgated by John L. Nevius, American Presbyterian missionary to Shandong, China, though in large part it was borrowed from the Welsh Baptist missionary, Timothy Richard.

12. Timothy S. Lee, *Born Again: Evangelicalism in Korea* (Honolulu: University of Hawaii Press, 2010), 24.

13. See Daniel J. Adams, "Church Growth in Korea: A Paradigm Shift From Ecclesiology to Nationalism," in *Perspectives on Christianity in Korea and Japan: The Gospel and Culture in East Asia*, ed. Mark R. Mullins and Richard Fox Young (Lewiston, Queenston, and Lampeter: Edwin Mellen Press, 1995), 13–28.

14. Kim and Kim, *History of Korean Christianity*, 93; see also Kenneth M. Wells, *New God, New Nation: Protestants and Self-Reconstruction Nationalism in Korea 1896–1937* (Honolulu: University of Hawaii Press, 1990), 96.

15. Kim and Kim, *History of Korean Christianity*, 121; Michael Edson Robinson, *Cultural Nationalism in Colonial Korea, 1920–1925* (Seattle: University of Washington Press, 1988), 44.

16. Adams, "Church Growth in Korea," 22–3; Kim and Kim, *History of Korean Christianity*, 121; Lee, *Born Again in Korea*, 43.

17. Roy Watson Curry, *Woodrow Wilson and Far Eastern Policy 1913–1921* (New York: Bookman Associates, 1957), 210–11.

18. Manela, *The Wilsonian Moment*, 205–6.

19. Ibid., 208–11.

20. Don Baker, "Christianity 'Koreanized'," in *Nationalism and the Construction of Korean Identity*, ed. Hyung Il Pai and Timothy R. Tangherlini (Berkeley, CA: University of California Berkeley Institute of East Asian Studies, 1998), 118.

21. *The Korea Mission Field* 15, 11 (1919): 239–40.

22. *Ibid.*, 15, 6 (1919): 131.

23. Ibid., 15, 12 (1919): 245–53.

24. Ibid., 16, 1 (1920): 1. The other two mighty "revivals" were listed as the incarnation of Christ and the Day of Pentecost.

25. Ibid., 16, 2 (1920): 26–27.

26. Kim and Kim, *History of Korean Christianity*, 124; Wi Jo Kang, "Church and State Relations in the Japanese Colonial Period," in *Christianity in Korea*, eds. Robert E. Buswell Jr. and Timothy S. Lee, (Honolulu: University of Hawaii Press, 2006), 106.

27. Kim and Kim, *History of Korean Christianity*, 139–34; Park Heon-Wook, "The Korean Christian Church in Japan: A Study of the Gospel, Indigenization, and Nationalism," in Mullins and Young, eds., *Perspectives on Christianity in Korea and Japan*, 51.

28. James H. Grayson, "The Shintō Shrine Conflict and Protestant Martyrs in Korea, 1938–1945," *Missiology: An International Review* 29, no. 3 (2001): 287–305 (at p. 294).

29. James H. Grayson, *Myths and Legends from Korea: An Annotated Compendium of Ancient and Modern Materials* (Richmond, Surrey: Curzon Press, 2001), 56–57.

30. Lee, *Born Again in Korea*, 65.

31. Ibid., 65.

32. Kim and Kim, *History of Korean Christianity*, 185.

33. Ibid., 275.

34. Kim and Kim, *History of Korean Christianity*, 261. The term used was *Man*, the Chinese character for 10,000, which can simply mean "a large number." I owe this point to Professor James Grayson.

35. Brian Porter-Szűcs, *Faith and the Fatherland: Catholicism, Modernity, and Poland* (New York: Oxford University Press, 2011), 4–15; Jerzy Kloczkowski, *A History of Polish Christianity* (Cambridge: Cambridge University Press, 2000), 269, 338.

36. Manela, *The Wilsonian Moment*, 60.

37. Porter-Szűcs, *Faith and the Fatherland*, 12; Kloczkowski, *A History of Polish Christianity*, 330, 338–9.

38. Kloczkowski, *A History of Polish Christianity*, 319.

39. Norman Davies, *God's Playground: A History of Poland in Two Volumes*, rev. ed. (Oxford: Oxford University Press, 2005), I, ix–xi.

40. Porter-Szűcs, *Faith and the Fatherland*, 361.

41. Davies, *God's Playground*, I, 4, 15–16; Christopher Garbowski, *Religious Life in Poland: History, Diversity and Modern Issues* (Jefferson, NC: McFarland & Co., 2014), 63.

42. Song of Solomon 1:5; Jaroslav Pelikan, *Mary through the Centuries: Her Place in the History of Culture* (New Haven, CT: Yale University Press, 1996), 25–26, 78–79.

43. George Huntson Williams, *The Mind of John Paul II: Origins of His Thought and Action* (New York: Seabury Press, 1981), 39; Miri Rubin, *Mother of God: A History of the Virgin Mary* (London: Allen Lane, 2009), 306.

44. Porter-Szűcs, *Faith and the Fatherland*, 272–327, 369, 392–95.

45. Ibid., 365–9; Brian Porter, "*Hetmanka* and Mother: Representing the Virgin Mary in Modern Poland," *Contemporary European History* 14, no. 2 (2005), 151–70 (at pp. 155–56); Cathelijne de Busser and Anna Niedźwiedź, "Mary in Poland: A Polish Master Symbol," in *Moved by Mary: The Power of Pilgrimage in the Modern*

World, ed. Anna-Karina Hermkens, Willy Jansen and Catrien Notermans (Farnham: Ashgate, 2009), 89.

46. Porter, "*Hetmanka* and Mother," 166–67.

47. Garbowski, *Religious Life in Poland*, 63–64; De Busser and Niedźwiedź, "Mary in Poland," 91.

48. George Weigel, *Witness to Hope: The Biography of Pope John Paul II* (New York: Harper Collins, 2001), 248–9; for the influence of the sometimes unorthodox tradition of Polish Romantic messianism on John Paul II see Williams, *The Mind of John Paul II*, 42–47.

49. In October 1982 Kolbe was canonized by John Paul II, who overruled his advisers in insisting that Kolbe had fulfilled the canonical conditions to be venerated as a martyr.

50. Weigel, *Witness to Hope*, 305–20.

51. Kloczkowski, *A History of Polish Christianity*, 287–8; Davies, *God's Playground*, II, 162.

52. Cited in Garbowski, *Religious Life in Poland*, 8.

53. Weigel, *Witness to Hope*, 323.

54. Kloczkowski, *A History of Polish Christianity*, 334–36.

55. Elzbieta Halas, "Symbolic Politics of Public Time and Collective Memory. The Polish Case," *European Review* 10, no. 1 (2002):125; de Busser and Anna Niedźwiedź, "Mary in Poland," 98.

56. Porter-Szűcs, *Faith and the Fatherland*, 272–327, 391–96.

Chapter 3. The Power of the Word and Prophecy

1. Kenneth Scott Latourette, *A History of the Expansion of Christianity*, 7 vols. (London: Eyre & Spottiswoode, 1938–47), titles to vols. IV, V, and VI.

2. Johnson and Zurlo, *World Christian Database* http://www.worldchristian database.org/wcd/ (Accessed October 10, 2017). Tables on "Global Religion over Time" and "Africa: Religion over Time."

3. Daniel H. Bays, *A New History of Christianity in China* (Chichester: Wiley-Blackwell, 2012), 77, 147, 169.

4. For one such voice see V. Y. Mudimbe, *The Idea of Africa* (Bloomington and Indianapolis: Indiana University Press, 1994), 105–10; idem, *The Invention of Africa; Gnosis, Philosophy and the Order of Knowledge* (Bloomington and Indianapolis: Indiana University Press, 1998), 47–48.

5. Adrian Hastings, *The Church in Africa 1450–1950* (Oxford, Clarendon Press, 1994), 560.

6. Hastings, *Church in Africa*, 601–2; Willy De Craemer, *The Jamaa and the Church: A Bantu Catholic Movement in Zaire* (Oxford: Clarendon Press, 1977).

7. Lamin Sanneh, *Translating the Message: The Missionary Impact on Culture*, rev.ed. (Maryknoll, NY: Orbis Books, 2009); Adrian Hastings, *The Construction of Nationhood: Ethnicity, Religion and Nationalism* (Cambridge: Cambridge University Press, 1997); J. D. Y. Peel, *Religious Encounter and the Making of the Yoruba* (Bloomington, IN: Indiana University Press, 2000); Andrew F. Walls, *The Missionary Movement in Christian History: Studies in the Transmission of Faith* (Maryknoll, NY:

Orbis Books, 1996) and *The Cross-Cultural Process in Christian History: Studies in the Transmission and Appropriation of Faith* (Maryknoll, NY: Orbis Books, 2002).

8. Acts 2:11 (KJV).

9. Jost Zetzsche, *The Bible in China: The History of the Union Version or the Culmination of Protestant Missionary Bible Translation in* China (Sankt Augustin: Monumenta Serica Institute, 1999).

10. Brian Stanley, *The History of the Baptist Missionary Society 1792–1992* (Edinburgh: T. & T. Clark, 1992), 126, 340. The Swedish Svenska Missionförbundet in fact published a complete Kikongo Bible in 1905, but it was in the Mazinga dialect rather than the Mbanza Kongo dialect spoken by the early followers of Simon Kimbangu.

11. For a South African example, see Deborah Gaitskell, "Hot Meetings and Hard Kraals: African Biblewomen in Transvaal Methodism, 1924–60," *Journal of Religion in Africa* 30, no. 3 (2000): 277–309.

12. Brian Stanley, "The Re-Shaping of Christian Tradition: Western Denominational Identity in a Non-Western Context," in *Unity and Diversity in the Church. Studies in Church History*, vol. 32, ed. R. N. Swanson (Oxford: Blackwell for the Ecclesiastical History Society, 1996), 323–4; idem, *The World Missionary Conference, Edinburgh 1910* (Grand Rapids. MI: Eerdmans, 2009), 324.

13. Luke 24:25 (KJV).

14. Adam Mohr, "Out of Zion and into Philadelphia and West Africa: Faith Tabernacle Congregation, 1897–1925," *Pneuma* 32, no. 1 (2010): 56–79.

15. Brian Stanley, "Edinburgh and World Christianity," *Studies in World Christianity* 17, no. 1 (2011): 84.

16. Bengt Sundkler, *Zulu Zion and Some Swazi Zionists* (London: Oxford University Press, 1976), 14, 68; David Maxwell, "Historicizing Christian Independency: The Southern African Pentecostal Movement," *Journal of African History* 40, no. 2 (1999): 243–64; idem, *African Gifts of the Spirit: Pentecostalism and the Rise of a Zimbabwean Transnational Religious Movement* (Oxford: James Currey, 2006).

17. Joel Cabrita, *Text and Authority in the South African Nazaretha Church* (New York: Cambridge University Press, 2014).

18. On Braide see Frieder Ludwig, "Elijah II: Radicalisation and Consolidation of the Garrick Braide Movement 1915–1918," *Journal of Religion in Africa* 23, no. 1 (1993): 296–317; G. O. M. Tasie, "The Prophetic Calling: Garrick Sokari Braide of Bakana (d. 1918)," in Elizabeth Isichei, ed., *Varieties of Christian Experience in Nigeria* (London: Macmillan, 1982), 99–115; idem, *Christian Missionary Enterprise in the Niger Delta, 1864–1918* (Leiden: E. J. Brill, 1978), 166–201; H. W. Turner, "Prophets and Politics: A Nigerian Test-Case," *Bulletin of the Society for African Church History* 2, no. 1 (1965): 97–118.

19. M. A. Kemmer, "The Truth about Garrick Braide Lately Designated Elijah II. How Garrick Was Introduced to the World Outside the Delta Pastorate Church or Extracts from the Delta Pastorate Chronicle for the Year 1909," reprinted in *Lagos Weekly Record*, 24 February 1917. Kemmer gives several examples of Braide's abilities in rain-making, prophetic judgment, and foretelling the future.

20. Ludwig, "Elijah II," 296. Tasie, "The Prophetic Calling," 109–11, dates this encounter in February 1916.

21. Ludwig, "Elijah II," 308–9.

22. Tasie, "The Prophetic Calling," 112; Turner, "Prophets and Politics," 105–14.

23. Ludwig, "Elijah II," 309–14.

24. On Harris see Gordon A. Haliburton, *The Prophet Harris: A Study of an African Prophet and his Mass-Movement in the Ivory Coast and the Gold Coast, 1913–1915* (London: Longman, 1971); David A. Shank, *Prophet Harris, the "Black Elijah" of West Africa* (Leiden: E. J. Brill, 1994).

25. Mark 9: 12–13.

26. Shank, *Prophet Harris*, 186.

27. For a contemporary account of Harris's baptismal ministry see J. E. Casely Hayford, *William Waddy Harris. The West African Reformer. The Man and His Message* (London: C. M. Phillips, 1915).

28. Shank, *Prophet Harris*, 212–16.

29. D. J. Mackay, "Simon Kimbangu and the B.M.S. Tradition," *Journal of Religion in Africa* 17, no. 2 (1987): 113–71.

30. P. H. J. Lerrigo, M.D., "The 'Prophet Movement' in Congo," *International Review of Missions* 11 (1922), 272.

31. For first-hand Protestant missionary accounts see W. B. Frame, "Prophets on the Lower Congo," *Congo Mission News* 37 (Oct. 1921): 6–9; Lerrigo, "The 'Prophet Movement' in Congo," 270–77. Catholic missionary reaction is summarized in Damaso Feci, *Vie cachée et vie publique de Simon Kimbangu selon la littérature coloniale et missionnaire Belge* (Brussels: Cahiers du Cedaf, 1972).

32. Feci, *Vie cachée*, 36, 81; Lerrigo, "The 'Prophet Movement'," 272; Efraim Andersson, *Messianic Popular Movements in the Lower Congo*, Studia Ethnographica Upsaliensia (Uppsala: Almqvist & Wiksells, 1958), 54–55.

33. Letter to G. R. R. Cameron, June 2, 1923, printed in Cecilia Irvine, "Birth of the Kimbanguist Movement in the Bas-Zaire," *Journal of Religion in Africa* 6, no. 1 (1974): 75.

34. Stanley, *History of the BMS*, 343.

35. Probably Mark 16:17–18 is meant: "And these signs will accompany those who believe: in my name they will cast out demons; they will speak in new tongues; they will pick up serpents, and if they drink any deadly thing, it will nor hurt them; they will lay their hands on the sick, and they will recover (RSV)."

36. The reference is to Luke 9: 49–50, where Jesus instructs the disciples not to forbid a man casting out demons in the name of Christ who "does not follow with us."

37. Letter to G. R. R. Cameron, June 2, 1923, in Irvine, "Birth of the Kimbanguist Movement," 74–75.

38. Joshua D. Broggi, *Diversity in the Structure of Christian Reasoning: Interpretation, Disagreement, and World Christianity* (Leiden, E. J. Brill, 2015), 56–87.

39. David Barrett, George Kurian, and Todd Johnson, *World Christian Encyclopedia: A Comparative Survey of Churches and Religions in the Modern World*, vol. 1 (Oxford: Oxford University Press, 2001), 216.

40. Raeburn Lange, *Island Ministers: Indigenous Leadership in Nineteenth Century Pacific Islands Christianity* (Christchurch and Canberra: Macmillan Brown Centre for Pacific Studies, Canterbury University, and Pandanus Books, 2005), 291.

41. On Keysser see Charles W. Forman, *The Island Churches of the South Pacific: Emergence in the Twentieth Century* (Maryknoll, NY, Orbis Books, 1982), 59–60;

NOTES TO PAGES 72-75 [379]

Timothy E. Yates, *Christian Mission in the Twentieth Century* (Cambridge: Cambridge University Press, 1994), 44–49, 53–56. In East Africa, Bruno Gutmann of the Leipzig Mission applied a similar *Volkskirche* approach in his work among the Chagga of what is now Tanzania.

42. David Hilliard, *God's Gentlemen: A History of the Melanesian Mission 1849–1942* (St. Lucia: University of Queensland Press, 1978), 275.

43. Ross Weymouth, "The Unevangelised Fields Mission in Papua, 1931–1981," *Journal of Pacific History* 23, no. 2 (1988): 175–90. The UFM was established in 1931 in a break-away from the Worldwide Evangelization Crusade (WEC), formed by C. T. Studd in 1913. In 1970 its Australian branch became the Asia Pacific Christian Mission.

44. Darrell L. Whiteman, ed., *An Introduction to Melanesian Cultures: A Handbook for Church Workers* (Goroka, Papua New Guinea: Melanesian Institute for Pastoral and Socio-Economic Service, 1984), 89.

45. James Moulton Roe, *A History of the British and Foreign Bible Society 1905–1954* (London: British and Foreign Bible Society, 1965), 125–26.

46. Ian Breward, *A History of the Churches in Australasia* (Oxford: Oxford University Press, 2001), 342; Philip Cass, "Fr Francis Mihalic and *Wantok* Niuspepa in Papua New Guinea," *Pacific Journalism Review* 17, no. 1 (2011): 211–26; Geoff P. Smith, *Growing up with Tok Pisin: Contact, Creolization and Change in Papua New Guinea's National Language* (London: Battlebridge Publications, 2002), 4–5.

47. Breward, *History of the Churches in Australasia*, 347–48.

48. Tony Swain and Garry Trompf, *The Religions of Oceania* (London and New York: Routledge, 1995), 140–3; G. W. Trompf, *Melanesian Religion*, rev. ed. (Cambridge: Cambridge University Press, 2010), 12–13, 84–5; idem, *Payback: The Logic of Retribution in Melanesian Religions* (Cambridge: Cambridge University Press, 2008), 56–77; idem, "Christianity in Melanesia," in *Introducing World Christianity*, ed. Charles E. Farhadian (Chichester: Wiley-Blackwell, 2012), 247.

49. Swain and Trompf, *Religions of Oceania*, 176–77; Trompf, *Melanesian Religion*, 129–32.

50. Alan R. Tippett, *Solomon Islands Christianity: A Study of Growth and Obstruction* (London: Lutterworth Press, 1967), 219–66; Garry Trompf, "Independent Churches in Melanesia," *Oceania* 54, no. 1 (1983): 51–54; "Eto, Silas (c. 1905-1984)," *Solomon Islands Historical Encyclopedia 1893–1978* (2013), http://www.solomonencyclopaedia.net/biogs/E000442b.htm (Accessed March 31, 2017). "Mama" paradoxically means "Father."

51. On Kopuria and the Melanesian Brotherhood see Hilliard, *God's Gentlemen*, 227–32; Brian Macdonald-Milne, *The True Way of Service: The Pacific Story of the Melanesian Brotherhood 1925-2000* (Leicester: Christians Aware and the Melanesian Brotherhood, 2003).

52. Macdonald-Milne, *True Way of Service*, 85.

53. Ibid., 53.

54. Tippett, *Solomon Islands Christianity*, 51.

55. Charles Wilde, "Acts of Faith: Muscular Christianity and Masculinity among the Gogodala of Papua New Guinea," *Oceania* 75, no. 1 (2004): 32–48; Trompf, "Christianity in Melanesia," 253.

56. Ross M. Weymouth, "The Gogodala Society: A Study of Adjustment Movements since 1966," *Oceania* 54, no. 4 (1984): 269–88.

57. Alison Dundon, "Dancing around Development: Crisis in Christian Country in Western Province, Papua New Guinea," *Oceania* 72, no. 3 (2002): 215–30.

58. Papua New Guinea became independent in 1975, the Solomon Islands in 1978, and Vanuatu in 1980.

59. For an early assessment of such movements see John Barr, "A Survey of Ecstatic Phenomena and 'Holy Spirit Movements' in Melanesia," *Oceania* 54, no. 2 (1983): 109–32.

60. As argued by Weymouth, "Gogodala Society."

61. Joel Robbins, *Becoming Sinners: Christianity and Moral Torment in a Papua New Guinea Society* (Berkeley: University of California Press, 2004). Robbins describes them (p. 1) as comprising approximately 390 people.

62. Ibid., 37–39, 122–25.

63. Bambi B. Schieffelin, "Tok Bokis, Tok Piksa: Translating Parables in Papua New Guinea," in *Social Lives in Language: Sociolinguistics and Multilingual Speech Communities. Celebrating the Work of Gillian Sankoff*, ed. Miriam Meyerhoff and Naomi Nagy (Amsterdam: John Benjamins B.V., 2008), 112, 116.

64. De Craemer, *The Jamaa and the Church*, 136–74.

65. Yates, *Christian Mission in the Twentieth Century*, 55, 214–19.

Chapter 4. Making War on the Saints

1. Steve Bruce, *God Is Dead: Secularization in the West* (Oxford: Blackwell, 2002), 30.

2. Steve Bruce, *Secularization: In Defence of an Unfashionable Theory* (Oxford: Oxford University Press, 2011), 201.

3. Bruce, *God Is Dead*, 3, 41–3.

4. Edward E. Roslof, *Red Priests: Renovationism, Russian Orthodoxy, and Revolution, 1905–1946* (Bloomington and Indianapolis: Indiana University Press, 2002), 12.

5. James F. McMillan, "Religion and Gender in Modern France: Some Reflections," in *Religion, Society and Politics in France since 1789*, ed. Frank Tallett and Nicholas Atkin, (London: The Hambledon Press, 1991), 56–59.

6. John Anderson, "Out of the Kitchen, out of the Temple: Religion, Atheism and Women in the Soviet Union," in *Religious Policy in the Soviet Union*, ed. Sabrina Petra Ramet (Cambridge: Cambridge University Press, 1992), 206–28.

7. Maurice Larkin, *Church and State in France after the Dreyfus Affair* (London: Macmillan, 1974), 103.

8. Nicholas Atkin, "The Politics of Legality: The Religious Orders in France, 1901–45," in Tallett and Atkin, *Religion, Society and Politics in France since 1789*, 152–53.

9. Larkin, *Church and State in France after the Dreyfus Affair*, 140–41, 152, 227, 236.

10. Ibid., 170–73, 180, 209–10.

11. Kevin Passmore, "Catholicism and Nationalism: The *Fédération républicaine, 1927–39*," in *Catholicism, Politics and Society in Twentieth-Century France*, ed. Kay Chadwick (Liverpool: Liverpool University Press, 2000), 56, 59.

12. Larkin, *Church and State in France after the Dreyfus Affair*, 212.

13. Atkin, "The Politics of Legality," 153.

14. Passmore, "Catholicism and Nationalism," 54.

15. Larkin, *Church and State in France after the Dreyfus Affair*, 213; Fernand Boulard (fondateur), *Matériaux pour l'histoire religieuse du people français, XIXe–XXe siècles*, 3 vols. (Paris: Éditions de l'École des Hautes Études en Sciences Sociales; Presses de la Fondation Nationale des Sciences Politiques; Éditions du Centre National de la Recherche Scientifique, 1982, 1987, 1992), II, 9–10.

16. James F. McMillan, "Catholicism and Nationalism in France: The Case of the Fédération Nationale Catholique, 1924–39," in *Catholicism in Britain and France since 1789*, ed. Frank Tallett and Nicholas Atkin (London: The Hambledon Press, 1996), 151–63.

17. Larkin, *Church and State in France after the Dreyfus Affair*, 219–22.

18. Nicholas Atkin, "The Politics of Legality: The Religious Orders in France, 1901–45," in Tallett and Atkin, *Religion, Society and Politics in France since 1789*, 159; and W. D. Halls, "Church and State: Prelates, Theologians and the Vichy Regime," in Tallett and Atkin, *Religion, Society and Politics in France since 1789*, 175.

19. Michael Kelly, "Catholics and Communism in Liberation France, 1944–47," in Tallett and Atkin, *Religion, Society and Politics in France since 1789*, 187–202.

20. Maurice Larkin, *Religion, Politics and Preferment in France since 1890: La Belle Époque and Its Legacy* (Cambridge: Cambridge University Press, 1995), 202.

21. Nicholas Beattie, "Yeast in the Dough? Catholic Schooling in France, 1981–95," in Chadwick, *Catholicism, Politics and Society in Twentieth-Century France*, 197–98.

22. Colin Roberts, "Secularisation and the (Re)formulation of French Catholic Identity," in Chadwick, *Catholicism, Politics and Society in Twentieth-Century France*, 267.

23. Gabriel Le Bras, "Statistique et histoire religieuse: pour un examen detaillé et pour une explication historique de l'état de Catholicisme dans les diverse regions de France," *Revue d'histoire de l'église de France* 17, no. 77 (1931): 425–49.

24. H. Godin and Y. Daniel, *La France pays de Mission?* (Paris: Les Éditions du Cerf, 1943).

25. Fernand Boulard, *Introduction to Religious Sociology: Pioneer Work in France*, English transl. (London: Darton, Longman, & Todd, 1960), 4–5, and map between pp. 36 and 37.

26. Ralph Gibson, *A Social History of French Catholicism 1789–1914* (London: Routledge, 1989), 173.

27. Ibid., 185–88.

28. Ruth Harris, *Lourdes: Body and Spirit in the Secular Age*, new ed. (Harmondsworth: Penguin Books, 2000), 10–12, 247, and *passim*.

29. Gibson, *A Social History of French Catholicism*, 266.

30. McMillan, "Religion and Gender in Modern France," 55–66.

31. Gibson, *A Social History of French Catholicism*, 183.

32. Boulard, *Matériaux pour l'histoire religieuse du people français, XIXe–XXe siècles*, vol. I, 69–70.

33. Larkin, *Church and State in France after the Dreyfus Affair*, 8; Gibson, *A Social History of French Catholicism*, 173.

34. Y.-M. Hilaire, "La sociologie religieuse du Catholicisme français au vingtième siècle," in Chadwick, *Catholicism, Politics and Society in Twentieth-Century France,* 252.

35. Larkin, *Church and State in France after the Dreyfus Affair,* 7, 225, 255 n. 5–6.

36. Larkin, *Religion, Politics and Preferment in France since 1890,* 199.

37. The decline has continued in the present century. By 2009 regular Sunday attendance was down to 4.5%, according to *Le Figaro,* December 12, 2009, at http:// www.lefigaro.fr/actualite-france/2009/12/29/01016-20091229ARTFIG00292-les -francais-boudent-la-messe-.php (Accessed May 19, 2017).

38. Hilaire, "La sociologie religieuse du Catholicisme français au vingtième siècle," 255–57.

39. For Spain and the Netherlands, see Hugh McLeod, *Religion and the People of Western Europe* (Oxford: Oxford University Press, 1981), 137–40, 143; for Quebec and Australia, see his *The Religious Crisis of the 1960s* (Oxford: Oxford University Press, 2007), 168–69. For Britain, see Callum G. Brown, *The Death of Christian Britain: Understanding Secularisation, 1800–2000* (Routledge: London, 2001).

40. Evelyn Diébolt, "Les femmes catholiques: entre église et société," in Chadwick, *Catholicism, Politics and Society in Twentieth-Century France,* 219–20, 240.

41. Gérard Cholvy and Yves-Marie Hilaire, *Histoire religieuse de la France contemporaine,* 3 vols. (Toulouse: Bibliothèque historique Privat, 1985–1988), III, 395–96.

42. McLeod, *The Religious Crisis of the 1960s,* 148.

43. Ibid., 236; Danièle Léger, *Le féminisme en France* (Paris: Éditions Le Sycomore, 1982).

44. Cholvy and Hilaire, *Histoire religieuse de la France contemporaine,* III, 390–2; see also Roberts, "Secularisation and the (Re)formulation of French Catholic Identity," 277.

45. Dimitry V. Pospielovsky, *The Russian Church under the Soviet Regime, 1917–1982,* 2 vols. (Crestwood, NY: St Vladimir's Seminary Press, 1984), vol. I, 31–32.

46. Gregory L. Freeze, "Subversive Atheism: Soviet Antireligious Campaigns and the Religious Revival in Ukraine in the 1920s," in *State Secularism and Lived Religion in Soviet Russia and the Ukraine,* ed. Catherine Wanner (Oxford: Oxford University Press; and Washington: Woodrow Wilson Center Press, 2012), 30, 51 n. 12.

47. See Roslof, *Red Priests.*

48. Pospielovsky, *The Russian Church under the Soviet Regime, 1917–1982,* vol. I, 38.

49. Ibid., vol. I, 93–9; Freeze, "Subversive Atheism," 31–32.

50. Freeze, "Subversive Atheism," 40–42, 48.

51. Ibid., 44.

52. Pospielovsky, *The Russian Church under the Soviet Regime, 1917–1982,* vol. I, 103; Daniel P. Peris, *Storming the Heavens: The Soviet League of the Militant Godless* (Ithaca, NY: Cornell University Press, 1998), 2.

53. Walter Sawatsky, *Soviet Evangelicals since World War II* (Kitchener, ON: Herald Press, 1981), 47; Peris, *Storming the Heavens,* 89–90.

54. Anna Dickinson, "Quantifying Religious Oppression: Russian Orthodox Church Closures and Repression of Priests 1917–41," *Religion, State & Society* 28, no. 4 (2000): 329.

55. Ibid., 329–30. Much lower figures can be found in other sources, e.g., Nathaniel Davis, *A Long Walk to Church: A Contemporary History of Russian Orthodoxy* (Boulder, CO: Westview Press, 1995), 13, estimates that only 200–300 churches remained open in the entire USSR in 1939.

56. Davis, *A Long Walk to Church*, 12.

57. Tatiana A. Chumachenko, *Church and State in Soviet Russia: Russian Orthodoxy from World War II to the Khruschev Years*, edited and translated by Edward E. Roslof (New York: M. E. Sharpe, 2002), 85.

58. Karpov's full account of this meeting is printed in Felix Corley, ed., *Religion in the Soviet Union: An Archival Reader* (Basingstoke and London: Macmillan, 1996), 139–47.

59. The indispensable source here is Chumachenko, *Church and State in Soviet Russia*.

60. Ibid., 50–1, 71.

61. Ibid., 67 and 59 (Table 1.1). It is not easy to reconcile these statistics with the much lower figures cited above (p. 382, n. 55) for numbers of Orthodox churches that remained open in Russia itself in 1940.

62. Ibid, 187–88. This paragraph summarizes chapters 2 and 3 of Chumachenko's book.

63. William C. Fletcher, *Religion and Soviet Foreign Policy 1945–1970* (London: Oxford University Press for the Royal Institute of International Affairs, 1973), 16–19.

64. W. A. Visser 't Hooft, *Memoirs* (London: SCM Press, 1973), 275.

65. Corley, ed., *Religion in the Soviet Union*, 361; see also 359–82 for numerous other examples.

66. Christopher Andrew and Vasili Mitrokhin, *The Sword and the Shield: The Mitrokhin Archive and the Secret History of the KGB* (New York: Basic Books, 2001), 487–88, 491–92. On the Soviet manipulation of the WCC through the Orthodox hierarchy see also Gerhard Besier, Armin Boyens, and Gerhard Lindemann, *Nationaler Protestantismus und Ökumenische Bewegung: Kirchliches Handeln im Kalten Kreig (1945–1990)* (Berlin: Duncker & Humblot, 1999), passim, and W. R. Ward, "Peace, Peace and Rumours of War," *Journal of Ecclesiastical History* 51, no. 4 (2000): 767–70.

67. Andrew and Mitrokhin, *The Sword and the Shield*, 490–91.

68. Michael Bourdeaux, "The Russian Church, Religious Liberty and the World Council of Churches," *Religion in Communist Lands* 13, no. 1 (1985): 4–27.

69. John Anderson, *Religion, State and Politics in the Soviet Union and Successor States* (Cambridge: Cambridge University Press, 1994), 83–87; Dimitry V. Pospielovsky, *Soviet Studies on the Church and the Believer's Response to Atheism.* Volume 3 *of A History of Soviet Atheism in Theory and Practice, and the Believer* (Basingstoke: Macmillan, 1988), 202–4.

70. The Evangelical Christians originated in the 1870s as a result of the evangelistic work in the St. Petersburg region of the English evangelical peer, Lord Radstock. They joined the Russian Baptists in 1903 to form the Union of Evangelical Christians-Baptists, but in 1909 a substantial number of the Evangelical Christians formed their own All-Russian Union of Evangelical Christians under the leadership of Ivan S. Prokhanov. Various abortive attempts were made to unite the two groups until unity was finally achieved under state pressure in 1944.

71. Sawatsky, *Soviet Evangelicals*, 37, 39.

72. Alexander Kashirin, "Protestant Minorities in the Soviet Ukraine, 1945–1991" (PhD diss., University of Oregon, 2010), 10, 35.

73. The fullest account of the 1944 union is in Sawatsky, *Soviet Evangelicals*, 78–99; see also Kashirin, "Protestant Minorities in the Soviet Ukraine," 102–8.

74. Minority Rights Group, *Religious Minorities in the Soviet Union, Report No. 1, 1984* (London: MRG, 1984), 20–22, 24.

75. For a detailed study of how CARC operated as "an ombudsman for believers" in the Ukraine, see Kashirin, "Protestant Minorities in the Soviet Ukraine," especially 82–94.

76. Ibid., 110–11.

77. Ibid., 115–22.

78. Arnold T. Ohrn, ed., *Baptist World Alliance Golden Jubilee Congress (Ninth World Congress) London, England 16th–22nd July, 1955: Official Report* (London: Carey Kingsgate Press, n.d. [1955]), 261.

79. Sawatsky, *Soviet Evangelicals*, 201, 364–65. Stoian had studied at Bristol Baptist College from 1957 to 1959.

80. Ibid., 368.

81. An exhaustive account of the Baptist schism that resulted in the formation of the CECB is found in Kashirin, "Protestant Minorities in the Soviet Ukraine," 590–748.

82. For a retrospective reflection by a British Baptist leader on the attempt to maintain relationships with both the AUCECB and the CECB see David S. Russell, "Church/State Relations in the Soviet Union: Recollections and Reflections on the 'Cold War' Years," *Baptist Quarterly* 36, no. 1 (1995): 21–28.

83. Walter Sawatsky, "Protestantism in the USSR," in Ramet, *Religious Policy in the Soviet Union*, 342–43.

84. Sabrina Petra Ramet, "Epilogue: After the Collapse," in Ramet, *Religious Policy in the Soviet Union*, 352; Minority Rights Group, *Religious Minorities in the Soviet Union*, 24.

85. Viktor Yelensky, "The Revival before the Revival: Popular and Institutionalized Religion in Ukraine on the Eve of the Collapse of Communism," in Wanner, *State Secularism and Lived Religion in Soviet Russia and the Ukraine*, 302–30.

86. Dimitry V. Pospielovsky, *Soviet Studies on the Church and the Believer's Response to Atheism*. Volume 3 *of A History of Soviet Atheism in Theory and Practice, and the Believer* (Basingstoke: Macmillan Press, 1985), 197.

Chapter 5. Contrasting Patterns of Belonging and Believing

1. Hugh McLeod, *Secularisation in Western Europe, 1848–1914* (Basingstoke: Macmillan, 2000), 285.

2. This chapter interprets the term "Scandinavia" in a broad geographical sense, to include Finland and Iceland.

3. Grace Davie, *Religion in Britain since 1945: Believing without Belonging* (Oxford: Blackwell, 1994).

4. Grace Davie, *Religion in Britain: A Persistent Paradox*, 2nd ed. (Chichester: Wiley-Blackwell, 2015), xi, 6.

5. Grace Davie, *Europe: The Exceptional Case: Parameters of Faith in the Modern World* (London: Darton, Longman & Todd, 2002); idem, "Religion, Territory, and Choice: Contrasting Configurations, 1970–2015," in *Secularization and Religious Innovation in the North Atlantic World*, ed. David Hempton and Hugh McLeod (Oxford: Oxford University Press, 2017), 323.

6. Grace Davie, *Religion in Modern Europe: A Memory Mutates* (Oxford: Oxford University Press, 2000), 17.

7. The French sociologist of religion, Danièle Hervieu-Léger, has argued that the phrase "belonging without believing" should in fact be applied to European religion as a whole: "Religion und Sozialer Zusammenhalt in Europa," *Transit: Europäische Revue* 26 (2004): 101–19.

8. Rodney Stark and Roger Finke, *Acts of Faith: Exploring the Human Side of Religion* (Berkeley: University of California Press, 2000). For the debate between secularization theorists and "supply-siders" see Steve Bruce, ed., *Religion and Modernization: Sociologists and Historians Debate the Secularization Thesis* (Oxford: Clarendon Press, 1992).

9. David Martin, *A General Theory of Secularization* (Oxford: Blackwell, 1978).

10. David Martin, *On Secularization: Towards a Revised General Theory* (Aldershot: Ashgate, 2005), 3.

11. José Casanova, "Rethinking Secularization: A Global Comparative Perspective," *The Hedgehog Review* 8, nos. 1–2 (Spring–Summer 2006): 7–22.

12. David Goodhew, "Growth and Decline in South Africa's Churches, 1960–1991," *Journal of Religion in Africa* 30, no. 3 (2000): 344–69.

13. Sebastian C. H. and Kirsteen Kim, *A History of Korean Christianity* (Cambridge: Cambridge University Press, 2015), 274–75, 282–87; Sung-Ho Kim, "Rapid Modernisation and the Future of Korean Christianity," *Religion* 32, no. 1 (2002): 27–37.

14. Ian Breward, *A History of the Churches in Australasia* (Oxford: Oxford University Press, 2001), 411–14.

15. Ibid., 361.

16. Joy L. K. Pachau, *Being Mizo: Identity and Belonging in Northeast India* (New Delhi: Oxford University Press, 2014), 136–37, 182 n. 2; see also Frederick S. Downs, *Christianity in North-East India: Historical Perspectives* (New Delhi: ISPCK, 1983), 151–55.

17. McLeod, *Secularisation in Western Europe*.

18. Hempton and McLeod, eds. *Secularization and Religious Innovation in the North Atlantic World*, 187–88, 306, 335, 343.

19. Bruce, ed., *Religion and Modernization*.

20. World Values Survey, 1981–2001, cited in Pippa Norris and Ronald Ingelhart, *Sacred and Secular: Religion and Politics Worldwide* (Cambridge: Cambridge University Press, 2004), 74.

21. Cited in Davie, *Europe: The Exceptional Case*, 6. Norway was not included.

22. For example, Norris and Ingelhart also reproduce on p. 72 a table from the Mannheim Eurobarometer Trend File showing weekly church attendance in the European Union between 1970 and 1998 that indicates a much lower figure for Britain, though roughly comparable data for Scandinavia. They offer no explanation of the discrepancies between the two sets of data.

23. Martin Schwartz Lausten, *A Church History of Denmark*, translated by Frederick H. Cryer (Aldershot: Ashgate, 2002), 314.

24. Inger Furseth, "Nordic Countries," in *Encyclopedia of Global Religion*, eds. Mark Juergensmeyer and Wade Clark Roof (Los Angeles: SAGE Reference, 2012), 931.

25. The phrase "belonging without believing" has been applied to Scandinavia by Ole Riis, "Patterns of Secularization in Scandinavia," in *Scandinavian Values: Religion and Morality in the Nordic Countries*, ed. Thorleif Pettersson and Ole Riis (Uppsala: ACTA Universitatis Upsaliensis, 1994), 99.

26. Davie, *Europe: The Exceptional Case*, 7; Norris and Ingelhart, *Sacred and Secular*, 90.

27. Richard F. Tomasson, "How Sweden Became so Secular," *Scandinavian Studies* 74, no. 1 (2002): 62, 68.

28. Furseth, "Nordic Countries," 931.

29. Isabella Kasselstrand, "'Tell the Minister not to Talk about God': A Comparative Study of Secularisation in Protestant Europe" (PhD thesis, University of Edinburgh, 2013), 136. Kasselstrand has summarized her argument in "Nonbelievers in the Church: A Study of Cultural Religion in Sweden," *Sociology of Religion* 76, no. 3 (2015): 275–94.

30. Phil Zuckerman, *Society without God: What the Least Religious Nations Can Tell Us about Contentment* (New York: New York University Press, 2008), 150–55.

31. Steve Bruce, "The Supply-Side Model of Religion: The Nordic and Baltic States," *Journal for the Scientific Study of Religion* 39, no. 1 (2000): 35.

32. Martin, *A General Theory of Secularization*, 65.

33. Kasselstrand, "'Tell the Minister not to Talk about God'," 32.

34. Lausten, *Church History of Denmark*, 263; Nicholas Hope, *German and Scandinavian Protestantism, 1700–1918* (Oxford: Clarendon Press, 1999), 536.

35. Neil Kent, *The Soul of the North: A Social, Architectural and Cultural History of the Nordic Countries, 1700–1940* (London: Reaktion Books, 2000), 43; Leslie Stannard Hunter, ed., *Scandinavian Churches: A Picture of the Development and Life of the Churches of Denmark, Finland, Iceland, Norway and Sweden* (London: Faber & Faber, 1965), 29.

36. Zuckerman, *Society without God*, 120–27; see also Kasselstrand, "'Tell the Minister Not to Talk about God'," 171; Martin, *On Secularization*, 125.

37. Kasselstrand, "'Tell the Minister not to Talk about God'," 38; Dag Thorkildsen, "Scandinavia: Lutheranism and National Identity," in *World Christianities, c. 1815–c. 1914: The Cambridge History of Christianity*, vol. 8, ed. Sheridan Gilley and Brian Stanley (Cambridge: Cambridge University Press, 2006), 350–51; Jonas Alwall, "Religious Liberty in Sweden: An Overview," *Journal of Church and State* 42, no. 1 (2000): 147–71.

38. Kent, *The Soul of the North*, 370.

39. Furseth, "Nordic Countries," 930.

40. Göran Gustafsson, "Sweden: A Folk Church under Political Influence," *Studia Theologica—Nordic Journal of Theology* 44, no. 1 (1990): 3–16; Kasselstrand, "'Tell the Minister not to Talk about God'," 37–38.

41. Maciej Zaremba, November 28, 1999, cited in Tomasson, "How Sweden Became so Secular," 80; see also Kasselstrand, "'Tell the Minister not to Talk about God'," 38–39.

42. Lausten, *Church History of Denmark*, 283–85.

43. Martin, *A General Theory of Secularization*, 71.

44. Peter Berger, Grace Davie and Effie Fokas, *Religious America, Secular Europe? A Theme and Variations* (Aldershot: Ashgate, 2008), 26.

45. Kasselstrand, "'Tell the Minister not to Talk about God'," 34–35.

46. Ibid., 220.

47. Robert Wuthnow, *The Restructuring of American Religion: Society and Faith since World War II* (Princeton, NJ: Princeton University Press, 1988), 159; Steve Bruce, *God Is Dead: Secularization in the West* (Oxford: Blackwell, 2002), 205.

48. Wuthnow, *The Restructuring of American Religion*, 36–38.

49. James Hennesey, S.J., *American Catholics: A History of the Roman Catholic Community in the United States* (New York: Oxford University Press, 1981), 283, 286.

50. Grant Wacker, *America's Pastor: Billy Graham and the Shaping of a Nation* (Cambridge, MA: The Belknap Press of Harvard University Press, 2014), 23.

51. Wuthnow, *The Restructuring of American Religion*, 159.

52. Frank Hobbs and Nicole Stoops, *Demographic Trends in the Twentieth Century: Census 2000 Special Reports*, U.S. Census Bureau, Census 2000 Special Reports, Series CENSR-4 (Washington, DC: US Government Printing Office, 2002), 13 https://www.census.gov/prod/2002pubs/censr-4.pdf (Accessed May 26, 2017).

53. Wuthnow, *The Restructuring of American Religion*, 161–62.

54. Hennesey, *American Catholics*, 329.

55. Ibid., 329.

56. Tobin Grant, "Mainline Decline? Depends on What You are Counting," Religion News Service, June 2, 2015, http://tobingrant.religionnews.com/2015/06/02 /mainline-decline-depends-on-what-youre-counting/ (Accessed May 26, 2017); see also Edwin S. Gaustad and Philip L. Barlow, *New Historical Atlas of Religion in America* (New York: Oxford University Press, 2001), Figures C.16 (p. 375), and C.21 (p. 388). The United Church of Christ was formed in 1957 by a merger of the Congregational Church and the Evangelical and Reformed (German) Church. Gaustad and Barlow were interested primarily in the geographical patterns of historic American denominational Christianity, and their Atlas is of limited value in charting the switching of church affiliation to other groups in the late twentieth century.

57. Roger Finke, "An Unsecular America," in Bruce, ed., *Religion and Modernization*, 153.

58. Hugh McLeod, "'Religious America, Secular Europe': Are They Really So Different?" In Hempton and McLeod, *Secularization and Religious Innovation in the North Atlantic World*, 350.

59. Gaustad and Barlow, *New Historical Atlas of Religion in America*, Figure 4.16, p. 349.

60. Wuthnow, *The Restructuring of American Religion*, 192.

61. Ibid., 177, 192; Joel Carpenter, *Revive Us Again: The Reawakening of American Fundamentalism* (New York: Oxford University Press, 1997), 158–59.

62. Grant Wacker, *Heaven Below: Early Pentecostals and American Culture* (Cambridge, MA: Harvard University Press, 2001), 271–72.

63. Lawrence N. Jones, "The Black Churches: A New Agenda," in *African American Religious History: A Documentary Witness*, ed. Milton C. Sernett, 2nd ed. (Durham, NC: Duke University Press, 1999), 585.

64. Bryan R. Wilson, *Religion in Secular Society: A Sociological Comment* (London: C. A. Watts & Co., 1966), 114; see also David Hempton, "Organizing Concepts and 'Small Differences' in the Comparative Secularization of Western Europe and the United States," in Hempton and McLeod, *Secularization and Religious Innovation in the North Atlantic World*, 363.

65. Bruce, *God Is Dead*, 207–9.

66. R. Laurence Moore, *Selling God: American Religion in the Marketplace of Culture* (New York: Oxford University Press, 1994).

67. Wade Clark Roof, *Spiritual Marketplace: Baby Boomers and the Remaking of American Religion* (Princeton, NJ: Princeton University Press, 1999), 183.

68. John G. Turner, *Bill Bright and Campus Crusade for Christ: The Renewal of Evangelicalism in Postwar America* (Chapel Hill, NC: University of North Carolina Press, 2008), 98–103.

69. Carpenter, *Revive Us Again*, 25, 216.

70. This paragraph is indebted to the research of my Edinburgh PhD student, Amber Thomas.

71. Colleen McDannell, *Material Christianity: Religion and Popular Culture in America* (New Haven, CT: Yale University Press, 1995), chapter 8; Moore, *Selling God*, 255.

72. Hempton, "Organizing Concepts and 'Small Differences' in the Comparative Secularization of Western Europe and the United States," in Hempton and McLeod, *Secularization and Religious Innovation in the North Atlantic World*, 360–61.

73. McDannell, *Material Christianity*, 229–46.

74. Moore, *Selling God*, 275.

75. Ibid., 275–76.

76. Patrick Allitt, *Catholic Intellectuals and Conservative Politics in America, 1950–1985* (Ithaca, NY: Cornell University Press, 1993), 270–88.

77. Barry Hankins, *Francis Schaeffer and the Shaping of Evangelical America* (Grand Rapids, MI: Eerdmans, 2008); Brian Stanley, *The Global Diffusion of Evangelicalism: The Age of Billy Graham and John Stott* (Downers Grove, IL: Inter-Varsity Press, 2013), 133–39.

78. Richard John Neuhaus, *The Naked Public Square: Religion and Democracy in America* (Grand Rapids, MI: Eerdmans, 1984).

79. "Evangelicals and Catholics Together: The Christian Mission in the Third Millennium." *First Things* (May 1994), http://www.firstthings.com/article/1994/05/evangelicals—catholics-together-the-christian-mission-in-the-third-millennium-2 (Accessed April 20, 2017).

80. Molly Worthen, *Apostles of Reason: The Crisis of Authority in American Evangelicalism* (New York: Oxford University Press, 2014), 244–5. For Notre Dame's Marian devotion and links to Lourdes see McDannell, *Material Christianity*, chapter 5.

81. Robert E. Webber, *Evangelicals on the Canterbury Trail: Why Evangelicals Are Attracted to the Liturgical Church* (Waco, TX: Word Books, 1985), 10–17; Worthen, *Apostles of Reason*, 161–6; Stanley, *Global Diffusion*, 239–43; D. Oliver Herbel, *Turning to Tradition: Converts and the Making of an American Orthodox Church* (New York: Oxford University Press, 2014), 103–45.

82. Worthen, *Apostles of Reason*, passim; Stanley, *Global Diffusion*, 243–47.

83. James Davison Hunter, *To Change the World: The Irony, Tragedy and Possibility of Christianity in the Late Modern World* (New York: Oxford University Press, 2010).

Chapter 6. Is Christ Divided?

1. Notably Horton Davies, *Worship and Theology in England*, vol. 5: *The Ecumenical Century 1900–1965* (Princeton, NJ: Princeton University Press, 1965).

2. For a full account of the World Missionary Conference see my *The World Missionary Conference, Edinburgh 1910* (Grand Rapids, MI, and Cambridge: Wm. B. Eerdmans, 2009).

3. For Bishop Bonomelli see J. M. Delaney, "From Cremona to Edinburgh: Bishop Bonomelli and the World Missionary Conference of 1910," *Ecumenical Review* 52, no. 3 (2000): 418–31 [quotation at p. 420].

4. Stanley, *World Missionary Conference*, 49.

5. W. R. Hogg, "Edinburgh, 1910—Ecumenical Keystone," *Religion and Life* 29, no. 3 (1960): 349.

6. J. J. Willis and others, *Towards a United Church 1913–1947* (London: Edinburgh House Press, 1947), 28–32.

7. J. H. Shakespeare, *The Churches at the Crossroads: A Study in Church Unity* (London: Williams and Norgate, 1918).

8. J. G. Lockhart, *Cosmo Gordon Lang* (London: Hodder & Stoughton, 1949), 268; G. K. A. Bell, *Randall Davidson*, 2nd ed. (London: Oxford University Press, 1938), 1012.

9. G. K. A. Bell, ed., *Documents on Christian Unity: A Selection from the First and Second Series 1920–30* (London: Oxford University Press, 1920), 3–4. The best account of the origins of the Lambeth Appeal is David M. Thompson, "Church Unity in Twentieth-Century England: Pleasing Dream or Common Calling?" in *Unity and Diversity in the Church. Studies in Church History*, vol. 32, ed. R. N. Swanson (Oxford: Blackwell for the Ecclesiastical History Society, 1996), 511–20.

10. Bell, ed., *Documents on Christian Unity 1920–30*, 46. For the origins of this distinction between the fact and theory of episcopacy, see p. 135.

11. For a helpful summary of the Malines conversations see Adrian Hastings, *A History of English Christianity 1920–1985* (London: Collins, 1986), 208–12.

12. Bell, ed., *Documents on Christian Unity 1920–30*, 36–39.

13. Figures compiled from *Addresses and Records: International Missionary Council Meeting at Tambaram, Madras, December 12th to 29th, 1938* (London: Oxford University Press, 1939), 181–202. The figure for the younger churches is estimated, as it is not always possible to determine with certainty the nationality of a particular name.

14. F. A. Iremonger, *William Temple Archbishop of Canterbury: His Life and Letters* (London: Oxford University Press, 1948), 387.

15. W. A. Visser 't Hooft, *Memoirs* (London: SCM Press, 1973), 311–12.

16. Ruth Rouse and Stephen Charles Neill, eds., *A History of the Ecumenical Movement 1517–1948* (London: SPCK, 1954), 498. The Church of Christ in China (1927) oddly does not feature on Rouse and Neill's list, presumably because they regarded it as "a federation rather than as a church" (see pp. 459–60).

17. Gordon Hewitt, *The Problems of Success: A History of the Church Missionary Society 1910–1942*, 2 vols. (London: SCM Press, 1971, 1977), II, 168–69.

18. However, Tamil Anglicans in the Jaffna diocese had in 1947 voted to affiliate to the CSI, thus dividing the Anglican community in Sri Lanka.

19. *Ecumenical Review* 36, no. 4 (October 1984): 409–10.

20. *Anglican-Methodist Unity: Report of the Anglican-Methodist Unity Commission. Part 2 The Scheme* (London: SPCK and Epworth Press, 1968), 29, 127.

21. Owen Chadwick, *Michael Ramsey: A Life* (Oxford: Oxford University Press, 1991), 338–41.

22. See Gavin White, *How the Churches Got to Be the Way They Are* (London: SCM Press, 1990), 104.

23. In the Netherlands in 2004 the Dutch Reformed Church, the Reformed Churches, and the Evangelical Lutheran Church united to form the Protestant Church in the Netherlands.

24. G. S. Eddy, "A National Church for India," *The Harvest Field* 31 (1911): 213–19. The George Sherwood Eddy papers in the Special Collections of Yale Divinity School Library (RG32-6-102) contain an offprint of this article annotated by Eddy in later life with a comment that traces the church union movement in India back to the Edinburgh conference. For Eddy's vision of a revived primitive and constitutional episcopate see Bengt Sundkler, *Church of South India: The Movement towards Union 1900–1947*, rev. ed. (London: Lutterworth Press, 1965), 66–67; and Brian Stanley, "The Reshaping of Christian Tradition: Western Denominational Identity in a Non-Western Context," in Swanson, *Unity and Diversity in the Church*, 411.

25. Sundkler, *Church of South India*, 62–67, 364. Sundkler notes that there is some doubt over the date of the Madras meeting, but late 1910 seems the most likely.

26. *Records of the South India United Church* (1908), 48–51.

27. Sundkler, *Church of South India*, 102; cf. W. R. Huntington, *The Peace of the Church* (London: James Nisbet, 1891), 204–6, cited in David M. Thompson, "Church Unity in Twentieth-Century England," in Swanson, *Unity and Diversity in the Church*, 524.

28. Sundkler, *Church of South India*, 128–30. The Mar Thoma Church was formed in 1889 by a group within the Jacobite Church who had links with the CMS and wished to combine Syrian Orthodox tradition with evangelical faith.

29. Special Collections, Yale Divinity School Library, George Sherwood Eddy Papers, RG 32-3-66, report letter dated August 15, 1919.

30. K. T. Paul, "The Lambeth Advance and the Viewpoint of India," "An Indian Form of Episcopacy," and "Indianise the Church?" *The Young Men of India* 32 (1921): 313–21, 381–89, 548–53.

31. Stanley, "The Reshaping of Christian Tradition," 411.

32. Paul, "The Lambeth Advance and the Viewpoint of India," 317. Sundkler, *Church of South India*, 133, oddly misreads Paul's view as being that episcopacy was so much in accordance with the genius of India that it would be wise to opt for democratic polity instead.

33. Sundkler, *Church of South India*, 290.

34. Ibid., 205–6.

35. Cited in ibid., 143.

36. G. V. Job and others, *Rethinking Christianity in India* (Madras: A. N. Sudarisanam, n.d. [1938]), 138.

37. Ibid., 196.

38. Ibid., 188. The Lutheran churches did not in fact join the CSI.

39. Sundkler, *Church of South India*, 326–28.

40. For a detailed narrative see ibid., 315–22.

41. H. P. Thompson, *Into All Lands: The History of the Society for the Propagation of the Gospel in Foreign Parts, 1701–1950* (London: SPCK, 1951), 595–98.

42. *American Board of Commissioners for Foreign Missions Report* (1947), 21.

43. David B. Barrett, George T. Kurian, Todd M. Johnson, eds., *World Christian Encyclopaedia*, 2nd ed. (New York: Oxford University Press, 2001), 369, 371, gives adult membership of the CSI in 1995 as 1,471,000 and total adult membership of all churches in India in 1995 as 32,643,646.

44. The North India plan also embraced the new nation of Pakistan created by the partition of India in 1947, but on the understanding that two autonomous united churches would be formed, sharing a common constitution.

45. For a full account of the negotiations from the point of view of the Baptist community, see Brian Stanley, *The History of the Baptist Missionary Society 1792–1992* (Edinburgh: T. & T. Clark, 1992), 412–19.

46. The nation of Bangladesh (formerly East Pakistan) was formed in 1971.

47. Roger E. Hedlund, ed., *The Oxford Encyclopaedia of South Asian Christianity*, 2 vols. (New Delhi: Oxford University Press, 2012), II, 428.

48. Kenneth S. Latourette, *A History of Christian Missions in China* (New York: Macmillan, 1929), 667–9.

49. Marina Xiaojing Wang, "The Church Unity Movement in Early Twentieth-Century China: Cheng Jingyi and the Church of Christ in China" (PhD thesis, University of Edinburgh, 2012), 82.

50. Wang, "Church Unity Movement," 88–89. The Bible Training Institute in Glasgow survived into the twenty-first century as the International Christian College, which closed in 2015.

51. Stanley, *World Missionary Conference*, 108.

52. F. Rawlinson and others, eds., *The Chinese Church as Revealed in the National Christian Conference Held in Shanghai, Tuesday, May 2, to Thursday, May 11, 1922* (Shanghai: The Oriental Press, n.d.), 5–12, 524.

53. Zhonghua ji du jiao hui, *Let Us Unite! The Church of Christ in China and Church Unity in China* (Peiping: General Assembly, Church of Christ in China, n.d [1935]), 19–21.

54. Ryan Dunch, *Fuzhou Protestants and the Making of a Modern China* (New Haven, CT: Yale University Press, 2001), 115.

55. Daniel H. Bays, *A New History of Christianity in China* (Chichester: Wiley-Blackwell, 2012), 112.

56. Kevin Xiyi Yao, *The Fundamentalist Movement among Protestant Missionaries in China, 1920–1937* (Lanham, MD: University Press of America, 2003), 63.

57. Ibid., 215–16. The League had c. 75,000 members by 1932; the communicant membership of the Church of Christ in China in 1933 was c. 130,000 (*Let us Unite!*, 9).

58. Daniel H. Bays, "The Growth of Independent Christianity in China, 1900–1937," in *Christianity in China from the Eighteenth Century to the Present,* ed. Daniel H. Bays (Stanford: Stanford University Press, 1996), 310.

59. For a powerful and controversial missionary statement of this diagnosis see David M. Paton, *Christian Missions and the Judgment of God* (London: SCM Press, 1953).

60. SOAS, CIM archives, Minutes of British Council, December 6, 1951.

61. Wang, "Church Unity Movement," 241–43, 270–71, 283.

62. For an interpretation in support of their view see Philip Wickeri, *Seeking the Common Ground: Protestant Christianity, the Three-Self Movement, and China's United Front* (Maryknoll, NY: Orbis Books, 1988), 127–33.

63. The original title (from 1951–4) was "Three-Self Reform Movement."

64. See Daniel H. Bays, "Foreign Missions and Indigenous Protestant Leaders in China, 1920–1955: Identity and Loyalty in an Age of Powerful Nationalism," in *Missions, Nationalism, and the End of Empire,* ed. Brian Stanley, 144–64 (Grand Rapids, MI: Wm. B. Eerdmans, 2003); idem, *New History of Christianity in China,* 138–40, 166–68.

65. Lian Xi, *Redeemed by Fire: The Rise of Popular Christianity in Modern China* (New Haven, CT: Yale University Press, 2010), 250, estimates that by 2010 the total Protestant community numbered approximately 50 million, whereas official figures for TSPM membership in 2006 were only 16 million.

66. Paul P. Mariani, *Church Militant: Bishop Kung and Catholic Resistance in Communist Shanghai* (Cambridge, MA: Harvard University Press, 2011), 16.

67. Ibid., 61–62, 77.

68. Ibid., 87–91, 107.

69. Ibid., 110.

70. Ibid., 138.

71. Ibid., 200.

72. Philip Wickeri, *Reconstructing Christianity in China: K. H. Ting and the Chinese Church* (Maryknoll, NY: Orbis Books, 2007), 223–25.

73. Mariani, *Church Militant,* 214–15.

74. See Lian Xi, *Redeemed by Fire.*

75. James T. Myers, *Enemies without Guns: The Catholic Church in the People's Republic of China* (New York: Paragon House, 1991), 202.

76. Bays, *New History of Christianity in China,* 192–3; Mariani, *Church Militant,* 220–3.

77. Wickeri, *Reconstructing Christianity in China,* 355–6.

78. John Kent, *The Unacceptable Face: The Modern Church in the Eyes of the Historian* (London: SCM Press, 1987), 203.

79. Korean Ministry of Culture, Sports and Tourism, *The Present Condition of Religions in Korea* (Seoul: 2011), 38–47. I owe this reference to Dr Kyo Seong-Ahn of the Presbyterian University and Theological Seminary, Seoul. For a discussion of the wider issue of Presbyterian disunity in Korea, see Dr Ahn's thesis: K. S. Ahn, "Mission in Unity: An Investigation into the Question of Unity as it has Arisen in the Presbyterian Church of Korea and its World Mission" (PhD thesis, University of Cambridge, 2008).

Chapter 7. The Voice of Your Brother's Blood

1. Samantha Power, *"A Problem from Hell": America and the Age of Genocide* (New York: Basic Books, 2002), 4–14.

2. M. Zimmermann, *Wilhelm Marr: The Patriarch of Anti-Semitism* (New York: Oxford University Press, 1986), 89–92.

3. *Oxford English Dictionary*, 2nd ed. (Oxford, 1989), vol. XIII, 74.

4. Magnus Hirschfeld, *Racism* (1938), translated and edited by Eden and Cedar Paul, new ed. (Port Washington, NY: Kennikat Press, 1973).

5. Raphael Lemkin, *Axis Rule in Occupied Europe. Laws of Occupation. Analysis of Government. Proposals for Redress* (Washington, DC: Carnegie Endowment for International Peace, 1944), xi and 79, cited in John Cooper, *Raphael Lemkin and the Struggle for the Genocide Convention* (Basingstoke: Palgrave Macmillan, 2008), 56–57.

6. Donna-Lee Frieze, ed., *Totally Unofficial: The Autobiography of Raphael Lemkin* (New Haven, CT: Yale University Press, 2013).

7. For the ambiguity of Hume's and Kames's views on polygenesis see Colin Kidd, *The Forging of Races: Race and Scripture in the Protestant Atlantic World, 1600–2000* (Cambridge: Cambridge University Press, 2006), 93–100.

8. See Bruce Baum, *The Rise and Fall of the Caucasian Race: A Political History of Racial Identity* (New York: New York University Press, 2006).

9. J. J. Carney, *Rwanda before the Genocide: Catholic Politics and Ethnic Discourse in the Late Colonial Era* (New York: Oxford University Press, 2014), 53, 192.

10. Nicholas Godfrey, "Understanding Genocide: The Experience of Anglicans in Rwanda, c. 1921–2008" (PhD thesis, University of Cambridge, 2009), 3–7.

11. Ernest Renan, *The Life of Jesus* (English translation, London: Trübner & Company, 1864), 74. Susannah Heschel, *The Aryan Jesus: Christian Theologians and the Bible in Nazi Germany* (Princeton, NJ: Princeton University Press, 2008), 33–38; Shawn Kelley, *Racializing Jesus: Race, Ideology and the Formation of Modern Biblical Scholarship* (London: Routledge, 2002), 64–88; Maurice Olender, *The Languages of Paradise: Race, Religion, and Philology in the Nineteenth Century* (Cambridge, MA: Harvard University Press, 1992), 51–81.

12. T. R. Glover, *The Conflict of Religions in the Early Roman Empire* (London: Methuen & Co, 1909), 132–3, 167.

13. *Pan-Anglican Congress, 1908*, vol. VI, section E: *Missions in Christendom, Speeches and Discussions Together with the Papers Published for the Consideration of the Congress* (London: SPCK, 1908), 82–141 (quotation at 91–92); for similar statements at Edinburgh see Brian Stanley, *The World Missionary Conference, Edinburgh 1910* (Grand Rapids, MI, and Cambridge, 2009), 193–98.

14. G. Spiller, ed., *Papers on Inter-Racial Problems Communicated to the First Universal Races Congress Held at the University of London July 26–29, 1911* (London: P. S. King & Son, 1911), 309–10.

15. J. S. Conway, *The Nazi Persecution of the Churches 1933–45* (London: Weidenfeld & Nicolson, 1968), 1–2, 328–30.

16. E. H. Robertson, *Christians against Hitler* (London: SCM Press, 1962).

17. Carlo Falconi, *The Silence of Pius XII* (Eng. trans. London: Faber, 1970).

18. John Cornwell, *Hitler's Pope, the Secret History of Pius XII* (London: Penguin, 2000), 298–318.

19. For a defence of Pius XII on the basis of lack of information see Owen Chadwick, "The Pope and the Jews in 1942," in *Persecution and Toleration, Studies in Church History*, vol. 21, ed. W. J. Sheils (Oxford: Basil Blackwell for the Ecclesiastical History Society, 1984), 435–72; idem, *Britain and the Vatican during the Second World War* (Cambridge: Cambridge University Press, 1986), 198–221.

20. Michael Phayer, *The Catholic Church and the Holocaust, 1930–1965* (Bloomington, IN: Indiana University Press, 2000), 57–61, 219–21. For the most virulent attack on Pius see Daniel Jonah Goldhagen, *A Moral Reckoning: The Role of the Catholic Church in the Holocaust and Its Unfulfilled Duty of Repair* (London: Little, Brown, 2002); for more recent surveys of the debate see José M. Sánchez, *Pius XII and the Holocaust: Understanding the Controversy* (Washington, DC: Catholic University Press of America, 2001); Patrick J. Gallo, ed., *Pius XII, the Holocaust, and the Revisionists: Essays* (Jefferson, N.C.: McFarland & Co., 2006); David Bankier, Dan Michman and Iael Nidam-Orvieto, ed., *Pius XII and the Holocaust: Current State of Research* (Yad Vashem and Jerusalem: The International Institute for Holocaust Research, 2012).

21. Derek Hastings, *Catholicism and the Roots of Nazism: Religious Identity and National Socialism* (New York: Oxford University Press, 2010).

22. Wolfgang Gerlach, *And the Witnesses Were Silent: The Confessing Church and the Persecution of the Jews* (Lincoln, NE: University of Nebraska Press, 2000), 14.

23. Cited in Robertson, *Christians against Hitler*, 49.

24. Gerlach, *And the Witnesses Were Silent*, 73–76.

25. Werner Ustorf, *Sailing on the Next Tide: Missions, Missiology, and the Third Reich* (Frankfurt: Peter Lang, 2000), 22, 53–78.

26. Robert P. Ericksen, *Theologians under Hitler: Gerhard Kittel, Paul Althaus and Emanuel Hirsch* (New Haven, CT: Yale University Press, 1985), 35, 54–55.

27. Peter M. Head, "The Nazi Quest for an Aryan Jesus," *Journal for the Study of the Historical Jesus* 2, no.1 (2004): 72, n. 73.

28. Victor Farías, *Heidegger and Nazism*, Eng. translation (Philadelphia: Temple University Press, 1989); Hugo Ott, *Martin Heidegger: A Political Life*, Eng. translation (London: HarperCollins, 1993); Kelley, *Racializing Jesus*, 89–128.

29. Ericksen, *Theologians under Hitler*, 31, 189.

30. Richard Steigmann-Gall, *The Holy Reich: Nazi Conceptions of Christianity, 1919–1945* (Cambridge: Cambridge University Press, 2003), 134–40, 267.

31. Ibid., 39–41.

32. Head, "The Nazi Quest for an Aryan Jesus," 63–64.

33. Doris L. Bergen, *Twisted Cross: The German Christian Movement in the Third Reich* (Chapel Hill: University of North Carolina Press, 1996), 2, 229.

34. Daniel Goldhagen, *Hitler's Willing Executioners: Ordinary Germans and the Holocaust*, rev. ed. (London: Abacus Books, 1997), 49–51.

35. Ibid., 68–71.

36. Ibid., 115.

37. Heschel, *The Aryan Jesus*.

38. Head, "The Nazi Quest for an Aryan Jesus," 70–71.

39. Ibid., 75–86; Heschel, *The Aryan Jesus*, 152–5, 263–64.

40. Baum, *The Rise and Fall of the Caucasian Race*, 133–41.

41. Carney, *Rwanda before the Genocide*, 11-12; Timothy Longman, *Christianity and Genocide in Rwanda* (Cambridge: Cambridge University Press, 2010), 60-1; cf. Kidd, *The Forging of Races*, 247-54.

42. For an effective critique of the view that Hutu-Tutsi antagonism was the creation of European colonialism see Johan Poitier, *Re-Imagining Rwanda: Conflict, Survival and Disinformation in the Late Twentieth Century* (Cambridge: Cambridge University Press, 2002).

43. Christian P. Scherrer, *Genocide and Crisis in Central Africa: Conflict Roots, Mass Violence and Regional War* (Westport, CT: Praeger, 2002), 4-5, 21.

44. Longman, *Christianity and Genocide in Rwanda*, 44 n. 29.

45. M. Catharine Newbury, *The Cohesion of Oppression: Clientship and Ethnicity in Rwanda 1860-1960* (New York: Columbia University Press, 1988), 10-13; Poitier, *Re-Imagining Rwanda*, 13-15.

46. John D. Y. Peel, *Religious Encounter and the Making of the Yoruba* (Bloomington, IN: Indiana University Press, 2000).

47. Carney, *Rwanda before the Genocide*, 36, 39.

48. Kevin Ward and Emma Wild-Wood, eds., *The East African Revival: History and Legacies* (Farnham: Ashgate, 2012).

49. Longman, *Christianity and Genocide in Rwanda*, 63.

50. Carney, *Rwanda before the Genocide*, 49-53, argues that this was the crucial motivation.

51. The above account is indebted to the masterly analysis in Carney, *Rwanda before the Genocide*, 121-61.

52. Godfrey, "Understanding Genocide," 43-5, 49, 55-58; Carney, *Rwanda before the Genocide*, 273 n. 156; Longman, *Christianity and Genocide in Rwanda*, 89, 144-45.

53. Carney, *Rwanda before the Genocide*, 198.

54. Longman, *Christianity and Genocide in Rwanda*, 194-96.

55. Godfrey, "Understanding Genocide," 105-8.

56. Carney, *Rwanda before the Genocide*, 203.

57. Hans Luckey, editor of the German Baptist monthly *Der Hilfsbote*, in 1938, cited in Nicholas M. Railton, "German Free Churches and the Nazi Regime," *Journal of Ecclesiastical History* 49, no. 1 (1998): 126; see also Bernard Green, *European Baptists and the Third Reich* (Didcot: Baptist Historical Society, 2008).

58. Godfrey, "Understanding Genocide," 135-49.

59. Doris L. Bergen, "Catholics, Protestants and Christian Antisemitism in Nazi Germany," *Central European History* 27, no. 3 (1994): 329; cited in Longman, *Christianity and Genocide in Rwanda*, 196.

60. Carney, *Rwanda before the Genocide*, 208.

61. Adrian Hastings, *The Shaping of Prophecy: Passion, Perception and Practicality* (London: Geoffrey Chapman, 1995), 29.

62. Carney, *Rwanda before the Genocide*, 199-202.

Chapter 8. Aliens in a Strange Land?

1. An earlier version of this chapter was published as "Christians, Muslims and the State in Twentieth-Century Egypt and Indonesia," in *Christians and Religious*

Plurality. Studies in Church History, vol. 51, ed. Charlotte Methuen, Andrew Spicer, and John Wolffe (Woodbridge: Boydell and Brewer for the Ecclesiastical History Society, 2015), 412–34.

2. Alan Race, *Christians and Religious Pluralism: Patterns in the Christian Theology of Religions*, 2nd ed. (London: SCM Press, 1993), 1–9, 149, and Stanley J. Samartha, *One Christ—Many Religions: Towards a Revised Christology* (Maryknoll, NY: Orbis Books, 1991), 1, both rightly affirm that what is new about the contemporary world is not the fact of religious pluralism, but the widespread perception of this fact. Yet Samartha goes on (120) to call for a radically revised Christology on the grounds that the creeds were formulated "under very different circumstances than what obtains in the religiously plural world today."

3. Hugh Goddard, *A History of Christian-Muslim Relations* (Edinburgh: Edinburgh University Press, 2000), 4; see also 177–94.

4. Sidney H. Griffith, *The Church in the Shadow of the Mosque: Christians and Muslims in the World of Islam* (Princeton, NJ: Princeton University Press, 2008), 3–4, 22, 176–79.

5. Herbert Butterfield, *The Whig Interpretation of History* (London: G. Bell & Sons, 1931).

6. I. A. Rehman, "A Critique of Pakistan's Blasphemy Laws," in *Pakistan: Between Secularism and Islam*, edited by Tarik Jan, et al. (Islamabad: Institute of Policy Studies, 1998), 200–201; Farhana Nazir, "Offences Relating to Religion in British India and Their Implications in Contemporary Pakistan," (PhD thesis, University of Edinburgh, 2013). For the Utilitarian and pragmatic foundations of Macaulay's Indian Penal Code see Eric Stokes, *The English Utilitarians and India* (Oxford: Clarendon Press, 1959), 190–233.

7. S. M. Zwemer, "The City of Cairo," *Moslem World* 10, no. 3 (1920): 266–73.

8. Otto F. A. Meinardus, *Christians in Egypt: Orthodox, Catholic and Protestant Communities Past and Present* (Cairo: The American University in Cairo Press, 2006). The French Orientalist, Louis Massignon, estimated that c. 95% of Egyptian Muslims are of Coptic ancestry; see Anthony O'Mahony, "The Coptic Orthodox Church in Modern Egypt," in *Eastern Christianity in the Modern Middle East*, ed. Anthony O'Mahony and Emma Loosley, (London: Routledge, 2010), 62.

9. Todd M. Johnson and Brian J. Grim, eds. *World Religion Database* (Leiden: E. J. Brill), www.worldreligiondatabase.org (Accessed March 3, 2017). Table on "Religions and sub-Religions," pp. 77–8 and 154, estimates for Indonesia and South Korea in 2000.

10. Heather J. Sharkey, *American Evangelicals in Egypt: Missionary Encounters in an Age of Empire* (Princeton, NJ: Princeton University Press, 2008), 65.

11. Decree No. 2466 Issued by the Minister of Justice [in the Egyptian government], February 28, 1913, printed in Helen Clarkson Miller Davis, comp., *Some Aspects of Religious Liberty in the Near East: A Collection of Documents* (New York: Harper & Bros., 1938), 104.

12. Special Collections, Yale Divinity School Library, *Minutes of Egypt Inter-Mission Council*, 1921, Appendices II and III.

13. Samuel M. Zwemer, *Across the World of Islam: Studies in Aspects of the Mohammedan Faith and in the Present Awakening of the Moslem Multitudes* (New York: Fleming H. Revell Co., 1929), 33, 48–50.

14. It is important to draw the distinction between modern Islamic political theory and the political thought of early Islam, which had no doctrine of the Islamic state and was based on the equality of relations within the kinship group made up of those who followed Muhammad; see Richard Sudworth, "Christian Responses to the Political Challenge of Islam," http://repository.berkleycenter.georgetown.edu/120711 SudworthChristianResponsesPoliticalChallengeIslam.pdf (Accessed April 27, 2017).

15. Bruce Masters, *Christians and Jews in the Ottoman World: The Roots of Sectarianism* (Cambridge: Cambridge University Press, 2001), 134–41; Fiona McCallum, *Christian Religious Leadership in the Middle East: The Political Role of the Patriarch* (Lewiston, ME: Edwin Mellen Press, 2010), 69–70.

16. See Peter B. Nockles, *The Oxford Movement in Context: Anglican High Churchmanship, 1760–1857* (Cambridge: Cambridge University Press, 1994), 44–79.

17. Masters, *Christians and Jews in the Ottoman World*, 195.

18. D. B. Macdonald, "Anno Domini 1919," *Moslem World* 9, no. 1 (1919), 1.

19. I am indebted here to the analysis of Samir Khalil Samir, "The Christian Communities, Active Members of Arab Society Throughout History," in *Christian Communities in the Arab Middle East: The Challenge of the Future*, ed. Andrea Pacini (Oxford: Clarendon Press, 1998), 67–91; also to the summary of the exposition in 1983 by Yūsuf al-Qaraḍāwī, a member of the Muslim Brotherhood, of the question of non-Muslims in a Muslim state, in Yvonne Yazbeck Haddad, "Christians in a Muslim State: The Recent Egyptian Debate," in *Christian-Muslim Encounters*, ed. Yvonne Yazbeck Haddad and Wadi Z. Haddad (Gainesville, FL: University Press of Florida, 1995), 381–95.

20. Fiona McCallum, "Muslim-Christian Relations in Egypt: Challenges for the Twenty-first Century," in *Christian Responses to Islam: Muslim-Christian Relations in the Modern World*, ed. Anthony O'Mahony and Emma Loosley, 74 (Manchester: Manchester University Press, 2012).

21. W. H. T. Gairdner, "The Christian Church as a Home for Christ's Converts from Islam," *Moslem World*, 14, no. 3 (1924), 238; Sharkey, *American Evangelicals*, 67–8; Constance E. Padwick, *Temple Gairdner of Cairo*, 2nd ed. (London: SPCK, 1929), 264.

22. Andrew Watson, *The American Mission in Egypt, 1854–1896*, 2nd ed. (Pittsburgh: United Presbyterian Church Board of Publication, 1904), 58, cited in Heather J. Sharkey, "American Missionaries, the Arabic Bible, and Coptic Reform in Late Nineteenth-Century Egypt," in *American Missionaries and the Middle East: Foundational Encounters*, ed. Mehmet Ali Doğan and Heather J. Sharkey (Salt Lake City: The University of Utah Press, 2011), 239.

23. See Padwick, *Temple Gairdner*, 267–68; Eugene Stock, *The History of the Church Missionary Society*, vol. IV (London: Church Missionary Society, 1916), 113–14; see John Stuart, "Empire, Mission, Ecumenism, and Human Rights: 'Religious Liberty' in Egypt, 1919–1956," *Church History* 83, no.1 (2014): 116.

24. Samuel M. Zwemer, *The Law of Apostasy in Islam: Answering the Question Why There Are so Few Moslem Converts, and Giving Examples of their Moral Courage and Martyrdom* (London: Marshall Brothers, n.d. [1924]), 18.

25. See Todd M. Thompson, "J. N. D. Anderson, Nationalism, and the 'Modernisation' of Islamic Law, 1932–1984" (PhD thesis, University of Cambridge, 2010), 88–89; and Thomas S. Kidd, *American Christians and Islam: Evangelical Culture and*

Muslims from the Colonial Period to the Age of Terrorism (Princeton, NJ: Princeton University Press, 2009), 71.

26. Sharkey, *American Evangelicals*, 71, 77.

27. Samuel M. Zwemer, *Islam: A Challenge to Faith: Studies on the Moham-medan Religion and the Needs and Opportunities of the Mohammedan World from the Standpoint of Christian Missions* (New York: Student Volunteer Movement for Foreign Missions, 1907), 172; idem, *Across the World of Islam*, 48.

28. McCallum, *Christian Religious Leadership in the Middle East*, 74-75.

29. *The United Presbyterian*, June 12, 26, and July 3, 1919; *Triennial Report of the Board of Foreign Missions of the United Presbyterian Church of North America*, 1919-1921, 63, 81. Missionary sources tended to give the impression that all non-Muslims were under attack; for a retrospective account, see Earl E. Elder, *Vindicating a Vision: The Story of the American Mission in Egypt 1854-1954* (Philadelphia: Board of Foreign Missions of the United Presbyterian Church of North America, 1958), compare pp. 151-54 with 195-96.

30. For a brief Muslim eyewitness account of the 1919 revolution, see Arthur Gold-schmidt, Jr., ed., *The Memoirs and Diaries of Muhammad Farid, an Egyptian National-ist Leader (1868-1919)* (San Francisco: Mellen University Research Press, 1992), 507-9. For brief scholarly treatments see Leland Bowie, "The Copts, the Wafd, and Religious Is-sues in Egyptian Politics," *Muslim World* 67, no. 2 (1977): 108; Vivian Ibrahim, *The Copts of Egypt: Challenges of Modernisation and Identity* (London: I. B. Tauris Publishers, 2011), 64-65; S. S. Hasan, *Christians versus Muslims in Modern Egypt: The Century-Long Struggle for Coptic Equality* (New York: Oxford University Press, 2003), 36.

31. Special Collections, Yale Divinity School Library, George Sherwood Eddy Pa-pers, RG 32-3-67, report letter dated October 21, 1920.

32. *Triennial Report of the Board of Foreign Missions of the United Presbyterian Church of North America*, 1919-1921, 64; W. T. Fairman, "Nationalism and Evange-lism in Egypt," *Moslem World* 13, no. 3 (1923): 234.

33. McCallum, *Christian Religious Leadership in the Middle East*, 81-3; Hasan, *Christians versus Muslims in Modern Egypt*, 104.

34. Hasan, *Christians versus Muslims in Modern Egypt*, 71-3; Sharkey, *American Evangelicals*, 45.

35. On Girgīs see Habib Badr, ed., *Christianity: A History in the Middle East* (Beirut: Middle East Council of Churches Studies and Research Program, 2005), 781. Girgīs remained principal of the seminary until his death in 1951.

36. Hasan, *Christians versus Muslims in Modern Egypt*, 73-5; Otto F. A. Mein-ardus, *Two Thousand Years of Coptic Christianity* (Cairo: The American University in Cairo Press, 1999), 93.

37. Hasan, *Christians versus Muslims in Modern Egypt*, x, 82, 85; cf. Michael Walzer, *The Revolution of the Saints: A Study in the Origins of Radical Politics* (Lon-don: Weidenfeld and Nicolson, 1966).

38. McCallum, *Christian Religious Leadership in the Middle East*, 132.

39. Dina El Khawaga, "Political Dynamics of the Copts: Giving the Community an Active Role," in Pacini, *Christian Communities in the Arab Middle East*, 179.

40. El Khawaga, "Political Dynamics of the Copts," 183n; J. D. Pennington, "The Copts in Modern Egypt," *Middle Eastern Studies* 18, no. 2 (1982): 162, 167.

41. Hasan, *Christians versus Muslims in Modern Egypt*, 216–19; O'Mahony, "The Coptic Orthodox Church in Modern Egypt," 75; McCallum, *Christian Religious Leadership in the Middle East*, 130–1 follows John W. Watson in estimating the number of monks at 2,000 in 2004.

42. Mark Francis Gruber, "The Monastery as the Nexus of Coptic Cosmology," in *Between Desert and City: The Coptic Orthodox Church Today*, ed. Nelly van Doorn-Harder and Kari Vogt (Oslo: Novus forlag, 1997), 67–82.

43. Hasan, *Christians versus Muslims in Modern Egypt*, 22–25; Otto F. A. Meinardus, *Christian Egypt Ancient and Modern*, 2nd rev. ed. (Cairo: The American University in Cairo Press, 1977), 75.

44. The number of 144,000 is taken from Revelation 14:1; Nora Stene, "Becoming a Copt," in van Doorn-Harder and Vogt, *Between Desert and City*, 205, 210; Edward Wakin, *A Lonely Minority: The Story of Egypt's Copts*, 2nd ed. (Lincoln, NE: Authors Guild BackinPrint.Com, 2000), 7.

45. McCallum, "Muslim-Christian Relations in Egypt," 69.

46. Hasan, *Christians versus Muslims in Modern Egypt*, 108–9; McCallum, *Christian Religious Leadership in the Middle East*, 127; Shenouda maintained this stance even in the less polarized religious politics of the Mubarak era, vowing in 2000 that "we will not enter Jerusalem except with our Muslim brethren"; see idem, "Muslim-Christian Relations in Egypt," 79.

47. Hasan, *Christians versus Muslims in Modern Egypt*, 105–13; McCallum, *Christian Religious Leadership in the Middle East*, 133.

48. John W. Watson, *Among the Copts* (Brighton: Sussex Academic Press, 2000), 103, 109.

49. Ibid., 113–14.

50. Ibid., 104–5.

51. Ibid., 116.

52. McCallum, *Christian Religious Leadership in the Middle East*, 147.

53. Jan Sihar Aritonang and Karel Steenbrink, ed., *A History of Christianity in Indonesia* (Leiden: E. J. Brill, 2008), 165. Although this book presents itself as an edited volume, the authors of the individual chapters are not identified.

54. Ibid., 166–67, 170.

55. Ibid., 173. On Catholicism in Flores see Susanne Schröter, "The Indigenisation of Catholicism on Flores," in *Christianity in Indonesia: Perspectives of Power*, ed. Susanne Schröter, (Berlin: Lit Verlag, 2010), 137–57. On the vexed relations between the Christian Dani of West Papua and the Indonesian state see Charles E. Farhadian, *Christianity, Islam, and Nationalism in Indonesia* (New York: Routledge, 2005).

56. Lorraine V. Aragon, *Fields of the Lord: Animism, Christian Minorities and State Development in Indonesia* (Honolulu: University of Hawaii Press, 2000), 24–25; Rita Smith Kipp and Susan Rodgers, ed., *Indonesian Religions in Transition* (Tucson: University of Arizona Press, 1987), 23.

57. Hendrik Kraemer, *From Missionfield to Independent Church: Report on a Decisive Decade in the Growth of Indigenous Churches in Indonesia* (London: SCM Press, 1958), 146.

58. Ibid., 32–34.

59. Aritonang and Steenbrink, *A History of Christianity in Indonesia*, 174.

60. Ibid, 167.

61. I owe this point to Wilbert Van Saane of the University of Utrecht; see C. Howard Hopkins, *John R. Mott 1865–1955: A Biography* (Grand Rapids, MI: Eerdmans, 1979), 652–53.

62. Kraemer, *From Missionfield to Independent Church*, 65.

63. Aritonang and Steenbrink (eds.), *A History of Christianity in Indonesia*, 180–87.

64. Ibid., 187.

65. English sources on Sjarifoeddin are sparse. There is a biography in Indonesian: Frederiek D. Wellem, *Amir Sjarifoeddin: Tempatnya Dalam Kekristenan dan Perjuangan Kemerdekaan Indonesia* (Jakarta: Pernebit, 2009).

66. Gerry van Klinken, *Minorities, Modernity and the Emerging Nation: Christians in Indonesia, a Biographical Approach* (Leiden: KITLV Press, 2003), 115–23. On Schepper (1887–1967) see also Aritonang and Steenbrink, *A History of Christianity in Indonesia*, 178–79; and Th. Van der End in *Biografisch Lexicon voor de geschiedenis van het Nederlands protestantisme*, vol. 6, 276–78, http://resources.huygens .knaw.nl/retroboeken/blnp/#page=0&accessor=accessor_index&view=imagePane (Accessed April 27, 2017).

67. T. B. Simatupang, *Report from Banaran: Experiences during the People's War*, Eng. translation (Ithaca, NY: Modern Indonesia Project, Southeast Asia Program Cornell University, 1972), 78.

68. Ibid., 78–9.

69. Van Klinken, *Minorities, Modernity and the Emerging Nation*, 198–201.

70. Ibid, 205.

71. See Simatupang, *Report from Banaran*, 81–83.

72. Both the order and the precise wording of the *Pancasila* were amended between their first enunciation by Sukarno in a speech of 1 June 1945 and their eventual embodiment in the Indonesian constitution.

73. Aritonang and Steenbrink, *A History of Christianity in Indonesia*, 188–90; Muhammad Rasjidi, "The Role of Christian Missions: The Indonesian Experience," *International Review of Mission* 65, no. 260 (1976): 435. T. B. Simatupang in World Council of Churches, Sub-Unit on Dialogue with the People of Living Faiths and Ideologies, *Christian Presence and Witness in Relation to Muslim Neighbours* (Geneva: World Council of Churches, 1981), 30. For an argument that the Muslim acceptance of *Pancasila* was indebted to a Javanese tradition of cultural tolerance yet superiority, see Franz Magnis-Suseno, "Pluralism under Debate: Muslim Perspectives," in Schröter, *Christianity in Indonesia*, 353–55.

74. For English-language sources on Simatupang see his autobiography, *The Fallacy of a Myth*, Eng. translation (Jakarta: Pustaka Sinar Harapan, 1996); and Frank L. Cooley, "In Memoriam: T. B. Simatupang, 1920–1990," *Indonesia* 49 (April 1990): 145–52.

75. Cited in Cooley, "T. B. Simatupang," 148.

76. Kipp and Rodgers, *Indonesian Religions in Transition*, 21–25.

77. Avery T. Willis, Jr., *Indonesian Revival: Why Two Millions Came to Christ* (South Pasadena, CA: William Carey Library, 1977), 63–64, 103–4, 210–11. Willis was

a disciple of Donald McGavran's church growth theory, which was not afraid to cite political and sociological factors behind Christian conversion movements.

78. Aragon, *Fields of the Lord*, 14–15, 33; Aritonang and Steenbrink, *A History of Christianity in Indonesia*, 204–7.

79. Aritonang and Steenbrink, eds., *A History of Christianity in Indonesia*, 207–9; Cooley, "T. B. Simaputang," 149; Rupert Shortt, *Christianophobia* (London: Rider Books, 2012), 135–37.

80. Karel A. Steenbrink, "Muslim-Christian Relations in the *Pancasila* State of Indonesia," *Muslim World* 88, nos. 3–4 (1998): 338.

81. Simatupang, *The Fallacy of a Myth*, 209–13.

82. For two assessments of the situation as of 2010 see Hassan Noohaidi, "The Radical Muslim Discourse on Jihad, and the Hatred Against Christians," and Magnis-Suseno, "Pluralism Under Debate: Muslim Perspectives," in Schröter, *Christianity in Indonesia*, 323–46 and 347–59 respectively.

83. For example, the number of Christians in Iraq declined from at least 1.2 million in 1990 to under 200,000 in 2012; see Shortt, *Christianophobia*, 27.

Chapter 9. That the World May Believe

1. Nathan Showalter, *The End of a Crusade: The Student Volunteer Movement for Foreign Missions and the Great War* (Lanham, MD: Scarecrow Press, 1998), 182; see also Michael Parker, *The Kingdom of Character: The Student Volunteer Movement for Foreign Missions (1886–1926)* (Lanham, MD: American Society of Missiology and University Press of America, 1998).

2. Thomas S. Kuhn, *The Structure of Scientific Revolutions* (Chicago: University of Chicago Press, 1962).

3. Konrad Raiser, *Ecumenism in Transition: A Paradigm Shift in the Ecumenical Movement?* (Geneva: WCC Publications, 1991), 54, 96; see Mark T. B. Laing, *From Crisis to Creation: Lesslie Newbigin and the Reinvention of Christian Mission* (Eugene, OR: Pickwick Publications, 2012), 199–201. Raiser was general secretary of the WCC from 1992 to 2004.

4. John Flett, *The Witness of God: The Trinity, Missio Dei, Karl Barth, and the Nature of Christian Community* (Grand Rapids, MI: Eerdmans, 2010), 131. Flett's study is now indispensable in tracing the complex origins of *missio Dei* theology.

5. World Council of Churches Department on Studies in Evangelism, *The Church for Others, and the Church for the World: A Quest for Structures for Missionary Congregations* (Geneva: World Council of Churches, 1967), 14, 17, 69–70, cited in part in Flett, *The Witness of God*, 53.

6. Lesslie Newbigin, "Ecumenism in Transition," *International Bulletin of Missionary Research* 18, no. 1 (1994): 2–5; see also Raiser's rejoinder and Newbigin's reply in 18, no. 2 (1994): 50–52.

7. David F. Wright, "The Great Commission and the Ministry of the Word: Reflections Historical and Contemporary on Relations and Priorities," *Scottish Bulletin of Evangelical Theology* 25, no. 2 (2007): 132–57. The widespread influence of the Scofield Bible, published in 1909, which affixed the label "The Great Commission" to

Matthew 28, but not to the parallel passage in Mark 16, may well be partly responsible for this usage.

8. Angelyn Dries, *The Missionary Movement in American Catholic History* (Maryknoll, NY: Orbis Books, 1998), 108, 304; J. I. Parker, ed., *Interpretative Statistical Survey of the World Mission of the Christian Church* (New York: International Missionary Council, 1938), 87, 91.

9. See Werner Ustorf, *Sailing on the Next Tide: Missions, Missiology, and the Third Reich* (Frankfurt am Main: Peter Lang, 2000).

10. Albert Monshan Wu, *From Christ to Confucius: German Missionaries, Chinese Christians, and the Globalization of Christianity* (New Haven, CT: Yale University Press, 2016), 152.

11. Ernest P. Young, *Ecclesiastical Colony, China's Catholic Church and the French Religious Protectorate* (New York: Oxford University Press, 2013), 212–14; Wu, *From Christ to Confucius*, 62, 125, 190–205.

12. Adrian Hastings, "The Clash of Nationalism and Universalism within Twentieth-Century Missionary Christianity," in *Missions, Nationalism, and the End of Empire*, ed. Brian Stanley (Grand Rapids, MI: Eerdmans, 2003), 17.

13. Ibid., 18.

14. For a discussion from a sociological perspective of Mother Teresa's iconic global status see Gëzim Alpion, *Mother Teresa: Saint or Celebrity?* (London: Routledge, 2007).

15. John G. Turner, *Bill Bright and Campus Crusade for Christ: The Renewal of Evangelicalism in Postwar America* (Chapel Hill: The University of North Carolina Press, 2008), 98–103.

16. See J. Waskom Pickett, *Christian Mass Movements in India: A Study with Recommendations* (New York: The Abingdon Press, 1933).

17. Christian Keysser, *A People Reborn*, Eng. translation (Pasadena, CA: William Carey Library, 1980), ix; see Timothy Yates, *Christian Mission in the Twentieth Century* (Cambridge: Cambridge University Press, 1994), 54–55; Donald A. McGavran, *The Bridges of God: A Study in the Strategy of Missions* (New York: Friendship Press, 1955).

18. Giuseppe Alberigo and Joseph A. Komonchak, eds., *History of Vatican II*, vol. I: *Announcing and Preparing Vatican Council II: Toward a New Era in Catholicism* (Maryknoll, NY: Orbis Books, 1995), 3–4.

19. Ibid., 42–43.

20. Ibid., 40.

21. Giuseppe Alberigo and Joseph A. Komonchak, eds., *History of Vatican II*, vol. II: *The Formation of the Council's Identity. First Period and Intersession. October 1962–September 1963* (Maryknoll, NY: Orbis Books, 1997), 5, 200.

22. *Lumen Gentium*, chapter III, art. 21. All references to the Vatican II decrees are to the translated text in Austin Flannery, ed., *Vatican Council II: The Conciliar and Post Conciliar Documents* (Wilmington, DE: Scholarly Resources Inc., 1975).

23. Giuseppe Alberigo and Joseph A. Komonchak, eds., *History of Vatican II*, vol. IV: *Church as Communion. Third Period and Intersession September 1964–September 1965* (Maryknoll, NY, Orbis Books, 2003), 66–70, 418–44.

24. *Lumen Gentium*, chapter III, arts. 22, 25.

25. E.g. Eamon Duffy, *Saints and Sinners: A History of the Popes*, 2nd ed. (New Haven, CT: Yale University Press, 2001), 360–61.

26. Alberigo and Komonchak, *History of Vatican II*, vol. IV, 2–27, 325.

27. *Ibid.*, vol. II, 47–49.

28. *Ibid.*, vol. I, 211–15, 221–3; vol. II, 120–1.

29. *Constitutio de Sacra Liturgia*, chapter I, art. 47.

30. Alberigo and Komonchak, *History of Vatican II*, vol. 1, 326.

31. *Lumen Gentium*, chapter 1, art. 8; see Herbert Vorgrimler et al., *Commentary on the Documents of Vatican II*, vol. I (London: Burns & Oates 1967), 149–51.

32. *Lumen Gentium*, chapter 1, art. 9; see Gerald O'Collins, S.J., *The Second Vatican Council on Other Religions* (Oxford: Oxford University Press, 2013), 71.

33. *Decree on Ecumenism*, chapter II, art. 21 [my italics].

34. Alberigo and Komonchak, *History of Vatican II*, vol. IV, 416.

35. *Nostra Aetate*, art. 4.

36. *Nostra Aetate*, arts. 2–3.

37. *Ad Gentes*, art. 11.

38. *Lumen Gentium*, art. 16.

39. O'Collins, *The Second Vatican Council on Other Religions*, 150–1 and *passim*.

40. *Gaudium et Spes*, chapter II, arts. 22, 26.

41. *Gaudium et Spes*, chapter II, art. 26, and chapter IV, art. 41.

42. Duffy, *Saints and Sinners*, 361–62.

43. On Hoekendijk see *Biographical Dictionary of Christian Missions*, ed. Gerald H. Anderson (New York, Macmillan Reference, 1998), 297; Bert Hoedemaker, "The Legacy of J. C. Hoekendijk," *International Bulletin of Missionary Research* 19, no. 4 (1995): 166–70.

44. J. C. Hoekendijk, "The Church in Missionary Thinking," *International Review of Missions* 41, no. 163 (1952): 332.

45. Mark T. B. Laing, "'The Calling of the Church to Mission and Unity': Bishop Lesslie Newbigin and the Integration of the International Missionary Council with the World Council of Churches" (PhD thesis, University of Edinburgh, 2010), 204; Laing, *From Crisis to Creation*, 84.

46. World Council of Churches Department on Studies in Evangelism, *The Church for Others*, 20, 26.

47. Norman Goodall, ed., *The Uppsala Report 1968: Official Report of the Fourth Assembly of the World Council of Churches Uppsala July 4–20, 1968* (Geneva: World Council of Churches, 1968), xvii, 38.

48. Lesslie Newbigin, *Honest Religion for Secular Man* (London: SCM Press, 1966).

49. Lesslie Newbigin, *Unfinished Agenda: An Updated Autobiography* (Edinburgh: St Andrew Press, 1993), 219; Laing, *From Crisis to Creation*, 211–13, 217, 233–43.

50. Owen Chadwick, *Michael Ramsey: A Life* (Oxford: Oxford University Press, 1991), 256–57, 266, 276–77.

51. Wheaton College, Billy Graham Center, BGCA 46, Box 30/27, International Congress on World Evangelization. Meeting of the consultative conference, Vero Beach, Florida, March 23–24, 1972. The account of the Lausanne Congress that follows is an abridgement of chapter 6 of my *The Global Diffusion of Evangelicalism: The Age of Billy Graham and John Stott* (Downers Grove, IL: IVP, 2013).

52. René Padilla, "Evangelism and the World," in *Let the Earth Hear his Voice. International Congress on World Evangelization Lausanne, Switzerland: Official Reference Volume: Papers and Responses*, ed. J. D. Douglas (Minneapolis: World Wide Publications, 1975), 116–33 at p. 126.

53. *Crusade*, September 1974, 26; *Church of England Newspaper*, July 26, 1974, 3.

54. Douglas, ed., *Let the Earth Hear His Voice*, 134–36 at pp. 136 and 144.

55. Ibid., 303–18.

56. Ibid., 319–26, at pp. 322 and 326.

57. John Stott, "The Significance of Lausanne," *International Review of Mission* 64, no. 255 (1975): 289.

58. Douglas, *Let the Earth Hear His Voice*, 675–94 at p. 682. Freire's book was published in Portuguese in 1968 and first appeared in English translation in 1970.

59. *Christianity Today*, September 13, 1974, 66.

60. "A Response to Lausanne," *International Review of Mission* 63, no. 252 (1974): 574–76; the Anglican evangelical clergyman Jack Dain described the Theology and Radical Discipleship group as comprising "mainly younger men and women" in *Church of England Newspaper*, August 9, 1974, 2.

61. Alister Chapman, *Godly Ambition: John Stott and the Evangelical Movement* (New York: Oxford University Press, 2012), 11–31.

Chapter 10. Good News to the Poor?

1. Gustavo Gutiérrez, *A Theology of Liberation: History, Politics and Salvation*, Eng. translation by Sister Caridad Inda and John Eagleson, 1973. British ed. (London: SCM Press, 1974), 11.

2. Juan Luis Segundo, *The Liberation of Theology* (Dublin: Gill and Macmillan, 1977), 3.

3. Otto Maduro, "Introduction," in *The Future of Liberation Theology: Essays in Honor of Gustavo Gutiérrez*, eds. Marc H. Ellis and Otto Maduro (Maryknoll, NY: Orbis Books, 1989), xvi. Vol. 11:

4. Giuseppe Alberigo and Joseph A. Komonchak, eds., *History of Vatican II*, vol. 11: *The Formation of the Council's Identity. First Period and Intersession. October 1962–September 1963* (Maryknoll, NY: Orbis, and Leuven: Peeters, 1997), 171–2.

5. Johannes Baptist Metz, *Theology of the World* (London: Burns & Oates, 1969), Eng. translation of *Zur Theologie der Welt* (Mainz: Mathias-Grünewald-Verlag, 1968).

6. Jürgen Moltmann, *Theology of Hope: On the Grounds and Implications of a Christian Eschatology* (London: SCM Press, 1967), Eng. translation of *Theologie Der Hoffnung: Untersuchungen zur Begründung und zu den Konsequenzen einer christlichen Eschatologie* (München: C. Kaiser, 1964).

7. Rebecca S. Chopp, "Latin American Liberation Theology," in *The Modern Theologians*, ed. David F. Ford, 2nd ed. (Oxford: Blackwell, 1997), 411–12.

8. Christian Smith, *The Emergence of Liberation Theology: Radical Religion and Social Movement Theory* (Chicago: University of Chicago Press, 1991), 104–5.

9. Manuel A. Vásquez, *The Brazilian Catholic Church and the Crisis of Modernity*, rev. ed. (Cambridge: Cambridge University Press, 2008), 32–37.

10. Gutiérrez, *A Theology of Liberation*, 81.

11. For a pungent rebuttal of dependency or underdevelopment theory from the perspective of strict Marxist theory see Bill Warren, *Imperialism: Pioneer of Capitalism* (London: Verso Books, 1980).

12. Alistair Kee, *Marx and the Failure of Liberation Theology* (London: SCM Press, 1990), 137, 168, 257.

13. S. M. Lipset and S. S. Wolin, eds., *The Berkeley Student Revolt: Facts and Interpretations* (Garden City, NY: Doubleday & Co, Anchor Books: 1965), 6. However, Lipset and Wolin rightly point out (p. 8) that the majority of the student population in Latin American universities was apolitical.

14. Juan Luis Segundo, *Signs of the Times: Theological Reflections* (Maryknoll, NY: Orbis Books, 1993), 68–69.

15. Christopher Rowland, ed., *The Cambridge Companion to Liberation Theology*, 2nd ed. (Cambridge: Cambridge University Press, 2007), 315.

16. Mario Aguilar, *The History and Politics of Latin American Theology*, 3 vols. (London: SCM Press, 2007–8).

17. David Tombs, *Latin American Liberation Theology* (Leiden: E. J. Brill, 2002), 84–85 (fn. 68), 112, 142 (fn. 21).

18. Daniel Salinas, *Latin American Evangelical Theology in the 1970's: The Golden Decade* (Leiden: E. J. Brill, 2009), 56.

19. Sergio Torres, "Gustavo Gutiérrez: A Historical Sketch," in Ellis and Maduro, eds., *The Future of Liberation Theology*, 97.

20. Gustavo Gutiérrez and M. Richard Shaull, *Liberation and Change*, edited and introduced by Ronald H. Stone (Atlanta, GA: John Knox Press, 1977).

21. Mark L. Taylor, "M. Richard Shaull: A Tribute," *Princeton Seminary Bulletin* 24, no. 3 (2003): 343–7.

22. Smith, *The Emergence of Liberation Theology*, 254, n. 54.

23. Rubem Alves, *A Theology of Human Hope* (New York: Corpus Publications, 1969), 11, 13, 15, 169–70. See Paulo Freire, *Educação como Prática de Liberdade* (Rio de Janeiro: Editora Civilização Brasileira, 1967).

24. Alves, *A Theology of Human Hope*, 15, 98–99.

25. Ibid, 89–91, 178; G. Ernest Wright, *The Old Testament against Its Environment* (London: SCM Press, 1960), 49–50; idem, *God Who Acts: Biblical Theology as Recital* (London: SCM Press, 1952), 55.

26. Gustavo Gutiérrez, "Toward a Theology of Liberation" (July 1968), in *Liberation Theology: A Documentary History*, ed. Alfred T. Hennelly (Maryknoll, NY: Orbis Books, 1990), 70.

27. Paulo Freire, *La Educación como Práctica de la Libertad*, Spanish translation (Montevideo: Tierra Nueva, 1969; and Santiago de Chile: ICIRA, 1969). Compare Gutiérrez, *A Theology of Liberation*, 98.

28. Gutiérrez, "Toward a Theology of Liberation," 70, 71, 76.

29. On this theme see John Coffey, *Exodus and Liberation: Deliverance Politics from John Calvin to Martin Luther King, Jr.* (Oxford: Oxford University Press, 2014), chapter 5; Albert J. Raboteau, "African Americans, Exodus and the American Israel," in *Religion and American Culture: A Reader*, ed. David H. Hackett (New York: Routledge, 1995), 73–86.

30. James Cone, *A Black Theology of Liberation*, 40th anniversary ed. (Maryknoll, NY: Orbis Books, 2010), xvi, 49; see also 2, 31, 50, 57, 72.

31. Smith, *The Emergence of Liberation Theology*, 151–53, 160; Segundo, *The Liberation of Theology*, 193.

32. See the extended extracts in Hennelly, ed., *Liberation Theology*, 90–118. The exodus is mentioned in paragraph 6 of the introduction (p. 96).

33. Smith, *The Emergence of Liberation Theology*, 21, 176–77.

34. Gustavo Gutiérrez (Merino), "The Meaning of Development (Notes on a Theology of Liberation)," in *In Search of a Theology of Development: Papers from a Consultation on Theology and Development Held by Sodepax in Cartigny, Switzerland, November, 1969* (Geneva: Committee on Society, Development and Peace, n.d. [1970]), 116–79. In June 1970 Gutiérrez published a substantially revised version of his Cartigny paper in the Jesuit scholarly journal, *Theological Studies*, under a slightly different title: Gutiérrez, "Notes for a Theology of Liberation," *Theological Studies* 31, no. 2 (1970): 243–61.

35. *In Search of a Theology of Development*, 22; Gutiérrez, "The Meaning of Development," 169, n. 21; Gutiérrez, *A Theology of Liberation*, 91–92, 98 n. 47.

36. Gutiérrez, "The Meaning of Development," 145–47.

37. Alves, "Theology and the Liberation of Man," in *In Search of a Theology of Development*, 75–92, at pp. 80 and 91 (n. 14).

38. Gutiérrez, *A Theology of Liberation*, 151, 196–203.

39. Ibid., 159.

40. Ibid., 155.

41. Gutiérrez, "The Meaning of Development," 146.

42. Gutiérrez, *A Theology of Liberation*, 156–57, and 181, n. 24. Gutérrez also cites a work by the Nicaraguan Jesuit, Arnaldo Zenteno, *Liberación social y Christo: Apuntes para una teología de la liberación* (Mexico, D.F.: Secretariado Social Mexicano, 1971).

43. Gutiérrez, *A Theology of Liberation*, 182, n. 41 and 217.

44. Smith, *The Emergence of Liberation Theology*, 176–77.

45. J. Severino Croatto, *Liberación y libertad: Pautas hermenéuticas* (Buenos Aires: Nuevo Mundo, 1973); English translation, *Exodus: A Hermeneutics of Freedom* (Maryknoll, NY: Orbis Books, 1981), 14–15. It is worthy of note that Croatto had worked on archaeological digs with G. Ernest Wright; see Samuel Almada, "An Obituary and a Tribute to J. Severino Croatto," *JOLAH, Journal of Latin American Hermeneutics* Year 2005 /2 at https://www.researchgate.net/publication/265654040.

46. Michael Walzer, *Exodus and Revolution* (New York: Basic Books, 1985), 4, 7, 9–10, 32, 47, 48, 160, n. 47.

47. Segundo, *The Liberation of Theology*, 110, 112.

48. John Eagleson and Philip Scharper, eds., *Puebla and Beyond: Documentation and Commentary* (Maryknoll, NY: Orbis Books, 1979), 146, 147, 163, 200, 264, 265; the document extends from p. 123 to p. 285. See also Hennelly, ed., *Liberation Theology*, 245, 254.

49. Cardinal Joseph Ratzinger, "Liberation Theology," in Hennelly, ed., *Liberation Theology*, 374.

50. "Instruction on Certain Aspects of the 'Theology of Liberation,'" in Hennelly (ed.), *Liberation Theology*, 407–8.

51. "Instruction on Christian Freedom and Liberation," in Hennelly, ed., *Liberation Theology*, 474.

52. Smith, *The Emergence of Liberation Theology*, 204.

53. Naim Stifan Ateek, *Justice and Only Justice: A Palestinian Theology of Liberation* (Maryknoll, NY: Orbis Books, 1989), 74.

54. Ibid., xii.

55. Ibid., 77.

56. Naim S. Ateek, *A Palestinian Christian Cry for Reconciliation* (Maryknoll, NY: Orbis Books, 2008), 54–5, 71.

57. Ibid., 5–6; see Rosemary Radford Ruether and Herman J. Ruether, *The Wrath of Jonah: The Crisis of Religious Nationalism in the Israeli-Palestinian Conflict* (San Francisco: Harper & Row, 1989), 186–88.

58. Estimates of the number of Palestinian Christian refugees vary quite widely. Compare Anthony O'Mahony, "The Vatican, Palestinian Christians, Israel, and Jerusalem: Religion, Politics, Diplomacy, and Holy Places, 1945–1950," in *The Holy Land, Holy Lands, and Christian History. Studies in Church History*, vol. 36, ed. R. N. Swanson (Woodbridge: The Boydell Press for the Ecclesiastical History Society, 2000), 358, with Bernard Sabella, "Palestinian Christians: Realities and Hopes," in the same volume, 373–97, at p. 374. See also Mitri Raheb, *Sailing through Troubled Waters: Christianity in the Middle East* (n.p.: Diyar Publisher, 2013), 97.

59. Samuel J. Kuruvilla, *Radical Christianity in Palestine and Israel: Liberation and Theology in the Middle East* (London: I. B. Tauris, 2013), 104.

60. Marc H. Ellis, "Theologies of Liberation in Palestine-Israel and the Struggle for Peace and Justice," in *Theologies of Liberation in Palestine-Israel: Indigenous, Contextual, and Postcolonial Perspectives*, eds. Nur Masalha and Lisa Isherwood (Eugene, OR: Pickwick Publications, 2014), 39–56.

61. Naim S. Ateek, Marc H. Ellis, and Rosemary Radford Ruether, eds., *Faith and the Intifada: Palestinian Christian Voices* (Maryknoll, NY: Orbis Books, 1992), xi.

62. Naim Ateek and Michael Prior, ed., *Holy Land Hollow Jubilee: God, Justice and the Palestinians* (London: Melisende, 1999), 17.

63. Edward W. Said, *Out of Place: A Memoir* (London: Granta Books, 1999), 5, 15, 22, 31, 107, 112–14, 118–19, 143–44, 225–33.

64. Mitri Raheb, *Faith in the Face of Empire: The Bible through Palestinian Eyes* (Maryknoll, NY: Orbis Books, 2014), 27–28.

65. Sabella, "Palestinian Christians," 373.

66. Ibid., 374, 391.

67. Inger Marie Okkenhaug, *The Quality of Heroic Living, of High Endeavour and Adventure: Anglican Mission, Women and Education in Palestine, 1888–1948* (Leiden: E. J. Brill, 2002), 41.

68. Y. Porath, *The Emergence of the Palestinian-Arab National Movement 1918–1929* (London: Frank Cass, 1974), 295.

69. Okkenhaug, *The Quality of Heroic Living*, 82.

70. Donald M. Lewis, *The Origins of Christian Zionism: Lord Shaftesbury and Evangelical Support for a Jewish Homeland* (Cambridge: Cambridge University Press, 2010).

71. Ibid., 107–9.

72. Kuruvilla, *Radical Christianity in Palestine and Israel*, 53–4.

73. O'Mahony, "The Vatican, Palestinian Christians, Israel, and Jerusalem," 359–60, n. 6; Michael Christopher King, *The Palestinians and the Churches*, vol. I: *1948–1956* (Geneva: WCC, 1981).

74. Larry Ekin, *Enduring Witness: The Churches and the Palestinians*, vol. II (Geneva: World Council of Churches, 1985), 130–35.

75. Uwe Gräbe, "Mission and Proselytism, Presence and Witness," in *Christian Witness between Continuity and New Beginnings: Modern Historical Missions in the Middle East*, eds. Martin Tamcke and Michael Marten (Berlin: Lit Verlag, 2006), 249–50.

76. Kuruvilla, *Radical Christianity in Palestine and Israel*, 75–78.

77. Ibid., 75–80.

78. Coffey, *Exodus and Liberation*, passim.

79. Alistair Kee, *The Rise and Demise of Black Theology* (Aldershot: Ashgate, 2006), 82–84.

80. Gina Lende, "A Quest for Justice: Palestinian Christians and their Contextual Theology" (M.Phil. thesis, University of Oslo, 2003), cited in Kuruvilla, *Radical Christianity in Palestine and Israel*, 71.

Chapter 11. Doing Justice in South Africa and Canada

1. Mary Ann Glendon, *A World Made New: Eleanor Roosevelt and the Universal Declaration of Human Rights* (New York: Random House, 2001), 42–43, 176.

2. Glendon, *A World Made New*, 154, 168; John Nurser, *For All Peoples and All Nations: Christian Churches and Human Rights* (Washington, DC, and Geneva: Georgetown University Press and WCC Publications, 2005), 160–69; O. Frederick Noble, *Free and Equal: Human Rights in Ecumenical Perspective* (Geneva: World Council of Churches, 1968), introduction by Charles Habib Malik, 10, and 42–46; Samuel Moyn, *The Last Utopia: Human Rights in History* (Cambridge, MA: The Belknap Press of Harvard University Press, 2010), 65, 256–57 n. 38.

3. Peter Marshall, "Smuts and the Preamble to the United Nations Charter," *Round Table; The Commonwealth Journal of International Affairs* 90, no. 358 (2001): 55–65.

4. Owen Chadwick, *The Christian Church in the Cold War* (London: Penguin Books, 1993), 67–71.

5. Moyn, *The Last Utopia*, 76–79.

6. Maurine H. Beasley, *Eleanor Roosevelt: Transformative First Lady* (Lawrence: University Press of Kansas, 2010), 110, 120–2, 127–31, 134–35, 138–40, 154–57, 193–98.

7. Martin Luther King, "Letter from a Birmingham Jail," April 16, 1963, http://okra.stanford.edu/transcription/document_images/undecided/630416-019.pdf (Accessed March 10, 2017).

8. James F. Findlay, Jr., *Church People in the Struggle: The National Council of Churches and the Black Freedom Movement, 1950–1970* (New York: Oxford University Press, 1993), 3, 33–4.

9. "Black Manifesto," http://www.episcopalarchives.org/Afro-Anglican_history/exhibit/pdf/blackmanifesto.pdf (Accessed March 10, 2017); Jerry K. Frye, "The 'Black Manifesto' and the Tactic of Objectification," *Journal of Black Studies* 5, no. 1

(1974): 72; Findlay, *Church People in the Struggle*, 200–201; for a contemporary assessment in 1969 see Robert S. Lecky and H. Elliott Wright, eds., *Black Manifesto: Religion, Racism and Reparations* (New York: Sheed and Wright, 1969).

10. Riverside Church is affiliated both to the American Baptist Churches USA and the United Church of Christ.

11. Findlay, *Church People in the Struggle*, 202–3.

12. Howard Schomer, " The Manifesto and the Magnificat," *The Christian Century*, June 25, 1969, 866; Findlay, *Church People in the Struggle*, 203–4.

13. Findlay, *Church People in the Struggle*, 206.

14. Thomas C. Reeves, *The Empty Church: The Suicide of Liberal Christianity* (New York: Free Press, 1996), 140; Findlay, *Church People in the Struggle*, 212–19.

15. Findlay, *Church People in the Struggle*, 220–23.

16. J. Robert Nelson, "Preparation for Reparation and Separation: The Churches' Response to Racism?," *The Christian Century*, June 25, 1969, 862–65.

17. The seven points are reproduced in Claude E. Welch, Jr., "Mobilizing Morality: The World Council of Churches and its Programme to Combat Racism, 1969–1994," *Human Rights Quarterly* 23, no. 4 (2001): 878.

18. Lecky and Wright, eds., *Black Manifesto*, 26–27; Elisabeth Adler, *A Small Beginning: An Assessment of the First Five Years of the Programme to Combat Racism* (Geneva: World Council of Churches, 1974), 14–15, 95.

19. Trevor Huddleston, *Naught for Your Comfort* (London: Collins, 1956).

20. Nelson, "Preparation for Reparation and Separation," 862.

21. Håkan Thörn, *Anti-Apartheid and the Emergence of a Global Civil Society* (Basingstoke: Palgrave Macmillan, 2006), 6–7, 10.

22. Figures of the number of casualties vary slightly; see Ambrose Reeves, *Shooting at Sharpeville: The Agony of South Africa* (London: Victor Gollancz, 1960), 55; John S. Peart-Binns, *Ambrose Reeves* (London: Victor Gollancz, 1973), 206–15.

23. Peart-Binns, *Ambrose Reeves*, 235–36; Michael E. Worsnip, *Between the Two Fires: The Anglican Church and Apartheid* (Pietermaritzburg: University of Natal Press, 1991), 149–51.

24. On Loram (1879–1940) see *Dictionary of South African Biography*, vol. III (Pretoria: Talfelbeg-Uitgewers for the Human Sciences Council, 1977), 537–8; Richard D. Heyman, "C. T. Loram: a South African Liberal in Race Relations," *International Journal of Historical Studies* 5, no. 1 (1972): 41–50; Richard Elphick, *The Equality of Believers: Protestant Missionaries and the Racial Politics of South Africa* (Charlottesville: University of Virginia Press, 2012), 184–85.

25. Elphick, *The Equality of Believers*, 117–19, 154–56.

26. Ibid., 191–93; on Brookes (1897–1979) see also *Dictionary of South African Biography*, vol. V (Pretoria: Chris Van Rensburg Publications for the Human Sciences Research Council, 1987), 92–94.

27. Saul Dubow, "Afrikaner Nationalism, Apartheid and the Conceptualization of 'Race'," *Journal of African History* 33, no. 2(1992): 209–37; Elphick, *The Equality of Believers*, 222–57.

28. Cited in "World Council of Churches' Consultation with Member-Churches in South Africa: Cottesloe, Johannesburg, 7–14 December, 1960," *The Ecumenical Review* 13, no. 2 (1961), 246; see W. A. Visser 't Hooft, *Memoirs* (London: SCM Press,

1973), 285, 295 n. 4. The original NGK memorandum limited the right of democratic participation "in the government of which [they were] a subject" to those non-whites who were "economically integrated," i.e., those in white urban areas who had no residence in a black homeland.

29. On Naudé see Charles Villa-Vicencio and John W. de Gruchy, *Resistance and Hope: South African Essays in Honour of Beyers Naudé* (Grand Rapids, MI: Eerdmans; and Cape Town: David Philip, 1985); John W. de Gruchy with Steve de Gruchy, *The Church Struggle in South Africa*, 3rd ed. (London: SCM Press, 2004), 101–12.

30. *Final Report of the Commission of Inquiry into Certain Organisations: Christian Institute of Southern Africa* (Pretoria: Government of the Republic of South Africa, n.d. [1974]).

31. "Beyers Naudé on Trial," *Christian Institute News*, December 1973, p. 3; International Committee of Jurists, Geneva, ed., *The Trial of Beyers Naudé: Christian Witness and the Rule of Law* (London: Search Press, in conjunction with Ravan Press, Johannesburg, 1975).

32. Ian Mcqueen, "Students, Apartheid and the Ecumenical Movement in South Africa, 1960–1975," *Journal of Southern African Studies* 39, no. 2 (2013): 447–63; Philippe Denis, "Seminary Networks and Black Consciousness in the 1970s," *South African Historical Journal* 62, no. 1 (2010): 162–82; I owe the latter reference to Dr. Denis.

33. Pete Lowman, *The Day of His Power: A History of the International Fellowship of Evangelical Students* (Leicester: Inter-Varsity Press, 1983), 28–29, 272–75. The SCM did not formally affiliate to IFES.

34. Anthony Butler, *Cyril Ramaphosa* (Oxford: James Currey, 2008), 26–9, 50–1.

35. Ibid., 86–87; Frank Chikane, *No Life of My Own: An Autobiography* (London: Catholic Institute for International Relations, 1988), 37–39; Caesar Molebatsi with David Virtue, *A Flame for Justice* (Oxford: Lion Publishing, 1991), 94–97.

36. Allen James Goddard, "Invitations to Prophetic Integrity in the Evangelical Spirituality of the Students' Christian Association Discipleship Tradition: 1965–1979" (PhD diss., University of KwaZulu-Natal, 2016), chapter 5. This paragraph is indebted to Dr. Goddard's dissertation.

37. Butler, *Cyril Ramaphosa*, 56.

38. Ibid., 392. In February 2018 Ramaphosa became president of South Africa.

39. Chikane, *No Life of My Own*, 43–44, 50–51, 61–64, 76. At the time of writing (in 2017) Chikane was the president of Apostolic Faith Mission International.

40. Peter Walshe, "South Africa: Prophetic Christianity and the Liberation Movement," *Journal of Modern African Studies* 29, no. 1 (1991): 48.

41. "The Kairos Document (1985)," in Andrew Bradstock and Christopher Rowland, eds., *Radical Christian Writings: A Reader* (Oxford: Blackwell, 2002), 285–304, at 304.

42. Church membership in 1995 was estimated at 78 percent of the population; *World Christian Encyclopedia*, eds. David B. Barrett, George T. Kurian and Todd M. Johnson, 2nd ed. (Oxford: Oxford University Press, 2001), 675.

43. Butler, *Cyril Ramaphosa*, 72.

44. Elphick, *The Equality of Believers*, 181–93.

45. John W. de Gruchy, "Grappling with a Colonial Heritage: The English-Speaking Churches under Imperialism and Apartheid," in *Christianity in South Africa: A Political, Cultural, and Social History*, ed. Richard Elphick and Rodney Davenport (Oxford: James Currey; and Cape Town: David Philip, 1997), 161–62; for

the Social Gospel tradition in South Africa see Richard Elphick, "The Benevolent Empire and the Social Gospel: Missionaries and South African Christians in the Age of Segregation," in ibid., 347–69.

46. John Webster Grant, *Moon of Wintertime: Missionaries and the Indians of Canada in Encounter since 1534* (Toronto: University of Toronto Press, 1984), 177.

47. Compare J. R. Miller, *Shingwauk's Vision: A History of Native Residential Schools* (Toronto: University of Toronto Press, 1996), 142, and John S. Milloy, *"A National Crime": The Canadian Government and the Residential School System* (Winnipeg: University of Manitoba Press, 1999), 208.

48. Milloy, *"A National Crime,"* 3.

49. Brian Clarke, "English-Speaking Canada from 1854," in Terrence Murphy and Roberto Perin, eds., *A Concise History of Christianity in Canada* (Toronto: Oxford University Press, 1996), 304–5.

50. Miller, *Shingwauk's Vision,* 350–51.

51. Ibid., 169.

52. For the Oblates' advocacy of agriculture see Brian Titley, "A Troubled Legacy: The Catholic Church and Indian Residential Schooling in Canada," *Paedagogica Historica: International Journal of the History of Education* 31, Supplement 1 (1995): 335–49.

53. Grant, *Moon of Wintertime,* 184.

54. Miller, *Shingwauk's Vision,* 415–16; Titley, "A Troubled Legacy," 342–43.

55. Grant, *Moon of Wintertime,* 186.

56. Ibid., 198.

57. Milloy, *"A National Crime,"* 220–21; Grant, *Moon of Wintertime,* 199.

58. Titley, "A Troubled Legacy," 344–48.

59. Grant, *Moon of Wintertime,* 191–92.

60. Miller, *Shingwauk's Vision,* 199–200.

61. Eric Bays, *Indian Residential Schools: Another Picture* (Ottawa: Baico Publishing, 2009), 39–52.

62. On Blake (1835–1914), see *Dictionary of Canadian Biography: Volume XIV (1911–1920)* (Toronto: University of Toronto Press, 1998), 85–88. Blake was a prime mover in the foundation in 1877 of the Protestant Episcopal Divinity School (later named Wycliffe College) as an evangelical response to the High Church Trinity College, Toronto.

63. Megan Sproule-Jones, "Crusading for the Forgotten: Dr. Peter Bryce, Public Health, and Prairie Native Residential Schools," *Canadian Bulletin of Medical History* 13 (1996): 199–224.

64. Samuel Hume Blake, *Don't You Hear the Red Man Calling?* (Toronto: publisher not known, 1908), 11–16, 18, 22; in "Our Roots: Canada's Local Histories Online," http://ourroots.ca (Accessed March 10, 2017).

65. Grant, *Moon of Wintertime,* 194–96.

66. P. H. Bryce, *The Story of a National Crime: An Appeal for Justice to the Indians of Canada* (Ottawa: James Hope & Sons, 1922). The title of Bryce's pamphlet is reflected in one of the standard modern histories of the residential schools by John S. Milloy, *"A National Crime"* (1999).

67. Charles T. Loram, "The Fundamentals of Indian White Contact in the United States and Canada," in *The North American Indian Today: University of Toronto—Yale*

University Seminar Conference: Toronto, September 4–16, 1939, ed. C. T. Loram and T. F. McIlwraith (Toronto: University of Toronto Press, 1943), 8–9.

68. Grant, *Moon of Wintertime,* 185.

69. Clarke, "English-Speaking Canada from 1854," 353.

70. A. E. Caldwell, "Indian Education Today," in *No Vanishing Race: The Canadian Indian Today,* ed. George Dorey and others (Toronto: The Committee on Missionary Education of the United Church of Canada, 1955), 59.

71. James E. Milord, "Genocide in Canada: We Call It Integration," *United Church Observer,* August 1970, 24–6; cited in Phyllis D. Airhart, *A Church with the Soul of a Nation: Making and Remaking the United Church of Canada* (Montreal: McGill-Queen's University Press, 2014), 232.

72. Cited by Benjamin G. Smillie, "The Missionary Vision of the Heart," in *Visions of the Heart: Canadian Aboriginal Issues,* eds. David Alan Long and Olive Patricia Dickason (Toronto: Harcourt Brace & Company, 1996), 27–28.

73. Miller, *Shingwauk's Vision,* 328–29.

74. The only large Canadian denomination that did not have residential schools was the Baptists, who were opposed on principle to the receipt of state financial aid for church or mission work.

75. Ronald Niezen, *Truth and Indignation: Canada's Truth and Reconciliation Commission on Indian Residential Schools* (Toronto: University of Toronto Press, 2013), 44–45.

76. Niezen, *Truth and Indignation,* 52–53, 59.

77. Ibid., 18–19; Pauline Regan, *Unsettling the Settler Within: Indian Residential Schools, Truth Telling, and Reconciliation in Canada* (Vancouver: University of British Columbia Press, 2010), 193.

78. Kevin N. Flatt, *After Evangelicalism: The Sixties and the United Church of Canada* (Montreal: McGill-Queen's University Press, 2013).

79. Mark A. Noll, "What Happened to Christian Canada?," *Church History* 75, no. 2 (2006): 245–73.

80. By the end of 1974 the PCR had awarded 22,500 US dollars to three First Nations organizations; Adler, *A Small Beginning,* 93.

81. Grant, *Moon of Wintertime,* 202–4; Bays, *Indian Residential Schools,* 168.

Chapter 12. A Noise of War in the Camp

1. The important exception was the anti-slavery movement, which, at least in principle, was gender-neutral in its determination to liberate human beings from bondage.

2. David John Frank and Elizabeth H. McEneaney, "The Individualization of Society and the Liberalization of State Policies on Same-Sex Sexual Relations, 1984–1995," *Social Forces* 77, no. 3 (1999): 911–44; Daniel Hurewitz, *Bohemian Los Angeles and the Making of Modern Politics* (Berkeley, CA: University of California Press, 2007), 5–6.

3. Randall T. Davidson, *The Six Lambeth Conferences 1867–1920. Compiled under the Direction of the Most Reverend Lord Davidson of Lambeth Archbishop of Canterbury, 1903–1928,* new ed. (London: SPCK, 1929), "Resolutions Formally Adopted by

the Conference of 1920," resolution 48, p. 44; *The Lambeth Conference 1930: Encyclical Letter from the Bishops with the Resolutions and Reports* (London: SPCK, n.d. [1930]), 89–92.

4. Alexandra Nikolchev, "A Brief History of the Birth Control Pill," http://www.pbs.org/wnet/need-to-know/health/a-brief-history-of-the-birth-control-pill/480/ (Accessed May 2, 2017).

5. The Alliance of the Reformed Churches Holding the Presbyterian System was formed in 1875; the World Methodist Council in 1881; the International Congregational Council in 1891; the Baptist World Alliance in 1905. The Presbyterian and Congregational world bodies merged in 1970 to form the World Alliance of Reformed Churches (which in 2010 amalgamated with a more conservative body, the Reformed Ecumenical Council, to form the World Communion of Reformed Churches).

6. See especially Philip Jenkins, *The Next Christendom: The Coming of Global Christianity*, 3rd ed. (Oxford: Oxford University Press, 2011). The language of "culture wars" derives from James Davison Hunter, *Culture Wars: The Struggle to Define America* (New York: Basic Books, 1991).

7. See Timothy Larsen, *Christabel Pankhurst: Fundamentalism and Feminism in Coalition* (Woodbridge: The Boydell Press, 2002).

8. David Hilliard, "Pluralism and New Alignments in Society and Church: 1967 to the Present," in *Anglicanism in Australia: A History*, ed. Bruce Kaye (Carlton South, Victoria: Melbourne University Press, 2002), 135–36.

9. Hilliard, "Pluralism and New Alignments in Society and Church," 127.

10. Patrick O'Farrell, *The Catholic Church in Australia: A Short History: 1788–1967* (London: Geoffrey Chapman, 1968), 2, 243.

11. Muriel Porter, *Sydney Anglicans and the Threat to World Anglicanism* (Farnham: Ashgate, 2011), 30, 32, 34.

12. See David Goodhew, "The Rise of the Cambridge Inter-Collegiate Christian Union, 1910–1971," *Journal of Ecclesiastical History* 54, no. 1 (2003): 62–88.

13. On Hammond see Geoffrey R. Treloar, *The Disruption of Evangelicalism: The Age of Torrey, Mott, McPherson and Hammond* (Downers Grove, IL: Inter-Varsity Press, 2016), 199–200.

14. Marcus L. Loane, *Archbishop Mowll: the Biography of Howard West Kilvinton Mowll Archbishop of Sydney and Primate of Australia* (London: Hodder & Stoughton, 1960), 143–8; Stephen Judd and Kenneth Cable, *Sydney Anglicans: A History of the Diocese* (Sydney: Anglican Information Office, 1987), 238–40.

15. Ian Breward, *A History of the Churches in Australasia* (Oxford: Oxford University Press, 2001), 304.

16. *The Six Lambeth Conferences 1867–1920*, resolutions 48 and 50, p. 40.

17. *The Lambeth Conference 1930*, 177–9; see Sean Gill, *Women and the Church of England from the Eighteenth Century to the Present* (London: SPCK, 1994), 219, 238.

18. Breward, *A History of the Churches in Australasia*, 210–11.

19. Nora Tress, *Caught for Life: A Story of the Anglican Deaconess Order in Australia* (Araluen, NSW: Nora Tress, 1993), 91, cited in Timothy Willem Jones, *Sexual Politics in the Church of England, 1857–1957* (Oxford: Oxford University Press, 2013), 100.

20. Anne O'Brien, *God's Willing Workers: Women and Religion in Australia* (Sydney: University of New South Wales Press, 2005), 107, 111, 116–18.

21. Jacqueline Field-Bibb, *Women Towards Priesthood: Ministerial Politics and Feminist Praxis* (Cambridge: Cambridge University Press, 1991), 134–35.

22. *The Lambeth Conference 1968: Resolutions and Reports* (London: SPCK, 1968), 39–40, 106; cited in Field-Bibb, *Women Towards Priesthood*, 103. The section report reflected the views of its chairman, Archbishop Donald Coggan of York, an evangelical supporter of the ordination of women.

23. O'Brien, *God's Willing Workers*, 239.

24. Porter, *Sydney Anglicans and the Threat to World Anglicanism*, 115.

25. Piggin, *Evangelical Christianity in Australia*, 205.

26. Robert J. Banks, "The Theology of D. B. Knox: A Preliminary Estimate," in *God Who Is Rich in Mercy: Essays Presented to Dr. D. B. Knox*, ed. Peter T. O'Brien and David G. Peterson (Homebush West, NSW: Lancer Books, 1986), 377–403.

27. Stuart Piggin, *Evangelical Christianity in Australia: Spirit, Word and World* (Melbourne: Oxford University Press, 1996), 204.

28. Piggin, *Evangelical Christianity in Australia*, 208–9; David Hilliard, "Pluralism and New Alignments in Society and Church," 134; see obituary of Dr. Patricia Brennan in *Sydney Morning Herald*, April 8, 2011.

29. David Robarts, "A Tolerable Pluralism?" in *Women Priests in Australia? The Anglican Crisis*, ed. David Wetherell (Melbourne: Spectrum Publications, 1987), 57.

30. David Hilliard, "Defending Orthodoxy: Some Conservative and Traditionalist Movements in Australian Christianity," in *Making History for God: Essays on Evangelicalism, Revival and Mission in Honour of Stuart Piggin, Master of Robert Menzies College 1990-2004*, ed. Geoffrey R. Treloar and Robert D. Linder (Sydney: Robert Menzies College, 2004), 284; Piggin, *Evangelical Christianity in Australia*, 209–10; Brian Stanley, *The Global Diffusion of Evangelicalism: The Age of Billy Graham and John Stott* (Downers Grove, IL: Inter-Varsity Press, 2013), 218–19.

31. Piggin, *Evangelical Christianity in Australia*, 203, 210–13.

32. *Sydney Morning Herald*, April 18, 1992.

33. Gill, *Women and the Church of England*, 258.

34. Piggin, *Evangelical Christianity in Australia*, 220.

35. Hilliard, "Defending Orthodoxy," 286.

36. On the Ordinariate see "The Personal Ordinariate of our Lady of the Southern Cross," http://www.ordinariate.org.au/ (Accessed May 2, 2017).

37. Nicholas C. Edsall, *Toward Stonewall: Homosexuality and Society in the Modern Western World* (Charlottesville: University of Virginia Press, 2003), 3–5, 8–9, 13, 71, 221–2; John d'Emilio, *Sexual Politics, Sexual Communities: The Making of a Homosexual Minority in the United States 1940-1970* (Chicago: The University of Chicago Press, 1983), 4. The late eighteenth-century French court is the only clear example of a pre-nineteenth-century lesbian subculture identified by historians. Homosexual culture in ancient Greece idealized male homosexual relationships as a form of noble pleasure, but without any clear sense of a compulsion arising from the innate homosexual identity of certain individuals.

38. *LIFE* magazine, 26 June 1964, 68; Les Wright, "San Francisco," in *Queer Sites: Gay Urban Histories since 1600*, ed. David Higgs (London: Routledge, 1999), 164–76.

39. Les Wright, "San Francisco," 173, 185.

40. Ibid., 178, 180.

41. D'Emilio, *Sexual Politics, Sexual Communities*, 33–37; John D. Skrentny, *The Minority Rights Revolution* (Cambridge: MA: The Belknap Press of Harvard University Press, 2002), 322, 447 n. 206.

42. Alfred T. Kinsey, Wardell B. Pomeroy, and Clyde E. Martin, *Sexual Behavior in the Human Male* (Philadelphia: W. B. Saunders, 1948), 638–41, 647, 650. While Kinsey found (p. 651) that 10% of white males were "more or less exclusively homosexual" for at least three years between the ages of 16 and 55, he also found that only 4 percent were "exclusively homosexual throughout their lives" after the onset of adolescence. The parallel figures for women were much lower: see Alfred C. Kinsey, Wardell B. Pomeroy, Clyde E. Martin, Paul H. Gebhard, and others, *Sexual Behavior in the Human Female* (Philadelphia: W. B. Saunders, 1953), 473–74.

43. Ronald Bayer, *Homosexuality, and American Psychiatry: The Politics of Diagnosis* (New York: Basic Books, 1981); Maarit Jänterä-Jareborg, "A Scandinavian Perspective on Homosexuality, Equal Rights, and Freedom of Religion," in *Religious Freedom and Gay Rights: Emerging Conflicts in the United States and Europe*, ed. Timothy Samuel Shah, Thomas F. Farr, and Jack Friedman (New York: Oxford University Press, 2016), 251.

44. D'Emilio, *Sexual Politics, Sexual Communities*, 193–95, 214.

45. Ronald M. Enroth and Gerald E. Jamison, *The Gay Church* (Grand Rapids, MI: Eerdmans, 1974), 29–30.

46. Enroth and Jamison, *The Gay Church*, 74–75, 82.

47. *Christianity Today* 18, no. 15 (1974): 13–14, cited in Didi Herman, *The Antigay Agenda: Orthodox Vision and the Christian Right* (Chicago: University of Chicago Press, 1997), 45–6.

48. Enroth and Jamison, *The Gay Church*, 91.

49. Mark D. Jordan, *The Silence of Sodom: Homosexuality in Modern Catholicism* (Chicago: University of Chicago Press, 2000), 249–50. McNeill developed his articles published in the *Homiletic and Pastoral Review* for July, August, and September 1970 into a book, *The Church and the Homosexual* (London: Darton, Longman & Todd, 1977), which, after considerable delay, received the *imprimi potest* from the provincial of the Jesuit order.

50. Jordan, *The Silence of Sodom*, 31–32, 251; Robert Nugent and Jeannine Gramick, *Building Bridges: Gay and Lesbian Reality and the Catholic Church* (Mystic, CT: Twenty-Third Publications, 1992), 169–70.

51. Caroline J. Addington Hall, *A Thorn in the Flesh: How Gay Sexuality is Changing the Episcopal Church* (Lanham: MD: Rowman & Littlefield, 2013), 45, 48–49.

52. *Time*, 109, no. 4 (January 24, 1977): 58. Barrett denied the accuracy of the report.

53. Paul Moore, Jr., *Take a Bishop Like Me* (New York: Harper & Row, 1979), 133–35, 143; Hall, *A Thorn in the Flesh*, 54–57.

54. Hall, *A Thorn in the Flesh*, 59–60.

55. John Shelby Spong, *Living in Sin: A Bishop Rethinks Human Sexuality* (San Francisco: Harper & Row, 1988), 204; see also Hall, *A Thorn in the Flesh*, 76.

56. Hall, *A Thorn in the Flesh*, 79–82.

57. Ibid., 85, 89.

58. Miranda K. Hassett, *Anglican Communion in Crisis: How Episcopal Dissidents and Their African Allies Are Reshaping Anglicanism* (Princeton, NJ, and Oxford: Princeton University Press, 2007), 77–79.

59. Hall, *A Thorn in the Flesh*, 61–74, 107–24; Kevin Ward, *A History of Global Anglicanism* (Cambridge: Cambridge University Press, 2006), 313, 315. For a more journalistic treatment of the broader subject see S. Bates, *A Church at War: Anglicans and Homosexuality* (London: I. B. Tauris, 2004).

60. *The Christian Century*, December 2, 1992, 1097, cited in *The Sexuality Debate in North American Churches, 1988–1995: Controversies, Unresolved Issues, Future Prospects*, ed. John J. Carey (Lewiston, ME: Edwin Mellen Press, 1995), xiii.

61. Hassett, *Anglican Communion in Crisis*, 243.

62. The incompatibility clause was first introduced in 1972, and the accompanying prohibitions in 1976; Amanda Udis-Kessler, *Queer Inclusion in the United Methodist Church* (London, Routledge, 2008), 2.

63. Ibid., 67–72, 76–77, 85.

64. James D. Anderson, "The Lesbian and Gay Liberation Movement in the Presbyterian Church (U.S.A.), 1974–1996," *Journal of Homosexuality* 34, no. 2 (1997–98): 37–65.

65. Carey, *The Sexuality Debate in North American Churches, 1988–1995*, 44–46.

66. Udis-Kessler, *Queer Inclusion in the United Methodist Church*, 38, 40.

67. Hilliard, "Defending Orthodoxy," 280–82.

Chapter 13. The Spirit and the spirits

1. For a fuller account of the diffusion of charismatic renewal in evangelical Protestantism see my *The Global Diffusion of Evangelicalism: The Age of Billy Graham and John Stott* (Downers Grove, IL: Inter-Varsity Press, 2013), chapter 7.

2. Richard J. Bord and Joseph E. Faulkner, *The Catholic Charismatics: The Anatomy of a Modern Religious Movement* (University Park: The Pennsylvania State University Press, 1983), 8.

3. See especially *Lumen Gentium*, chapter 1, para. 7.

4. Katharine L. Wiegele, *Investing in Miracles: El Shaddai and the Transformation of Popular Catholicism in the Philippines* (Honolulu: University of Hawai'i Press, 2005), 4. Wiegele dates the inception of the radio program from 1981, but the movement's own former website, now no longer accessible, gave August 1983.

5. Grant Wacker, *Heaven Below: Early Pentecostals and American Culture* (Cambridge, MA: Harvard University Press, 2001), 161.

6. J. E. Lesslie Newbigin, *The Household of God: Lectures on the Nature of the Church* (London: SCM Press, 1953), 87–88.

7. Walter J. Hollenweger, *The Pentecostals* (London: SCM Press, 1972).

8. Allan Anderson, *An Introduction to Pentecostalism* (Cambridge: Cambridge University Press, 2004), 34.

9. Allan Anderson, *Spreading Fires: The Missionary Nature of Early Pentecostalism* (London: SCM Press, 2007), 57–65.

10. Anderson, *Spreading Fires*, 59; Wacker, *Heaven Below*, 232.

11. Brian Stanley, *The History of the Baptist Missionary Society 1792–1992* (Edinburgh: T. & T. Clark, 1992), 68–69.

12. Wacker, *Heaven Below*, 231.

13. Anderson, *Spreading Fires*, 28–29, 47–48, 79–89; Christian Lalive d'Epinay, *Haven of the Masses: A Study of the Pentecostal Movement in Chile* (London: Lutterworth Press, 1969), 7–14.

14. Allan Anderson, *To the Ends of the Earth: Pentecostalism and the Transformation of World Christianity* (New York: Oxford University Press, 2013), 5–6.

15. *Oxford English Dictionary*, 3rd online ed. (Oxford: Oxford University Press, 2005), citing *New York Times*, June 23, 1927, p. 1.

16. Adam Mohr, "Out of Zion into Philadelphia and West Africa: Faith Tabernacle Congregation, 1897–1925," *Pneuma* 32 (2010): 56–79.

17. Bengt Sundkler, *Zulu Zion and Some Swazi Zionists* (London: Oxford University Press, 1976), 14–43; David Maxwell, "Historicizing Christian Independency: The Southern African Pentecostal Movement," *Journal of African History* 40, no. 2 (1999): 243–64; idem, *African Gifts of the Spirit: Pentecostalism and the Rise of a Zimbabwean Transnational Religious Movement* (Oxford: James Currey, 2006), 38–45.

18. Mohr, "Out of Zion into Philadelphia and West Africa," 56–79.

19. David Killingray, "A New 'Imperial Disease': The Influenza Pandemic of 1918–9 and Its Impact upon the British Empire," *Caribbean Quarterly* 39, no. 4 (2003): 30–49; Adam Mohr, *Enchanted Calvinism: Labor Migration, Afflicting Spirits, and Christian Therapy in the Presbyterian Church of Ghana* (Rochester, NY: University of Rochester Press, 2013), 61, 68.

20. J. D. Y. Peel, *Aladura: A Religious Movement among the Yoruba* (London: Oxford University Press, 1968), 132–3; Adrian Hastings, *The Church in Africa 1450–1950* (Oxford: Clarendon Press, 1996), 516.

21. Gordon Lindsay, *The Life of John Alexander Dowie whose Trials-Tragedies and Triumphs are the Most Fascinating Object Lesson of Christian History* (n.p.: Voice of Healing Publishing Company, 1951), 22–25; Philip L. Cook, *Zion City, Illinois: Twentieth-Century Utopia* (Syracuse, NY: Syracuse University Press, 1996), 8.

22. L. G. McLung, Jr., "Exorcism," in *Dictionary of Pentecostal and Charismatic Movements*, eds. Stanley M. Burgess and Gary B. McGee (Grand Rapids, MI: Zondervan, 1988), 292.

23. J. E. Casely Hayford, *William Waddy Harris. The West African Reformer: The Man and His Message* (London: C. M. Phillips, 1915), 11; David A. Shank, *Prophet Harris: The "Black Elijah" of West Africa* (Leiden: E. J. Brill, 1994), 177–78.

24. See chapter 3.

25. Peel, *Aladura*, 91, 95, 141 [*my italics*].

26. Mohr, *Enchanted Calvinism*, 69–70.

27. Shank, *Prophet Harris*, 180; J. Kwabena Asamoah-Gyadu, *African Charismatics: Current Developments within Independent Indigenous Pentecostalism in Ghana* (Leiden: E. J. Brill, 2005), 43.

28. On the use of sacred objects as a dividing line between Spiritual and Pentecostal churches in Ghana see Birgit Meyer, *Translating the Devil: Religion and Modernity among the Ewe in Ghana* (Edinburgh: Edinburgh University Press for the International African Institute, 1999), 116–17, 136.

29. Asamoah-Gyadu, *African Charismatics*, 25; Mohr, "Out of Zion into Philadelphia and West Africa," 78.

30. Meyer, *Translating the Devil*, 106; Mohr, *Enchanted Calvinism*, 81.

31. This is the theme of Mohr, *Enchanted Calvinism*.

32. Asamoah-Gyadu, *African Charismatics*, 64–95.

33. Paul Gifford, *Ghana's New Christianity: Pentecostalism in a Globalising African Economy* (London: Hurst & Co., 2004), 11.

34. Emmanuel Kingsley Larbi, *Pentecostalism: The Eddies of Ghanaian Christianity* (Accra: Centre for Pentecostal Studies, 2001), 301.

35. Gifford, *Ghana's New Christianity*, 86, 88; idem, *African Christianity: Its Public Role* (London: Hurst & Co., 1998), 105.

36. Kate Bowler, *Blessed: A History of the American Prosperity Gospel* (Oxford: Oxford University Press, 2012).

37. Larbi, *Pentecostalism*, 308.

38. Ibid., 335–60; Gifford, *Ghana's New Christianity*, 135, 139, 197.

39. Derek Prince, *Life's Bitter Pool* (Harpenden: Derek Prince Ministries, 1984), 43.

40. Prince's obituary in *King's College Cambridge Annual Report* (2004), 50, notes the particular significance of audiocassettes for the dissemination of his teaching.

41. Gifford, *African Christianity*, 100, 346–7.

42. Opoku Onyinah, *Pentecostal Exorcism: Witchcraft and Demonology in Ghana* (Blandford Forum: Deo Publishing, 2012), 172.

43. Gifford, *Ghana's New Christianity*, 89; see also Larbi, *Pentecostalism*, 393.

44. Paul Gifford, *Christianity, Development and Modernity in Africa* (London: Hurst & Co., 2015), 118–19; idem, *African Christianity*, 227; James M. Collins, *Exorcism and Deliverance Ministry in the Twentieth Century: An Analysis of the Practice and Theology of Exorcism in Modern Western Christianity* (Milton Keynes: Paternoster, 2009), 57, 61, 63.

45. Collins, *Exorcism and Deliverance Ministry in the Twentieth Century*, 64–65, 87–90.

46. King's College Cambridge archives (KCAC/4/11/1), P. D. V. Prince, "The Evolution of Plato's Philosophical Method" (Fellowship dissertation, n.d. [1940]). Prince acknowledges his debt to Wittgenstein three times, on pp. 7, 12, and 130.

47. Prince's popular biographer, Stephen Mansfield, is the only commentator who has noted the marked Platonic influence on Prince's cosmology; see *Derek Prince: A Biography* (Baldock: Derek Prince Ministries and Authentic Media, 2005), 274.

48. Derek Prince, *Blessing or Curse: You Can Choose!* (Bletchley: Authentic Media, 2005), 18–19; see also his *Lucifer Exposed: The Devil's Plan to Destroy Your Life*, new ed. (Baldock: Derek Prince Ministries, 2007). Cf. Plato, *Phaedo*, transl. David Gallop (Oxford: Clarendon Press, 1975), 27.

49. Prince, *Blessing or Curse*, 32–42, 62; Plato, *Phaedrus*, transl. Robin Waterfield (Oxford: Oxford University Press, 2002), 244d–e, pp. 26–27.

50. Kwame Bediako, *Theology and Identity: The Impact of Culture upon Christian Thought in the Second Century and Modern Africa* (Oxford: Regnum Books, 1992), 108–9, 144–45.

51. Paul Freston, "Contours of Latin American Pentecostalism," in *Christianity Reborn: The Global Expansion of Evangelicalism in the Twentieth Century*, ed.

Donald M. Lewis (Grand Rapids, MI: Eerdmans, 2004), 224; Ari Pedro Oro and Pablo Semán, "Pentecostalism in the Southern Cone Countries: Overview and Perspectives," *International Sociology* 15, no. 4 (2000): 609.

52. Gastón Espinosa, "The Pentecostalization of Latin American and U.S. Latino Christianity,"*Pneuma* 26, no. 2 (2004): 267.

53. Albert Wardin, Jr., ed., *Baptists around the World: A Comprehensive Handbook* (Nashville, TN: Broadman & Holman, 1995), 331–32, 336–37.

54. Freston, "Contours of Latin American Pentecostalism," 228; idem, "The Future of Pentecostalism in Brazil: The Limits to Growth," in *Global Pentecostalism in the Twenty-First Century*, ed. Robert W. Hefner (Bloomington: Indiana University Press, 2013), 64.

55. For estimates for Latin America as a whole in 2010 see Todd M. Johnson and Kenneth R. Ross, eds., *Atlas of Global Christianity* (Edinburgh: Edinburgh University Press, 2010), 91. For census figures for Brazil in 2000 see Freston, "The Future of Pentecostalism in Brazil," 70.

56. Anderson, *Spreading Fires*, 200, 204; idem, *To the Ends of the Earth*, 177.

57. Anderson, *To the Ends of the Earth*, 177–78; R. Andrew Chesnut, *Born Again in Brazil: The Pentecostal Boom and the Pathogens of Poverty* (New Brunswick, NJ: Rutgers University Press, 1997), 27–28.

58. Anderson, *Spreading Fires*, 204–5; Paul Freston, "Pentecostalism in Brazil: A Brief History," *Religion* 25, no. 2 (1995): 121–5.

59. John Burdick, *Looking for God in Brazil: The Progressive Catholic Church in Urban Brazil's Religious Arena* (Berkeley: University of California Press, 1993), 4. Freston, "Pentecostalism in Brazil," 124, estimates 7–8 million in 1995.

60. Freston, "Contours of Latin American Pentecostalism," 241, 252–53.

61. Freston, "Pentecostalism in Brazil," 126.

62. Ibid., 127–8; André Corten, *Pentecostalism in Brazil: Emotion of the Poor and Theological Romanticism* (Houndmills, Basingstoke: Macmillan, 1999), 49.

63. Freston, "Pentecostalism in Brazil," 130; Ari Pedro Oro and Pablo Semán, "Brazilian Pentecostalism Crosses National Borders," in *Between Babel and Pentecost: Transnational Pentecostalism in Africa and Latin America,* ed. André Corten and Ruth Marshall-Fratani (London: Hurst & Co., 2001), 183; Ole Jakob Løland, "The Position of the Biblical Canon in Brazil: From Catholic Rediscovery to Neo-Pentecostal Marginalisation," *Studies in World Christianity* 21, no. 2 (August 2015): 101.

64. Anderson, *Introduction to Pentecostalism*, 73–74; Calvin L. Smith, "The Politics and Economics of Pentecostalism," in *The Cambridge Companion to Pentecostalism*, ed. Cecil M. Robeck, Jr., and Amos Yong (Cambridge: Cambridge University Press, 2014), 177; Paul Freston, "The Transnationalisation of the Universal Church of the Kingdom of God," in Corten and Marshall-Fratani, *Between Babel and Pentecost*, 196–215.

65. David Lehmann, *Struggle for the Spirit: Religious Transformation and Popular Culture in Brazil and Latin America* (Cambridge: Polity Press, 1996), 152.

66. Chesnut, *Born Again in Brazil*, 83.

67. Lehmann, *Struggle for the Spirit*, 136–37, 139–41.

68. Løland, "The Position of the Biblical Canon in Brazil," 98–118; Freston, "Pentecostalism in Brazil," 130–31.

69. The saying is usually attributed to "an unnamed Latin American theologian."

70. Chesnut, *Born Again in Brazil*, 4.

71. Lehmann, *Struggle for the Spirit*, 197–99; for the best-known exposition of this theme see Elizabeth E. Brusco, *The Reformation of Machismo: Evangelical Conversion and Gender in Colombia* (Austin, TX: University of Texas Press, 1995).

72. Chesnut, *Born Again in Brazil*, 67–72.

73. Antônio Flávio Pierucci and Reginaldo Prandi, "Religious Diversity in Brazil: Numbers and Perspectives in a Sociological Evaluation," *International Sociology* 15, no. 4 (2000): 630–31.

74. R. Andrew Chesnut, *Competitive Spirits: Latin America's New Religious Economy* (New York: Oxford University Press, 2003), 5, 64–101 (especially 79, 94–95).

75. Espinosa, "The Pentecostalization of Latin American and U.S. Latino Christianity," 271–72; Edward L. Cleary, *The Rise of Charismatic Catholicism in Latin America* (Gainesville, FL: University Press of Florida, 2011), 27, citing David Barrett and Todd Johnson, "The Catholic Charismatic Renewal, 1959–2025," in Oreste Pesare, ed., *Then Peter Stood Up* . . . (Vatican City: International Catholic Charismatic Renewal Services, 2000), 118–31, gives a figure of 33.7 million charismatic Catholics in Brazil in 2000.

76. Espinosa, "The Pentecostalization of Latin American and U.S. Latino Christianity," 277. Espinosa draws his statistics from Todd M. Johnson of the Center for the Study of Global Christianity at Gordon-Conwell Seminary. Compare Freston, "The Future of Pentecostalism in Brazil," 70.

77. Freston, "Pentecostalism in Brazil," 131.

78. Freston, "The Transnationalisation of Brazilian Pentecostalism," 198.

79. Freston, "The Future of Pentecostalism in Brazil," 71–72.

Chapter 14. The Eastern Orthodox Church and the Modern World

1. Vasilios N. Makrides, "The Enlightenment in the Greek Orthodox East: Appropriation, Dilemmas, Ambiguities," in *Enlightenment and Religion in the Orthodox World*, ed. Paschalis M. Kitromilides, (Oxford: Voltaire Foundation, 2016), 32; Nikos Chrysoloras, "Why Orthodoxy? Religion and Nationalism in Greek Political Culture," *Studies in Ethnicity and Nationalism* 4, no. 1 (2004): 40–61.

2. "Fellowship of St Alban & St Sergius: Our History," http://www.sobornost.org/about.php (Accessed May 5, 2017), Ken Parry et al., eds., *The Blackwell Dictionary of Eastern Christianity* (Oxford: Blackwell, 1999), 89–91.

3. Timothy Ware, *The Orthodox Church*, new ed. (London: Penguin Books, 1997), 181.

4. For the rate of growth of Orthodoxy in the USA see D. Oliver Herbel, *Turning to Tradition: Converts and the Making of an American Orthodox Church* (New York: Oxford University Press, 2014), 8–9, 160 n. 19; for a sociological treatment of recent conversions see Amy Slagle, *The Eastern Church in the Spiritual Marketplace: American Conversions to Orthodox Christianity* (DeKalb, IL: Northern Illinois University Press, 2011), passim.

5. Heather Jones and Uta Hinz "Prisoners of War (Germany)," in *1914–1918-online. International Encyclopedia of the First World War*, ed. Ute Daniel et al., Berlin: Freie Universität Berlin, 2014. DOI: 10.15463/ie1418.10387.

6. Ware, *The Orthodox Church*, 173; Christopher D. L. Johnson, *Globalization of Hesychasm and the Jesus Prayer: Contesting Contemplation* (London: Continuum, 2010), 41.

7. Thomas Bremer, *Cross and Kremlin: A Brief History of the Orthodox Church in Russia* (Grand Rapids, MI: Eerdmans, 2013), 102–3.

8. Bryn Geffert, "Anglicans and Orthodox Between the Wars" (PhD thesis, University of Minnesota, 2003), 154, n.7; Nicolas Zernov, *Sunset Years: A Russian Pilgrim in the West* (London: The Fellowship of St Alban & St Sergius, 1983), 85–86.

9. Stephen K. Batalden, *Russian Bible Wars: Modern Scriptural Translation and Cultural Authority* (Cambridge: Cambridge University Press, 2013), 197.

10. "Fellowship of St Alban & St Sergius: Our History," http://www.sobornost.org/about.php (Accessed May 5, 2017).

11. Zernov, *Sunset Years*, 15–16; idem, *The Russians and their Church*, 3rd ed. (Crestwood, NY: St Vladimir's Seminary Press, 1994), 1.

12. Nicolas Zernov, *The Russian Religious Renaissance of the Twentieth Century* (London: Darton, Longman & Todd, 1963), 260–61, 327; idem, *Sunset Years*, 28–39.

13. Kallistos Ware, foreword to "A Monk of the Eastern Church" [Archimandrite Lev Gillet], *The Jesus Prayer* (Crestwood, NY: St Vladimir's Seminary Press, 1987), 6–7, 76–77, 81; Johnson, *Globalization of Hesychasm and the Jesus Prayer*, 31–45.

14. Johnson, *Globalization of Hesychasm and the Jesus Prayer*, 41, 52.

15. Ibid., 57–58.

16. Élisabeth Behr-Sigel, *Lev Gillet, Un Moine de l'Église d'Orient: un libre croyant universaliste, évangélique et mystique* (Paris: Les Éditions du Cerf, 1993), 36, 453.

17. Behr-Sigel, *Lev Gillet*, 313–70.

18. Ibid., 411–29; see chapter 10.

19. For an American example see the brief account in chapter 5 of Peter Gillquist and the New Covenant Apostolic Order. In Britain, one of the leading pioneers of charismatic renewal in the Church of England, Rev. Michael Harper, was received into the Antiochian Orthodox Church in 1995. See Brian Stanley, *The Global Diffusion of Evangelicalism: The Age of Billy Graham and John Stott* (Downers Grove, IL: InterVarsity Press 2013), 239–43.

20. Ware, foreword to *The Jesus Prayer*, 7–14.

21. Ware, *The Orthodox Church*, 176.

22. Victor Roudometof, "The Evolution of Greek Orthodoxy in the Context of World Historical Globalization," in *Orthodox Christianity in 21st Century Greece: The Role of Religion in Culture, Ethnicity and Politics*, ed. Victor Roudometof and Vasilios N. Makrides (Farnham: Ashgate, 2010), 22–23.

23. Dimitri Pentzopoulos, *The Balkan Exchange of Minorities and Its Impact on Greece*, new ed. (London: Hurst & Co., 2002), 25–27, 38; Richard Clogg, *A Short History of Modern Greece*, 2nd ed. (Cambridge: Cambridge University Press, 1986), 114.

24. Clogg, *Short History of Modern Greece*, 118; Pentzopoulos, *The Balkan Exchange of Minorities*, 47.

25. Renée Hirschon, ed., *Crossing the Aegean: An Appraisal of the 1923 Compulsory Population Exchange between Greece and Turkey* (New York: Berghahn Books, 2003), 14.

26. Clogg, *Short History of Modern Greece*, 120–21; Bruce Clark, *Twice a Stranger: How Mass Expulsion Forged Modern Greece and Turkey*, rev. ed. (London: Granta Books, 2007), 219, 223.

27. "The Genocide of Ottoman Greeks, 1914–1923," Rutgers Center for the Study of Genocide and Human Rights, http://www.ncas.rutgers.edu/center-study-genocide -conflict-resolution-and-human-rights/genocide-ottoman-greeks-1914-1923 (Accessed May 5, 2017).

28. Hirschon, ed., *Crossing the Aegean*, 15.

29. Clark, *Twice a Stranger*, 219.

30. Ibid., 232.

31. Chrysoloras, "Why Orthodoxy?" 42.

32. Roudometof, "The Evolution of Greek Orthodoxy in the Context of World Historical Globalization," 27.

33. Anastassios Anastassiadis, "An Intriguing True-False Paradox: The Entanglement of Modernization and Intolerance in the Orthodox Church of Greece," in Roudometof and Makrides, *Orthodox Christianity in 21st Century Greece*, 47, n. 7.

34. This paragraph is indebted to Anastassiadis, "An Intriguing True-False Paradox," 39–60.

35. For divergent estimates see Chrysoloras, "Why Orthodoxy?" 49; Vrasidis Karilis, "Greek Christianity after 1453," in *The Blackwell Companion to Eastern Christianity*, ed. Ken Parry (Oxford: Blackwell, 2007), 175; Ware, *The Orthodox Church*, 138.

36. Graham Speake, *Mount Athos: Renewal in Paradise* (New Haven, CT: Yale University Press, 2002), 2–3.

37. Constantinos A. Vavouskos, "Church and State in Modern Greece: A Review Article," *Balkan Studies* 9, no. 1 (1968): 211–12.

38. Speake, *Mount Athos*, 182–83.

39. Clogg, *Short History of Modern Greece*, 121; Robert Byron, *The Station. Athos: Treasures and Men* (London: Duckworth, 1928), 57; Veronica della Dora, *Imagining Mount Athos: Visions of a Holy Place from Homer to World War II* (Charlottesville: University of Virginia Press, 2011), 7–8.

40. Byron, *The Station*, 283, mis-cited in della Dora, *Imagining Mount Athos*, 6.

41. "Women Invade Athos Despite 1,000-Year Ban," *New York Times*, April 26, 1953, p. 67.

42. Della Dora, *Imagining Mount Athos*, 235–37.

43. Eleni Sotiru, "'The Traditional Modern': Rethinking the Position of Contemporary Greek Women in Orthodoxy," in Roudometof and Makrides, *Orthodox Christianity in 21st Century Greece*, 131–53.

44. Speake, *Mount Athos*, 6, 168, 184–85.

45. Ibid., 174.

46. OrthodoxWiki contributors, "Sophrony (Sakharov)," *OrthodoxWiki*, https:// orthodoxwiki.org/index.php?title=Sophrony_(Sakharov)&oldid=112984 (Accessed May 5, 2017).

47. Speake, *Mount Athos*, 175–79.

48. Ibid., 177.

49. Stephen Hayes, "Orthodox Mission in Tropical Africa," *Missionalia* 24, no. 3 (1996): 396.

50. Ciprian Burlacioiu, "Expansion without Western Missionary Agency and Constructing Confessional Identities: The African Orthodox Church between the United States, South Africa, and East Africa (1921–1940)," *The Journal of World Christianity* 6, no. 1 (2016): 90; Herbel, *Turning to Tradition*, 77–78.

51. The fullest account of the tangled story of Vilatte is in Elias Farajajé Jones, *In Search of Zion: The Spiritual Significance of Africa in Black Religious Movements* (Bern: Peter Lang, 1990), 132–33.

52. Burlacioiu, "Expansion without Western Missionary Agency," 82–98; Gavin White, "Patriarch McGuire and the Episcopal Church," *Historical Magazine of the Protestant Episcopal Church* 38, no. 2 (1969): 109–41; Theodore Natsoulas, "Patriarch McGuire and the Spread of the African Orthodox Church to Africa," *Journal of Religion in Africa* 12, no. 2 (1981): 81–104.

53. Burlacioiu, "Expansion without Western Missionary Agency," 85.

54. Natsoulas, "Patriarch McGuire and the Spread of the African Orthodox Church to Africa," 93–9, 103, n. 61; Jones, *In Search of Zion*, 147–52.

55. F. B. Welbourn, *East African Rebels: A Study of Some Independent Churches* (London: SCM Press, 1961), 77–81, 87–88. http://www.worldchristiandatabase.org/wcd/

56. Ibid., 83–84.

57. Ibid., 88–92; Joseph William Black, "Offended Christians, Anti-Mission Churches and Colonial Politics: One Man's Story of the Messy Birth of the African Orthodox Church in Kenya," *Journal of Religion in Africa* 43, no. 3 (2013): 261–96. Black gives Vlachos's name as Ulachos.

58. Francis Kimani Githeya, *The Freedom of the Spirit: African Indigenous Churches in Kenya* (Atlanta, GA: Scholars Press, 1997), 96–103; Black, "Offended Christians, Anti-Mission Churches and Colonial Politics," 270–71, 274–75; Burlacioiu, "Expansion without Western Missionary Agency," 90–91.

59. Black, "Offended Christians, Anti-Mission Churches and Colonial Politics," 275–9; Githeya, *The Freedom of the Spirit*, 106–7; Welbourn, *East African Rebels*, 91–92.

60. Black, "Offended Christians, Anti-Mission Churches and Colonial Politics," 280–4; Githeya, *The Freedom of the Spirit*, 107–16; Athanasios N. Papathanasiou, "Missionary Experience and Academic Quest. The Research Situation in Greece," in *European Traditions in the Study of Religion in Africa*, ed. Frieder Ludwig and Afe Adogame (Wiesbaden: Harrasowitz Verlag, 2004), 305–6.

61. *World Christian Database*, eds. Todd M. Johnson and Gina A. Zurlo (Leiden: E. J. Brill, 2007), "Orthodox by Country," Kenya (p. 11) and Uganda (p. 21) (Accessed August 26, 2016). For the claim of one and a half million Kenyan members (by 1997), see Githieya, *The Freedom of the Spirit*, 116.

62. Hayes, "Orthodox Mission in Tropical Africa," 391–97.

63. Papathanasiou, "Missionary Experience and Academic Quest," 305.

Chapter 15. Migrant Churches

1. Adam McKeown, "Global Migration, 1846–1970," *Journal of World History* 15, no. 2 (2004): 155–89.

2. Ken Parry et al., eds., *The Blackwell Dictionary of Eastern Christianity* (Oxford; Blackwell, 1999), 122; Wilhelm Baum and Dietmar W. Winkler, *The Church of the East: A Concise History* (London: RoutledgeCurzon, 2003), 135–39, 150–57.

3. Stephen Hunt and Nicola Lightly, "The British Black Pentecostal 'Revival': Identity and Belief in the 'New' Nigerian Churches," *Ethnic and Racial Studies* 24, no. 1 (2001): 104–124, estimated the UK membership of the Redeemed Christian Church of God at 200,000, but this seems a gross over-estimate in the light of membership figures published by the church itself, which recorded a membership of 80,200 a decade later; see Babatunde Adedibu, *Coat of Many Colours: The Origin, Growth, Distinctiveness and Contributions of Black Majority Churches to British Christianity* (n.p.: Wisdom Summit, 2012), 71.

4. Marilyn Halter, "Africa: West," in *The New Americans: A Guide to Immigration since 1965*, ed. Mary C. Waters and Reed Ueda (Cambridge, MA: Harvard University Press, 2007), 289; Mark R. Gornik, *Word Made Global: Stories of African Christianity in New York City* (Grand Rapids, MI: Eerdmans, 2011), 62.

5. Timothy Tseng, "Trans-Pacific Transpositions: Continuities and Discontinuities in Chinese North American Protestantism since 1965," in *Revealing the Sacred in Asian and Pacific America*, ed. Jane Naomi Iwamura and Paul Spickard (New York: Routledge, 2003), 258.

6. Irma Watkins-Owens, *Blood Relations: Caribbean Immigrants and the Harlem Community, 1900–1930* (Bloomington, IN: Indiana University Press, 1996), 1, 4; Peggy Levitt, "Dominican Republic," in Waters and Ueda, *The New Americans*, 399; Milton Vickerman, "Jamaica," in ibid., 479.

7. Jehu J. Hanciles, *Beyond Christendom: Globalization, African Migration and the Transformation of the West* (Maryknoll, NY: Orbis Books, 2008), 310–11.

8. For the religious dimensions of African immigration to the United States see Hanciles, *Beyond Christendom*; Jacob K. Olupona and Regina Gemignani, eds., *African Immigrant Religions in America* (New York: New York University Press, 2007).

9. David Killingray, "Transatlantic Networks of Early African Pentecostalism: The Role of Thomas Brem Wilson, 1901–1929," *Studies in World Christianity* 23, no. 3 (2017): 218–36.

10. Parry et al., eds., *The Blackwell Dictionary of Eastern Christianity*, 23.

11. Rae Rosen, Susan Wieler, and Joseph Pereira, "New York City Immigrants: The 1990s Wave," *Current Issues in Economics and Finance* 11, no. 6 (2005): 3–4; Hanciles, *Beyond Christendom*, 311.

12. Joaquin L. Gonzalez III and Andrea Maison, "We Do Not Bowl Alone: Social and Cultural Capital from Filipinos and Their Churches," in *Asian American Religions: The Making and Remaking of Borders and Boundaries*, ed. Tony Carnes and Fengang Yang (New York: New York University Press, 2004), 345.

13. Timothy Matovina, *Latino Catholicism: Transformation in America's Largest Church* (Princeton, NJ: Princeton University Press, 2011), 38.

14. Milton C. Sernett, *Bound for the Promised Land: African American Religion and the Great Migration* (Durham, NC: Duke University Press, 1997); Wallace D. Best, *Passionately Human, No Less Divine: Religion and Culture in Black Chicago, 1915–1952* (Princeton, NJ: Princeton University Press, 2005), 7–8.

15. The African Methodist Episcopal Church was formed in 1818 following the secession of black members from white Methodist Episcopal churches in Philadelphia and Baltimore.

16. The African Methodist Episcopal Church Zion was formally constituted in 1821 but traces its origins to the formation in New York in 1796 of a black Methodist Episcopal congregation called Zion Church.

17. Jennifer Holdaway, "China: Outside of the People's Republic of China," in Waters and Ueda, *The New Americans*, 365.

18. Fengang Yang, *Chinese Christians in America: Conversion, Assimilation, and Adhesive Identities* (University Park: Pennsylvania State University Press, 1999), viii, 7; Jenna Weissman Joselit, Timothy Matovina, Roberto Suro and Fenggang Yang, "American Religion and the Old and New Immigration," *Religion and American Culture: A Journal of Interpretation* 22, no. 1 (2012): 26.

19. Carolyn Chen, *Getting Saved in America: Taiwanese Immigration and Religious Experience* (Princeton, NJ: Princeton University Press, 2008), 39.

20. Pyong Gap Min, "Korea," in Waters and Ueda, *The New Americans*, 491–503; Weissman Joselit et al., "American Religion and the Old and New Immigration," 26.

21. Pei-te Lien and Tony Carnes, "The Religious Demography of Asian American Boundary Crossing," in Carnes and Fengang Yang, *Asian American Religions*, 50.

22. Matovina, *Latino Catholicism*, 29–31.

23. Ibid., 35.

24. Ibid., 39, 136, 177, 188; Joselit et. al., "American Religion and the Old and New Immigration," 8–9.

25. Sernett, *Bound for the Promised Land*, 56; Best, *Passionately Human, No Less Divine*, 23.

26. Best, *Passionately Human, No Less Divine*, 51–59.

27. Ibid., 11, 149–53, 174–82; Sernett, *Bound for the Promised Land*, 188–195; Lucy Smith Collier Papers, Chicago Public Library, http://www.chipublib.org/fa-lucy-smith-collier-papers-2/ (Accessed May 8, 2017).

28. Best, *Passionately Human, No Less Divine*, 166–70.

29. Sernett, *Bound for the Promised Land*, 184–86.

30. Kip Richardson, "Gospels of Growth: The American Megachurch at Home and Abroad," in *Secularization and Religious Innovation in the North Atlantic World*, ed. David Hempton and Hugh McLeod, (Oxford: Oxford University Press, 2017), 291–92.

31. See Cleveland Gaillard to Bethlehem Baptist Association, April 1, 1917, http://www.umbc.edu/che/tahlessons/pdf/Understanding_the_Great_Migration_RS_02.pdf (Accessed May 8, 2017).

32. Best, *Passionately Human, No Less Divine*, 46–47; Wallace Best, "Olivet Baptist Church," *Encyclopedia of Chicago*, http://www.encyclopedia.chicagohistory.org/pages/929.html (Accessed May 8, 2017); "Olivet Baptist Church (OBC) [Chicago],

1850–," http://www.blackpast.org/aah/olivet-baptist-church-obc-chicago-illinois-18501 (Accessed May 8, 2017); Steven A. Reich, ed., *Encyclopedia of the Great Black Migration*, 3 vols. (Westport, CT, Greenwood Press, 2006), vol. 1, 443–44. James R. Grossman, *Land of Hope: Chicago, Black Southerners, and the Great Migration* (Chicago: The University of Chicago Press, 1989), 74, 94, 102, 104, 132, 156.

33. Best, *Passionately Human, No Less Divine*, 13–19; Grossman, *Land of Hope*, 230.

34. Sam Hitchmough, "Missions of Patriotism: Joseph H. Jackson and Martin Luther King," *European Journal of American Studies* 6, no. 1 (2011): 1–19.

35. F. Burton Nelson, "The Life of Dietrich Bonhoeffer," in *The Cambridge Companion to Dietrich Bonhoeffer*, ed. John W. de Gruchy (Cambridge: Cambridge University Press, 1999), 29, 31–32; Reggie L. Williams, *Bonhoeffer's Black Jesus: Harlem Renaissance Theology and an Ethic of Resistance* (Waco, TX: Baylor University Press, 2014), 1–5, 122–32.

36. Sernett, *Bound for the Promised Land*, 132–3; Kenneth T. Jackson, ed., *The Encyclopedia of New York City* (New Haven, CT: Yale University Press, 1995), 3–4.

37. Timothy George, James Earl Massey, and Robert Smith, Jr., eds., *Our Sufficiency is of God: Essays on Preaching in Honor of Gardner C. Taylor* (Macon, GA: Mercer University Press, 2010); Edward Gilbreath, "The Pulpit King," *Christianity Today*, December 11, 1995, 25–28 (quotation at p. 28).

38. "Rev. Ethelred Brown: He Mixed Religion with Politics," *The Gleaner*, September 4, 2011, http://jamaica-gleaner.com/gleaner/20110904/focus/focus11.html (Accessed May 8, 2017); see also Egbert Ethelred Brown papers, The New York Public Library Archives and Manuscripts, http://archives.nypl.org/scm/20552 (Accessed May 8, 2017).

39. Watkins-Owens, *Blood Relations*, 59–60.

40. Ibid., 74; Philip Kasinitz, *Caribbean New York: Black Immigrants and the Politics of Race* (Ithaca, NY: Cornell University Press, 1992), 39–48.

41. Jackson, *The Encyclopedia of New York City*, 611–12; Kasinitz, *Caribbean New York*, 55.

42. Kasinitz, *Caribbean New York*, 61, 64, 97–98.

43. Jackson, *The Encyclopedia of New York City*, 221–22, claims a membership of 3,000, but the *New York Times*, February 27, 1994, p. CY10, mentioned a peak of 1,000 and a rapid decline to 400 by 1994, owing to a sexual scandal associated with the priest.

44. For a sociological study of these two congregations see Janice A. McLean-Farrell, *West Indian Pentecostals: Living Their Faith in New York and London* (London: Bloomsbury Academic, 2016).

45. Brian Stanley, *The History of the Baptist Missionary Society 1792–1992* (Edinburgh: T. & T. Clark, 1992), 68–70, 96–97.

46. Nicole Rodriguez Toulis, *Believing Identity: Pentecostalism and the Mediation of Jamaican Ethnicity and Gender in England* (Oxford: Berg, 1997), 106, 109; William Wedenoja, "Modernization in the Pentecostal Movement in Jamaica," in *Perspectives on Pentecostalism: Case Studies from the Caribbean and Latin America*, ed. Stephen D. Glazier (Washington, DC: University Press of America, 1980), 30.

47. Church of God in Christ (UK),"History of COGIC UK," http://cogic.org.uk/?q=node/3 (Accessed May 8, 2017).

48. New Testament Church of God (UK), "Our History," https://ntcg.org.uk/about /history (Accessed May 8, 2017).

49. Toulis, *Believing Identity*, 114–18; "Rev Dr Oliver Lyseight—Blue Plaque Unveiling," http://www.obv.org.uk/news-blogs /rev-dr-oliver-lyseight-blue-plaque-unveiling (Accessed May 8, 2017); "Dr O. A. Lyseight," http://www.100greatblackbritons.com /bios/dr_oa_lyseight.html (Accessed May 8, 2017).

50. Fenggang Yang, *Chinese Christians in America*, 5.

51. Shehong Chen, "Republicanism, Confucianism, Christianity, and Capitalism in American Chinese Ideology," in *Chinese American Transnationalism: The Flow of People, Resources, and Ideas between China and America during the Exclusion Era*, ed. Sucheng Chan (Philadelphia: Temple University Press, 2006), 175; Fengang Yang, *Chinese Christians in America*, 35. These figures exclude Alaska and Hawaii.

52. Fenggang Yang, *Chinese Christians in America*, 6.

53. Shehong Chen, "Republicanism, Confucianism, Christianity, and Capitalism in American Chinese Ideology," 186–87.

54. Horace R. Cayton and Anne O. Lively, *The Chinese in the United States and the Chinese Christian Churches: A Statement Condensed for the National Conference on the Chinese Christian Churches* (National Council of the Churches of Christ in the U.S.A. Bureau of Research and Survey, 1955), 55–57.

55. Ibid., 55–73 (quotation at p. 69).

56. Tseng, "Trans-Pacific Transpositions," 253–56.

57. Fenggang Yang, *Chinese Christians in America*, 6; Tseng, "Trans-Pacific Transpositions," 244, 262. The higher figures are those cited by Tseng and drawn from the *Directory of Chinese Churches, Bible Study Groups, Organizations in North America*, published by Ambassadors for Christ, Inc., and thus include some Chinese Christian bodies that were not strictly churches.

58. H. Leon McBeth, *The Baptist Heritage* (Nashville, TN: Broadman Press, 1987), 746–48.

59. Tseng, "Trans-Pacific Transpositions," 246–58.

60. R. G. Tiedemann, *Reference Guide to Christian Missionary Societies in China: From the Sixteenth to the Twentieth Centuries* (London: Routledge, 2016), 128–29.

61. Lian Xi, *Redeemed by Fire: The Rise of Popular Christianity in Modern China* (New Haven, CT: Yale University Press, 2010), 132. The first Chinese woman to obtain an M.D. degree in the USA was Dr Ida Kahn, who attended the World Missionary Conference in Edinburgh in 1910 as an unofficial delegate.

62. Ibid., 151; on Sung see Leslie T. Lyall, *John Sung: Flame for God in the Far East* (London: Overseas Missionary Fellowship, 1954) and Daryl R. Ireland, "John Sung: Christian Revitalization in China and Southeast Asia" (PhD diss., Boston University, 2015).

63. Daniel H. Bays, *A New History of Christianity in China* (Chichester: Wiley-Blackwell, 2012), 137.

64. Andrew Gih, *Twice-Born—and Then? The Autobiography and Messages of Rev. Andrew Gih, Litt.D., F.R.G.S.*, 2nd ed., edited by Ruth J. Corbin (London: Marshall, Morgan & Scott, 1954), 65.

65. Tseng, "Trans-Pacific Transpositions," 259; Andrew Gih, *Into God's Family: A Fascinating Account of the Lives and Work of Members of the Bethel Evangelistic*

Bands and Some of Their Inspiring Messages, rev. ed. (London: Marshall, Morgan & Scott, 1955), 111.

66. Fenggang Yang, *Chinese Christians in America*, 64–65.

67. Tseng, "Trans-Pacific Transpositions," 260–61; Chinese Christian Mission, "Brief History of CCM," http://ccmusa.org/engl/aboutus/history_en.aspx (Accessed May 8, 2017).

68. Tseng, "Trans-Pacific Transpositions," 263.

69. Ibid., 263–65.

70. Diana L. Eck, *A New Religious America: How a "Christian Country" Has Become the World's Most Religiously Diverse Nation* (San Francisco: HarperSan Francisco, 2001), 46–47, 65–77.

71. Fenggang Yang, in Joselit et al., "American Religion and the Old and New Immigration," 24.

Conclusion

1. Joshua D. Broggi, *Diversity in the Structure of Christian Reasoning: Interpretation, Disagreement, and World Christianity* (Leiden: E. J. Brill, 2015).

2. Derek R. Peterson, *Ethnic Patriotism and the East African Revival: A History of Dissent, c. 1935–1972* (Cambridge: Cambridge University Press, 2012).

3. Joel Robbins, *Becoming Sinners: Christianity and Moral Torment in a Papua New Guinea Society* (Berkeley, Los Angeles, and London: University of California Press, 2004), 37–39, 122–25.

Archives

Egbert Ethelred Brown papers, The New York Public Library Archives and Manuscripts. Listed at http://archives.nypl.org/scm/20552.

King's College Cambridge archives (KCAC/4/11/1), P. D. V. Prince, "The Evolution of Plato's Philosophical Method." Fellowship dissertation, n.d. [1940].

Lucy Smith Collier Papers, Chicago Public Library. Listed at http://www.chipublib .org/fa-lucy-smith-collier-papers-2/.

School of Oriental and African Studies, London. Overseas Missionary Fellowship (China Inland Mission) archives, Minutes of British Council.

Yale Divinity School Library, Special Collections, George Sherwood Eddy Papers, RG 32.

Primary Source Periodicals and Newspapers

American Board of Commissioners for Foreign Missions Reports
The Christian Century
Christian Institute News
Christianity Today
Church of England Newspaper
Confidence
Congo Mission News
Crusade
Ecumenical Review
The Gleaner (Jamaica)
The Harvest Field
International Review of Mission[s]
King's College Cambridge Annual Report
The Korea Mission Field
Lagos Weekly Record
Life
Moslem World
New York Times
The Presbyterian
Records of the South India United Church
Religion and Life
Sydney Morning Herald
Time
Triennial Reports of the Board of Foreign Missions of the United Presbyterian Church of North America
The United Presbyterian
The Young Men of India

Books, Articles, Electronic Resources, and Unpublished Dissertations

Adams, Daniel J. "Church Growth in Korea: A Paradigm Shift from Ecclesiology to Nationalism." In Mark R. Mullins and Richard Fox Young, eds., *Perspectives on Christianity in Korea and Japan: The Gospel and Culture in East Asia*, 13–28. Lewiston, ME: Edwin Mellen Press, 1995.

Addresses and Records: International Missionary Council Meeting at Tambaram, Madras, December 12th to 29th, 1938. London: Oxford University Press, 1939.

Adedibu, Babatunde. *Coat of Many Colours: The Origin, Growth, Distinctiveness and Contributions of Black Majority Churches to British Christianity.* n.p.: Wisdom Summit, 2012.

Adler, Elisabeth. *A Small Beginning: An Assessment of the First Five Years of the Programme to Combat Racism.* Geneva: World Council of Churches, 1974.

Aguilar, Mario. *The History and Politics of Latin American Theology*, 3 vols. London: SCM Press, 2007–8.

Ahn, K. S. "Mission in Unity: An Investigation into the Question of Unity as it has Arisen in the Presbyterian Church of Korea and its World Mission." PhD thesis, University of Cambridge, 2008.

Airhart, Phyllis D. *A Church with the Soul of a Nation: Making and Remaking the United Church of Canada.* Montreal: McGill-Queen's University Press, 2014.

Alberigo, Giuseppe, and Joseph A. Komonchak, eds., *History of Vatican II.* 5 vols. Maryknoll, NY: Orbis Books, 1995–2006.

Allitt, Patrick. *Catholic Intellectuals and Conservative Politics in America, 1950- 1985.* Ithaca, NY: Cornell University Press, 1993.

Almada, Samuel. "An Obituary and a Tribute to J. Severino Croatto," *JOLAH, Journal of Latin American Hermeneutics,* Year 2005/2 at https://www.researchgate.net /publication/265654040 (Accessed November 14, 2014).

Alpion, Gëzim. *Mother Teresa: Saint or Celebrity?* London: Routledge, 2007.

Alves, Rubem. "Theology and the Liberation of Man." In *In Search of a Theology of Development*: *Papers from a Consultation on Theology and Development Held by Sodepax in Cartigny, Switzerland, November, 1969*, 75–92. Geneva: Committee on Society, Development and Peace, n.d. [1970].

Alves, Rubem. *A Theology of Human Hope.* New York: Corpus Publications, 1969.

Alwall, Jonas. "Religious Liberty in Sweden: An Overview," *Journal of Church and State* 42, no. 1 (2000): 147–71.

Anastassiadis, Anastassios. "An Intriguing True-False Paradox: The Entanglement of Modernization and Intolerance in the Orthodox Church of Greece." In Victor Roudometof and Vasilios N. Makrides, eds., *Orthodox Christianity in 21st Century Greece*: *The Role of Religion in Culture, Ethnicity and Politics*, 39–60. Farnham: Ashgate, 2010.

Anderson, Allan. *An Introduction to Pentecostalism.* Cambridge: Cambridge University Press, 2004.

Anderson, Allan. *Spreading Fires: The Missionary Nature of Early Pentecostalism.* London: SCM Press, 2007.

Anderson, Allan. *To the Ends of the Earth: Pentecostalism and the Transformation of World Christianity*. New York: Oxford University Press, 2013.

Anderson, James D. "The Lesbian and Gay Liberation Movement in the Presbyterian Church (U.S.A.), 1974–1996." *Journal of Homosexuality* 34, no. 2 (1997–98): 37–65.

Anderson, John. "Out of the Kitchen, Out of the Temple: Religion, Atheism and Women in the Soviet Union." In Sabrina Petra Ramet, ed., *Religious Policy in the Soviet Union*, 206–28. Cambridge: Cambridge University Press, 1992.

Anderson, John. *Religion, State and Politics in the Soviet Union and Successor States* Cambridge: Cambridge University Press, 1994.

Andersson, Efraim. *Messianic Popular Movements in the Lower Congo*, Studia Ethnographica Upsaliensia. Uppsala: Almqvist & Wiksells, 1958.

Andrew, Christopher, and Vasili Mitrokhin. *The Sword and the Shield: The Mitrokhin Archive and the Secret History of the KGB*. New York: Basic Books, 2001.

Anglican-Methodist Unity: Report of the Anglican-Methodist Unity Commission. Part 2: The Scheme. London: SPCK and Epworth Press, 1968.

Aragon, Lorraine V. *Fields of the Lord: Animism, Christian Minorities and State Development in Indonesia*. Honolulu: University of Hawaii Press, 2000.

Aritonang, Jan Sihar, and Karel Steenbrink, ed., *A History of Christianity in Indonesia*. Leiden: E. J. Brill, 2008.

Asamoah-Gyadu, J. Kwabena. *African Charismatics: Current Developments within Independent Indigenous Pentecostalism in Ghana*. Leiden: E. J. Brill, 2005.

Ateek, Naim Stifan. *Justice and Only Justice: A Palestinian Theology of Liberation*. Maryknoll, NY: Orbis Books, 1989.

Ateek, Naim Stifan. *A Palestinian Christian Cry for Reconciliation*. Maryknoll, NY: Orbis Books, 2008.

Ateek, Naim Stifan, Marc H. Ellis, and Rosemary Radford Ruether, eds. *Faith and the Intifada: Palestinian Christian Voices*. Maryknoll, NY: Orbis Books, 1992.

Ateek, Naim Stifan, and Michael Prior, eds. *Holy Land Hollow Jubilee: God, Justice and the Palestinians*. London: Melisende, 1999.

Atkin, Nicholas. "The Politics of Legality: The Religious Orders in France, 1901–45." In Frank Tallett and Nicholas Atkin, eds., *Religion, Society and Politics in France since 1789*, 149–65. London: The Hambledon Press, 1991.

Atkin, Nicholas, and Frank Tallett. *Priests, Prelates and People: A History of European Catholicism since 1750*. London: I. B. Tauris, 2003.

Badr, Habib, ed. *Christianity: A History in the Middle East*. Beirut: Middle East Council of Churches Studies and Research Program, 2005.

Baker, Don. "Christianity 'Koreanized.'" In Hyung Il Pai and Timothy R. Tangherlini, eds., *Nationalism and the Construction of Korean Identity*, 108–25. Berkeley, CA: University of California Berkeley Institute of East Asian Studies, 1998.

Ballantyne, Tony. "The Persistence of the Gods: Religion in the Modern World." In Antoinette Burton and Tony Ballantyne, eds., *World Histories from Below: Disruption and Dissent*, 137–67. London: Bloomsbury Academic, 2016.

Bankier, David, Dan Michman, and Iael Nidam-Orvieto, ed. *Pius XII and the Holocaust: Current State of Research*. Yad Vashem and Jerusalem: The International Institute for Holocaust Research, 2012.

Banks, Robert J. "The Theology of D. B. Knox: A Preliminary Estimate." In Peter T. O'Brien and David G. Peterson, eds., *God Who is Rich in Mercy: Essays Presented to Dr. D. B. Knox*, 377–403. Homebush West, NSW: Lancer Books, 1986.

Barnes, Andrew. *Making Headway: The Introduction of Western Civilization in Colonial Northern Nigeria.* Rochester, NY: University of Rochester Press, 2009.

Barr, John. "A Survey of Ecstatic Phenomena and 'Holy Spirit Movements' in Melanesia." *Oceania* 54, no. 2 (1983): 109–32.

Barrett, David, and Todd Johnson. "The Catholic Charismatic Renewal, 1959–2025." In Oreste Pesare, ed., *Then Peter Stood Up . . .* 118–31. Vatican City: International Catholic Charismatic Renewal Services, 2000.

Barth, Karl. *The Epistle to the Romans.* Translated from the sixth edition by Edwyn C. Hoskyns. London: Oxford University Press, 1933.

Batalden, Stephen K. *Russian Bible Wars: Modern Scriptural Translation and Cultural Authority.* Cambridge: Cambridge University Press, 2013.

Batalden, Stephen K., Kathleen Cann, and John Dean, eds. *Sowing the Word: The Cultural Impact of the British and Foreign Bible Society.* Sheffield: Phoenix Press, 2004.

Bates, S. *A Church at War: Anglicans and Homosexuality.* London: I. B. Tauris, 2004.

Baum, Bruce. *The Rise and Fall of the Caucasian Race: A Political History of Racial Identity.* New York: New York University Press, 2006.

Baum, Wilhelm, and Dietmar W. Winkler. *The Church of the East: A Concise History.* London: RoutledgeCurzon, 2003.

Bayer, Ronald. *Homosexuality, and American Psychiatry: The Politics of Diagnosis.* New York: Basic Books, 1981.

Bays, Daniel H. "Foreign Missions and Indigenous Protestant Leaders in China, 1920–1955: Identity and Loyalty in an Age of Powerful Nationalism." In Brian Stanley, ed., *Missions, Nationalism, and the End of Empire*, 144–64. Grand Rapids, MI: Eerdmans, 2003.

Bays, Daniel H. "The Growth of Independent Christianity in China, 1900–1937." In Daniel H. Bays, ed., *Christianity in China from the Eighteenth Century to the Present*, 307–16. Stanford: Stanford University Press, 1996.

Bays, Daniel H. *A New History of Christianity in China.* Chichester: Wiley-Blackwell, 2012.

Bays, Eric. *Indian Residential Schools: Another Picture.* Ottawa: Baico Publishing, 2009.

Beasley, Maurine H. *Eleanor Roosevelt: Transformative First Lady.* Lawrence: University Press of Kansas, 2010.

Beattie, Nicholas. "Yeast in the Dough? Catholic Schooling in France, 1981–95." In Kay Chadwick, ed., *Catholicism, Politics and Society in Twentieth-Century France*, 197–219. Liverpool: Liverpool University Press, 2000.

Bebbington, David W. "The Advent Hope in British Evangelicalism since 1800." *Scottish Journal of Religious Studies* 9, no. 2 (1988): 103–14.

Bebbington, David W. "Baptists and Fundamentalism in Inter-War Britain." In David W. Bebbington and David Ceri Jones, eds., *Evangelicalism and Fundamentalism in the United Kingdom in the Twentieth Century*, 95–114. Oxford: Oxford University Press, 2013.

Bebbington, David W. *Evangelicalism in Britain: A History from the 1730s to the 1980s*. London: Unwin Hyman, 1989.

Bebbington, David W. "Martyrs for the Truth: Fundamentalism in Britain." In Diana Wood, ed., *Martyrs and Martyrologies. Studies in Church History*, vol. 30, 417–51. Oxford: Blackwell Publishers for the Ecclesiastical History Society, 1993.

Bebbington, David W., and David Ceri Jones, eds. *Evangelicalism and Fundamentalism in the United Kingdom in the Twentieth Century*. Oxford: Oxford University Press, 2013.

Bediako, Kwame. *Theology and Identity: The Impact of Culture upon Christian Thought in the Second Century and Modern Africa*. Oxford: Regnum Books, 1992.

Behr-Sigel, Élisabeth. *Lev Gillet, Un Moine de l'Église d'Orient: un libre croyant universaliste, évangélique et mystique*. Paris: Les Éditions du Cerf, 1993.

Bell, G. K. A. *Randall Davidson: Archbishop of Canterbury*, 2nd ed. London, New York, and Toronto: Oxford University Press, 1938.

Bell, G. K. A., ed., *Documents on Christian Unity: A Selection from the First and Second Series 1920–30*. London: Oxford University Press, 1920.

Bergen, Doris L. "Catholics, Protestants and Christian Antisemitism in Nazi Germany." *Central European History* 27, no. 3 (1994): 329–48.

Bergen, Doris L. *Twisted Cross: The German Christian Movement in the Third Reich* Chapel Hill: University of North Carolina Press, 1996.

Berger, Peter, Grace Davie, and Effie Fokas. *Religious America, Secular Europe? A Theme and Variations*. Aldershot: Ashgate, 2008.

Besier, Gerhard, Armin Boyens, and Gerhard Lindemann. *Nationaler Protestantismus und Ökumenische Bewegung: Kirchliches Handeln im Kalten Kreig (1945–1990)*. Berlin: Duncker & Humblot, 1999.

Best, Wallace D. *Passionately Human, No Less Divine: Religion and Culture in Black Chicago, 1915–1952*. Princeton, NJ: Princeton University Press, 2005.

Black, Joseph William. "Offended Christians, Anti-Mission Churches and Colonial Politics: One Man's Story of the Messy Birth of the African Orthodox Church in Kenya." *Journal of Religion in Africa* 43, no. 3 (2013): 261–96.

"Black Manifesto." http://www.episcopalarchives.org/Afro-Anglican_history/exhibit /pdf/blackmanifesto.pdf (Accessed April 29, 2017).

Blake, Samuel Hume. *Don't You Hear the Red Man Calling?* Toronto: publisher not known, 1908. In "Our Roots: Canada's Local Histories Online." http://ourroots.ca (Accessed March 10, 2017).

Bord, Richard J., and Joseph E. Faulkner. *The Catholic Charismatics: The Anatomy of a Modern Religious Movement*. University Park: The Pennsylvania State University Press, 1983.

Boulard, Fernand. *Introduction to Religious Sociology: Pioneer Work in France*, English translation. London: Darton, Longman, & Todd, 1960.

Boulard, Fernand (fondateur). *Matériaux pour l'histoire religieuse du people français, XIXe-XXe siècles*. 3 vols. Paris: Éditions de l'École des Hautes Études en Sciences Sociales; Presses de la Fondation Nationale des Sciences Politiques; Éditions du Centre National de la Recherche Scientifique, 1982, 1987, 1992.

Bourdeaux, Michael. "The Russian Church, Religious Liberty and the World Council of Churches." *Religion in Communist Lands* 13, no. 1, 1985: 4–27.

Bowie, Leland. "The Copts, the Wafd, and Religious Issues in Egyptian Politics." *Muslim World* 67, no. 2 (1977): 106–26.

Bowler, Kate. *Blessed: A History of the American Prosperity Gospel*. Oxford: Oxford University Press, 2012.

Bradstock, Andrew, and Christopher Rowland, eds. *Radical Christian Writings: A Reader*. Oxford: Blackwell, 2002.

Bremer, Thomas. *Cross and Kremlin: A Brief History of the Orthodox Church in Russia*. Grand Rapids, MI: Eerdmans, 2013.

Breward, Ian. *A History of the Churches in Australasia*. Oxford: Oxford University Press, 2001.

"The British-Israel-World-Federation: Our History." http://www.britishisrael.co.uk/history.php (Accessed March 10, 2017).

Broggi, Joshua D. *Diversity in the Structure of Christian Reasoning: Interpretation, Disagreement, and World Christianity*. Leiden: E. J. Brill, 2015.

Brown, Callum. *The Death of Christian Britain: Understanding Secularisation 1800–2000*. London: Routledge, 2001.

Brown, Judith M. *Gandhi: Prisoner of Hope*. New Haven, CT: Yale University Press, 1989.

Bruce, Steve. *God Is Dead: Secularization in the West*. Oxford: Blackwell, 2002.

Bruce, Steve, ed. *Religion and Modernization: Sociologists and Historians Debate the Secularization Thesis*. Oxford: Clarendon Press, 1992.

Bruce, Steve. *Secularization: In Defence of an Unfashionable Theory*. Oxford: Oxford University Press, 2011.

Bruce, Steve. "The Supply-Side Model of Religion: The Nordic and Baltic States." *Journal for the Scientific Study of Religion* 39, no. 1 (2000): 32–46.

Brusco, Elizabeth E. *The Reformation of Machismo: Evangelical Conversion and Gender in Colombia*. Austin, TX: University of Texas Press, 1995.

Bryce, P. H. *The Story of a National Crime: An Appeal for Justice to the Indians of Canada*. Ottawa: James Hope & Sons, 1922.

Burdick, John. *Looking for God in Brazil: The Progressive Catholic Church in Urban Brazil's Religious Arena*. Berkeley: University of California Press, 1993.

Burlacioiu, Ciprian. "Expansion without Western Missionary Agency and Constructing Confessional Identities: The African Orthodox Church between the United States, South Africa, and East Africa (1921–1940)." *The Journal of World Christianity* 6, no. 1 (2016): 82–98.

Burton, A. H., et al. *Further Advent Testimony Addresses: Meetings at Queen's Hall and All Souls' Church, Langham Place, December 4th, 1918: Authorised Report*. London: Chas. J. Thynne, 1919.

Busch, Eberhard. *Karl Barth: His Life from Letters and Autobiographical Texts*. Translated by John Bowden. London: SCM Press, 1976.

Busser, Cathelijne de, and Anna Niedźwiedź. "Mary in Poland: A Polish Master Symbol." In Anna-Karina Hermkens, Willy Jansen, and Catrien Notermans, eds., *Moved by Mary: The Power of Pilgrimage in the Modern World*, 87–100. Farnham: Ashgate, 2009.

Butler, Anthony. *Cyril Ramaphosa*. Oxford: James Currey, 2008.

Butterfield, Herbert. *The Whig Interpretation of History*. London: G. Bell & Sons, 1931.

Byron, Robert. *The Station. Athos: Treasures and Men*. London: Duckworth, 1928.

Cabrita, Joel. *Text and Authority in the South African Nazaretha Church*. New York: Cambridge University Press, 2014.

Cannadine, David. "War and Death, Grief and Mourning in Modern Britain." In Joachim Whaley, ed., *Mirrors of Mortality: Studies in the Social History of Death*, 187–242. London: Europa Publications, 1981.

Carey, John J., ed. *The Sexuality Debate in North American Churches, 1988–1995: Controversies, Unresolved Issues, Future Prospects*. Lewiston, ME: Edwin Mellen Press, 1995.

Carnes, Tony, and Fengang Yang, eds. *Asian American Religions: The Making and Remaking of Borders and Boundaries*. New York: New York University Press, 2004.

Carney, J. J. *Rwanda before the Genocide: Catholic Politics and Ethnic Discourse in the Late Colonial Era*. New York: Oxford University Press, 2014.

Carpenter, Joel. *Revive Us Again: The Reawakening of American Fundamentalism*. New York: Oxford University Press, 1997.

Casanova, José. "Rethinking Secularization: A Global Comparative Perspective." *The Hedgehog Review* 8, nos. 1–2 (Spring–Summer 2006): 7–22.

Cass, Philip. "Fr Francis Mihalic and *Wantok* Niuspepa in Papua New Guinea." *Pacific Journalism Review* 17, no. 1 (2011): 211–26.

Cayton, Horace R., and Anne O. Lively. *The Chinese in the United States and the Chinese Christian Churches: A Statement Condensed for the National Conference on the Chinese Christian Churches*. National Council of the Churches of Christ in the U.S.A. Bureau of Research and Survey, 1955.

Chadwick, Kay, ed. *Catholicism, Politics and Society in Twentieth-Century France*. Liverpool: Liverpool University Press, 2000.

Chadwick, Owen. *Britain and the Vatican during the Second World War*. Cambridge: Cambridge University Press, 1986.

Chadwick, Owen. *The Christian Church in the Cold War*. London: Penguin Books, 1993.

Chadwick, Owen. *Michael Ramsey: A Life*. Oxford: Oxford University Press, 1991.

Chadwick, Owen. "The Pope and the Jews in 1942." In W. J. Sheils, ed., *Persecution and Toleration, Studies in Church History*, vol. 21, 435–72. Oxford: Basil Blackwell for the Ecclesiastical History Society, 1984.

Chapman, Alister. *Godly Ambition: John Stott and the Evangelical Movement*. New York: Oxford University Press, 2012.

Chen, Carolyn. *Getting Saved in America: Taiwanese Immigration and Religious Experience*. Princeton, NJ: Princeton University Press, 2008.

Chesnut, R. Andrew. *Born Again in Brazil: The Pentecostal Boom and the Pathogens of Poverty*. New Brunswick, NJ: Rutgers University Press, 1997.

Chesnut, R. Andrew. *Competitive Spirits: Latin America's New Religious Economy*. New York: Oxford University Press, 2003.

Chikane, Frank. *No Life of My Own: An Autobiography*. London: Catholic Institute for International Relations, 1988.

Chinese Christian Mission, "Brief History of CCM." http://ccmusa.org/engl/aboutus/history_en.aspx (Accessed May 8, 2017).

Cholvy, Gérard, and Yves-Marie Hilaire. *Histoire religieuse de la France contemporaine*. 3 vols. Toulouse: Bibliothèque historique Privat, 1985–1988.

Chopp, Rebecca S. "Latin American Liberation Theology." In David F. Ford, ed., *The Modern Theologians*, 2nd ed., 409–25. Oxford: Blackwell, 1997.

Chrysoloras, Nikos. "Why Orthodoxy? Religion and Nationalism in Greek Political Culture." *Studies in Ethnicity and Nationalism* 4, no. 1 (2004): 40–61.

Chumachenko, Tatiana A. *Church and State in Soviet Russia: Russian Orthodoxy from World War II to the Khruschev Years*, edited and translated by Edward E. Roslof. New York: M. E. Sharpe, 2002.

Church of God in Christ (UK)."History of COGIC UK." http://cogic.org.uk/?q=node /3 (Accessed May 8, 2017).

Clark, Bruce. *Twice a Stranger: How Mass Expulsion Forged Modern Greece and Turkey*, rev. ed. London: Granta Books, 2007.

Clarke, Brian. "English-Speaking Canada from 1854." In Terrence Murphy and Roberto Perin, eds., *A Concise History of Christianity in Canada*, 261–360. Toronto: Oxford University Press, 1996.

Cleary, Edward L. *The Rise of Charismatic Catholicism in Latin America*. Gainesville, FL: University Press of Florida, 2011.

Clements, Keith W. *Faith on the Frontier: A Life of J. H. Oldham*. Edinburgh: T. & T. Clark, 1998.

Clements, Keith W. *Lovers of Discord: Twentieth-Century Theological Controversies in England*. London: SPCK, 1988.

Clogg, Richard. *A Short History of Modern Greece*, 2nd ed. Cambridge: Cambridge University Press, 1986.

Coffey, John. *Exodus and Liberation: Deliverance Politics from John Calvin to Martin Luther King, Jr*. Oxford: Oxford University Press, 2014.

Coletta, Paolo E. *William Jennings Bryan III. Political Puritan 1915–1925*. Lincoln: University of Nebraska Press, 1969.

Collins, James M. *Exorcism and Deliverance Ministry in the Twentieth Century: An Analysis of the Practice and Theology of Exorcism in Modern Western Christianity*. Milton Keynes: Paternoster, 2009.

Committee of Enquiry on the Army and Religion. *The Army and Religion: An Enquiry and its Bearing upon the Religious Life of the Nation. With a Preface by the Bishop of Winchester*. London: Macmillan & Co., Ltd., 1919.

Cone, James. *A Black Theology of Liberation*, 40th anniversary ed. Maryknoll, NY: Orbis Books, 2010.

Conway, J. S. *The Nazi Persecution of the Churches 1933–45*. London: Weidenfeld & Nicolson, 1968.

Cook, Philip L. *Zion City, Illinois: Twentieth-Century Utopia*. Syracuse, NY: Syracuse University Press, 1996.

Cooley, Frank L. "In Memoriam: T. B. Simatupang, 1920–1990." *Indonesia* 49 (1990): 145–52.

Cooper, John. *Raphael Lemkin and the Struggle for the Genocide Convention*. Basingstoke: Palgrave Macmillan, 2008.

Corley, Felix, ed. *Religion in the Soviet Union: An Archival Reader*. Basingstoke and London: Macmillan, 1996.

Cornwell, John. *Hitler's Pope, the Secret History of Pius XII*. London: Penguin, 2000.

Corten, André. *Pentecostalism in Brazil: Emotion of the Poor and Theological Romanticism*. Houndmills, Basingstoke: Macmillan, 1999.

Corten, André, and Ruth Marshall-Fratani, eds. *Between Babel and Pentecost: Transnational Pentecostalism in Africa and Latin America*. London: Hurst & Co., 2001.

Craemer, Willy De. *The Jamaa and the Church: A Bantu Catholic Movement in Zaire*. Oxford: Clarendon Press, 1977.

Croatto, J. Severino. *Exodus: A Hermeneutics of Freedom*. English translation. Maryknoll, NY: Orbis Books, 1981.

Currie, Robert, Alan Gilbert, and Lee Horsley. *Churches and Churchgoers: Patterns of Church Growth in the British Isles since 1700*. Oxford: Clarendon Press, 1977.

Curry, Roy Watson. *Woodrow Wilson and Far Eastern Policy 1913–1921*. New York: Bookman Associates, 1957.

Davidson, Randall T. *The Six Lambeth Conferences 1867–1920. Compiled under the Direction of the Most Reverend Lord Davidson of Lambeth Archbishop of Canterbury, 1903–1928*, new ed. London: SPCK, 1929.

Davie, Grace. *Europe: The Exceptional Case: Parameters of Faith in the Modern World*. London: Darton, Longman & Todd, 2002.

Davie, Grace. *Religion in Britain since 1945: Believing without Belonging*. Oxford: Blackwell, 1994.

Davie, Grace. *Religion in Britain: A Persistent Paradox*, 2nd ed. Chichester: Wiley-Blackwell, 2015.

Davie, Grace. *Religion in Modern Europe: A Memory Mutates*. Oxford: Oxford University Press, 2000.

Davie, Grace. "Religion, Territory, and Choice: Contrasting Configurations, 1970–2015." In David Hempton and Hugh McLeod, eds., *Secularization and Religious Innovation in the North Atlantic World*, 309–26. Oxford: Oxford University Press, 2017.

Davies, Horton. *Worship and Theology in England, vol. 5: The Ecumenical Century 1900–1965*. Princeton, NJ: Princeton University Press, 1965.

Davies, Norman. *God's Playground: A History of Poland in Two Volumes*, rev. ed., 2 vols. Oxford: Oxford University Press, 2005.

Davis, Helen Clarkson Miller, comp. *Some Aspects of Religious Liberty in the Near East: A Collection of Documents*. New York: Harper & Bros., 1938.

Davis, Nathaniel. *A Long Walk to Church: A Contemporary History of Russian Orthodoxy*. Boulder, CO: Westview Press, 1995.

Dayton, Donald W., ed. *The Prophecy Conference Movement, vol. 4*. New York: Garland, 1988.

De Gruchy, John W. "Grappling with a Colonial Heritage: The English-Speaking Churches under Imperialism and Apartheid." In Richard Elphick and Rodney Davenport, eds., *Christianity in South Africa: A Political, Cultural, and Social History*, 155–72. Oxford: James Currey; and Cape Town: David Philip, 1997.

De Gruchy, John W., with Steve de Gruchy. *The Church Struggle in South Africa*, 3rd ed. London: SCM Press, 2004.

Delaney, J. M. "From Cremona to Edinburgh: Bishop Bonomelli and the World Missionary Conference of 1910." *Ecumenical Review* 52, no. 3 (2000): 418–31.

Della Dora, Veronica. *Imagining Mount Athos: Visions of a Holy Place from Homer to World War II*. Charlottesville: University of Virginia Press, 2011.

D'Emilio, John. *Sexual Politics, Sexual Communities: The Making of a Homosexual Minority in the United States 1940–1970*. Chicago: University of Chicago Press, 1983.

Denis, Philippe. "Seminary Networks and Black Consciousness in the 1970s." *South African Historical Journal* 62, no. 1 (2010): 162–82.

Dickinson, Anna. "Quantifying Religious Oppression: Russian Orthodox Church Closures and Repression of Priests 1917–41." *Religion, State & Society* 28, no. 4 (2000): 327–35.

Diébolt, Evelyn. "Les femmes catholiques: entre église et société." In Kay Chadwick, ed., *Catholicism, Politics and Society in Twentieth-Century France*, 219–43. Liverpool: Liverpool University Press, 2000.

Dixon, A. C. et al. *Advent Testimony Addresses: Delivered at the Meetings at Queen's Hall, London, W.C., December 13th, 1917: Authorised Report*. London: Chas. J. Thynne, 1918.

Doorn-Harder, Nelly van, and Kari Vogt, ed. *Between Desert and City: The Coptic Orthodox Church Today*. Oslo: Novus Forlag, 1997.

Dorey, George, et al., eds. *No Vanishing Race: The Canadian Indian Today*. Toronto: The Committee on Missionary Education of the United Church of Canada, 1955.

Douglas, J. D., ed. *Let the Earth Hear his Voice. International Congress on World Evangelization Lausanne, Switzerland: Official Reference Volume: Papers and Responses*. Minneapolis: World Wide Publications, 1975.

Downs, Frederick S. *Christianity in North-East India: Historical Perspectives*. New Delhi: ISPCK, 1983.

Dries, Angelyn. *The Missionary Movement in American Catholic History*. Maryknoll, NY: Orbis Books, 1998.

"Dr O. A. Lyseight." http://www.100greatblackbritons.com/bios/dr_oa_lyseight.html (Accessed May 8, 2017).

Dubow, Saul. "Afrikaner Nationalism, Apartheid and the Conceptualization of 'Race'." *Journal of African History* 33, no. 2 (1992): 209–37.

Duffy, Eamon. *Saints and Sinners: A History of the Popes*, 2nd ed. New Haven, CT: Yale University Press, 2001.

Dunch, Ryan. *Fuzhou Protestants and the Making of a Modern China*. New Haven, CT: Yale University Press, 2001.

Dundon, Alison. "Dancing around Development: Crisis in Christian Country in Western Province, Papua New Guinea." *Oceania* 72, no. 3 (2002): 215–30.

Eagleson, John, and Philip Scharper, eds. *Puebla and Beyond: Documentation and Commentary*. Maryknoll, NY: Orbis Books, 1979.

Eck, Diana L. *A New Religious America: How a "Christian Country" Has Become the World's Most Religiously Diverse Nation*. San Francisco: HarperSan Francisco, 2001.

Edsall, Nicholas C. *Toward Stonewall: Homosexuality and Society in the Modern Western World*. Charlottesville: University of Virginia Press, 2003.

Ekin, Larry. *Enduring Witness: The Churches and the Palestinians, vol. II*. Geneva: World Council of Churches, 1985.

Elder, Earl E. *Vindicating a Vision: The Story of the American Mission in Egypt 1854–1954.* Philadelphia: Board of Foreign Missions of the United Presbyterian Church of North America, 1958.

Ellis, Marc H. "Theologies of Liberation in Palestine-Israel and the Struggle for Peace and Justice." In Nur Masalha and Lisa Isherwood, eds., *Theologies of Liberation in Palestine-Israel: Indigenous, Contextual, and Postcolonial Perspectives,* 39–56. Eugene, OR: Pickwick Publications, 2014.

Ellis, Marc H., and Otto Maduro, eds. *The Future of Liberation Theology: Essays in Honor of Gustavo Gutiérrez.* Maryknoll, NY: Orbis Books, 1989.

Elphick, Richard. "The Benevolent Empire and the Social Gospel: Missionaries and South African Christians in the Age of Segregation." In Richard Elphick and Rodney Davenport, eds., *Christianity in South Africa: A Political, Cultural, and Social History,* 347–69. Oxford: James Currey; and Cape Town: David Philip, 1997.

Elphick, Richard, and Davenport, Rodney, eds. *Christianity in South Africa: A Political, Cultural, and Social History.* Oxford: James Currey; and Cape Town: David Philip, 1997.

Elphick, Richard. *The Equality of Believers: Protestant Missionaries and the Racial Politics of South Africa.* Charlottesville: University of Virginia Press, 2012.

Enroth, Ronald M., and Gerald E. Jamison. *The Gay Church.* Grand Rapids, MI: Eerdmans, 1974.

Epinay, Christian Lalive d'. *Haven of the Masses: A Study of the Pentecostal Movement in Chile.* London: Lutterworth Press, 1969.

Ericksen, Robert P. *Theologians under Hitler: Gerhard Kittel, Paul Althaus and Emanuel Hirsch.* New Haven, CT: Yale University Press, 1985.

Espinosa, Gastón. "The Pentecostalization of Latin American and U.S. Latino Christianity." *Pneuma* 26, no. 2 (2004): 262–92.

"Evangelicals and Catholics Together: The Christian Mission in the Third Millennium." *First Things* (May 1994). https://www.firstthings.com/article/1994/05/evangelicals-catholics-together-the-christian-mission-in-the-third-millennium (Accessed May 26, 2017).

Falconi, Carlo. *The Silence of Pius XII.* English translation. London: Faber, 1970.

Farhadian, Charles E. *Christianity, Islam, and Nationalism in Indonesia.* New York: Routledge, 2005.

Farías, Victor. *Heidegger and Nazism,* English translation. Philadelphia: Temple University Press, 1989.

Feci, Damaso. *Vie cachée et vie publique de Simon Kimbangu selon la littérature coloniale et missionnaire Belge.* Brussels: Cahiers du Cedaf, 1972.

"Fellowship of St Alban & St Sergius: Our History." http://www.sobornost.org/about.php (Accessed May 5, 2017).

Fengang Yang. *Chinese Christians in America: Conversion, Assimilation, and Adhesive Identities.* University Park: The Pennsylvania State University Press, 1999.

Field-Bibb, Jacqueline. *Women Towards Priesthood: Ministerial Politics and Feminist Praxis.* Cambridge: Cambridge University Press, 1991.

Figgis, John Neville. *Hopes for English Religion.* London: Longman, Green & Co., 1919.

Final Report of the Commission of Inquiry into Certain Organisations: Christian Institute of Southern Africa. Pretoria: Government of the Republic of South Africa, n.d. [1974].

Findlay, James F., Jr. *Church People in the Struggle: The National Council of Churches and the Black Freedom Movement, 1950–1970.* New York: Oxford University Press, 1993.

Finke, Roger. "An Unsecular America." In Steve Bruce, ed., *Religion and Modernization: Sociologists and Historians Debate the Secularization Thesis*, 145–69. Oxford: Clarendon Press, 1992.

Flannery, Austin ed. *Vatican Council II: The Conciliar and Post Conciliar Documents.* Wilmington, DE: Scholarly Resources Inc., 1975.

Flatt, Kevin N. *After Evangelicalism: The Sixties and the United Church of Canada.* Montreal: McGill-Queen's University Press, 2013.

Fletcher, William C. *Religion and Soviet Foreign Policy 1945–1970.* London: Oxford University Press for the Royal Institute of International Affairs, 1973.

Flett, John. *The Witness of God: The Trinity, Missio Dei, Karl Barth, and the Nature of Christian Community.* Grand Rapids, MI: Eerdmans, 2010.

Forman, Charles W. *The Island Churches of the South Pacific: Emergence in the Twentieth Century.* Maryknoll, NY: Orbis, 1982.

Forsyth, P. T. *The Justification of God: Lectures for War-Time on a Christian Theodicy.* London: Duckworth & Co., 1916.

Forsyth, P. T. *Lectures on the Church and the Sacraments.* London: Longmans, Green & Co., 1917.

Fosdick, Harry Emerson. *Shall the Fundamentalists Win? A Sermon Preached at the First Presbyterian Church, New York, May 21, 1922.* New York: 1922.

Fox, Richard Wightman. *Reinhold Niebuhr: A Biography.* Ithaca, NY, and London: Cornell University Press, 1996.

Frank, David John, and Elizabeth H. McEneaney. "The Individualization of Society and the Liberalization of State Policies on Same-Sex Sexual Relations, 1984–1995." *Social Forces* 77, no. 3 (1999): 911–44.

Freeze, Gregory L. "Subversive Atheism: Soviet Antireligious Campaigns and the Religious Revival in Ukraine in the 1920s." In Catherine Wanner, ed., *State Secularism and Lived Religion in Soviet Russia and the Ukraine*, 27–62. Oxford: Oxford University Press; and Washington: Woodrow Wilson Center Press, 2012.

Freire, Paulo. *Educação como Prática de Liberdade.* Rio de Janeiro: Editora Civilização Brasileira, 1967.

Freire, Paulo. *La Educación como Práctica de la Libertad.* Spanish translation. Montevideo: Tierra Nueva, 1969; and Santiago de Chile: ICIRA, 1969.

Freston, Paul. "Contours of Latin American Pentecostalism." In Donald M. Lewis, ed., *Christianity Reborn: The Global Expansion of Evangelicalism in the Twentieth Century*, 221–70. Grand Rapids, MI: Eerdmans, 2004.

Freston, Paul. "The Future of Pentecostalism in Brazil: The Limits to Growth." In Robert W. Hefner, ed., *Global Pentecostalism in the Twenty-First Century*, 63–90. Bloomington: Indiana University Press, 2013.

Freston, Paul. "Pentecostalism in Brazil: A Brief History." *Religion* 25, no. 2 (1995): 119–33.

Freston, Paul. "The Transnationalisation of the Universal Church of the Kingdom of God." In André Corten and Ruth Marshall-Fratani, eds., *Between Babel and Pentecost: Transnational Pentecostalism in Africa and Latin America*, 196–215. London: Hurst & Co., 2001.

Frieze, Donna-Lee ed. *Totally Unofficial: The Autobiography of Raphael Lemkin*. New Haven, CT: Yale University Press, 2013.

Frye, Jerry K. "The 'Black Manifesto' and the Tactic of Objectification." *Journal of Black Studies* 5, no. 1 (1974): 65–76.

Fullerton, W. Y. *F. B. Meyer: A Biography*. London: Marshall, Morgan & Scott, n.d.

Furseth, Inger. "Nordic Countries." In Mark Juergensmeyer and Wade Clark Roof, eds., *Encyclopedia of Global Religion*, 929–34. Los Angeles: SAGE Reference, 2012.

Gaitskell, Deborah. "Hot Meetings and Hard Kraals: African Biblewomen in Transvaal Methodism, 1924–60." *Journal of Religion in Africa* 30, no. 3 (2000): 277–309.

Gallo, Patrick J. ed. *Pius XII, the Holocaust, and the Revisionists: Essays*. Jefferson, NC: McFarland & Co., 2006.

Garbowski, Christopher. *Religious Life in Poland: History, Diversity and Modern Issues*. Jefferson, NC: McFarland & Co., 2014.

Gardner, W. J. *William Massey*. Wellington: A. H. and A. W. Reed, 1969.

Gaustad, Edwin S., and Philip L. Barlow, *New Historical Atlas of Religion in America*. New York: Oxford University Press, 2001.

George, Timothy, James Earl Massey, and Robert Smith, Jr., eds. *Our Sufficiency is of God: Essays on Preaching in Honor of Gardner C. Taylor*. Macon, GA: Mercer University Press, 2010.

Geffert, Bryn. "Anglicans and Orthodox between the Wars." PhD thesis, University of Minnesota, 2003.

"The Genocide of Ottoman Greeks, 1914–1923." Rutgers Center for the Study of Genocide and Human Rights. http://www.ncas.rutgers.edu/center-study-genocide -conflict-resolution-and-human-rights/genocide-ottoman-greeks-1914-1923 (Accessed May 5, 2017).

Gerlach, Wolfgang. *And the Witnesses Were Silent: The Confessing Church and the Persecution of the Jews*. Lincoln: University of Nebraska Press, 2000.

Gibson, Ralph. *A Social History of French Catholicism 1789-1914*. London and New York: Routledge, 1989.

Gifford, Paul. *African Christianity: Its Public Role*. London: Hurst and Company, 1998.

Gifford, Paul. *Christianity, Development and Modernity in Africa*. London: Hurst and Company, 2015.

Gifford, Paul. *Ghana's New Christianity: Pentecostalism in a Globalising African Economy*. London: Hurst and Company. 2004.

Gih, Andrew. *Into God's Family: A Fascinating Account of the Lives and Work of Members of the Bethel Evangelistic Bands and Some of Their Inspiring Messages*, rev. ed. London: Marshall, Morgan & Scott, 1955.

Gih, Andrew. *Twice-Born—and Then? The Autobiography and Messages of Rev. Andrew Gih, Litt.D., F.R.G.S.*, 2nd ed. edited by Ruth J. Corbin. London: Marshall, Morgan & Scott, 1954.

Gill, Sean. *Women and the Church of England from the Eighteenth Century to the Present*. London: SPCK, 1994.

Gillet, Lev. ["A Monk of the Eastern Church"]. *The Jesus Prayer*. Crestwood, NY: St Vladimir's Seminary Press, 1987.

Githeya, Francis Kimani. *The Freedom of the Spirit: African Indigenous Churches in Kenya*. Atlanta, GA: Scholars Press, 1997.

Glendon, Mary Ann. *A World Made New: Eleanor Roosevelt and the Universal Declaration of Human Rights*. New York: Random House, 2001.

Glover, T. R. *The Conflict of Religions in the Early Roman Empire*. London: Methuen & Co, 1909.

Goddard, Allen James. "Invitations to Prophetic Integrity in the Evangelical Spirituality of the Students' Christian Association Discipleship Tradition: 1965–1979." PhD diss., University of KwaZulu-Natal, 2016.

Goddard, Hugh. *A History of Christian-Muslim Relations*. Edinburgh: Edinburgh University Press, 2000.

Godfrey, Nicholas. "Understanding Genocide: The Experience of Anglicans in Rwanda, c. 1921–2008." PhD thesis, University of Cambridge, 2009.

Godin, H., and Y. Daniel. *La France pays de Mission?* Paris: Les Éditions du Cerf, 1943.

Goldhagen, Daniel Jonah. *Hitler's Willing Executioners: Ordinary Germans and the Holocaust*, rev. ed. London: Abacus Books, 1997.

Goldhagen, Daniel Jonah. *A Moral Reckoning: The Role of the Catholic Church in the Holocaust and Its Unfulfilled Duty of Repair*. London: Little, Brown, 2002.

Goldschmidt, Arthur Jr., ed. *The Memoirs and Diaries of Muhammad Farid, an Egyptian Nationalist Leader (1868-1919)*. San Francisco: Mellen University Research Press, 1992.

Gonzalez, Joaquin L. III, and Andrea Maison. "We Do Not Bowl Alone: Social and Cultural Capital from Filipinos and Their Churches." In Tony Carnes and Fengang Yang, eds., *Asian American Religions*: *The Making and Remaking of Borders and Boundaries*, 338–59. New York: New York University Press, 2004.

Goodall, Norman, ed. *The Uppsala Report 1968: Official Report of the Fourth Assembly of the World Council of Churches Uppsala July 4-20, 1968*. Geneva: World Council of Churches, 1968.

Goodhew, David. "Growth and Decline in South Africa's Churches, 1960–1991," *Journal of Religion in Africa* 30, no. 3 (2000): 344–69.

Goodhew, David. "The Rise of the Cambridge Inter-Collegiate Christian Union, 1910–1971." *Journal of Ecclesiastical History* 54, no. 1 (2003): 62–88.

Gornik, Mark R. *Word Made Global: Stories of African Christianity in New York City*. Grand Rapids, MI: Eerdmans, 2011.

Gräbe, Uwe. "Mission and Proselytism, Presence and Witness." In Martin Tamcke and Michael Marten, eds., *Christian Witness between Continuity and New Beginnings: Modern Historical Missions in the Middle East*, 247–54. Berlin: Lit Verlag, 2006.

Grant, John Webster. *Moon of Wintertime: Missionaries and the Indians of Canada in Encounter since 1534*. Toronto: University of Toronto Press, 1984.

Grant, Tobin. "Mainline Decline? Depends on What You are Counting," Religion News Service, June 2, 2015. http://religionnews.com/2015/06/02/mainline-decline-depends-on-what-youre-counting/ (Accessed May 26, 2017).

Grayson, James H. *Myths and Legends from Korea: An Annotated Compendium of Ancient and Modern Materials*. Richmond, Surrey: Curzon Press, 2001.

Grayson, James H. "The Shintō Shrine Conflict and Protestant Martyrs in Korea, 1938–1945." *Missiology: An International Review* 29, no. 3 (2001): 287–305.

Green, Bernard. *European Baptists and the Third Reich*. Didcot: Baptist Historical Society, 2008.

Gribben, Crawford. *Evangelical Millennialism in the Trans-Atlantic World, 1500–2000*. Basingstoke: Palgrave Macmillan, 2011.

Griffith, Sidney H. *The Church in the Shadow of the Mosque: Christians and Muslims in the World of Islam*. Princeton, NJ: Princeton University Press, 2008.

Grimley, Matthew. *Citizenship, Community, and the Church of England: Liberal Anglican Theories of the State between the Wars*. Oxford: Clarendon Press, 2004.

Grimley, Matthew. "The Religion of Englishness: Puritanism, Providentialism, and 'National Character', 1918–1945." *Journal of British Studies* 46, no. 4 (2007): 884–906.

Grossman, James R. *Land of Hope: Chicago, Black Southerners, and the Great Migration*. Chicago: University of Chicago Press, 1989.

Gruber, Mark Francis. "The Monastery as the Nexus of Coptic Cosmology." In Nelly van Doorn-Harder and Kari Vogt, eds., *Between Desert and City: The Coptic Orthodox Church Today*, 67–82. Oslo: Novus Forlag, 1997.

Gunstone, John. *Lift High the Cross: Anglo-Catholics and the Congress Movement*. Norwich: Canterbury Press, 2010.

Gustafsson, Göran. "Sweden: A Folk Church under Political Influence." *Studia Theologica—Nordic Journal of Theology*, 44, no. 1 (1990): 3–16.

Gutiérrez, Gustavo (Merino). "The Meaning of Development (Notes on a Theology of Liberation)." In *In Search of a Theology of Development*: *Papers from a Consultation on Theology and Development Held by Sodepax in Cartigny, Switzerland, November, 1969*, 116–79. Geneva: Committee on Society, Development and Peace, n.d. [1970].

Gutiérrez, Gustavo. "Notes for a Theology of Liberation." *Theological Studies* 31, no. 2 (1970): 243–61.

Gutiérrez, Gustavo. *A Theology of Liberation: History, Politics and Salvation*, English translation by Sister Caridad Inda and John Eagleson, 1973. British ed. London: SCM Press, 1974.

Gutiérrez, Gustavo. "Toward a Theology of Liberation" (July 1968). In Alfred T. Hennelly, ed., *Liberation Theology: A Documentary History*, 62–76. Maryknoll, NY: Orbis Books, 1990.

Gutiérrez, Gustavo, and M. Richard Shaull. *Liberation and Change*, edited and introduced by Ronald H. Stone. Atlanta, GA: John Knox Press, 1977.

Haddad, Yvonne Yazbeck. "Christians in a Muslim State: The Recent Egyptian Debate." In Yvonne Yazbeck Haddad and Wadi Z. Haddad, eds., *Christian- Muslim Encounters*, 381–95. Gainesville, FL: University Press of Florida, 1995.

Halas, Elzbieta. "Symbolic Politics of Public Time and Collective Memory. The Polish Case." *European Review* 10, no. 1 (2002): 115–29.

Haliburton, Gordon A. *The Prophet Harris: A Study of an African Prophet and his Mass-Movement in the Ivory Coast and the Gold Coast, 1913-1915*. London: Longman, 1971.

Hall, Caroline J. Addington. *A Thorn in the Flesh: How Gay Sexuality is Changing the Episcopal Church.* Lanham: MD: Rowman & Littlefield, 2013.

Halls, W. D. "Church and State: Prelates, Theologians and the Vichy Regime." In Frank Tallett and Nicholas Atkin, eds., *Religion, Society and Politics in France since 1789*, 167–86. London: The Hambledon Press, 1991.

Hamilton, Michael S. "The Interdenominational Evangelicalism of D. L. Moody and the Problem of Fundamentalism." In Darren Dochuk, Thomas S. Kidd and Kurt W. Peterson, eds., *American Evangelicalism: George Marsden and the State of American Religious History*, 230–80. Notre Dame, IN: University of Notre Dame Press, 2014.

Hanciles, Jehu J. *Beyond Christendom: Globalization, African Migration and the Transformation of the West.* Maryknoll, NY: Orbis Books, 2008.

Hankins, Barry. *Francis Schaeffer and the Shaping of Evangelical America.* Grand Rapids, MI: Eerdmans, 2008.

Harris, Ruth. *Lourdes: Body and Spirit in the Secular Age*, new ed. Harmondsworth: Penguin Books, 2000.

Hasan, S. S. *Christians versus Muslims in Modern Egypt: The Century-Long Struggle for Coptic Equality.* New York: Oxford University Press, 2003.

Hassett, Miranda K. *Anglican Communion in Crisis: How Episcopal Dissidents and their African Allies are Reshaping Anglicanism.* Princeton, NJ: Princeton University Press, 2007.

Hastings, Adrian. *The Church in Africa 1450–1950.* Oxford: Clarendon Press, 1994.

Hastings, Adrian. "The Clash between Nationalism and Universalism in Twentieth-Century Christianity." In Brian Stanley, ed., *Missions, Nationalism, and the End of Empire*, 15–33. Grand Rapids, MI: Eerdmans, 2003.

Hastings, Adrian. *The Construction of Nationhood: Ethnicity, Religion and Nationalism.* Cambridge: Cambridge University Press, 1997.

Hastings, Adrian. *A History of English Christianity 1920–1985.* London: Collins, 1986.

Hastings, Adrian. *The Shaping of Prophecy: Passion, Perception and Practicality* London: Geoffrey Chapman, 1995.

Hastings, Derek. *Catholicism and the Roots of Nazism: Religious Identity and National Socialism.* New York: Oxford University Press, 2010.

Hayes, Stephen. "Orthodox Mission in Tropical Africa." *Missionalia* 24, no. 3 (1996): 383–98.

Hayford, J. E. Casely. *William Waddy Harris. The West African Reformer. The Man and His Message.* London: C. M. Phillips, 1915.

Hazelgrove, Jenny. *Spiritualism and British Society between the Wars.* Manchester: Manchester University Press, 2000.

Head, Peter M. "The Nazi Quest for an Aryan Jesus." *Journal for the Study of the Historical Jesus* 2, no. 1 (2004): 55–89.

Heeney, Brian D. *The Women's Movement in the Church of England, 1850–1950.* Oxford: Clarendon Press, 1988.

Hempton, David. "Organizing Concepts and 'Small Differences' in the Comparative Secularization of Western Europe and the United States." In David Hempton and Hugh McLeod, eds., *Secularization and Religious Innovation in the North Atlantic World*, 351–73. Oxford: Oxford University Press, 2017.

Hempton, David, and Hugh McLeod, eds. *Secularization and Religious Innovation in the North Atlantic World*. Oxford: Oxford University Press, 2017.

Hennelly, Alfred T., ed. *Liberation Theology: A Documentary History*. Maryknoll, NY: Orbis Books, 1990.

Hennesey, James, S.J. *American Catholics: A History of the Roman Catholic Community in the United States*. New York: Oxford University Press, 1981.

Henson, Hensley. *Retrospect of an Unimportant Life*, 3 vols. London: Oxford University Press, 1942–1950.

Herbel, D. Oliver. *Turning to Tradition: Converts and the Making of an American Orthodox Church*. New York: Oxford University Press, 2014.

Herman, Didi. *The Antigay Agenda: Orthodox Vision and the Christian Right*. Chicago: University of Chicago Press, 1997

Hervieu-Léger, Danièle. "Religion und Sozialer Zusammenhalt in Europa." *Transit: Europäische Revue* 26 (2004): 101–19.

Heschel, Susannah. *The Aryan Jesus: Christian Theologians and the Bible in Nazi Germany*. Princeton, NJ: Princeton University Press, 2008.

Hewitt, Gordon. *The Problems of Success: A History of the Church Missionary Society 1910–1942*, 2 vols. London: SCM Press, 1971, 1977.

Heyman, Richard D. "C. T. Loram: a South African Liberal in Race Relations." *International Journal of Historical Studies* 5, no. 1 (1972): 41–50.

Hilaire, Y.-M. "La sociologie religieuse du Catholicisme français au vingtième siècle." In Kay Chadwick, ed., *Catholicism, Politics and Society in Twentieth-Century France*, 244–59. Liverpool: Liverpool University Press, 2000.

Hilliard, David. "Defending Orthodoxy: Some Conservative and Traditionalist Movements in Australian Christianity." In Geoffrey R. Treloar and Robert D. Linder, eds., *Making History for God: Essays on Evangelicalism, Revival and Mission in Honour of Stuart Piggin, Master of Robert Menzies College 1990–2004*, 273–92. Sydney: Robert Menzies College, 2004.

Hilliard, David. *God's Gentlemen: A History of the Melanesian Mission 1849–1942*. St. Lucia: University of Queensland Press, 1978.

Hilliard, David. "Pluralism and New Alignments in Society and Church: 1967 to the Present." In Bruce Kaye, ed., *Anglicanism in Australia: A History*, 124–48. Carlton South, Victoria: Melbourne University Press, 2002.

Hine, Edward. *Twenty-seven Identifications of the English Nation with the Lost House of Israel*. London: G. J. Stevenson, 1869.

Hirschfeld, Magnus. *Racism* (1938). Translated and edited by Eden and Cedar Paul, new ed. Port Washington, NY: Kennikat Press, 1973.

Hirschon, Renée, ed. *Crossing the Aegean: An Appraisal of the 1923 Compulsory Population Exchange Between Greece and Turkey*. New York: Berghahn Books, 2003.

Hitchmough, Sam. "Missions of Patriotism: Joseph H. Jackson and Martin Luther King." *European Journal of American Studies*, 6, no. 1 (2011): 1–19.

Hobbs, Frank, and Nicole Stoops, *Demographic Trends in the Twentieth Century: Census 2000 Special Reports*. U.S. Census Bureau, Census 2000 Special Reports, Series CENSR-4. Washington, DC: US Government Printing Office, 2002. https://www.census.gov/prod/2002pubs/censr-4.pdf (Accessed May 26, 2017).

Hoedemaker, Bert. "The Legacy of J. C. Hoekendijk." *International Bulletin of Missionary Research* 19, no. 4 (1995): 166–70.

Hollenweger, Walter J. *The Pentecostals*. London: SCM Press, 1972.

Hong, Harold S., Won Yong Ji, and Chung Choon Kim, eds. *Korea Struggles for Christ: Memorial Symposium for the Eightieth Anniversary of Protestantism in Korea*. Seoul: Christian Literature Society of Korea, 1966.

Hope, Nicholas. *German and Scandinavian Protestantism, 1700–1918*. Oxford: Clarendon Press, 1999.

Hopkins, C. Howard. *John R. Mott 1865–1955: A Biography*. Grand Rapids, MI: Eerdmans, 1979.

Huddleston, Trevor. *Naught for Your Comfort*. London: Collins, 1956.

Hunt, Stephen, and Nicola Lightly. "The British Black Pentecostal 'Revival': Identity and Belief in the 'New' Nigerian Churches." *Ethnic and Racial Studies*, 24, no. 1 (2001): 104–124.

Hunter, James Davison. *To Change the World: The Irony, Tragedy and Possibility of Christianity in the Late Modern World*. New York: Oxford University Press, 2010.

Hunter, Leslie Stannard, ed. *Scandinavian Churches: A Picture of the Development and Life of the Churches of Denmark, Finland, Iceland, Norway and Sweden*. London: Faber & Faber, 1965.

Huntington, W. R. *The Peace of the Church*. London: James Nisbet, 1891.

Hurewitz, Daniel. *Bohemian Los Angeles and the Making of Modern Politics*. Berkeley, CA: University of California Press, 2007.

Ibrahim, Vivian. *The Copts of Egypt: Challenges of Modernisation and Identity*. London: I. B. Tauris, 2011.

Il Fermo Proposito: Encyclical of Pope Pius X on Catholic Action in Italy Addressed to the Bishops of Italy. 1905, http://www.vatican.va/holy_father/pius_x/encyclicals/documents/hf_p-x_enc_11061905_il-fermo-proposito_en.html (Accessed March 24, 2017).

Inglis, K. S. *Sacred Places: War Memorials in the Australian Landscape*. Carlton South: Melbourne University Press, 1998.

In Search of a Theology of Development: Papers from a Consultation on Theology and Development Held by Sodepax in Cartigny, Switzerland, November, 1969. Geneva: Committee on Society, Development and Peace, n.d. [1970].

International Committee of Jurists, Geneva, ed. *The Trial of Beyers Naudé: Christian Witness and the Rule of Law*. London: Search Press, in conjunction with Ravan Press, Johannesburg, 1975.

Ireland, Daryl R. "John Sung: Christian Revitalization in China and Southeast Asia." PhD diss., Boston University, 2015.

Iremonger, F. A. *William Temple Archbishop of Canterbury: His Life and Letters*. London: Oxford University Press, 1948.

Irvine, Cecilia. "Birth of the Kimbanguist Movement in the Bas-Zaire," *Journal of Religion in Africa* 6, no. 1 (1974): 23–76.

Jänterä-Jareborg, Maarit. "A Scandinavian Perspective on Homosexuality, Equal Rights, and Freedom of Religion." In Timothy Samuel Shah, Thomas F. Farr, and Jack Friedman, eds., *Religious Freedom and Gay Rights: Emerging Conflicts in the United States and Europe*, 246–68. New York: Oxford University Press, 2016.

Jenkins, Philip. *The Next Christendom: The Coming of Global Christianity*, 3rd ed. Oxford: Oxford University Press, 2011.

Job, G. V., et al. *Rethinking Christianity in India*. Madras: A. N. Sudarisanam, n.d. [1938].

Johnson, Christopher D. L. *Globalization of Hesychasm and the Jesus Prayer: Contesting Contemplation*. London: Continuum, 2010.

Jones, Elias Farajajé. *In Search of Zion: The Spiritual Significance of Africa in Black Religious Movements*. Bern: Peter Lang, 1990.

Jones, Lawrence N. "The Black Churches: A New Agenda." In Milton C. Sernett, ed., *African American Religious History: A Documentary Witness*, 2nd ed., 580–88. Durham, NC: Duke University Press, 1999.

Jones, Timothy Willem. *Sexual Politics in the Church of England, 1857–1957*. Oxford: Oxford University Press, 2013.

Jordan, Mark D. *The Silence of Sodom: Homosexuality in Modern Catholicism*. Chicago: University of Chicago Press, 2000.

Joselit, Jenna Weissman, Timothy Matovina, Roberto Suro, and Fenggang Yang. "American Religion and the Old and New Immigration." *Religion and American Culture: A Journal of Interpretation* 22, no. 1 (2012): 1–30.

Judd, Stephen, and Kenneth Cable. *Sydney Anglicans: A History of the Diocese*. Sydney: Anglican Information Office, 1987.

Juergensmeyer, Mark, and Wade Clark Roof, eds. *Encyclopedia of Global Religion*. Los Angeles: SAGE Reference, 2012.

Kanya-Forstner, A. S. "The War, Imperialism, and Decolonization." In Jay Winter, Geoffrey Parker, and Mary R. Habeck, eds., *The Great War and the Twentieth Century*, 231–62. New Haven, CT and London: Yale University Press, 2000.

Karilis, Vrasidis. "Greek Christianity after 1453." In Ken Parry, ed., *The Blackwell Companion to Eastern Christianity*, 156–85. Oxford: Blackwell, 2007.

Karl, Rebecca E. *Staging the World: Chinese Nationalism at the Turn of the Twentieth Century*. Durham, NC: Duke University Press, 2002.

Kashirin, Alexander. "Protestant Minorities in the Soviet Ukraine, 1945–1991." PhD diss., University of Oregon, 2010.

Kasinitz, Philip. *Caribbean New York: Black Immigrants and the Politics of Race*. Ithaca, NY: Cornell University Press, 1992.

Kasselstrand, Isabella. "Nonbelievers in the Church: A Study of Cultural Religion in Sweden." *Sociology of Religion* 76, no. 3 (2015): 275–94.

Kasselstrand, Isabella. "'Tell the Minister Not to Talk about God': A Comparative Study of Secularisation in Protestant Europe." PhD thesis, University of Edinburgh, 2013.

Kay, William K. "Pentecostalism and Fundamentalism." In David W. Bebbington and David Ceri Jones, eds., *Evangelicalism and Fundamentalism in the United Kingdom in the Twentieth Century*, 309–27. Oxford: Oxford University Press, 2013.

Kee, Alistair. *Marx and the Failure of Liberation Theology*. London: SCM Press, 1990.

Kee, Alistair. *The Rise and Demise of Black Theology*. Aldershot: Ashgate, 2006.

Kelley, Shawn. *Racializing Jesus: Race, Ideology and the Formation of Modern Biblical Scholarship*. London: Routledge, 2002.

Kellogg, Vernon L. *Headquarters Nights: A Record of Conversations and Experiences at the Headquarters of the German Army in France and Belgium*. Boston: The Atlantic Monthly Press, 1917.

Kelly, Michael. "Catholics and Communism in Liberation France, 1944–47." In Frank Tallett and Nicholas Atkin, eds., *Religion, Society and Politics in France since 1789*, 187–202. London: The Hambledon Press, 1991.

Kent, John. *The Unacceptable Face: The Modern Church in the Eyes of the Historian*. London: SCM Press, 1987.

Kent, Neil. *The Soul of the North: A Social, Architectural and Cultural History of the Nordic Countries, 1700–1940*. London: Reaktion Books, 2000.

Keysser, Christian. *A People Reborn*, English translation. Pasadena, CA: William Carey Library, 1980.

Khawaga, Dina El. "Political Dynamics of the Copts." In Andrea Pacini, ed., *Christian Communities in the Arab Middle East: The Challenge of the Future*, 172–90. Oxford: Clarendon Press, 1998.

Kidd, Benjamin. *The Science of Power*. London: Methuen, 1918.

Kidd, Colin. *The Forging of Races: Race and Scripture in the Protestant Atlantic World, 1600–2000*. Cambridge: Cambridge University Press, 2006.

Kidd, Thomas S. *American Christians and Islam: Evangelical Culture and Muslims from the Colonial Period to the Age of Terrorism*. Princeton, NJ: Princeton University Press, 2009.

Killingray, David. "A New 'Imperial Disease': The Influenza Pandemic of 1918–9 and its Impact upon the British Empire." *Caribbean Quarterly* 39, no. 4 (2003): 30–49.

Killingray, David. "Transatlantic Networks of Early African Pentecostalism: The Role of Thomas Brem Wilson, 1901–1929." *Studies in World Christianity*, 23, no. 3 (2017): 218–36.

Kim, Sebastian C. H., and Kirsteen Kim. *A History of Korean Christianity*. Cambridge: Cambridge University Press, 2015.

King, Martin Luther. "Letter from a Birmingham Jail," April 16, 1963. http://okra .stanford.edu/transcription/document_images/ undecided/630416-019.pdf (Accessed March 10, 2017).

King, Michael Christopher. *The Palestinians and the Churches. Vol. I: 1948–1956*. Geneva: WCC, 1981.

Kinsey, Alfred T., Wardell B. Pomeroy, and Clyde E. Martin. *Sexual Behavior in the Human Male*. Philadelphia: W. B. Saunders, 1948.

Kinsey, Alfred C., Wardell B. Pomeroy, Clyde E. Martin, Paul H. Gebhard, et al. *Sexual Behavior in the Human Female*. Philadelphia: W. B. Saunders, 1953.

Kipp, Rita Smith, and Susan Rodgers, eds. *Indonesian Religions in Transition*. Tucson, AL: University of Arizona Press, 1987.

Klinken, Gerry van. *Minorities, Modernity and the Emerging Nation: Christians in Indonesia, a Biographical Approach*. Leiden: KITLV Press, 2003.

Kloczkowski, Jerzy. *A History of Polish Christianity*. Cambridge: Cambridge University Press, 2000.

Korean Ministry of Culture, Sports and Tourism. *The Present Condition of Religions in Korea*. Seoul: 2011.

Koschorke, Klaus, and Adrian Hermann, eds. *Polycentric Structures in the History of World Christianity/Polyzentrische Strukturen in der Geschichte des Weltchristentums.* Wiesbaden: Harrasowitz Verlag, 2014.

Kraemer, Hendrik. *From Missionfield to Independent Church: Report on a Decisive Decade in the Growth of Indigenous Churches in Indonesia.* London: SCM Press, 1958.

Kuhn, Thomas S. *The Structure of Scientific Revolutions.* Chicago: University of Chicago Press, 1962.

Kuruvilla, Samuel J. *Radical Christianity in Palestine and Israel: Liberation and Theology in the Middle East.* London: I. B. Tauris, 2013.

Laing, Mark T. B. "'The Calling of the Church to Mission and Unity': Bishop Lesslie Newbigin and the Integration of the International Missionary Council with the World Council of Churches." PhD thesis, University of Edinburgh, 2010.

Laing, Mark T. B. *From Crisis to Creation: Lesslie Newbigin and the Reinvention of Christian Mission.* Eugene, OR: Pickwick Publications, 2012.

The Lambeth Conference 1930: Encyclical Letter from the Bishops with the Resolutions and Reports. London: SPCK, n.d. [1930].

The Lambeth Conference 1968: Resolutions and Reports. London: SPCK, 1968.

Lange, Raeburn. *Island Ministers: Indigenous Leadership in Nineteenth Century Pacific Islands Christianity.* Christchurch and Canberra: Macmillan Brown Centre for Pacific Studies, Canterbury University, and Pandanus Books, 2005.

Larbi, Emmanuel Kingsley. *Pentecostalism: The Eddies of Ghanaian Christianity.* Accra: Centre for Pentecostal Studies, 2001.

Larkin, Maurice. *Church and State in France after the Dreyfus Affair.* London: Macmillan, 1974.

Larkin, Maurice. *Religion, Politics and Preferment in France since 1890: La Belle Époque and Its Legacy.* Cambridge: Cambridge University Press, 1995.

Larsen, Timothy. *Christabel Pankhurst: Fundamentalism and Feminism in Coalition* Woodbridge: The Boydell Press, 2002.

Latourette, Kenneth S. *A History of Christian Missions in China.* New York: Macmillan, 1929.

Latourette, Kenneth Scott. *A History of the Expansion of Christianity,* 7 vols. London: Eyre & Spottiswoode, 1938–47.

Lausten, Martin Schwartz. *A Church History of Denmark,* translated by Frederick H. Cryer. Aldershot: Ashgate, 2002.

Le Bras, Gabriel. "Statistique et histoire religieuse: Pour un examen detaillé et pour une explication historique de l'état de Catholicisme dans les diverse regions de France." *Revue d'histoire de l'église de France* 17, no. 77 (1931): 425–49.

Lecky, Robert S., and H. Elliott Wright, eds. *Black Manifesto: Religion, Racism and Reparations.* New York: Sheed and Wright, 1969.

Lee, Timothy S. *Born Again: Evangelicalism in Korea.* Honolulu: University of Hawaii Press, 2010.

Leed, Eric J. *No Man's Land: Combat & Identity in World War I.* Cambridge: Cambridge University Press, 1979.

Léger, Danièle. *Le féminisme en France.* Paris: Éditions Le Sycomore, 1982.

Lehmann, David. *Struggle for the Spirit: Religious Transformation and Popular Culture in Brazil and Latin America.* Cambridge: Polity Press, 1996.

Lemkin, Raphael. *Axis Rule in Occupied Europe. Laws of Occupation. Analysis of Government. Proposals for Redress*. Washington, DC: Carnegie Endowment for International Peace, 1944.

Lende, Gina. "A Quest for Justice: Palestinian Christians and their Contextual Theology." MPhil thesis, University of Oslo, 2003.

Lenin, V. I. "The Socialist Revolution and the Right of Nations to Self- Determination" (1916). In his *Collected Works*, vol. 22, 143–56. 45 vols. Moscow: Progress, 1960–70.

Levine, Lawrence W. *Defender of the Faith. William Jennings Bryan: The Last Decade 1915-1925*, 2nd ed. New York: Oxford University Press, 1968.

Lewis, Donald M., ed. *Christianity Reborn: The Global Expansion of Evangelicalism in the Twentieth Century*. Grand Rapids, MI: Eerdmans, 2004.

Lewis, Donald M. *The Origins of Christian Zionism: Lord Shaftesbury and Evangelical Support for a Jewish Homeland*. Cambridge: Cambridge University Press, 2014.

Lian Xi. *Redeemed by Fire: The Rise of Popular Christianity in Modern China*. New Haven, CT: Yale University Press, 2010.

Lienesch, Michael. *In the Beginning: Fundamentalism, the Scopes Trial, and the Making of the Antievolution Movement*. Chapel Hill: University of North Carolina Press, 2007.

Lindsay, Gordon. *The Life of John Alexander Dowie Whose Trials-Tragedies-and Triumphs are the Most Fascinating Object Lesson of Christian History*. n.p.: Voice of Healing Publishing Company, 1951.

Lipset, S. M., and S. S. Wolin, eds. *The Berkeley Student Revolt: Facts and Interpretations*. Garden City, NY: Doubleday & Co, Anchor Books: 1965.

Livingstone, David N. *Darwin's Forgotten Defenders: The Encounter between Evangelical Theology and Evolutionary Thought*. Grand Rapids, MI: Eerdmans, 1987.

Loane, Marcus L. *Archbishop Mowll: the Biography of Howard West Kilvinton Mowll Archbishop of Sydney and Primate of Australia*. London: Hodder & Stoughton, 1960.

Lockhart, J. G. *Cosmo Gordon Lang*. London: Hodder & Stoughton, 1949.

Løland, Ole Jakob. "The Position of the Biblical Canon in Brazil: From Catholic Rediscovery to Neo-Pentecostal Marginalisation." *Studies in World Christianity* 21, no. 2 (August 2015): 98–118.

Longfield, Bradley J. *The Presbyterian Controversy: Fundamentalists, Modernists, and Moderates*. New York: Oxford University Press, 1991.

Longman, Timothy. *Christianity and Genocide in Rwanda*. Cambridge: Cambridge University Press, 2010.

Loram, Charles T. "The Fundamentals of Indian White Contact in the United States and Canada." In *The North American Indian Today: University of Toronto - Yale University Seminar Conference: Toronto, September 4–16, 1939*, ed. C. T. Loram and T. F. McIlwraith, 3–18. Toronto: University of Toronto Press, 1943.

Lowman, Pete. *The Day of His Power: A History of the International Fellowship of Evangelical Students* Leicester: Inter-Varsity Press, 1983.

Ludwig, Frieder. "Elijah II: Radicalisation and Consolidation of the Garrick Braide Movement 1915-1918." *Journal of Religion in Africa* 23, no. 1 (1993): 296–317.

Lyall, Leslie T. *John Sung: Flame for God in the Far East*. London: Overseas Missionary Fellowship, 1954.

Macdonald-Milne, Brian. *The True Way of Service: The Pacific Story of the Melanesian Brotherhood 1925–2000*. Leicester: Christians Aware and the Melanesian Brotherhood, 2003.

Machen, J. Gresham. *Christianity and Liberalism*. New York: Macmillan, 1923.

Mackay, D. J. "Simon Kimbangu and the B.M.S. Tradition." *Journal of Religion in Africa* 17, no. 2 (1987): 113–71.

Makrides, Vasilios N. "The Enlightenment in the Greek Orthodox East: Appropriation, Dilemmas, Ambiguities." In Paschalis M. Kitromilides, ed., *Enlightenment and Religion in the Orthodox World*, 17–47. Oxford: Voltaire Foundation, 2016.

Magee, Malcolm D. *What the World Should Be: Woodrow Wilson and the Crafting of a Faith-Based Foreign Policy*. Waco, TX: Baylor University Press, 2008.

Magnis-Suseno, Franz. "Pluralism under Debate: Muslim Perspectives." In Susanne Schröter, ed., *Christianity in Indonesia*: *Perspectives of Power*, 347–59. Berlin: Lit Verlag, 2010.

Maiden, John. *National Religion and the Prayer Book Controversy, 1927–1928*. Woodbridge: Boydell Press, 2009.

Manela, Erez. *The Wilsonian Moment: Self-Determination and the International Origins of Anticolonial Nationalism*. New York: Oxford University Press, 2007.

Mansfield, Stephen. *Derek Prince: A Biography*. Baldock: Derek Prince Ministries and Authentic Media, 2005.

Mariani, Paul P. *Church Militant: Bishop Kung and Catholic Resistance in Communist Shanghai*. Cambridge, MA: Harvard University Press, 2011.

Marsden, George M. *Fundamentalism and American Culture: The Shaping of Twentieth-Century Evangelicalism*. New York: Oxford University Press, 1980.

Marshall, Peter. "Smuts and the Preamble to the United Nations Charter." *Round Table; The Commonwealth Journal of International Affairs* 90, no. 358 (2001): 55–65.

Martin, David. *A General Theory of Secularization*. Oxford: Blackwell, 1978.

Martin, David. *On Secularization: Towards a Revised General Theory*. Aldershot: Ashgate, 2005.

Martin, T. T. *Evolution or Christ? Christ or Hell?* (n.p., n.d. [1923]), http://moses.law.umn.edu/darrow/documents/T_T_Martin_Evolution_or_Christ.pdf (Accessed October 10, 2017).

Martin, T. T. *Hell and the High Schools: Christ or Evolution, Which?* Kansas City: Western Baptist Publishing Co, 1923,

Marty, Martin E. *Modern American Religion, vol. 2: The Noise of Conflict 1919–1941*. Chicago: University of Chicago Press, 1991.

Masters, Bruce. *Christians and Jews in the Ottoman World: The Roots of Sectarianism*. Cambridge: Cambridge University Press, 2001.

Mathews, Shailer. *The Faith of Modernism*. New York: Macmillan, 1924.

Matovina, Timothy. *Latino Catholicism: Transformation in America's Largest Church*. Princeton, NJ: Princeton University Press, 2011.

Maximum Illud: On the Propagation of the Faith throughout the World, 1919, paragraphs 19 and 41. http://data.over-blogkiwi.com/0/51/25/32/201309

/ob_74799f42d52fa3a430ded78eef31e7c4_maximum-illud-en.pdf (Accessed March 10, 2017).

Maxwell, David. *African Gifts of the Spirit: Pentecostalism and the Rise of a Zimbabwean Transnational Religious Movement*. Oxford: James Currey, 2006.

Maxwell, David. "Historicizing Christian Independency: The Southern African Pentecostal Movement." *Journal of African History* 40, no. 2 (1999): 243–64.

McBeth, H. Leon. *The Baptist Heritage*. Nashville, TN: Broadman Press, 1987.

McCallum, Fiona. *Christian Religious Leadership in the Middle East: The Political Role of the Patriarch*. Lewiston, ME: Edwin Mellen Press, 2010.

McCallum, Fiona. "Muslim-Christian Relations in Egypt: Challenges for the Twenty-first Century." In Anthony O'Mahony and Emma Loosley, eds., *Christian Responses to Islam: Muslim-Christian Relations in the Modern World*, 66–84. Manchester: Manchester University Press, 2012.

McConnachie, John. *The Barthian Theology and the Man of Today*. London: Hodder & Stoughton, 1933.

McDannell, Colleen. *Material Christianity: Religion and Popular Culture in America*. New Haven, CT: Yale University Press, 1995.

McGavran, Donald A. *The Bridges of God: a Study in the Strategy of Missions*. New York: Friendship Press, 1955.

McKeown, Adam. "Global Migration, 1846–1970." *Journal of World History* 15, no. 2 (2004): 155–89.

McLean-Farrell, Janice A. *West Indian Pentecostals: Living Their Faith in New York and London*. London: Bloomsbury Academic, 2016.

McLeod, Hugh. *Religion and the People of Western Europe*. Oxford: Oxford University Press, 1981.

McLeod, Hugh. "'Religious America, Secular Europe': Are They Really So Different?" In David Hempton and Hugh McLeod, eds., *Secularization and Religious Innovation in the North Atlantic World*, 329–50. Oxford: Oxford University Press, 2017.

McLeod, Hugh. *The Religious Crisis of the 1960s*. Oxford: Oxford University Press, 2007.

McLeod, Hugh. *Secularisation in Western Europe, 1848–1914*. Basingstoke: Macmillan, 2000.

McMillan, James F. "Catholicism and Nationalism in France: The Case of the Fédération Nationale Catholique, 1924–39." In Frank Tallett and Nicholas Atkin, eds., *Catholicism in Britain and France since 1789*, 151–63. London and Rio Grande: The Hambledon Press, 1996.

McMillan, James F. "Religion and Gender in Modern France: Some Reflections." In Frank Tallett and Nicholas Atkin, eds., *Religion, Society and Politics in France since 1789*, 55–66. London: The Hambledon Press, 1991.

McNeill, John J. *The Church and the Homosexual*. London: Darton, Longman & Todd, 1977.

Mcqueen, Ian. "Students, Apartheid and the Ecumenical Movement in South Africa, 1960–1975." *Journal of Southern African Studies* 39, no. 2 (2013): 447–63.

Meinardus, Otto F. A. *Christian Egypt Ancient and Modern*, 2nd rev. ed. Cairo: The American University in Cairo Press, 1977.

Meinardus, Otto F. A. *Christians in Egypt: Orthodox, Catholic and Protestant Communities Past and Present*. Cairo: The American University in Cairo Press, 2006.

Meinardus, Otto F. A. *Two Thousand Years of Coptic Christianity*. Cairo: The American University in Cairo Press, 1999.

Metz, Johannes Baptist. *Theology of the World*. English translation, London: Burns & Oates, 1969.

Mews, Stuart Paul. "Religion and English Society in the First World War." PhD thesis, University of Cambridge, 1974.

Meyer, Birgit. *Translating the Devil: Religion and Modernity among the Ewe in Ghana*. Edinburgh: Edinburgh University Press for the International African Institute, 1999.

Miller, J. R. *Shingwauk's Vision: A History of Native Residential Schools*. Toronto: University of Toronto Press, 1996.

Milloy, John S. *"A National Crime": The Canadian Government and the Residential School System*. Winnipeg: University of Manitoba Press, 1999.

Minority Rights Group. *Religious Minorities in the Soviet Union, Report No. 1, 1984* London: MRG, 1984.

Mohr, Adam. *Enchanted Calvinism: Labor Migration, Afflicting Spirits, and Christian Therapy in the Presbyterian Church of Ghana*. Rochester, NY: University of Rochester Press, 2013.

Mohr, Adam. "Out of Zion and into Philadelphia and West Africa: Faith Tabernacle Congregation, 1897–1925." *Pneuma* 32, no. 1 (2010): 56–79.

Molebatsi, Caesar, with David Virtue. *A Flame for Justice*. Oxford: Lion Publishing, 1991.

Moltmann, Jürgen. *Theology of Hope: On the Grounds and Implications of a Christian Eschatology*. English translation. London: SCM Press, 1967.

Moore, James R. *The Post-Darwinian Controversies: A Study of the Protestant Struggle to Come to Terms with Darwin in Great Britain and America 1870–1900*. Cambridge: Cambridge University Press, 1979.

Moore, Paul, Jr. *Take a Bishop Like Me*. New York: Harper & Row, 1979.

Moore, R. Laurence. *Selling God: American Religion in the Marketplace of Culture* New York: Oxford University Press, 1994.

Morgan, D. Densil. *Barth Reception in Britain*. London: T. & T. Clark, 2010.

Moyn, Samuel. *The Last Utopia: Human Rights in History*. Cambridge, MA: The Belknap Press of Harvard University Press, 2010.

Mudimbe, V. Y. *The Idea of Africa*. Bloomington, IN: Indiana University Press, 1994.

Mudimbe, V. Y. *The Invention of Africa; Gnosis, Philosophy and the Order of Knowledge*. Bloomington, IN: Indiana University Press, 1998.

Mullins, Mark R., and Richard Fox Young, eds. *Perspectives on Christianity in Korea and Japan: The Gospel and Culture in East Asia*. Lewiston, ME: Edwin Mellen Press, 1995.

Murray, Harold. *Dinsdale Young the Preacher: An Intimate Sketch of Dr Dinsdale T. Young*. London: Marshall, Morgan & Scott, n.d. [1938].

Myers, James T. *Enemies without Guns: The Catholic Church in the People's Republic of China*. New York: Paragon House, 1991.

Natsoulas, Theodore. "Patriarch McGuire and the Spread of the African Orthodox Church to Africa." *Journal of Religion in Africa* 12, no. 2 (1981): 81–104.

Nazir, Farhana. "Offences Relating to Religion in British India and Their Implications in Contemporary Pakistan," PhD thesis, University of Edinburgh, 2013.

Nelson, F. Burton. "The Life of Dietrich Bonhoeffer." In John W. de Gruchy, ed., *The Cambridge Companion to Dietrich Bonhoeffer*, 22–49. Cambridge: Cambridge University Press, 1999.

Neuhaus, Richard John. *The Naked Public Square: Religion and Democracy in America*. Grand Rapids, MI: Eerdmans, 1984.

Newbigin, J. E. Lesslie. "Ecumenism in Transition," *International Bulletin of Missionary Research* 18, no. 1 (1994): 2–5.

Newbigin, J. E. Lesslie. *Honest Religion for Secular Man*. London: SCM Press, 1966.

Newbigin, J. E. Lesslie. *The Household of God: Lectures on the Nature of the Church*. London: SCM Press, 1953.

Newbigin, Lesslie. *Unfinished Agenda: An Updated Autobiography*. Edinburgh: St Andrew Press, 1993.

Newbury, M. Catharine. *The Cohesion of Oppression: Clientship and Ethnicity in Rwanda 1860–1960*. New York: Columbia University Press, 1988.

New Testament Church of God (UK). "Our History." At https://ntcg.org.uk/about /history (Accessed May 8, 2017).

Niebuhr, Reinhold. *The Nature and Destiny of Man: A Christian Interpretation*. 2 vols. New York: Scribner's and Sons, 1941, 1943.

Niezen, Ronald. *Truth and Indignation: Canada's Truth and Reconciliation Commission on Indian Residential Schools*. Toronto: University of Toronto Press, 2013.

Nikolchev, Alexandra. "A Brief History of the Birth Control Pill." http://www.pbs.org /wnet/need-to-know/health/a-brief-history-of-the-birth-control-pill/480/ (Accessed May 2, 2017).

Noble, O. Frederick. *Free and Equal: Human Rights in Ecumenical Perspective*. Geneva: World Council of Churches, 1968.

Nockles, Peter B. *The Oxford Movement in Context: Anglican High Churchmanship, 1760–1857*. Cambridge: Cambridge University Press, 1994.

Noll, Mark A. "What Happened to Christian Canada?" *Church History* 75, no. 2 (2006): 245–73.

Norris, Pippa, and Ronald Ingelhart. *Sacred and Secular: Religion and Politics Worldwide*. Cambridge: Cambridge University Press, 2004.

Nugent, Robert, and Jeannine Gramick. *Building Bridges: Gay and Lesbian Reality and the Catholic Church*. Mystic, CT: Twenty-Third Publications, 1992.

Numbers, Ronald L. *The Creationists: The Evolution of Scientific Creationism*. Berkeley: University of California Press, 1993. First published 1992 by Alfred A. Knopf.

Nurser, John. *For All Peoples and All Nations: Christian Churches and Human Rights*. Washington, DC, and Geneva: Georgetown University Press and WCC Publications, 2005.

O'Brien, Anne. *God's Willing Workers: Women and Religion in Australia*. Sydney: University of New South Wales Press, 2005.

O'Collins, Gerald, S.J. *The Second Vatican Council on Other Religions*. Oxford: Oxford University Press, 2013.

O'Farrell, Patrick. *The Catholic Church in Australia: A Short History: 1788–1967*. London: Geoffrey Chapman, 1968.

Ohrn, Arnold T. ed. *Baptist World Alliance Golden Jubilee Congress (Ninth World Congress) London, England 16th–22nd July, 1955: Official Report*. London: Carey Kingsgate Press, n.d. [1955].

Okkenhaug, Inger Marie. *The Quality of Heroic Living, of High Endeavour and Adventure: Anglican Mission, Women and Education in Palestine, 1888–1948*. Leiden: E. J. Brill, 2002.

Oldham, J. H. *Christianity and the Race Problem*. London: Student Christian Movement, 1924.

Olender, Maurice. *The Languages of Paradise: Race, Religion, and Philology in the Nineteenth Century*. Cambridge, MA: Harvard University Press, 1992.

Olupona, Jacob K., and Regina Gemignani, eds. *African Immigrant Religions in America*. New York: New York University Press, 2007.

O'Mahony, Anthony. "The Coptic Orthodox Church in Modern Egypt." In Anthony O'Mahony and Emma Loosley, eds., *Eastern Christianity in the Modern Middle East*, 56–77. London: Routledge, 2010.

O'Mahony, Anthony. "The Vatican, Palestinian Christians, Israel, and Jerusalem: Religion, Politics, Diplomacy, and Holy Places, 1945–1950." In R. N. Swanson, ed., *The Holy Land, Holy Lands, and Christian History. Studies in Church History*, vol. 36, 358–72. Woodbridge: The Boydell Press for the Ecclesiastical History Society, 2000.

O'Mahony, Anthony, and Emma Loosley, eds. *Christian Responses to Islam: Muslim-Christian Relations in the Modern World*. Manchester: Manchester University Press, 2012.

Onyinah, Opoku. *Pentecostal Exorcism: Witchcraft and Demonology in Ghana*. Blandford Forum: Deo Publishing, 2012.

Oro, Ari Pedro, and Pablo Semán. "Brazilian Pentecostalism Crosses National Borders." In André Corten and Ruth Marshall-Fratani, eds., *Between Babel and Pentecost: Transnational Pentecostalism in Africa and Latin America*, 181–95. London: Hurst & Co., 2001.

Oro, Ari Pedro, and Pablo Semán. "Pentecostalism in the Southern Cone Countries: Overview and Perspectives." *International Sociology* 15, no. 4 (2000): 605–27.

Ott, Hugo. *Martin Heidegger: A Political Life*. English translation. London: HarperCollins, 1993.

Pachau, Joy L. K. *Being Mizo: Identity and Belonging in Northeast India*. New Delhi: Oxford University Press, 2014.

Pacini, Andrea. *Christian Communities in the Arab Middle East: The Challenge of the Future*. Oxford: Clarendon Press, 1998.

Padwick, Constance E. *Temple Gairdner of Cairo*, 2nd ed. London: SPCK, 1929.

Pan-Anglican Congress, 1908, vol. VI, section E. Missions in Christendom, Speeches and Discussions Together with the Papers Published for the Consideration of the Congress. London: SPCK, 1908.

Papathanasiou, Athanasios N. "Missionary Experience and Academic Quest. The Research Situation in Greece." In Frieder Ludwig and Afe Adogame, eds., *European Traditions in the Study of Religion in Africa*, 301–12. Wiesbaden: Harrasowitz Verlag, 2004.

Park Heon-Wook. "The Korean Christian Church in Japan: A Study of the Gospel, Indigenization, and Nationalism." In Mark R. Mullins and Richard Fox Young, eds., *Perspectives on Christianity in Korea and Japan: The Gospel and Culture in East Asia*, 47–59. Lewiston, ME: Edwin Mellen Press, 1995.

Parker, J. I., ed. *Interpretative Statistical Survey of the World Mission of the Christian Church*. New York: International Missionary Council, 1938.

Parker, Michael. *The Kingdom of Character: The Student Volunteer Movement for Foreign Missions (1886–1926)*. Lanham, MD: American Society of Missiology and University Press of America, 1998.

Passmore, Kevin. "Catholicism and Nationalism: The *Fédération républicaine*, 1927–39." In Kay Chadwick, ed., *Catholicism, Politics and Society in Twentieth-Century France*, 47–73. Liverpool: Liverpool University Press, 2000.

Paton, David M. *Christian Missions and the Judgment of God*. London: SCM Press, 1953.

Peart-Binns, John S. *Ambrose Reeves*. London: Victor Gollancz, 1973.

Peel, J. D. Y. *Aladura: A Religious Movement among the Yoruba*. London: Oxford University Press, 1968.

Peel, J. D. Y. *Religious Encounter and the Making of the Yoruba*. Bloomington, IN: Indiana University Press, 2000.

Pei-te Lien, and Tony Carnes. "The Religious Demography of Asian American Boundary Crossing." In Tony Carnes and Fenggang Yang, eds., *Asian American Religions: The Making and Remaking of Borders and Boundaries*, 38–51. New York: New York University Press, 2004.

Pelikan, Jaroslav. *Mary through the Centuries: Her Place in the History of Culture* New Haven, CT: Yale University Press, 1996.

Pennington, J. D. "The Copts in Modern Egypt." *Middle Eastern Studies* 18, no. 2 (1982): 158–79.

Pentzopoulos, Dimitri. *The Balkan Exchange of Minorities and its Impact on Greece*. New ed. London: Hurst & Co., 2002.

Peris, Daniel P. *Storming the Heavens: The Soviet League of the Militant Godless*. Ithaca, NY: Cornell University Press, 1998.

"The Personal Ordinariate of our Lady of the Southern Cross." At http://www.ordinariate.org.au/ (Accessed May 2, 2017).

Peterson, Derek R. *Ethnic Patriotism and the East African Revival: A History of Dissent, c. 1935–1972*. Cambridge: Cambridge University Press, 2012.

Phayer, Michael. *The Catholic Church and the Holocaust, 1930–1965*. Bloomington, IN: Indiana University Press, 2000.

Pickering, W. S. F. *Anglo-Catholicism: A Study in Religious Ambiguity*. Rev. ed. London: SPCK, 1991.

Pickett, J. Waskom. *Christian Mass Movements in India: A Study with Recommendations*. New York: The Abingdon Press, 1933.

Pierard, R. V. "John R. Mott and the Rift in the Ecumenical Movement during World War I." *Journal of Ecumenical Studies* 23, no. 4 (1986): 601–20.

Pierucci, Antônio Flávio, and Reginaldo Prandi. "Religious Diversity in Brazil: Numbers and Perspectives in a Sociological Evaluation." *International Sociology* 15, no. 4 (December 2000): 629–39.

Piggin, Stuart. *Evangelical Christianity in Australia: Spirit, Word and World*. Melbourne: Oxford University Press, 1996.

Piper, John F., Jr. *Robert E. Speer: Prophet of the American Church*. Louisville, KY: Geneva Press, 2000.

Pirouet, Louise M. "East African Christians and World War I." *Journal of African History* 19, no. 1 (1978): 117–30.

Plato, *Phaedo*. transl. David Gallop. Oxford: Clarendon Press, 1975.

Plato, *Phaedrus*. transl. Robin Waterfield. Oxford: Oxford University Press, 2002.

Poitier, Johan. *Re-Imagining Rwanda: Conflict, Survival and Disinformation in the Late Twentieth Century*. Cambridge: Cambridge University Press, 2002.

Pollard, John F. *The Unknown Pope: Benedict XV (1914–1922) and the Pursuit of Peace*, new ed. London: Geoffrey Chapman, 2000.

Porath, Y. *The Emergence of the Palestinian-Arab National Movement 1918–1929*. London: Frank Cass, 1974.

Porter, Andrew N. *Religion versus Empire? British Protestant Missionaries and Overseas Expansion, 1700–1914*. Manchester: Manchester University Press, 2004.

Porter, Brian. "*Hetmanka* and Mother: Representing the Virgin Mary in Modern Poland." *Contemporary European History* 14, no. 2 (2005): 151–70.

Porter, Muriel. *Sydney Anglicans and the Threat to World Anglicanism*. Farnham: Ashgate, 2011.

Porter-Szűcs, Brian. *Faith and the Fatherland: Catholicism, Modernity, and Poland*. New York: Oxford University Press, 2011.

Pospielovsky, Dimitry V. *Soviet Studies on the Church and the Believer's Response to Atheism: Volume 3 of A History of Soviet Atheism in Theory and Practice, and the Believer*. Basingstoke: Macmillan Press, 1988.

Pospielovsky, Dimitry V. *The Russian Church under the Soviet Regime, 1917–1982*. 2 vols. Crestwood, NY: St Vladimir's Seminary Press, 1984.

Power, Samantha. *"A Problem from Hell": America and the Age of Genocide*. New York: Basic Books, 2002.

President Woodrow Wilson's Fourteen Points. http://avalon.law.yale.edu/20th _century/wilson14.asp (Accessed December 20, 2016).

Prince, Derek. *Blessing or Curse: You Can Choose!* Bletchley: Authentic Media, 2005.

Prince, Derek. *Life's Bitter Pool*. Harpenden: Derek Prince Ministries, 1984.

Prince, Derek. *Lucifer Exposed: The Devil's Plan to Destroy Your Life*, new ed. Baldock: Derek Prince Ministries, 2007.

Raboteau, Albert J. "African Americans, Exodus and the American Israel." In David H. Hackett, ed., *Religion and American Culture: A Reader*, 73–86. New York: Routledge, 1995.

Race, Alan. *Christians and Religious Pluralism: Patterns in the Christian Theology of Religions*, 2nd ed. London: SCM Press, 1993.

Raheb, Mitri. *Faith in the Face of Empire: The Bible through Palestinian Eyes*. Maryknoll, NY: Orbis Books, 2014.

Raheb, Mitri. *Sailing Through Troubled Waters: Christianity in the Middle East*. n.p.: Diyar Publisher, 2013.

Railton, Nicholas M. "German Free Churches and the Nazi Regime." *Journal of Ecclesiastical History* 49, no. 1 (1998): 85–139.

Railton, Nicholas M. "God and Magog: The History of a Symbol." *Evangelical Quarterly* 75, no. 1 (2003): 23–43.

Raiser, Konrad. *Ecumenism in Transition: A Paradigm Shift in the Ecumenical Movement?* Geneva: WCC Publications, 1991.

Raiser, Konrad. "Is Ecumenical Apologetics Sufficient? A Response to Lesslie Newbigin's 'Ecumenical Amnesia.'" *International Bulletin of Missionary Research*, 18, no. 2 (1994): 50–51.

Ramet, Sabrina Petra. "Epilogue: After the Collapse." In Sabrina Petra Ramet, ed., *Religious Policy in the Soviet Union*, 350–54. Cambridge: Cambridge University Press, 1992.

Ramet, Sabrina Petra, ed. *Religious Policy in the Soviet Union*. Cambridge: Cambridge University Press, 1992.

Randall, Ian M. *The English Baptists of the Twentieth Century*. Didcot: The Baptist Historical Society, 2005.

Rasjidi, Muhammad. "The Role of Christian Missions: The Indonesian Experience." *International Review of Mission* 65, no. 260 (1976): 427–38.

Rawlinson, F., Helen Thoburn, and D. MacGillivray, eds. *The Chinese Church as Revealed in the National Christian Conference Held in Shanghai, Tuesday, May 2, to Thursday, May 11, 1922*. Shanghai: The Oriental Press, n.d.

Reeves, Ambrose. *Shooting at Sharpeville: The Agony of South Africa*. London: Victor Gollancz, 1960.

Reeves, Thomas C. *The Empty Church: The Suicide of Liberal Christianity*. New York: Free Press, 1996.

Regan, Pauline. *Unsettling the Settler Within: Indian Residential Schools, Truth Telling, and Reconciliation in Canada*. Vancouver: University of British Columbia Press, 2010.

Rehman, I. A. "A Critique of Pakistan's Blasphemy Laws." In Tarik Jan, et al., eds., *Pakistan: Between Secularism and Islam: Ideology, Issues, and Conflict*, 196–204. Islamabad: Institute of Policy Studies, 1998.

Renan, Ernest. *The Life of Jesus*. English translation, London: Trübner & Company, 1864.

Report of the First Anglo-Catholic Congress London, 1920. London: SPCK, 1920.

"Rev Dr Oliver Lyseight—Blue Plaque Unveiling." At http://www.obv.org.uk/news -blogs /rev-dr-oliver-lyseight-blue-plaque- unveiling (Accessed May 8, 2017).

Richardson, Kip. "Gospels of Growth: The American Megachurch at Home and Abroad." In David Hempton and Hugh McLeod, eds., *Secularization and Religious Innovation in the North Atlantic World*, 291–308. Oxford: Oxford University Press, 2017.

Riis, Ole. "Patterns of Secularization in Scandinavia." In Thorleif Pettersson and Ole Riis, eds., *Scandinavian Values: Religion and Morality in the Nordic Countries*, 99–128. Uppsala: ACTA Universitatis Upsaliensis, 1994.

Robarts, David. "A Tolerable Pluralism?" In David Wetherell, ed., *Women Priests in Australia? The Anglican Crisis*, 50–69. Melbourne: Spectrum Publications, 1987.

Robbins, Joel. *Becoming Sinners: Christianity and Moral Torment in a Papua New Guinea Society*. Berkeley: University of California Press, 2004.

Roberts, Colin. "Secularisation and the (Re)formulation of French Catholic Identity." In Kay Chadwick, ed., *Catholicism, Politics and Society in Twentieth-Century France*, 260–79. Liverpool: Liverpool University Press, 2000.

Robertson, A. T. *The New Citizenship: The Christian Facing a New World Order*. New York: Fleming H. Revell, 1919.

Robertson, E. H. *Christians against Hitler.* London: SCM Press, 1962.

Robinson, Michael Edson. *Cultural Nationalism in Colonial Korea, 1920–1925.* Seattle: University of Washington Press, 1988.

Rodgers, John H. *The Theology of P. T. Forsyth: The Cross of Christ and the Revelation of God.* London: Independent Press, 1965.

Roe, James Moulton. *A History of the British and Foreign Bible Society 1905–1954.* London: British and Foreign Bible Society, 1965.

Roof, Wade Clark. *Spiritual Marketplace: Baby Boomers and the Remaking of American Religion.* Princeton, NJ: Princeton University Press, 1999.

Rosen, Rae, Susan Wieler, and Joseph Pereira. "New York City Immigrants: The 1990s Wave." *Current Issues in Economics and Finance* 11, no. 6 (2005): 1–7.

Roslof, Edward E. *Red Priests: Renovationism, Russian Orthodoxy, and Revolution, 1905–1946.* Bloomington, IN: Indiana University Press, 2002.

Roudometof, Victor. "The Evolution of Greek Orthodoxy in the Context of World Historical Globalization." In Victor Roudometof and Vasilios N. Makrides, eds., *Orthodox Christianity in 21st Century Greece: The Role of Religion in Culture, Ethnicity and Politics*, 21–38. Farnham: Ashgate, 2010.

Roudometof, Victor, and Makrides, Vasilios N. eds. *Orthodox Christianity in 21st Century Greece: The Role of Religion in Culture, Ethnicity and Politics.* Farnham: Ashgate, 2010.

Rouse, Ruth, and Stephen Charles Neill, eds. *A History of the Ecumenical Movement 1517–1948.* London: SPCK, 1954.

Rowland, Christopher, ed. *The Cambridge Companion to Liberation Theology*, 2nd ed. Cambridge: Cambridge University Press, 2007.

Rubin, Miri. *Mother of God: A History of the Virgin Mary.* London: Allen Lane, 2009.

Ruether, Rosemary Radford, and Herman J. Ruether. *The Wrath of Jonah: The Crisis of Religious Nationalism in the Israeli-Palestinian Conflict.* San Francisco: Harper & Row, 1989.

Russell, David S. "Church/State Relations in the Soviet Union: Recollections and Reflections on the 'Cold War' Years." *Baptist Quarterly* 36, no. 1 (1995): 21–28.

Sabella, Bernard. "Palestinian Christians: Realities and Hopes." In R. N. Swanson, ed., *The Holy Land, Holy Lands, and Christian History. Studies in Church History*, vol. 36, 373–97. Woodbridge: The Boydell Press for the Ecclesiastical History Society, 2000.

Said, Edward W. *Out of Place: A Memoir.* London: Granta Books, 1999.

Sale-Harrison, L. *The Remarkable Jew: His Wonderful Future. God's Great Timepiece*, 7th ed. Harrisburg, PA: Evangelical Press, 1928.

Salinas, Daniel. *Latin American Evangelical Theology in the 1970's: The Golden Decade.* Leiden: E. J. Brill, 2009.

Samartha, Stanley J. *One Christ—Many Religions: Towards a Revised Christology.* Maryknoll, NY: Orbis Books, 1991.

Samir, Khalil Samir. "The Christian Communities, Active Members of Arab Society Throughout History." In Andrea Pacini, ed., *Christian Communities in the Arab Middle East: The Challenge of the Future*, 67–91. Oxford: Clarendon Press, 1998.

Sánchez, José M. *Pius XII and the Holocaust: Understanding the Controversy.* Washington, DC: Catholic University Press of America, 2001.

Sandeen, Ernest R. *The Roots of Fundamentalism: British and American Millenarianism 1800–1930*. Chicago: University of Chicago Press, 1970.

Sanneh, Lamin. *Translating the Message: the Missionary Impact on Culture*, rev.ed. Maryknoll, NY: Orbis, 2009.

Sawatsky, Walter. "Protestantism in the USSR." In Sabrina Petra Ramet, ed., *Religious Policy in the Soviet Union*, 319–49. Cambridge: Cambridge University Press, 1992.

Sawatsky, Walter. *Soviet Evangelicals since World War II*. Kitchener, ON: Herald Press, 1981.

Scherrer, Christian P. *Genocide and Crisis in Central Africa: Conflict Roots, Mass Violence and Regional War*. Westport, CT: Praeger, 2002.

Schieffelin, Bambi B. "Tok Bokis, Tok Piksa: Translating Parables in Papua New Guinea." In Miriam Meyerhoff and Naomi Nagy, eds., *Social Lives in Language: Sociolinguistics and Multilingual Speech Communities. Celebrating the Work of Gillian Sankoff*, 111–34. Amsterdam: John Benjamins B.V., 2008.

Schröter, Susanne. "The Indigenisation of Catholicism on Flores." In Susanne Schröter, ed., *Christianity in Indonesia: Perspectives of Power*, 137–57. Berlin: Lit Verlag, 2010.

Schröter, Susanne, ed. *Christianity in Indonesia: Perspectives of Power*. Berlin: Lit Verlag, 2010.

Segundo, Juan Luis. *The Liberation of Theology*. Dublin: Gill and Macmillan, 1977.

Segundo, Juan Luis. *Signs of the Times: Theological Reflections*. Maryknoll, NY: Orbis Books, 1993.

Sernett, Milton C. *Bound for the Promised Land: African American Religion and the Great Migration*. Durham, NC: Duke University Press, 1997.

Shakespeare, J. H. *The Churches at the Cross-Roads*. London: Williams & Norgate, 1918.

Shank, David A. *Prophet Harris, the "Black Elijah" of West Africa*. Leiden: E. J. Brill, 1994.

Sharkey, Heather J. *American Evangelicals in Egypt: Missionary Encounters in an Age of Empire* Princeton, NJ: Princeton University Press, 2008.

Sharkey, Heather J. "American Missionaries, the Arabic Bible, and Coptic Reform in Late Nineteenth-Century Egypt." In Mehmet Ali Doğan and Heather J. Sharkey, eds., *American Missionaries and the Middle East: Foundational Encounters*, 237–59. Salt Lake City: The University of Utah Press, 2011.

Shehong Chen. "Republicanism, Confucianism, Christianity, and Capitalism in American Chinese Ideology." In Sucheng Chan, ed., *Chinese American Transnationalism: The Flow of People, Resources, and Ideas between China and America during the Exclusion Era*, 174–93. Philadelphia: Temple University Press, 2006.

Shepherd, Peter. *The Making of a Modern Denomination: John Howard Shakespeare and The English Baptists, 1898–1924*. Carlisle: The Paternoster Press, 2001.

Shortt, Rupert. *Christianophobia*. London: Rider Books, 2012.

Showalter, Nathan. *The End of a Crusade: the Student Volunteer Movement for Foreign Missions and the Great War*. Lanham, MD: Scarecrow Press, 1998.

Simatupang, T. B. *The Fallacy of a Myth*, English translation. Jakarta: Pustaka Sinar Harapan, 1996.

Simatupang, T. B. *Report from Banaran: Experiences During the People's War*, English translation. Ithaca, NY: Modern Indonesia Project, Southeast Asia Program Cornell University, 1972.

Skrentny, John D. *The Minority Rights Revolution*. Cambridge: MA: The Belknap Press of Harvard University Press, 2002.

Slagle, Amy. *The Eastern Church in the Spiritual Marketplace: American Conversions to Orthodox Christianity*. DeKalb, IL: Northern Illinois University Press, 2011.

Smillie, Benjamin G. "The Missionary Vision of the Heart." In David Alan Long and Olive Patricia Dickason, eds., *Visions of the Heart: Canadian Aboriginal Issues*, 21–39. Toronto: Harcourt Brace & Company, 1996.

Smith, Calvin L. "The Politics and Economics of Pentecostalism." In Cecil M. Robeck, Jr., and Amos Yong, eds., *The Cambridge Companion to Pentecostalism*, 175–94. Cambridge: Cambridge University Press, 2014.

Smith, Christian. *The Emergence of Liberation Theology: Radical Religion and Social Movement Theory*. Chicago: University of Chicago Press, 1991.

Smith, Geoff P. *Growing up with Tok Pisin: Contact, Creolization and Change in Papua New Guinea's National Language*. London: Battlebridge Publications, 2002.

Snape, Michael. "Civilians, Soldiers, and Perceptions of the Afterlife in Britain during the First World War." In Peter Clarke and Tony Claydon, eds., *The Church, the Afterlife and the Fate of the Soul, Studies in Church History*, vol. 45, 371–403. Woodbridge: The Boydell Press for the Ecclesiastical History Society, 2009.

Snape, Michael. *God and the British Soldier: Religion and the British Army in the First and Second World Wars*. London: Routledge, 2005.

Sotiru, Eleni. "'The Traditional Modern': Rethinking the Position of Contemporary Greek Women in Orthodoxy." In Victor Roudometof and Vasilios N. Makrides, eds., *Orthodox Christianity in 21st Century Greece: The Role of Religion in Culture, Ethnicity and Politics*, 131–54. Farnham: Ashgate, 2010.

Speake, Graham. *Mount Athos: Renewal in Paradise*. New Haven, CT: Yale University Press, 2002.

Spiller, G. ed. *Papers on Inter-Racial Problems Communicated to the First Universal Races Congress Held at the University of London July 26–29, 1911*. London: P. S. King & Son, 1911.

Spong, John Shelby. *Living in Sin: A Bishop Rethinks Human Sexuality*. San Francisco: Harper & Row, 1988.

Sproule-Jones, Megan. "Crusading for the Forgotten: Dr. Peter Bryce, Public Health, and Prairie Native Residential Schools." *Canadian Bulletin of Medical History* 13 (1996): 199–224.

Stanley, Brian. *The Bible and the Flag: Protestant Missions and British Imperialism in the Nineteenth and Twentieth Centuries*. Leicester: Apollos, 1990.

Stanley, Brian. "Edinburgh and World Christianity." *Studies in World Christianity* 17, no. 1 (2011): 72–91.

Stanley, Brian. *The Global Diffusion of Evangelicalism: The Age of Billy Graham and John Stott*. Downers Grove, IL: Inter-Varsity Press, 2013.

Stanley, Brian. *The History of the Baptist Missionary Society 1792–1992*. Edinburgh: T. & T. Clark, 1992.

Stanley, Brian, ed. *Missions, Nationalism, and the End of Empire*. Grand Rapids, MI: Eerdmans, 2003.

Stanley, Brian. "The Re-Shaping of Christian Tradition: Western Denominational Identity in a Non-Western Context." In R. N. Swanson, ed., *Unity and Diversity in the Church. Studies in Church History*, vol. 32, 399–426. Oxford: Blackwell for the Ecclesiastical History Society, 1996.

Stanley, Brian. "Twentieth-Century World Christianity: A Perspective from the History of Missions." In Donald M. Lewis, ed., *Christianity Reborn: The Global Expansion of Evangelicalism in the Twentieth Century*, 52–86. Grand Rapids, MI: Eerdmans, 2004.

Stanley, Brian. *The World Missionary Conference, Edinburgh 1910*. Grand Rapids, MI: Eerdmans, 2009.

Stark, Rodney, and Roger Finke, *Acts of Faith: Exploring the Human Side of Religion*. Berkeley: University of California Press, 2000.

Steenbrink, Karel A. "Muslim-Christian Relations in the *Pancasila* State of Indonesia." *Muslim World* 88, nos. 3–4 (1998): 320–52.

Steigmann-Gall, Richard. *The Holy Reich: Nazi Conceptions of Christianity, 1919–1945*. Cambridge: Cambridge University Press, 2003.

Stene, Nora. "Becoming a Copt." In Nelly van Doorn-Harder and Kari Vogt, eds., *Between Desert and City, The Coptic Orthodox Church Today*, 191–212. Oslo: Novus Forlag, 1997.

Stock, Eugene. *The History of the Church Missionary Society*, vol. IV. London: Church Missionary Society, 1916.

Stokes, Eric. *The English Utilitarians and India*. Oxford: Clarendon Press, 1959.

Strachan, Hew. *The First World War*, vol. I: *To Arms*. Oxford: Oxford University Press, 2001.

Straton, John Roach. *Evolution versus Creation: Second in the Series of Fundamentalist-Modernist Debates*. Nashville, TN: Sunday School Board: Southern Baptist Convention, 1924.

Stuart, John. "Empire, Mission, Ecumenism, and Human Rights: 'Religious Liberty' in Egypt, 1919–1956." *Church History* 83, no. 1 (2014): 110–34.

Sudworth, Richard. "Christian Responses to the Political Challenge of Islam," http://repository.berkleycenter.georgetown.edu/120711SudworthChristian ResponsesPoliticalChallengeIslam.pdf (Accessed April 27, 2017).

Sundkler, Bengt. *Church of South India: The Movement towards Union 1900–1947*, rev. ed. London: Lutterworth Press, 1965.

Sundkler, Bengt. *Zulu Zion and Some Swazi Zionists*. London: Oxford University Press, 1976.

Sung-Ho Kim. "Rapid Modernisation and the Future of Korean Christianity." *Religion*, 32, no. 1 (2002): 27–37.

Swain, Tony, and Garry Trompf. *The Religions of Oceania*. London and New York: Routledge, 1995.

Swanson, R. N., ed. *The Holy Land, Holy Lands, and Christian History. Studies in Church History*, vol. 36. Woodbridge: The Boydell Press for the Ecclesiastical History Society, 2000.

Sykes, Stephen. "P. T. Forsyth on the Church." In *Justice the True and Only Mercy: Essays on the Life and Theology of Peter Taylor Forsyth*. Edited by Trevor Hart, 1–15, Edinburgh: T. & T. Clark, 1995.

Tallett, Frank, and Nicholas Atkin, eds. *Religion, Society and Politics in France since 1789*. London: The Hambledon Press, 1991.

Tasie, G. O. M. *Christian Missionary Enterprise in the Niger Delta, 1864–1918*. Leiden: E. J. Brill, 1978.

Tasie, G. O. M. "The Prophetic Calling: Garrick Sokari Braide of Bakana (d. 1918)." In Elizabeth Isichei, ed., *Varieties of Christian Experience in Nigeria*, 99–115. London: Macmillan, 1982.

Taylor, Mark L. "M. Richard Shaull: A Tribute." *Princeton Seminary Bulletin* 24, no. 3 (2003): 343–47.

Thompson, David M. "Church Unity in Twentieth-Century England: Pleasing Dream or Common Calling?" In R. N. Swanson, ed., *Unity and Diversity in the Church. Studies in Church History*, vol. 32, 511–20. Oxford: Blackwell for the Ecclesiastical History Society, 1996.

Thompson, H. P. *Into All Lands: The History of the Society for the Propagation of the Gospel in Foreign Parts, 1701–1950*. London: SPCK, 1951.

Thompson, James J. *Tried by Fire: Southern Baptists and the Religious Controversies of the 1920s*. Macon: GA: Mercer University Press, 1982.

Thompson, Todd M. "J. N. D. Anderson, Nationalism, and the 'Modernisation' of Islamic Law, 1932–1984." PhD thesis, University of Cambridge, 2010.

Thorkildsen, Dag. "Scandinavia: Lutheranism and National Identity." In Sheridan Gilley and Brian Stanley, eds., *World Christianities, c. 1815-c. 1914: The Cambridge History of Christianity, vol. 8*, 342–58. Cambridge: Cambridge University Press, 2006.

Thörn, Håkan. *Anti-Apartheid and the Emergence of a Global Civil Society*. Basingstoke: Palgrave Macmillan, 2006.

Throntveit, Trygve. "The Fable of the Fourteen Points: Woodrow Wilson and National Self-Determination." *Diplomatic History* 35, no. 3 (2011): 445–81.

Tiedemann, R. G. *Reference Guide to Christian Missionary Societies in China: from the Sixteenth to the Twentieth Centuries*. Armonk, NY: Taylor and Francis, 2016.

Tippett, Alan R. *Solomon Islands Christianity: A Study of Growth and Obstruction*. London: Lutterworth Press, 1967.

Titley, Brian. "A Troubled Legacy: The Catholic Church and Indian Residential Schooling in Canada." *Paedagogica Historica: International Journal of the History of Education* 31, Supplement 1 (1995): 335–49.

Tomasson, Richard F. "How Sweden Became so Secular," *Scandinavian Studies* 74, no. 1 (2002): 61–88.

Tombs, David. *Latin American Liberation Theology*. Leiden: E. J. Brill, 2002.

Torres, Sergio. "Gustavo Gutiérrez: A Historical Sketch." In Ellis and Maduro, *The Future of Liberation Theology*, 95–101.

Toulis, Nicole Rodriguez. *Believing Identity: Pentecostalism and the Mediation of Jamaican Ethnicity and Gender in England*. Oxford: Berg, 1997.

Treloar, Geoffrey R. *The Disruption of Evangelicalism: The Age of Torrey, Mott, McPherson and Hammond*. Downers Grove, IL: Inter-Varsity Press, 2016.

Tress, Nora. *Caught for Life: A Story of the Anglican Deaconess Order in Australia.* Araluen, NSW: Nora Tress, 1993.

Trompf, G. W. "Christianity in Melanesia." In Charles E. Farhadian, ed., *Introducing World Christianity*, 244–58. Chichester: Wiley-Blackwell, 2012.

Trompf, G. W. "Independent Churches in Melanesia." *Oceania* 54, no. 1 (1983): 51–72.

Trompf, G. W. *Melanesian Religion*, rev. ed., Cambridge: Cambridge University Press, 2010.

Trompf, G. W. *Payback: The Logic of Retribution in Melanesian Religions.* Cambridge: Cambridge University Press, 2008.

Tseng, Timothy. "Trans-Pacific Transpositions: Continuities and Discontinuities in Chinese North American Protestantism since 1965." In Jane Naomi Iwamura and Paul Spickard, eds., *Revealing the Sacred in Asian and Pacific America*, 242–72. New York: Routledge, 2003.

Turner, H. W. "Prophets and Politics: A Nigerian Test-Case." *Bulletin of the Society for African Church History* 2, no. 1 (1965): 97–118.

Turner, John G. *Bill Bright and Campus Crusade for Christ: The Renewal of Evangelicalism in Postwar America.* Chapel Hill, NC: University of North Carolina Press, 2008.

Udis-Kessler, Amanda. *Queer Inclusion in the United Methodist Church.* New York: Routledge, 2008.

Ustorf, Werner. *Sailing on the Next Tide: Missions, Missiology, and the Third Reich.* Frankfurt: Peter Lang, 2000.

Vásquez, Manuel A. *The Brazilian Catholic Church and the Crisis of Modernity*, rev. ed. Cambridge: Cambridge University Press, 2008.

Vavouskos, Constantinos A. "Church and State in Modern Greece: A Review Article." *Balkan Studies* 9, no. 1 (1968): 200–26.

Villa-Vicencio, Charles, and John W. de Gruchy. *Resistance and Hope: South African Essays in Honour of Beyers Naudé.* Grand Rapids, MI: Eerdmans; and Cape Town: David Philip, 1985.

Visser 't Hooft, W. A. *Memoirs.* London: SCM Press, 1973.

Vorgrimler, Herbert, ed. *Commentary on the Documents of Vatican II.* 5 vols. London: Burns & Oates, 1969–89.

Wacker, Grant. *America's Pastor: Billy Graham and the Shaping of a Nation.* Cambridge, MA: The Belknap Press of Harvard University Press, 2014.

Wacker, Grant. *Heaven Below: Early Pentecostals and American Culture.* Cambridge, MA: Harvard University Press, 2001.

Wakefield, Gavin. *The First Pentecostal Anglican: The Life and Legacy of Alexander Boddy.* Cambridge: Grove Books, 2001.

Wakin, Edward. *A Lonely Minority: The Story of Egypt's Copts*, 2nd ed. Lincoln, NE: Authors Guild BackinPrint.Com, 2000.

Walls, Andrew F. *The Cross-Cultural Process in Christian History: Studies in the Transmission and Appropriation of Faith.* Maryknoll, NY: Orbis Books, 2002.

Walls, Andrew F. *The Missionary Movement in Christian History: Studies in the Transmission of Faith.* Maryknoll, NY: Orbis Books, 1996.

Walshe, Peter. "South Africa: Prophetic Christianity and the Liberation Movement." *Journal of Modern African Studies* 29, no. 1 (1991): 27–60.

Walzer, Michael. *Exodus and Revolution*. New York: Basic Books, 1985.

Walzer, Michael. *The Revolution of the Saints: A Study in the Origins of Radical Politics*. London: Weidenfeld and Nicolson, 1966.

Wang, Marina Xiaojing. "The Church Unity Movement in Early Twentieth-Century China: Cheng Jingyi and the Church of Christ in China." PhD thesis, University of Edinburgh, 2012.

Wanner, Catherine, ed. *State Secularism and Lived Religion in Soviet Russia and the Ukraine*. Oxford: Oxford University Press; and Washington: Woodrow Wilson Center Press, 2012.

Ward, Kevin. *A History of Global Anglicanism*. Cambridge: Cambridge University Press, 2006.

Ward, Kevin, and Emma Wild-Wood, eds. *The East African Revival: History and Legacies*. Farnham: Ashgate, 2012.

Ward, W. R. "Peace, Peace and Rumours of War." *Journal of Ecclesiastical History* 51, no. 4 (2000): 767–70.

Wardin, Albert, Jr., ed. *Baptists around the World: A Comprehensive Handbook*. Nashville, TN: Broadman & Holman, 1995.

Ware, Timothy. *The Orthodox Church*, new ed. London: Penguin Books, 1997.

Warren, Bill. *Imperialism: Pioneer of Capitalism*. London: Verso Books, 1980.

Waters, Mary C., and Reed Ueda, eds. *The New Americans: A Guide to Immigration since 1965*. Cambridge, MA: Harvard University Press, 2007.

Watkins-Owens, Irma. *Blood Relations: Caribbean Immigrants and the Harlem Community, 1900–1930*. Bloomington, IN: Indiana University Press, 1996.

Watson, Andrew. *The American Mission in Egypt, 1854–1896*, 2nd ed. Pittsburgh: United Presbyterian Church Board of Publication, 1904.

Watson, John W. *Among the Copts*. Brighton: Sussex Academic Press, 2000.

Webber, Robert E. *Evangelicals on the Canterbury Trail: Why Evangelicals Are Attracted to the Liturgical Church*. Waco, TX: Word Books, 1985.

Weber, Timothy P. *Living in the Shadow of the Second Coming: American Premillennialism, 1875–1982*, rev. ed. Chicago: University of Chicago Press, 1987. First published 1979 by Oxford University Press.

Wedenoja, William. "Modernization in the Pentecostal Movement in Jamaica." In *Perspectives on Pentecostalism: Case Studies from the Caribbean and Latin America*, edited by Stephen D. Glazier, 27–48. Washington, DC: University Press of America, 1980.

Weigel, George. *Witness to Hope: The Biography of Pope John Paul II*. New York: HarperCollins, 2001.

Welbourn, F. B. *East African Rebels: A Study of Some Independent Churches*. London: SCM Press, 1961.

Welch, Claude E., Jr. "Mobilizing Morality: The World Council of Churches and its Programme to Combat Racism, 1969–1994." *Human Rights Quarterly* 23, no. 4 (2001): 863–910.

Wellem, Frederiek D. *Amir Sjarifoeddin: Tempatnya Dalam Kekristenan dan Perjuangan Kemerdekaan Indonesia*. Jakarta: Pernebit, 2009.

Wells, Kenneth M. *New God, New Nation: Protestants and Self-Reconstruction Nationalism in Korea 1896–1937*. Honolulu: University of Hawaii Press, 1990.

Weymouth, Ross M. "The Gogodala Society: A Study of Adjustment Movements since 1966." *Oceania* 54, no. 4 (1984): 269–88.

Weymouth, Ross M. "The Unevangelised Fields Mission in Papua, 1931–1981." *Journal of Pacific History* 23, no. 2 (1988): 175–90.

White, Gavin. *How the Churches Got to Be the Way They Are*. London and Philadelphia: SCM Press and Trinity Press International, 1990.

White, Gavin. "Patriarch McGuire and the Episcopal Church." *Historical Magazine of the Protestant Episcopal Church*, 38, no. 2 (1969): 109–41.

Whiteman, Darrell L., ed. *An Introduction to Melanesian Cultures: A Handbook for Church Workers*. Goroka, Papua New Guinea: Melanesian Institute for Pastoral and Socio-Economic Service, 1984.

Wickeri, Philip. *Reconstructing Christianity in China: K. H. Ting and the Chinese Church*. Maryknoll, NY: Orbis Books, 2007.

Wickeri, Philip. *Seeking the Common Ground: Protestant Christianity, the Three-Self Movement, and China's United Front*. Maryknoll, NY: Orbis Books, 1988.

Wickham, E. R. *Church and People in an Industrial City*. London: Lutterworth Press, 1957.

Wiegele, Katharine L. *Investing in Miracles: El Shaddai and the Transformation of Popular Catholicism in the Philippines*. Honolulu: University of Hawai'i Press, 2005.

Wi Jo Kang. "Church and State Relations in the Japanese Colonial Period." In Robert E. Buswell Jr. and Timothy S. Lee, eds., *Christianity in Korea*, edited by 97–115. Honolulu: University of Hawaii Press, 2006.

Wilde, Charles. "Acts of Faith: Muscular Christianity and Masculinity among the Gogodala of Papua New Guinea." *Oceania* 75, no. 1 (2004): 32–48.

Wilkinson, Alan. *The Church of England and the First World War*. London: SPCK, 1978.

Williams, George Huntson. *The Mind of John Paul II: Origins of His Thought and Action*. New York: Seabury Press, 1981.

Williams, Reggie L. *Bonhoeffer's Black Jesus: Harlem Renaissance Theology and an Ethic of Resistance*. Waco, TX: Baylor University Press, 2014.

Willis, Avery T., Jr. *Indonesian Revival: Why Two Millions Came to Christ*. South Pasadena, CA: William Carey Library, 1977.

Willis, J. J., J. W. Arthur, and S. C. Neill. *Towards a United Church 1913–1947*. London: Edinburgh House Press, 1947.

Wilson, Bryan R. *Religion in Secular Society: A Sociological Comment*. London: C. A. Watts & Co., 1966.

Wilson, Bryan R. *Sects and Society: A Sociological Study of Three Religious Groups in Britain*. London: Heinemann, 1961.

Wilson, H. A. *Received With Thanks of P. E. Tindall, M. E. Atlay, Frank Weston, Richard Wilson, H. F. B. Mackay, H. A. Pollock*. London and Oxford: A. R. Mowbray, 1940.

Wilson, John. "British Israelism: The Ideological Restraints on Sect Organisation." In *Patterns of Sectarianism: Organisation and Ideology in Social and Religious Movements*, edited by B. R. Wilson, 345–76. London: Heinemann, 1967.

Wilson, John. *Our Israelitish Origin: Lectures on Ancient Israel and the Israelitish Origin of the Modern Nations of Europe*, 3rd ed. London: James Nisbet, 1844.

Winter, J. M. *The Great War and the British People*, 2nd ed. Basingstoke: Palgrave Macmillan, 2003.

Winter, J. M. *Sites of Memory: Sites of Mourning: The Great War in European Cultural History*. Cambridge: Cambridge University Press, 1998.

"World Council of Churches' Consultation with Member-Churches in South Africa: Cottesloe, Johannesburg, 7–14 December, 1960." *The Ecumenical Review* 13, no. 2 (1961), 244–50.

World Council of Churches Department on Studies in Evangelism. *The Church for Others, and the Church for the World: A Quest for Structures for Missionary Congregations*. Geneva: World Council of Churches, 1967.

World Council of Churches, Sub-Unit on Dialogue with the People of Living Faiths and Ideologies. *Christian Presence and Witness in Relation to Muslim Neighbours*. Geneva: World Council of Churches, 1981.

Worsnip, Michael E. *Between the Two Fires: The Anglican Church and Apartheid*. Pietermaritzburg: University of Natal Press, 1991.

Worthen, Molly. *Apostles of Reason: The Crisis of Authority in American Evangelicalism*. New York: Oxford University Press, 2014.

Wright, David F. "The Great Commission and the Ministry of the Word: Reflections Historical and Contemporary on Relations and Priorities," *Scottish Bulletin of Evangelical Theology* 25, no. 2 (2007): 132–57.

Wright, G. Ernest. *God Who Acts: Biblical Theology as Recital*. London: SCM Press, 1952.

Wright, G. Ernest. *The Old Testament against its Environment*. London: SCM Press, 1960.

Wright, Les. "San Francisco." In David Higgs, ed., *Queer Sites: Gay Urban Histories since 1600*, 164–76. London: Routledge, 1999.

Wu, Albert Monshan. *From Christ to Confucius: German Missionaries, Chinese Christians, and the Globalization of Christianity*. New Haven, CT: Yale University Press, 2016.

Wuthnow, Robert. *The Restructuring of American Religion: Society and Faith since World War II*. Princeton, NJ: Princeton University Press, 1988.

Yao, Kevin Xiyi. *The Fundamentalist Movement among Protestant Missionaries in China, 1920–1937* Lanham, MD: University Press of America, 2003.

Yates, Timothy E. *Christian Mission in the Twentieth Century*. Cambridge: Cambridge University Press, 1994.

Yelensky, Viktor. "The Revival before the Revival: Popular and Institutionalized Religion in Ukraine on the Eve of the Collapse of Communism." In Catherine Wanner, ed., *State Secularism and Lived Religion in Soviet Russia and the Ukraine*, 302–30. Oxford: Oxford University Press; and Washington: Woodrow Wilson Center Press, 2012.

Young, Ernest P. *Ecclesiastical Colony: China's Catholic Church and the French Religious Protectorate*. New York: Oxford University Press, 2013.

Zenteno, Arnaldo. *Liberación social y Christo: Apuntes para una teología de la liberación*. Mexico, D.F.: Secretariado Social Mexicano, 1971.

Zernov, Nicolas. *The Russian Religious Renaissance of the Twentieth Century*. London: Darton, Longman & Todd, 1963.

Zernov, Nicolas. *The Russians and Their Church*, 3rd ed. Crestwood, NY: St Vladimir's Seminary Press, 1994.

Zernov, Nicolas. *Sunset Years: A Russian Pilgrim in the West*. London: The Fellowship of St Alban & St Sergius, 1983.

Zetzsche, Jost. *The Bible in China: the History of the Union Version or the Culmination of Protestant Missionary Bible Translation in China*. Sankt Augustin: Monumenta Serica Institute, 1999.

Zhonghua ji du jiao hui. *Let us Unite! The Church of Christ in China and Church Unity in China*. Peiping: General Assembly, Church of Christ in China, n.d. [1935].

Zimmermann, M. *Wilhelm Marr: The Patriarch of Anti-Semitism*. New York: Oxford University Press, 1986.

Zuckerman, Phil. *Society Without God: What the Least Religious Nations Can Tell Us About Contentment*. New York: New York University Press, 2008.

Zwemer, Samuel M. *Across the World of Islam: Studies in Aspects of the Mohammedan Faith and in the Present Awakening of the Moslem Multitudes*. New York: Fleming H. Revell Co., 1929.

Zwemer, Samuel M. *Islam: A Challenge to Faith: Studies on the Mohammedan Religion and the Needs and Opportunities of the Mohammedan World from the Standpoint of Christian Missions*. New York: Student Volunteer Movement for Foreign Missions, 1907.

Zwemer, Samuel M. *The Law of Apostasy in Islam: Answering the Question Why There Are So Few Moslem Converts, and Giving Examples of their Moral Courage and Martyrdom*. London: Marshall Brothers, n.d. [1924].

Works of Reference

1914–1918-online. International Encyclopedia of the First World War. Edited by Ute Daniel, Peter Gatrell, and Oliver Janz. Berlin: Freie Universität Berlin, 2014. DOI: 10.15463/ie1418.10387. http://www.1914-1918-online.net/. (Accessed October 27, 2017).

Atlas of Global Christianity, edited by Todd M. Johnson and Kenneth R. Ross. Edinburgh: Edinburgh University Press, 2010.

Biografisch Lexicon voor de geschiedenis van het Nederlands protestantisme. http://resources.huygens.knaw.nl/retroboeken/blnp/#page=0&accessor=access or _index&view=homePane (Accessed April 27, 2017).

Biographical Dictionary of Christian Missions, edited by Gerald H. Anderson. New York: Macmillan Reference, 1998.

The Blackwell Dictionary of Eastern Christianity, edited by Ken Parry, David J. Melling, and Dimitri Brady. Oxford: Blackwell, 1999.

Dictionary of Canadian Biography. 12 vols. Toronto: University of Toronto Press, 1966–91.

The Dictionary of New Zealand Biography. 5 vols. Wellington: Department of Internal Affairs, 1990–2000.

Dictionary of Pentecostal and Charismatic Movements, edited by Stanley M. Burgess and Gary B. McGee. Grand Rapids, MI: Zondervan, 1988.

Dictionary of South African Biography. 5 vols. Cape Town: Nasionale Boekhandel for the National Council for Social Research, Department of Higher Education, 1968–1987.

Encyclopedia of Chicago. Chicago Historical Society: Chicago, 2005. http://www.encyclopedia.chicagohistory.org/pages/700000.html (Accessed May 8, 2017).

Encyclopedia of the Great Black Migration, edited by Steven A. Reich. 3 vols. Westport, CT, Greenwood Press, 2006.

The Encyclopedia of New York City, edited by Kenneth T. Jackson. New Haven, CT: Yale University Press, 1995.

OrthodoxWiki. https://orthodoxwiki.org/index.php?title=Main_Page&oldid=124632 (Accessed May 5, 2017).

Oxford Dictionary of National Biography. Oxford: Oxford University Press.

The Oxford Encyclopaedia of South Asian Christianity, edited by Roger E. Hedlund, 2 vols. New Delhi: Oxford University Press, 2012.

Oxford English Dictionary. 3rd online ed. Oxford: Oxford University Press, 2005.

Solomon Islands Historical Encyclopedia 1893–1978 (2013). At http://www.solomonencyclopaedia.net/index.html (Accessed March 31, 2017).

World Christian Database, edited by Todd M. Johnson and Gina A. Zurlo. Leiden: E. J. Brill. http://www.worldchristiandatabase.org/wcd/ (Accessed February 27, 2017).

World Christian Encyclopaedia, edited by David B. Barrett, George T. Kurian, Todd M. Johnson, 2nd ed. New York: Oxford University Press, 2001.

A NOTE ON THE TYPE

THIS BOOK has been composed in Miller, a Scotch Roman typeface designed by Matthew Carter and first released by Font Bureau in 1997. It resembles Monticello, the typeface developed for The Papers of Thomas Jefferson in the 1940s by C. H. Griffith and P. J. Conkwright and reinterpreted in digital form by Carter in 2003.

Pleasant Jefferson ("P. J.") Conkwright (1905–1986) was Typographer at Princeton University Press from 1939 to 1970. He was an acclaimed book designer and AIGA Medalist.

The ornament used throughout this book was designed by Pierre Simon Fournier (1712–1768) and was a favorite of Conkwright's, used in his design of the *Princeton University Library Chronicle*.